W9-AED-706

70258

M
125
.G64
1925

DATE DUE			
Jan 18 '71			
Apr 25 '74			
May 9 '74			
Dec 9 '75			
GAYLORD M-2			PRINTED IN U.S.A.

DISCARDED

GREAT WORKS OF MUSIC

GREAT WORKS
OF
MUSIC

[SYMPHONIES AND THEIR MEANING]

BY

PHILIP H. GOEPP

Three Volumes in One

GARDEN CITY PUBLISHING CO., INC.
GARDEN CITY   NEW YORK

CARL A. RUDISILL LIBRARY
LENOIR RHYNE COLLEGE

M
125
.G64
1925

FIRST VOLUME
COPYRIGHT, 1897, BY J. B. LIPPINCOTT COMPANY
COPYRIGHT, 1925, BY PHILIP H. GOEPP

SECOND VOLUME
COPYRIGHT, 1902, BY J. B. LIPPINCOTT COMPANY

THIRD VOLUME
COPYRIGHT, 1913, BY J. B. LIPPINCOTT COMPANY

70258

June, 1970

PRINTED IN UNITED STATES OF AMERICA

TO

MRS. A. J. D. DIXON

WHO ENCOURAGED THE LECTURES
FROM WHICH IT GREW
THIS BOOK
IS
DEDICATED

Musicus qui numerans nescit se numerare

PREFACE

THE plan of this book is very simple It is really the reverse of the traditional. Little is here told of the lives of the masters; of a composer's ancestry, of the painful scale of his career, even of the date of his works. Concrete events have, in themselves, no place. And yet, it is believed, instead of a loss, there is in this very omission a great gain of personal interest, of insight into the essence of a master's individual quality, of his poetic character.

The plan is to open the book and see what is there, without discovering subtle stories or graphic pictures, avoiding, too, a mere technical analysis. There may be, in such an account of the impression of a master work, a discovery here and there of symbolic significance. The exact nature of this middle road cannot well be predicated. It is here that the book must stand its own defence, which lies in the fulfilment, not in the words of the promise.

There is, at the outset, no value whatever in a mere theoretic exposition of themes and development. Undoubtedly the subjective intensity of the impression is strongly to be reckoned with. But there must be the balance, the rein which resists allegory run riot.

In such a view is the true mirror of the master. It is an unfailing, perfect test. From such a quiet, all-surveying study, as one looks at a painting standing off, it is possible to see the pervading quality, if it is there, or to detect its lack. The beauty will ever appear more clearly, or the faultiness, the meretricious deceit, the patched pretence of homogeneous whole.

Another word about the " meaning" of the symphonies. In the title this word has a negative intent, quite as strong as the positive. The book is meant to restrain the wrong interpretation, as to urge the right. True listening lies in the balance of intense enjoyment and clear perception. There must be no clouding by the one, nor too much interference of translating thought. In a simple setting forth of a serious enjoyment will be all the "meaning" that the master will claim for his work, or the musician for his art. But to tell just how far the music gives the spirit of the master were idle in a preface, as it is the purpose of the book.

Thus the aim is primarily to set forth the impression of each of certain chosen symphonies, and through them to get, at first hand, a clear glimpse of the individuality of each of the great masters. Secondarily, it is intended to suggest, by the mode presented, an attitude in the listener which will increase his enjoyment by an intelligent perception of the intent of the master, or which, for critical purposes, may serve in testing a new work. An ultimate object, which it is not intended to pursue categorically, is the suggestion of an underlying purpose in the art, and, similarly, of its scope, wherein will be involved certain incidental questions of the connection between the art-work and the intent or unconscious thought, the personal tone, even the *morale*, of the master.

FIRST SERIES

CONTENTS

CONTENTS

SECOND SERIES
CONTENTS

CONTENTS

THIRD SERIES

CONTENTS

CONTENTS

GREAT WORKS OF MUSIC

SYMPHONIES

AND THEIR MEANING

I

INTRODUCTORY

THERE are some truths concerning the right attitude of listening to music, which had best be mentioned at the outset. They are not to be proved, like a theorem, in the pages which follow; there is no such deliberate or definite intent. On the contrary, they seem almost axiomatic; they are fundamental in all discussion and enjoyment of music. But they have been so long forgotten that they have a new look. The present generation may well be reminded of them.

In so far as they will be regarded as necessarily true, they may stand as the landmarks of the view, here presented, of the great masterpieces. In so far as they may be challenged, the succeeding chapters are offered as exemplifications from which their truth may be concluded by a kind of inductive proof. For, unhappily, the time has not come for a systematic philosophy of art, or even of the tonal branch.

Agreement is wanting as to basic principles. No one dares to define the real purpose of art, the method of its working, or even the meaning of the word. This youngest of the sisters, music, has utterly disturbed traditional views. Aristotle's definitions of art will not fit with Beethoven's symphonies. So, in music especially, we are too near, so to speak, to take a general view. We are still groping in the bewilderment of a new paradise of sense impressions for some first principle, for the fruit of the tree of knowledge, whereby we may discern the good from the evil.

The first of these axioms is most in need of assertion, though its simple statement would probably pass an easy muster. But the attack is always subtle, indirect, and wide-spread.

There is truth in art, resting on fundamental principles; its landmarks exist; without them there is no true perception, no just criticism. Very likely

14

the point of this statement will be clearest
from the opposite fallacy, which we often hear,
that everything is good that sounds good. It
does seem that this is a critical time for the art
of music. It is, one might say, the hour for
the declaration of independence, and, strangely,
not of the many from the leaders, but of the
leaders from the many. In prose and in poetry
we do not hesitate to apply the searching test
of sound art, with clear principles and highest
ideals. And we are wont to listen with respect to those who are trained to know and
to judge. There is a natural leadership of the
few critics in literature, in painting, and in architecture. Yet in the most complex of all
the arts we insist on this rampant democratic
dictum, that it is all a rude question of taste.
Nay, we dare to hold that precisely just because we are not trained, we are better quali-
fied to judge ; that it is the very knowledge that
unfits the critic.

This is surely a strange condition for a great
art. It is not wise to dispute such a position,
to do more than show its absurdity. All will
agree that it is one of the primeval purposes of
art to develop a sense of beauty. But how

will the first step ever come, if our taste in the original condition of ignorance is to be the touchstone? There can be no progress, either in argument or in fact.

The fault lies, in reality, in that phase of modern art which casts to the winds sound principle, clear process, and rests all in the sensational and emotional effect, in utter indifference to the true or the false, the right or wrong of the workmanship.

We do not intend, surely, to let music be to us a mere narcotic, to affect us in a passive, unreasoning state. Therefore, I say, now more than ever there is need for true leaders, to save us from the false; but far more still, for each to become his own critic,—to master the principles which underlie true art, and the right attitude of reception and of perception.

In the classical past it was our good fortune to have none but true leaders. We learned to trust them unconsciously as well as implicitly. But with later democratic stirring there came inevitable demagoguism. Men appealed over the heads of those who had the true, the saner intuition to the ruder mob to whom clear thought was naught, sensational amusement

16

all. Democratic as we must be in government, there is no doubt that the bursts of
popular will throughout the nineteenth century
have had a sinister effect upon art. The lower
instincts with the lower classes have broken
away from the higher. Within the right
meaning, the true democrat in government not
only can, he must be the true aristocrat in art.
And thus we may explain much of what is commonly charged of late against art, under such
words as *degeneration* and *decadence*. Our only
cure is, as we must act as a democracy, to
have the feeling and thought of true aristoc-
racy.

We must pay art, in general and special,
the respect of an intelligent attitude, which we
can only acquire by mastering its process, the
mode of its working, and its intent. A century ago all this could not have been seriously
thought in need even of suggestion.

The second premise relates to a question
which has always raged with much uncertainty: the connection between the master's
thought and his art-work. How far does
he translate a "meaning" into his music?
How far has he an intent that must be re-

garded? Or is it merely a pretty amusement, a delight of the senses, by nice combinations of beauty in tone, in color, and in outline? And this latter alternative cannot be disregarded, when it seems to be held by one who is accounted the greatest German critic of the day. Gradually, however, the truth is breaking, that, while the apparent purpose is that of mere delight, *the true essence of music is its unconscious subjective betrayal of a dominant feeling*, in contrast with the conscious, objective depiction in poetry and in the plastic arts. At once the charm and mystery is the stress on the unconsciousness of purpose. And yet it is not strange. Throughout life consciousness of action or of utterance is not only not needful; its effect is actually weakening as a useless diversion of the mind. It is this very absence of self-observation which gives music its overwhelming power as a means of expression. This is in harmony, too, with that modern experience which believes more and more in personal force and influence, which, without materialism, believes less and less in the virtue of definite dogma.

In a talk with a friend, the spoken word is

not essential, rather the personal attitude unconsciously betrayed. So in a symphony of Beethoven the ultimate purpose is the utterance of the high thought or feeling of a great man. However unconscious this aim may be, I think it may justly be called the true intent of the master.

It may be thought, however, that there is here too little stress on the art proper, in its perfection of form and detailed beauty. The answer is, perhaps subtle: between the intensity and nobility of the feeling which dominates the poet, and its artistic expression is a close and curious connection, and, further, an analogy. As, after all, the apparent, the conscious purpose is a beautiful work of art, the nobility of the poet is measured by the nobility of his work; his clearness of vision, by the perfection of detail. The truth is, a high feeling compels a great utterance; and conversely, where there is a beautiful expression there must be nobility of the prompting thought. Thus the greatest poets will have the purest form. In proportion as the feeling or thought is intense, its utterance will be sustained in a work of high structure. A true poet does not roar himself into a state, in order to convey his emotion; that is not the kind the world cares to hear. Therefore it follows, of course, that the feeling at the source is only reached by a perception of the beauty of the art-work. And the object must always be so to study the master-works as to feel most keenly the unconscious intent, the mood-purpose of the creator.

It is clear how the first premise leads to the second as a natural preliminary, and how each reinforces the other. So the third will prove but a larger view of the second; and all are but different phases of the whole truth.

In poetry we do not hesitate to regard the moral quality of the poet. In music this seems never to be thought of. Yet in music this personal tone of the poet is more potent far than in the other arts; it is more subtly conveyed, and needs most to be watched. All moral influence is exerted, we know, not so much logically or intellectually, as emotionally. Music, which affects the feelings most powerfully, most easily conveys the personal influence of the poet to the hearers. We all know the moral force of companionship, of mere neighborhood. Yet how could this personal tone be conveyed more directly than by a word uttered in living figures of sound.

The mystery, of course, is how we are to detect this moral quality, where there are no tell-tale words and story. Impossible, however, as it is to sum up in systematic philosophy, nothing is so clear to the persistent and open-minded listener in both phases, the good and the bad, the moral and unmoral. I have pointed above to the curious connection or analogy between honesty of art and honesty of feeling. It is equally true between the dishonesty of the one and of the other. In an unbiassed and intelligent attitude, no category of evidence in court is clearer than from the four corners of the document of symphony or opera. For thoroughly following out such a plan it might be well to embrace works of both kinds. It must follow that if we glow in tune with the high aspiration of a Beethoven, we must be ready to discern the trick of the false prophet. But in a work like the present the negative phase of criticism cannot be more than suggested.

It is just here that musical criticism has been lacking. It has followed an even tenor of so-called catholic tolerance of good and bad, of the false and the true. Again, it has lost all thought, it has taken no account whatever, of any element beyond the mere æsthetic. In fact, it is the moral that rouses the greatest enthusiasm, in art as well as in life. The charming, after all, gives mere temporary pleasure. It is precisely in so far as the moral element has been forgotten that music has not been highly regarded.

Thus, then, in the attitude of the intelligent point of view first insisted on, we see, from the second, how the intent, the feeling of the master is reflected from the particular work; and finally, from the third, how, from a broader view even than the second (rather from a succession of such impressions), the *morale* of the master shines clear throughout his art.

II

THE SYMPHONY

ART, it would seem, begins its career, like man, by leaning on another. Thus, sculpture was first subordinate to architecture. Painting, in turn, was the foster-child of sculpture, in the beginning merely tracing outlines and features, much like an infant writing with guided hand.

Music in Greece followed slavishly the metre of the poetry.* In the early church, before Gregory, the words of the liturgy were intoned with complete subservience to the rhythm of the verse, so that agreement of singing was possible only when the chorus followed the arbitrary leader.

It is most valuable to see clearly the final

---

* With all the "discoveries" of Pindaric odes, nothing has ever established the fact of a Greek conception of musical rhythm independent of that of the verse. Greek "music" lacked the first requisite for a tonal art.

23

evolution of the independent art of absolute instrumental music as the latest link in this chain. Leaning on the words and story of the drama, music developed, on the stage of the opera, melody, and its accompaniment in tones colored by various blending and contrasting instruments. She was preparing her pallet. In the church, following the lead of the service, music was exploring all the possibilities of polyphonic combination and of architectural complexity by algebraic computation. But in neither church service nor in opera was she progressing unaided. Of course, walking with a cane is different from depending on a guiding parent. So differs the music of Palæstrina from that of Ambrose. But even in the great Bach's works music had not thrown away all her supports. She first learned to tread her independent course, speaking her message purely in her own language of tones unaided by words, when she lisped the first sonata, which, in orchestral dress, is the symphony.

It must be remembered that the entire growth of the art of music, and what was really the slow manufacture of its elements and forms, was wrought within the Church.

This development began when to the unison chant was added the servile accompaniment of a second voice, keeping always its unaltered respectful distance. It ended when all the changes of fugal counterpoint had been rung with mathematical ingenuity. But until modern centuries there had not been a thought of music without words, of unsung music. When the absurdly artificial forms were abandoned by mutinous singers, the organ took the place of the unwilling voice, and invited further composition for its special performance.

But this had nothing in common with secular instrumental music and its origin. For the elements, we must go back to the strange attempts at opera by Italian amateurs. The very convenient date of the first opera— 1600—is an excellent landmark in gauging the growth of unsung secular music,—the year when Peri's "Eurydice" was produced in Florence. It is in the formless preludes and interludes of the players that the germ of the symphony lies. The first conception of flowing *cantabile* melody, which is the very fibre and tissue of every movement, came in the early opera. (There is absolutely no kinship between this *melody* and the fugal *theme* of the church school.) With these the dance, of obscure origin, completes the foundation on which sonatas and symphonies were reared.

If we enter the forge in which these materials were being welded into the great forms of the symphony,—in other words, if we study the precursors of the masters,—we find, indeed, little promise of intellectual significance, or, for that matter, of pleasurable amusement. But, in art, periods of exclusively formal growth always lack imaginative power. It is like latent heat, when ice changes to water. Great men, it would seem, are content with the form they find, hiding the lines with their fulness of thought. Shallower minds, sensitive to popular demand, tinker at new devices of outward novelty. Thus, Sebastian Bach did not find the sonata sufficiently perfected. Haydn was the first master to approve. Therefore, in a review of the history of musical thought rather than of musical structure, it may fairly be said that the sonata and the whole school of secular instrumental music did not begin before Haydn.

The analogy between Bach and the secular

masters is striking. In his earlier generation he found nothing but the strict forms of the church school. He gave them their essential artistic purpose ; he crowned their development by endowing them with the highest expression of religious feeling. When a master thus reaches the greatest height, a lower level must be started in another direction, leading to a second master.

If we take a survey of this new stream of worldly composition—melodies with artificial accompaniment, digressions of rippling scales or tripping arpeggios and suddenly intruding crashes of full chords—and contrast it with what is found in the church school with its precise, dignified, and elaborate structure of voices, independent in melody, yet interdependent in harmony, the question comes, What new spirit moves here? How can there be, almost at the same time, two opposite phases of the same art, both honored by the greatest masters?

Clearly, here is the latest, though not the weakest, wave of the Renaissance pulse. The same rebellion against the all-absorbing intellectual domination of the Church, the same resistless wave of earthly feeling and its expression, apparent in painting and in the literatures of England, France, and Italy, is here manifest in the youngest of the arts. Why the movement is so late in music need not be discussed beyond again saying that the art was jealously and exclusively fostered by the Church. All its forms, its whole framework had been devised solely for worship. An entirely new garb must be created before it could venture from the cloister into the gay world without great awkwardness and stiffness. Much depth of feeling or intellectual emphasis must not be expected of the first century of this new phase. The early works show their reactionary origin by utter frivolity and shallowness. Until an actual fitting form was obtained, there was a constant striving after a satisfaction of this very need, a self-conscious kind of emphasis of mere sound ; the composer sought to fill in as many black notes as possible.

The beginning of Haydn's career marks the final attainment of this form, and at the same time a sudden spring of true poetic feeling. The result was what is commonly called the sonata, which is really what we are considering; for a symphony is nothing else than a sonata written for the orchestra. In the light of the absolute newness of unsung music is seen the fitness of the name " sonata," that which is merely sounded, in contrast with that which is sung, the " cantata." Nowhere, I venture to say, in any phase of art, is the shock greater than of this burst from the sombre, confined, careful, intellectual process of the cloister to the free, irresponsible fancy dancing first over the meadows and in the forests, then into the life of men, the turmoil and the triumph of war, the romance and ecstasy of human affection.

It is clear, then, why the expected order— first of the less defined, second of the more clearly significant phase of the art—should be reversed. Within the cloister music had reached a high and complex power of expression of those feelings which were there sanctioned. Without, all was new and vague; there were no words or forms of expression for the new life. It must begin with the A B C of a new language. To condemn the first fruits of this stage for lack of definiteness of meaning would be to misunderstand the very purpose of all art. While definite language is not impossible to art, this is not its chief function; no more is mere beauty of outline. If a sentiment be expressed and transmitted, the medium of its transmission will be entitled to its place as an art of form. The language of prose has not the power thus to express and transmit all sentiment, though it may entitle its field in a rough sort of way. What prose cannot, the other arts must do, each in its peculiar region, not, perhaps, without encroaching mutually. Each art, beginning with primordial feelings, will translate more and more delicate shades in a constantly refining process, the form always reacting on the sentiment and suggesting an advance.

This must account for the vagueness of the earlier great works for instruments. But even in Haydn the pastoral element, the poetry of nature, discovered anew, is unmistakable, as is the peculiar playfulness of his humor. In fact, the appearance of humor of any kind in music in the eighteenth century is as absolutely new as anything can be under the sun. Imagine how utterly inconceivable it would have been to the long line, stretching through many centuries, of the worthy fosterers of music in the Church.

The sonata was said by a German critic to be intended by the earliest writers to show in the first movement what they could do, in the second what they could feel, in the last how glad they were to have finished. The simplicity of this interpretation—and no doubt it is accurate—emphasizes the vagueness of the real sentiment. In the hands of great men the form very soon attained a much more dignified plan.

In technicalities the essence is often lost. There is no value in analysis in itself. Yet a clear view of the general purpose is not dimmed by a glance at those elements which have in them more than mere technical value. The question is not merely what is the general purpose of the symphony, but what is the special value of the accepted model in carrying out this purpose. And, as has been said above, the first requisite in the listener is an intelligent grasp of the work.

In short, what is the essential of the much-mentioned sonata form; of the outline of the other movements; indeed, of the structure of the whole? A few relentless *wherefores* will bring us to the right point of attack. Nor can the answer lie in a technical statement of theme, of development, of tonality, and so on. But the one clear and grateful approach is by an historic view, where we see the need—the real *raison d'être*—of each cardinal element.

In the first place, the main stress of the symphony—indeed, of most absolute music—is centred on what is called the sonata form. It is the mould in which is cast the first movement: the serious burst of aspiring thought. The second, to be sure, is of no less dignity. But it is in complete contrast with the stress and strife, the stirring progress of the first. It is a calm lyric utterance from the high level to which the first mood has ascended. It does not need the discussion of the other. Simplicity of statement in the verses of a song is its natural utterance. Nowhere is the depth of genius of the highest master better shown than in the Andante,—that profound, broad sympathy of Beethoven, distinct from the statuesque pathos of Haydn, or the stately grace of Mozart. Here was reflected Beethoven's

32

highest trait, that which bound men to him most strongly. In the third phase the feeling of relaxation is undoubted, and, fittingly, the form, even in the highest flights, is based on the dance. The mood has passed from the spirit's stir and spring through pathos to humor. In its original conception this effect of relief, of restraint from the tension of the early movements, was continued in the last. A form peculiarly fitting for careless joy existed in the Rondo, where the melody appeared and vanished with graceful interludes, which later developed into lesser tunes. Discussion was supplanted by a constant, playful alternation of the various melodies. As the symphony grew a more serious utterance of poetic feeling, the last movement often rose to a second climax; and—here appears the meaning of form and of detail—the rondo yielded then to the Sonata type.

What, then, was this sonata form? What are the elements of its power for this new poetic expression?

Again, in the historic view, it is at once amusing, pathetic, and enlightening to see the struggles which preceded the great discovery. In Bach's time the approved form was the suite of dances, transplanted from the itinerant street-players to the new clavichord or newer piano-forte. At best this was a mere series of unrelated dances, idealized, to be sure, with expansion and polyphonic treatment. It was the holiday music of the learned musician, his only secular vent; and it afforded the special form for a kind of public tournament between rival players and composers. But, with the best intention to be worldly, there was over it the stern, ascetic, intellectual stamp of the Church spirit. What was the reaction of treatment which must answer the reaction of secular feeling?

The peculiar quality, as in the strict Church forms, was an unrelieved *monothemism*. Impressed with the traditional simple theme of counterpoint, men could not escape it; they lacked the artistic conception of the dual element, of balance, of contrast. The mystery, the strangeness, is that, not to speak of the eventual solution, the need itself was not clear. And unless we can see the very need, we cannot grasp the full meaning of the sonata and symphony.

SYMPHONIES AND THEIR MEANING

In a general way, it was felt, there must be
rebellion against the Church process,—no more
learned counterpoint; no textual theme frugally
sounded without harmonic surroundings, like
the verse of a sermon ; no eternal ringing of
its relentless burden, like the doom of dogma
without a hint of repose, of cadence,—on and
on, the voices ever multiplying the warning
phrase to a final massive climax of solemn
architecture. Away with it all! There must
be no taint of fugue in the new spirit. The
whole machinery of church forms seemed designed and fitted to an impersonal, a self-
effaced contemplation of high dogmatic truth
of the utmost solemnity. Here, out of the
Church, men dare to be happy and gay in their
individual joy ; they dare to celebrate the woods
and the green things of the earth. They want
a complete summer holiday from the damp air
of the Church.

Now see the features of this new expression
as they carry out this new feeling. There
must be a better and simpler meaning for our
technical big words. What seems the first,
the most significant, the most potent, is a clear
sense of harmonic residence, what the musicians

call tonality, as against the gray color, in the fugue, of a key vague until the end. Again, it seems, there is the impulse to utter a sense of worldly repose, in defiance of the constant strife in the fugue, which knew no rest until the final end.

Nowhere is this contrast clearer than in the piano works of Sebastian Bach and of Domenico Scarlatti. They were contemporaries, almost to the year. But Scarlatti had caught the earthly spirit in sunny Italy, under the inspiration of his father Alessandro, the founder of the new *aria*. Bach, somehow, could never get clear of the shadow of the cloister. With the German his dance-moods are still o'ercast with the pale hue of meditation. He was glancing out of doors through the windows of his study. The Italian was roving with a firm foot in the fields; he was ringing out his tintinnabulations with clearest note of tonal serenity and certainty,—still always the same one tune. He could have but a single idea at a time; no broad sense of balance, of contrast, of perspective. On such a basis there could never rise a structure of much serious dignity. But this is not all.

We must see, too, the strange alternative of the qualities of *Bach* and of *Scarlatti:* of vague reflection and of clear tonal simplicity. It seems that tonality must be at the expense of depth. The voices were borrowed for harmonic subservience, and must cease to discuss the theme. In a sense they were degraded from counsellors to train-bearers. So, in an ideal sense, there was a temporary loss of dignity. But this simplicity was after all a gain.

So far the elements are the same of the other secular moulds, of the song, the dance and the rondo. We have not yet come to the final typical trait of the strict sonata. It was a reconciliation of the various needs : first, of this tonality, the sense of certain harmonic location ; second, of relief from monotony of single melody, a sense of duality ; finally, of a quality which had been too completely lost with the fugue.

And this very stirring search has shown what a peculiar place the fugue filled. Let us return, for a thought, before the days of unsung music. Our art is still walking hand in hand with her older sister Poetry, but unmanageable, restless.

37

SYMPHONIES AND THEIR MEANING

One day a master dreams his melody for the instrument alone. Now it is clear that music must somehow atone for the new want of words. A song deprived of words is and remains incomplete. The clear meaning is gone, there is mere vacant beauty. Here begins the stir for a definite language of pure tones. And this is significant, too: none of the older forms were the achievement of music itself, its self-found utterance. They are foreign; they belonged to poetry, like the song, or to the dance, like the minuet. See, therefore, how this new *sonata* form is actually the first proper mode of expression of the pure art of music. *It says something in mere tones.*

From another point of view, the half-conscious want of the early masters in their search was this: they were dissatisfied with mere lyric burst, mere singing of the tune; *they must talk about it; they must get somewhere.* They quickly felt that melody was, after all, mere theme or text; there was no progress until you discussed it.

This element of discussion, of progress, which, in a sense, had been lost in the fugue, now achieved in a novel way, was the crowning

virtue of the new form for sonata and symphony. So here is the problem: to express
the definiteness which had been lost with the
words; to go beyond mere striking of the
melody; to start the pace for a genuine art,
which, beyond creating pretty phrases, will find
a language for ever deepening and ever differ-
entiating shades of feeling, approaching the
clearness of verbal thought. Finally, in the
structure of the whole work will lie the art-
form, which will build and co-ordinate in
supplementary moods one homogeneous expression of a great emotional idea.

How this special purpose of discussion was
carried out, the need being clear, will be easily
seen; further, too, how each element—of
tonality, of duality, of discussion—reinforced
the other.

The final achievement was this:

A melody begins with clear intonation of
the key, by harmonic sounding of the main
chord. It is succeeded presently by a second,
which is contrasted in every way,—in character,
in movement, and in key. Now see how duality
helps tonality. Black is black, after all, only
in contrast with white. So the original tonic

key is not really clear, until a departure into the complementary dominant, with the second melody. Thus the contrast, with well-marked cadence, sharpens the effect of each.

When the two melodies have been stated, there is, of course, a sojourn, a cadence, in the complementary key, the dominant. This in itself invites a return homeward to the original, or tonic. At the same time, the clearness of stated melodies is assured by a repetition from the beginning. And now the story really begins: the characters are described; now they act and talk; the several musical ideas are discussed, singly or together, to new surprises of climax and beauty; they take on the guise often of new melodies, or melodies of kindred beauty are suggested. Thus (not to bind ourselves beyond the hint of analogy) the themes pass from the mere phase of lyric utterance to that of epic narrative, not without strong dramatic power. Now must come the close; and see once more the interrelation of key and theme, of tonality and duality. The melodies reappear in the original order, but with change in key; for the second must close in the tonic. And, again, the balance is maintained;

for, while the earlier melody had the advantage of first appearance, the second has the last word in this, the principal tonal territory.*

And thus a symphony (which, etymologically, means a sounding together, using, as it did, all the resources of instrumental sound, and in Beethoven's Ninth even pressing voices into service) had, from the time of Mozart, the ambitious purpose of expressing a sort of modulation through three or four moods of one dominant feeling. I use the word "feeling" for lack of a better. In its highest phase, this purpose sometimes is a kind of poetic view of life, colored by what is at the time the individuality of the composer.

---

* The association of the first melody with the tonic key has in most sonata movements prevailed over the need of contrast of tonality. In these the final statement of melodies has the first in the tonic, followed by the second in the same key.

III

HAYDN

PERHAPS the distinguishing trait and charm of Haydn is a certain out-of-doors feeling after church or school, a dancing exuberance of childlike humor and hilarity, what the Germans call *Ausgelassenheit*. Haydn never lost this note. And we must mark that it was to express this feeling first and foremost that the symphony was invented. Later, to be sure, the symphony and fugue approached each other—were even blended—in spirit and in form.

This discovery has a double view,—one, that Haydn was the first to put a mood into the symphony: he was the first great secular tone-poet. In him feeling first mastered form, a feeling of pure joyousness; yet he could rise to a serious height of solemn devotion. There was not the subsequent note of defiance, of awful depth or sublimity. But Haydn had a serene profundity of his own, and, moreover, a true lyric beauty.

SYMPHONIES AND THEIR MEANING

The other view is the original simplicity of the purpose of the symphony, its note of reaction from stern complexities to a holiday mood. There is no breath of philosophy in the beginning,—mere childlike abandon. This finds naturally its symptoms and proof in the early form and treatment. And yet we should be farthest from the truth if we ascribed to Haydn a lack of mastery. The striking fact that the change was one of feeling, is clearest in the voluntary simplicity of the masters who could, at the proper hour, write the most profound counterpoint. Indeed, the tradition of the older school compelled a thorough training of the musician.

But the earliest bent of structural creation was in a horizontal direction, not vertical; was in melody and outline rather than in simultaneous polyphonic combinations. As soon as the form was achieved, the deepening process, in both senses, began with Haydn. In fact, Haydn in his long career (he wrote his first symphony before Mozart's birth, his greatest after the latter's death) shows very well the various phases of the whole movement.

In his later works the depth of treatment, united to light simplicity, is a most wonderful blending, a most delightful alternation of serious playfulness and playful seriousness. It is impossible to see how Haydn can fail to be perennial.

Aside from his undoubted absolute value, Haydn's importance is in some degree historic in his position as the pioneer in the expression in great art-works of purely secular feeling. A clear outward sign of this is his creation of the modern orchestra. It is not unjust to say that the orchestra, with predominance of strings, was the original conception of Haydn.

With Bach the orchestra belonged to the spirit of the Church, of frugal Protestant piety; with Handel it was devoted to the dramatic celebration of biblical themes, or, as in Gluck, of mythological heroes. With all it was stiff, undeveloped, and harsh, under the shrill domination of the classic pipe and reed. With Haydn, as the strings uttered the soft hum of woods and meadows, it was a joyous, exultant praise of nature. And see the significance of the titles of Haydn's oratorios, the " Creation,"

the " Seasons ;" contrast them with earlier subjects.

But with all this relative position, there is
no question of Haydn's absolute value. His
adagios may have a mock-heroic, a pseudo-
pathetic air ; but his andantes are true lyric
feeling.

With Haydn the symphony began as *salon*
amusement, and soon reached the height of
poetic expression of exuberant joyousness, of
playful humor, and of a certain idyllic, lyric
utterance. With Mozart it deepened in intensity and broadened in scope. Losing the limitations of *bourgeois* humor and joy, it took a
more cosmic view. We shall see later a great
step over both masters. In Haydn and Mozart
music still had strongly the entertaining attitude ; it was there principally to give pleasure.
There was no suggestion of prophecy, of warning, of defiant proclamation of truth in general,
or of any definite truth in particular. Music
did not, as yet, in Beethoven's words, " strike fire
from the soul of man." Haydn's holiday spirit,
complete in contrast with the Church school,
was limited in comparison with his successors.
In Mozart a classic depth and balance was

gained. Boyish exuberance yielded to maturer serenity. Depth of pathos was first explored. Haydn's was the song of the child; Mozart's of the youth; Beethoven's of the man. When, in Beethoven, feeling controls the form, the advance in poetic expression of passion seems as great as Haydn's original step.

Symphony in D.

(Peters Edition, No. 3.)

Haydn must always begin with the grave *Adagio*, which is as solemn as it is short. Often it seems hardly meant seriously. One cannot help thinking of the king of France and twenty thousand men. All this majestic striking of attitudes, to run off, after a few bars, into the sprightliest of *Presto* themes:

Presto. STRINGS.

The bass, as commonly doubled below.

46

reversed later, as countertheme:

The ascending melody in thirds.

All fits so perfectly that every one is unconsciously dancing alone, yet in perfect agreement
with the rest. Everything is so simple,—the
theme, the rhythm, the most obvious modulations, that one cannot see the secret of the
eternal freshness. In the most natural way, a
new melody and rhythm is made from the

47

countertheme by merely shifting the accent, using question for answer.

The second melody brings no great change of feeling:

STRINGS.

No one has succeeded, like Haydn, in being childlike, and, withal, fundamental; joyful, hilarious even, yet cosmic; light and simple, with pervading complexity.

After statement and repetition of melodies, the *Presto* continues, according to tradition, to discourse on the second theme. Here we may expect the highest polyphony, or contrapuntal discussion between the voices; and we are not disappointed. As in string quartet, the violins each have their say on the text of the melody, —now successively, now by alternate interruption, or, again, in dual agreement. Later the fagots put in their word, then all the woodwind; finally the brass and all join in the jolly countertheme, with much irresponsible

With higher octaves.........

Strings doubled below. Harmony in higher wind.

merriment in related phrases. The re-entrance of melodies in original order begins in the accustomed way, but suddenly turns, against all rule, into the developing episode of the second subject, and ends, naturally though irregularly, with final singing of the principal theme. The whole movement shows how the masters who first moulded the forms of the symphony, were, in a way, least bound by its shackles,—had the most perfect freedom of utterance.

The *Andante* is German folk-song of the purest and simplest. It seems that the most natural intervals and harmonies are the proper utterance of the Germans; all other "folk" must take up with the strange and eccentric. The nearer they are akin to the Germans, the more they share in the rights of the tonic and dominant. Like many of Haydn's slow movements, this is largely a variation of one melody,

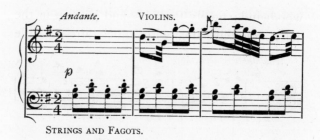

STRINGS AND FAGOTS.

with but a single foreign episode,—the *Minore*.
The latter, in its fragmental phrases, its pompous and eccentric stride of principal and lesser
figures, in the general clatter and noise, seems
intended mainly to give relief to the simplicity
of the principal melody,—perhaps to add a
tinge of dignity.

Haydn's scherzos always have a strong "out
of school" feeling,—this one especially; only
it is a short recess. The themes of the two
middle movements are plainly discernible at

first hearing.   But mark, after the first burst of
the whole orchestra :

the playfulness of the answer, whispered by
strings and flutes :

and the comic mocking of basses and trebles
in the first cadence.   The Trio in its first eight
bars has always been somewhat of a mystery :
why Haydn should have used what seems the
most modern of bizarre effects,—a continuous
sounding of the tonic chord in the strings,
with a melody in the flutes, which almost
craves a momentary glimpse of the dominant.

Haydn probably wanted a touch of the hurdy-
gurdy. It must be well marked that the second
time he clearly yields to the demands of the
dominant, though still keeping a tonic pedal-
point. The development of the Trio is much
more important than of the Scherzo, discoursing on a more suggestive theme, a phrase from
the Trio melody:

It is full of a humor and spirit of its own.

Strange to say, the Finale (marked *Vivace*) is
quite the most serious phase of the symphony.
Recess is quite over; we are back in school—
not to say church. For the violins, like a well
trained choir, are striking up a melody that
sounds much like a good old chorale:

FINALE. *Vivace.*

Simply stated, without a note of extended cadence, it is strictly repeated as if to make sure we know it. It is like the preacher who states his text with all serious unction, and repeats it, to give warning of the great sermon which is to follow. We are sure it is a rondo, mainly because it is not sonata-form; the cardinal theme, in its constant rounds, never lets us forget the text of the sermon. After some playing of themal phrases, there comes one of those dynamic passages, where all join to make a noise, and finally drop exhausted into a cadence; whereupon the strings, with a little help from the wood, gently toss about snatches of the melody, and the rest pitch in again in general turbulence. At last the strings rehearse the theme in really serious manner, with but slight *obligato* variation. The rest, too, join properly and respectfully in singing the hymn in its original harmonies. Soon comes another of those terrible phases, another *Minore*, where Papa Haydn tries so hard to look very fierce, without anything special to say; merely general muttering, with the same old faces. We all know it is only to break the more pleasantly into his own benignant smile.

Here is the fugue, which we knew was coming from the emphatic way the theme was first enounced. With such a theme it could not be resisted. It begins in the first violins, with the seconds tripping in *obligato* behind, before, and all around, until they finally take up the theme, and the violas " hold the candle." Best of all is when the cellos come in and the rest all play about. Of course, the violas have their turn, too. Finally, the wood make a trial at the theme, while the violins go on without attending to their ineffective attempts, and finally run away from them on a side path. At last the whole orchestra joins in the fugue with all possible magnificence and solemnity, until the last verse, which is sung once more as at first.

SYMPHONIES AND THEIR MEANING

Symphony in E♭.

(Peters Edition, No. 1.)

Here, again, is Haydn's beginning *Adagio*,—very beautiful; yet somehow it seems a mere " attention," or the formal prayer on entering church; or it is like the child's game, where

serious pretence but leads to frivolous surprise. Perhaps it does give a certain serious tone to the whole. But pathos was never Haydn's strong point. So he is glad to give way to the merry dance of the *Allegro*, like a monk's disguise thrown off by the dancer. Of course, our symphony has not quite emerged from the frivolous stage.

The melody is at once delightful in itself, and promising for " talking about " later on:

all in Haydn's favorite strings, while the woodwind merely answer in a noisy acclaim in a
rather unimportant way, with loud calls and
echoes,—very playfully, too, as when oboes,
fagots, and strings softly sound the theme,
and then all answer in frightening chorus:

There is a queer bustling figure which looks
as though we had heard it before:

56

Bass doubled below.

but we are sure we have not.

At last, a dancing melody comes along in not too foreign a key, quite as a merry afterthought, and sets the whole orchestra dancing with it:

And now, after repeated statement of both melodies, begins Haydn's typical phase of architectural lightness. Complexity usually suggests seriousness. But with Haydn it is the mood of old madrigals, of general merry-making. Yet the depth of treatment, when analyzed, is greater than of fugues; only it is spontaneous, and therefore the more perfect. There is a delicious conflict of rhythm; and so profound is the architecture that we must abandon minute perception. We can merely enjoy the general daze of varied harmony and structure.

Again enters the curiously familiar strain which we cannot place; more of playful and sometimes solemn repartee of higher and lower strings on the main theme; introducing, again, with delicious surprise, the dance of the second melody in a new light, while the woodwind are pertly talking back.

Then in orthodox simplicity the melodies enter in the original order, until—something strange happens. Out of a noisy tumult, closing in hushed cadence, the monkish figure reappears; the first melody is sung again. And now we see the secret of the strange

58

melody ; for, following immediately upon the former, it proves to be nothing but its mocking echo in very quick rhythm. The likeness between monk and dancer does not appear until the strain is rung in the successive variations, *penseroso* and *allegro*. On the whole, it does seem that Haydn, though he is charged here with serious intent, has again sacrificed all to his mood of friendly humor half unconsciously, like an amiable person turning off a severe word with a pleasantry.

But the *Andante* is, for Haydn, unusually solemn. The playing by strings, however, restores the typical quality. There is some of the stateliness that Papa Haydn would almost deliberately assume : " Now we must be very serious."

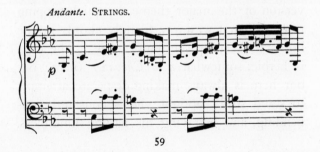

Andante. STRINGS.

But it has the fine, strong diatonic simplicity which marks all great music; and this appears especially in the major guise, later on.

It is all a series of variations on this melody. The first, in the major, has much of that German simplicity of intimate sentiment. In the

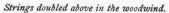

Strings doubled above in the woodwind.

second, there is a curious dramatic effect of the original minor, by a simple addition of a melody in the oboe. The third is a jolly version of the major theme, in quick-tripping runs, with a few warm, friendly chords in the horns, to keep up the temperature. The next is heroic, somewhat *a la Chevalier Gluck;* but our hero is always making desperate attempts to stand stiffly upright; he is constantly unbending, and betraying his natural kindliness.

But he is doing his best to look ferocious, and the next minute he is apologizing all the more sweetly. Now the major alternative has a special pastoral feeling, with the melody in the oboes, and counterphrases in the flutes, which later join the main song.

The end is impressive. First the voices steal in one by one, making, unconscious one of the other, a harmony of four melodies. Then they spruce up, and all march in best uniform, in full pride of their combined magnificence, not without an occasional lapse into quaint naturalness of feeling.

Here, in the third movement, is the ideal minuet feeling; the dear, old-fashioned stateliness and formality; the pretty, prim quaintness, with naïve reiterations of the last phrase, high and low:

Menuetto. Tutti (the melody an octave above in the flutes).

But presently it breaks into a treatment much too broad for the old minuet, where the voices, instead of strumming stiffly in rhythmic accompaniment, answer back with the theme in their own independent way.

The Trio seems a flight from the restraint of the rigid dance. In a gracefully free melody, indeterminate in tune and rhythm:

the strings enter in turn, on their own sweet
will. It is a little interlude in the dance; a
quiet *tête-à-tête*; at the end formalities and attitudes are again assumed.

In the *Finale*, one of the broadest of Haydn's
rondos, there is from the beginning a fine
duality. From the first phrase there is the
stamp of highest mastery. Every voice comes
in with something important to say, not a mere
polite accompaniment of " Yes, yes," " So say
we all." So there is from the start a profundity
which almost makes us fear what the climax
must be. At the outset there are two distinct
melodies,—one a fundamental motto in the
horns, the other a gay, careless phrase in the
strings :

CLARIONET.

Then, while these are ringing in our ears, a third adds to the sweet bewilderment. But before the third appears, the various strings enter in "Three Blind Mice" fashion, each without waiting for the other to finish, and, what is more wonderful, they sing the answer in the same way.

Ever and again, in the true rondo spirit, the friendly motto comes, in highest simplicity. There is a big, ponderous episode, where the motto, sounded loud, does not stop in strict conclusion, but, like a philosophic proposition, deduces itself at length. The whole is like dogma solemnly proclaimed on church organ (in the bass the second melody is marching), where over all lesser interests the great truth shines and dims the others :

Higher wood and strings doubled below in the brass.

Cellos, violas, and fagots doubled above in clarionets.

Basses added.

But with Haydn this mood never lasts long; the earthly, human quickly breaks through.

To the duet of motto and melody is added a smooth-running *obligato* in strings. Presently, after a noisy close of the whole orchestra, comes what seems the gem of the whole. In simple monomelodic statement it seems entirely new, sonorously sung by the cellos, while the upper strings strike the chord:

5

There is a complete lyric contrast with the former dramatic polyphony. The cellos are answered by flutes, and then, again replying, soar into one of those romantic modulations which we thought were of a later master. It foreshadows clearly the poetry of Schubert's Unfinished.

Then through a noisy chorus of lesser importance by a quiet cadence, like an informal conversation, we come back to the original duet of motto and melody. But here is still more bewildering architecture, — more and more massive, overpowering, until suddenly reappears the single romantic figure in a new color of light. At the end of the phrase, however, there is something new,—the round bassoon quietly chimes a note of assent, almost too unimportant to mention; but, after all, there are two instead of one. Again the Schubert modulation, that makes us think of *Erl-king* and *Death and the Maiden*. A loud acclaim brings us to our original key and beginning; again the delicious duality. But in this, the real return to the first part, everything is reinforced; all the reserves are called out; so that the first seemed but preliminary to this magnificence and to the enchanting confusion. Once more the Schubert melody. And see the number of mere strumming beats we must wait for the melody,—just so many. We must have good patience, and be ready at the exact time; otherwise we are out of tune,—a fine example of the musician, the unconscious arithmetician. Twelve meaningless strums, and then the melody, divinely ordained to come just at this moment. Now there is more beautiful duo singing in friendly quarrel.

At the end, like a blessing, the motto is broadly sounded by all the wind but the flutes, as if they really meant it as final conclusion, while the strings are loyal to their wordly counter-tune.

IV

MOZART

Until to-day, Mozart's greatness has been unquestioned. It devolves upon our generation to uphold him against voices that with faint praise or slurring epithet are seeking to relegate him to a mere historic shelf.

Mozart suggests the question which constantly arises in Art between perfect form or beauty of outline, and intensity of emotional content. Where must the stress be? Is he the greater master who charms with external beauty and cunning skill in detail,—to whom a harsh note is impossible? Or is it the poet who recklessly breaks the fetters of form, ruthlessly violates sacred canons; who shocks our ears with discord, and yet fills us with the sense of meaning, a vital feeling which impels to resolution and action. The question is perhaps not of the kind that can be answered directly. It is to some extent a matter of temperament. We can conceive of great poets of both kinds.

SYMPHONIES AND THEIR MEANING

It is the fashion of a Romantic age to decry
the Classic. The same question arises between
Schumann and Mendelssohn, between Tennyson and Browning. Nor must it be solved.
Rather is it important not to rush impetuously
to a conclusion which unjustly excludes. Yet
it bears on the question of the ultimate purpose
of Art, and it may be well to take some side
here. From Aristotle to a very recent time it
has been thought that beauty was the one aim
of Art, its creation the only function. This
was more natural in an age that knew chiefly
the plastic arts of sculpture and architecture.
There lies the reason why the transgressions of
a Beethoven were so bitterly resented. If he
was not beautiful, he was nothing. Through
Beethoven, mainly, it has become clear that
beauty is merely the means; that the chief end
of Art is the communication of feeling through
the medium of works of beauty; that beauty is
indispensable as test of true feeling; that high
thought compels a noble utterance. But the
feeling is, after all, the main end; for its expression there may be a temporary *hiatus*, a
violation of æsthetic sense, in order to deepen,
by contrast, the final effect. The element

of sequence, of musical sense, has arisen as paramount, if not supreme. It is clear how the same passage may be beautiful in one connection, impossible in another. Everything lies in the idea, the intent; nothing in the absolute independent beauty of separate sounds.

But, it must always be remembered, violation may never be in ignorance of rule,—only by the master who, knowing its reason and spirit, has a higher purpose in his conscious transgression of the letter.

It is certainly unquestionable that mere cunning of workmanship can never, in itself, be assurance of highest art. In so far as this is commonly the basis of Mozart's supremacy as master, we must withhold our homage. But, in reality, there is a better reason. Mozart does not stand simply for graceful perfection of detail and outline; there is expressed in his works the spirit which gives life to all this beauty, including with the humor of a Haydn something of the cosmic scope of a Shakespeare, to whom he is often likened. His very completeness of form is typical and expressive of the breadth of his sympathy. In Bach the broadest view of the religious spirit finds utterance in the highest development of the Church style, strongest in resistance to poetic emotion. Mozart crowns the secular outburst, deepening its pathos, idealizing its humor, adding a serious, heroic note which Beethoven afterwards expanded. The symphony passed in these masters from the stage of amusement to poetic expression and the utterance of a stern message.

We remember the note of simplicity of Haydn, in natural reaction from the complexity of the Church school. It is very important to see that this in no wise suggests a lack of learning; on the contrary, that it was a purely voluntary choice of a means of expression. Simplicity was necessary to express the new secular feeling, and, furthermore, a primitive clearness was needed to convey in absolute music—the *sonata*—what had before depended upon words,—in the *cantata*. And, then, the achievement of a new form, proper to instrumental music, involved a stress on horizontal structure, at the expense of the vertical, of counterpoint.

Soon these temporal needs were filled. The

melody or *aria* was attained, with full swing
and clear tonality; and, likewise, the basis of
a form of wonderful fitness for the exposition
and discussion of melodic thoughts. Now
the note of simplicity had been rung enough.
Even in Haydn we have seen a new profundity which somehow does not mar his childlike
lightness. But Mozart had an altogether
broader view and a profounder sense. He
reflects in music the cosmic breadth and the
mystic depth of his great contemporary, the
poet Goethe, and of the best German thought
of his time.

In Mozart the special prominence of any
typical feeling is less striking than in Haydn.
Therefore his music seems less characteristic.
But this comes not so much from a lack of
intensity as from greater breadth,—an equal
intensity in various moods.

Symphony in G Minor.
(Breitkopf and Haertel, No. 40.)

Is there anywhere more poetry or art, or
more of the blending of both, than in this
work of Mozart's? It is always a recurring
question whether Mozart's symphonies are not

the greatest, partly because of their very simplicity, of their childlike innocence of a burden of meaning,—because of their pure beauty and formal perfection. It does seem that in this respect, of pure beauty, the G Minor is the highest of all; and beauty is, after all, paramount in the purpose of art, even in these latter days. There is a fine Hellenic lack of strife and strain, a high serenity.

It is observable that Mozart's limitations do not appear in themselves, but only in negative comparison with other masters; and yet in this very comparison some of the highest traits appear. The true symphonic mastery is hardest to describe. It may break upon us during the course of this book. But whatever it is, Mozart certainly possessed it in a peculiar degree. His was the time when pure beauty, unalloyed with pale thought or dim meaning or grim woe, was filling men's minds. Schubert's Unfinished Symphony falls within this period.

But the special type of this phase is Mozart's G Minor, which begins with the entrancing melody, like a dashing brook in early spring, with the delicacy of gentlest rain:

Allegro molto. STRINGS. *With lower octaves.*

There is no lack of the foil of strong melodic contrast. But the motion and sequence of the whole is so subtly perfect that we cannot stop to label the themes. Immediately after the first comes a transitional theme:

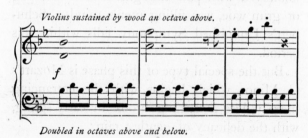

Violins sustained by wood an octave above.

Doubled in octaves above and below.

74

that is really more important than the regular
second, because it lends the quality of stiff-
ening lime. It is curiously noteworthy that
neither of the secondary themes has any part
in the discussion after the repeat of subjects,
which is entirely on the text of the principal
melody. It is what might be called a live
counterpoint, where the bass is as individual
as the soprano, a real discussion, a very logical exchange of retorts and repartees. Here
we are nearer the secret of true symphonic
mastery, when, after the melodies have made
their rounds and courtesies, the best is yet to
come.

Your lyricist, who expends himself upon his
melodies, worries through the period of treatment, the *Durchfuehrung*, as best he can. The
master feels the real purpose of themes : for

discussion. Mozart's development in the beginning *Allegro* of the G Minor is not, as in the
Jupiter, peculiarly contrapuntal or architectural,
but is typically a discussion. It is strange what
a dogmatic, pugnacious quality appears in so
graceful a theme by this alternative assertion
between violins and bassos. Its peculiar beauty
seems better fitted for the lighter retorts, best
of all for the simple, unchallenged song, after
all strife is over.

The *Andante* is in Mozart's most serious
mood. Surely any musician, hearing it for the
first time uninformed, would say Beethoven,
which again proves Mozart's versatility and
surprising depth. After all, it seems often
that Beethoven in his profoundest feeling is
grounded directly upon Mozart. We cannot
shelve Mozart as yet. He must go down
with the nineteenth century on the first line of
classics. As the Finale of this symphony is
prototype of Beethoven's Scherzo in the Fifth,
so this Andante strikes the serious note of the
slow movement of the same Beethoven symphony. And the Finale of the Jupiter has its
like nowhere save, perhaps, in Brahms.

SYMPHONIES AND THEIR MEANING

See how subtly the melody steals in, almost beyond exact quotation. It lies somewhere between the violin-voices, as they quietly enter in canon order, and the basses, in the graceful, mysterious curve of their ascent:

Andante. [IN STRINGS AND HORNS.]

But in all there is something of the prophetic sternness which we think of in Beethoven as against Mozart. To be sure, it is instantly relieved in the lighter answer:

but it is renewed with an added *ripieno* voice in the high violins over the recurring first melody.

The second melody has a tripping phrase in its constant wake,

which, later, added to the first, increases the solemn complexity. It is, after all, more than mere fine art,—a broad, deep, poetic thought. Or, rather, does not, in fact, art best express the real profundity?

After the clangor of discussion, the main melody steals in with even greater solemnity. It grows ever more complex, more human, more big with meaning, significant in its many voices, its many phrases, all singing to the same end.

It seems almost greatest of all *Andantes*—certainly of Mozart's—in point of depth and mastery. There, as in the last movement of the Jupiter symphony, is seen how by high and profound art you approach, *ipso facto*, nearer to clear meaning,—at least, to a clear definition of the feeling. We can understand Mendelssohn's remark that music is a more exact language than prose or poetry. This must, of course, depend upon some such premises as: that the highest and best of man's thought has in it more of feeling than of dogma; that in proportion as it is more precious it is less capable of statement in set terms. As part of this musical language of feeling, *counterpoint*, such as this of Mozart's, *is like a variety of symbols or illustrations of the same idea; but they are peculiarly reinforcing, as they are simultaneous, and harmonious in the beauty of their union.*

It seems as if Mozart must have lived in

these six weeks, in which he wrote his three greatest works, as never before or after. Are we curious what his thoughts were? The true answer is here, in the symphonies themselves, —far better than any verbal account that even he himself could give. And this only leads us back to the discussion we thought we had just taken leave of.

With all the bright humor of the *Menuetto*, what a masterful ring! A kind of Titans' dance, perfect in its easy, heavy, strange

MENUETTO. *Allegro.*

For strings, wood, and horns, with fuller harmony.

rhythm,—lacking grace only if lightness be necessary.

And then at last—in the Trio—the purely

TRIO. STRINGS.

human, all tenderness, delicacy, especially in the dainty ending:

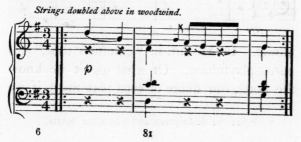

Strings doubled above in woodwind.

The coincidence has often been mentioned between the theme of this Finale and that of Beethoven's Scherzo in the Fifth Symphony.* It is, to be sure, exact in the first eight notes, disregarding the rhythm. But here is our opportunity. With all the literal similarity there is an absolute unlikeness in essence. This shows many things, and, first, the wrongness of our literal way of looking at music, as if a man could have a monopoly or patent on a succession of notes merely because he was first to light upon them. It shows, too, how the essence of music is different from the common belief: how it is purely one of mood and feeling. The Beethoven theme, with the grim irony of the dance-step (to quote, for the nonce, in another key), is in austerest, sardonic

humor. In Mozart, in "common time," it is purest playfulness. Of what use, if we know the notes, can quote or even play them, if we

---

* See the description and quotation below.

FINALE. *Allegro assai.*

STRINGS.

f Tutti, with harmony in higher wind.

lack the perception of feeling which makes
identical themes really antipodal. With Mozart,
it is all a jolly, wild revel of childlike joy, well
earned after the profound, serious absorption of
the earlier symphony. After the depths of
the *Weltschmerz*, after big thoughts of a universe, it is good to be dancing, like pure children. So the second melody is in simplest
Haydn humor.

STRINGS.

p   *mfp*

Was there ever anything so brilliant as the
development. Pompous, eccentric striding

about, as if terrible things were impending, and then—the most impish dancing under the very noses of the same figures that looked so solemn. But soon the imps get in a wild maze of dance. We are dizzy looking at them; we can no longer follow the leader. Each seems independent of all the rest, yet they never even jostle. Somehow, they all make a perfect picture; they seem to dance as a curious, complex whole, a simulation of wild disorder. Gradually they simmer down to a lull. It all ends in the joyous simplicity of the beginning.

The G Minor does seem the greatest of all symphonies—when we hear it. But, then, it is really the test of a symphony that you prefer it to all others when you hear it, and this must be an excuse for a subjective treatment. There is a right and wrong, a false and true in art, but there is no necessary gradation in rank of the masterpieces.

The "Jupiter" Symphony, in C Major.

(No. 41 of Breitkopf and Haertel.)

Were Mozart and Haydn as conscious of the high dignity and capacity of the symphony as Beethoven? They worked towards it, but they were, in a sense, still in the formative period. But this was, again, their strength, both in point of unconsciousness and of formal beauty.

The contrast is very complete from the G Minor. We miss the fine depth of sentiment. But instead there is a certain intellectual breadth, profundity, and vigor. In nothing is the contrast sharper than in the general plan. We have seen the early climax of the G Minor, and the gentle descent in the Finale. In the Jupiter the first three movements seem mere prelude of the last.

The first, *Allegro Vivace*, begins with an electric burst of the whole orchestra in a sparkling phrase, which with its inversions seems to unite the whole symphony in a common conception.

Allegro vivace.
Tutti.

f Doubled in upper and three lower octaves.

There is no defined melody. It is all like a broad *fanfare*, to show the breadth of scope and the intellectual pitch of the whole. There is a constant tendency to short, terse legends in tone. Not until the keen air of the original key is forsaken is there a lapse into gently swinging melodies, of which the second, in particular, is a grateful gliding into a more placid, a more human, perhaps a more frivolous mood.

STRINGS (the melody in octaves).

But the development begins in light humor, with charming counterpoint. And this shows an innocence of anything profounder than a vague cheeriness. Neither the first nor second movement has the profound feeling of the G Minor. But the whole symphony deepens as it proceeds. And so in the Andante, as the first theme is rather formal and stately in

its mood, the second is fairly steeped in senti‑ ment:

SYMPHONIES AND THEIR MEANING

There begins the real song,—the poetry of
the story; and from this point the treatment
of the first theme is richer and fuller.

The *Menuetto*, with all its charm of lightness
and dainty swing, cannot compare with that of
the G Minor in vigor or depth. It is a pure
dance, while the other was more than was bar-
gained for.

But in the *Finale*, the reverse of the G Minor,
there is the most thrilling architecture, all out
of a theme of four notes, united, augmented,

FINALE. *Allegro molto.*
STRINGS.

diminished. The vagueness of the first movement is justified; the whole is with a broadly
poetic conception, which is really much more
Greek than Gothic. There is *Jupiter Tonans.*
The view is always Olympian and manifold,
taking on a great cosmic complexity. In the
wake of the main subject come other phrases.
One in the bass recalls the beginning of the
whole work:

Woodwind with octave below and above.

Violins with upper octave.

Cellos, with violas above and basses above.

After a full cadence rings out what has been called the " hammer theme,"—might be called the " thunderer :"

In strings and wood, doubled in octave below.

carried on in two voices, one a third above the other.

At the end of this rumbling energy in the forge of the gods comes a fugal fabric in five separate voices from the strings on the motto, sung in quiet fancy, each entering voice shutting off the last word of its forerunner, thus :

so all the violins come in, from first to basso.
Then echoes the blast of the full orchestra,
with the theme above and the hammer phrase
below. Then a new counter-figure of importance is developed:

also entering fugally.

Then comes the sudden change to the gentle
second melody, still in the violins. But, see,

it is of the same flesh and bone with the first, a stolen rib. Around its disguised entrance the former phrases are constantly hovering.

Presently there is a compact forceful passage in the (inverted) second theme, without a moment's loss of melodic swing, without a suspicion of the lamp; on the contrary, with constantly added strength and vigor, and a peculiar sense of economy and mathematical perfection, so that we cannot but recall the " unconscious arithmetician." Now follows the most royal counterpoint, the sparks flying from the shock of discord, all with surest touch and perfect harmony.

The development (*Durchfuehrung*) begins more reflectively. But the counterpoint is so dazzling, so overwhelming, that only by intense expectancy, looking again and again, the sunlight is too bright, you can discern the components, shading the eyes and standing farther back. But perhaps the general dazzle is the real intent, rather than spelling out each theme. A wonderful work, with the stunning alternative of hammer themes in contrary motion, and a subtle insinuation of the motto! At last the motto appears boldly in its original guise in the basses, with enchanting, Schubert-like modulation from mystery to certainty.

At the end, after a *reprise* in the respective keys, there is the most marvellous episode of all. The motto, inversion, and diminution in one, and the other two themes, all in perfect harmony, are enough to give Bach a headache. There is an unquenchable thirst for new statements, new guises. The conception is of the boldest intellectual span. It stamps Mozart's as one of the most broadly constructive minds the world has possessed. It is indeed the *ne plus ultra* of Art.

V

BEETHOVEN

Two great traits stand out as we view the advance over the masters we have been considering, by the one who stands at the height of secular expression, if not of all.

To use technical words seems like travelling in a circle; for they must always be explained. Yet there is a certain indispensable rough convenience about them. *Development*, then, is, after all, that which gives life and reality to music, as to all human thought. It seems sometimes as if any one could make a tune by thinking hard enough or long enough. Then, melody may be reminiscent; it is always partly so. But if you can talk with sequence and coherence, you are a master of the magic language; it is, then, all your own. Bother the theme,—you can say something logically, deductively, consecutively.

This Beethoven carried to an undreamt power; Schumann developed it later wonderfully in certain narrower lines. Sometimes it seems as if, by comparison, Haydn and Mozart tied the melodic sections together; or used the devices of counterpoint, however masterfully, for their own sake; or, at least, while they wrote with sequence, they did so with a certain consciousness, with more emphasis on utterance than on content. In Beethoven, for the first time, everything becomes subordinate to the expression of a great, continuous, homogeneous thought or feeling. Still, in all justice, certain fundamental differences of the masters must be reckoned with. Mozart liked perfection of form in itself; he had a keener sense than Beethoven for the beauty of the utterance. He did not, therefore, like Beethoven, rebel against form for the sake of rebelling. There may possibly be a tendency to consider each succeeding master too distinctly as overshadowing those before him. Mozart and Beethoven were diametrically opposite in temperament, and the former is not merely a stepping-stone to the latter. In certain moods, Mozart reaches an expression than which a more perfect cannot be imagined. But in reality and force of passion, Beethoven undoubtedly far surpassed him.

SYMPHONIES AND THEIR MEANING

The first trait seems to lead immediately to the second, though at first glance they do not seem so closely akin. In other words, it is *Meaning* which now becomes more important than *Beauty* in itself. Beethoven first became less conscious of the dignity of detail than of the general plan or mood-purpose. In Beethoven we first see the gray hue of a distinct significance; or, better, perhaps, of a defined kind of feeling, instead of the vague prattling of Haydn and Mozart. The latter were content to be in an irresponsible, joyous state, or else they had the tears ready. They accepted their fate, their surroundings, their institutions unmurmuringly. They remained little above menials in the houses of the nobility. They were content, like good children, to be happy out of doors, in the woods and meadows; to go to the established church and sing its service; to obey the authorities,—glad to be allowed their wages, to please their patrons. They were in the Grubb Street stage of music. To be sure, at times there were, in the younger, moments of solemn wandering, even of bold revel. But this, too, was in the established order.

SYMPHONIES AND THEIR MEANING

Now comes a man, a counter-figure, only nobler, of that other man of the time across the Rhine, whom the former celebrated in a symphony. But in their high loyalty to his ideals, the works of Beethoven, as compared with the degeneration of Napoleon, show something of the nobility of art as compared with statesmanship.

Beethoven was *first* a thinking man. He took seriously himself, his surroundings, and institutions, social and political. In deed and fact he was true to the ideal of his thought. He recognized the real mission of art—but slowly dawning upon us—to utter the highest, profoundest emotions only *by means* of beauty of expression. He dethroned Beauty and set up Feeling. Thus for himself and for art he achieved the energy, the power, which rouses to action, does not lull to sleep.

His personal behavior betrayed his temper, not innocent of rudeness, when he completely reversed the accustomed relations of the nobility and the artist. Politically, he was in strongest sympathy with the struggles in France for individual freedom, for the principles on which stand our American republic and national life. This was the prompting motive of the *Eroica* Symphony. Napoleon then was the champion of Justice, Equality, Democracy, Common Sense, even of Universal Brotherhood. What Schiller dreamed in his " *Freude*," here was thought a heavenly reality. Thus Beethoven found in the opposite sphere of action the echoing voice to his half-conscious mutterings and rebellion against the tawdry and tyrannous feudal system, under which the European continent languished. In the Fifth Symphony is, perhaps, most distinctly the utterance of this spirit; though, wherever Beethoven boldly and knowingly breaks the fetters of form, he shows by unconscious analogy the quality of his democratic, iconoclastic temper.

Before proceeding to the symphonies themselves, it is necessary to touch on the true limits of meaning in music. We are apt today to become supercilious about " programme music." Its nobility lies in the fact that the inner content rises superior to the outward beauty. But the question is as to this meaning. As it was once thought translatable into human prose, the language of commonplace, useless for permanent things, and as it was found wanting, the reaction was natural to the modern theory of an Hanslick: that music is a mere whimsical combination of tonal figures without inner content or significance.

The meaning is certainly there, and it is the true kernel; but it is an emotional, not an intellectual meaning,—the kind that is the essence of poetry, religion, and all good things in the world,—the personal element which makes affection. And no other form of utterance is so powerful for its expression as is music. In reality, it seems to exist least where there is most intellectual meaning, as in a treatise, perfect in logic.

But the danger of seeking an exact meaning in music is great. Of the two errors, the negative attitude is infinitely the safer; it at least brings no ridicule upon the art. As we have said before, the true essence of music is its unconscious subjective betrayal of a dominating emotion, in contrast with the conscious, objective depiction in poetry and in the plastic arts. And it is in this unconsciousness that lies its overwhelming strength.

Symphony No. 3, in E♭ (Eroica).

Much has been said by critics to reconcile Beethoven's inscription "to celebrate the memory of a great man," to explain the apparent irrelevance of the *Scherzo* and *Finale*. They cannot see the fitness of humor and triumph after the funeral. Marx sees pictures of a busy camp and "the joys of peace." Berlioz finds in the Scherzo the solemn rites of Greek warriors at the grave of their leader. If you must have a scenic whole, Wagner's is the best,— Action, Tragedy, Serenity, Love.*

It seems clear that all the commentators insisted on a series of pictures; they must be told a story about each movement. No work could be fitter to test the true limits of meaning in music. Taking a natural view of the composer's attitude, he wrote, in the first place, a symphony (not a series of illustrations, not a narrative), of which the burden was A Great Man. All pictorial or narrative association must be abandoned, even of a chronological order. It is a symphony with the dominating

---

* A good account of the various interpretations is given in Upton's "Standard Symphonies."

feeling of a *Hero*, in its various moods. His death was, after all, as an event, a small element. The song of mourning must come, if at all, in the second movement, not merely according to tradition, but by the highest sense of fitness. In the whole "celebration" the mourning note must be subordinate. It is somewhat the thought of Hawthorne that death is an incident of our lives of far less importance than many a thought of an uneventful day. The lightness of rhythm of the Scherzo only gives the touch of highest joy, opening into the triumphant Finale.

In the dangerous task of technical description, the question is, How close is the relation between music and meaning? In proportion to greatness it seems that the conception is apart from the details. In lesser masters there is little below the sound. With the great you must stand off as from a canvas of larger scope ; you must not be too near the individual figures to catch the general plan.

While the beginning is almost graceful, the serious intent is soon disclosed where the orchestra enters united ; the dance of the violins

CARL A. RUDISILL LIBRARY
LENOIR RHYNE COLLEGE

ceases in the abrupt, severe *tutti* chords, with a rough syncopation which we think original in Brahms. Still, this may be a temporary contrast. The question is which is to predominate. Then the melody sounds solemnly in united basses and trebles, with full orchestra; but suddenly it drops all severity in the gliding grace of the second melody, which is sung in successive and responsive snatches by the woodwind and strings:

CARL A. RUDISILL LIBRARY
LENOIR RHYNE COLLEGE

SYMPHONIES AND THEIR MEANING

There is certainly nothing here but careless serenity, whatever the title, the warning sound of the first melody, and other omens may threaten. Throughout there seems to be a tense balance or rivalry between solemn foreboding and exultant dance, predominating respectively in the two melodies in a constant struggle, so uncertain that one is often in a curious mixture of terror and joy, save in occasional climaxes of clear triumph or in cadences of idyllic tranquillity.

If we remember the *raison d'être* of the sonata form,* we must see that the first statement of melodies must in itself give a strong clue to the whole symphony. In its clear enunciation, coming to a full emphatic close, followed by a complete repetition, it must be a prologue, as it were; nay more, as it contains the substance of the most important of the four chapters. And so in this strange vibrating between exuberance and seriousness, this curious balance between childlike abandon and succeeding vigorous, even harsh, solemnity and profundity is the typical feeling of the *Heroic* symphony.

---

* See Chapter II.

103

After the joyous and boisterous appearance of the two melodies enters the ominous mystery of modulation, uncertain whispering of fragments of the themes, followed by brief tranquillity in the second melody. Then gloomy minor mutterings of the first in the bass, increasing and reiterating like some fundamental fate, with fitful, hysterical breaking into the lightness of the second. But its own theme is bent to serve the stern humor of the whole ; and soon the whole orchestra is striking united hammer-blows in eccentric rhythm with overwhelming power, until suddenly relieved by a phrase of delicate pathos in the woodwind, with violins still sustaining the rhythm :

Back again to the fateful legend in the basses, reiterated in minor, suddenly relieved again, as

before. But the new phrase expands in clarionets and fagots

into a new song, sung responsively between
flutes and violins:

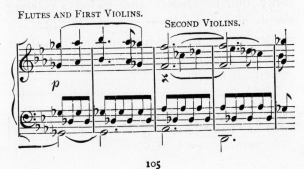

SYMPHONIES AND THEIR MEANING

Now comes the real discussion of the main subject, the vigorous strife in clear *stretto* of woodwind, with rhythmic stress:

too mazed for our sight, until it is merely the light oboe striking the phrase with resounding echo of the rest:

Then more hammer-blows on the chord, suddenly quieting before the melody, entering simply and cheerfully as at first. But here is a sudden serene humor for our moody subject in jolliest duet between horns and basses:

with the other strings humming away to the dancing rhythm; the duet is taken up by flutes and violins, then through loud cadence into a return to the first part of the movement, with all its themes and phrases, principal and secondary, and its changing moods, enriched with fuller treatment.

Withal there is the elemental simplicity and childlike exuberance of Beethoven. It is wrong to think him o'ercast with intellectual motives. At once he seems charged with profoundest emotion and lightest joy. It is the balance of depth and of humanity that makes Beethoven great. All doubt of the mood of the *Allegro* is gone with the audacious descent in three succeeding chords *en bloc*, defying the laws of musical progression, and in this defiance showing the intent.* Though often done afterwards, it never had the same Promethean ring.

Immediately thereafter is dancing revel and a serious joy, though with greatest lightness. The whole understanding of the Third Sym-

---

* Yet the musician feels how the spirit of his law is not disturbed.

phony depends upon distinguishing profound joy, even with wild revel, from a careless, irresponsible abandon,—the joy of the Hero in an universal cause, who, in his revel, feels a clear right to his exultation.

The intensity of Beethoven's feeling in his conception of Napoleon's ideals may be measured by the reaction, when he tore up the title-page on hearing of the emperor's coronation.

In the second movement, the *Funeral March*, he would go far astray who would listen merely for the main melody. It is a fine illustration of the relative unimportance in high art of the melody in itself. Throughout we are disappointed, if we tie our interest to mere melodic beauty here and there. The greatness lies somehow in the exalted tone, in the symbolic depth and unity to which the melodic details are quite subordinate, although they are of course the integral elements of the whole. So it is truly a symphonic work.

The initial melody, all in the strings, is evidently designed less for its individual, independent effect than for its fitness with the whole plan.

Marcia Funebre. *Adagio assai.*

After it is rehearsed by the whole chorus, comes the first of those smoothly gliding, soothing episodes, which are almost more beautiful than the subject itself, in the phrase

after a climax, descending by another gentle motive, sung responsively by strings:

breaking into the funeral march proper, as at first; but while the drum-beats go on, the gliding phrases are mainly sung, soothing the sorrow of the stiffly solemn subject. After another climax of the latter is a striking contrast: of quietest even gliding of strings, followed by sharpest clang of the wind and dull beating of drums.

The first part, in minor, of course closes distinctly. The *Maggiore*, in C major, is at first mysterious. What is this serene moving of oboe in one phrase, succeeded by the flute, with *violas* and *cellos* in another, of evenest rhythm, while the violins are humming in simplest strumming of pastoral placidity? It

would be cheerful, but for the complexity of the polyphony. Before eight bars comes an overpowering crash of whole orchestra, followed again by the former quiet, self-contained singing of joint voices, now serenely continuing, with no funereal strain save the beating of drums, with very gradual climax into the former crash. But with all the awfulness, the startling terror has been avoided.

It is surely clear. We are lifted away from the objective grief of mourning into the empyrean of a subjective exaltation of the Hero. After all, the mourning is not for him ; for him there is naught but serenity and triumph.

Back to the thud of drums and the awe of the original minor. But only for a strain. Here is the profoundest of all, whether technically or in its general meaning. Fagot and violin strike out in noisy, dogmatic counterpoint on dimly familiar themes, of which the most important must be the sombre guise (in minor) of one of the former quietly gliding phrases :

In succession, all the voices strike into the fateful chant. When the basses have it, we are overwhelmed as in a cathedral with the convincing mass of its awing architecture. In its closing climax the now hurried phrase is nothing but the old theme doubled in time. It is all surely a mingling of the feeling of Religion, of the deep enigma, in all this complexity; of life and death, and life thereafter. But the lull and return to the Funeral March is but for a moment. After a wail of violins in the main melody, brass and strings strike crashing into a strange chord. Again enters in the bass a reminder of the dogmatic theme carried on and on, until suddenly we hear in its very climax the original funeral melody marching in the woodwind, quite as if a secondary after-thought, all in complete song. The rest is as at first, but enriched and extended, with former separate themes now united in common pæan, with bolder acclaim of rhythmic strings. Where the end might be there is a sudden lull. In quietest song is a new melody with new swing. In its novelty, its strange simplicity, it suggests a feeling of transfiguration or apotheosis of the Hero.

The ending is solemn and subdued, save a single triumphant burst at the last. There is a curious touch in the final singing of the melody, with its original rhythm all distorted. It gives a strange effect of reality, as if the essence of the poetry, spoken without the flesh.

In the Scherzo, *Allegro Vivace*, we must not pretend to find anything but boisterous abandon. There is no note of the sombre, of the sinister, save possibly a suggestion of terror in the very vehemence of the mad delight.

The beginning seems all mere rhythmic preparation in the *staccato* strings until first violins and oboe break into the melody:

The low strumming of the first bass is surely
mere foil to the bright humor of the main theme.
The fine haste of the incessant tripping, a sort
of *perpetuum mobile*, is enhanced when the voices
leap one over the other in canon form:

overturning melodies head over heels, losing
accent in their mad haste. And, later, a still
more splendid *stretto*, in whole orchestra, between the measures of trebles and of basses:

Basses an octave below.

higher and higher in the chasing game, until they all fall together in headlong rhythm:

On their feet again and off tripping as before. No depth or complexity, save quite incidentally where the simultaneous phrases of first and second violins were reversed, the lower above the higher,—a master-stroke (what the scholars call double counterpoint), all quickly in passing.

The TRIO accents the deeper humor in a horn melody that savors unmistakably of the chase.

But its sustained tones only imply the pre-

TRIO. HORNS.

vious rhythm, and soon run into its wild gait; back again into the sonorous horn theme,— finally occasional lapses, as if sighing for a moment's thought before the Scherzo, which rushes past with the same melodies in close texture extended in a coda, where we are hovering uncertain between humor and serious triumph.

There can be no question about the mood of the Finale, *Allegro molto*. We need not speculate nor philosophize deeply, yet there is a rare chance for a mistake.

SYMPHONIES AND THEIR MEANING

There is no doubt about the unreined joyous elation of the whole. And yet it is most natural at first hearing to find nothing profounder than lightest romp and revel. But there is no music where there is closer relation between the notes and the sense, this higher content. Therefore, with no more ado to the reading. The opening bars are of course a mere *fanfare* of strings in preparatory (dominant) chord for the melody (in the tonic). What a strange theme! All in *pizzicato*, unison strings:

Strings doubled in two lower octaves.

almost a jest in its simplicity, and repeated in eccentric echoing of woodwind, and ended with comic, loud striking of common note, and lightly tripping off with the same stealthy pace.

Next the melody is sounded by one set of strings in sustained half-notes, instead of timid *staccato*, while the others dance about with snatches and phrases which seem to fit as well above the melody as below. We now see the deeper design which gradually breaks on us, that lends a profounder dignity,—a feeling of completeness, of universality. And yet the design is not conscious, but that curious star-guided intention of the master. And the unconsciousness but gives it the greater dignity and meaning.

What seemed the main melody is now relegated to insignificant basses, and a new chrysalis of tune gently dances aloft in wood-wind, reckless of its dethroned predecessor under its feet:

WOODWIND (with a running figure in violins).

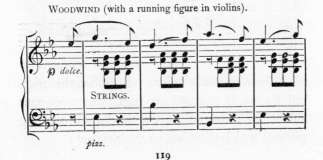

There is no mere reminiscent pretence, but the whole melody with the second above, the answer, even, with the heavy chords, and the final phrase

all in heaven-made union. But now the original theme is restored to dignity as sonorous subject of serious fugue, with the surrounding phrases which give life to the rhythm:

through the four strings down to the fundamental bassi, with attempts of woodwind to have their say.

It is clear that the theme has that peculiar quality of basic motto which we saw in the *Finale* of the Jupiter, and which we shall see further in Beethoven's symphonies. In it the masters expressed the sense of profound groping for fundamental truth which is strong in their compatriot and contemporary poets, which gave that peculiar charm and strength of blended philosophy and fancy to the works of Goethe.

The plot thickens as the theme enters diminished in *tempo* and in close *stretto*,—still further diminished, and we wonder what comes next in the maze, when suddenly out of the sombre dogmatic learning dances forth, like fairy queen, with quick surprise of modulation, the second melody in a minor key, where it loses none of its lightness, gaining a novel charm of mystery :

rehearsed with daintily comic change of rhythm in woodwind:

After some clownish horseplay in the strings, applauded by the rest, all join in a big, ponderous cosmic dance:

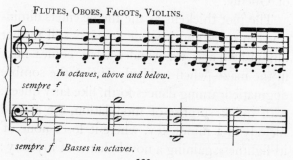

cosmic because of its primeval simplicity, and because we hear the same fundamental motto in the basses.

It has somehow the spirit and ring of universality of Schiller's Ode to Joy, proven in its simple completeness. The new dance extends its melody, with the motto both above and below, coming to what seems a complete close of full orchestra. But suddenly off again into unexpected regions of tone on the wings of the second melody, then into the mysterious phases of the minor, the motto always present above or below. Once more we are in the fugue, in the dogmatic humor; but now it builds more broadly and fully in a joyous climax, which suddenly drops into a religious chant of the woodwind in the scarce recognizable second melody :

OBOE, CLARIONETS.
Poco andante.

p con espressione.

FAGOTS.

123

in sustained, solemn organ tones, softened in spirit, echoed by the strings. The answer in second part is in more graceful lyric feeling. Suddenly into vehement clanging of tutti, with the same melody in basses ; here again a lull in volume and rhythm, only to end through the original *fanfare*, in furious galloping of the theme, in various rhythmic guises, in loudest, most emphatic close.

VI

BEETHOVEN (Continued)

The Seventh Symphony.

In spite of the remark in the last chapter on the new quality of Beethoven, in advance of Haydn and Mozart, of the element of a *meaning*, it is very necessary to mark the purely sentient, naïve, non-intellectual (I should rather not say emotional) character of Beethoven. And this is best seen in the seventh symphony, especially as against the third, the fifth, the sixth, and the ninth. On the whole, the untitled symphonies are much to be preferred.

We must be careful to reject absolutely any theory of story or description, except where the master himself gives it. And there, as in the sixth, it is not a success,—the highest proof of the superiority of absolute music. The test, after all, is the purely musical impression, but not in an unthinking attitude. Beethoven's greatness (and that of Brahms, too) is shown by his refusal to be categoried, to have his emotion narrowed and whittled down to answer a picture or story. In a very large degree, programme music is, after all, a pretty, intellectual game, a subtle flattery, a mental feat, a guess at conundrums. Generally, there is a real loss in the apparent gain. If the emotional is the true attitude, it can be seen how the title, by absorbing attention, prevents a pure enjoyment and the test by natural perception. Creating a false interest, the label withdraws the normal, unbiassed attention from the music itself, preconceiving the mind to an *a priori*, arbitrary connection or significance. In one way, entitled music is like the clever juggler who tricks by diverting attention from the real to a pretended act; in another, it is like the poor painter who holds the witless mind by the strength, not of his art, but of the printed label.

Schumann's view of programme music was the true one,—the title distinctly and literally an after-thought. If the impelling feeling must be unconscious, the poet cannot know, until he has finished, the word that explains his mood. This is the true view of the ninth symphony,— a spontaneous burst into song, not beautifully preconceived and prearranged, as of voices that could no longer contain the feeling stirred by the earlier music.

Implication of meaning came largely from ultra-radicals like Berlioz, who wanted, mistakenly, to raise the dignity of music by imputing to it a power which it could not, in the nature of things, possess. Their artistic sense was blurred by the philosophical. They confused the true limits of music and prose. Hence their incomplete work (as in all opera), seeking to eke out their music with a "meaning." Our genuine gain in joyousness from an untitled work of pure music is much greater than the temporary flattery of seeing, or seeming to see, a subtle significance.

For this reason, it seems well for this once to choose a work absolutely free from the taint of attempted translation; deliberately to avoid pictured or storied explanations; simply to get the true musical impression, not without keen study, at once as a rare example and an illustration of the real attitude of the listener. Or, if we hear of explanations, let us take them only to reject, with presumption against all; for, at most, but one of them can be true.

Such an ideal symphony is the seventh. It is impossible to escape the din of the critics who shout their labels at us,—their "Rustic Wedding," "Moorish Knighthood," "Masked Ball," "Pastoral Scenes."* But men will forget that the more a work refuses definition, the greater it is. In proportion as the interpretation is general, it is apt to be true. It is all part of our human impulse to limit, to circumscribe everything and everybody but ourselves, in order to make clear and easy to understand.† We are in too great haste to solve all puzzles by force, to cut the Gordian knot. One more observation on these critics: How each one understands or receives exactly according to his capacity, just like so many vessels of varying size, is nowhere so clearly shown as in symphonic commentaries. And this is a great truth, and the best view of criticism. Thus each has a right, without pretence of judicial

---

* If I had to join in the chorus, I should call it "The Earthly Symphony,"—Goethe's

> "Wirklich ist es wunderschön
> Auf der lieben Erde."

† Also, I fear, from a less worthy motive of depreciation.

authority, to tell the other how he feels about
it ; and each one is giving something of himself.

One common quality has been read in the
seventh symphony by so many commentators,
that the latest critic must naturally emphasize
an opposite element which seems to him to have
been overlooked. All agree in the bewitching
rhythmic spell that shines through every bar of
the symphony. But where we must differ with
many interpreters is in the degree of lightness
(or of seriousness) which they find. It seems
as if many view merely the fact of the dance-
rhythm, and of the simple melodies, without
feeling the bigness, the fundamental depth of
the orchestral treatment. But, avoiding the
danger from preconceived theory, let us listen :

The beginning is serious, the slow *Sostenuto*
of Haydn,—of Brahms, too. But Beethoven
could not, with the light intent of an Offenbach, sound a solemn prelude, only to dance
away into frivolity for the rest of the evening.
Therefore this beginning is significant. Then,
a symphony must begin simply, alone to show
its scope.

Out of heavy bursts of chords floats a quiet, legend-like theme, in primal intervals (somewhat as in the *Eroica*), in succeeding strains of the woodwind:

In both is that German, profound philosophical impulse to find the mystic formula, the pervading cosmic principle, as in the second part of Faust; the feeling, too, of Mozart's favorite motto,* in the Jupiter symphony and elsewhere. The literal musician, the " Fachmann," will say that these themes are chosen for their capacity for development. But this is exactly the wrong idea. He fails to see below the black notes on the surface. He treats music as a branch of mathematics, for-

---

* See Chapter IV.

getting entirely our definition of the Unconscious Arithmetician.

After a few bars of solemn chanting of the
legend, there is a gentle stir of motion in the
strings, which gradually infects the rest. With
the quiet theme still pervading, the whole slowly
gathers movement,—this is the clearest impression ; still, the motto constantly completing and
rounding out. As it grows to overpowering dimensions, there suddenly breaks through a melody, not of dance, but of the most tensely pent
desire for rhythm, in harmony of woodwind :

a call for the dance, oft repeated, high in the
woodwind and low in the strings (interrupted
by the earlier phase). Then there is a gradual
joining of hands, getting ready. Some begin ;
all are still moving imperfectly. Soon the

whole movement grows strong and united into a *Vivace* dance, led by the woodwind:

The strings at first merely strum lightly in time. But soon they take a higher part, in echoing response:

Woodwind in octaves.

Strings in double octaves below.

As the bass strings thus dance the time in counter-movement, the whole is too ponderous for frivolity; it becomes deep. This must be seen throughout. If the basses gave a mere rhythmic step, it would be otherwise. Their active vocal part gives a cosmic color to the whole. The dancing melody is so continuous that it seems impossible as well as needless to distinguish first and second themes. It is all so clear. Like a great round dance, they stop, and, gathering with a run, begin again the more furiously, now holding with a long step to return to the rhythm, suddenly in quietest, daintiest skipping, still softer, then in bold, loud chorus,

133

always this united feeling of a mass in unison, not of a small group,—a dancing song with changing phases ; sometimes the song is everything, then it is a mere dance again.

We must remember, here as ever, this dance is merely symbolic. We must not try to find a picture of it, nor to see it everywhere. It is only a figure, a passing image of a much greater idea or feeling. The joint dance of all is the common uniting of mankind in joy, as was proclaimed in those days by poets in verse and tone, and might well be proclaimed now anew. In another view, it shows how Beethoven combined purest exuberance with profoundest sympathy.

And, after the repeated statement, the period of discussion (to avoid the hated "development") shows the symbolic quality most strongly. For here, in the much weakened, almost halting rhythm, is the separate individual wandering off, clearest in the contrapuntal process. The hue of metaphysics is on. Up and down, one against the other, in the gray, colorless straying of independent individuals, the common bond is relaxed and forgotten, only to join once again, with gradual uniting, in the universal rhythm. If the dance is symbolic, the wandering is separate thought and action, independent, though not without interdependence. But ever again, after the tendency to stray apart in disunion and discord, comes the magnificent joining in the common movement and song.

Allegretto is the nearest approach Beethoven can make to the mood of pathos in this poem of Earth and Humanity. In this balance of rhythm with solemnity is, to us, one of the highest of all inspirations. It is in a vein rare to Beethoven, wherein we see much kinship with Schubert. The spirit of this *Allegretto* must have stirred in the younger master when he thought his famous melody of the song, "Death and the Maiden." We cannot escape, again, the mystic German groping for fundamental truth in a single motto; as, first, the essential harmonic and rhythmic plan is simply stated in lower strings, with sombre, broken sounds:

VIOLA, CELLI, BASSI.

and then the melodic song surges above in

clear, sustained tones, while the former fateful
dirge continues its solemn, unaltered march.

The second melody, in major, abandons the
solemn vein, in a strain of purest lyric feeling,
human and mortal, not of eternal truth.
Strangely, it reminds us of quite another
vein of Schubert, frequent in his impromptus.
But there is no complete escape from the
old rhythmic beat which keeps dinning on
in the bass against the swinging melody of
violins:

136

The lyric love-song is over, and now we are alone with the mournful hymn, but this is sung with greater freedom and lightness. Suddenly the strings alone strike into a monkish fugue on the original theme in thin, ominous tones, with unceasing course of the monotonous, rhythmless countertheme, all in pious submission to fate. But now fugal and countertheme both are rung with overwhelming power by the whole orchestra. Once more the strain of human longing is heard. Then comes the end in the same dull, broken, fateful sounds, with a strange wail in the violins with the closing chord, as of a dying soul.

Scherzo.   Presto.

Now for the dance in earnest. It is the natural climax for such a symphony, this third phase ; the very acme and essence of rhythm. All the pent-up motion is let loose, yet not in wild disorder, but all in unconscious though perfect obedience to a subtle swing. As elsewhere, the highest sum or quantity of motion is only possible with regularity and harmony simultaneously and successively, as of horses drawing a chariot. They must all race in one united agreement of a common speed, for real achievement of motion. And never was Offenbach or Strauss half so light as this profoundly serious master of ours.

Presto.
Tutti.   Woodwind in octave below.

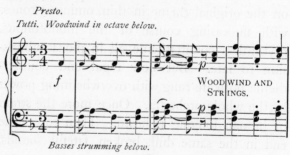

Basses strumming below.

And were long-sustained notes ever so inviting to the dance, so subtly alive with motion :

or in the oft-repeated humming in flute and
clarionets, like hovering insects :

But much greater is this subtle implication of motion in the *Trio*, where with violins sustaining a long *A* in octaves, the droning horns, fagots, and clarionets are singing, in diminished speed, a new theme:

It is a typical union of highest feeling and art. With violins sustained on a high tone, giving merely a rare quiver, it is like the constant buzzing of forest bees, but so subtle that it is for ruder ears really a rest with highest motion, much as the humming-bird, with wings vibrating in invisible motion, seems to rest on hidden threads, or like the pulse of sound itself, which is so rapid that it becomes one sustained tone. But this is only around and about. Through the midst comes the quiet, intimate song of the woodwind; emerging

from nature sounds, it speaks human sentiment. There is no mistaking this in the quiet,
definite notes of the song. It is too articulate in its contrast with the vaguely quivering,
buzzing wood-notes. And later the song is
ever more human, almost pleading, save for its
quiet, constant rhythm :

The horns begin a gradual stir of rhythm;
more and more enter, until all the world, man
and nature, with overwhelming power, have
joined in our sweetly solemn song.

It is really, all this Trio, a sort of idyllic
rest in the woods, from which we are whirled
by a sudden shock back to the impersonal
frolic of the original scherzo, with all its romping joy, in full career to the end, not without
several returns to the musing revery of the

song of the Trio. And withal there is never a break in the relentless, resistless motion, intensely rhythmic in all its disguise.

The Finale is a big, almost a serious abandon. With the infectious, resistless dance is a certain ponderousness,—above all, a simplicity which betrays its universality. It is greater than national, though there is the suggestion of national song. The primitive simplicity is shown in the absence of defined melody, of varied tonality, of contrast of rhythm. It is hard to find any official themes in the whole melodious tissue, and the complementary chords, of tonic and dominant, are rung with almost barbarous plainness. Magnetic as is the dance, it is in the simplest conceivable rhythm:

There are no contrasts, save in the sudden light tripping after the ponderous clog of the whole orchestra.

If any theme can be called the subject, it

is in the pervading figure (first in the violins),
after rhythmic chords :

Allegro con brio.

(With harmony in the strings.)

FLUTES AND OBOES.

CLARIONETS, FAGOTS.

where all the woodwind comes dancing in on
ponderous, eccentric skip at the end of the
bar. It is in the very lack of pretence, of
conscious beauty of outline, or of significance
in the melodies, that consists the feeling of
romp. And yet we must always come back
to that quality of joy which we saw in the first
movement, which seems special to our master,
as it is to the highest poetic feeling : of profundity. Nothing could be more reckless,
irresponsible in its abandon, than this rollicking Finale; but no one can think of it as

frivolous, can escape its stamp of universality and eternity.

On it goes, after first repeating of melody, foliowed by mere running up and down of all the wind, with strings beating the time. They change about. Then a bandying of the original phrase in the strings:

STRINGS.

with a mere suspicion of logic, of discussion, followed immediately by the simplest, most childlike dancing up and down in the primitive rhythm (cited above), as if to reject the

very suggestion of conscious thought, all together, hand in hand, in unison step, until the
first contrast, to which we alluded above.

As all stop on a sudden chord, the violins
trip lightly along, to the strumming of strings
alone, with sudden shock of interrupting chorus,
like clownish attempts at frightening :

The finest romping on, all stamping heavily
together, with eccentric thud, followed by
lightest tripping chase of strings up and down,

the very ideal of frolic. After repetition of all of this, we are curious how far the master will ascend (or descend) to the region of reflective thought in what German technique calls the *Durchführung*. But all we can discover is, after careering and coursing of the leading figure, a little wondering pause in violins, echoed or mimicked by lower strings:

plunging back into the rollicking swing. Later, as the high woodwind echoes the dance, there is a queer effect of mockery of this reflecting figure in the violins, in quick successive answers, after which there is a return to the original festivity, with deepening and extending of the little discussion (above quoted). The ending corresponds in increased boisterousness, with a full sounding of the pervading phrase, together with an answer developed in the discussion above described, which seems to vent the bursting feeling in an almost articulate phrase of exultation:

The Fifth Symphony.

We have so far conceived a symphony as an expression of a dominant feeling, from a subjective stand-point, or, objectively, as a view of life, in four typical phases or moods, of which the first is of aspiring resolution, the second of pathos, the third of humor, the the fourth of triumph. With such a plan, which was gradually and unconsciously developed from Haydn to Beethoven, we could not expect a great number of symphonies from one master. A man's pervading, fundamental feeling or view could not change so as to permit him to write two such symphonies in quick succession.* But this purpose may be called the highest. There are really two kinds of symphonies, the titled, and the untitled, where the range of feeling is narrowed, more or less, in some way. And we might even distinguish a third class, where there is a mere suggestion, by inscription or by a cursory remark of the composer, of the prevailing mood, contrasted with those works in which there is an expressly limited field from the beginning. Of course, we must never forget the unconsciousness of masters of these general or special purposes.

A very striking example of the specially titled symphony is Beethoven's Sixth, the Pastoral, "on the memories of life in the country." We have described the Heroic Symphony, written "to celebrate the memory of a great man." In more modern works such titles as Spring, Forest, Winter, Rhine are prominent.

It is doubtful whether the importing of titles

---

* Mozart's rapid composition of his three great symphonies must be viewed rather as the completion of earlier sketches.

into the symphony, the introduction of what is called programme music, in itself has added to its dignity or power. Perhaps the best type is Beethoven's Pastoral, which is annotated thus: First Movement, Pleasant Feelings awakened on arriving in the Country; Second, Scene at the Brook; Third, Jovial Meeting of Country People, interrupted by Fourth, Thunder and Storm, in turn interrupted by the final movement, entitled Sentiments of Benevolence and Gratitude to God after the Storm. Of course, it is impossible not to accept the composer's interpretation. But it must be remembered that in his sketches an appended note was found, directing the hearer to find the situations for himself; and, further, that in the final programme Beethoven added to the title the words, "Rather an Expression of Feeling than a Picture." If we should be obliged to dispense with any of Beethoven's symphonies, I venture to say that in the Pastoral least would be lost. It is not overbold to say that Beethoven himself was not consciously aware of the true dignity and power of the symphony. Truth in art is determined, not by reasoned *a priori* deduction, but by an irregular course of experiment, where much error must be expected.

In choosing from the rich field a single work as a type for illustration, from the limits of the untitled class, the Fifth, in C Minor, seems the most broadly representative. The work was produced in 1808, having been for years in course of composition. No title appears in the programme, except

Symphony No. 5, in C Minor, op. 67.

1. *Allegro con Brio.*
2. *Andante con Moto.*
3. *Allegro (Scherzo).*
4. *Allegro. Presto.*

There is, perhaps, one prejudice to the unassisted interpretation. It is Beethoven's reported casual suggestion of a meaning of the principal motive; but for the present that may be disregarded. The symphony is characterized by a sublime dignity, vigor, and breadth. At the first hearing it is impossible not to feel that there is a very real purpose behind the notes. The entire absence of frivolous dallying with themes, the striking contrast of succeeding melodies (especially towards the end of the third and fourth movements, which, against all tradition, follow each other without a stop), above all, the iteration from beginning to end of a certain short passage, but four notes:

with the whole orchestra at times hidden in the basses and drums, now in its grim, terrible severity, again in a dancing measure, then in timid, mysterious discord, until it ends in the clearest note of triumph,—can it be said that all this means nothing, until or unless it be translated word for note into the language of commonplace?

As in all truly great works of the human mind, there must be a certain degree of intelligent perception. Further, a certain maturity is absolutely necessary to understand Beethoven. He is not for the young; above all, not for the shallow. For these he is often no more than ugly and ominous noise, which makes them uneasy. They should shun him. His listeners must be capable of feeling the grimness, the terror, the fight of life. Then they can exult with him in the triumphant joy of the undaunted.

The recurring problem of musical study is the mode of this perception. There has always been a dilemma between a mere sympathetic, emotional attitude and that of technical analysis. Neither is adequate. The answer must be in analogy to the truth of the mode of creation, which is a blending of feeling and of high art, where the latter is subordinate, yet indispensable as unconscious means of expression. So the listener cannot expect to perceive unless he know this high language of the master. Yet in mere analysis he will not find the message; for art does not communicate propositions by logical proof. The listener must be in sympathetic, expectant attitude, not closed like a fortress to the besieger, not disdaining the utmost knowledge of the art-medium, with mind fully intent on the emotional meaning, by a similar blending, as of the original composer.

We might revert briefly to some special step in Beethoven's advance. It was in the third movement that Beethoven made the greatest change in outline. Originally, with

Haydn and Mozart, it was an idealized dance; Beethoven made it a humorous phase, fitting with the whole plan. But the humor was typically sardonic. He changed its name, too, from minuet to scherzo. But more significant is the change in the treatment of the theme. The era of childlike simplicity had passed. A more intellectual and more virile age had arrived, in which the leading melody in itself is not so important as its use literally and strictly as a theme; an age of musical thinking as against dreaming; of cerebration as against mere inspiration; of a logical sequence of thought rather than a blunt alternative; of a tendency which has resulted in a school where the theme is no more an integral part of a work than is the title of a story.

There is no more convincing evidence of the peculiar power of music, which we have been trying to define, than in the comparison of such works as the seventh and the fifth symphonies; of this graphic portrayal, not of pictures, not of stories, not of doctrines, but of feelings. And while saying the word we are aware of its utter weakness; for feeling may mean the emptiest, the most frivolous, the most useless thing, as, indeed, it may be the weightiest, the most precious, the most powerful. For when traced thoroughly, feeling such as prompts great artworks is the spring of all else in life worth recording. It is the original fount of all heroic action, of statesmanship, of ethics, of poetry, of humanity ; indeed, these are but the cold expression of that which is the living, sentient fire. It would not be difficult for a historian to find in the revolution of France, in the Constitution of America, the crystallized result of the passion which began to rouse men in unconscious beginnings from the first years of Humanism in Italy. And, useful as these organized institutions must be, the most precious forms of expression will be those which show most of the unconscious fire and vehemence of the original impelling feeling. In proportion as they take on practical shapes, they will lose their natural vigor. Thus it is that a medium like music, which, without pretence of articulate definition of the prose language of human makeshift, of so-called practical adjustment to the externals of changing conditions, still rears the highest structure of Art, on figures of enthralling beauty, will be the most perfect human utterance of our feelings, those all-powerful, noblest stirrings in man's nature. There is no corollary here of depreciation of logic, of significant language. There must be divers modes of utterance, varying in nobility, suited to differing natures and differing conditions of creation and of reception. In the various utterance of emotion, of whatever shade of Art or of differentiated meaning, constituting human intercourse, lies the seed or stimulus for ever new and nobler feelings, which in turn need newer utterance, and lead in their expression to improvement and ennoblement of outward conditions of human life.

Not only in their separate song, but in their contrast, are seen the varying qualities of those two great symphonies, and thereby of the versatile power of the language of music that Mendelssohn meant when he said that music was much more definite than prose, the very quality which laymen—those who live in externals—are fully persuaded is absolutely non-existent.

The Seventh is a mighty pæan of joy, in utterance of subjective feeling. The Fifth is burdened with the stern awfulness of the external power, with which the strongest can but struggle. Most of us run, as from the rain, or hide, as from the lightning, and gratefully bask in intermittent sunshine. The solitary Prometheus can at highest express the sense of struggle, or—— But let the symphony be its own evangel.

At the very beginning, the ominous motto strong, but in stern, hollow octaves:

then lightly dancing in the strings, with the rhythm which it first lacked, it rises, a melody

in its responsive singing, ending in massive chords and in a pause that adds to the solemnity of legendary utterance. The first pages

are full of stern, sombre melody, yet without
lack of resistless motion. Strange this constant, vital impulse, without joyousness. And
striking here, the contrast in sentient meaning
of the Fifth and the Seventh Symphonies, the
merciless drive of objective, external destiny as
against internal, subjective joy.

After a more decided, rational sounding of
the motto by the horns, follows the quiet,
pious second melody in the violins, in soothing
major, unmistakable in its sense of beseeching,
of refuge from the first,—cherishing peace and
solace. But it cannot resist anxiety stealing in

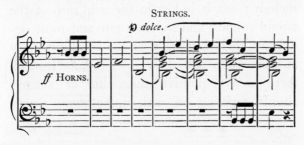

and increasing, as the four notes are approaching in the background of the basses, on to a
climax, where the repeated statement ends
with a determined ringing of the motto. No
greater contrast can be imagined than of the

SYMPHONIES AND THEIR MEANING

two melodies. It is like the dialogue of different persons; of stern necessity and pleading
spirit, with a quality of pious trust.

Here is the phase of discussion, with austerest warning, and then on with the rhythmical melody and the same theme, first gentle

STRINGS, CLARIONET, AND HORNS.

ff in doubled octaves.

and light, soon fitful and feverish, into furious
hammering. The more rational phase appears,
which promises to bring in the plaint of second
melody; but it is lost in the wild rush of the
fateful sounds, and so, most rare and most significant, there is no sign of the second melody
in the whole period of discussion. Instead,
there is a responsive succession of solemn
chords, tapering off with monotonous repeti-

WOODWIND AND BRASS.

STRINGS.

ff

tion, like the stillness of Egyptian temple, into timid expectancy before the renewed shocks of the terrible hammers, ringing their incessant, fateful thud, without peace and solace, in the original motto, followed by the original succession of melodies, where the second sounds more helpless and pitiful than ever. In the coda the main theme still predominates, with a brief fugue, suggestive of priest and church, but above all filled with the gloom of ruthless Doom. There is no mercy as yet.

Andante con moto. It might well have been called *Andante Religioso.* There is an entire change with the first note; in the first impression, rest from turbulence and anxiety; but soon we cannot be quite sure whether it is really rest or still a seeking for rest; like the distinction of Lessing's " Truth and Search for Truth," of which he preferred the latter. There seems to be a distinct feeling of prayer about the Andante. Perhaps the best word would be Faith,—a trustful reliance, which varies in strength as the attacks from without vary in intensity, which are clear in the dim reminders of the haunting motive.

But the predominant feeling is contained in

the leading melody, first announced in the
violas and in the celli.   It is that kind of mel-

ody where Beethoven strikes his deepest note ;
the tone of profoundest sympathy, which bound
men to him most.

It is not without interest that Beethoven is
known to have toiled on this theme, much as a
sculptor chisels his vision out of the marble.
It shows that there is no necessary connection
between the beauty of a melody and the ease
with which it was first uttered, which is often
called spontaneity.   On the contrary, there is
reason to think that the musical thoughts of
highest value were not without a certain corresponding labor in their final perfection.   The

manner of writing is thus often of high interest
in gauging, by comparison, the special quality
of each master. Thus, for example, this is a
melody which Schubert could not write. And
we remember how Schubert wrote with absolute freedom from toil, as if delivering himself
of a pressing burden. High and rare as was
Schubert's fancy, he had not that vein of deep
personal human sympathy which marks Beethoven not only as of the greatest among human
poets, but of the greatest among the men of all
time. There is a tendency to value too highly
the quality of ease of utterance. It would be
better to err on the other side.

This melody is the main tissue of the whole
movement. It is varied only by a secondary
one, which is contrasted neither in key nor in
theme, serving, in its simplicity, for quick

With obligato of Violas.

modulation into triumphant bursts, or preceded often by timid drooping before a suggestion of the terrible motto :

VIOLINS WITH SUSTAINING CLARIONETS.

pp VIOLINS AND VIOLAS.

First it rushes into a bold cadence in a new tonal atmosphere ; but, quickly relapsing, wanders, still pursued by the motto, an anxious suppliant, into the refuge of the first melody. The predominance of the chief melody is veiled by new figures of rhythm and of setting, and by intervening touches of eloquent pleading or of austere solemnity. At the last verse there is a decided joyfulness in the prayer,—a vision of coming victory, where woodwind and higher strings unite in loudest acclaim on the melody, the horns sound the harmony, the drums the rhythm, and the lower strings strum in rapid accompaniment. The end is in a spirit of reassurance.

Probably nothing in all musical literature offers such a subtle and irresistible temptation

to find a hidden content, as this third movement, where the name *Scherzo* seems to have
been omitted only because it was not needed;
although the humor is of a kind that, in its
sombre profundity, is as peculiarly Beethoven's
as is the pathetic or sympathetic quality of the
Andante. The temptation comes, I suppose,
from the curious atmosphere which one feels
immediately on entrance, like that of a magician, when the lights are lowered and terrible
things are going to happen.* There is a brilliant though dark-hued dramatic color about it
all, as in some ideal *Freischuetz*, without interfering words.

At the risk of seeming rhapsodical to some,
pedantic to others, I must recur to some well-
worn philosophical terms, for lack of better
ones. I can find nothing more expressive than
subjective and objective for a certain quality
or relation of themes. I cannot escape them;
for, more than suggestive or symbolic, they

---

* It may be interesting for the reader to compare the
impression Berlioz gives of this Scherzo somewhere in
his writings. The author has purposely refrained from
reading it anew, in order to present an unbiassed impression of his own.

represent accurately the truth of the composer's
intent.   Thus, nothing can be clearer than this
relative significance of question and answer in
the first theme, where the former rises from
the sombre depths of the basses, like a sinister

message, while the answer, in higher harmony,
is as unmistakably, as against the outer danger,
the inner deprecation.   Whatever any one may
read of story or meaning, according to his
sensible or inflammable state, no one who can

feel music at all, can deny this sharp relation
of a foreign omen and a personal plaint.   It is
good to have some bed-rock truth.

Now, after the repeated phrase and pause,
what shall we say to this entering figure? How
shall we take it?   For, as for simply accepting
a tripping theme in three-quarter time, and no
more,—that is, once for all, out of the question.
This is not that kind of music.   For those who
can or will feel nothing more, we can express
mere pity.   The horns sound, in curious
three-quarter dance time, a kind of iambic

waltz, while strings are thrumming the harmony, a theme of which all but the end is
nothing but groups of successive *G's*, with pe-
riodical halts, all with utmost vehemence, immediately answered and extended by the whole
orchestra, with martial vigor. None can fail
to see the hidden relation with the original
motto of the symphony; only it has the guise

of a newer rhythm; for it dances along with
infectious, resistless swing, instead of the dull
thud, with awing pause.

But how shall we take it, even so? Sometimes there is almost a touch of sardonic pro-
fanity, almost of blasphemy, of unholy jesting
with unspeakable things. Critics have been
sure of the ring of defiance here.

But we must remember several things.
Some of them we are always forgetting. For
one, it is the paradox of musical literature that
the composer is less conscious of his intent than
is the intelligent hearer. And the reason is not
far. The poet's mind is too intensely absorbed

with his creation to have an undercurrent thought for the quality of his mood. That will take care of itself, will express itself in the art, the better for being unwatched. But for the listener it is otherwise; he must by all means get as near as he can to the mood of the master.

And then we must not expect to see this sentient meaning (as it might be called) constant and interlinear, word for note. There must be often great uncertainty. And yet, within large limits, there may be the most absolute certainty. Thus there may be an indefinable border-land between the subjective and objective attitudes, while at times the two are clearly distinguished.

It is sometimes difficult to tell whether a writer or a speaker is in earnest or in jest. It is not strange if we cannot be absolutely certain of the intent of a composer, especially if he himself could not tell us. If Beethoven had written "*Scherzo*," there might be enough ground for the ring of defiant humor which many critics hear.* But, altogether, to us

---

* Literal questions and questioners for each phrase must be shunned with the same horror as the terrible people who ply you for categorical answers of *yes* or *no*.

the hue of seriousness prevails, what with the gloom of the minor, the vehemence of the chords, notwithstanding the constant tripping movement. Still suggesting the former correlatives, it is the old burden of external omen. The light rhythm, which for some means grim defiance, seems rather merely a new phase for the former threatening evil. But in the middle episode, commonly called the *Trio*, there can be no such doubt.

As the lowest strings start alone in a rumbling dance movement, here is the spirit of

Cellos and Basses (in octaves).

purest, roughest humor, boisterous,—not horseplay, much too ponderous. One thinks of the elephant dance in the jungle book. In the second part the humor is still clearer in the successive broken attempts of the basses before

Basses alone.

they once more find their feet and rumble away in the dance. But the humor has the profound, eternal quality, fitting with highest art, first ending in a great *bacchanale*. The second time it dwindles away, until we are suddenly back in the sinister, cavernous gloom of the first melody; again, in the puzzling beat of tripping motto, whether human or superhuman, descending into still lower depths of sombrest gloom, with demoniacal perversion of the melody, when suddenly a turn of the major lets in a clear ray of hope, and then comes the heroic lift from the abode of devils to that of angels, from hell to heaven, from sinister, overwhelming evil to moral triumph, to emancipation of the spirit, as the final Allegro, awaiting no pause, throwing off the shackles of the tripping pace, bursts in exult-

Allegro.
FULL ORCHESTRA.

ant marching chords in brightest major. It
is all clear as the spelled word,—nay, clearer;
a striking example, again, of Mendelssohn's
mot about music and prose. Your poly-
syllable from the Latin, with devious derivation, has a cold convention of meaning:
the music here is the meaning itself, is the
living and beautiful embodiment of this very
spirit of achieved freedom from outward conditions.*

Curiously, yet naturally, the feeling does not
break at first into a pronounced melody, as if
the joy were too great to find, for a while, a
clear utterance. So there are really two principal melodies, of which, when the first has exhausted its boisterous exuberance, the second
sings a clearer and quieter chant, while the
noisy basses are ever interrupting with turbu-
lent coursing up and down. So plain is the
chant, that you can almost hear the voices, as
of some great, comprehensive choral hymn:

---

* Again, it is suggested that Berlioz's comment be
read of the whole symphony. There is also one by Sir
George Grove in a book on Beethoven's Nine Symphonies. There must be other descriptions.

Oboe, Clarionet, and Horns.

Basses.

especially in the farther extending of the melody, still in clear notes of song. At last he has found articulate praise. And so he glides into a serener melody in a milder at-

Strings.

171

mosphere (the official second melody in dominant key), with less defiant, more feminine ring, more of pure, joyous abandon, joined in refrain of the whole orchestra, growing quite conversational. Then, as if something must still be said, a little postscript melody, in wood-

wind and strings, likewise sanctioned by full acclaim of all. All of which is repeated, as integral text and tissue of the whole, not as mere incidental thoughts. The latter of the secondary melodies is more serious than the former; but there is no uncertainty or drooping. In fact, the note of confident joy is maintained continuously in the discussion (all, of the first of the secondary themes), varying in profundity, in sparkling humor, ending in renewed burst of exultant triumph, where articulate tune is again lost in the vague intensity,—when suddenly, without a warning, the mysterious tripping of the furious movement re-enters with its early stealth, and leads, as before, to the burst of the final Allegro. It is, I suppose, a sort of reminiscence of the early terror, in order to make more sure of the reality of the victory. Again, the triumphant song sounds, first vague, then defined; as the third melody appears in the tonic key, instead of the complementary, we have a queer feeling of nearing home; still more with the fourth in the same familiar region. But we must return once more to the happy strain of the episode. Then a bright, hilarious peal of the second theme, with new rhythmic charm. From here on the movement is ever faster and faster; not feverish; mere festal assurance of highest joy; until the last theme is rehearsed with doubled speed. Still faster, into a final re-

affirmance of the original theme of assured victory, extended into a complete close; but we cannot stop. We rush on, until, after endless vague reiterations, the end at last may merely come, because it must.

I have said that Beethoven is reported to have given casually an interpretation of his motto, "*So klopft das Schicksal an die Pforte*" ("Thus Fate knocks at the door"). I almost wish he had said nothing; that there might be a perfect test and example of the power of music to define sentient truth, truth of feeling. Starting with Beethoven's words, it is quite possible to build up a complete picture of the strife of spirit with fate. But as soon as the mind occupies itself with the details of an imaginative picture, the musical attention flags. It cannot be literally translated. The purpose of the master is not a picture for entertainment; it is the communication of a sentiment such as that under which great deeds are done and genuine greatness is achieved, which does not depend for its force upon its minute definability. The more closely we follow the music, the less we can stray from this true meaning, this content of sentiment.

Remarkable as is the contrast of the Fifth with the Seventh Symphony, its difference from the Third is even more striking. Rebellion against existing conventional tyranny and oppression is not rare in Beethoven, whether in words or in notes. But there is something far more, far deeper, in the Fifth Symphony. Whatever Beethoven may or may not have said, there is no resisting the convincing impression of a sense of dull, superhuman, overpowering external evil,—of hopeless supplication, of prayerful faith, of assured triumph. Whether we have labels or not, we feel that the burden is that greatest of man's problems, as in the tragedies of the Greeks, or in the religion of Jew and Christian. And the solution is no less convincing, nay, far more so, than if set forth in Kantian logic. It is as clear as words could make it a triumph, moral, not physical, and so much the more real. Fate has no power over man himself, the inner man. It cannot control character. The book of Job is not more specific in its content. But beyond all is the overwhelming power of music, which makes us feel it, not as a mere cold symbol, a statement, but as truth itself.

VII

SCHUBERT

Schubert is at once the most understandable and the most mysterious of tone-poets. It is not eccentric to begin thus with a paradox, for he himself was a living paradox, and the puzzle has never been solved. His music always speaks direct to the feelings. There is not the psychological abstruseness of Bach and Beethoven, although there is much suggestion of the mystic charm of deep searching for truth. Schubert is, without any doubt, far the most "popular" of the great masters, and in this position, it seems, he will probably never be displaced. We do not knit our brows in listening to him; we do not wonder at his meaning. We sit content in quiet ecstasy, like children listening to entrancing fairy stories.

But when we consider the poet himself, the machinery of the creation, so to speak, there seems to be no clue whatever. With all other composers it is possible analytically to discover so-called causes, inheritances, traditions, influences, from far and near, personal and national, broad and narrow. With Schubert we stand absolutely baffled. Since the earliest years of his career he has been the great mystery. To his daily companions, with all the free abandon of his good-fellowship, he was still " der Einzige," the only one, the unexplained. The mystery was increased by the lack of correspondence between his person and his genius. Schubert's presence is reported as insignificant. He had none of the heroic qualities of Beethoven, the delight in making an awful impression. But in any man the quality of pouring forth exquisite melody at such an extraordinary rate would be marvellous. It seems just like some *Tarnhelm*, or magic gift in legend. Schubert had, it would seem, the most remarkable natural endowment for musical creation of all. The only one to suggest close comparison here is Mozart. Alike they had this untiring, almost voracious impulse to write, Schubert in greater measure, however. He would write four and five songs in a day. He would finish one and straightway begin another, often never seeing them again, once failing to recognize one a few

178

weeks old. The thinnest poetry was enough
to start this golden flow of melody. Schubert
seems almost a passive instrument, obedient to
the voice of some restless external genius.
He seemed to do hardly more than hold the
pen. He utterly lacked the element of toil of
a Beethoven, a Schumann, or a Brahms. And
this very difference, as we have suggested, and
shall repeat later, is not at all an unmixed
advantage. Absolutely there seemed no limit
to the flow of his thought. As Schumann
said, he could have set a placard to music.
And, indeed, it is curious that while in his six
hundred and thirty-four songs he duly recognized the greatest poets, yet he set one after
another of utterly worthless *libretti* for opera,
actually burying reams of great music in the
rubbish of bad verse.

The difference from Mozart is for good and
ill. Schubert rarely reached the Olympian
mastery of Mozart, the fruit of early appren-
ticeship. So he lacked the control, the sense
of completeness. But Mozart had not that
magic virtue of Schubert, of lighting on some
touch of undreamt beauty which crowns the
mystery.

After all, it is not the mere velocity of creation that strikes us most. Much lesser men
have been equally industrious.* It is the utterly
new beauty that Schubert surprises us with in
songs, piano, and chamber works, and in symphonies.† While Beethoven slowly chiselled
out his utterance, Schubert found his without
searching. And it is this that seems to make
Schubert's art less part of himself, less subjective, more a wonderful gift, separate from his
own thought.

But it is curious and significant how Beethoven has that other quality which Schubert
lacks. Schubert has been called feminine
in contrast with Beethoven. This does not
seem happy. There is no loss of vigor, no
absence of virility and fire. But the broad
human sympathy that Beethoven breathes in

---

* Schubert might have written as much on a lower
plane, and have been deservedly forgotten. Part of his
work is on such a plane.

† Of course, once a high point attained, a poet is
seldom content with a lower level. But the wonder with
Schubert is how he could rest so long on a mediocre level.
Apparently he trusted quite passively to the arrival of
the true thought.

his *Andantes* comes only from the hero who has struggled and conquered, and looks on in sympathy. Schubert lacks this almost entirely; but we may be firmly persuaded that if he had lived longer he would certainly have achieved it. The reason we shall see later in his symphonies. But in the youthful career, which was, alas! the whole, he was the unconscious seer rather than the moral prophet and teacher. In so far as Beethoven marks an advance from Mozart to a stage where music expresses a higher degree of profound meaning, Schubert relapses into a state of purely spontaneous inspiration.

And yet, in our hopeless paradox, Schubert has elsewhere a striking resemblance to Beethoven. We have suggested in the Seventh Symphony the subtle kinship between the Allegretto and Schubert's melody in the song, "Death and the Maiden," on which he discourses at length in one of his famous quartets. To this same kind of magic melody belongs the Andante of Schubert's great C Major Symphony. It is of the vein, too, in which, as we have seen, Beethoven often begins his symphonies, especially the third and the seventh, the quality so difficult to express in English: the sense of mystic depth and meaning, that filled German poetry and philosophy early in the century, which must be true of all times and of all nations, utterly opposed to modern English traditions of a philosophy built on geology. It is quite apparent in the beginning of Schubert's Unfinished Symphony; indeed, in a sense, it permeates the whole. It expresses not so much a German national feeling as a certain national mission, or message of the Germans to the world through their philosophy, poetry, and music. And here is seen again the resistless power of Music in such things, in intensifying the deep poetry of Goethe, of Herder, of Schiller; in beautifying, in idealizing their sentiment, in glorifying their profound vision. Thus, through Schubert (and Beethoven) we actually understand better and feel much more strongly the thought of Fichte and Schelling, of German Romantic philosophy. He gives of that period of awakening the very essence of what Novalis is searching for.

But the note in Schubert is not quite the same as in Beethoven; it is more delicate, less sombre, softer, but true and sound, never morbid or weak. As we have said, if Bee-thoven is prophet, Schubert is seer. He has less of ethical leaven. But his genius is intensely poetic; it is the essence of lyric inspiration. Hence his greatness in song, not merely German; his perfect settings of the highest lyric flights of a Goethe and a Shakespeare. But his quality was less adapted to symphony, wherefore his true symphonies are all the more wonderful.

Like Weber in fresh romanticism, he is utterly unlike him in needing no outward objects or stories for his fancy. Yet he had an entirely different subjectivity from Beethoven's, purely lyric as against the heroic and epic. Schubert in his moments mounted higher than any. He was the Shelley and Keats combined of music; but they were usually mere moments, not continuous thought, on a high plane, save in these two wonderful symphonies.

We cannot put Schubert down as mere lyricist. He is not lacking in the philosophic insight of Goethe and of Beethoven. But with all his poetic impulse he had not so powerful a grasp of poetic analysis as Beetho-

ven, though he had a keener lyric intuition.
This is seen in his endless, sometimes fruit-
less, strivings,—the vacuous stretches in the C
Major Symphony and in many piano works.
It seems as if he writes waiting for an inspiration to come while writing; while Beethoven writes directly to the point of melody
or climax.

Some light on Schubert's indefinable personal quality comes from the feeling and
poetry of historic and national surroundings.
It is an age which, in music, philosophy, and
poetry is commonly given the name " Romantic." This seems very like a blind guide; for
if there is anything indeterminate, it is the
" Romantic" in art. Various definitions are
given which do not even suggest the same
idea. One from an intense Romanticist of that
day—Novalis, the poet-philosopher—a very
mild description, is the art of surprising in a
pleasing manner. If we think of men who
shared the spirit (and of others who lacked it),
we shall stumble upon a foothold. A pioneer
in this field, who was then thought far more
important than Schubert, was Weber. From
him we have a clearer idea of the reaction. But,

first of all, we must not confine Romanticism
to any one period. There is nothing fixed
in time or space about this pair of correlatives,—Classic and Romantic. We must remember that Mozart was once Romantic, and
Mendelssohn is generally thought Classic. Yet
the term has so striking a significance at the
beginning of this century, the contrast between
Schubert and Weber and their predecessors was
so great that the former will probably be for
all time typical Romanticists.

There is a curiously ponderous sort of analysis
by Philipp Spitta of the Romantic in Opera, in
four ingredient elements,—the imaginative, the
national, the comic, and the realistic. This is,
of course, too definite for general use. It will
fit but one period, which, to be sure, we are
now considering. The truth is, each master is
dual in this respect: he is romantic towards
the past and classic for the future. He works
for change in traditions and for permanency for
all time; otherwise he is merely reactionary.
The same thought, the same feeling cannot
be uttered twice in succession with the same
freshness and spontaneous beauty. So, without derogation to the past, a new poet must

create anew.* As against the permanent classic poetry of the earlier masters there was room and need for Schubert's fancy. And while all are classics for posterity, yet the striking change in Schubert from the masters, who were almost of his generation, makes him peculiarly and perennially Romantic.

We might very well in the last two chapters have called Beethoven Romantic, in reaction from Mozart, perhaps with as great accuracy as any other master. Indeed, Beethoven is often termed so. We saw him the exponent of that remarkable shock given to men's minds by the French Revolution, which affected staid statesmen as well as sensitive poets in verse and in tone. There was a violent awakening from the peaceful, childlike, playful writing of sonatas for the *salon*. Men were forced to be serious. This suggests one of the salient qualities of the Romantic which Novalis ignores and Spitta at most may imply in his element of realism. It is that in the Romantic, external beauty of form and outline is over-

---

* If Schubert had in any measure dethroned Beethoven (not to impute to him iconoclastic motives), he would have become the supreme classic.

shadowed by the urgent intensity of mere emotional content. This might be called a rebellion of realism against formalism, but with great caution. The realism is of feeling, of inner meaning, and this formalism implies no slur on real beauty of form, which is an indispensable symptom and test of true feeling.

After all, is not every master's youth strikingly his Romantic age, when he reacts against the formal dominance of his predecessor? Later he himself matures; his form corresponds to his new meaning; in turn he becomes, in his very pre-eminence, blighting to younger poets. In Schubert's earlier works, especially for piano, we see a flight from the tyranny of sonata-formality,* we see neglect of structural regularity and beauty of proportion for the sake of some stray nugget of golden melody, or of lesser figure or turn. It was again an emphasis on inner content as against outer symmetry. Later, Schubert undoubtedly approached a finer unconscious proportion between feeling and utterance. But he neither lived nor wrought

---

* Of course, this was unconscious again, for he wrote many " Sonatas."

long enough to become in his turn a top-heavy master of musical ceremony. And we must not forget—we shall be reminded of it later— his final absorption and mastery of the symphony; most significant, whether in the view of Schubert the master, or of the Symphony, as perennial channel of pure tonal poetry.

In the typical Romantic reaction there is necessarily less of the repose which conduces to homogeneous, finished treatment, with a certain conscious stress on its own beauty. In the Romantic there is the new emotion or idea which burdens the mind, drives it to a more definite utterance at all hazards, at the expense of conventional precept. With the true master this leads to wrenching and bursting the fetters of tradition without real violation of fundamental artistic principle, without actual formal weakness. Form in the abstract must never be confused with concrete conventional forms. But with less than complete mastery, its special strength which Romantic inspiration imports of melodic fulness or power of intimate definite utterance, almost inevitably involves some weakness in outline, in development, in discussion. We have here, uninten-

tionally, come upon a striking shortcoming
of Schubert. But this weakness which shines
through six or seven insignificant symphonies,
which nearly neutralizes the glorious melody
of many piano works, was finally conquered
in the achievement of two symphonies, that
may fitly and fairly rank with Beethoven's nine.

But we were thinking, in the Romantic reaction of highest mastery, of Beethoven. With
him it was a cosmic movement. With Schubert and Weber the feeling was rather a national one, and it is so expressed in the new
quality of their melody. Beethoven's melodic
scope was larger ; his most potent means lay in
profound power of treatment and discussion.

The national vein of Schubert and Weber
expressed a state of things which is now historic. It came from the same impulse which
stirred the first beginnings of German literature in a Lessing, a Wieland, a Herder, and a
Goethe, culminating in the united burst of
nationalism on the downfall of Napoleon.
Indeed, its final political expression is but an
event of yesterday. Music suffered under a
different tyranny from the French influence on
German literature. There it was the Italian

domination (not unlike the German glamour to-day in America), and, through the Italian, of the revived legends and heroes of Greek and Roman mythology. Mozart, in *Don Giovanni*, at last left the tiresome procession of shadowy Greeks, who had filled all early opera; as did Beethoven in *Fidelio*. But neither had the courage to write a pure German name. The strong sense for reality of sentiment and for dramatic truth in these operas does not constitute a distinct reaction; the tendency is too gradual. The Romantic rebellion came in Weber. He boldly threw over the Welsh suzerainty. Everything is freshly Teutonic,— language, titles, legends. characters.

But language, titles, legends, heroes do not concern us in pure music. The question is of melody. No one can deny the Italian quality lingering in Mozart; the achievement in Beethoven of a more catholic or cosmic strain; finally, in Schubert and Weber, the full blossoming of German lyric song in music, as with Goethe in verse. All this applies most directly to Schubert's *Lieder*. His realm, where he was long supreme, is the German folk-song, as against the Italian Aria of earlier opera. It scems that

Schubert, with all his personal genius, came at the mathematical point of time to voice in song the unuttered German national feeling.

But the German quality of Schubert goes far deeper. And here we cannot escape the question how far the symphony is dependent upon the folk-song. I can see no other answer than an immediate relation,—one that tends to mark the limits of original creation in art. In this sense, Goethe did not create his lyrics, nor did Burns. Neither invented the form, the metre of their song. They simply wrote in the manner of their own national folk-song. Thus each new lyric is but a variation on some old fundamental type.

In music this national quality is equally essential and pervasive. The symphony, as a group of great utterances in high art, can be sifted to a discussion of a few melodies or themes. All else is in a sense subsidiary. The theme is the substance, the text. Thus the bearing of folk-song on the greatest masterpieces is clearly all-important. (The meaning of such a relation for Americans is significant; we may return to it later.) We have treated above, as we describe below in detail, how Schubert expressed in his symphonies a feeling which had a strong relation to a spirit in German poetry and philosophy.

Far the most important trait of Schubert's career is what seems his moral evolution through mastery of the symphony. And here appears a wonderful, an entrancing, and a profoundly important mystery in the relation of art and ethics. Schubert was gifted with the talent which made sustained utterance in rounded, perfect, unconscious outline a difficulty; so he was morally endowed to make most difficult a certain balance, a thoroughgoing completeness. If he had yielded to his weakness, if he had become what moderns call a degenerate, he would have followed the line of least resistance, have written still more songs, have perhaps devised some new shift of form, eminently suited to his capacities and defects. But this is exactly what Schubert did not do. He struggled through seven ineffective symphonies, where there is no rounding out into unconscious completeness, where the melodic inspirations are not justified. But he did not yield in the double fight,—of artistic and moral self-realization. And, finally, none too soon, he achieved the double victory. In March, the C Major symphony was begun; in November Schubert died. This, his tenth symphony, is in every way typical, symbolic, directly eloquent of this greatest of heroic struggles, which ought to come to every man, whereby the artistic victory becomes an expression of the moral, and whereby the corresponding art-work has perhaps, as its greatest value, this stamp of ethical achievement. I should even say that, where this is not attained in artist or poet, the art or poetry cannot be of permanent value. Lacking this moral stamp, it cannot have lasting beauty; or rather in converse statement the principle is more clearly borne out. And this is the most striking value of Schubert's career. All this, too, must bring with it a correction of the prevailing monstrous theory that genius involves abnormality.

Symphony, B Minor. (*Unfinished.*)

(Allegro Moderato. Andante con moto.)

The Unfinished Symphony is equally remarkable, whether viewed in the whole literature of music, or merely in the group of Schubert's works. In the first place, it is not, as might be thought, his last work; it is in no way to be likened to the unfinished romances of great novelists. Yet, while written six years before the end of his short career, it seems, with perhaps one exception, absolutely his highest level, which he did not distantly approach for a long time. Then it is somehow strangely free from characteristic defects which troubled Schubert before and afterwards. Nay, it seems marked by the very qualities essential to the symphony which he most lacked elsewhere; so that, of all his nine symphonies, the unfinished, and the last, in *C Major*, are the only ones generally performed.

The work begins in a way like nothing save some touches of Beethoven (in the third and in the seventh symphonies), where the bass mysteriously foreshadows the melody. It is, after all, the bass to which you must look for the symphonic quality. Schubert's lyric leaning is betrayed by a too frequent tendency to run into accompanied melody. But here Schubert, with all the contrast, shows his strong affinity for Beethoven. We cannot put him off as a mere lyricist. The legend-like melody in the bass strings:

194

Allegro moderato.

is preparatory. But the melody is too subtle for formal statement. First comes a quivering in the strings (with rhythmic bass), where somewhere an indefinable melody is hovering. But presently, like a royal figure after his noble precursors, the real theme sounds high and clear, though in softest tone, in the woodwind:

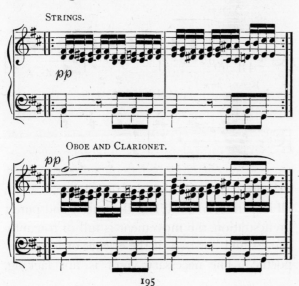

195

while the herald-figures lapse into attendants. Melodic separation seems, somehow, wrong. To drop theoretic phraseology for once, the whole is like a continuous flow of melody where each phrase seems chief until it pales before its successor.

So, after some overpowering clashes, which preserve the prevailing tone of delicacy and lightness from monotonous sweetness, there glides in, borne by the cellos, the most charming melody in all music:

delicately echoed high in the violins. With all its perfect melody, and the softest and purest orchestration, the movement is full of romantic shocks and bursts, as if the essence of legendary poetry. The necessary vigor is not lacking,

nor the true relation and balance of *dolce* and
forte. It is a mistake to view the crashing
chords as mere interlude between the verses;
they are quite as real a part of the poem as
any other. But with all the beauty of the
melodies and of the modulation (which was
Schubert's special secret), what is called the
development, after the repeated statement of
melodies, is somehow perhaps of the highest
spontaneity, although just here we might expect the greatest weakness.

A motive from the first phrase:

treated in canon, rises to a dramatic climax in
which, added to the dynamic effect, is an overpowering surprise of modulation. Again and
again the tempest seems about to subside into
the enchantment of the second melody, but

each time it rises to a new height. Now the whole orchestra sound the answering phrase in unison; then with the motive in the basses, the strings accompanying in *tremolo* figure, a wild perversion of their original melody, the whole orchestra thunders and storms in mad tossing about of the motive, where the secret of counterpoint is unconsciously invoked for the most dramatic of passages. Suddenly we are in the delicate, mysterious atmosphere of the first melody, and so on through the second, with a final repetition of the original bass figure to the end. The whole is the final essence of romance, the feeling of Arabian tales, with quick, sharp succession of happenings, good and ill, with no room for prosaic reflection.

The *Andante* begins more quietly, but it is in the same vein. At the outset there is the same melodic bass:

Andante con moto.

HORNS AND FAGOTS.

Basses an octave lower.

presaging the melody in the strings:

STRINGS (with melody doubled above).

pp

Indeed, the very quality of the tonal change of scene is characteristic of Schubert's modulation. Throughout, the duet between the active *staccato* bass figure and the quiet gliding of the violins is sustained. Perhaps it is its dainty surprises of modulation that somewhat take the place of the dynamics in the *Allegro*. Yet here in the second page is a sudden martial sound in the trebles, with a noisy lumbering in the bass like the tread of giants, suddenly thinning away into the original *pianissimo* melody. The whole episode of the first theme departs with the same phrase which introduced it. Equally complete is that of the second. Preceded by a curiously promising rhythm in the strings, the clarionets sing a melody so simple that you wonder where the charm lies.

Quoting will not show it; the secret must be in large part in the accompanying rhythm and in the exquisite turn of modulation. Indeed, it is not a strict melody at all, but melodic speech which might go on as long as the urging rhythm will hold out. In its later career it develops even more beauty, so that the beginning seems mere introduction. Suddenly the vision—at its loveliest—is rudely broken by loud crashes, where we lose all sense of connection with the past until we recognize a noisy minor of the basses, which is a gloomy memory of the second melody; the storm rages furiously, but in a trice ends with the enchanting rhythm which again promises the second melody in its true guise, this time exquisitely given in canon duet by cellos and violins. Again there is here one of the highest passages in all music; because to all his genius of melody, harmony, modulation, and rhythm, Schubert adds the unconscious mastery of counterpoint. Quietly the scene glides to the first melody, and then, as at first, through the various phases, gentle and wild, not without many new touches with which Schubert never fails to surprise.

SYMPHONIES AND THEIR MEANING

C Major Symphony.

The pervading trait of this greatest of Schubert's works is the large scale of its design, and with this a certain breadth and depth. Indeed, not only does it seem the shallowest judgment to call some modern work the tenth symphony, so clear is the superiority of Schubert's last to all its successors, I am even tempted to hold that in a still higher (and more perilous) ranking of masterpieces, Schubert's C Major belongs in a small group which would not contain all of Beethoven's symphonies. The C Major is certainly far superior to Beethoven's Pastoral, not to go further.

So complete is this unity in Schubert's symphony, a unity transparent in its very breadth and depth and continuous purpose, that the first movement, with all its dimensions and supreme perfection of form, seems like a great *fanfare*, prelude to the rest.

The movement itself begins with a prologue, *Andante*, in a curious prophetic way (like the Impromptu for piano in C Minor), without charm of rhythm or wealth of harmony, alone in solemn horns:

As the strain is taken up by others, and the strings sing an answer in many-voiced hymn, it is like an invocation. Soon there is a loud confident chorus in the original strain. Then a dainty answering melody from the oboe, with strange irruptions on the gentle song by the

whole orchestra, ever and again in eccentric alternation,—a kind of refusal to be committed to either humor. The echoes, continuing through gray changes of tonal color, finally break into a clear melodious close in the original key; slowly the prophetic atmosphere changes to one of joyful confidence. The first phrase is sung by the woodwind, with new movement in accompanying strings. The whole has some of that promise of coming rhythm which we saw in the prelude of the Seventh Symphony, and a similar gradual gathering of all to join in the great dance of the Allegro. There seemed to be in Beethoven and Schubert in the beginning of their symphonies a common feeling of solemn dedication to high purpose, which broke gently and with increasing momentum into exuberant song.

Suddenly there is a burst into that indefinite joyousness, just like the *Finale* of Beethoven's Fifth in its vague and boisterous turbulence. The literal mind must have its concrete traditions. It is uneasy without the official themes. Otherwise, there is too much barbaric high spirits. Indeed, this work is to some symphonies, above all to the Unfinished, what certain scenery of the Rocky Mountains is to other of the Italian Alps. You must view it more broadly, with larger angle of sight.

Here the noisy strum of the strings comes from an earlier phrase, alternating with a swelling vibration of the woodwind and horns:

But the only definite mood is just at the close, whence more light and more delight are

shed on the rehearsing of earlier melody. On goes the constant motion of the original strain in the strings, with continual breaking in of the jolly twittering of woodwind and horns, with

answering trumpet-calls, which increase in
vehemence, with an occasional descent into
melody. Then back to the main rhythmic

strain, when suddenly a new tune, with strange

Oboes, doubled below in Fagots ; Brass sustaining the harmony.

206

swing and accent, is heard in the oboes and
fagots. It is immediately taken up by flutes
and clarionets in higher pitch. Then both
groups fight for the word, shouting and answering back. Later there is a new accent in
whimsical humor.

Once in a certain swinging pace of answering
strains, with occasional intrusion of chord or
cadence from the whole chorus, and of straying
through cycles of tonal scenery, there seems to
be no end, as if all time were before us,—what
made Schumann speak of the "heavenly length."
At last, before returning to the beginning, we
enter on a broad, sweeping, universal cadence,
where the strings give the support of quivering
rhythm. Thrice the phrase is sung, each time
with greater emphasis; the last, ascending to
the highest summit, is absolutely conclusive:

SYMPHONIES AND THEIR MEANING

Full Orchestra.

Violins vibrating in unison with the respective wind-parts;
Fagots doubling the melody below.

Bass doubled below.

I think there is no mistaking a Hungarian flavor in the second melody. This rhythmic touch of the Slavonic constantly appears, as elsewhere in Schubert. It serves to lend a greater breadth to the Teutonic vein; it helps us unconsciously to transcend the limits of mere national feeling.

Sometimes there seems to be a characteristic tendency towards extension instead of depth. But in reality we have both; there is surely no lack of the maze of discoursing themes. In the discussion proper, which begins after repeated singing of melodies, there is at first a predominance of the Hungarian elfish (second) melody, with an added touch of Midsummer Night's Dream through Mendelssohn eyes.

But the rhythm of the first melody constantly

Oboes, doubled above in Flutes.

Strings with lower bass-note.

Oboes and Clarionets (joined by Fagots below).

Strings.

intrudes in the strings, always alternating with
the strain of the elves through magic changes
of light. But the rougher rhythm is reinforced,

Violins and Violas.

Cellos and Basses.

striding up and down in contrary motion, each way in double ranks, until with its multitudinous movement it seems to triumph, although the daintier rhythm is never lost. On through all sorts of lights and shades of tonal landscape, into a series of delicious suspended discords (of which Schumann later learned the special trick), while the rough motion of the first theme is drawn out in length until against the various dance of the rest the bass in strings and brass is solemnly sounding its legend:

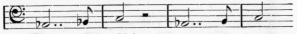

ff *Doubled above and below.*

In a sudden lull from the resounding chorus the same series of exquisite discords is heard most lightly, with melodious question and answer between voices in woodwind and strings:

211

p CELLOS AND BASSES.

Finally, again the lower strings, joined later by higher clarionets, sing the solemn chant against quivering violins, in a cadence whence the

FAGOTS sustaining the harmony.

pp

Doubled above and below.

original song of melodies is rehearsed to the end. It is all quite the same as at first, but magnified and heightened in the brilliancy of responsive song of tunes, in the mad *abandon* of movement; above all in the wonderful play of what musicians call modulation, of tonal color, like the magician's dazzling change of chromatic light. All is the same except the last word, best of all. Where we expect the final chord, the whole chorus break in confident, joyful tone into the melody of the invocation. Somehow, timidity, questioning, is gone. With the clear assurance of its rounded close, it is no longer Invocation; it is the Fulfilment.

Andante con Moto.

At last Schubert's long restrained melody has a vent. As the Allegro was all vague motion, this is pure, continuous melody,—one golden fabric.

To " explain" this lyric gem seems impertinent for two opposite reasons,—its simplicity and its mystery. It is the typical paradox of the master himself. There is, throughout, the puzzling blending of lightest humor with deep meaning. At the outset it seems clearly a restrained dance. But there is no escaping the sense of secret meaning, as in Beethoven's Allegretto of the seventh symphony, and espe-

cially in these first six bars, where, similarly, the
tuneful bass foreshadows the coming melody :

Then to the same sprightly step comes the
song of principal melody by oboe :

With sustaining Fagots and Horns.

If we cared to analyze more technically, we could see how the mixture of minor mood with sprightly gait helps the mystery. But, usually, in groping for ingredients, in tearing apart the rose-petals, the main fragrance is lost.

But the curious impersonal quality of the melody is seen by contrast in the little con-cluding strain in friendly major, with a clear, sudden touch of human feeling. Again, it is like the Trio in the Beethoven Allegretto:

215

But in the next boisterous blast of the whole band and in the striding of strings in mock heroic dignity, there is no doubt the childlike,

playful humor, pure fun, whence, through warning signs to hold our faces, we return to the serious beauty of the first melody. Still, it is now not the first song in doubling duet;

but there is the daintiest interplay between the
phrases of gentlest mockery:

OBOE AND CLARIONET.

STRINGS.

In octaves.

How wonderful is the versatile power of
music for mirroring humor. Could any words,
spoken or written, possibly approach remotely
its delicate changes? Here, while the boisterous
merriment is so apparent, yet, after these four
accented warning *E's*, with all the delicious
lightness of fancy, there is not a touch of
Teuton fun. It is all Oriental fantasy. Those
phases move through various contrasting rounds
until a third mood is upon us. Again there
is no doubt of the meaning. And, again, it is
what we had thought a special Schumann feeling. It is, too, a good instance of the way the
greatest masters are constantly using the simplest

themes,—the proverbial union of simplicity
with highest art.

Nothing is more natural than this descent of
four notes. To be sure, the preliminary step
of the bass down two full tones has much to
do with it all.

Now all mystery of spirit land is absolutely
gone. Here is an intimate, human dialogue,—
unter vier Augen, as the Germans say; and the

little endings, always recurring like repeated friendly greetings, with assurance of good-will:

Woodwind doubled above.

But immediately with the descent into minor, there is the momentary slight transition to the hazier realm. For the moment there is a refuge in a playful strain, hiding the head in ostrich fashion. Then through curiously repeated warn-

Clarionet and Fagot below.

ing notes held unchanged, through shifting harmonic scenery, in the horns, heralds of

legends, we are back in another canto of our
Arabian fairy story.

Now to the original mysterious melody of
oboe is added in horns and trumpets, later in
violins, a still lighter playfulness. It is a little
like a child playing in the midst of danger,—
Media in vita, etc. :

The side tunes grow ever more melodious.
So again come the other phases, similarly enriched. When next the humorous episode
comes round, with the sudden noisy burst and
the strutting of strings, it is much extended.
The woodwind in a minor blast seems to have
a difference of opinion with the strings in the
major. All through there is the evident tendency to amplify, to repeat, to hold the floor :
inevitably the old Schubert trick of talking for

an inspiration. There are strange strokes of the
whole orchestra in unison, alternating with an
ominous chord, which interrupt the merry skipping up and down :

Strings doubled above.

Strings doubled below.

This continues in almost pure iteration, with
hardly perceptible variation, always with interrupting chords arresting the skipping movement, until we feel ourselves unexpectedly rushing somewhere, with increasing violence, at last
leaping furiously on a final height.

And here is again that best of all, that golden
nugget. We knew it would come if Schubert
would hold on, like the angler playing patiently
for his trout. Of a sudden, out of the wild,
insistent chord of mad questioning, after a
complete pause, comes a transformation of
scene or mood. Instinctively we feel we must
not inquire into the magic of the master. A
sudden change of tonal color, whose like is
nowhere in music, brings a new strain in the

cellos on a former subject in simplest confidence.

There was a subtle way of transition by smallest step as through secret spring; the slighter the outer change or journey, the greater the transformation. No one knew this secret spring save Schubert; with him it died.

The first time, the close is in dreamily mournful minor; the second, with the same confiding song, the close is the clearest reassurance of serene major, whence we continue directly into another verse in the friendly strain of the second melody, with its artless, homely phrase.

A keen man of literary power has suggested, among his friends, a classing of composers in some such way as : 1st, The Prophet; 2d, The Counsellor; 3d, The Friend; 4th, The Tempter. It is exactly true. And we are reminded of it by the analogous variety of relation in one master. Clearly Schubert has at first more of the impersonal seer, even stern monitor, and then quickly glides into friendliest, soothing speech. So comes again the momentary strain of playfulness; again the warning herald notes in the horn of the final verse of the fanciful legend. There is now a curious chariness in ornament and rhythm, a halting in the last words, as if to add a certain insistent sincerity. The dance has almost ceased. It is no longer the child playing in the lightning. It is more reflective, with a fine little *envoi*, a minor memory of an old strain. With kindly humor, it marches up the hill—and down again:

OBOE (joined by Clarionet and Flute).

STRINGS (*pizzicato*).

Scherzo, Allegro Vivace.

We are so accustomed to humor in words that it is difficult to think of its utterance through another medium. To some, I suppose, humor in music is almost incredible. To discuss such a question is to be drawn into an endless perambulation, losing our way utterly from the central purpose. The trouble lies largely in the scope of the word humor. Sometimes it does seem that, while for the expression of feeling music is far the most powerful of the arts, humorous utterance is easiest in prose. But here it would become necessary to distinguish elements of humor, or at least different kinds, where the danger of straying looms greater than ever. It may not be too broad to say that when humor is largely compact of light, merry sentiment, music is still the more natural medium. Much of the humor we are accustomed to, seems largely a game, with a jumbling together of concrete things, where by accident a striking contrast results. There is much more of chance here than of original, creative feeling. It necessarily lies out of the bounds of music, which has naught to do with visible realities.

Humor, as in a conventional sense, the rut of common minds, is no more important than a meaningless game; in another sense it may need the highest power of human thought and utterance.

The instinct for surprise, for sudden contrast of opposites, has certainly a free field in music. The very first of the secular masters, Haydn, was eminently a humorist. I have seen a musical child laugh involuntarily over a Haydn scherzo. Beethoven's humor we have studied. It was not altogether amusing. It is that rare compounding of serious latent purpose with the show of lightness. It is not cynical; for a warped, a hopeless sentiment cannot be uttered in high art. If it could, Offenbach would be a classic. Sardonic it can fairly be called; and thus music again shows a distinction of feeling more clearly than any words. Between the qualities of humor of Beethoven and of Offenbach, not to speak at all of the strength, is an infinite gulf. Sinister, even, Beethoven appears often. But it is all, like other universal minds, like Aristophanes, like Cervantes, like Shakespeare, it is discoursing, in apparent play, on the highest themes. It is in central purpose neither light nor despondent. The frivolous dance in the seventh symphony is really a cosmic joy; the temporary gloom of the fifth makes the final triumph all the brighter.

We cannot pretend that Schubert has herein any similarity to Beethoven. Nor can it be said that Schubert had striking humor; we should not call him humorist. He had not the keen power of conjuring strange opposites; the comic was not his favorite element. He was not disciplined in its special expression. So it seems his *scherzo* mood lapses into mere merriment, not sharply distinct from other *allegro* feeling save perhaps in its irresponsible lightness:

SCHERZO.
Allegro vivace.

STRINGS.
Doubled below in two octaves.

This theme of the scherzo strikes us, in its unison, with a certain clownish heaviness, lightly answered in the woodwind, with playful drums beating clumsily at the theme:

It rushes with headlong speed to a climax in a cousin key, whence, while clarionets and fagots are still chattering away at the theme, the violins and cellos have a duet in a melody where play is more blended with romance. But again the boisterous spirit dominates. Its further career, the bass ponderously dancing to the quick theme, seems all committed to noisy motion, when suddenly the *elf* feeling, which gleamed here and there in the first movement, dances forth alone from the earlier turbulence:

228

And so through jolly mocking of piping, laughing wood and buzzing strings. All at once the latter have dwindled to strumming of dance beat, and the flute sings aloft a clear,

WOODWIND.

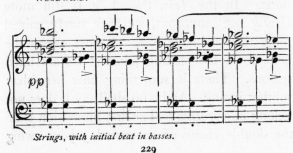

Strings, with initial beat in basses.

229

gentle song, and in a new scene in the forest, by one of those unpremeditated tone changes of the poet's.

And now the same song is heard in another corner of the wood, from the oboe, but more boisterously, until the dance can no longer be restrained, and the old fun breaks out much more freely and stormily than before. With the Titanic horse-play there is the sharp alternation of daintiest talk of sprites, mostly of violins, each having his say in turn in the

phrase, ending the *scherzo* much in the original burst. In the *Trio*, though it is still more clearly not humorous, we have surely gained more than we have lost. A poet cannot be held down to cracking jokes at certain fixed seasons. There is something finer here than subtlest jesting. And who shall say it does not belong in a *scherzo*? The first impression is of the double charm of an eternal, joyous swing and a clear, simple song. It is one of those places where we suddenly hear human singing in the orchestra. In every way there is contrast with the preceding,—in the gentle gliding, in the sweet simplicity of the song, in every way save one; though we cannot clearly see. Somehow, the rate of movement is exactly the same as before, under different guise. The charm of the constant, swinging, sweeping motion, of greatest speed with least show of effort, is indescribable,—like the march of a big Niagara, like the planets themselves. Distinct from the song, the swinging pace is double, the even gliding phrase of violins, ever ending with the skip of the brass. Or rather it is the constant mingling of two distinct paces, the glide and the skip, where now one, now the other is in relief, according to the ear of the hearer. One supplies the continuous element of perennial go, the other gives the perpetual fillip of new impulse. And in united woodwind, blending the various motion is the broad sweep of the great universal love-song, too big for fragmental discussion, pouring out verse after verse, a stream of purest melody, without economy of themal logic :

And with this faithful accompaniment of motion the song continues:

Then off into the minor, always with the loyal satellites, with the same sweep, and with all the events of a song, surprises of tonal color, of closes that do not end, of those special intimate asides of Schubert's:

233

Here a broader swing than ever bursts forth:

Woodwind, doubled above and below.

Earlier double rhythm in strings and brass.

all with pervading completeness and perennial freshness, that is hopeless to suggest without full quotation. Always the dainty reserve and the broad pealing forth, each inviting the other in turn. There seems no reason why it should end, except that all things end. In all this never varying continuity of subsidiary motion, and the constant swing of the song, changing only in its own burden, there is a great sense of freedom from restraint and commotion.

Never before or since has a master so ignored the element of discussion. We feel we have reached an empyrean of lyric song which is above all mystery, above even questioning and the need of discourse. The fall to the scherzo is almost that of the proverb,—certainly from the sublime to the humorous.

Finale, Allegro Vivace.

We have followed the symphony so far, saying little of a general plan. It is perhaps less
apparent than in the great Beethoven poems,
the Eroica, the Fifth and Seventh Symphonies.
But while we might easily have guessed a general meaning earlier, it is, after all, our rule to
cloud the evidence of the music itself as little
as possible with our own preconception,—
rather to have the pervading quality break
upon us unwitting, convincing us with the
reinforced evidence from all regions of the
work.

But inevitably the first sounds of the *Finale*
bring us back to the broad scale of the beginning. It is the same vague carelessness of

Doubled above and two octaves below.

articulate tune ; fearlessness of endless iteration of an expressive strain ; a perpetual go ; an ever-impelling drive that knows no rest ; a vagueness of utterance for its own sake.

The first approach to definite phrase (strange how in defined expression there is at once a descent from the very joy we are uttering !) is in the oboes, doubled by fagots below, while the violins keep up the ceaseless flow of motion, and the basses and the horns give the motive impulse, adding something of the pulsing rhythm of the *Trio :*

236

STRINGS (the melody played in quarter-notes by Oboes, and Fagots below).

Most of the charm must lie in the sense of endless, pleasant motion, like the first railroad journey or ocean voyage. And, as in the *Trio*, the accompanying movement once established, the song sweeps freely along, singing its burden, without heed of other voices:

soaring boldly into higher and still higher flights, and ever the unceasing rush of coursing violins and pelting horns until there is an unheard of, overpowering momentum. Suddenly we are in the first phrase, with answering cadences, whence we find ourselves in episodes of sheer drive :

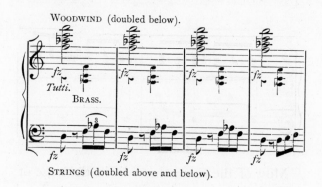

The profound discourse of polyphony, even the lyric distinctness of melody, are all forgotten in this onward, restless, and ceaseless coursing. At most, there are some such answering strains as that which immediately follows the last quoted phrase. Oft reiterated are these pounding passages of pure, rushing rhythm all carried to a furious climax, where the wind hold a long

WOODWIND (doubled an octave above and below).

STRINGS (doubled an octave above and below).

chord, while strings and drums are exhausting
their momentum on the simplest figure, ending
abruptly in a crash:

Doubled twice below.

After a lull, during which you can almost
hear the drive as you see the sun with closed

eyes, suddenly here is the melodic germ, the
heart of the movement, always sure to come,
like gold to the miner, after those long ham-
merings of Schubert. It is a miniature of
the old gigantic thumping, as of shadowy
imps. But the grace is rarer than before, and,
above all, here, out of the four long notes,
a song proceeds, clear and human:

All the pent-up vagueness has found speech, in which it glories, exults, revels, first timidly whispering, then with involuntary burst, retiring again into almost inaudible recesses and hidden scenes; suddenly breaking forth into clear light with glad presence, with unrestrained shouts, and all supported with this irresistible dance. Indeed, we cannot let it go. When the poet returns to the older, stiffer movement, we cry out for the gladder step, as for a native element, and—we get it. Just those four hammering notes with the clattering course. And we are happy in the mere motion, in all guises, higher and higher; now thundering near by, now humming far off,—at last with a seeming end in the broad cadence, while the violins are vibrating

WOODWIND AND BRASS (doubled above and below).

to the same tune and the low horns and strings are holding up the harmony.   But instead of ending, the latter basses are shouting out the tune a little varied, while the others are not so

Doubled below.

important, diminishing in violence and repeating more softly, while the high woodwind soon take courage and join the tune in piping pitch. But soon we are in a mere vague hum of the low strings, while some wood and brass notes are hopping faintly at the old dance.* And thus dying down to a murmur, we are willing to wake suddenly and, returning to the beginning, go through the glad frolic again.   When that is over we sit down and think it over.   We can now be a little reflective.   So we toss the fine tune, now our own by long search, about here and there, while movement is reduced to the least shuffling in the strings, suggestive, it is true, of the old rhythm.   Very softly, in a new

---

* The hearer must not be literal nor too consistent. He must follow about with quick sympathy of insight.

scenic spot, we sing the song and quietly add
an answering strain:

The whole atmosphere is changed. There is a shadowy gloom of deepening woods, of coming dusk. The air is cooler. There is a half sadness of reflection as bits of the theme occur here and there,—in minor, too, in confused, jumbling comparison with others. In the dreaminess the dance is almost gone. But soon a new energy appears. The high violins sing the melody with a kind of trembling anxious-

ness, still higher, more plaintively and insistently, the wind gradually joining in sympathy, finally, almost in triumph. And now the glorious old pæan sounds out in basses and brass (giving increased assurance), while the rest shout in fervent acclaim:

STRINGS.

Basses in Strings and Brass.

Tutti, with octave below.

Here it is one long triumphal procession. Nothing can describe the terrible magnificence of this elemental dance. The very ground under us is rocking to the rhythm, not to speak of the increasing maze of voices singing the answering phrases in disjointed confusion. When at its height, the cellos are discovered very softly but firmly sustaining the marching song, while the violins are mockingly strutting about; oboes and fagots are gently singing a new melody in unconscious harmony with the rest. The only ominous figures are the drums beating softly and continuously. They soon betray their purpose, when, first faintly, then more insistently, the motive is

heard summoning all gradually back, trooping more and more tumultuously, once again to the original chorus;

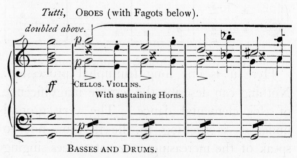

Tutti, OBOES (with Fagots below).

246

The final refrain of the old order of melodies is in the usual broad spirit. The first smooth melody of the woodwind is often rehearsed in minor, to ascend the more joyfully into corresponding major. After all the prelude and actual entrance of the great phrase of childlike triumph, there is the loud singing of the smooth melody in the basses, again dying down to a lull. But from here on it is little more than ever eager cries of the great melody, in first part and second. Towards the end, the former comes in four mighty thumps in sheer hard unison tones (almost unmusical), followed by four chords shouting in answer,—question and answer recurring again and again, lapsing at last into the broad cadence. Then the whole symphony ends in the trumpet calls which begin the last Allegro, and in the spirit of *fanfare* which began and pervades the whole.

247

VIII

SCHUMANN

It is a most interesting question just what and where is the greatest work of any poet or musician, and it is, of course, closely akin to the secret, perhaps unfathomable, of Art itself.

We are apt to fall into a rather palpable error ; to confound greatness in dimensions with greatness in substance ; to think that the longest works, or those on the largest scale, or those on which the poet has most toiled, or of which he was most ambitious, are necessarily his master-pieces. We have all heard the famous advice to destroy whatever seems in the writing most happy.

The question is, it seems, much more subtle than has been supposed. There is no doubt that just as some men, very like others in most respects, perhaps in many inferior, for hidden reasons will utter thoughts infinitely more valuable to the world, just so the same man, for reasons occult to himself, will at times be a prophet, at others a bore. Much of Schubert, much of Beethoven, is not the real Schubert, is not the real Beethoven. Perhaps it all comes back, after all, to the quality we have so often given stress,—unconsciousness. It is the strange, almost contradictory element of tonal art in particular. It seems that the best of man's thought is uttered when he is not watching himself; that no man can work his highest, with a perfect knowledge of the existing conditions of his art; so that it seems almost true advice to a poet to reject his own judgment. There seems to be a secret magic in the lack of conscious deliberation. Yet, we are asked, Where is then our *art*, our hard achieved mastery, if we are not to use it as resource in our design? The answer comes with inevitable iteration; all this past struggle and mastery has full weight, but only as unconscious resource, as experience rather than study. So there is no advice here to dispense with toil, to shout forth our first wild emotion, without care of clear and true expression; for the more we toil in reverent pursuit of our art, the more powerful we are for unpremeditated utterance. It is, on the contrary, the one who lacks the patience for mastery, who fails in this respect to his art, that is most often driven to deliberate calculation and padding labor. It is the early discipline that, never relaxed, produces the perfect mastery of language, which is indispensable for true spontaneity. The element of work, which must enter into all art, at first was toil, later is forgotten in the joy of utterance. While founded on this hidden basis of early apprentice-ship, a true art work must spring from an invol-untary feeling, must not be too compact of conscious care.

It is thus an absorbing question : Where is the greatest Schumann ? It seems, sometimes, that his genius did not find perfect content in the forms hallowed by the highest art before him ; that he may have turned to them in a spirit of challenge, to show his mettle. To show the maze of such a problem,—it is quite possible to hold that whole passages of his symphonies are more beautiful than any of his shorter works, and yet that, as a whole, the latter may be superior. There is a tremendous responsibility about large dimensions ; so that a long episode of the greatest perfection may be actually neutralized by failure in proportion and relation of the rest.

Schumann's was a poet nature of the sharpest individuality, yet, withal, so deep and versatile, that we have no sooner found the typical trait than we seem to see it with equal truth in each of several other qualities. One of the most striking is his power of definite characterization. Of course, the mention of such a thing brings us back to the old question of the purpose of the art. And it suggests the query whether, if feeling be constantly refined to an ever more delicate shade, the final result will be as clear as the verbal thought. Only we must never forget that the mere outward significance, the guessing of the word-title, is of no value in itself.

After the climax of the classic masters, there seems to have been a tendency towards exploring the limits of the power of music to specialize a " meaning." Direct utterance of simple feeling yielded to this dazzling experiment. Berlioz is probably the most typical representative of this tendency; yet how simple seems the refutation of his own labels which he would intersperse through the pages. Opera was given a new impulse. It is most grateful to find in

Schumann just the right perception of this power of music; and it is interesting to see how his nature and his training led to the distinguishing quality of his poetry.

Schumann and Mendelssohn were the first of the masters born and bred in a social class whose main function was not the service of another; to whom education and culture were their own right and need. So Schumann was early steeped in poetry; more so, indeed, than in music. And his mind, thus inclined towards a more reflective art, was confirmed in this direction by a course, however irregular, in jurisprudence. The taste for meditation is hard to abandon. In music its effect was to lead men to prefer to explore hidden recesses of thought and of special sentiment, national, legendary, or local, rather than to utter naïve bursts of untitled feeling. It is not until our day, of Brahms in particular, that we have returned to the more natural attitude.

Schumann was the first master who had the distinction not to be an infant phenomenon. The most wonderful musical feat told of his youth was a mimicry of friends at the piano; and it is characteristic, too, of his later genius.

SYMPHONIES AND THEIR MEANING

There was here an early temptation to translate ideas into music. The boy's channels of influence were literary; it was thus that impressions came to him. Music was not his first native element in which he lived, breathed, listened, and spoke unconsciously. He received in verse and gave out in tones. It seems that this habit found a strong introspective quality in his nature to build upon.

It cannot be difficult to see his aims by sympathetic intuition. To educated men the feeling for logical thought is almost the stay of life. To abandon it is like selling the soul. It is here that religion so often fails to hold the most honest minds. But a generation or two ago this leaning on the saving grace of reason was stronger far than to-day. The further we go from the mediæval sway of deductive philosophers, the less faith we have in the final power of mere reasoned knowledge to win salvation. Modern science, equally in its achievements and in its disappointments, has changed us. We have certainly become more agnostic, and we have been led beyond the true line by riotous fads and follies in all the arts, by abandonment of ethical and artistic ideals.

SYMPHONIES AND THEIR MEANING

We have gone far astray, forgetting that, while deductive reasoning can never give original or final truth of itself, it is, yet, the only sure way to arrive from one truth to its successor. Indeed, the virtue lies not in the logic of words, but goes back to the saving principle of true *sequence*.

It is this word, more perhaps than any other, which tells the supreme achievement of Schumann. He felt unconsciously bound to add to the honor of his art in thus increasing her power of clear utterance. It is even now the common charge we hear brought against music by those who are rather proud of their ignorance, that music means nothing, is therefore a mere matter of the senses. Every musician, until he sees the truth, must feel the sting. But the fact is that in its own perfect sequence lies the clearest test of the truth of its thought and utterance, —more clear far than the test of logic textbook. It is in the perfect mastery of the art in all its lines, of melodic phrase, of combined agreement of several strains, of the rounding out of the whole, in the verification of perfect beauty of the complete art work, that lies the security for real truth. For this mastery of the language gives the power of uttering honest feeling; indeed, the connection is double, for the mastery itself is based originally on the fundamental honesty of artistic purpose.

It is the inner perfection of workmanship, not the outer evidence of signs and labels, that bears witness to the truth of the tonal art.

Schumann can be seen striving in all kinds of ways for this hidden power of music. One was a curious device of themes from the musical letters of names of special significance. For instance, almost all the scenes of the " Carnival " are based on notes which represent the musical letters of his own name, S c h a. They happened to be the same as those of the town *Asch*, which at one time had a romantic meaning for Schumann. Thus, by the German nomenclature, *Asch* would be *A*, *Es* (E♭), *C*, *H* (B):

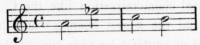

A splendid example of this sort of musical punning are the inspiring fugues on the name *Bach*. Sometimes this seems a mere unimportant amusement; at others it betrays an undoubted sense of symbolism. Another view, which at once answers two separate needs of Schumann's nature, is that, however unimportant the themes are in themselves, the stress is laid on their treatment. In other words, no matter what your theme, you can talk about it musically. Thus we can talk about Bach and others in music. It must be admitted, of course, that there is here too little importance of its own beauty allowed to the theme. Yet all the more genius and power of sequential thought is required in this discussion. And this element of discussion, extended greatly even beyond Beethoven, explored vast fields in the power of music for more definite significance. It is best to regard all this writing as experimental in the possibilities of themal development.

Of much higher dignity are those poems of musical characterization like the Children's Scenes and the Forest Scenes, where he conjures up in simplest touches the quintessence, not of the outward situation or event, but of the peculiar feeling which enshrouds them. The superficial critic, who speaks too quickly, says, "Of what use are the titles, if the music tells the story?" He cannot forget that the mere conjecture of the particular title in the poet's mind is of no gain. The music is not a picture of this and of nothing else. There is a feeling here uttered which is certainly associated with this situation, in however many others it may also reside. The feeling is all we care for. Rather pertinent here is Beethoven's experience in the Pastoral Symphony. It is well known how at first he directed the reader to find the situations for himself. But on completion, he gave precise labels everywhere, and added, "Rather an expression of feeling than a picture." The poet is bound to help us to this enjoyment by telling us all he knows; it is not a guessing match. In agreement with this is Schumann's own admission that he always wrote the title after composition. He never set out deliberately to translate a certain subject into tonal language. It was undoubtedly in this mood and with this equipment that Schumann wrote his songs, which, independent of their wealth of beauty and depth of sentiment, came to the world as absolutely new conceptions of the power of music to mirror the particular emotional significance of the words.

But these are relatively the less important

elements of Schumann's art, though to discuss
them thus categorically is to ignore the inseparable totality with which they express his genius.
So when we have spoken of his sense of sequence
in music, we have said but little unless we take
into account some of the strongest influences
of his youth. In the fore of these must be
placed the great German prose-poet, Jean Paul
Richter. So direct and overwhelming was his
power over Schumann's thought, that one
might almost say, Who does not know Jean
Paul, does not know Schumann. Undoubtedly,
reading the former throws the brightest light
upon the intent of the latter.

In Jean Paul we feel the sole prominence of
pure sentiment, the ruthless, almost cynical
subordination of everything material; the extravagant contempt of facts, of objective personalities, of events, of plot, in riotous revel of
unalloyed feeling. Then we remember the
sudden succession of humor and pathos, all
part of this plan of revolt from the tyranny of
concrete externals; and, too, we know that
with all this whim of sudden change there is
not only no lack of connection, on the contrary, there is in the very contrast of emotions

and in the freedom from hostile realities of outward sense, the closest continuity, one unbroken
fibre of emotional experience.

It seems as if Schumann was almost conscious of his mission as the Jean Paul of music.
The nature of his art left him free from the
intrusion of the world of concrete sense. This
influence of Jean Paul's strikingly reinforced
Schumann's other tendency towards musical
meaning and sequence. It gave him a peculiar
power of consecutive musical thought, a sense
of development quite beyond that of Beethoven,
although in his path. The theme being relegated
to mere text, all vital stress was laid on the
following out of the emotional thread wherever
it may lead. Wedded to this power was an
intensity of abandon to an absolute subjective
emotion (utterly reckless of a conventional
world), which bears most indubitably the
stamp of sincerity beyond even the faintest
suspicion of conscious attempt to please. Thus
lost in the concentration of his emotion, he
gives its essence, turning music away from its
supposed vocation of mere beauty to the most
powerful utterance of high feeling, becoming
almost definite by this very intensity.

The most direct examples here are the Novelettes, which are not only greatest among Schumann's works, but of the greatest of all piano literature. By this wonderful threading of the theme, and by these magic contrasts of feeling, there is the clearest sequence of narrative, so that you can almost read off the story. At any rate you have the same essential gain,—all but the dry, dead weight of facts and names. For the very pleasure of reading a story, I should turn as eagerly to Schumann's Novelettes as to any prose-writing. And then it is always equally fresh, with ever new changes of unimportant details. It is not at all the mere tempest of on-rushing drive in one theme ; the best is always some sudden exquisite phase of new tender feeling, that by its contrast shows the closest continuity. There is probably no work in all the literature of music so aptly named as Schumann's Novelettes.

The only other influence to be compared with that of Jean Paul's was one within the domain of his own art. To be sure, there can be traced in Schumann's works more or less pervading traces of several musical personalities. Schubert is very distinct in the intimate touches, the *naïveté* of melodic flow, the surprises of modulation. But it seems that one other master affected not merely Schumann's style, but, more deeply, his mode of musical thought. And with him we come to what bids fair to be a perennial mystery in musical literature. The posthumous career of Bach's influence is not only striking as a type of the final triumph in art of the good, by its inherent power; it must appeal to us, alone from its dramatic pathos. To our modern democracy, it seems that all salvation for the artist, all true and final judgment must ultimately lie with that awful tribunal, the people, quite without regard to its capacity, not of judging, but merely of understanding. Thus a critic in a recent book* actually advises the musician to bow to the triumph of the composer who has conquered "his quarter of the globe," swallowing all convictions of right. Thus it does seem that the greatest danger to music comes from its friends, who yield a certain sacred trust. With them the old ideal of truth, of right in itself, has absolutely ceased to inhabit the uni-

---

* Apthorp's "Musicians and Music-Lovers."

verse. The only result can be a mad, vulgar scramble for the nod of the mob.

Bach stands as the eternal denial of all this. When the rest of the world was revelling in the delights of the new toy, opera, which all but upset the grave beauty of church music, which drove out the ideal of high art, and left sensuous melody the sole usurper, this master quietly wrote his German oratorios, his organ music, and other instrumental forms in the spirit of the high art of strict discipline, all within the limits of a German province, harassed by the worries of an ill-paid organist. The true value of Bach is still enigmatic. His is, strangely, a rising influence, which cannot even now be justly gauged. There seems to be no doubt that in his peculiar mastery of the art he is not only highest of all, but he is almost incredible in the achieved power of his equipment. But, to return to the man, to show the absolute isolation of the artist from the applauding crowd, he wrote on to a good old age in his modest rut of outer life, with a family of twenty children forming probably the main nucleus of his following, and then died and was forgotten. Let the modern world of sudden *furore*, of mad

popular judgment, think how long was the sleep
of his spirit. Just one hundred years after the
first performance of his great work, " The Passion according to St. Matthew," it was unearthed
and brought to light and living sound by Mendelssohn. And ever since, Bach's power has
been steadily waxing,—only over the minds of
musicians and masters, never with the people
directly,—growing absolutely by the sole force
of its inherent truth and nobility. It cannot
down, though it can never, in its nature, be
popular. It is almost like a decalogue in art.
And so, be it fate, or, better, the force of truth
direct, there is preserved the work of this giant
hero, who single-handed upheld the traditions
of highest art in the time of its greatest peril.

It seems inevitable that this influence of
Bach's is destined to be borne indirectly through
other masters, like some high truth of Egyptian
priesthood. We can see some reason for this.
The forms of Bach's writing are, save one, not
adapted to popular hearing on any great scale.
Even in Germany, it is probably only his oratorios, sung in church, that are known directly
by the people. And it seems that there is some
limitation here in Bach's genius itself, although

it is almost profane to attempt individual judgment. But by the nature of the spirit of religious mystery and man's self-effaced devotion that Bach uttered, he was driven rather to an altitude of deep, high meditation than of free individual expression. So in his writings, almost paradoxically, the actual total effect of separate works seems less important than the quality of his musical thought. And therefore Bach has ever needed a mediator for his final assertion; a new master who will reconcile the profound vein of his thought with modern ideas of art forms. But the great compensation, we might say, is that, while the horizon of all others seems limited, the latent power of Bach seems in an unending increase.

The paradox of Bach's art is a most tempting one; but its final pursuit does not belong here. We remember how, in the first emergence of music from the school-days in the cloister, there was a period of utter abandon from meditation to exuberant revel of individual feeling. Bach's art came before all this. Later, the crowning masters of the secular epoch sought a return to the profundity of the early cloister days. But even in Beethoven this was never

quite attained. There is always a great difference between the analytic meditation (what
musicians call counterpoint) of Beethoven and
of Bach. There is lacking a certain psychological, introspective quality. After all, with all
the later complexity of Beethoven, his whole
art is on a different basis from that of Bach.
It is originally secular, lyric, monomelodic;
only later did it turn towards polyphony. Bach
was meditative to the core.

While Mendelssohn brought Bach's works
to the surface, Schumann was the great master
who absorbed his spirit and thought. Almost
a man, Schumann turned to Bach as the highest
artistic oracle. This influence throws a double
light on each master. It makes Bach clearer
and Schumann. In both is the strong, reflective hue of thought, and the polyphonic mode
of expression. In Schumann's symphony we
seem almost to see how Bach would have gone
about it. It might be said that as Bach is the
Religious Meditator, Schumann is the Romantic
Psychologist. Just one example, out of all
this mass of theoretic speculation, will at once
give proof and throw light. It is a lightest
touch, but I believe it is typical. In one of the

Forest Scenes, "Lonely Flowers," the whole picture is the literal intertwining of two slight, graceful themes. Throughout there is hardly a note that is not of individual voice, that is not what the wise men call polyphonic. It is the pure Bach art applied, almost idealized, in secular poetry.

It is not difficult to see how this influence reinforced a native trait of Schumann, of introspection that was sometimes morbid. But again we must see how it affected merely the process of thought, not the outward shape of art work. Mendelssohn followed Bach in the external outline. It could not be expected of Schumann. He wrote no oratorio, no organ sonata. And we are thus brought to the final and the paramount view of Schumann's art.

Too much stress cannot be laid upon the entire difference of *form* as an abstract conception, as an element of art, like melody or harmony, and *forms* as mere conventional examples of the other. No ideas are so relentlessly confused. The commonest answer to the charge that a musician lacks the power of form is to decry traditional types like the sonata or the symphony. You might as well confine the idea of dress to the pantaloons. It is utterly forgotten that form is a quality of creative thought, not a prescribed law. Musicians otherwise of the soundest will constantly tell students that the recipe of composition consists simply in the filling of the classic moulds with original themes,—nothing more. The fact is that true form is absent exactly as this prescriptive form is present. The sonata and the symphony can live on only as long as poets feel their exigence for their thought; they will die as soon as they are obeyed as mere authority.

Schumann in the respect of form has been much misunderstood. It was in the nature of the poetry of his time to forsake temporarily (for its own sake) the great models of the classics. In the German prose literature of the day is seen the chaotic impulse, delighting in disorder, in overthrowing the old, in chasing madly after some butterfly sentiment, and yet, in all the loose mass of disconnected episodes, having a very decided continuous thread. Only the thread is not external, of story or plot; it is a unity of feeling in one subjective personality through contrasting situations. This sort of book was the prototype of Schumann's *Humor-*

eske and *Kreisleriana*, where apparently all idea
of form is abandoned; one piece hardly ends
when an utterly irrelevant one begins. But our
highest delight is to find the subtle connection
which pervades the whole. And thus, with all
his independence of earlier models, perhaps by
reason of it, Schumann seems strongest in this
very power of weaving subtly initial themes to
a climax which crowns the work with its own
justification and true ultimate meaning.

As to Schumann's symphonies, it must seem
at first thought that all these elements and
early influences promise little. The art and
thought of Bach were remote, and equally the
chaotic method of dominant literature.

It must be seen, too, that the universal tendency of all musical thought in the nineteenth
century was special. In Beethoven was the
colossal climax. In Schubert came the national
reaction and assertion. Berlioz went far beyond
the true limits of graphic depiction. Wagner
cannot escape his Teutonic flavor. Mendelssohn seemed to find most inspiration in local
romance,—at any rate in the suggestion of
special subjects.

Schumann seems to us the greatest poet of

the time ; but he was representative of its spirit. And so there is in him, too, as compared with the classic height, a descent into narrower lines of feeling. He is under the domination of ideals and thought of contemporary German poetry, pervaded with the spirit of German legend. Under all these poets of the century, one theme has become predominant beyond its due, has had too much conscious stress. Schumann's treatment, to be sure, has been of the highest in tone,—far higher than Wagner's. But in all, the field is too narrow, too full of special subjects ; there is no approach to the noble height of Beethoven's cosmic, universal thought.

The symphony, as the highest known mode of utterance in music, is always greatest with the widest scope. Indeed, it might be said, in a very strict humor, that the true symphony can have no limitation whatever of special subject, whether expressed or implied. We are thus dangerously near a prejudiced view of Schumann's symphonies. It is better to take our usual course, forming our opinion in the very reading of the work.

IX

SCHUMANN (Continued)

WITH no master is it more urgent that we approach with absolute honesty, free from pre-judgment, above all from the presumption that his symphonies are masterpieces. We may hope, but we must fear for symphonies in a Romantic period.

The second symphony has no title or even association. We are not inclined in any direction. It begins not unlike the characteristic prelude of Beethoven and Schubert, which we have often noticed. With them it was a mystic vein. Now, Schumann is of all poets in verse or tone most lost in his peculiar subjectivity. He does not paint objects (though he will give with subtle power the true sentiment suggested in outward situations), and he is not at all philosophical. It would be a great gain to discern this distinction between the element of mystic philosophy in music with a certain universal scope, and what might be called the

meditative, the psychological, the purely introspective. Bach and Schumann were the latter.
Bach was tied fast to the moorings of his creed.
He could not roam and grope freely for the
lowest foundations. Schumann's temper was
for romantic meditation, but his feeling was
intensely and passionately special. For him the
wealth of emotion in the individual man was
too great to stray into the bleaker regions of
general impersonal speculation. And yet Schumann was neither materialist nor sentimentalist.

He might, by some, be called a link between
the high, impersonal tone of his great predecessors and the sentimentalism of his day and the
later materialism. But that is only because he
himself held the true balance. He had the
right mean ; he did not run into riotous, irresponsible hedonism. In the vehemence of his
sentiment he held to the lode-star of highest
ethical ideals. He reached, of all German
poets, the highest conception of woman. With
the passionate intensity of his feeling, he had
the leaven of idealism, a sense of responsibility and of profundity. If he had lived into a
vigorous middle age, it seems that he would
probably have matured into the highest poetic

quality. Unfortunately, the very intensity of his early romanticism, his absorption in individual emotion, made irreparable havoc on his mental powers.

In his symphonies we have glimpses, and more, of the height to which he was tending. Ever deeper his sympathies were growing, ever wider his horizon ; and there is no loss of intensity of feeling. Yet his symphonies seem to remain still in the field of special and individual interest ; they are not what we have so often praised in Beethoven and sometimes in others : they are not cosmic. It is not simply that the third symphony is, in truth and in title, a poem of the Rhine. We are thinking of the music itself.

Here, in the second symphony, begins the legendary tone in the horns, with quiet, prime-

val simplicity, while the violins add an accompanying serene meditation. It is distinctly Teutonic. It has not the universality of the Beethoven Fifth, or even of Schubert's C Major.

Gradually others join. The discussion grows in a more human, a more personal vein. It leads somewhere. Yet, all through, the deep-toned legend resounds. Between its verses the wind sings quite naturally and naïvely:

But as soon as the horns return, the strings fall again into their revery. Now with gentle, not sudden awakening, the strings striking into

a quivering hum, a new strain is heard from
discoursing woodwind, with a kind of heavily
springing gait, after the musing walk of the
Sostenuto.

The light answer:

grows brighter, more insistent and vehement,
but disappears when the legend of the horns
returns. But the other phrase, equally eccentric
though more serious, follows along:

through a full and broad conclusion and
a free, rhetorical flourish of violins, into the
Allegro, where the text is the little answering
theme that before piped its timid attempts and
now sings a steady chant of joy, with that
power for endless sequence and flow, which
we have seen lurking in Schumann and in his
themes:

Allegro ma non troppo.
STRINGS (doubled in unison and upper octave by Wood).

Eventually a climax is reached in this jolly, skipping song, with some change of locality; and now, for the rest of the preliminary statement of melodic subjects, there is a quiet talk, with much regularity of question and answer, on a theme that is not too high pitched, that contrasts pleasantly with the first in the even glide of its motion:

Doubled above and below.

Wood (reinforced by *tremolo* strings).

Doubled below.

All this chatting is wound up by (what seems really best of all) a broad, authoritative conclusion, in simple terms (see page 278), presently confirmed below in echoing basses. A final verse of the theme closes the statement.

Discussion is natural to Schumann. But instead of the dramatic, boisterous fray of many voices fighting out their conclusion of peace and concord, it is a meditation, a curious internal reflection. The melodic voices seem like

WOODWIND AND STRINGS.

Rhythmic figure doubled in octaves.

impersonal shades rather than the living figures
which laugh and talk in the earlier masters.
Poetical it is in the highest degree. But it is
less easily perceived as a graphic symbolism of
mundane, every-day persons and doings. It is
more a dreamy haze of imaginings, which has
its artistic place and need as much as any other
mood; but it is perhaps better adapted to the

solitary handling of a single instrument than to the orchestral world of sounds.

Here the united strings make repeated descent of three steps, while above in the woodwind the first *Allegro* is still keeping us in good cheer with a little answering phrase of violins:

Now the maze of these three phrases continues. A duet in the violins is see-sawing:

while the flutes are still piping at the skipping song, and the brass, aided by fagots and oboes, are ever descending into lower and lower depths, and new subterranean scenes. When the violins cross each other's path, there is a strange pinch, a narrow escape from quarrel, which keeps us in pleasantly increasing suspense. Soon the second *Allegro* theme is the bone of contention between mixed parties of wood and strings. Still, the anxious suspense, soothed a little by a new thought:

280

echoed above at each utterance, then advancing
again with assenting voices:

and now through a strain of clearer serenity:

to higher and still more delicate refrains of the
anxious phrase:

wandering on through echoing stretches, interrupted by strains of the old maze of descending
basses and answering strings. Always there is
this balance between joy and pain, this dulcet
anxiety; throughout, of course, the joyful dance
of the first melody is absent. Now the mood
grows firmer, more confident, gradually lifting

out of the depths; then, with more nervous
step, rising more and more impetuously, a new
energy in the answering phrase of the strings
(which has been hitherto vaguely wandering in
and out):

STRINGS (sustained in unison and above by Wind).

And so, soaring into gladder heights, we
reach at last the swing of the first *Allegro*
melody, but merely the dancing movement.
It is again the trio of voices which began the
discussion, and the sky is still o'ercast with
minor clouds. When we thought we were out

of the wilds, back we must go to the dim, sweetly-sad uncertainty, until we despair of reaching the old pleasant places before dark. In gliding strings, while the woodwind above is lightly piping along, is that earlier strain of anxious soothing.

But at the end of the climax, after a few departing wails, we are at last gambolling again in our sunny meadows to the tune of the old dancing song. It is all as at first, only noisier and more spirited. But when the melodies have been sung again, and the strings descend as in the beginning of the discussion, the wood, instead of replying with the skipping phrase, answer with equally steady, gliding sweep, in contained serenity :

And so through one more descent, when the

ascent begins *con fuoco* with nervous energy of phrase:

and with extended rehearsing of other earlier phrases and cadences, all dominated by the insistence of the principal melody, with springing gait.

Scherzo.

We are not pretending to set forth a plan. Frankly, we have not discovered it. We prefer to search for it in company with the reader.

Special connection with the Scherzo is not apparent,—mere general sympathy of mood. By itself, it is one of the most deliciously melodious, magically rhythmical bits of music. But in the symphony, separate charm is almost irrelevant,—is far behind germane pertinence.

The theme is a type of one of Schumann's diverse humors, utterly opposite to his more common sombre sternness. And it has the quality, rare in extended subjects, of great versatility for discussion. The melody, seem-

Allegro vivace.

STRINGS (the chords doubled in lower Woodwind).

ingly without thought of a necessary end, bounds along through scene after scene. A little later the wood, which have been chattering along, make gay retort to the first phrase of violins:

The dialogue continues in varying pitch. In the midst of it comes a most delicate bit of play, at hide and seek, between strings and

wind. Then both go tripping together back to the original dance, whence all is repeated. Here the swing of the first melody has an increased vigor, almost the swoop of wind.

After a friendly touch at the close, the first Trio is contrasted in a confidential, informal, intimate way, peculiarly Schumann's, breaking

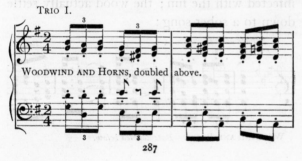

287

STRINGS, doubled above.

formal rhythm. Though quietly playful, it is reflective compared with the bubbling Scherzo.

All in graceful swing, the woodwind sing their song laughingly; the strings answer more seriously. The wood continue frivolous; the strings now discourse freely without much attention to the mischievous wood, humming away without constraint of period, as if to themselves, reiterating, lengthening out the phrases at sweet will into a sincere, friendly conclusion, broken into by the impish woodwind, when the melody is repeated. And now the strings are quickly infected with the fun; the wood actually settle down to a sober song:

Higher octaves.

WOOWIND AND BRASS. *Bass doubled below.*

Then, after returning to the earlier Trio, they gradually are drawn again into the whirl of the Scherzo. But the Trio was evidently not enough of a brown study. Schumann must have his recoil from hilarity,—must retreat into his shell for a good hour by himself. In the second Trio, after the merriment of the Scherzo has faded away, we leave dancing and shouting and settle into a quiet current of bitter-sweet dreaming. There is no glad rhythm, no sparkling tune, but a continuous song, charged with mingled longing and content:

TRIO II. STRINGS.

Bass 8va lower...............

The revery deepens when the melody subtly steals in in the basses, before the oboes have finished, and similarly the flutes break in before the latter end. Soon the dreamy plot thickens, with manifold play of initial phrases. Later

the full song returns with complete swing.
Then, after repeated timid attempts, the jolly
Scherzo steals in and soon spreads its cheer all
about, ending in a romp.

The *Adagio* is the real lyric point of the
symphony. Like the Scherzo, in its way it is
an inspiration of the highest beauty. And
with the Scherzo the relation of contrast enhances its meaning. If it were not for the
stern standard we have set, we could rejoice
with glad assurance in one of the greatest of
all symphonies. But we cannot lose sight of
the one highest requisite,—the dominance of
one feeling throughout; and by this standard
we must measure.

It is not simply in the majestic, simple grace
and fervid pathos of the melody, it is quite as

much the ingenuous charm with which a new voice ever slips in with the subject, before we are prepared, without any fuss or ceremony of introduction,—like members of a family group stealing in around the hearth one by one; and before you know it, all are gathered, cosily talking. At the end of a verse of the great melody, the wood and horns have a simple introduction with the strings in a discussion on a phrase that seems insignificant, but breaks out into a most moving cadence:

STRINGS (with occasional Woodwind).

   Then on the first two bars of the melody,
rung at ever higher pitch by the violins, rises
an insistent plaint of speaking beauty, ending at last serenely in a (major) key of contentment. Now creeps in pure meditation, who
must have her moment. Even from pathetic
utterance Schumann must retire to chew the
cud of quiet reflection. The visible cud is a
fugal theme discussed by monkish strings in
strict impersonal solemnity, from the gloomy
maze of which the expressive woodwind relieves us by unceremoniously entering with
the main melody. Again the discussion of
the strings; again the insistent plaint; and
the end, in profound musing, with the lowest
strings humming bits of the tune again and
again.

We come to the *Finale*. Here, if anywhere, must be the justification. Let us pursue our quietly expectant way. We have had, so far, a spirited *Allegro*, introduced in truly naïve musing, broken ever by legend-toned horns; a sparkling *Scherzo*, with its shy retreating and periodic reserve; and an *Adagio* of rarest beauty. Here is at first a mere signalling strum and blast. Then what seems the main melody, queerly starting in a subordinate key, sounds with all the band but drums and low brass, all in *Allegro molto vivace :*

WHOLE ORCHESTRA (save Drums and Trombones).

and so, long in continuous, spirited melody, bandying about one phrase :

more extended :

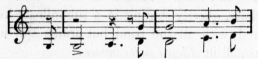

and breaking out again in simple, hearty chorus, ever adding some new touch of quaint variation :

All but Trombones, with higher octaves.

Then comes in the strings what seems almost pedantic for so glad a song. As violas and fagots trip leisurely along, the violins simply course up and down the scale, with no special

significance, continuing in mild playfulness. Soon horns and other wind join. Now is the meaning clear. Through the network of running strings and coursing woodwind sings from the depth of cellos and fagots, reinforced by violins and clarionets, the stately melody of the

OBOES AND HORNS below.

VIOLAS, CLARIONETS, CELLOS, AND FAGOTS.

SYMPHONIES AND THEIR MEANING

Adagio, with serener majesty, and a little less of sadness, in long notes, making a basic theme for the whole.

All is on a great scale and with a certain reserve. Once the legend has sounded, it does not forthwith sound again, but lets the voluble strings chatter away the more lightly for its absence. But it is always gathering for a new utterance. And so it returns, enounced in a higher scenic region; it sings more frequently:

Responsive play of mixed groups of Woodwind and Strings. Doubled in octaves above and below.

Doubled below. HORNS.

Now all are started singing fragments in a great medley.

The pathos is all gone, but not the depth or majesty. Finally, as half the instruments are coursing furiously, the others sing the conclusive phrase with true assured finality:

Strings doubled above in Woodwind.

Strings doubled below.

Thence back to the first melody, but not at all with formal exactness. For after the refrain of this theme comes the unmistakable psycho-

Harmony in the Woodwind.

STRINGS.

Doubled above and below.

297

logical moment which stamps Schumann. All sentiment aside, we must down for a good hard think on the phrase of the original strum of the movement.

The collision of the running forces, roughly jostling by, shows the argumentative reflection, —*Æneas multa diu jactans animo.* The jar of altercating contradictions is undeniable. We can see the parties getting into technicalities. Out of it suddenly is a more placid, but more

STRINGS AND CLARIONETS.   FLUTES in octave above.
RHYTHMICAL   *marcato.*
HORNS AND FAGOTS.

absorbed revery; eyes turned inward; a rapt musing; no resultant feeling as yet; still wandering and wondering.

The strumming run, too, adds its opposing course, though, to be sure, the other voices, differing before, now unite against the intruder:

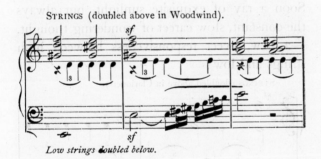

And presently we are in the very valley of the shadow of darkest groping,—ominous:

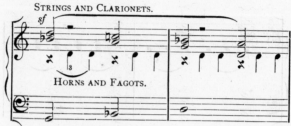

Soon a ray of exquisite sunlight, but always the constant, slow career of wondering thought, —a new, sweet responsiveness between high strings and low:

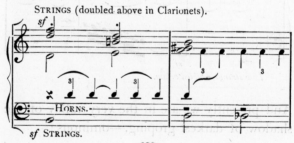

And now, at last, a more friendly, home-like, reassuring word:

SYMPHONIES AND THEIR MEANING

Then we fight our way out of the gloom in triumphant struggle, crowned by the song in big swinging rhythm of the Adagio melody, more soothing than ever, spreading its soaring chant,

302

with answering voice far down in smooth-toned bass, in peaceful duo, singing away with no thought of end. And right from the serene song there is that special, intimate touch of none but Schumann.

And when the melody begins again, descending instead of ascending, we have reached the best again, the purest trust, unshaken because deepest laid, answered above, and again uttered with a broadly worded conclusion, maintained with big, still pauses.

And here is a phase that no Beethoven ever conceived; certainly, never in the heart of an Allegro. It is the poet of Romance, the Jean Paul of music, of unforeseen surprises of mood; and yet, in the most abrupt change, you never feel the lack of inner essential connection and significance.

It is somewhat the feeling of the second Trio. Absolutely without traditional prescription of form, more than half-way through, the storm of the Allegro ceases, and an entirely new melody—outwardly!—begins, charged with that deepening feeling which has so strong a resemblance to the devotional. We might call it a secular chorale. It was the mood in

which Schumann wrote himself "Eusebius";
and it follows here with the usual fitting
inconsequence upon the heels of Florestan.
Chorale-like it is in the half-notes of the wood-

wind, followed by strings descending in hollow
unison:

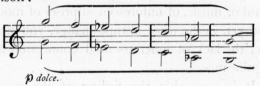

and then the idyllic chorale in a new quarter of
the wood. It is strange how merely external is
this irrelevance. In reality, it is felt as a closest
part of the whole texture. You are perplexed
with a haunting sense that it has sung before.

For a moment there breaks in a stirring pulse
from an earlier verse; but slowly we descend

into a reflective vein on the chorale. Still, it is not the psychological moment of Schumann. That is a conscious mental spinning; this is mere pensive, sentient dreaming, free of algebraic thought, but with the more perfect sequence of unwitting logic, running on as if with infinite measure of verse:

WOODWIND AND STRINGS.

Then as the run of strings reappears, the earthly hymn takes on a new spring, and we are back in the old discussion on the strumming phrase, with abrupt, authoritative ending of the dispute in a pause that sets all wondering, expectant that Florestan with his boisterous train is coming to say the final word. Instead, the gentle, pensive Eusebius once again enters. He has a new note in his song, a turn of quaint assurance. See how the melody now descends, without the old questioning:

Again the strange retort in timid unison. Then the chorus enter with firm, conclusive strain, still strongly charged with a pious spirit. At the end of one of the final refrains of the chorale, before we have discovered it, an old figure has stolen in; the primeval legend of horns is sounding its perennial phrase, as though it had not been silent all along. And now another old memory rises from the musing of the earliest beginning:

WOODWIND (doubled above and below).

Sempre crescendo.

Low strings.

Somehow it does not fit ill with the Eusebius melody. And now see how, while this sings in three-measured rhythm, the legend sounds in the brass in perfect accord of independent rhythm, the old one of four paces. While the former vanishes, the latter continues, with slight intervals, until the end, and, all in unconscious agreement, the Eusebius melody floats above in triumph; below the strings are still striding in the strange three-paced rhythm.

Then in the last great verse, a big phrase takes command; it reminds us a little of the first Allegro in its eccentric gait, and somehow suggests, too, the song, though more broadly, of the first melody of the last movement. Still, Eusebius has not subsided; he is paramount in the great throng. Indeed, he has the very last word of clear song. He seems to broaden, almost to smile a gentle blessing at the end. But the big melody does, indeed, reconcile the feeling of the first and last canto of our epic.

.

What shall we say to it all? Surely so much beauty can only come from sincerity. The unity is here; we must bow our head. It is a true, a great symphony. Yet next comes the trying question: What is this feeling whose unity is proclaimed? It is certainly not the clear mood of the great Beethoven poems that we found words for; not of the earlier Mozart; not of the later Schubert. It is less definable than all these. It has not their universality, their bigness of conception. It is in romantic recoil from their classic cosmic completeness. But in its narrower roaming among romantic dells, bold heights, and shaded valleys, it makes a smaller, but hardly less perfect circle of its own. In its delving and dreaming it goes beyond the reach even of our attempt at entitling or summing. And here it is, perhaps, lesser than the earlier symphonies, where, it seems, the intensity of message forces the meaning clear of mystery. It finds, somehow,

SYMPHONIES AND THEIR MEANING

apart from the broad careers of its great predecessors, a new cycle of untrodden path. It has not, perhaps, their bigness of view, nor their breadth. It is somewhat confined within the poetic fancy of the Teutonic nation. Yet it marks the truest circle of its own beauty and justification.

In its recoil from the classics, it necessarily lacks their completeness of view. Therefore its very purpose from the beginning is more special. It is a symphony, not of Man in the broadest sense, nor of Life, but rather of a certain very high conception of the Teuton poet, complete within the limits of nationality, and of a more idyllic sentiment, which was, after all, lost in the broad scope of the older masters.

309

X

SCHUMANN (Continued)

Third Symphony.

Our first sense is of vigor; then it has something to say. It is clearly not joyful, like so many symphonies; a certain stern strength forbids. It seems to have some special poetic content, which it is struggling to express with more definiteness than the usual vague symphony. So it suggests three kinds of works: first, the entitled; lastly, those that are untitled and vague even to the composer; between them are those that, while untitled, are definite to the composer, and are meant to show a meaning purely on the musical merits and by musical means, without help of verbal label.

The question rises: Is it right to set the mind puzzling? Music is not a graphic art, nor explanatory, nor logical, but purely emotional. Hence, why should not the master tell all he knows, and let the hearer enjoy. Still, to withhold the literal label does seem to save

music from the ridiculous position of being
eked out by words in its purpose. What is
the answer? We must get over the fact that
music is not meant to be graphic. Even if
music were to paint you a perfect picture with
all the details, or tell you a thrilling story, it
would really do nothing. You would catch it
much better in colors or in words. Therefore
the element of making clear an outside meaning must be abandoned as, after all, frivolous,
irrelevant, unworthy. Even if we are accused
of false pretence in writing down a title, we
must simply bear it. But, of course, we must
not really try this tonal painting. Only in so
far as we may, in writing, be burdened with the
sense of a subject, may we tell the hearer this
in words, and ask him to feel with us, at every
risk of false accusation. All the time we set
him guessing is wasted. We must never try to
ennoble our art by setting it on a throne of
verbal significance. If it communicates a
poetic mood, it does enough and the highest.
Whether you call your work a Rhine Symphony or a Legendary Symphony or Feudal or
Primeval, anything within the great field suggestive of the particular direction of the soaring

thought or the color of the spirit's mood will be enough. Whether it be just the Rhine or the Ganges is not necessarily a real gain.

Music must not fear to be irrelevant even with itself; for instance, to rush off into an apparently frivolous by-way. For the very unconscious impulse that suggests the flight is more relevant than any carefully conscious plan and keeping to the plan. And thus the very attempt at consistent picturing defeats the whole object of spontaneous expression of feeling. It will take care of itself, and prove its own verification.

In this symphony, for example, knowing the " Rhine" title (which Schumann suggested), we should describe our impressions in certain words; not knowing it, with certain others. But in any case, these words are not the symphony itself. They would change at each writing. They are only meant to suggest. And whether we know the title or not, if we are faithful to the feeling and intelligent in our art, we are bound to reflect the mood, in whatever words. In some we come nearer to the original feeling than in others.

Of course, there is no doubt that in some

cases the particular mood, if specially defined, may be more difficult to catch than in others; for instance, where there is a dream of particular national legend or locality, to a foreign ear. And here again the answer must be to the composer: Don't waste time in puzzling the hearer. Tell him all possible. Let him enjoy with you.

But in any case it ought to be purely beautiful. Only in so far as a special subject dances before the mind of the writer, may the uninformed listener puzzle to a certain degree. Beauty and meaning are blended to an undistinguishable degree. Where the meaning is vaguest for definite words,—as in Mozart—we are apt to talk merely of beauty; where significance has the stress, beauty is almost lost sight of. There is no dividing line. Beauty ought not to be in itself the only purpose,—nor significance to threaten to usurp its sway. Significance must be unconscious, unstriving. But both are equally important. Meaning of poetic mood leavens the vague beauty of sound to a wholesome message.

It is not unfair, then, to take every hint the master gives. So, first, we must see how every title is German. "Dritte Symphonie" it is, and begins "Lebhaft,"—no foreign *Allegro*. This is all not really essential.

Strong and rugged is the central quality, firmly standing on the basic tone, which it is loth to part with, which holds a lingering pedal point beyond its natural domain. The melody is strongly grounded in the tonic chord. It is

Lebhaft.

FULL ORCHESTRA (Woodwind in higher octaves).

not flowing, almost severe and rough ; resolute, not insinuating.

But the less *cantabile* the melody, the more continuous and unending,—the compensation in all things. Striking melody must have an early end by the very requirement of its symmetric beauty ; in its charm lies the necessity for its early conclusion. So, conversely, the less of melodic rotundity, the more spontaneous and unlimited the progress. So here there is much of that special power for sequence, for the course of narrative, that Schumann was

foremost to develop. These sequences (from the end of the first quotation) seem as if they might well go on forever.

Soon the original refrain is taken up with greater chorus than before. The brass, with sonorous solemnity, is strongly present throughout the symphony. In the repetition, a phrase of new vivacity appears in the answer:

Bass doubled below.

all carried along with that logic of sequence and narrative that makes all seem equally worth quoting. Almost the essence of the movement is contained in the rhythm which appears everywhere, especially in horns and basses:

Now the subject enters again with wonderful depth of device, as the oboes, clarionets, and fagots are singing the melody a whole beat behind flutes, brass, and violins, and yet, instead of conflict, there is but a richer magnificence. The feeling of depth of unconscious design is growing upon us, in step with the symbolic music. Again comes the fluent phrase, which helps to a cadence, simmering down to the quiet lyric feeling of the second melody, mostly in woodwind, with but faintest reminders of more solemn background.

WOODWIND (with the low strings sustaining the harmony).

Then it swings with bolder plaint out into the major, but quickly returns to the stern theme of the beginning. There is a very similar relation of objective and subjective, of fate and

victim, to the first Allegro of Beethoven's Fifth
Symphony, though we have no thought of a
similar extension of such an idea. But the
repeated prayer of the second and the stern
progress of the first melody suggest the analogy
for the moment. But right here there is a
sudden glad complexion of the main figure,
that spoils the continuing symbol, while it
enhances the charm of the poem. From the
high-spirited burst—on through a phrase which
sustains the feeling in more meditative vein.
Then suddenly back to stern business, with the
rapid run, with relentless power, in *fff*, interrupted anon with curious, delicate cogitations
on the echoed phrase. Now follows the second
melody with a new profundity. For, as it
sings on high in woodwind, out of the depths

WOODWIND.

STRINGS.

rises an interrupting echo, both voices chanting independently. They grow, mutually reinforcing, losing the plaint, to a climax of
power, in which is blended the vigor of the
rapid phrase. When the first subject reappears
in the basses, it comes no longer in terrible
interruption, but rather by natural expectation.
The element of passive subject is not lost; but
by the courage of companionship he has gradually nerved himself to meet the nearing fate.
We must not commit ourselves to one image.
All are shifts to utter the general mood. Here
there is a new spring. If forced to a single
phrase, I should say the whole had the feeling
of some Stern High Festival,—big with deep
omen, but still festive. Hear this solemn echo
de profundis :

Throughout there is this feeling of High Festival with solemn undertone, where the bass is constantly speaking, and finally breaks out into the subject, joined later by the whole chorus. The second melody now sounds more human than ever in the contrast, with slight change of higher swing. Soon reflection appears in the dual discussing voices; and now, after a climax (where, before, the subject

sounded powerfully) is the "best" again. In surprise of harmony, trembling in high strings and wood, in softest tones, sings, down in sacred horns, not the melody itself, but its essence in simple, drawn-out sounds.

It is the very spirit and voice of ancient legend sounding through the hallowed woodland,—in the whole passage, where the horns, at last rising to a high note, gradually sink, dim meditation hovering about, down and away into unseen depths, as suddenly the clarion woodwind ring out irregular, conflicting cries through the forest :

Then higher uncertain calls are answered below in united horns and lower wood; later is the simple cry of this legend-spirit, twice re-echoed from highest woodwind to lowest brass.

The echoes continue on broader phrase to highest possible grandeur, emerging in the beginning melody, itself the echoing phrase, in fullest, loudest union of all. For some time the original verse is rehearsed. In its midst is a gloomy, uneasy dying away of broken phrases in the wood. Out of it anon come cries from the pleading melody. It might be the *Loreley* witch and her victim caught in the forest:

"Kommst nimmermehr aus diesem Wald."

But presently sounds again the firm note of main theme. And now all is in gladder strain. There is a new glow of epic joy, with a crowning burst at the end. It is the clearest epitome of Teutonic legendary poetry.

Scherzo. Sehr Mässig.

We are surer than ever that we have caught the spirit, when we come to the second movement,—the only one in which Schumann has descended from his sacred German to a foreign word. That shows its importance; and so there is no doubt of the humor. I should call it an heroic ballad with humorous edge. The national color is here of the sharpest. To one who has not known and felt the German ballad of the Rhine, it may be somewhat of a riddle. But then it is all the clearer from its very limitations :

Sehr mässig.
In strings and lower horns.

Fagots and low strings.

You can almost see the words under the score, beginning, say :

"Im hohen Burgverliess,"

and so spinning along to the drive of the song. But it must be a sombre old ballad; of dread danger, and some impossible happenings, not without a grim sort of ancient humor. We think of such tales as of the old robber knight with seven sons on the scaffold; how his last request of the Emperor to spare his sons was answered in cruel jest: that he should be saved whom the father's headless trunk should approach; and how the condition was fulfilled with all seven.

Of course, there is no absolute need of all this interpretation. In any case, there is no mistaking the sprightly beauty and poetic treatment. But there is surely much added charm in the knowledge of the special association in the composer's mind.

The melody is finely varied in other verses, and returns with telling climax to the original one. Then comes a more puzzling canto of our ballad. A curious theme, made for musing mystery:

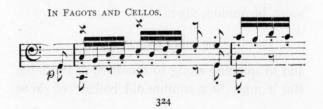

IN FAGOTS AND CELLOS.

begins in basses and threads its mystic and complex way through the varying voices. It is not simply that the poet's thinking-cap is on, after the lyric burst. It is a wandering strain of ancient prehistoric things,—" eine alte Rune," —tracing its fateful paths in the dim world of gods and men, in the days when fate hung heavy o'er both races. It is not the pondering on these things. For this is a ballad. It is the things themselves.

The dark phrase winds on its destined course:

IN STRINGS AND WOODWIND.

Doubled below.

and now merges into the heroic strain, where, however, it still holds equal sway.

In the third canto is a new element,—the human, personal, the purely lyric. But anon the ancient saying sends a warning reminder,

and the glamour of legend is not lost. It is all
poetic in the highest degree:

It sings in a more modern vein.

Now the first verse returns in a brighter key,
with more brilliant resonance. Then it sinks
into the mood of the third phase, and emerges
once again as at the beginning. Towards the
end are quaint, primitive refrains of the beginning of the first melody, with its answer, a

kind of "Yes, yes," again and again, and sug-
gestions of the third. The ominous second
strain has vanished, for good, indeed.

In its absolute isolation from the rest of the
symphony the Scherzo is all the greater. Free
from attempts of connected meaning by reminiscent theme, it is really all the more relevant
to the general plan.

In the third division the air of legends has
gone. Its very absence here proves their reality
before, and acquits us of rhapsody. Clearly,
the scope of the symphony broadens. It might,
so far, have been all in the realm of the myth.
Here we are in the clear sunlight of idyllic
human feeling. And it is absolutely German
to the core. So, probing for bearings, we think
perhaps of a "German Symphony," like the
"Scotch" of Mendelssohn. Nor would this be
far wrong. But Schumann's has a higher and
profounder national significance.

The Andante melody here—*Nicht schnell*—
is pure German folk-song. There is a placid
rest from earlier mysticism.

As national song it reminds us of Schubert.
But it has that special vein the Germans call

" innig," which was Schumann's own, although it in nowise touched his leaning towards musing thought. And here, too, is contrast with the earlier symphony. There was nothing " innig" about primitive legends.

Like most Andantes, this is of lyric simplicity. No profound depths are stirred, as in the first movement; and no bold heights are gained. The first melody is merely followed in and out by another of equal simplicity, with hardly a change of tonal color:

328

STRINGS with accompanying HORNS AND FAGOTS.

In the middle they both sing together, and a new answer leads into a phase of gentle, intimate discourse, of which this new strain, a simple, descending figure, is the principal subject, with many digressions and lesser topics. The second melody, too, is evident throughout, so that, at the end of the talk, the first one returns with a new freshness. The end has some of the friendly touches of the former, and of the dialogue. It is all clearly a ray of earthly sunlight before entering the cathedral, in the fourth division.

The second slow movement is marked "*Feierlich.*" If our object be to prove the existence of a meaning, we need say little. The very direction—"solemnly,"—a single glance at the score, show the intent most plainly. And see at the outset the utter contrast of the solemnity at the beginning of the symphony and here, though, in both, expressed by the brass. For there it was the quality of Waldhorn, sacred to the religion which lurks in the forest from earliest Teuton ages. Here the brass is the stern dogma, the overwhelming power of cathedral organ, where the visible architecture is mirrored in the massive polyphony. We remember Schelling's definition of architecture: frozen music. Not only is there solemnity of feeling in both these movements, but in both it is religious. Yet could there be a greater actual contrast? Again we must bow before this power of music to make us feel the strength and quality of these influences. And the fortunate tone-poet can simply give forth directly their essence, without the words which, in sacred things, might offend others, or rouse the prejudice of bigotry. Not only is he safer in music, but much more powerful. And so he can actually show through his tone-poetry the soundness that still lingers of the old religion, and the stern truth of the new.

To be just, however, there is undoubtedly in

this episode of Schumann's symphony rather a picture of mediæval German church spirit than a direct utterance of personal religion, like Bach's Passion music. There is clearly a sense of the picturesque; and the greater stress is perhaps upon nationality. There are local and temporal limitations in the religious poem. There is, throughout, the constant sense of dogma; no personal melody; all fitting in a perfect system of priest-lore; the main theme discoverable being a short fugal one, beginning in trom-

bones in awful minor. At the end of a sentence all join in a loud assenting phrase, which is surely nothing but the quickened theme; it suggests an overwhelming Amen from the multitude in the body of the church, eagerly

WHOLE ORCHESTRA EXCEPT OBOES.
Flutes in upper octaves.

responding to the liturgy of chancel and choir.
Then the doctrinal structure really begins with
its colossal, dazzling, massive net-work. If
it is puzzling on the score to the lingering
glance (which is the wrong attitude), what
must it be in transient sound. And there is
no end,—no gentle cadence of secular tune,—
on and on voices enter, breaking in one upon
the other, make an eternal progress. These
curious changes of movement, all with the
same theme : first, in simple, march-like rhythm,
suddenly twice as fast a motion, but with great,
heavy, three-paced swing ; and, finally, with the
same rate, but in even movement again,—what
are they ? Different doctrines about the same
central truth ? Or varying attitudes of worship ?
But there is always one central, single idea.

332

SYMPHONIES AND THEIR MEANING

We cannot, however, ignore the constant gain in intensity, together with actual speed, of a certain eagerness, betrayed in strings trembling in the theme, with sustaining horns; more and more a personal reality of feeling,— and then, suddenly, before the end, a breaking off of the fateful progress, and a human cry in united burst in new key or color of tone; then back to the former march, and again the interrupting burst. Strangely, the end is not in massive architectural climax. Rather, the last human cry has prevailed to soften the former rigor, and the first phrase has a certain simplicity and sincerity of Lutheran *chorale*, with much diminished conflict of voices, with hymn-like cadence.

Finale

There is ever the danger for writer and reader to forget the true weight of interpreting phrases and figures; that there is no translation of fixed subject; that the real content is the general spirit perceived by simple enjoyment of the beauty of the art-work. With this in mind, we have really much more freedom; we are re-minded of this and of that; many things are suggested. But none of them are really essen tial. Where they are thought of by the composer; where they are mentioned by him or even set down as governing subject, there is the best reason for holding still to the same view that they are not absolutely needful to the right perception. And yet, for the purpose of suggesting the beauty, the sentient meaning, they may be of the highest use. Once having entered on the essay of telling in words of the value of a work of art, we are hopelessly cramped if we are restricted to the mere setting forth of technical structure. Therefore, our figures are indispensable for suggestion; for literal interpretation they are worthless.

It is well to think of this once more in this fifth and last division of our Symphony,—mainly because of the great danger of definite and final association, to which we are lured by the fine relevance of this movement with the first four. Having given fair warning, we shall not fear to deck our impressions freely with suggested figures.

At the very beginning, with this strong, simple, virile song, with eminent brass, and free, rolling bass, there is one German word that ever recurs, to which we can find no English equiv-

Lebhaft.
STRINGS, FLUTES, CLARIONETS, FAGOTS AND HORNS.
(Flutes in higher octave.)

alent, which we can only describe,—*burschikos*.
It is the spirit of German university life. As it
is a "Rhine" symphony, by the master's admission, as he did celebrate the old minster at
Cologne, we are probably near to his own conscious idea with our word. In such a symphony, teeming with the typical ideal life of
the German, this element, of the university
spirit, would hardly be absent. At any rate, its
main qualities are here, the stirring, soaring

spirit, fearless of the cynical world, firm with manly tread, and the rough humor, too; they are all here.

But this is not all. And it is not all so simple of content. Nor is it necessary to restrict our suggestion to the academic life, properly. It is a larger view of the bustling doings and thought of the old German Rhine city, sacred to higher interests and ideals.

The choral song is for a while simple in its course, and needs no study but the hearing. But at the end of its full refrain emerge the four horns with more than casual theme, while the violas are supporting in their own livelier way:

The rest all take it up, not exactly fugally, though it savors strongly of the cloister. Surely it is a reminder of the solemn old cathedral phrase:

IN TROMBONES.

but much faster. Then as answer comes the
pert humor of this phrase:

STRINGS AND WOODWIND. (Doubled above in Flutes.)

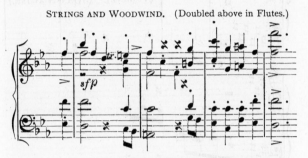

treated with the same fugal suggestiveness;
ending with a good, honest blare from the
horns. Now we are back in the march spirit
of the beginning. And here is a longer extension of an earlier episode of quieter feeling,
which did not seem important before. It certainly takes away from the masculine harshness
of the rest, or heightens it as foil. From its
close succeeds a fine antiphonal shout of chords,
as all the wind responds to wood and strings.
Suddenly this is tempered to hushed minor

chords; in their midst we hear something like the old cathedral theme, in its lighter phase:

STRINGS AND WOODWIND.

Then the comic theme struts in again, here and there, high in piping wood, while our last quoted, more serious motive is singing low in alternating strings.

No apology is needed for seeing here the master touch of quaint, mediæval, scholasticism, with comic hue,—below the pious priest, above the flippant *studiosus*,—much like the famous scene of the monk in Schiller's " Wallenstein's Camp." Alas! as soon as the word is said, it seems too much. The humor is not expressed, of course. Perhaps Schumann did not ever dare to think it to himself. But it was there, the more truly, in a less conscious stage. Comic may be too strong for sprightly. There is certainly the quaint neighborhood of the monastic and of the secular, and the latter seems to predominate, finally ending the episode in a melodious blast in the brass of true, honest German feeling:

WOODWIND AND STRING. (Doubled above.)

Added to all these themes, really the sinew of the whole, is a certain constant movement from the quieter middle of the first song, which softens the saucy wit of the one, and the serious tone of the other, and gives to the whole a friendly kind of sincerity, which is specially caught and summed in the (last quoted) strain of the horns,—more than ever at the last time, from full heart and lungs.

And so straight on into the first chorus, with the same vehement sincerity, with its succeeding joyful and friendly phrases. The brass have more and more to do. Sometimes they are given free room to themselves alone,—answered by strident strings. When we seem to see the end, they all stop for the last verse, which begins with the starting of a heavier and more vehement pace in low strings, in stern fugue led off by ïagots and two horns, followed at proper intervals by other groups, all in the old theme:

WOODWIND, BRASS AND STRINGS.

CELLOS.

In they come, four groups and more, until we can no longer see or hear them distinct. Just as we lose the sense of bearings in the architectural mass, they join into a closer body, and soon are snouting united a last acclaim, all in a great hymn, which is neither religious nor

340

secular. Too broad for either, it includes them both.

So in this German Symphony of the Rhine seem to merge all the inspiring influences of the nation. But it does not need its title. It speaks not of localities, rather of memories and of aspirations, which, though they may have special association, belong to us all.

MENDELSSOHN

THE critic cannot always be optimist and eulogist. The kind of catholicity is not good that tries to accept, to approve everything. The truth is that, whether we will or no, we cannot say our honest say without some implied disparagement. If it is impossible to admire without exaggeration, it is easy to blame by mere silence. Our vehement praise of one is often the severest word against another. If we were treating of music in general, our praise of Mendelssohn would be unbounded. If he had written no symphonies, we should not, in omitting, ignore him. But in our special field, there is danger that by faint praise we may do some damning. The very high place we are guarding for the symphony, holds us to an honest telling of our impression. After all, what the man may lose, the art must gain.

Mendelssohn was all but master in the highest sense. It may be unwise to make shelves of lesser and greater poets; it certainly is to try a rigid ranking. But we must be clear in mind about the word we are often using, that implies such a mastery of the art medium, that artisanship is merged in clear poetry, where we can no longer see the lines of conscious toil. This is, indeed, most rare. Then there are lesser and greater forms. There may be writers of most expressive songs. Others may have the power over profound architecture of simultaneous voices. But this must be quickly seen. Those works wherein the whole structure is of another art, not created by the musician, cannot test and prove the true master like those which, absolute, independent in tones alone, evolve with inner power a perfect structure all their own. Thus a writer merely of greatest song, of oratorio, or of opera, has not measured his power in the pure tonal art, which is most difficult because of the very absence of words. Here the very perfection of form, rounded by a certain unconscious process of crystallization, attests its truth and greatness.

A common mistake as to this special power, this question of form, must not be passed over, Strange to say, it is a mistake found as often with good musicians as with laymen, perhaps oftener. A very respectable composer of national note once gave the author his recipe, which was: Get your themes and fit them in the established moulds. In other words, be original about your melodic subjects, and, in harmonic treatment, too, be your sincere self; but in form follow the strict directions of tradition. There are no other forms in the music world than these sacred ones: the sonata, rondo, dance, and song; and, of course, there never will be.

It is most strange this, because it betrays utter lack of the very idea of composition. So there is this constant, almost hopeless confusion of *form*, the abstract quality, and special, concrete *forms* and moulds. Just so, by exact parallel, is the confusion of *thought*, the process, with special *thoughts*, so that the scholar, who has never wondered beyond his precise, literal logic, can see none of this highest of man's process, unless it be uttered in the verbal language of makeshift. It is, this, the main cause for the low conception of music. What does it mean? he says. You cannot tell me precisely in words; therefore it means nothing.

344

SYMPHONIES AND THEIR MEANING

He does not see that all that his literal language does is to suggest by the shifts of a limited lot of conventions, by vain labels aimed at high ideas, by combining these in rough images, the inner thought that is sorely struggling for true utterance. He cannot see, or he surely will not, that this very utterance is far clearer, more joyous in the language, not of conventional shifts, but of pure tonal beauty. Finally, he has never reflected that in his logic, sacred to the language of prose, the true essence and secret power is the sequence ; that this sequence may be where the terms and premises are other than verbal ; indeed, that there can be no greater scope for this sequence of man's highest thought than in melodies, their contrast, the depth and complexity of their combination, and in the complete cycle of their roaming career within a tonal poem.

To return to the former question, we find such a mistake, not of the layman, but of the respected musician. Originality he praises in theme and in the agreement of simultaneous tones. But this quality of all, which is the final test of the master, he makes a mere matter of school-boy's cramming. So we can never remember too often that the quality of spontaneous utterance in form true to the subject, is utterly distinct from memorized schedules. Indeed, it is hostile in this sense, that every true composition must vary somewhat from the outline of any earlier work for its own individuality. A man had far better take prosaic themes and let them flow by their own vital motion to an organic whole, than lay new melodies, however beautiful, in the dead mould of older works. So many evils spring from this that great stress must here be allowed. For men will either insist on the rigid, fatal formalism, or, revolting, will welcome all abandon of complete structure.

The true reason, I suppose, lies in the difficulty of perception. And it is not very different in architecture. Just as this quality is the highest to conceive, so it is hardest to perceive. In the " frozen music," a child may admire, in a cathedral, the embossing of outer doors, or the beauty of interior detail; a youth will catch the bold leap of the tower; a man will feel the massive dignity of vaulted aisle. But he must be almost a builder himself who will prove the completeness of rounded whole. Now in music it is actually still more difficult.

SYMPHONIES AND THEIR MEANING

For the cathedral is ever before us. But in the symphony, the first tones have vanished; enchanted with the present, we forget the past; and how shall we ever conjure it all together to feel the test of perfect sequence and relevance? Still, hard or easy, we cannot lose sight of this greatest of elements. And, indeed, it may not be so bad a problem. We are apt to proceed too much on the need of conscious study. We forget that the greatest enjoyment is most unstudied. The truth is here almost a paradox. The more the hearer knows, the more he has a basis of earlier study, the more careless may be his enjoyment. The beauty of melody, the fitness of contrasting subjects, the cycle of rounded path he will feel without the need of more consciousness than the creating master. But let there be no false notion of the ignorant. High art requires mind to enjoy as well as to create. Once for all, would there were an end to those nauseous phrases of the Philistine, proud of his ignorance, that he does not understand music, but knows what he likes. It must not be thought that there is something inherent in the natural man more than in the natural animal, whereby he may catch great thoughts without thinking. It would be a very false gospel to preach that great music is very easy to see by a certain trick. The masterpieces of music must be approached in far humbler spirit. It is all part of the original purpose of the art, whether of entertainment or of highest moral message. If it is the former, it were an unworthy kind of materialism to spend so much time in mere preparation for an amusement. So, again, this talk of the Philistine about the lack of meaning in music, this easy judgment of the blissful ignorant on what they like, is all irrelevant. They do not know because they have not looked. If they were not so serious, they would remind us of the famous Sam Weller, who did not see his father in court when looking straight at the ceiling.

Mendelssohn is the very type to test this mastery. He seemed to have all the qualities, if any one ever did. And, indeed, many of them, of all but highest value, are sadly out of vogue in modern days, such as the much neglected elements of absolute clearness, and of thoroughgoing refinement in detail and in spirit. He is charged with lack of depth and of intensity of feeling. In reality, he was most sincere in his very freedom from that pseudo-passion that seeks, in its false whirl, to throw a cloud of dust, covering great, primal faults.

Mendelssohn was most lucid in many-voiced building and strong in massive treatment; his power over the palette of orchestral colors was bred in his very fibre. With all these, which led to success in other paths, he lacked in personal quality to employ them in their highest use. In his wonderful expression of local color and his objective depiction, he was more affected by an outward stimulus than by his own subjective feeling. Mendelssohn made no advance in the outline of the symphony over Haydn. It is, therefore, significant that, correspondingly, he shows no inherent strength in his symphonic feeling or ideas. On the contrary, he was driven to find emotional content in historic sentiment or in scenic description. These subjects belong more properly to the lesser overture, and here Mendelssohn was in the first rank.

It is under the head of form that, it seems, Mendelssohn falls short of the measure of master. And here he serves wonderfully to illustrate the great virtue of the symphony. If we could use another word, we should be glad,—one less coldly technical. After all, it is exactly the same quality we have been searching for in each succeeding master, that of live continuity, of agreement of all regions of the work in the common purpose. There is nothing mysterious about it; nor is it the trick of handicraft. It is all a matter of sincerity, intensity of purpose. If a child has a message to give, and he is absorbed in its truth and value, he will say it without faltering to many people. The halting will come when the natural impulse of communication is weakened. The principle is exactly the same as to the clear, continuous homogeneity of a work of art. In the master symphonies the motive purpose was strong enough to sustain a clear thread and plan throughout.

The real trouble is not the lack of form, but the want of feeling, of the content of the message. The outward incoherence is merely the sign of original weakness. None of the elements of the art of music are so keen a test of sincerity of the prompting feeling as that of harmony of outline. It is, in the spontaneous sense, the true justification of the whole,—like the final answer in algebra, which verifies the proposition.

It will, of course, be said: How may this spontaneous perfection be distinguished from the mere imitation of old exemplars? It is much the same question as in other imitations, of greater or lesser art, from poetry to lace. Sometimes the earmark of the false is the very strictness of its adherence to the true. Thus, when we said above that Schumann's *Noveletten* were, perhaps, his greatest work, it was from this very conviction of the powerful coherence of the various episodes in a plan of radical novelty.

Finally, in a symphony, in the very highest meaning, our quality of form does not relate so much to the completeness of the several move-ments, as to their mutual relation in the whole. It is something like the old truth, that two halves do not make a whole, that of four perfect sym-phony movements the whole may be actually less than each of the parts, in poetic value.

There is, then, no technical lack nor want of detailed beauty that we find in Mendelssohn. The greatest charge we can bring against him is that his symphonies do not fulfil our highest idea of the form. Even so, there is no denying their enchanting beauty; the sincerity of their clearness, thoroughness, self-restraint; the high purity of their tone; the poetic charm and brilliance of treatment. We must merely withhold that highest of all qualities, a strong, pervading, uniting, subjective feeling.

In other ways Mendelssohn showed that he had not that intensity of personal feeling which expresses itself in highest form, breaking, in the hands of later masters, the fetters of the earlier, and extending their limits. Rather he genially reflected other poetic conceptions, as in his rare music for the Midsummer Night's Dream.

But, on the other hand, Mendelssohn was sincere in his very moderation. He had none of the false prophet, who works himself into a conscious state of false passion. In his balance of fine mean, he differs strikingly from most of the masters we have treated. He had not the profound sympathy of Beethoven; but he had more than Schubert. The quality which is somewhat opposed, that of light fancy, where imagination runs away with personal feeling, he shared with Schubert not unequally. But he had not the bold scope of Schubert's mind. He was rather the orthodox musician of his century, setting its sacred dramas and services, celebrating picturesque scenes and striking history. But the writing of oratorios in the great sense had been accomplished in the previous century. Here he was, after all, a follower. He was original, individual, chiefly in his special extension of Programme Music. We have seen Schumann's attitude. Mendelssohn's was poetic in the highest degree. But it was not of sufficient dignity for the great forms of pure instrumental music. It fitted better the looser overture. Therefore it seems that his greatest works are his scenes from the Midsummer Night's Dream and his striking overtures with scenic and historic titles. Mendelssohn had little touch with the great stirring spiritual and intellectual discoveries of his time. He did not utter and represent them as did Beethoven and Schubert in their age, and Schumann in a lesser, national way in his. But, then, neither did Mendelssohn represent certain downward tendencies.

The symphony must demand, once for all, the subjective vein. This does not say that there may not be a special title, implied or expressed. But the treatment is of the inner, individual view, not the mere outward depiction.

Here the Scotch Symphony falls short. Its only continuous purpose is the Scotch character of the melodies. This is a purely external unity; it does not affect the personal conception of the poet. However exquisitely beautiful and tempting with its rich depth and brilliant complexity, we must not invite the reader to a hopeless search for such an inner meaning as the symphony, in our view, must have. But the Italian Symphony here stands distinct. Evidently the intent here was not the outward, national likeness of tunes. There must have been a certain Teutonic subjective conception in the musician's mind, which pervades most of the work. It has the true plan, if not the complete fulfilment. It was not a mere reflection of Italian skies. It is rather the inner picture which every German poet has of the ideal land of beauty and art. Mendelssohn has certainly suggested this.

Italian Symphony (No. 4).

The name "Italian," unlike many musical titles, was constantly used by the composer. The work is a direct expression of that enchantment for the ideal land of beauty, joy, and art which has held Germans captive from the earliest invasions of Goths, through the attempts at conquest of a Barbarossa, to the poetry of a Goethe.

Exactly opposed to the " Scotch," there is no actual trace of Italian nationalism in the music. It is German, a pure German expression of delight. So the symphony is not graphic or picturesque; it is a highly poetical utterance of the German idea of Italy.

The first theme, in *Allegro Vivace*, gives the

355

stamp of simple joyousness to the whole movement. It strikes the leading note, which is reflected in various lesser melodies. The texture
of the whole is wonderfully close. It is impossible to trace outwardly the subtle similarity
and relation of melodies. The first builds in
the very beginning a stirring climax on its
own theme, resounding at last vigorously in
the basses. Throughout, there is the element
of airiest lightness. This is first suggested by
a fluent phrase at the close of the main
melody. By deft turns and by the trick of
sequence it evolves ever new phrases, hardly
like the first save in the merry pace. It
gives the whole movement a wonderful freshness. Ever it bubbles forth in a new guise.
You cannot mistake its hidden personality.
The second melody, which continues the
spirit of the first, is sacred to the woodwind,

CLARIONETS AND FAGOTS.

356

though the strings are lightly dancing about playfully.

The melody extends into purest song, quite merging the dance at times. Faintly a solo clarionet calls from the distance, and presently the merry chorus of the first theme are all about, quite drowning with their festive bustle the more delicate note of the second.

The best of it is the sparkling discussion after this presenting of themes has been repeated. It begins with a restless phrase which has threaded its way, we cannot tell how, from its source in the cadence of the first melody. But it is too volatile, too incessant in its shallow chatter to take the lead; so it soon subsides into mere companionship with a theme of greater dignity and distinction, which now enters. Again we feel its kinship to the others, and its fitness in the whole; but we cannot trace it outwardly:

Around it develops, in the strings alone, an episode purely fugal, yet without the least odor of the lamp, nay, with all the fragrance of the wood, full of the truest poetry. The minor gives it a touch of sombre romance. From the almost prosaic hilarity of the beginning we have plunged into the land of strange legends, into dim mystery of history that merges into myth. Into the midst the first theme bursts, first in the wood, then in the brass, alternating; still the fugal play continuing, yet all so spontaneous, fresh, and smooth that you do not think of counterpoint unless you look at the score. It is, indeed, that highest art, which makes least show of means and of difficulties, concealing them beneath the wealth of feeling.

This stage of the two themes is of highest interest, as it is fought now with successive

WOODWIND AND STRINGS (doubled above).

CELLOS AND BASSES.

assertion of one and the other, now with equal insistence of both at the same time.

They are so different in humor: the fugal, full of dark romance, the first melody mere holiday gladness.

Strange to say, the official second theme has no part in the discussion. But later, when, after a lull, the original order of tunes re-enters, the second appears in a new way, sung as duet of cellos above violas. But even here the darker-hued fugal theme intrudes its humor, first lightly in the minor. But as it grows more vehement, it is squarely attacked by the first melody in the original key. After a struggle of a few bars, the latter triumphs, and holds its cheery sway to the end.

The melody of the second movement is a perfect lyric embodiment of a phase of Italian poetry as it appears to the German mind. Burdened with a wealth of legendary feeling, it belongs to a rare type which is indefinable; in folk-song it is sometimes a setting of a strange ballad of foreign land. We remember that other type we found common in Beethoven and Schubert, in the Seventh and in the C Major, and we wonder at the idea of thus arraying all great melodies. I believe you would find the melody of mystic, almost philosophic search; another class of dim legend or ballad as here; another of intimate, friendly confidence. We might try to analyze what makes this legendary sound, but we prefer intuition to hard proof.

Andante con moto.

FAGOTS AND VIOLAS (doubled an octave above in Oboes).

CELLOS (doubled an octave below in Basses).

Much of the charm lies in the stately move-ment of strings, while the song proceeds above in the wood. Later, the violins take up the theme, and the flutes join the *obligato*, somehow picking out a shadowy counter-melody in the movement. Indeed, it is all melody, like the simple verses of a ballad, telling its sad story, without reflection or overflowing emotion. So the next verse is mysteriously told by strings alone, in the minor, the violins singing the story to the fateful, ever present accompaniment of the lower strings:

In Strings alone.

There is a queer bit of humor at the end,—pure Mephistophelian. He must have sold his soul. Immediately follows a touching strain, all in human major,—a new melody in the clarionets.

As it flows along in more and more intimate vein, it is rudely stopped by minor strokes which herald the original ballad, though not in regular verse,—mere vague memories. Once more the human strain enters with all the contrast of

sharpest colors. The whole ends in the full atmosphere of legendary mystery.

The *Scherzo* is bucolic and playful, with idyllic humor. But the relevance is not clear. There is, to German ears, unmistakably something of their own folk-song in the melody, and this more specially because the cadence is that of a well-known *Volkslied*. Indeed, the Scherzo seems a mere setting for the gem, the

Trio, with its intensely romantic melody, for horns and bassoons. It supplies all that we crave in the placid simplicity, almost plainness of the former. And as if to convince us that the Scherzo is but foil to the Trio, the latter pervades the close of the movement.

TRIO. HORNS AND FAGOTS.   VIOLINS.

But of the whole it must be admitted that its place in the general plan is not clear. It does not seem to have a value of its own, proportioned to each of the other movements.

363

The *Saltarello* is conceived in that special vein of Mendelssohn's, of lightest fancy and rhythm, so different from the humor of Beethoven. Mendelssohn's dance seems that of an imaginary race, which knows of nothing but joyousness; Beethoven's is of human beings.

Illustrations and examples are dangerous, tying the listener to accidental association. Yet the temptation is too great to suggest in the *Saltarello* the humor and poetic antics of Hawthorne's "Faun." It is based largely on the rhythm of the main melody:

It is one of those phrases that, lacking in definite beauty, seem capable of endless extension and variation. In the incessant motion we are almost reminded of the Finale of Schubert's

great symphony.   But we dismiss the thought
before it is uttered.   The intermediate episodes
are of no special importance.   In the middle is
a striking passage, very similar in conception
and construction to the fugal one in the first
movement, where, on the figure, imitated in

strict canon, there is built what is really an old-
fashioned round in dance-rhythm, at first only
in strings, gradually embracing the woodwind,
the whole forming one of the longest episodes
in the symphony,—an orgy of dance and of
counterpoint.

Altogether it seems that a noble plan is suggested and sustained with vigorous feeling and
high art through the first two movements.   In
the third it seems to halt.   The fourth has a
certain clear agreement with the name " Italian."
In its purely objective, almost graphic treatment
it might stand with more perfect fitness as the
last of a suite of independent tone-pictures,
than as the conclusion of a subjective poem,
such as the first half of the work promises.

XII

BRAHMS

THE symphony was not in agreement with the reactionary attitude of the Romanticists. With the return to Classicism it finds its original importance again. Mendelssohn showed his lack of the true symphonic thought. Correspondingly, his form was largely mere imitation of the old. By this double test, Schumann is more nearly in line with the symphonic masters. As his untitled works expressed truer symphonic feeling, so his freedom in treatment and in structure was path-breaking. Still, one often feels that he was only *about* to realize the highest grasp. He was finding his way. He was transplanting his Romantic spirit in broader, classic fields. In so far as this spirit is reactionary, impulsive, intense, specialized, its forms are, needs, abrupt, fragmental. There must be this perfect correspondence between form and feeling. You cannot pour new wine into old bottles. The writing of symphonies by the

Romanticists was a little too conscious. Chopin wisely refrained entirely. They wrote because they felt a challenge rather from without than from within. Schumann, however, the most profound of them, gradually as his sentiment was deepening and his vision broadening, was growing to fit the mantle of the classic masters.

The real heir, it is often said, was to be another, a younger, coming at a time ripe for mature survey of the great preceding schools which group about Bach, Beethoven, and Schumann. Instead of reacting from the classic and its forms, he mastered them from the outset. He grasped more thoroughly than any other the polyphonic depth of Bach's style. He was the first to unite it with the structural freedom and boldness of Beethoven. We have seen how the vein of Bach's musical thought, profoundest of all, had never found a worthy outline in pure, unsung music.* Brahms gave it the new dress of secular form. Finally, he absorbed the spirit of the Romanticists, which was still crying for more complete utterance; so that, while classic in his form, he is often

---

* See chapters on Schumann.

367

called a disciple of Schumann. His work is strictly in fulfilment of Schumann's ideals.

It sometimes seems that in a purely Romantic period there can be little of final truth. And thus the symphony does not specially suit it. It is the age for fragmental bursts, breaking the leading strings of a too limited classicism.

When first you come into a garden, unknown in boundary and contents, you dash here and there in reckless enjoyment, like the bee sipping irresponsibly. This is Romanticism, with its singing of separate beauties, its predominance of pure feeling. When once you begin to trace outlines, limits, order, a meaning, you enjoy the garden as a whole, not in wild, fragmental profusion. This is classicism, with predominance of form. Of the two, the latter is final; the former necessarily precedes.

The symphony is a final summing, a complete view. It is, in its true nature, cosmic, not national. Here lies the reason for that strange lack of patriotism in the poet Goethe. Now, there must be in a classic period a classic reaction, a strong element of intellectuality. There is, besides the mere utterance of emotion, the problem of reconciliation. As against intensity of feeling there must be breadth of vision. Depth is more needful than velocity.

Romanticism is like the minus quantity in algebra. The natural reaction from it, romantic rebellion from romanticism, brings back classicism. The more novel and fresh Brahms is in his feeling, the more he suggests the serene classic repose. But it is in the style, the manner of his working, that we must expect the sharpest difference. And it is here that he is, perhaps, most inspiring. Schumann wrote of Brahms's youthful works under the title " New Paths." It is quite possible that, in a narrower sense, he is merely breaking paths for others. But he is heroically pointing and urging the right way, though the narrow. He insists on uttering his truth within the perfect language of one of the arts, not in the polyglot of all. It is by internal mastery in all its dimensions,— in linear melody, in extent of form, in depth of architectural polyphony that he raises the art, strongest and profoundest of all, to a plane higher than ever before.

Brahms seems, at times, greatest for this very direction of his art, for the courage of his intellectuality. Every one is afraid nowadays of high art and of its defence. We dread the slur of pedantry. Low art seems to be the cry. Let us not believe it, though the masses are against us. In art, democracy does not count. If a man is charged with intellectual stress, that ought to bring a presumption of greatness, not of weakness. Romanticism pays the penalty for its mad rebound in the extreme abandon of the principles and quality of high art. The looseness of Schubert, the intensity of Schumann, the realism of Berlioz, were naturally followed by modern amorphism and sensationalism.

Because a man is difficult to perceive, is felt by the few, is no reason against his greatness. On the contrary, it speaks something for his originality, for his freshness and truth. It was Brahms's great deed to lead back to the high level of the masters,—the only vantage-ground from which music can answer the charge of lack of meaning and worse. Yet, by inherent vigor, the novelty of his poetry, on his first appearance, was such as to flatter the extreme Romanticists, led by Liszt, that a new hero had joined their ranks. No outward act of artist is so impressive as this resolute step of the youthful Brahms in turning sharply away from that dominant school of shallow aims.

His life and work are a rebuke to the common modern idea of art which has brought it such reproach, so that it is commonly heard that a poet is necessarily abnormal. The work of Brahms is of the kind to show that high art is the very essence, the true abiding-place of pure reason. We have heard too much of the linking of art and poetry with irresponsible abandon to overwrought feeling, too much dissociation of art and ethics. It is time the world sees that the highest of all, the most permanent, though not the first to reach applause, is the art which, yoking profound intellectual mastery with wealth of feeling, stands for fulness of experience, held in rein by a clear sight and a moral balance.

Just how this quality appears concretely and actually in the music, we shall see later in the reading of the symphony. In general, it is by an almost complete return to the mode of writing of Bach, except in the matter of structural outline. We remember how, with the great master of the church style, music was a perfect polyphonic tissue of themal voices.

371

Then came the sharp secular reaction, with pure monophony: a single melody with impersonal accompaniment, of itself without meaning. After all, there can be, ideally, little dignity in a stereotyped harmonic figure, however beautiful the melody.

So far as an ideal theory of music goes, there can be no doubt of the superiority of the church style. The question is of its test in the reality and truth of its poetic content. We saw a return in the great secular masters to architectural polyphony. But with all its grandeur, it was not a permeating element of their art, which was still based on the idea of a single melody with harmonic support. Duality or plurality of themes existed merely successively, or horizontally; with the Churchmen it was simultaneous, or vertical. We saw, too, how none of the secular masters were affected by Bach's influence and example before Schumann, who absorbed it far more than Mendelssohn or Chopin. So far as the quality of style may be summed in a word, that of Brahms is, in essence,

372

a reconciliation of Bach's mode of thought with secular freedom of outline, that is well-nigh ideal in its perfection. It goes, in this respect, as far beyond Schumann as the latter went beyond Mendelssohn. One is tempted to view a Brahms as a possible Bach symphony.

Still, one cannot gauge the artistic value and power of Brahms in proportion to this twofold master, however impressive. It must be, first, a question of the poetic reality. You cannot write music or measure it by a theory, however ideal. A man may have a perfect outward mastery and lack poetic content; though this is always found in imitators, who follow the outer manner of another. Brahms was no disciple; for Bach had written no symphonies. Again, however, we remember that in periods of formal development poetry often lagged. So it may be that Brahms has prepared the way for a greater.

Even of Bach the highest value seems to be an influence which reaches the world only through the works of other masters. So it may be with Brahms. His indirect power may be the greatest. There is no possible denying the nobility of his aim and attitude in modern days.

SYMPHONIES AND THEIR MEANING

There is a modern striving for unrest, for cyclonic effect, for barbaric brute force, for emotion with a capital E. All true sentiment must be unconscious; and so the effect upon the hearer must be unpremeditated. You cannot expect to *see* the emotion; it must not be too palpable. We must not be able to say, pointing, here it is; else we must also say, here it is not. We must not regard it as a frenzy, as some definite, individualized thing. The truest emotion is one which is most subtle, not seeking to trumpet its war-cry, to conquer an audience by the violence of its noise. On the contrary, careless of immediate reception, it is the expression of the personal feeling, soberly controlled, not roused to unmanageable excess. We do not care to see a man make big eyes or roar himself into a state, either at home or in the concert.

We must not get into a false way of measuring emotion by its brute force. A work is not great in proportion to the number of kettledrums, as Berlioz seemed to think. The true feeling is like the still small voice; it is the essence of a great personality unconsciously betrayed by highest art.

374

SYMPHONIES AND THEIR MEANING

We recur thus naturally at our close to a vital point of the beginning: the ethical phase of the musical art. Many deny this view to art generally. Few will persist as to poetry. It seems clear that if we agree that the content, not the mere language, is all-important, we must insist on its soundness. In music this has been entirely ignored. If a noble personality can be expressed in music, so can an ignoble. In music as in poetry it is possible by an extravagance of outward beauty to bribe an audience to listen to the morbid, unsound outpourings of a weak spirit. This is another modern danger. We listen too much with exclusive attention to the rapturous beauty of the sound. We do not think of the ethical quality, nor of the ethical effect. If we did, we should give less prominence to music, for example, of a Chopin. The question is all one. The strong, sound spirit, like the true sentiment, is tested by thorough mastery of the art. It proves the quality by its divine patience.

Brahms stands out strangely cold against the intense extremism of moderns. But the nobility of his position lies in a classic rebuke, contemptuously indifferent, to the hysterical men of tears and sighs, of rage and storms, in his perfection of form, in plan and in detail. There is a giant power, a reposeful mastery without strain, without lack of a corresponding strength and breadth of feeling. The manner of his writing is the result of his poetic personality; the latter is not fitted to the former.

At times there is a preponderance of the workman over the poet, as there was in Bach and in Mozart. This suggests that he may be a Mozart for a future Beethoven. Yet there is a pervading personality in the originality of his melodic thought, and in the homogeneity of his style. He it is who has rescued the art from the abuse of false schools by following the toilsome path which all masters must tread.

XIII

BRAHMS (Continued)

Symphony (No. 2) in D Major.

Once more let us strictly carry out our constant plan, reading the new master purely and absolutely from the score of one of his works, taken at random, seeing no comments on the music nor on the man, so that from the most perfect evidence we may get our impression, first of the symphony, then of the poet. This new figure, writing in the clear air of to-day, who is spoken of in the same breath with Beethoven and Schumann, what can he have to say that is comparable to their thought? And it must be new. To echo them, even to add corollaries to their truth, would not make him a master.

Our first sense is of blended simplicity and novelty,—the latter what Schumann meant by *neue Bahnen*. At the same time it is of an old primeval feeling. The expression is all new; the sentiment is of all time. But above all is that direct, unaffected simplicity of melody which we found stamped on Beethoven; the spontaneous thought, without pretence or evident effort. The color is the mellow, placid, legendary quality of horns and fagots.

The very beginning, the first three notes in the bass are most unpremeditated. Nationally, the melody is undoubtedly German,—that broad, even sweep, losing its accent in the syncopation of an endless cadence; an utter-

378

ance of the ancient Teutonic feeling of Wagner with the classic dignity of a master. It is not the modern romance; there is in the placid horns the suggestion of the heroic in repose.

Little is here of the vehement contrasts of the Schumann Romanticism. It is a calm neo-classicism, with all the workmanship of the Bach style. There is an entirely new poetry, clearer, more illumined, coming forth from Romantic caves and dells, enlightened by the revelations of a time that makes havoc with old fancies and illusions. It is distinctly broader, yet not quite with the humanity of a Beetho-ven,—lacking his strong *morale :* more national, too, in color than Beethoven, in spite of differ-ence in time, and in this respect more special and romantic. Yet it has more than the mere German spirit. There is a new breath in its conventional sentiment, as if including the Slavonic, with its freedom of tone and rhythm. But it is all northern; there is no recovery from the reaction against Italian domination. And there is always the tinge of Hungarian light-ness,—clear against German heaviness.

Soon appears a melody in the strings, there-fore human and more modern; the heroic quality is suspended. But the key is the same; there is no progress in tonal residence. It is all in the shadow of the first melody; it is, as yet, no new episode.

We know, however, that the themes here have not the official importance they had in Haydn and Mozart. Constantly we find several melodies where it is difficult to decide which has the clear title to the nominal rank. Often it seems that the function of the old second melody is divided among several. There is one, strictly second in succession, contrasting in character though not in key, whose main business later is to weave about the first melody, in simultaneous harmony, the architectural tissue of the discussion.

The real second melody comes after duly solemn preparation, down in cellos and violas. In mood, it is a return to the primeval air of the main subject, especially when repeated in the

STRINGS. (Melody in Cellos and Violas.)

woodwind, trebled in hollow octaves. It is distinctly the episode of the movement, an outing from the main theme. Though beginning gently, it has the germ of power, and rousing with its plain figure :

repeated through various syncopation:

it reaches a climax of heroic effect, with sharp and rough gait, with a strangely nervous motive

Doubled in Strings.

(of which we shall speak later), lapsing soon into rhythmic background before a phrase of slow, even swing:

RHYTHMIC CLARIONETS, HORNS, AND VIOLAS.
(*Violins, the second time.*)

FAGOT, CELLOS, AND BASSES.

382

Violins doubled below.

But slowly and dimly do we feel here, in the bass, another phase of the figure of the episodic melody. The effect is splendid, a kind of feudal, heroic pace, well set and maintained. It is like a crusaders' march, banners fluttering together, men tramping in step. Throughout is the spirit of Barbarossa and of mediæval story. Suddenly steals in the gentle flow of the second melody, now in serener major, through which we return to the beginning for a rehearsal of melodies.

With Brahms we must vary a little our attitude. The infinitesimal detail of this polyphonic net-work is such that the broad view, as in Schubert's C Major, loses too much of the beauty, especially in the age when Brahms is still, to many of us, a new enigma. There may, too, be an ulterior purpose with us to see something concrete of this novel style. It may be, as we have hinted, that there is more of the artisan than the poet. But the line cannot be drawn.

In any case, a nearer knowledge can but help. We must, then, magnify our view (or hearing) at least for a few periods, until we are accustomed to this new plan of highly defined detail. Indeed, if we once take account of the workmanship, as such, there is, I believe, more bewilderment of architecture in Brahms than in any other master of all time. Not only do you have this pervading unity of small detail, but at the same time the broad lines of the general plan, and the poetic unity of the whole work. It is as if Brahms had written his work once from the structural stand-point, and then had entirely worked over the whole, point by point, with minute, almost invisible perfection. It seems hardly possible for one creating mind to have at once this double sense: one pervading plan in the big, another in smallest execution. Brahms is probably far the greatest example of the saying that genius is an infinite capacity for work. Either kind of unity would seem to suffice even for our high standard. Brahms actually combines both. Yet, in itself, all this is mere workmanship. Its real value must lie in its unconscious use for utterance of a poetic conception.

A few glimpses will give a hint of this pervading perfection of detail. To show it in full would need almost a description of every note in the work.

We remember the innocent little phrase before the first melody :

In a curious way, with all our enjoyment of the melodies and their structure, the further we go, looking at lesser figures, the more we are magnetized by the constant reappearance of this motive in every guise, until we wonder whether this is a symphony in three notes. It is as if in a house of larger lines of beauty, we caught, at second and later views, the strange omnipresence of some arabesque curve, of hidden meaning, on ceiling, wall, and floor, large and small, now all but disguised.

In the first quotation we saw it creep in, at beginning and end, with least possible show.

SYMPHONIES AND THEIR MEANING

Throughout the cadence from the first melody we meet it. In the long drawn out chords we cannot escape it magnified:

Presently we see it, even where it is not, as when the sun is in our eyes. But surely the first three notes of the second melody are but a quicker pace of the same motto; for at its close the original *tempo* appears clearly. And now it comes thick and fast, until the second theme brings a rest. But the nervous phrase which

leads the crusaders' march is again a shorter form of those first three notes. It is not good to go farther in this analysis, which is too grammatical for real enjoyment. We can now have a dim consciousness of the significance of the master's constant treatment. Of course, with him it was the mere simplicity and economy of highest art. Somehow, it seems, more consciousness is needed to perceive than to create. We get, too, a sense of that strangely firm power of sequence, more subtle even than Schumann's, though without his passionate intensity. With Brahms it brings a hidden, yet strong connection of distant regions of the work, which is felt rather than thought. In a true symphony the various movements reinforce each other. We shall find a light, cast from the last movement upon the first.

It must be that in the discussion is the measure of his genius. But so complex is the fine filigree of his poetic diction that one needs the elbow-room of a book to tell of a single work. We must be content with a quicker and cruder view. His symphony is a kind of great modern fugue, where hardly a phrase is not a melodic fragment. Brahms has reduced to the minimum what we might call the irrelevant machinery, rhythmic and harmonic, as distinct from melodic text. Yet he is never dry; there is always the personal and poetic quality, though on a steady plane, with few picturesque heights. One of the traits that stamp him is the masterly sustaining of vein: the magnificence of his continuous and complete workmanship. He is very different from Schumann in temperament; much more equable; less intense. Wonderful are his vast Olympian levels; but they do not rise as high as Schumann's Gothic peaks.

Quickly we view, after repeated statement, how he slowly climbs from sombre minor of the first part of the original melody with steady insistence to a glorious march in the second:

More than ever are the images of that first motto, ever in new rhythmic guise. That broad multiplicity of rhythm is new with Brahms. Then comes the relief of the idyllic, flowing melody, the unofficial second, but in minor, answered by the motto on high, in full sway, almost in stern rebuke, in its slow sounding of the first three notes of the former. Suddenly break in thunderous unison strokes of an early phrase:

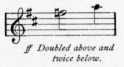

ff Doubled above and twice below.

Gradually, after faint efforts, the first melody flows along with all its old gentleness and a new soothing calm, now not succeeded but entwined by the liquid beauty of the second. And

CLARIONETS (with lower Horns).

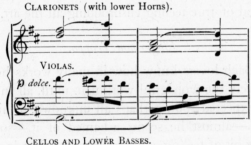

VIOLAS.

p dolce.

CELLOS AND LOWER BASSES.

thus we are in the last singing of themes in original manner, once more, too, with the grand march of crusaders. Later is a burst of great sweetness and power of modulation, followed by a most moving groping through uncertain worlds of thought. Once more breaks in the light of main melody, now in a new charm of *berceuse* swing,—still with the motto below:

Piu tranquillo. In STRINGS.

mp espressivo.

There is a great tenderness in the ending,—a flood of true feeling enshrouding all the art.

Adagio non Troppo.

Bach lovers know how in many works he is merely the wonderful workman, until, all in an unexpected spot, perhaps all unknown to himself,—almost he seems ashamed of it,—some true bit of feeling comes along, nigh lost in the mass of the other. Something of this there is in Brahms. He seems to begin almost indifferent to beauty of theme; and when we are nearly discouraged, in an unimportant place suddenly comes the human song. Brahms is a little like Wagner, as with both their song

seems merged into discourse, their poetry drawn
out into prose. But with Wagner the tissue is
too often iteration; with Brahms it is a continuous polyphonic woof.

The melody here seems to have the deceptive
quality,—a less promising beginning; the real
beauty comes in the answer. Here in the third
bar is that golden vein of diatonic melody, that
inexhaustible source of highest lyric utterance:

It is, after all, the true natural utterance. Then, too, it is that Brahms way of coming from dim uncertainty to clear light.

And so it flows on, pure, self-contained, melodic discourse. The horn takes up the thread of the last word of repeated theme, the rest join successively. You do not think of the fugue, but they are all talking, beginning in turn on the same subject. When the discussion is becoming technical, all are set at peace with that same altogether satisfying ending of the first melody (quoted above), just like the kindest word of wisest parent.

A curious *Adagio* quality this of Brahms. It is similar to that rare vein of Beethoven that we prized most. Brahms has not quite his deep sympathy. He is more impersonal, like Schubert. There is something of German folk-song here; but it seems broader, more ancient in source, almost Pagan. There is much of modern feeling for Teutonic legend. But the conception is higher and finer than most of such poetry.

A new verse comes now; hardly a clear-cut melody. Curiously, it has exactly the nature of the first. Beginning in a questioning mood,

it grows more anxious, and then is stilled by
another broad, soothing cadence:

VIOLINS, VIOLAS, AND CELLOS.

Once more the questioning, grubbing spirit
is roused, rearing now a stormy whirl of rebellious doubts.   He is laid by a last, calm, broad
verse of the main song.

Allegretto Grazioso (Quasi Andantino).

In Andantes there is a new Brahms.   Architectural depth must yield there to lyric direct-

ness. In the slow movement is the true poet who shows that German folk-song is not exhausted, as he does elsewhere in his glorious *Lieder;* that it has new strains, which come from the border-land of newer races. In these song-movements is tested the sentiment of the poet ; in the Allegros, the broad view and structural power.

In the Scherzos there is a second departure, almost as great as in the first. The humor of Brahms seems largely an expression of Hungarian lightness. There is complete absence of polyphony. He begins with child-like dance with odd accent:

Allegretto gracioso (*Quasi andantino*).

There is much, too, of Tyrolese drollery. It is all a jolly *bourgeois*, not to say peasant fun. There is none of the serious humor of Beethoven. Yet we do not mean at all that it does not belong as justly in the symphony. Such prohibition would be intolerable. A symphony even can bear no philosophic intent, unless it be quite unconscious. In the lightness of Brahms's pleasant frolic there is much real poetry.

The humor is in all kinds of smallest touches; sometimes it is a teasing play of voices; at others, of groups of instruments,—a humor of orchestration. You would not catch it in a piano arrangement, as there are sudden modulations or surprises of accent. From the dainty waltz melody of the beginning there darts out a queer, quick dance in even time:

Presto ma non assai.
VIOLINS, VIOLAS, AND CELLOS.

It is, of course, a prank at masquerading the first tune. Some touches defy telling. Right here, in the next bar, the strings try to run off to another key, another play-ground. The wood won't let them. The strings urge, the wood refuse. Then they run off and for a moment play strutting soldiers. But it is all too light for heavy words. On returning, the first waltz-like dance has a new, delicate pathos, where a second voice discourses sweetly in flowing measure fitted to the slow glide of the theme.

A rough bit of barbaric play interrupts in reckless Presto. It jangles in our Western ears. We lose our sense of tonal bearings, and are glad to return once more to the gentler pace of the German dance.

Allegro con Spirito.

In the Finale is undoubtedly the historic color and the mediæval swing of the beginning. With all the danger of finding fixed meanings, there is no doubt of this, that Brahms, of course, all unconscious in the creating, stands in the highest branch of the highest art for that modern return to the spirit of Teuton legend which has a strange power over our minds to-day, which has been almost a dominant poetic subject of the century. With Brahms it has a great breadth. He had much of the Ossian feeling. Undoubtedly his geographical position helped him. Born in the farthest north of Germany, he visited the South, and settled and died in the far East.

If we are asked to show evidence of this theme in Brahms's poetry, we may be helpless in a legal sense. To our own conviction appeals most the very quality of the melodies, which, instead of modern romantic sweetness, have a distinctive rough breadth, and a strangeness which cannot speak of modern things. Simplicity is, of course, of all ages; therefore, at the least, it does not jar on an archaic feeling. It is strange that with a similar breadth in Brahms and in Beethoven, we think of the latter as looking forward; in the former only do we feel the historic spirit. The truth is, these periods differ totally. There was no retrospection early in the century. It was all for new ideas and ideals. To-day there is a constant longing for the sanctity of old conceptions. The modern is the practical and stereotyped; in the ancient lies the poetic truth. Brahms realizes to the full this feeling. He is, thus, representative of his age; his was in pure music the unconscious impulse that drove Tennyson to the King's Idylls and Wagner to

the Nibelungen Epic; and this is the burden
of the symphony.

The first melody enters in bleak unison of
all the strings:

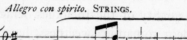

BASSES an octave below.

In its stiffness, its set, cramped energy, it has
the feudal feeling of the first *Allegro*. When
the melody has a learned counter-theme, the
atmosphere is more monastic. It has much of

complexity and close texture. But it is bubbling
with melody and rhythm.

We soon find that, strangely, the first four
notes correspond, as motto, to that of the first
movement. We do not know whether we
ought to notice that the first three notes are in
both movements the same. So we have everywhere, in all sorts of garb, this phrase:

Through a misty change of scene we are led
to the second melody, which is surely one of

Largamente. STRINGS.

399

the simple, diatonic kind. Still, the motto is ever present.

With smooth, sweeping flight it lightly wings aloft in successive curves into a climax of power that did not seem to lie in the germ of the theme. Now the motto has all the say, and there is a great rollicking of pairs of voices, each in duet, in the same motive coursing all about, losing all rein of regular pace, at last quieting down to the first melody.

The answer of the latter at the very beginning we cannot ignore. It has a certain ancient humor, sung as it is in barbaric unison, again and again, like some well-seasoned popular strain:

Strings, doubled below in Fagots and Cellos.

Basses sustaining low A.

As now the main melody is discussed in fragmentary perversions, this old refrain ever comes in with conclusive air, is even sung fugally. But it serves later to give one of the rarest touches of primeval humor of the sym-

phony. For when at last the final chant of
melodies has begun, as at first, and we look
above wondering, here is a strange sound from
the basses upward,—the inverted disguise of the
comic answering strain:

In Strings, doubled above and below.

And now we are rolling towards the end, the
first song of melodies fuller and more boisterous.
There is always the same feeling of march of
pious knights. And there are many touches
of the kinship of the main themes of first and
last movement. For instance, a sudden quiet
retreat (which is written *Tranquillo* in the score),
seems at first new with its strange, slow swing
in four-voiced woodwind:

Tranquillo.
WOODWIND, melody doubled above in Flutes.
(Echo in STRINGS.)

HORNS.

26   401

Now, this is, of course, primarily and poetically a romantic refuge from the din of strife. But in its melodic origin it comes not only from the first melody of the finale, but most clearly from the very motto of the original movement. It is, indeed, a melody in this very motto, pure and simple.

Strictly, we have here gone back, for a moment, before the *reprise* of melodies. Returning, after the final rollicking episode, there is a quaint droning of monks' fugue, in second melody, sung in pairs:

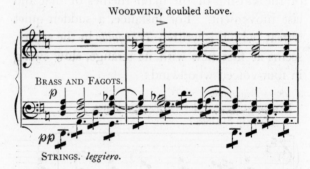

This broadens into a march of big idea and spirit, with complex swing, whence suddenly we are again in the timid Tranquillo, now the second legend droning in the bass:

STRINGS (Horns sustaining harmonic tones).

BASS an octave below.

Of course, this has the promise of power. And so the end comes in a martial burst with rapid iteration of this phrase from the second melody.

Brahms may have appeared to us, in all this, as composer rather than as poet. He is, perhaps, too near to see the big lines. He is, too, a recurrence of the simplicity of earliest masters. We must not expect romantic definiteness. But the unity of message is as clear as with any poet. Finally, he may be the pioneer of greater poetry in the paths he has broken.

Of course, this has the promise of power.
And so the 'ind comes in a martial burst with
rapid iteration of this phrase from the second
melody.

Brahms may have appealed to us, in all this,
as composer rather than as poet. He is, perhaps, too near to see the big lines. He is, too,
a reassurance of the simplicity of earlier masters. We must not expect romantic definiteness. But the unity of message is as clear as
with any story. Finally, he may be the pioneer
of greater poetry in the paths he has broken.

INDEX

Andante, 32, 45, 49.

Art: Purpose, 14, 19, 30, 68–9; limitations, 30; mode of creation, 249, 347. See also Preface.

Bach, 24, 26, 34, 36–7, 40, 70, 93, 177, 260 *et seq.*, 271, 367 *et seq.*

Beauty, 95, 96, 97, 313.

Beethoven, 14, 19, 32–3, 45–6, 69, 71, 76–7, 82, 85, Chaps. V.–VI., 177–183, 186, 189–90, 194, 201, 226–7, 268–70, 364

Berlioz, 100, 127, 163, 170, 251, 268.

Brahms, 76, 102, 125, 129, 179, 252.

Church school (of composition), 24–27, 31, 34–5, 44–5, 71, 377.

Classicism. (See Romanticism.)

Counterpoint (see Polyphony), 25, 35, 75, 79, 91, 265.

Criticism, 13 *et seq.*, 22, 342.

Dance (see Minuet, Scherzo), 26, 34, 36–8.

Development, 38 *et seq.*, 49, 75–6, 92, 94–5, 130, 134, 153.

Durchführung. (See Development.)

Ethics (in Music), Preface, 20 *et seq.*, 192, 371 *et seq.*

Folk-Song (see National Element), 49, 190, 191, 359.

Form, 95, 98, 192, 250 *et seq.*, 343 *et seq.*, 350 *et seq.*

Fugue, 42, 54, 58.

Goethe, 72, 128, 182–3, 189–91

405

INDEX

Handel, 44.

Haydn, 30, 32, Chap. III., 70–2, 83–4, 95–6, 125, 129, 147, 153, 226.

Humor (in Music), 30, 59, 70, 82, 104, 167 *et seq.*, 225 *et seq.*, 322, 338–9, 364.

Interpretation, 333–4.

Jean Paul Richter, 258 *et seq.*

Language. (See Prose.)

Listening, Chap. I., 152, 347–8.

Logic (in Music). See Sequence.

Master (Mastery), 249 *et seq.*, 342 *et seq.*, 350, 369 *et seq.*

Meaning (in Music), 17, 96, 98–9, 100–1, 125 *et seq.*, 148 *et seq.*, 154–5, 167 *et seq.*, 249 *et seq.*, 270 *et seq.*, 278, 308, 310 *et seq.*, 330, 333–34, 344 *et seq.*

Mendelssohn, 79, 155, 170, 185, 210, 252, 263, 265–6, Chap. XI.

Metaphysics (in Music), 134–5, 146, 177, 182, 270 *et seq.*, 289–299.

Minuet (see Dance, Scherzo), 38, 51, 60, 80, 89, 152 *et seq.*

Modulation, 104.

Mozart, 32, 43, 45–6, Chap. IV., 95–6, 125, 130, 153, 178–9, 181, 185, 190, 313.

Music (see Art, Meaning, Symphony, Master): Essence, 18, 99; limitations, 127, 310 *et seq.*; power and purpose, 153 *et seq.*, 330 *et seq.*, 345.

National Element (in Music) (see Folk-Song), 182, 189, 209, 309, 322 *et seq.*, 327, 331, 341.

Opera, 127, 188, 190, 251, 262.

Orchestra, 44, 349.

Overture, 349.

INDEX

THE END.

GREAT WORKS
OF
MUSIC

Volume Two

CLASSIC SYMPHONIES

PREFATORY

THIS book completes the whole survey of classic symphonies. The aim of the first volume was to find the mystery of symphonies, —not here, nor there, but of the ideal type; to see what tonal meaning really *means*, and, quite as clearly, what it does not mean. The quaint confusion ever will intrude that only that is definite that finds a term in common speech. And so the lay-world seldom dreams that music, pure and simple, in highest form of art, will tell a message clearer far and richer, nobler and more human, too (in its own field), than one may hope of prose or even verse.

In this design the special symphonies described were the mere proof and evidence. A later thought, helped by the kind response to the first volume, was to test these hidden truths in other classic symphonies that varied in their plan and quality, and lastly to survey the whole field of the great tonal works of art.

PREFATORY

In thus returning to the earlier masters, the third of Mozart's group of masterworks remained to be included. With Haydn the problem is a special one. The long list of his symphonies implies two consequences, really two in one. First, they are all much alike in inner content,—in that which here is sought to bring to clearer light. Then, for the same reason, this very message is a lesser one, does not so well invite or quite deserve, nor does it surely need the verbal sketch. The aim was to amuse and cheer in highest sense. While they do cheer, each in a novel way, they do not vary in significant degree within the original mood of merry humor.

Of Beethoven's symphonies all are here discussed except the three of volume one. The question there must face us of Beethoven's earlier art,—the true degree of independence, the share of Mozart (and of Haydn) in the younger master's thought. And this must touch the other problem, ever rising new to view, of highest rank.

In face of warning proverb of odious comparisons, there are some questions that will never down. You cannot cure the world of having

its greatest—poet or soldier. It does not want a
democracy of genius; it tends, however wrong,
to feel with Odysseus : " One must be foremost."
The later Beethoven compels two subjects of
profoundest interest and moment, where reasoning may well confirm the test of great experiment. In the " Pastoral" we wonder at the
bounds of tonal art, in actual graphic copying
of nature; in the Ninth we are aroused to take
sides as to the highest ultimate effect of instruments alone, or of joint orchestra and chorus.

The works of Raff bring a new phase of
titled symphonies; and here the " Scotch" of
Mendelssohn belongs. And so the whole field
of programme music opened forth with Berlioz's
Fantastic Symphony, the literal story of an
artist's woes. Liszt's " Faust" must show the
touches of the great dramatic school; Tschaikowsky's Pathétique is here in line of clear
descent. At the same time, the symphonies of
Schumann and of Brahms preserved the standard of highest tonal epic, of pure subjective
quality.

The raging quarrel of the two great modern
schools can somehow not be all ignored. There
the new word of latest instrumental poet

must surely shed a ray of brilliant light on coming lines. And so, though Richard Strauss has not as yet chosen the strict symphony, his broadest, latest work, *Ein Heldenleben*, could not be resisted.

At this point came a certain strong desire to include in all this view each individual symphony that has uttered its new note of sincere poetic message. As there must doubtless be dispute in such a list of those composers whose final laurels are not yet secure, at least one work of each is treated. So, in appended note, Gade and Goetz disclose a narrower vein, though still of truest art. The charming " Country Wedding" of Goldmark shows well the limits of the symphony. Another work, by Gilchrist, is an instance of the form transplanted in a newer field.*

The description is really all symbolic, and must be taken as such, for any value whatever. We might, in a sense, have printed in the inside of our book on the meaning of symphonies,—

---

* There is a group of American symphonies, by such composers as Paine and Chadwick, that would well repay an exposition. Lack of space forbids the choice of more than one.

nothing. It would be true in a way. Music means nothing that can definitely be put in words. It means so much to the musician, indeed it seems often to hold all truth, that he could talk about it indefinitely in more than one sense.

And it is certainly worth helping others to the same joy of intelligence, even though he can only eagerly point to the glorious beauties, anxious for responsive agreement, as at sight of fleeting clouds in waning light of sunset one would catch at this figure and that to fix it to the eye of a friend. So if ordered beauty as well as delight of golden touches can be brought in some measure to fellow ears and minds, it will be the main object,—at least of the descriptions.

But, somehow, there is a little more than mere chance imagery; for there is real truth in the symbolism of the moral strife of individual, of debate and dispute, drawing truth from the dregs, rising to final enlightenment. Every phase of life is here idealized. Again, the symbol has real truth. Beauty, strength, each have their figures. The moral, not the external life of man finds in music its full play and mirror. The true essence of life is in its emotions, and these play in tones as do fish in the waters. The highest problems are ethical, emotional, of experience; science is but a lesser helpmeet. In music their utterance is so real that they seem to be there themselves in the life of the tonal stream.

Given the type of pleading, of defiance, of plaint, of dim foreboding akin to objective omen, of prayerful trust, of triumphant joy,—given all these, together with the full play of dispute and strife,—and you have all the resources, unconscious and therefore the more genuine and convincing, for the utterance of man's most vital thought. So you have in the Fifth Symphony actually as stirring a refrain of the same high truth as in the book of Job.

The elements of rhythm, pace, and melody, of single song and polyphonic or mere hymnal chorus, the lesser, of orchestral color, are all quickly caught; they need no technical account. Even the element of form, the highest in the mastery of the art, can be suggested in recurrence of the themes. One phase there is that seems more difficult to show in direct meaning. The schoolmen call it modulation, the change of tonality. The latter we have agreed is scene or tonal residence. The key may thus be said in simplest truth to be the home of a tune,— where it begins and ends, whence it may wander for a long or shorter journey. It were, indeed, idle to speak of tunes or lesser figures without this sense of residence. They would be as shadowy as the spirits of the unreal world. It is the tonal color that gives the living hue.

If a key is the home of a tune, what then is the grateful change? Whether you regard yourself as going about subjectively, wandering tonally from scene to scene with conclusion in each, returning finally home to the first, or whether you are resting and it all passes before you, is of no moment of difference. If we were to sit still and have the planets fly past us, it would be as much of a journey as if we were flying ourselves. In any case we are taking a tonal journey; that is as near the true state as a symbol will take us. All the motion is there of voyage, —all the incident, main and lesser, of the change.

So a modulation is literally change of scene, and it may be graded or sudden, as in wandering through a plain or over a mountain. Indeed, the quick surprise of new turn of view is just the same sort of pleasure as the charm of sudden shift of key. The symbol for us will be our own journey, or of picture moving before our eyes. We may even leave quite vague the figure each one chooses for himself. But we shall hope for ready response of the reader without need of literal fulness.

Suppose the symbol is of action, what then of the key? Where the first theme is type of energy, the second may be of passive apprehension, the state of joyous perception; in any case, under whatever guise, you must have a dual quality, not merely of tune but of tone. Contrast there must be in outer garb and colors as well as in actual lineaments of theme. Else, if the second follows in the same tone, there is no progress, no relation, no sequence, no contrast. One is mere continuation of the other, like a building all in one dimension. One figure belongs in one line and light, the second in another. The tonal color of melodic subjects is one of the main elements of musical enjoyment; it marks the difference of old fugue and new earthly sonata. What the tunes stand for, what they do, where they are aiming, none of it is more important than where they come from tonally, in what tonal quarter do they sing, what is the change of tonal scene from one tune to the other. It may, to be sure, be possible to stress too far this matter of the scene or light. It is the nearest word that comes for the idea. There may be a better that may fit in certain other symbols of the whole.

In all the discussion of the meaning and potency of musical works of art this cannot be lost. It is of first moment, though so intimate a matter that it is hard to separate from the nature of the melody itself. In the symbols of scene or journey it is all clear enough, and needs no further light. In the profounder figures of actual or moral struggle the matter is deeper and more difficult; it cannot be dismissed so easily. In any case the tonal shift serves as in lighter symbols to mark the change. Change there must be in garb, guise, point of entrance; in strife there is the more need of opposite directions in the fighters, complete separation of residence, even of origin. So the change may approach almost to realism of stage shifting, so as to give the new direction. The villain must enter on the other side.

But the music must show it all. Nevertheless

in all symbols it will be yielded that tone or key stands ever for residence ; carried to mathematics, for orientation or location. So whether tunes are lines of picture, or the traveller himself is moving about making his own scenes, or whether they are types of action and of strife, they must have each their quarter where they dwell, whence they emerge and advance. For music is a very real sort of human process. It is no shadowy, abstract allegory. It is all genuine, real existence and enjoyment. These musical figures must have their entity, their real being, and so their place. Further, music is all astir with living, thrilling beauty that ever transcends. So this residence is not of mathematics or topography, but rich in color,—beauty is again its main designation. And thus, as every bit of music has a home where it begins and where it ends, every melodic figure has its own nook or niche, and every idea, of whatever symbolic guise, has its own tonal vine and fig-tree.

The best excuse, it must be here admitted, for treating more than one of the included symphonies, was their strong evidence, in converse proof, by negative example. There is no truth more

urgently to be proclaimed than the absolute connection between a clear and honest art and a
high moral tone. Here music can be shown to
be the truest record of man's best intuition ; thus
it becomes the strongest power for moral incul-
cation. And so the author, with all desire to give
a fair account of every work, can somehow not
restrain the hope that the reader will subtly feel
how, where the whole poem lacks in true organic
growth, the strong pervading moral tone is absent, the impulse of display, of less sincere poetic
message, finds a special channel. For here we
see most clearly how the pure type of symphony
has won pre-eminence of all the forms as the
evangel of the highest truth.

No doubt there is most gain in positive approval. Disparaging attacks are on much lower
plane. Ring out the praise of all the best in the
world, and that which stands opposed, must meet
its own deserved fate, by its own force, that needs
no outer aid.

And yet no other field of human intellect, not
all dramatic poetry nor varying lines of other
arts do seem to hold so tense a moment and
concern as just this double question : the meaning of the greatest tonal works, as it has worked

its own solution through the century just passed, and as it must prove in that which has begun. For music is the art of latest age; it is the present self-expression of the race, the only channel where a creative vein runs still unchecked.

But music has a double power not merely for the good. The quality that brings the message home in warmest living tones may easily run riot in sensuous effect or meretricious sentiment. And so the question, What is good and what is permanently great? yields to no other in ultimate importance. It must affect the whole thought and ethics of the race. It has a greater urgency than the latest problems of theology. For here, in music, seems to lie the true creed and religion that has a common language clear to all

I

MOZART'S SYMPHONY IN
E FLAT

IT is ever an old question, like that of the lost
tribes of Israel, and some others that are never
settled, on which the world's judgment stays
poised. There are always people who believe
that Mozart reached an absolute pinnacle of
Parnassus,—that Beethoven marked a descent.
The problem is incapable of solution. Both
views are true, in a way. One thing is certain:
every man has a right, in more than legal sense,
to think Mozart the greatest. Von Ambros,
prince of historians, says of the group of Mozart's symphonies in C, E Flat, and G Minor:
"They are the *ne plus ultra* of art." Thus it
becomes a question whether there was more gain
or loss in a dominance of the emotional over the
purely æsthetic. It may belong to the dualism
of human things that both have their opposite,
correlative, eternal positions; that each must come
in its phase; that each is greatest in independence.
One is inclined to think that you cannot com-

pare Mozart and Beethoven any more than a lake and a mountain. One turns from the cold, smooth perfection of the elder with eagerness to the fire and wealth of sympathy of the younger master, and again from the wild, ruthless abandon and harshness of the latter with delight to the sane serenity and limpid art of the former. Perhaps each is needed in his time. Perhaps it were a better world if there were no cause for the fiery wrath of a Beethoven,—a perpetual Nirvana, where Mozart sings the theme of constant blessedness. But then, we might say, a world without the stress of moral strife very like is no world at all,—a state of non-existence. The chief business of the world, after all, is the moral strife and onward, upward course; we know no other and conceive of none. The angelic note of eternal praise fails of sustaining interest, suggests a lack of dignity, a somewhat pointless task for all the ages.

Of such a world of moral strife Beethoven is the great prophet; he is, therefore, the most human of all the tone poets.

But ought there to be a content at all? Is it a lowering of pure art when that begins? There is no reason for this fear. For, if the poet is not self-conscious in his special mood, absorption and concentration are more perfect. The beauty is used as means. There is less of material enjoyment. A wonderful wedding of joy and truth is this of art. To be sure, there is an immediate descent on the other side, where music has constant label in graphic account of detailed event or scene.

It is a simple problem, almost algebraic. If there is no emotional hue, there is too little absorption. If there is such a coloring, there must be a projection of subjective spirit, which immediately assumes a moral (or immoral) quality.

There is a constructive phase of art forms, where the tinkering is conscious,—is all there is. It seems to be a needed link; it has no other reason for existence; it is not interesting in itself. The consciousness of form forbids spontaneity. Then comes the phase of perfected form, where the facile master goes roving freely in the prepared pastures, plucking the flowers that are blossoming for him.

A period arrives when there is a certain relish of the perfect dwelling, when one eyes and touches the panels and pillars with a delight in the new design. But it is not as yet the sense of home, the quality of human association. In music, so long as consciousness of outer design is there, the high point is not reached. On the other hand, in the dwelling, association and special quality enter unwatched and unushered, one knows not when. So in the very master who has the sense of outer perfection, a strong quality of emotion, of sympathy, and secret moral spur may exist unreckoned by himself. Here we reach the three great symphonies of Mozart. He combines both phases. On the other hand, when the master gets wind of his own power of special utterance, comes the temptation wittingly to paint certain feelings. Here is Beethoven's design in the Sixth and Ninth. Thus broadly in the curve of the symphony we trace the formal growth to sudden height, to over-bold experiment across the bounds of tonal art to absolute depiction. We see a gentler later journey in the realms of more defined emotion, where intimate fragrance is gained with loss of primal truth. And at the latest do we have the brave return to biggest view, that reaps all gain of earlier experience and best contains the present message of the world, pointing the way and form of utterance of even greater, deeper thought.

MOZART'S SYMPHONY IN E FLAT

Mozart's Symphony in E Flat connects Haydn and the earlier Beethoven. The absolute innocence of purpose strikes us first. *Adagio* here in the beginning meant no mood, merely a decent suppression of spirits for ceremony's sake. It was a tradition in line with the old French overtures. Haydn follows it much of the time. It was the feeling of Gluck, Cimarosa, Paer, those worthies of the stiffer school. It has something in common, too, with the old prelude before the fugue. In a way it utters the sense of gravity of the coming epic,—an invocation for the right spirit. So these Adagios seem to be cast in the same mould. Yet this did not prevent a structure of solemn beauty with clear tracery of lesser figures; there are no eminent themes, no main ideas. There is a free-flowing sequence, and again,

FLUTES, VIOLINS & FAGOT.

CELLOS AND BASSES.
(See page 18, line 4.)

towards the end, a bold, clashing modern discord, all done in the polyphonic process. At the end the voices enter in turn (of canon) on a placid theme, which seems to have something of prophecy, and thence hurries instantly into one of those dancing melodies that were first conceived in Haydn's humor, but here with Mozart have an added inevitable quality. They cannot be imagined otherwise by smallest note. Yet they lie not in that voice or this, but consist in the interplay and imitation of several, mostly in strings:

The second verse has the tune all in the bass, much in the later Beethoven fashion, with new phrases to suit in the upper voices. Wonderful, too, how the bass follows it out, even in the answer. The upper voices seem to lead, but merely suit the song of original melody below. All this has been lightest drollery, almost whispering. Now breaks in the full chorus at the loudest, very much in Gluck's old martial effect, —pure, childlike pomp.

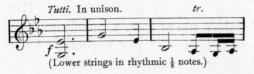

Tutti. In unison.

(Lower strings in rhythmic ⅛ notes.)

Next follows a period in livelier strumming motion; still the play of simplest sort of phrases, mere runs of strings and blasts of woodwind. But the sequence is charming, running gradually to neighboring tonal mooring, with jolly cadence

(See page 20, line 4.)

in cheery chirp of smaller figures. Then, on still lighter trip of foot, a prettily moving duet in strings is given a pert response in low cellos, with assenting chorus in the wood.

A new strain, more thoughtfully serene, just escaping sadness, moves in the strings.

Most charmingly, right against the expressive answer, woodwind follow (in canon) with the theme. A return to general tripping and trilling merriment ends the repeated statement. It all shows how in music the big man can ever be a child,—need never be ashamed to dance about

in all his corpulence like any schoolboy or
tot.

After the rehearsing, the discussion begins on

STRINGS.

one of the last lightest figures, as if with a "by-
the-way," then quickly returns to the graver second theme sung in the earlier manner,—a real
and thorough discussion, too, though short,
driving the theme home by logical process to
cadence of conclusive beauty. When the serious question is thus disposed of, we naturally
return to the lighter,—a mere line of retorts in
two former phrases, of skipping motion in strings
(that began the discussion) and blows of the
wind; or rather the retort is of the former alone
in trebles and basses of strings, the latter chiming
in with general lack of importance. But the
whole is ever moving tonally, shifting the scene
and light until it enters the original region with
scampering figures. A pause, a few touches of
the thoughtful vein, bring us back to the original

song of themes, which follows in the old lines. But, of course, the second melody plays in the home tone, and Mozart's wit never fails of a new way of saying old things. The ending is true to the pervading spirit of noisy mirth. It seems that in the very artisan perfection of the whole and of detail, that, least of all music, suggests verbal translation, lies the magic one vainly tries to utter in words.

The second movement, *Andante*, suggests how simplest utterance may be profoundest. It has the melody here of lyric pathos nearest akin (of all of Mozart's) to the great Beethoven type.

One must not forget to trace the origin to Mozart. The whole first period, repeated, too, is all given to the song of the reigning melody; not least is the moving sequence, against steady strum of viola, of the first phrase, with strange

taste of harmony, returning in free, almost playful, descent to the strict theme.

Now, after two bars that seemed irrelevant
preface,

WOODWIND AND HORNS.

(Fagots doubled below.)

that quaint pompous effect breaks out in full
chorus with no particular tune,—mere short

STRINGS.

(*f* chord of woodwind.)

(Basses in ₁⁄₁₆ notes on F.)

phrases that lend themselves easily to the play of
sequence and imitation. The whole is, frankly,
nothing but foil to the principal melody, a short
relief from the sustained strain of its pathos,
though to us it seems to have no great burden
of grief; there is a very sure undertone of con-

tentment. In those days the main business of music was to cheer and amuse. To us this loud striding and shouting seems like a sort of stage device,—a sudden change to rouse the mood from pathos, to prepare the better for its return. It is, it must be confessed, the least real of Mozart. It came from a tradition abounding in Haydn and vanishing entirely in Beethoven. It is a symptom that marks the evolution of music from workmanship, from conscious external effect, to emotional utterance. But very beautifully the gentle ascent on strain of first theme in the wood returns to the old strum of violas, this time answered in basses. As the phase repeats, a graceful curve of melody is suited above to the constant ascent of the former below:

(In 8ves of violins; rhythmic $\frac{1}{16}$ note chords in woodwind.)

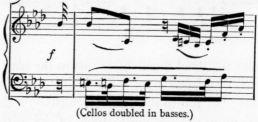

(Cellos doubled in basses.)

Strange, this Mozart genius! In our modern sensational way we are just smiling despisingly at his triteness, when here he does a bolder stroke, all with the innocence of a child playing with blocks. Right in the last free cadence on strain of first theme, in its very midst, a canon begins

(that is, a game of follow the leader) on a strange motive,—strange till we force our memory back to that irrelevant preface of second subject. Most curiously is blended the ending of one episode and the formal beginning of another, and on the same tone. And the almost ominous ring of the theme is repeated at each successive entrance of new voices. But in the end all is resolved on most primitive, nay, homely cadence, with a special touch of humor.

Sometimes it seems that music must be true to the old adage: "Still waters run deep." Where there is most blatant noise there is least thought. Again comes the quaint, serious canon leading in liveliest cadence back to original theme. Now

(Violins with lower 8ve.)

(Woodwind with lower 8ve ;
Basses of strings sustaining harmony.)

a full-fledged phrase grows over the lower subject, and other figures are coursing about the
former ascending strain. The whole song of
main melody sings with new fulness, here in
sombre minor, now in bright change of light,
followed by the second theme, pompous as before, but more brilliant in its shifting hues, with
now a most modern flourish. So magnificent is
this prismatic round of colors that the tune finds
here a new reason and a new beauty. And there
is little to add, save that in this recurring round
there is ever a greater richness of surrounding
figures, so that the whole is almost transformed
in mood. Indeed the lesser phrase threatens to
o'ermaster the theme in outer emphasis and in
humor. That might be, save that, after a return
of the canon, the main melody sings in original
simplicity, and the air of sincerity is heightened
as the theme, refusing to close in the usual way,

puts off the farewell in a few ingenuous words of extension.

For once the Minuet is a true minuet; there is no disguise nor idealized Platonic form with the original quality distilled away, but very frankly the old dance, though in magnificent equipment.

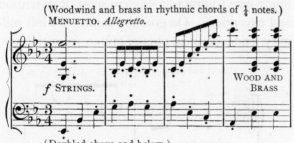

(Woodwind and brass in rhythmic chords of ¼ notes.)
MENUETTO. *Allegretto.*

f STRINGS.

WOOD AND BRASS

(Doubled above and below.)

There is no "meaning" whatever here beyond just this joy and sense of the dance; but it is a nobler movement than its lesser descendant the waltz. Assured strength there is in the slow, restrained swing, which is not merely a single skip, but three measured steps, the first being strongest. The grace is consummate, stately and ever brilliantly resplendent with full martial accoutrement,—brass, drums, and all. But this does not prevent a sudden soft gliding phrase in answer, as if soothing after the awe of the first.

Repeats come with due precision; there is absolutely no yielding to a modern spirit of extension
and exception.   On goes the dance with full mil-
itary stride on new phrase, gotten from the first,

(Wood and brass in rhythmic chords of ¼ notes.)

with a certain relentless attack of step, sweeping
a splendid curve back to main theme.   Again
comes the full ceremonial of rehearsal.

The Trio is very different.   It does approach
our later waltz.   But there is a blended sort of
cradle song and dance in the rocking of clarinets and skipping of strings.   Woodwind sing
the tune in pretty echo of cadence.   Here, too,

28

reigns the strict rule of repeat. Then the song winds along in freest phrase,—all trick of movement gone for once, in naïve discussion of the new melody. Thence we are led with greater formality to the main tune with due rehearsing, and back once more to the full pomp of majestic minuet. Again the absolute innocence of early symphony is surely proved.

Finale: Allegro. Sportiveness is the mood of this vehement chorusing of merry round dance, given out first by timidly jaunty strings. The

whole band almost frighten you with its mirth;
perhaps they intend it.   There is another charm
in the way the jolly jingle begins, not on strict

bass note, as a respectable melody ought to do,
but high in careless inverted chord at the very
beginning, like the informal word that betrays
friendly feeling.   There is again something of
the holiday from school in these final rondos,—of
the gay feeling that the task is nearly done and
well done, and the rest is merry-making.   For,
after the melody has sung twice, the band merely
prance about in almost infantile glee, with not a
sign of articulate theme, a kind of prolonged
musical laughter,—anything to keep the jingle
going.   But, looking deeper, it is significant and
curious how this Mozart *finale* sets the pace for

(Woodwind in rhythmic chords of ⅛ notes.)

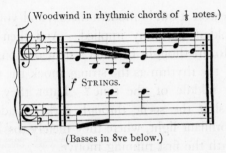

(Basses in 8ve below.)

the later Beethoven, even of profoundest symphony, as the Third and Seventh. It is the perfect link between earliest Haydn and latest Beethoven. For the childlike is ever an element of
profoundest art. Without it there is no art; just
as there is no ethics, no morals, without clinging
to simplest principle.

And all this vacant frolicking is repeated, too,
fearlessly. To be sure, these dancing figures do
gradually edge away into neighboring scene of
tone, whence they come to a full stop and give
the main tune a chance again. Now there are
new pranks. The highest note of the jingle is put
higher by most mischievous, charming touch.*

---

* To be sure, the original note is merely doubled an octave higher. But the boldness of harmonic touch, that was
almost lost in the quick flow of first verse, is here daringly
and repeatedly emphasized.

Yet, reason it out in modern theory, and you find the boldest harmony implied. And then who but Mozart thought of such a delicious pushing out of the rhythm as the strings mock the wood in the middle of the tune? Later they suddenly shift the scene through darker shades to more brilliant light, where they merely toss back and forth the first running motive.

After a boisterous but ever buoyant climax, the reigning motive is discussed more thoughtfully, to return the more gayly to a close on repeated song of tune.

In the hour of strict discussion, such as it is, the main theme is announced almost defiantly as the text for the evening, and there is a sudden complete pause. Instead of the expected, is a magical change of tone; the tune sings half through; then in another light the first motive above is echoed midway by basses again and again, ever trying a new tonal spot. Later the echo comes much closer on the heels of the call.

Finally the chase grows wilder, and all the voices join in the game, and again there is a stop. The search through varying scenes goes on in a new way; strings will start the reigning motive, and wood will answer in slow groping

(Violins doubled above.) CLAR. & FAGOTS.   VIOLINS.

CELLOS.

chords, though the bass is ever tripping away. Finally, the strings keep eagerly on and the home tone is reached, where the original verse is now sung again, the tune in all its fulness, the chorus shouting the refrain as at first, followed, too, by the merry, simple, inarticulate dance. All the round of tunes and scenes plays here, save that the path is of course homeward, not afield. At the very end the main motive runs down with sudden slam in reckless fun.

The sole prevalence of single theme throughout sonata movement can only be conceived with the blending of fulness and economy, of abandon and restraint, which seems indeed to belong to the highest reaches, the *ne plus ultra* of art.

BEETHOVEN'S FIRST SYM-PHONY

ONCE more bravely refusing to spy on date of writing, or age of composer, and thus by outer irrelevant aid to compound a view of the probable dominant influence, let us look at the notes themselves and hope thus for truest light.

Adagio molto was the old tradition for the beginning, which Haydn rarely broke. We have seen with him its innocent formality, a harmless ceremony, sometimes plunging into the *Allegro* with almost comic haste, like a hungry diner who cannot wait for grace. Here, with Beethoven, it does seem all free of this tinge of ceremony. The rhythm is so very solemn, the figures of vague outline, though the best is placidly playful in strings, pleasantly answered by a similar one in woodwind.

Finally, the brevity makes most strongly against deep import of the *Adagio*. The beginning and end seem a little obvious of phrase; still, we cannot judge the prelude without the

(Strings with higher 8ve.)　　(Flute with lower Fagot.)

(See page 34, line 16.)

whole; we cannot test a chance prophetic strain. Those first chords of simplest cadence (as of Amen), all in neighboring tones,—what can make them worthy of earliest invocation?

The *Allegro* has a theme of unusual nervous dash, that raps its accent on first tone with bold insistence, though in gentle sound of strings:

The theme is carried on in natural sequence of higher pitch, and ends in galloping descent of arpeggio, with big chords, in simplest cadence. Right here we cannot miss, withal, a subtle relation to the first and the last chords of

35

Adagio; a brave and vigorous simplicity is thus made to hold sway as far as we have heard. And it is strengthened by the continuing phrase (without change of tone), still in primitive chord of first scene, met by like notes of answer. They are just of the tissue of like Mozart phrases. They mean no more than the hearty greeting, with the inevitable response; they come from the earlier, artisan days of symphony and sonata, when the sound of simple chord was fresh to the ear. Men were like the child of to-day, that delights to find the "new" chord of oldest triad.

This very quality of opposite fitness of two great chords in every bit of music had to be rung and driven home. The older fugue gave no sense of tonal color in the æsthetic toil of its journey. But even to-day there is great doubt whether we feel the full depth of just these two main chords that are like the eternal duality of things, of yea and nay, of black and white, of good and bad.* In the Symphony, above all, this dual nature abounds, where there are two

---

* In England the Sonata is commonly called the "binary" form.

themes in contrasting tone.*   Nothing is clearer than the answer of first chord to the question of the other.   The modern view of true basis of many chords of supposed independence has greatly lowered their number.   It is a matter of wonder whether they must not narrow to the limits of these two.

Nor was this tonal emphasis the sole purpose. So in those early days of melodic discovery— when the sense was fresh of a tune at home and another abroad—the very clearness of setting needed a separation that was merely formal, a digression purely general of figure.   Thus the early Beethoven is timidly roaming to freer fields. By contrast, these simple phrases are surprising in melodic relevance ; yet we must not forget that the historical is not the true and final view.   A classic must be intrinsically great and beautiful.

---

* Tone is used at least in two big senses : first, of the home key which may change for a time ; second, as one of the seven harmonic bases in this key or tonal home.   Of these seven, the first and fifth have a striking trait of correspondence, as of question and answer,—finality resting with the original first tone.   Their technical names are tonic and dominant.   The dominant, throughout this volume, has been called the neighboring or nearest tone.

And there is no need to eke out here with ex-
planation; these figures, however primitive, have
a fresh vigor that will not fade merely because
the time has passed for saying them anew. What
is at any time a true expression will stay, without
regard to later growth and experience.

The text of main theme fits for big, spirited,
dashing close in neighboring tone, where the
second subject sings a graceful melody in woodwind to a soft dancing step of strings:

It is built on brief motive that is merely passed
along the voices of the wood in rising tones, so
that the whole gives outline of single tune.

If we have not over-preached the text, the
dual idea is still heightened here; for, best of all,
it is in their nature that the themes are most opposed. The sense of clear resolution of the first,
of restless drive, is met with type of innocent,
helpless grace that has a touch of timid appeal.
We have seen the full strength of this dual

38

meaning in the Fifth Symphony. And the true force must come, not in the first mention, but in the later story.

In its close and climax this feminine trait is quickly lost. And most striking is the quiet, dim passage of second theme far down in murmuring basses, while higher strings keep lightly dancing and oboe far aloft sings a brightening reply:

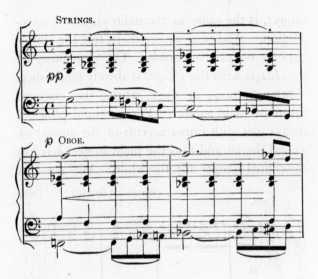

Striking it is how, with all the gentle volume, the passive hue here has vanished. The sense in lower theme is clear, of a certain masculine stern-

ness, returning through boisterous close to the
dash of first theme, both in refrain of tunes and in
the following discussion. But, with all danger of
too close a view, we must not forget the clear
source of cadence of the song of tunes. The line
of slow notes, lengthened from a strain of second

subject, is the same as the main phrase of introduction. And now we see there, too, the simple
response of massive chords. The clear unity of
the *Adagio* with the *Allegro* is already established.

Strange, now, in these retorts the changed
nature of main subject. For its timid phrase is
always met with firmer accents of the answer of
second theme, and thus the main subject has lost
its original temper for the while. We see that

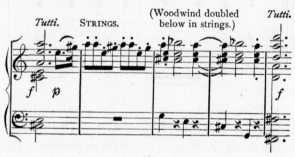

there is, after all, no final quality in a tune or theme of itself; it is all in the poetic handling. The childlike motive may get the sense of deepest import by a light touch of rhythmic bass.* Thus it is that, in a master's hands, tunes, as personal figures, may show big drama of experience, of emotion and moral strife; they are not stereotyped. Thus, as symbols, they give, to him who listens, clearest message of the deepest meaning that man may need; and it is not blurred with dogma, but comes with straightest force.

The anxious queries end in a new phrase (the last motive of main theme) that rises from below in sombre minor, with higher echo, curving in constant change of light.

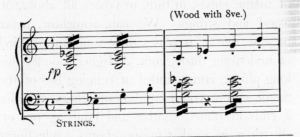

(Wood with 8ve.)

STRINGS.

---

* Compare the first theme of Beethoven's *Eroica* Symphony with a common nursery rhyme, Vol. I.

Simple though the harmonies be, they are marked with a clear flash that gives them the charm of novel boldness. After all, the inner thought is all, not the means of utterance. If the touch, the true ring of bold idea, be there, who cares how simple be the expression? So throughout this symphony, amid all the simplicity of tonal roaming, there are clear, varying shades of light and mood. Here, in the gloom of minor, there is a shifting between dim earnest and grim sort of playfulness. Through loudest clash of discord we rush into the doubled speed of the last cadent phrase. Up and down, crossing each other in the eager chase, joining in united run, they enter on a lesser function of quick-flitting figure, above which the first motive of theme enters, in turn, in voices all about, of wood and strings. We can, somehow, never be sure that it is play; there is an uneasy kind of undertone throughout. Higher mounts this long phrase, compounded of echoing bits of the theme with nervous trembling of strings. Finally it ends in united motive and coursing run of all strings in loudest unison chorus, while horns and trumpets hold a big blast on the main tone,

followed by broad, conclusive phrase of the wood. Hearty it would be but for this prevailing cast of minor that ever shuts out the song of cheery hope. In repeated phrase of climax we are led back to the whole round of themes, and though there we return to major, there is still a want of cheer and joy. The main theme goes straight-way wandering into higher, cloudier lights, and soon hurries its flight to find the magic spot. There is somehow, too, a hard, fitful rap in the first phrase of subject. The flight through higher tones is, we must confess, almost homely in the singleness of each slow step. The feeling is less of beauty than of relentless climb. At the top the sense of exultation breaks out in unpretend-ing phrase. The beauty of second theme enters as before, though now in original tone, and, too, the dim strain in basses, crowned by song of woodwind.

As we near the end, the old rollicking of wood returns and a long stride of arpeggic motive, from end of second theme, that closed the original verse of theme and has its rise in earliest *Adagio*.

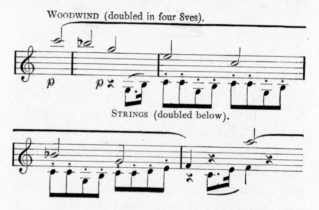

But this is now blended, rather welded, to a nervous song of most of main subject. The duet of contrasts winds its higher journey and ends in final shouts of glee, where the primitive chords of cadence are rung with a certain intent of elemental celebration. The last score of bars are in a single, unvaried tone. The simplicity

of introduction has thus a bearing on the first
Allegro.

Andante cantabile con moto. A melody, like a
flower, is perfect of its own reason, fulness, and
symmetry. The violet does not lack because it
has not the warmth and richness of the rose.
So there is an organic completeness that proves
the beauty of tune, as of flower. However simple the lines, we do not test or compare it herein.
All the question is: Is it beautiful of its own
agreement? And this perfection never comes
by toil, that tinkers at a mere chance phrase.
The first idea has the seed of the tune's beauty,
and finds thereby its own test of soundness.

We cannot compare the violet to the rose,
nor, often, to another violet. It is not size that
makes the flower. So we cannot compare our
Andante either to the Mozart kind or to the later
Beethoven. There is, in truth, much temptation here. If we were allowed comparison, we
should surely choose the *Andante* of Mozart's
G-Minor * Symphony. For the melody begins
very like this of Beethoven's; but the fragrance is
very different. The Mozart melody is of much

---

* See Vol. I. p. 77, third edition.

prouder bloom,—has, too, a certain impersonal beauty, almost awful in majestic moments. The Beethoven *Andante* is more modest in garb and dimensions, makes, throughout, a more direct human appeal, above all in the phrase of answer.

2d Violins.

pp

Violas and Cellos.

Possibly a fanciful question might be asked without impertinence: How would one prefer the first notes of the theme to be treated,—in the Beethoven or Mozart manner? The answer then at best would bring us back to the original problem. We can merely cite differences, not measure the relative rank.*

Instead of the pomp of second theme, here are the briefest bits of timid phrases, yet again answered in broad sympathetic strain, the second time with more of serene assurance:

---

* To follow out this idea, so far as it may be seriously conceived, we have but to trace the course of the Mozart *Andante* of the preceding chapter, especially in the episode of second theme.

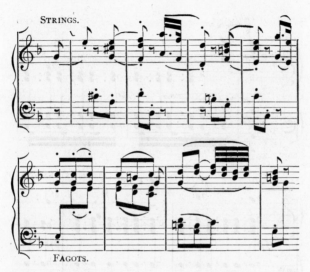

STRINGS.

FAGOTS.

The close here has a sudden joyous step, with a dancing beat of drum and simplest flowing refrain above.

After rehearsing of themes, our timid second melody creeps in, darkly clad, suddenly bursts into big flash of new light, and now, in gentle grace of the new restrained dance, trips along (in strings), while, in the wood above, voices pipe sweetly back and forth on the brief strain. At every two steps of the slow dance there is again a sudden crash of chord that almost frightens. With rare beauty this verse winds through deli-

47

(See page 47, line 9.)

cate tints of shifting shades, ever with a sudden swoop of sound. And that new lilt of slow, jaunty skip has come to stay, or else there is an even quicker pace for most of the song. After final climax it lightly leads the way back to the first verse. In all this rhythmic episode Beethoven has never lost the secret touch of pathos that is part of *andante*. There is here the happiest blending of dance and lyric plaint.

Again, if we are given leave to take an historic glance, Beethoven has here, in the first instance, wonderfully solved the question of tradition. Where Mozart (even in the *Andante* of G-Minor Symphony) breaks into tumultuous, vacant episode, in formal contrast with the pathos of tune, Beethoven has never lost the pervading vein, though he does not lack the dynamic touch and the sparkle of new rhythm.*

The trait of varied, quickened pace of *andante* became almost a habit with our master. Of course we must not forget that the new step lay all within the line of the original melody. Singing again all the themes with still richer rhythm (which never disturbs the basic mood), the *Andante* ends with almost passionate stress of first answer.

The third movement is called *Menuetto*, but is really *Scherzo*, and the first of its unmistakable kind, freed from the bond of dance,—pure glee, without the least need or heed of aught besides.

For theme, look at the line purely of scale, all

---

* See also the discussion of the *Andante* of Mozart's E-Flat Symphony in the preceding chapter.

the notes in successive steps, touched with magic wand of rhythm to most expressive song:

And the second part is really a full discussion of the mere rhythm itself:

driving along to boldest scenes, ending in full cadence far from familiar ground. Here, as the gay tripping of former bass sings overhead, the tune is down below, dinging away with most sonorous iteration,—all this inversion with the ease

of mature master. The trip now keeps on alone, most softly, broken by a sudden single skip of lower and echoing higher voices. These three in mischievous flight bring us suddenly to first tone, where all the chorus join in the loud song of main theme, carried on to brilliant pranks of tone and rhythm, ending in a step of unison clog.

The *Trio* has, first in Beethoven, the sense of tense, quivering rhythm, in sustained chords of woodwind, too, and clumsy brass, while running phrase of strings ever spurs the restless pulse:

TRIO.
WOODWIND AND HORNS.

(8ve of Violins & Violas.)

Almost greater is the hidden motion here, merely implied in the slow gurgling notes of wood and horn,—the finest, subtlest revel, with all economy of motion. In the second verse, on go the throbbing tones of wood and answering pulse of strings, calling back and forth like playing children,

CLARINETS AND HORNS.   STRINGS.

softer and softer, till the strings are coursing alone. Then the wind dance in again and end in biggest chorus, joined by strings in full career. Almost two motions here there are, if we cared to single the quaintly heavy clog of wind,—like an old person taking long steps to three of the younger. And so, back to the fling of earlier *scherzo.*

The *Finale* shows the capacity for highest exultation, in feeling and expression, which seems part of genius. There is a certain delight in finding all the ear-marks of the older master, and, withal, the freshness of the younger. The method is of Mozart; the bold, big rushing humor of late *Finale* is not dreamt of, yet.

There is no resisting a reminder of the *Finale* of Mozart's E-Flat Symphony.* Nor can the movement here be said to strike a deeper note of glee, nor to wing a broader course. In workmanship, too, there is a feeling of the great *Finale* of the Jupiter Symphony, as short phrases in long notes are combined in close architecture with quick coursing themes. Indeed, there is a likeness of actual phrase.

---

* See the preceding chapter.

BEETHOVEN'S FIRST SYMPHONY

First, after gradual approach from the pace of *Adagio*, comes the quick, flashing, jesting theme in running strings.

(With low C in the Bass.)

For answer (where fagots aid the cellos) we have, in slower notes, again a new rhythmic guise of scale, presently inverted and sealed in

full cadence. The next phrase has a certain flavor of Jupiter Symphony, indeed a much stronger, to trace farther back, of the *Finale* of

Haydn's in E-Flat,* where the very theme and part of answer are used. Nevertheless, of actual

borrowing there is none. For, first of all, it is here mere digressing phrase, which was supposed to consist of commonest figure (as we have shown above), where all the world had equal property. Nor is the answer brought on the heels of theme, as in Haydn with quite different effect. The resemblance does show a common phase of the three masters who guided the career of the Symphony. It shows Beethoven here in obedient suit of the other two. Moreover, the leadership was not, as we might think, with the oldest; for the Jupiter Symphony † preceded Haydn's in E Flat by seven years.

---

* Peters Edition, No. 1. See Vol. I., "Symphonies and Their Meaning."

† It was written with the others of the great trio in 1788.

The true importance lies in the fact that our poet was not yet free from a touch of formal phrase. Nor does the outward themal likeness prove it, but merely confirms the direct view. The spirit has not roamed far from the humor of Haydn.

This duet of long and short notes soon drops into a sort of canter on the trip of the quicker phrase, and leads to the neighboring tone, in which it closes with a most jovial entrance of answer of main subject in the basses, echoed in almost unison chorus.

The virtue of second verse, now in new tone, lies in the trick of rhythm, of easy stride of basses and constant quicker strum of violas on single note, whereby the tune has a witching sort of leisurely pleasantry :

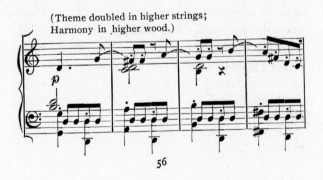

(Theme doubled in higher strings;
Harmony in higher wood.)

The climax is not overwhelming, and closing figures follow which do not show a strong creative effort. Indeed, the spirit of the whole is mere innocent humor—when a man was frankly glad to near the end of his work.

The themes repeated, the closing phrase is taken up, as if for serious thought, and twice considered in varying lights. But suddenly an unforeseen chorus bursts in with bouncing, heavy gait and unimportant message, leading quickly to a very pretty encounter of two phrases of first subject:

Then the main melody itself is tossed here and there, the upward phrase runs down for answer; all, musical quips and puns, and flashes of wit. There is no earnest intent, no serious mood. There is, too, little sequence; for here, when the dispute looks a bit fugal, a gentle dance from the woodwind comes to the relief; the phrases trip along with still gayer abandon, ending in the same jovial song of answer in the basses. Through merry climax we reach the original chain of tunes, the second appearing in the main tone. All the lesser phrases recur with an added verse of theme; the Haydn strain follows in quite a new guise.

The simplicity of first movement is all here in the last, and thus agrees with the introduction. But of the two *Allegros*, the stress is with the first. The *Andante* and even more the *Menuetto* suggest a far maturer stage. The latter seems, indeed, to point to a *Finale* of greater weight. It seemed as if the master here retreated into the safer shell of earlier tradition.

BEETHOVEN'S SECOND SYMPHONY

WE must think of the traditions existing: Haydn's playful idea; little real pathos; abundant mock heroics, however unwitting; but, of Mozart, a real Olympian force, even if there be no Promethean fire. The symphony and, with it, music and musicians have gained by degrees a breadth, a dignity, a respect, merging in awe.

A symphony no longer amuses and merely charms; the minstrel doffs the guise of clown; he takes the stand of prophet and of poet.

Hovering in this border-land is much of the second of Beethoven. When the fire appears, it comes unknown to the poet himself. There can never be aught of assumed dignity in the true poet. All his power is won with his own reluctance. He cannot help the greatness of his words; he can only prepare for his own best expression. This period, when an undreamt

moral force is first evolved in the very servants
of outer nobility, is truly dramatic,—the wonderful proof of the greatest kind of hidden truth,
—as in Scripture, the "evidence of things not
seen."

The full pause at the start, to call for "sacred
silence," is almost a formality. It means little
in itself; by tradition it may run straight into a

burst of merriment. There follows a placid
strain, in the wood, of gently flowing, thoughtful
song, hardly the note of pathos. Recurs the
pause and the strain, now in strings, with trilling
cadences. Climbing to higher perches, it does
strike, at the top, a blow of new force and
meaning in sudden new light of tone, of a certain stern reality. Through all dreamy haze a
new masterful phrase descends in strings, followed

in fugal chase by other voices, the first returning
in slow chords of harp to the heights. Against

Adagio molto.
STRINGS.

ff p

(Basses in lower 8ve.)

(Flutes doubled in fagots two 8ves below.)

sfp

sfp

the nervous quicker strum, the slower figure
grows to clearer song on seeming text of first
phrase. In the stirring pulse of movement, in
the authority of themal utterance, in the growing
maze of speaking voices, we see Beethoven
taking his prelude more seriously than was the
wont. All this profounder episode ends in a big
unison tone, descending in notes of minor chord.
Then follows another phase, gentle of volume,
but ever close-knit in the double canon, the exchange of higher air with lower. The basic

phrase is in the spirit, if not in the outline of original strain,—a kind of last refrain of its essential notes.

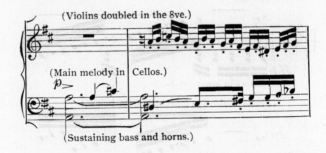

(Violins doubled in the 8ve.)

(Main melody in Cellos.)

(Sustaining bass and horns.)

Thence in vague, trembling chords, answered by trill of flutes with strange accents echoed below in strings, the voices hurry in eager though solemn swell of song to the new speed and dash of the *Allegro*. There is indeed a kind of prophetic quality of big overture in this true prelude, as we shall see clearly far on towards the end of the whole work.

One of those themes is this first of *Allegro*, where motion stands out more than outline. Beginning in basses of strings, the tune lifts the whole structure directly and powerfully on the momentum of its own current. That is the virtue of a melody in the bass: it is not cumbered with the duller weight of mere harmonic and rhythmic harness. There is a great economy and telling force in its whole utterance, rhythmic as well as harmonic,—the two elements of melody.

Strange how certain tunes need a translation through moving mass of cumbrous chords for real effect, while others mark their own harmony in the melodic path and ever bear above the tune the weight of other melodies. It is a little like the natural law, where more power is needed, the nearer it is applied to the basic point; and of course the effect is the more direct. Some such instant result has the melody which lies in its own bass. Were we to call on science, our simile would prove an example of the broad law itself. This basic quality continues, save in lighter phrases of answer (in high strings or wood). In its Titanic manner the tune descends,

without reck, into bold changes of ever lower
tonal base, then swings suddenly off into bustling phrase in high strings and wood, that might

be a second tune but for the paling melody that
soon sounds in neighboring tone, which has been
reached with due formality.

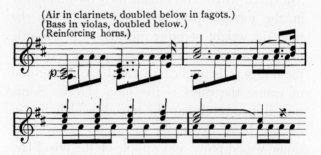

In notes of lower wood and horns this hunter
song sings brave and blithe, with quivering strings
below, acclaimed with full chorus, that ends the

(repeated) verse in still farther tonal station. Quite
a line or two are built on mere chance phrase of
the end of last cadence,—just to show how little
formal theme is needed if there be a good charge
of spurring rhythm. It is indeed rhythm alone
that will give to the outline of mildest tune the
most heroic figure. With its magnificent torrent of pace, the second melody comes to tumultuous close 'mid big plunging chords.

But, dispensing with formal end, the motive of
first theme steals whispering in, far down in strings,
on the same feverish pulse and leads in swelling
volume to final cadence of still greater power on
the tonal quarter of second melody, whence the
song of themes is repeated.

Two episodes stand out in the discussion, marking something of the later power of the poet.
Beginning in dim minor of strings, the basses
growl the strain of main theme with a clash of
bold jarring chords against trembling of high
violins, as they hold their sure, unyielding course.
Presently, out of the lower tune and the high
tremolo emerge at the same time two themes of
fugal hue and emphasis, which meet and exchange rôles, each standing as answer for the
other. A special relevance lies in the close like-

ness of upper phrase to the one we nearly mistook for second theme; but it has here a much more masculine look. Carried on in several steps of sequence, the whole has a very dogmatic air of stern logic. Later the woodwind, which had been silently watching the dual exposition, join in lighter kind of answers of less serious strain.

For some time the quick motive of main theme holds sway, while first the chords of basses strike lower steps with stern emphasis; later, chords in woodwind descend, through shifting tones, while the motion runs below. There is a sort of border-land of earnest and humor. Perhaps the serious intent is not quite attained. Now, in nearby tone, the second melody sings light versions of its main phrase. Then, as the climax is reached, comes the second of our episodes upon a basic phrase, strong of tone and active movement, again like the two former whose kinship we have traced. There sounds, above, a phrase in simple though sturdy notes of single chord,

ff STRINGS (the upper tune doubled in 8ve above, the lower below. Sustained octave chords of C sharp in the wood).

rising and descending much like the famous King of France, and, especially in downward motion, showing a clear origin in answer of main theme. The whole is an innocent phase, where the old play does not quite emerge to the later grim earnest, though it shows the tendency. From the resulting crisis the fall is quick to the entrance of main subject, as at first. The whole journey of tunes is much as before, save, of course, homeward; but there is an after-thought which marks a third period of mild discussion. A short phrase of quiet reflection, which had served to turn back to repeated song of themes, here sings at the corresponding spot; is taken up

WOODWIND.

(Strings in 3 octaves.)

with firm emphasis by the basses against bits of main theme; rises in higher and higher steps, doubling soon the speed of its tune, driving the themal phrase before it in eager chase. Before the ending frolic there is a strain of real profundity, when on the spur of main motive, darting into strange shades, in trembling strings and sustaining wood, there rises, in pent tension, through brilliant steps of changing light, the climax of movement, whence the descent is in shifting chords, as a while ago. In the ending frolic the unofficial (second) tune runs its jolly course in the basses against vague merry phrase above. Later the main motive very simply runs up and down, in full career, and ends with the usual harmonic farewell in big chords.

Larghetto. One might say these earlier Beethoven poems are Mozartian; if they are, they by no means measure Mozart; they merely show his influence on a very opposite spirit. We are inclined to think these Mozartian *Andantes* of Beethoven decidedly lower than their great models. Comparison has, here, less of odium, because it depends on the single measure of the elder master's art.

Poets cannot be compared. Even if two poets had the same strength and equipment, all things, in other words, being equal save the individual temper, they would certainly take different views of life and of the world; they would have no common unit of measure. Their supposed equality could never be determined. Now, as no two poets have just such equal endowment, the problem of comparison is so much the more difficult,—in short, is clearly impossible.

The Mozart *Andantes* are complete. The Beethoven *Larghetto* of the Second Symphony lacks something that we feel in the later symphonies. The lack is also in Mozart; but there it has a compensation.

As yet serenity has not lost its sway. There is no depth of world-woe in our flowing *Larghetto*. But there is a most charming folk-song of appealing pathos. There is no doubt that the glorious melody of the beginning might hold its own with any of the later ones:

STRINGS.
Larghetto.

It is really of the same mould of profound sympathy. It is in the rest of the movement that the difference of mood and basic purpose lies. The lowest depths of our *Larghetto* are reached at the beginning, in the first melody; the rest is relief, foil, almost apology for its seriousness. In the later symphonies, the first melody is but the principal figure of a tragedy.

But nothing can gainsay the beauty of our main subject; and it has a generous satisfying reach. After the first half, a full tune in itself, has come to rest in the neighboring tone, the second flows on with sense of anxious questions

which are answered with rare and deep solace.
But immediately, in the original tone, all strain
of pathos is lightened in simplest time of am-
bling to placidly dancing pace, with playful
answers, on smallest fragment of melody:

It rises, to be sure, quickly to big height of
tone and volume, in stern colors of chord, against
reversed motion in the bass, all echoed most
lightly, followed by bolts of big, bold harmony.
But all this must be half pretence, mock earnest.
For, on the tune goes dancing, saucily almost.
Immediately afterwards follows the second theme,

utterly reckless of anything else in the world but its own springing gait.

Later the tune sings in quicker variation, while high wood come piping in, fitly in place. Very soon, of course, against its minor note on high, lower voices press in rising stress with touch of original earnest, to the crisis.

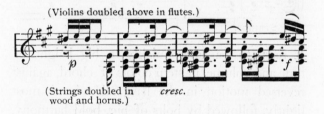

Quickly the stress is relieved in lightest run, now rises again with more urgency, where the echoes of phrases are less play than emphasis, to far bigger climax, awful for the moment. But once again the massed chords dance gently away from the stern height and the tune runs lightly down to lower, harmless plane, repeating all this easy descent in whispers. At the end, much like the coda of first theme, is an after-touch in pleasantest good humor, like a primitive peasant dance. It is evident that our poet will

(Cellos doubled above in violins.)

not harry our feelings in this *Andante*. But in this battledore and shuttlecock of moods we

are never safe; the end of the dance, comic in
its lumbering step, rings again and again, and
always louder until it quite frightens us in its full
height, when it runs down once more to the level
of first tone.   Thence the original melody sings
in minor, not so much to heighten the pathos,—
for this is neither needed nor achieved,—but as a
path towards stranger tones, where a new quality
of sternness is reached in spite of the light run
that ever answers the motive of main theme.
Now the lowest fathoms are touched, as always
in the discussion, where the dim line of the motive sounds far down in ominous bass, against
trembling strings, answered on high by fearsome
cries in the wood (in reversed theme), all in tune

(Cellos doubled below.)

of restless gloom.   Call and answer ring again
and again, and the volume swells to big cadence,
still in gloom of minor.   Once more sings the sad
duet, beginning now on high, answered below.

74

Here the swelling volume brings gladder cadence in brighter major, in distant scene, to be sure. Still the sense is most of power and striving, less of joyous triumph, as the treble and bass in eager canon rear big mass in thundrous toil of Titans, on the base of first motive. The hue of minor darkens the struggle for a moment before the big crisis. And no dancing step comes in for relief; instead, the former urging ascent of lower voices against higher note, that followed second theme. Here, too, the stress is sterner than before, and from the height that is reached, no playful skip descends, but a phrase of graver color. From this point we return to the original course of themes, main and lesser, official and incidental. Change there is, first in the richer suite of flowing phrases attending main melody, though they do not add to sense of pathos. The after-phrase, to be sure, attains a greater force in its deeper extension. Else there is no new note or mood. And so the prevalence of lighter dance, as at the beginning, must prevent a final sense of real profundity. The end is in note of main theme—a last word of the speaking solace of original cadence.

Scherzo. Full of childlike playfulness is the

Scherzo, dashing from loud strokes to light skip, like a game of "frightening:"

Most development is by faintest gradation; there is here nothing of the profound humor of the type of Beethoven *scherzo*. We might call it Haydn-like, but for a certain forcefulness of rhythm, a greater vigor of accent than Haydn cared to assert. Herein, however, it has no advantage over Mozart's great *menuettos* of E-Flat and G-Minor symphonies; and so, if we were forced to compare, we should place it thus in intermediate rank.

The second verse of *scherzo*, after a strain or two of first theme, runs in jolly, informal tune in freest abandon, without least serious undertone.

All the more vigorous is the stroke of returning theme. This time, instead of the stop in full chorus, it scampers away on trip of dance, really a very quick waltz. At the faintest, the high oboe sounds gently an unexpected lay, swaying to the broad swing of quicker trip,—answered in

bustling chords of strings, first up, then down,—
that extends to usual spirited close. The theme
of Trio, merely a new verse on the same buoyant
wing, is a most tuneful roundelay in its narrowest
limits :

(Oboes and fagots with horns.)

The second part merely keeps the rhythm humming alone in sustained trill of neighboring tone,
or in unison glide up and down the arpeggic
chord,—coming with a halt to the first tone and
tune of Trio. In the last refrain, the bass is
busily running along in quicker trip, and the

78

last cadence is sportively rung in constant canonic iteration.

There is little ground for holding these earlier symphonies as lesser because they do not strike the deeper note of sympathy or of humor. To be sure, they are in the Haydn and Mozart tradition ; yet they have their own spontaneous quality. Slowly the younger spirit moves to independent utterance ; but the growth itself is all of the real Beethoven, and perhaps the Mozart influence means a healthier feeling and art. Who shall say ? It is our old question. It is best to be glad of the purely joyous spring of the youthful master, and to take the maturer works with sombrer though profounder hue, as another phase of poetry. We may compare two forms of art that utter the same feeling, not two different kinds of thought.

Allegro molto. The first tune somehow, for right or wrong, carries us back to the prophetic trilling motive (the only phrase of the prelude of which we can find a literal trace in the later symphony).

BEETHOVEN'S SECOND SYMPHONY

It seems to suit with the big breadth of this true overture, more serious in plan than any earlier of symphony. That very first strain of all had a certain width of view, disdaining mere literal foretaste of tune. It did not give a glimpse of the *Andante*, though in similar spirit. It seemed like poetic forecast of the real meaning of the whole. The sense of strife of second phase, returning to quieter thought, ended with nervous figure of trill, spurring to the rush of first *Allegro*.

Unconsciously now the *Finale* returns to this figure for text, and binds the whole with faint semblance of outer theme:

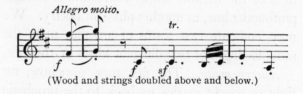

(Wood and strings doubled above and below.)

The timid expectant cry of wondering flutes finds here an assured utterance in the firm, unison phrase of masterful chorus of woodwind and strings.

In answer, strings run lightly in even trip of curve to simple cadence, while the bass moves in big, sweeping tones, almost of melody. After

repeating, the strings answer the skip of first notes with short, almost comic stride, that soon

doubles to gay cadence.

The whole is clearly restrained from rushing pace of *Scherzo*; the point of gravity, since the Jupiter Symphony, has veered towards the *Finale*. And then there is ever a compensation in the speed of beginning and end, of first movement and last. With all the quickness of *molto allegro*, there is a frequent breaking of the pace by recurring halts.

With all the speed, there is a poetic, almost dreamy touch in the second tune, whose motive is contained in four notes, beginning in bass, in close fugal woof of true pastoral madrigal, first in strings.

Soon the theme pipes higher in reeds, crossing the answer of strings in prettiest maze. After a more harmonious close, where the bass sings the motive in notes of double length, flutes and oboes ring the glee in higher pitch, against answers of lower strings and horns. Then all join in another friendly, gayer close in neighboring tone.

Our *Finale* seems all built on simplest themal lines. For, as strings strike a comfortable, rock-

ing gait, the tune of second subject starts with
mere notes of chord in low wood:

(Clarinet, doubled below in fagot.)

STRINGS.

OBOE. FLUTE. VIOLINS.

begun, again, as canon of wind, while violins
answer with almost flippant, chipper phrase that
is hardly part of the theme, which goes winding
on serenely, ever in alternating verses.   Now it
sounds in higher perch, now in minor, to wing
to still bolder height, where comes curving cadence of quaint beauty.   The idyl descends to

the first quarter, and ends, once more with active bustling of all the chorus, in phrases of general import, that gradually trip to the motion of first theme.

In the formal recurrence of noisy martial chorus is one of the strongest signs of the vigor of old tradition, that in later works merges into phases of graver meaning of truer symbol of strife.

The *Rondo* has no nominal claim of a period sacred to discussion. But the free course of later symphony blurred these formal lines of difference. The phase of themal disputation may come in song of *Andante,* even in dance of *Scherzo.* So here we cannot miss a certain serious intent, perhaps a little deliberate, to spin the stated themes to newer maze and meaning. The first theme is main text and, at the outset, the original motive ; then the answer, changed in uncertain hue of tone. And the curve of bass, that seemed at first melodic, now sings in treble in inverted guise, playing the pretty dispute of bass and air, that seems ever a part of Beethoven's art. Returns the first motive and dives into all shades of tonal light. Finally on the very ending bit of motive the higher voices gambol in closest chase,

while the strings keep up the strumming motion. A gliding phrase of unison voices leads to
a new subject of talk: the first two notes of
theme, which the voices toss saucily back and

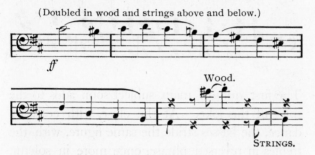

(Doubled in wood and strings above and below.)

forth in lighter spring of dance. A hush and a
belated note of the call bring us again to the
round of full tunes. In its time the second
theme appears in the tone of the first. That
tuneful close has now a newer curve, still with
the sweet and brave simplicity of old. All the
themes have fuller setting than before. When
we await the first in final close, here is a true jest,
in a way of subtlest, both, and simplest fun.
The comfortable swing of strings makes us look
at least for the broad curve of second theme.
Instead, the lower voices merely dance in softest
tread. It is all like mere accompaniment with-

out the song, when we see the basses, in mincing step, descending the simple motive that announced the second theme:

The first quip of main subject soon adds to the spice of the joke. At the close, with cease of dance, the basses stride the same figure, with the trebles in reversed phrase, once more in solemn length of halved subject. Then into universal merry-making, where the clearest figure is the first bit of main theme, with repetition of the whispered jest, to end in simplest mood of mirth.

BEETHOVEN'S FOURTH SYMPHONY

THE POET OF PATHOS AND HUMOR

BEETHOVEN'S Fourth Symphony, though often labelled of an "early period," shows some of his greatest traits. Most evident is a certain alternation of austere profundity and simplest hilarity. No one could be so severe as Beethoven, and, a moment after, so purely jolly.

It is an old and a new way to have a symphony begin *Adagio*. A man cannot always plunge right into the rush and strife of the first *Allegro*. Sometimes he must start the wheels slowly, have the figures of his stirring story grow gradually out of a certain mood of absorbed reflection. Haydn used to do it with a kind of conscious pose. But you have the true vein in the seventh, or in Schubert's C Major, and very specially in Schumann.

Here the poet begins his wandering thought in very simple phrases,—long tones descending in unison, answered by quick-breathed notes of violins. Right here is a bold touch in the minor ninth, sounded at the climax,—a chord that many think a later invention.

(Woodwind and lower strings.)
Adagio.

The quiet *Adagio* walk is wakened by the noisy, nervous snare of drum and the summons to the strings for a general gathering. Then forth breaks the main melody, first in violins:

Allegro vivace. STRINGS.

88

BEETHOVEN'S FOURTH SYMPHONY

How this grows out of the introduction, so that we are sure it was not patched in afterwards, like a modern preface! Right out of those halting Adagio notes of the violins comes the *Allegro* theme, soon taken up by the whole band. And we must not be too wise and overlook the primitive childlike humor of it. Indeed, the true poet must never be afraid of simplicity. Not to quote Scripture, the truth must be much like the old verse: "Out of the mouth of babes . . ." There must be a guileless directness about all great utterance. So we have at the very start, *de profundis*,—out of the depths of revery, springing the most sparkling joyous song. It runs along through purling strain of digressive tune into a varied verse, and then, turning the corner to neighboring scene (what is wisely called the second theme), here are fagot, oboe, and flute frisking about, talking back and forth on a strain of curious charm, with a certain taste of demon mischief.

All the rest are drawn into the game, and the first refrain of melodies ends in a kind of big Titanic gambol. As soon as it has sung again, the meditative hue appears in the thin color, the logical sequence of phrases. But soon these are

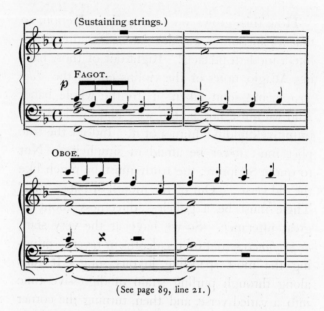

(See page 89, line 21.)

lulled and rocked by the magic of new rhythm.
Suddenly the chief melody bursts forth; but
together with its strain, taken up along the line,
is a new answer: there is something more to be
said on this question. And so you have the
very element of discussion.

Ever a new group enter with the song, while
the preceding or another sing the countertheme.
Magnificently the noisy chorus tapers down to a
still, sombre whisper, as if darkness had stolen

(Strings, with main theme in fagots.)

(See page 90, line 6.)

over, nothing staying of the big dance save the pattering of feet in the steady rhythm. And even that yields at last to solitary strains from strings. Now little responses are heard; the night is lifting; the sombre hue vanishes. Gradually all waken and join with full throat in the main tune, as they sang it at first, save that they cannot restrain new, varying conceits here and there. Again comes the mischievous dialogue of woodwind, with a step of the dance, wherein Beethoven ever touches earth, and shows or renews his humanity. With a final joyous verse, mostly in the vein of the main melody, the movement ends.

The *Adagio* is pure German folk-song, culled by Beethoven, and endowed with all his art to express another side, a quiet lyric human sympathy. It is all mere evident song,—needs simply listening, while all the time there is an accompanying tap of slow figure, to hold a certain grave dignity.

It is another instance of how the mere successive sounds of the scale seem an inexhaustible fount for noblest melody.

The secondary themes have in themselves no special emphasis. They are all in the same strain of beautiful simplicity and dignity as the first; but they seem hardly more than digressive or discursive; they are like interludes between the main verses. The second melody comes in the same tone as the main one, and herein shows a purpose of the poet to avoid contrast and novelty; the main phrase is hardly more than answering cadence to another that is a rhythmic reinforcement of first motive of the theme.

The whole is mere after-strain of theme, always in loyal emphasis of its dominant rhythm, as of ocean waves. A tune of new pathos, and beauty now sings in clarinets in neighboring tone. With all the distinction of its own tonal

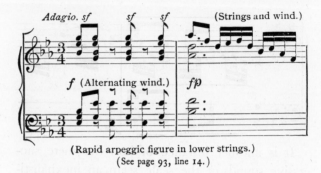

(Rapid arpeggic figure in lower strings.)
(See page 93, line 14.)

quarter, it seems again a mere version of main theme. But the melodic essence is in the text of variant, and not the rhythmic, as before.

BEETHOVEN'S FOURTH SYMPHONY

To break frankly from an old rut, this dubbing of themes is often all misleading, a purely false view. Thus in our *Adagio* the truth, apart from trite lines of formal chart, is that, the first song over, an after-strain of true feeling sings, as it were, in the ebb between recurring tides of the big rhythmic pulse. Again and again, in higher pitch of sound and pathos, this appeal is soothed by descending strain in high wood, affirmed from still higher point, while strings add greatly to the rhythmic course of simple phrase of wood. In big rise of song the basses take up this very bustling course of the descending strain, that almost turns its soothing into terror, then sinks to solemn hush. The melody of clarinet thus comes in guise of plaintive, shy appeal, answered once more by solacing motive, leading to friendliest cadence, in hearty volume, too. A last brief, timid word that seems blended of plaint and soothing, turns trustfully to the full sound and big pulse of recurring theme. We must not forget that it is not always the tune that tells the story. Here the first rhythm's oceanic pulse has a faint sense of stolid Fate, against the human voice of the tune. The verse over, the wave-beat rises in tumultuous height of all the voices,—and sinks before the returning song. We have seen how, when the main melody has ended, big tides come swelling in between the phrases of after-strain, and then how a rhythmic vehemence is added to soothing answer. In the soft plaint of clarinets the motion is all but lost, but returns, welling gently like lapping waters, to the friendly answer. The full first pulse, even strengthened with redoubled course of strings, comes with the after-word that preceded the return of main melody.

Henceforward the theme in its regular song is softened by new grace of setting. But in the midst of this verse there is a dramatic play of opposite elements, In fullest volume of all the chorus a stern phrase, like evil dæmon of the gentle melody, descends, to big strumming basses. Suddenly out of the cadence, in new light, two voices in higher strings alone flit about in timid canon of vague, homeless phrase. They seek for refuge here and there, while the first pulse sounds ill-boding in dim depths. Then presently the home tone is found, where all the full song flows along to the end, decked in still friendlier figure. The trait of dual idea, of external fate and subjective plaintive hope, that finds full room in the Fifth, here spreads a graver hue o'er the less tragic song of early symphony.

Again the native vigor of the poet rings in the *Scherzo*. There he has cast loose the leading-strings of the graceful minuet. A certain roughness, an element of Titan, there always is about Beethoven's humor, not wanting right in these first bars, with the rude strength of the theme:

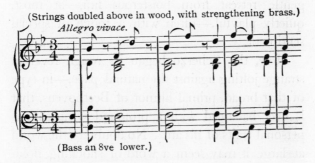

(Strings doubled above in wood, with strengthening brass.)

Allegro vivace.

(Bass an 8ve lower.)

in great contrast with the misty flight of impish answer, in flickering shift of tonal light.

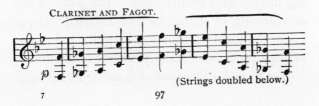

CLARINET AND FAGOT.

(Strings doubled below.)

After repetition, the first motive flies off to distant scene of romantic color, and there has the pace and air of elfish answer, dancing about in mazing change of light and figure, darting high in the wood, gliding deep in strings as if in chase of its own echo,—all a mystic gleam of fairy-land,— then bursting into the clear, bright humor of mortals, as at first. The answer leads to tumultuous cadence on the first tone.

The Trio, since early days, has come to be a gentle retreat from boisterous fun,—at most, quietly playful,—often with a touch of special sentiment.

Here, the Scherzo began its rough revel in strange jolting against the natural pace,—in type of that broad, primal humor of Beethovens, that is ever balanced with a profound sympathy, as personal traits of his art. No doubt, to the world at large it may seem a word of shocking boldness: that nowhere in the whole treasure-house of art and poetry are these two elements of feeling uttered with greater vigor. The world is not accustomed, in strange lack of rounded view, to count the tonal poet among its prime influences, perhaps because he is the youngest of them all.

Yet to find a like note of deepest, firmest sympathy, we must pass over whole literatures of nations, of Latin or of Teuton, with doubt of old Greek tragedy, and sureness only in the words of highest moral teacher. It is quite true, though again it may shock our unaccustomed ears, that the depth of soothing in Beethoven's great Andantes is nowhere passed save in the prophets of holy writ and in the later words of the great Preacher on the Mount. That broad sense of brotherhood seems to have sprung first in the prophetic song of the religious race, and next in its crowning figure, the moral Savior of mankind. The later formulations not merely clouded the precious basic love of kind; they served as special means and cause of men's recoil to artificial privilege, of this world and the next. In the great burst for freedom and like human rights, Beethoven was the tonal prophet. The setting of Schiller's "Ode to Universal Joy," in his ninth symphony, was not the only evidence. In the Andante of almost every symphony Beethoven stands the clear sturdy poet of fraternity. The other cause for which men strove—the lesser, of equality—is uttered with Titanic force in other parts of later symphony.

But one truth needs strongest proclamation,

that music bears the message of highest human need. In the great moral lines, Beethoven is the clearest prophet of the newer age. And once more we must not forget that one may feel the message without actual conscious sense of all its verbal import, although the knowledge will surely help the true reception.

The sense of justice and equality strikes in each least revolution. But the far deeper, underlying note of universal kinship sings a much rarer song. Here towers the stature of our master high o'er the mere Rousseaus, and rings his strain of keenest sense of kind, in deepest vein of all our Christian poetry.

It is here must lie the noblest trait of Beethoven and his work; and well it needs a noting in this very day. For, that greatest sense that man can have of other humankind, that final evolution from first stage of brute, as it is seldom felt, so it is most quickly lost. It could not come to Roman bard, against the conquering spirit of his race. Nor can it come to modern nation's poetry, where sways the brute pride of overpowering force. For, all opposed, a moral strife and victory is this, that joins both parties in the firmest bonds. The highest poets, whom otherwise the world acclaims, it is clear to all who read, have each touched on this great idea. Few they are in the force of message ; and, of them all, since the first stirring words of golden rule, Beethoven is both clearest and most human. (Nor can the true music lover fail to mind, that praise of the master brings the greater praise of the art itself.)

So, in the subtler element of humor, there is no doubt again that Beethoven stands as one of the chief creative spirits. In Titanic boldness of thought and contrast, in big comic sense of rollicking fun, we can hardly prefer an Aristophanes or a Shakespeare. One gets nearer the mystic element in the wild fancies of a Jean Paul Richter ; a Teuton sense of big truth, long suppressed through national neglect, is seen to emerge with irresistible vitality. The quality of this strange vein of all-embracing humor lies perhaps in bold surmounting of all human ills with the triumphant vigor of a resolute mirth. The woes and littleness of actual things are lost for them in the broad universal view. If we may rank poets as prophets, and mere seers, this humor is of the latter. The solace, of moral prophet, comes first ; second, the cheer of humor.

But there is more, still, in the vein of Beethoven Scherzo. The triumphant joy belongs more to last of word of *Allegro Finale*. There is, in *Scherzo*, an idea of pure amusement,—a common touch of oldest puppet-show. Here the stage is the great world of sparkling opposites, on which we look with perennial laughter. Spectators, here, we are, or seers. The cheer comes from the absorbed glance on this big cosmic comedy. Here lies the change from the mere joy of last *Allegro* phase, where we ourselves *act* in triumphant deed. The ethical phase here returns; the poet is prophet again. The change to earlier Menuet from the true Scherzo is almost to a vein of flippant fun. At least the strong, bold undertone is absent until the great symphonies of Mozart. It seems this a mighty step from mere effort to amuse and please, to a spontaneous, individual poet-vein. Most striking is the harvest of poetic thought that blossomed from the toil of formal workmanship.

In the *Trio*, as the rough jolting is gone, the tune seems to fly the smoother. With the lesser speed is more of intimate sentiment, as the boisterous fun recedes. Yet there is a sense of the pace that, in its height, approaches rest; the quickest flight does seem to bring all the delight of quiet ease. A very personal kind of confidence it is, too, with the utmost directness and naïveté.

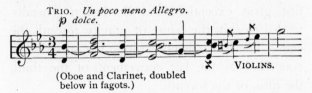

And here it is seen particularly in the quaint childlike cadences.

And the cheerful flute sings a laughing strain of assent after each phrase of the melody. Later, the strings make a primitive kind of lumbering bass, to which the simple song of the theme is repeated, still with the same quaint cadences. Then the whole orchestra rise to a fervent climax as of pious hymn.

In the *Finale* is the chief difference in im-

portance between this work and the more famous
symphonies. Beethoven here still followed the
older tradition, which was to leave the main stress
with the first *Allegro*. Mozart's Jupiter was the
first great exception, and Beethoven generally
tended to shift the centre of gravity towards the
end. The Finale is not so long nor so seriously
conceived as the last movement of the third,
the fifth, or the seventh.

It begins in a spirit of midsummer frolic, not
without great breadth, on a theme broken between first and second violins :

Then the strings run along in sequences on the first few notes until the leaders sing forth a real tune at last.

But soon they relapse into the whirling movement on the vigorous motive, until, resting on a neighboring scene, they listen to the song of the oboe with accompanying clarinet. It is carelessness itself, the second theme, a regular holiday tune.

(Clarinet, with sustaining strings.)

And then how fresh sounds the answer in simplest change of tonal scene!

(Clarinet with staccato strings in the harmony.)

On these strains the strings discourse a while, the tune singing in the bass with new melodic treble. The wood suggest a new idea to which all assent, and they ring out their nodding refrain to a climax of vehemence, where the original motive beats through the wild harmony. Twice this climax is relieved by a light cadence. The vehemence is lost, and the statement ends like an

(With *tremolo* of violas.)   (Added flute and horns.)
(See page 106, line 6.)

old round dance or song where opposite figures change places:

(Reinforcing wind.)

BEETHOVEN'S FOURTH SYMPHONY

After the discussion, the strings are chatting away quite aimlessly on a subject that seems not much weightier than the weather. Yet how relevant it proves to the main theme! But here are some curious things. As the garrulous strings keep running indefinitely on their old motive, suddenly there is a loud protesting single note, as if to say: this must really stop. Then the lower unison strings sing out the little answering air in boldest change of scene, actually without chords. All alone they sing the mere air alone, that, somehow, has its own implied harmony.

What is the mystery when single voice strikes change of tone, when single touch opens a new scene? It is the whole harmony of all the figures that marks the usual scene and color. One note may be of one or of the other,—as a single tree in landscape, though in the given region it may alone point the resting-place. It is in the relation of all the figures that lie the quality and charm of region.

In olden days, in grayest age of music's birth, there were but single tones; and so there was but one well-worn scene, or almost none at all. The word cannot be used without the sense of color. Here is the bold, charming touch of the stray voice groping back to friendly region, and then the others join in reassuring echo. Our voices may be of double symbol, of place and of inhabitant; yet the hidden feeling may become the clearer.

For a time there threatens a technical discussion by fugal rule. There is an echoing dispute, the simple and redoubled pace of new motive, that springs quite casually, though with melodic point, from phrase of bass while the original air is running in and out.

But the discussion is never very serious. It merely whets the desire for the rollicking dance in the whirling figure of the first phrase, which leads back to the main melodies. Once more come all the events of the first verse, not forgetting the little round, with exchange of figures. At last, quite needlessly, all join again in the main tune and dance to a fierce point. After the lull, as the basses stealthily hum the little run, like gentle drone of hurdy-gurdy, the high strings sing right at the same time the tuneful answer. A phrase of farewell has its timid say, answered by parting climax of the running theme. There is a pause. In pretty play of twice as slow a pace, the theme goes with deliberate step half-way and stops. The fagots sing four more notes to a halt, and so the low strings next. Then all the chorus with big festive noise and speed scamper down and—out.

BEETHOVEN'S EIGHTH SYM-
PHONY

AN EPIC OF HUMOR

THE Eighth Symphony has not the stress of the Fifth nor of the Seventh; its dimensions are less in every sense. Not that they measure the Symphony. It is frankly playful, teaches no lesson whatever. Almost, we might say, it came as apology for the sternness of the Fifth, the experiment of the Sixth, and even, as of future shadow, of the basic departure of the Ninth. It is most akin, in general cast, to the Seventh, but much simpler of pretence: one big *scherzo* of its own. It strikes no depth of profound sympathy. So it lacks a certain perspective or relief. As symphony, it is certainly not typical. The absence of true *andante* makes it exceptional. Its charm is therefore no less, rather greater, as undisturbed epic of merriment. There are no great contrasts of mood, few darker hues; the brightness has no help from contrasting shadows. Yet it has its broad reaches, bold flights, big views. In a way it is a reversion to the old type of Haydn, the jolly symphony of the *salon* of good old times, where the composer had no business to do aught but amuse. A higher sort of court fool after all, in a way, was our " Papa" Haydn.

In complete abandon, careless of all responsibility and expectation bred of the master's earlier designs, this work was born ; and in this defiant spontaneity lies assurance of its special charm. We may philosophize, if we feel we must. Just the right quantity of pathos cannot be determined by prescription to make a symphony. There may be a world all of humor,—a life-view all of merriment. There has been such a philosophy. For the sage who went about laughing at everything, this work is a special symphony, a mirror of his world. If we must have a tragic symphony or pathetic, why not a comic? Humor has as much right to over-emphasis as has pathos, perhaps a little more.

Clinging to our idea of the symphony as a kind of view of life of the poet, here the merry side has its own paramount place, a true comedy in the big sense of " Much Ado About Nothing," of " As You Like It." Secure, we listen, of no deaths or funerals,—a jolly carnival though quite serious and sober in scope, not fearing to touch the ground note. But for once, instead of a sympathy big for all sorrows (like the Fifth), it cozens you gently and cheerily out of your sadness, wrings a laugh from the tears, brushes away the frowns with lightest touch.

A type of jolly serenity is the first theme :

Allegro vivace e con brio.

Full orchestra, with redoubled theme and harmony.)

Allegro vivace e con brio. Nothing ominous or profound. The tradition of Haydn's light abandon has lingered in the theme through all the stress of the Fifth, the sternness of Third, and the brilliant completeness of Seventh. The list of instruments is of old economy; trombones are not used at all. After the first theme is started in gay canter, it is carried on by galloping strings and a pompous figure dimly drawn

8

from main subject, where again the motion is more than the tune, and you can go indefinitely on the fillip in constant sequence of the slight motion; for, the smaller the phrase, the better for rearing structure.

The woodwind do no more than shout a regular acclaim as often as they are allowed. All this simmers down pretty solemnly, when out of the hushed and halted motion the second theme sings cheerily, though gently, almost timidly, with a touch, too, of jaunty humor in grateful change of tonal scene.

Our second melody emerges in charming shift of quarter; but in its second verse approaches the more familiar scene. Then, starting for the moment in anxious, hushed trembling, in gathering ascent of volume, it finally bursts in chorus on simplest cadent figure:

(Redoubled in full orchestra.)

to which the answer is one of the most charming spots. It is gently sung

(Oboes and higher flutes.)

STRINGS.

p dolce.

FAGOTS.

in solo voices of wood, each of which takes up the verse in turn, where quicker figures are entwined in the strings. Again bursts forth the noisy chorus, just like Haydn's frightening places ; and once again a responsive episode leads gradually to a big climax in the old way.

Now all is duly repeated according to rule. Then, as the bass keeps softly jogging the former noisy gait, stray bits of first theme are gently discussed in woodwind in a clear way that is somehow lost of late. In bursts the last noisy cadence. This alternating game, a little old-fashioned, reminding of Gluck, goes on for some time, but always with scenal change. Indeed this is almost the whole of it. As first we stray into dim shadows and suddenly dart into brilliant sunshine, once more wander into gray shadows and emerge into boldest light of all. Here the game is stopped. Instead, against trembling strings and crashes of wood, loud basses rumble the theme in rough minor. Merely the first theme rushes along, not waiting for the former answer, impetuously, as new text of its own, ever followed by united plaudits of wood.

The motive is transferred to high wood, group echoing group in eager cries. On a new height of the structure all the trebles hold the motive, echoed far down in bass. Once more there is a whirling mass of excited cries of this incipient motive. At last, at the final climax, it is permitted to return to its original channel on full-blown theme. Only, it sings in resounding bass with trembling harmony above, though repeated in soft wood. But the basses are more important now ; have much more to say. The lesser figure, which followed the theme with rocking motion, is more of melodic phrase, and is echoed by the bass.

As before, the gently skipping, cheery second tune comes singing along and leads to the same short burst of chorus. Charmingly as before follows the madrigal of timidly trustful voices of wood, entwined by tuneful figure of strings. Instead of ending, in a dim distant quarter the first melody sings or whispers a verse in slow clarinets. The answer is softly mocked by strings. Then all the strings in four groups play whispering a kind of canon, or game of chase with snatches of this very answer. They get noisier. At last all the chorus take courage and sing the main melody lustily with all the responsive play, inverting tune if needs be both ways at once, all in big frolic. Once more the plaintive madrigal of second melody is sweetly sung. But soon it is caught in the drollery and noise, and the

whole ends in shouting and shuffling on the first
motive.

Allegretto. The great charm is this light
dancing shuffle all in regular sprightly time, like
chorus of dancers with the main figure behind
the scenes, which suddenly appears with all usual
grace. The most delightful prank in the world,
as if a good confessor or confidant, instead of
meeting you at the usual time, with long face

and responsive consoling grief, were gayly and roguishly to laugh you out of it all. For here is the second movement, the appointed time for pathos, sighs and tears maybe, and we are absolutely cheated out of our sad comfort and, what is more, made to dance a jolly turn instead with the gay deceiver himself. Can anything be more humiliating than to have to laugh at your own woes?

There is no resisting the mincing, dancing, rascally humor of the step. At the very start,— not too fast, a kind of deliberate, teasing, suppressed bit of humor, where wood are lightly shuffling and high strings are striking the tune, really a sort of duet as of mocked pedantry. It is marked all the more with a little echo way down in string basses.

On goes the sprightly strain with a slight change of tone and tune. A new prank comes, when, as the tune begins again, the whole chorus shout with most alarming volume, just for a moment, and then the tune goes singing right along with its old mock seriousness, as if nothing had happened or were ever to happen again. And here is another touch of drollery, as in dancing cadence high violins strike the light figure (which begins with the theme), and instantly the clumsy low basses imitate, sometimes coming in in a belated, ineffective way and the more comic. More frightening bursts and other queer surprises,—unexpected lulls and stops. Then on again with the tune in all its innocent pertness of teasing, mincing step. But here a new jolly song rings out lustily, the tune in strings, shuffling step in the wood; in the low basses still the old skipping figure as if they had forgotten to leave off:

At the end the basses make an utterly unnecessary, terrible noise, running up and down the strings, and do it again soon afterwards, rudely interrupting a very harmless discussion of timid voices in strings and wood on snatches they had just heard, though it isn't quite free from a suspicion of mischief as the voices softly whisper in quaintly broken snatches taken up here, there, and again, like dashing fire-flies. Now a broad, tuneful, sweetly serious sort of phrase

comes sweeping along for a moment's rest from the fun, a true human word, a quick assurance of real sympathy, though there is still a mincing step in the answer. But it is repeated and the feeling is sustained a while, as the voices gradually return from the neighboring tone to the old, and the fun begins again, all the fresher for the break. Now the former course of tune and tricks all returns. But as the main melody repeats, after the basses have had their first refrain far down, a jolly variation of the air sings out, prancing gayly across the old outline, like daring rope-dancer, and coming out all right.

But here with all the fun, as the tune goes swinging on, a new feeling is blended. Some-

thing of intimate appeal creeps into the dance as
the air beautifully extends and soon expands
into lusty second tune, where still the comic
basses are skipping away all alone in the old
step, and again, as before, come breaking in with
that frightful run in a most annoying way, with
their very strange idea of a joke. Later the
broad phrase of friendly assurance returns. Still
the roguish whispers on skipping figure are more
surprising than before, broken into by most tremendous shouts of every living throat about, all
in quickest possible step, too, all ending in one
more romp on the pure dance itself, though
some are going two and even four steps to
one, swelling once more from softest whisper to
loudest din.

Menuetto. The minuet has an unwonted
swing, though of course in three-step time, but
it seems less like a dance than a sweep of one
big motion for the three lesser ones, and the
tune is a regular song with a good burst in the
midst; you could sing words to it and forget
to dance. After it is repeated with a special
sense of freshness, it darts off to a neighboring
tone; but instead of the full tune the first
bit is passed down the line of strings by the

Tempo di Menuetto.

p

HORNS AND TRUMPETS.

FAGOTS.

cresc.

(Strings accented and doubled above.)

(See page 122, line 20.)

pleasantest sort of trick of retort, and then up again in a much jollier way still, getting noisily back to the first, the home tone.

Here the voices simmer down on playful phrase until the main tune returns, now down in fagots with low murmuring strings, with gently telling effect. Soon, of course, this mounts to another joyous height, where ends the first verse (the strict *scherzo*), with an odd sort of round clog on the first notes of theme, where one group strike in on the heels of another.

In the *Trio* the fun has pretty much vanished. It is merely a true German folk-song in simplest lines and mood. Mostly the horns lead with the air just like an old song of love or hunt.

Oboes answer, followed in kind of canon by horns and cellos. In the Trio's second part (each is repeated) the motive of melody is simply played in dimmer minor, while the preceding

124

canon phrase still goes threading its consecutive course.

Soon a darker, shadier scene is reached, where the folk-song now sounds in full strings, the thread still running in the horns, and reaches a hearty conclusion. Suddenly it shifts to the old scene, singing the same heart-felt strain, now in horns. Carried farther, the song, in responsive and successive step, has a fervent though gentle burst, while the first motive ever sounds far down in basses with its slight trip against the smooth appeal of a newer cadent figure. Oft rehearsed is this burst, then dies down to a hallowed hush of horns and strings, whence the *scherzo* sings once more its merrier strain.

Finale. In the Finale is a bigger rhythmic swing (a little too big, perhaps, for traditional notation), one of those great reaches that Beethoven seemed to call from a stranger, higher sphere, conceived in a freer flight than we are tuned to in our scientific, " practical" age:

(Doubled below.)

The theme seems mere rhythmic idea; but the answer is more articulate song of gladness, on big soaring wing, though, to be sure, all in softer strings:

which play a while with strange hollow effect on the first motive. Then, in loudest unison of all, the whole song is rehearsed; or rather the rehearsing came first and this is the regular full verse.

In a new stride the basses have worked themselves into, they march ahead without heed of concluded verse, in a kind of special melodic consciousness.

126

while strings are trembling on in the old way and bursts of wood point the pace. The high wood now have a feeling for the tune and sing it as it mounts reversed in the basses, while the strings tremble on in the first motion. The scene slightly darkens, and now the striding tune has lapsed into mere retorts *en masse* in full force. Suddenly, hushed in distant quarter, a real melody, that makes all the rest prelude to its song, sings rapturously in strings and, just before the close of phrase, the oboe chimes in a most sweetly concluding strain:

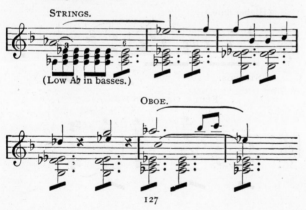

The song wings on its freer course and then, with a fresh delight of returning to home tone, sings against broader swaying of strings, while lower wood now join, like the former oboe, in the tuneful concluding medley. On the latter motive, wood and strings start in timid, anxious ascent in strange cross-purpose of rhythm, then descend. The same journey is taken up by all in bold spirit, and on safe return the manful stride resumes to original tonal region.

Here, after a few timid tries at the motive, the main theme sings again as at first; but instead of echoing chorus, timidity reigns again, and against trembling strings a long, anxious, whispered discussion follows on answer of main theme:

voices entering without waiting for others to
vanish. Three or four are attacking at once
the same strain in different kind of suit and
pitch; a few are singing bits reversed; the whole
subject is gone over. Then some kind of order
is restored and high cellos and low violins are
given the floor. To be sure, they start together in
opposite direction, but precisely agreeing in each
rhythmic turn. Soon another pair are champions; the middle strings are sent off discoursing
the same way. They cannot help getting tangled
later with others. The strings seem to have a
hopeless tendency to argue. For some time a
strange call in two long notes has been heard
again and again, here and there, above and below.
It enters often crashing against the clash of quarrelling strings. Dimly we are forced back to the
sounds of incipient second melody through all
the strife of first, and finally it triumphs and
brings order and a burst on united main theme
in new scene.

Presently we have its original course home
again. Of course it is enriched now with the
gain of newer figures, mainly of striding bass;
so the full refrain sounds far more triumphant,
bigger with wonderful complexity of rhythms,

warring for the moment. The old course, as after original verse, continues, of melody, bass and retorts of massed groups. The second melody in full queenly beauty follows, though still in newer scene of sound, with rich accoutrement of melodic vassals, and again, as before, returns to sing on familiar ground. The anxious ascent and descent of wood and strings into discordant gait all recur with a full choral pursuit. We ought to be glad we are home again and rest for good; but we stray once more.

An entirely new pace is set, a new course of ideas. Out of the silence, in dim religious light, violins sound a chant, descending in notes of dirge:

It is answered by oboes and fagots, starting in opposite direction, but the old trembling motion will not let go,—the one reminder of old frolic. Twice the chant is duly sung and answered, then in double pair of ascending woodwind against descending basses. They are met on high by a soft acclaim of the others; but the strings still tremble on. Now the motion is reversed. All this has been sung in dread hush of tones. Now it rings out as full religious pæan in four independent voices of strings against loud blasts of brass and clash of drum, while the woodwind shake a slower, though more solemn, vibrating call in big ecclesiastical magnificence. The chorus proceeds with solemn pomp. At last they break into quicker pace; the theme has a more playful ring; the trembling call quickens as of old. Then out flashes the old theme, but in strange, brilliant light.

Finally, in the gentle lull of the beginning it sings another verse. But a new spirit has somehow crept in; for anon all is stopped by full blast of chorus,—even the trembling motion ceases. Now, in overpowering mass the theme returns; but there is a strange tonal quality, an uneasy sense of omen. It is really a sort of mock fear. In the very height of triumphant joy, or rather on the eve of it, there is a note of uncertainty, merely to increase the assurance when it comes, as it promptly does, in the old familiar scene where now lesser themes go chasing helter-skelter to give the chief a rest before the final verse.

But before him his queenly mate once more pours forth her lovely song in the very home tone, where she has not yet sung, where he himself had hitherto held sway. The beauty infects even rough basses, which are given leave to sing a sonorous verse against the higher harmonies of the others; and all the rest is great rejoicing as on home-coming, that seems, after all, to be the main purpose and the best of all journeys,—that leaves some truth in the old pedant who describes the movements of ancient sonata in all earnest: "The first to show what the composer can do, the second what he can feel, the last how glad he is to have finished." All things earthly and even above are, after all, an eternal round.

BEETHOVEN'S SIXTH (PASTORAL) SYMPHONY

TONAL DEPICTION

"**A**WAKENING of Cheerful Feelings on arriving in the Country" is the title of the first movement.

"*Feelings*" here is the key-note that ought to pervade the whole symphony. If it did pervade, we should have a pastoral whole, as we have two real bucolics in tones. The first movement begins on simplest tune in the strings, that is like the song of a bird, if only in the leisurely pause before resuming, answered in four-voiced choir :

Allegro ma non troppo.

STRINGS. *p*
(Low C in basses.)

Later the tune steals into the wood, and soon rings out in full chorus with extended melody. At the end, as the accompanying clarinets and fagots pipe in triplet motion, the violins discourse freely on a strain of the tune, and glide with ideal ease into the second theme, really the first, so far as beauty lends dignity.

And here the wonderful art of the master appears. The most difficult feat comes without a seeming jot of toil. The perfect form does not appear at first, from its very perfection,—the soprano and bass are complementary tunes and at the end change places, without loss of a note, so that one does not know whether to find the melody above or below; it is all a double sort of melody. The highest art (what schoolmen call double-counterpoint) comes as naturally as the chirping of a bird. To write a second melody to a first is a feat of the older artisan; but to pour forth a double melody from the beginning, all uncon-scious of the feat, was highest of all, because done in a simple burst of feeling, not in pride of art.

Soon a third voice in high flutes strikes in the midst with the tune of the bass, and all the birds in the wood are singing bits of the double song, ending in half-unison, hymn-like cadence, dying down with a cheery call in strings and a carolling note in the woodwind. This leads

(Strings, later with treble and bass exactly inverted.)

(See page 134, line 20.)

back to a rehearsing of the tunes from the beginning.

The discussion proceeds, unhampered by labels,
on the original strain. You cannot possibly talk
freely in music if everything you say must have
a verbal title and meaning. Fearless of repetition,
the simple phrase runs along:

modulating through bright changes of tonal light and shade to a kind of chorus where the theme is in the bass. Then the call is sung back and forth with perfect childlike or birdlike freedom. For the nonce, the first tune interrupts in fugal, reflective guise, but merely for the moment. The call sings on again through new modulations of tonal light. After a like appearance of the first tune we have the answer of the four-voiced choir. Its theme is carried first in low duet with strings, then in single song of violins, again in duet, and now in full hymnal chorus. Though brief, this is the climax, and, dying down, it leads straight to the rehearsal of themes as at first, with a trill instead of the pause. The big chorus and the whole second melody follow in full beauty. To be sure, the ending duet with cheerful phrase and carolling wind is much extended in length and volume, and there is added a rollicking dance tune, at the end of which the first theme sings softly as possible in strings, then in high flute, all alone, answered mockingly by a playful burst of the whole band.

Feelings, scenes, events have all been attempted in music. They have their place, certainly, in art. Has not each kind its special branch? For scenes there is painting; for events there are words, measured or unmeasured, prose or verse. So once more, from a different point, though not, of course, by a strict proof, we come to our old truth: that music is specially the utterance of feeling. Other propositions, various in grade, are all related: first and clearest, that feeling is the main burden of music; whether exclusive, is another question. A converse of the first, that by no means follows by mere deductive logic, is whether music is the clearest utterance of feeling. That it is not its only language is almost absurd even to mention. In one sense, feeling is the final theme of every art. A scene in colors or threads, an action or event in ballad or story, to arouse the least interest must spring from emotional motive, however unconscious, beyond the mere design of exact depiction or narration. So, to tell an event without interest, however faithfully; to copy precisely an object without a meaning, implies no art. All art must have its rise in feeling and must make its appeal to feeling. When, therefore, we speak of the utterance of feeling in art as against scenes or events, we mean merely the direct utterance without the medium of outside objects, of nature or of human experience. Here the strength of music seems to lie in freedom from interfering subjects, finally in the primary beauty of its alphabet. To be sure, we have seen that even here the depiction of feeling ought not to be conscious; its best utterance is a kind of involuntary betrayal, where the main interest is on the musical design itself; for indeed all work comes best from concentration, from an absolute absorption. For the poet to trouble about the emotional hue of the whole is like talking with one eye on the mirror; it is a hopeless diversion, a dissipation of effort. So, as we have seen, the best basis of titles in music is, as Schumann discovered, a kind of postscript: a final touch after the whole untrammelled course of the poem.

But this does not argue the impossibility deliberately to celebrate special subjects. Indeed, it is not for the hearer to inquire when the title was written, before or after; all must be tested by the work itself. But a natural guess may be ventured as to difficulty and danger of preconceived subject, an almost fatal cramping of its limitations. Any fetter of the fancy of the

138

musician is a loss, and is never atoned for by the mere fidelity to a title. High art is the aim; the name, the label, is nothing. In the older arts, especially in verse, a name sprang from the necessity of conditions, because there must be an object. Prose and verse are themselves words; there a title is not derived outside of the art, it is part of the tissue of the work itself. Sculpture and painting stand midway. Names are not needed; but as they dealt always in outside objects, it was but natural to add the names that belonged to them. Most striking it is that more and more in modern plastic and chromatic art, of chisel and of brush, wholly fanciful subjects are vanishing, actual names are less and less employed.

In music, the necessary use of outside objects does not exist; with it the excuse, the reason for labels seems equally to be lost; they seem a mere vanity in every sense.

In Beethoven's day they were most pardonable; for the art was young, lusty, and unconscious of boundaries. Nay, the experiment, we may say, had to be made. If the greatest failed, the proof is the more complete. The very concentration of masters on their art left them witless of its philosophic theory. It was left for a

Bach—highest poet of man's religious sense—to write a crowing cock in the Passion of Christ.

Therefore in the "Scene at the Brook" the words will be taken not in the narrowest, but in the broadest sense. "Scene" must mean the feelings aroused by a visit to the brook. As we shall see elsewhere,* the agreement of actual incident and its subjective impression may be so close that the musical utterance will answer, as does positive to negative of a picture. As composers do not split hairs, the use of actual story or song is most natural ; their emotional meaning must, whenever possible, be implied.

The strings below are murmuring in steady course, the horns are droning in sense of quiet woodland, while the upper violins slowly sing themselves into articulate song :

(The accompaniment doubled in cellos and basses)

of which the close is clearer than the first notes. The lower background of vague strings soon

---

* See the "Lenore" Symphony, *infra*.

grows to richer waving and swaying; a high trill, sweetly discordant, is added in the branches above, while the lower woodwind now sing the melody. Throughout is the special charm of the gentle clash of nature-sounds. The fool (and critic) might say in his heart: a vain displacing of art with brutal touch of nature. The truth is, the poet everywhere merely foresees a future touch of pure art which to the lay ear has ever the sense of clash, the herald of new experience. (Of course, it adds to the immediate poetic impression of the scene.) It is all easily demonstrable with the numbers of exact science, and were worth doing if the convictions of art were not always those of intuition rather than of logic.

The song soon breaks into a verse of more human clearness, first in the high strings :

VIOLINS.

dolce.

(Murmuring cellos, violins and violas.)

now the cellos below and clarinets above take up the strain, while a like pair, violins and fagots, strike into the midst with a tune of the same fibre, aslant the skein of the first pair; and now even the high flutes add to the woof of song. Simply it ends and returns to the first murmuring tune of strings, spreading with new freedom of tonal moorings, and of melodic figure more cheerful of mood, ending in well-contented cadence of flute in a neighboring key:

(Full harmonies in strings, wood and horns.)

echoed by bassoons below. But the close is not real; a new scene gently appears with fagots starting afresh into song, while now higher strings alone are murmuring:

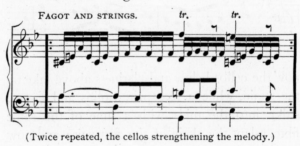

(Twice repeated, the cellos strengthening the melody.)

the lower are soon strengthening the fagots; the singers trip into a jolly measure. The clarinets come crosswise into the dance; others add to the maze; but the end is in united chorus. The verse is repeated with richer interlacing of lesser phrases, but throughout all is a rural simplicity; the complexity is not of conscious thought, it is the sweet whirl of woodnotes. The best of all comes at the end of the verse, when the close playfully runs into another maze, richer, broader, stronger than before, on the more human, tender strain of the end of the first verse. As the vein, though not the tune, of the first theme returns, gentle clashes of single notes of strings (against the whole stream of song) grow bolder, bold even for to-day,—a century later. It is a clear case of the weakness of theoretic law when once the mind surmounts it, mastering the intent, in open transgression, yet true to the spirit of order. It is in a way a mystery, but it shows how the idea is all,—the outward, visible or audible effect nothing. The same note, written in ignorance of the law and therefore in false intent, would be false, because the idea were false. And Beethoven's idea seems false to the ear that is rigidly attuned to primitive consonances, refusing heed to constant change, to ever-expanding truth. (So, perhaps, nothing is true in the sense of rigid force of written dogma, and nothing is false in so far as it may find somewhere its right relation.) From a narrow artistic view, it remains true that the value does not lie here in a brutal intrusion of a hostile note in graphic depiction of nature; the beauty of pure art must be there and thus establish the truth.

Coming back to our song, the sense is almost an illusion of the sweet conflict of forest sounds of insects, birds, and waters. A new verse, through all of the old tissue, now sings out, echoed higher in the flutes. To be sure, like the second, it merely digresses from the constant strain of the original song which now proceeds with more readiness and variety of principal and lesser figures, succeeded again by the maze of the speaking strain of the second verse. This now spreads through stronger climax into a new tonal scene of the first. By a similar turn, still a new scene is found for the same verse, and by still further subtle changes the original key is reached, where the verse is sung complete as before (after the second), though with much fuller acclaim of all the voices. The contented cadence comes now in the original key; but it is again elusive and leads as before into the third verse with a dancing clause. Then comes again the friendly strain of the second and a final harking back again to the first.

A few trills in high woodwind, entering one after the other, may disturb the philosophic interpretation. They are labelled in the score: the flute's trill, the nightingale; the call of the oboe, the quail; of the clarinet, the cuckoo. They are answered by one more verse of the friendly strain. Musically they do not change our enjoyment. Beethoven's intent undoubtedly, it is more and more evident, is actually to depict the forest scene. However, it is wise for us, even in defiance of his conscious purpose, to get the best of the music. A composer, we dare say, is not a good authority on the value of his own music; the musical intent is his, and there he is authority; not so the verbal label. For he utters his authority only by his music, not by words. Never ask a composer what he means by a piece of music, nor a painter by his picture; for the composer's unconscious musical mood may be at war with the vanity of his desire to force an external meaning on his music. And here we may, nay we must, side with the true though latent musical purpose.

In the third movement, "Joyful Gathering of Peasants" is the first title. Who shall say it is the outward bustle, the mere view, the external action, rather than the enjoyment of it, the joviality itself,—all to a most expressive jolly jingle in quickstep of a real tuneful jig:

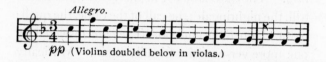

The answer has more of song than of dance. Later there are cross-figures; then all dance in unison, followed by a united burst almost of hymn, breaking off into a gay waltzing trip. Lightly as this constant skip recedes to softest, gentlest background, suddenly the ingenuous reed most naïvely blows a rustic air with all the bucolic freedom from measured limits:

Somehow it never strays far from the soft skip
of dancing feet. Again and again comes the
simple refrain, though never too often; and now
the clarinet breaks in, in lower pitch, the comic
bassoon even intrudes its three clumsy notes, and
the horns still lower. Soon others are caught
humming, even the lowest bass, when abruptly
strikes a rudest jingle in rough time and harsher
accord, in a primitive sort of tone common to all
nations in barbaric stage:

In tempo d' allegro.

(Violins, with sustained strings.)

True, a later, more civilized tune sings above the
receding jig and through a fine burst leads first
to the beginning, then to a final verse of the first
tune, whence again the united song breaks into
the tripping rustic waltz, to be harshly disturbed
by—"Rain and Storm."

Above the faint rumble of basses comes the
light patter of a sprinkling verse in the second,
and larger drops in the first violins; very soon
the full storm is on, in furious tempest on the
whole horizon of tone, with rough stride of de-

scending violins, the winds driving big things, tumbling in heavy fall. Now thunder growls from afar; now strikes the crash; now again; now more peals in quick suit; then the former patter leads to a more furious storm than before.

Two things are true: first, we must never lose the possible sense of mere subjective impression, not of actually described event. The correspondence will become more and more close and exact as the outward titles increase in number. Under one general title the fancy and feeling may roam with great, though not with unfettered freedom. But here is a second truth: as the labels multiply comes the perplexing need of still more. We are driven to ask what is this and that and even every least note. Here is the tremendous increasing danger of titles. They are fearful tyrants and hold the imagination bound.

Even if the musician means to give but touches here and there of realism, yet the whole is transformed from free feeling to a graphic account. The question of objective and subjective, action or impression, is soon the splitting of hairs,—a matter of technical phrase. We cannot get away from the multiplicity of detail. Now this is mere negative. Think of the loss of all we have seen and gained in the free musical discussion of lyric melodies soaring to utmost ranges of structural height without the least fear of transcending imposed barriers, and then rearing the greatest possible art from the seed of the melodies and the soil of the poet's mood. And the real meaning, though we cannot define it in common words, is it not far nobler than theatrical touch of rain and thunder? Think of the value and meaning to the world, if only during a single year, of Beethoven's Fifth Symphony, which is all untitled.

The thunder and storm all crash together; heavy bolts descend through the blinding rain and wind. Lightning still flashes throughout. Now the tempest retreats; low thuds of pelting rain strike more gently; here and there a loud bolt recurs. As the last growls recede, the higher strings and clarinet sound a few notes of hymnal song, which seem the first touches of pure untrained feeling. But it glides immediately into the " Shepherd's Song,"—" Glad and Grateful Feelings After the Storm."

We have *feelings* again; the worst is over. The structure of song form is just like lyric poem, where first verse recurs in refrain. Clarinets and horn strike the pitch in simple rhythmic chord, violins begin the song itself:

(Violins, with chords in woodwind and violas.)
Pizzicato. BASSES.

p dolce.

of simplest ancient kind; rehearsing to make doubly sure, that all may presently join in full chorus, where clarinets, horns, and low strings take the air, the rest holding long tones in the chord or keeping mere time with skipping step. Almost as good and as joyous is the little afterstrain:

VIOLINS. *ten.*

(Chords in wood.)
(Obligato accompaniment in lower strings.)

first in lower strings, answered by the higher. From out of this, as one subject of talk leads to the next, flows another separate verse of the song in neighboring pitch of tone, in mere mocking phrase, like things of the tree, ever higher in the branches, extending finally into an after-phrase almost finer than the main, and resting in the new home of tone, whence the quick return to the old leads back to the first verse with playful skip of lower figure. Hence quickly we turn in another direction to a third verse in another quarter of tonal scene. Broader swings the double air, broken ever by mischievous intrusion of chorus. Now we are carried into the freest phase, leaving the staid lines of rustic song playing about the end of the tunes, darting in strange colors of tone. Mostly the basses are humming in rough semblance of the main verse a tune of their own, while high strings are coursing furiously in rural bacchanale; but soon they all return to the simpler song, first of the original verse, though with whimsical changes, the strings still coursing lightly,—once more repeated with fullest chorus and followed by after-phrase and again by the second verse and its own postscript. And now a light carolling brings us to a formal round where our rustics try their skill, as one voice enters all alone, later a second in separate figure, the rest merely keeping time with hands and feet. The climax through another carolling strain leads to a feat of greater difficulty and complexity, where two separate groups are trying separate manœuvres, crowned by a tumult of loudest festivity.

Right at the close the old song sounds as devout hymn, all free of worldly dance, chanting its thanksgiving clearer than words:

It almost seems as if this were no longer our Shepherd's Song; as if, like the touch in the last movement, we had escaped from the title, we heard the poet's own finer thought of it all, his own purer note of thanksgiving.

BEETHOVEN'S NINTH (CHORAL) SYMPHONY

THE FINAL NEED OF WORDS

THE Ninth Symphony brings us to a question at once most simple and most profound. What is more natural than the gradual striving for definite utterance of highest feeling, like the child breaking from the cooing rhythm of the cradling nurse? On the other hand, does this burst into words actually bring the definiteness striven for? Does it crown the insufficient utterance of the wordless song of the earlier symphony? To lapse for a moment from our exclusive view of the work itself, there is no doubt that the fact that Beethoven at the end of his last Symphony broke into words, must be a doughty argument for those who contend for the greater definiteness of verbal utterance in music. But we must not forget that while Beethoven may reach the greatest heights as a master, he was not infallible as theorist on the nature of his art. He found the latter only by experiments, which were often failures, which we must test by our own intuition, which Beethoven himself would not have us accept in blind confidence in himself.

The last great work of big dimensions designed by Beethoven begins very freely, in vehement rhythmic strum :

(Strings doubled below.)
(The chord sustained in horns.)

that foreshadows rather than utters, soon breaking in loudest unison into a simple harmonic figure that is too frugal for melody :

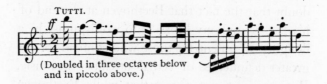

(Doubled in three octaves below and in piccolo above.)

Indeed it is all introduction, very like recitatives heralding the aria. At times it approaches the tune :

WOODWIND.

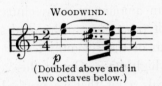

(Doubled above and in
two octaves below.)

but soon we wonder whether the whole movement is not introduction. Often even all three
movements seem prelude to the last. But presently a clearer phrase emerges:

(Flutes in 8ve of higher voice.)
WOODWIND.

(Doubled below.)

with antiphonal answer, and this but precedes a
still fuller melody, though it is disguised by dis-
tribution among several voices:

(Tune in woodwind.)

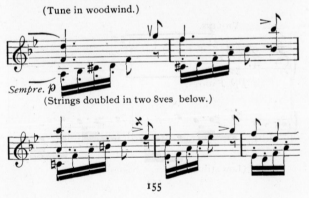

(Strings doubled in two 8ves below.)

There is an amount of noisy climax that does seem out of proportion to the modest tune; but it is all part of the solemnly festive humor that foretokens high rites. Out of this very burst of cadence steals a bit that we nearly lose, though it is of clearest ore. On the fillip of the previous clash :

(Augmented in full orchestra.)

now rung softly far down in basses, a kind of motto hovers high in strings and wood merely for the length of a breath, in four sustained notes :

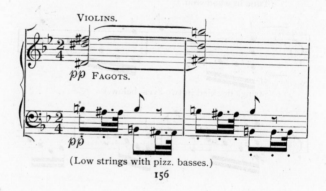

(Low strings with pizz. basses.)

156

But it is as integral as any fragment in this in-
choate, chaotic, inconsequent prelude, and presently another melodic snatch sings in softest
wood and strings, in outline like the reverse of
the main melody:

Lower strings, tripping rhythm in drums.

157

Indeed, the whole is largely compact in mosaic
of brilliant strains, all striving for dominance,
none with clear sovereignty. After a still more
furious climax, broken but heightened by momentary lulls, we enter again the stirring strum
of the beginning,—a shadowy discussion of very
shadowy subjects, where that earliest phrase in
simplest harmony assumes more dignity :

Other thoughts, too, are crowding in for the lead,
Here is one in cradling motion, which springs
from an earlier motive :

The main frugal theme seems the very type of vague striving. So the whole has more and more of fragmental effect; the striving alone is definite; the vagueness alone is clear; each thought is rejected for the next.

Now, beautifully blended of the cradling phrase and the cadence of the big theme, springs a verse that sings its larger career first in resounding bass of fagots and strings, with the cradling phrase always somewhere about in other voices than the leaders. Now the tune is in high flutes and in violins; lower strings are rocking to the rhythm; now tune and phrase are confused in high strings and wood; finally, the melody remains on high and the lesser phrase sinks to a perfect bass in strings where, by a sort of verification, the whole is crowned to a glorious conclusion, swinging along in full discussion, which never loses the rhythm in the dispute. When it seems to have died away, we are in a sort of madrigal of responsive refrains on the cradling phrase, with more song and swing and sweetness and less dispute than before, whence we return to the main melody (not the first theme) in the strings. But, instead of the noisy tempest, the tune runs smoothly: first above, answered below; then reversed; third, with new answer in the midst; and, finally, with redoubled answer dancing all above, drowning the song itself with very gayety. From out of the festive orgy the ominous strum of the beginning has suddenly driven the other figures.

It is wonderful, the magic of musical discussion. Is it the mere association of external similarity of phrases, hurled back and forth,—one view; or is it the marching in architectural array in magnificently prodigal profusion of ordered fragments, running by new dimension to massive structure?

Discussion shows the humble dignity of the separate lyric strain; it confirms the relevancy of the whole by the text and fibre of the motive, which is now merged into the infinite importance of the organic structure. The discussion from different melodic ends, fitting together, verifies and convinces far beyond the strongest force of man's logical proof. It is thus that poems and other forms of art stay longer than laws and institutions, which seem hedged in and buttressed by all the external means in the world. An unseen melody, a symphony that merely floats in the air, has the more powerful existence and permanence because it is fortified by truth,—it is truth itself.

And now comes the original suite of strains, save there is an angrier dispute of the rude phrases of the beginning, clashing in contrary stride, marching in prouder step, with broader swing, with redoubled countermarching and cadence. Heralded as before, the main melody is again divided among its choir of voices, followed by the noisy tumult. Once more the gentle motto in four long notes, the bustling ascent, the swinging third melody that came before in the wake of the motto, the big climax. Instead of rest there is new discussion, still in the vague humor, striving for ever better, newer expression, not content with the theme at hand. The original subject enters softly for the first time, and is answered in more rational fashion, other voices chiming in in independent time. Then follows the climax, in earlier vein, of crossing phrases, which has something of mystic brooding. Through another lusty fanfare it leads to one of the best moments. That little blended tune of cradling phrase and cadence of first subject enter softly in major in the horns, while oboes and fagots sweetly interfere with the tune.

(Sustained 8ves of A in strings.)
(See page 161, line 25.)

The whole is colored by a more joyous hue, though once again enters the dispute of contrary stride. So the whole is a paradox in that the main theme and phase are lesser, in inverse proportion to official rank; and the best is in obscurest corners,—mere after-thoughts, not of the main design or text, yet betraying, through the pain of striving, a secret joyousness of humor. It is of course but a type of life, where the best often comes least awaited in humblest places.

So, near the very end comes another episode full of resonant charm, as the basses march gently to the active pace of the previous blended melody, and the horns and wood strike a call and trilling cadence, gradually infecting most of the band, ending finally in triumphant close of original theme.

Scherzo. The first canto has not ascended

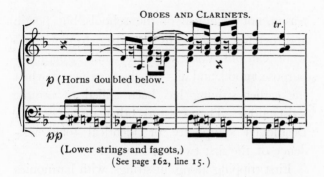

(See page 162, line 15.)

the heights of clear joy; the time for the calm lyric utterance has not come; the *Andante* must be deferred. Much clearer in tune than the *Allegro*, bright in tripping gait, the *Scherzo* is yet strongly intermixed with a mystic vein, a little like a dance of will-o'-the-wisps. It begins a dazzling filigree of five-voiced fugue on the theme:

which, most unusually, against its very nature is in the same tonal color (in the same key) with the preceding movement,—another sign of insufficiency, of an introductory function. It is this

163

reason, not technical of the schools, but poetic and therefore real. The departure to new tonal scene can only come when the whole structure—purpose, mood, and all—has been achieved, when the earlier striving has been stilled to utmost satisfaction. There is no other instance in a Beethoven symphony of identical tonal residence of the first two movements.

First tripping along in strings, with harmonies in the wood, the theme, no longer a fugue, plunges into full chorus in pure free dance with flowing answer. One continuous romp it seems—to the Trio. Still, one can distinguish, to the constant trip in the strings, the wood playing softly a slow hymn-like phrase:

(Long notes in woodwind; short notes in strings.)

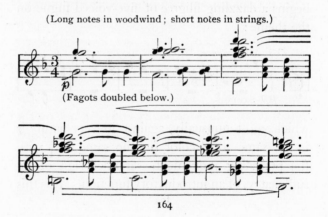

(Fagots doubled below.)

to which the whole chorus (all the brass but horns are omitted throughout) shout a tumultuous refrain :

(Tune doubled above and below in woodwind.)

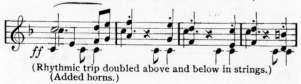

(Rhythmic trip doubled above and below in strings.)
(Added horns.)

The trip ever continues in the strings, soon prevails in playful repartee with the wood, and rushes through alternate gentle and noisy lines to a close. Whence first a complete repetition, then a discussion of the tripping motive, ever with mocking exchange between the choirs with playful pauses, climbing all the boughs of the tonal tree. Here is a new trick ; the fugue has the voices dancing in, every three measures instead of four ; so there is a double rhythm of dance, little and big, checking the great irresistible pace which must soon reappear when the voices restore the balance by entering, not on the fourth but on each successive measure. Finally, they let out their suppressed spirits and pace in pure repeated step, then burst once more into the former course of dance tunes with the same triumphant close. Thence the whole discussion and refrain are rehearsed.

In complete transformation of scene and rhythm the *Trio* sounds a pious hymn in organ tones of the wood:

Playful, perhaps, is the first note of solemn lay that is soon to reign,—a touch of eternal fate, with all simplicity and even humor. Hymn-like, the second seems a mere varied verse of the first, where with dazing art the voices are reversed again and again, and the themes to boot:

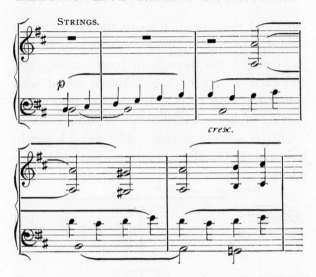

so that the pervading sense of the thought remains without a single actual repeated strain, all in even monkish measure, though the quicker second pause still reminds us of the old fun. Now the horns below have the tune, and the high strings sing the former bass reversed, sounding even more fitting than at first; and so tunes and countertunes flow along far up and down without reck which is bass or air.   An ascending play on the quick measure leads to the hymn in full canonicals, whence most of the Trio is repeated. In still greater array the hymn is borne to festive

close and the impish tune of the fugal scherzo
returns. In big equipment the course of the
gay dance is run through to heart's satisfaction,
and even a line of the hymn is added with
almost mocking effect. But we fear there is no
proving of heresy on musical evidence.

Adagio molto e cantabile. The mood is purely
lyric and the placid flow of tones has a noble simplicity:

Adagio molto e cantabile.

From the second line there is a special sense,
first of constant sequence, as in story; also there

is an informality of whispered echoes or refrains, breaking the stately flow of regular period.
While the song begins in many voices, it breaks
soon into passionate cadence of one prevailing
soprano :

Finally the old fragmental, tentative air is soon
felt as the pace of song halts, and presently
changes from even four to triple rhythm into a
verse beginning very like a lullaby :

The quality of the whole lies less in the melodies, but just in this discontent, moving with restless whim, scarce touching one beautiful, expressive strain before leaving it for another. After the second, the first returns much disguised in fitful figure of strings, though the clear tune is mostly seen in clarinets. As the lullaby re-enters in fuller numbers, it seems, as it were, joy cradled in extreme ecstasy, before abandon of outbreak. In the first there is more of calm, steady assurance of quiet content, though with strong-rising emotion and a stormy burst at the end. Indeed, they seem different phases almost of joyous suppression instead of utterance.

The next singing of the first verse is in dulcet fugue on the first four notes, between clarinet and horn, later between flute and fagot on a part of the theme, all in dim changing tonal light and halting figure of melody. But the twilight soon breaks into the clear first color and outline of the main tune in the wood, enriched by thread of strings coursing all about the song. But there is ever the conversing air, the quaint echoing refrain stopping the strict measure, the listlessness chafing against the bonds of rhythm, as when the melody is suddenly broken by trumpet blasts, which in turn are quickly hushed by timid whispered snatches, the fugue introducing the song as before. Again the trumpet blows, the scene and rhythm change for the moment, to return to the quiet flow of the placid song. Altogether, we do not find, as elsewhere, a clear quality. There are content and discontent, quiet delight and vague, almost mournful striving, and passionate outburst. We must be content with discontent. The sense, again, is clearly the very doubt of feeling, the uncertainty of its incomplete utterance; though the melody closes formally, it is still tentative.

Presto. In unrhythmic *fanfare*, in the escape from rhythm, we feel afresh the old disquiet; the phrase of recitative in formless figure shows a still stronger impulse towards new definiteness. The repeated fanfare leads to the stirring thrum that began the Symphony as a motto, —as a kind of password. Here it accents the tension for a new articulation. Again the recitative; now a strain of the dancing scherzo. Is it to return in search of the true word there; or is it a general view, a comparison of uttered ideas; or the mere sense, in this disjointed song, of comparison as the first basis of reasoning, of discus-

sion? Pure discussion, disputation, is unrhythmic. A new phrase, as of spoken words, marks
further casting off of the bonds of measured
melody; the quick changing of rhythm shows
the striving for verbal definiteness in the restless
harking back and forth to this idea and that.
Away with the fetters of mere rhythm to *things*,
exact ideas, free of the thrall of beauty's laws!
Tear the charming scales from the eyes! So in
review passes again the *Adagio* theme. Now a
more thoughtful, promising solo phrase. At last
a fleeting glimpse of a new song; back again to
the thoughtful herald phrase: now at last the full
course of the final song:

in basses alone without words; the refrain in
stately array of full-voiced, fugue-like polyphony,

finally in fervent simple setting of hymning chorus, ending, however, with full abandon of phrases of the song, flowing to a free climax.

But this is a mere foretaste, a mere fore-shadowing; for, once again the restless Presto breaks into the rhythmic course, ending with the first actual words sung on formless phrase of reci-tative,—words not of poet: "Not these tones, friends; rather let us strike a more pleasing and joyous strain." The words are not inspired; they are like a stage-direction, breaking into the text of the play; they are part of the scheme that renounces all previous attempts. Throwing off compunction and hesitation, the standards are flung aside; there is open desertion to the cause of verbal song. The resources of pure tones are abandoned for words: Schiller's "Ode to Joy," set to the new-found tune.

"Joy, thou spark of Heaven descended,
  Daughter of Elysian line,
 Drunk with ecstasy we enter,
  Goddess fair, thy sacred shrine.

"By thy magic charm is healed
  Despot Fashion's cruel pain;
 All mankind are clasped as brothers
  Under thy bewitching reign.

BEETHOVEN'S NINTH SYMPHONY

" Who hath won the highest venture,
    True friend's chosen friend to be ;
Who hath gained a noble woman,
    Let him join our jubilee,—

" Nay, whoe'er upon this planet
    Count a single soul his own.
And who may not, let him, grieving,
    Steal away and weep alone.

" Heavenly Joy all earthly creatures
    Drink, of Nature's fountain source,
Good and evil all pursuing
    Joy o'er a rose-scented course.

" Wine and kisses Joy hath given,
    And a proven Friend in death.
And the worm hath share in pleasure ;
    Cherub before God draws breath.

" Joyous as the suns are flying
    Through the heaven's vasty sphere,
Joyous as a hero conqu'ring,
    Brothers, run your high career !

" Be embraced, millions all ;
    This kiss for the world is meant !
Brothers, o'er the starry tent
Is a Father's kindly thrall.

BEETHOVEN'S NINTH SYMPHONY

" Ye lie prostrate, myriads all.
　　　Reck'st thou thy Creator, world ?
　　　Seek Him o'er the sky unfurl'd !
　　　Brothers, o'er the sky unfurl'd
　　Is a loving Father's thrall.''

There is here no homogeneous art; neither
fully developed song nor instrumental form,—
neither *cantata* nor *sonata*. There is a straining
of the one art to find expression beyond its
bounds in the language of another. The intent
seems very clearly to be a confession of weakness of mere instruments, and on highest authority. Think of the argument: on the side
of verbal song the great Bach masterpieces,
and Beethoven's final word of concession. And
yet all this weighs nothing against the proof of
the music itself. Not what it wishes to say,
this Ninth Symphony, what it wants to express
or to have expressed, not the conscious intent of
the poet, is our question, but simply and only:
What does it express by the force and beauty of
pure art? The words, borrowed from another
poet, announce *Joy* very clearly: they might as
clearly announce any other idea or emotion.
The words are no more convincing as to the
sense of the music than a clumsy boy's label of

a drawing. The prelude of the song seems theatrical,—a preconceived idea, imagined in philosophy and forced upon musical utterance, lacking the wholeness of a work of art. It is, probably, spontaneously and sincerely tentative. But all attempts in art are not convincing merely because they are beautiful in separate parts. It is not impossible, nor infrequent, in the later career of the poet, for mystic philosophy to halt and choke pure fancy. We come back to the true basis of art, which is independent of announced purpose, works not with labels, is ever unconscious of its verbal meaning. It is quite possible for Beethoven to say : For once I wish to reinforce my inarticulate cries with spoken, indisputable words of verbal poet. It is an admission, if you will, of his own temporary lack of power, not of his art ; it is really a reinforcement, a repetition in different terms, not one complete whole. Nor is it strange that the wonderful words of Schiller should occur to the modest composer as tempting crown to his symphony : the true composer never knows the full dignity and force of his work. Again, the composer's ideas of the nature of his art are of no value ; the involuntary spirit of his work alone moves us.

There is no reason in the world why Beethoven
should not wish to invoke Schiller's Ode in a
setting. There is no reason in the world to hold
his act as invoking the assistance of poetry to
music in general. The fact that it is his last symphony has no weight at all, even if he knew it
was to be his last. There is, therefore, no reason
in denouncing Beethoven's intent, in reading into
it a confession of weakness of the whole of music ;
although it cannot be said too often that the
greatest master's ideas on the theory of his art
are of small value, that he is very likely to go
astray in vain experiments, as did Bach. The
fact that the Ninth Symphony did not inspire a
train of successors is of the highest import to our
view. The only way the artist, after all, learns
the nature and limitations of his art is by experiment,—merely to a small, preliminary extent by
a priori theory. A Paradise Lost must have its
Paradise Regained. Almost every success of a
writer must be matched by a failure ; even Shakespeare has his worthless moments, his unworthy
designs ; even Homer nods. The poet is to be
measured by his best, not by a cool estimate of
average. In Schubert we have masses of ore to
a grain of gold. There is a Battle Symphony

of Beethoven that never reaches an audience, though the score be at hand. Haendel's wonderful melodies are not enough, even in the land of his special worship, to revive the ghosts of his ancient operas, though his oratorios hold the stage of sacred drama in the Anglo-Saxon world. There is absolutely nothing in the authority of the poet as to theory. It would be very convenient, indeed, if we had a text-book from Beethoven, like sacred articles of creed, telling us just what is good and right, what is to be liked, and what must not be enjoyed. Convenient it would be, but fatal to true art. The essence of enjoyment is ever the sense of discovery by personal discrimination. The sure knowledge that it is good takes away the true edge of delight and prompts contrariety. True enjoyment, like true creation, can never be gained by pure imitation. We must, therefore, find for ourselves as listeners the real value of every work, even of a Beethoven, taking nothing for granted from the halo of master or the tradition of past audiences. Indeed, the long run of public judgment, counted through the centuries, does do this, as we have shown,—has crowned this work of highest master and condemned that. But the process is too long and costly. A long course of false enjoyment, of self-delusion, will lead to eventual revulsion; but it is not the only way nor the best. It is like choosing food by first sickening of poison, by the brute process of elimination or exclusion. What we need and want is the positive, instant choice of the best by intuition, whetted by constant and sober vigilance. Thus the keen sense of the leader is shared by each member of the flock; the truth lies much safer in the combined and tested judgment of many, where each is equal member of the court.

Now Schiller's glorious "Ode to Joy" runs on to the resistless pace of simple hymn, borne by quartette of solo voices and by added chorus. The music from this point takes the second place, the words of the poem are first; this must never be forgotten. The label is not the picture, nor the poem the song. The setting may be gloriously apt, overpoweringly rich; it may be more movingly beautiful, it may be infinitely more important in its poetic wealth and burden, in the strength of emotion which it carries and conveys; but it does not usurp the place of verse in expressing the artistic purpose. It may not exceed this purpose; it may not start on an unhindered career to try its own independent burden. At best it is wedded to the verse in marriage of equal dignity as to beauty and power. As to meaning, it can no more than reinforce and enrich. The whole function of the meaning of independent music now loses its *raison d'être*, gives way to the definite tenor of the words. The meaning of music, as it can be given in pure instrumental forms, is dependent on the spontaneous, though inevitable flow of each part and of all the parts to a convincing whole, where the literal title is as small as the limitations are large. Little as it can be defined in prose words, it is overwhelming in its ethical import and its emotional power. The proof, as we have often said, lies in the verifying agreement of all parts in the whole.

All this, that clearly seems the noblest function of music, is least when refuge is taken to verse. So it is that from this point the symphonic quality, in the free instrumental development and discussion, disappears. As to form, we have merely separate verses of the hymn, set in varying shades of fulness, with no musical internal connection. The whole function of musical sequence, correspondence, development, discussion, and final convincing climax has vanished.

There is no reason, however, in the special instance, why the enriching beauties of the setting should be ignored, more than in a song of Schubert; but our own work becomes secondary, much easier, of much lesser dignity, the mere perception of this and that detail. The keen scent for profound musical significance takes a holiday.

As the strings follow the singers in the first verse, an opposite melody appears high in oboes; to which a choir of woodwind soon rears a song of new beauty on the hymn in the bass:

(Woodwind redoubled.)
(Brass, reinforcing the hymn.)

By thy mag-ic charm is heal-ed

now the voices themselves weave a fuller harmony, the bass freely rolling through a melodious course of lesser passing tones, to which the oboes and fagots give answering phrase :

SOLI ALTO, TENOR, BASS.

Who hath won the high - est ven - ture,

(Rhythmic chords in horns.)

True friend's cho - sen friend to be;

(Oboe, doubled in lower fagots.)

as the climax is reached, the whole orchestra join, either in redoubled melody or in enlivened rhythm. Then the voices disguise the tune in varied manner, though the harmonic character is never lost, under the mask of outer change. The instruments either follow and echo the voices or spur them with trills and other rhythmic tricks.

SOLI TENOR AND BASS.
(With very light assistance of wood, horns and basses.)

Hea - ven - ly Joy all earth-ly crea-tures

Drink, of Na - ture's fount - ain source,
(See page 182, line 7.)

Towards the end of this division the voices, of which the chorus and solo quartette have been singing alternate strains, leave to the woodwind the melodic text of the tune and sing a chorale to the line:

"Cherub before God draws breath,"

in phrase of utmost simplicity, ending in fervent climax.

Alla marcia allegro assai vivace. In spirit of march, in liveliest cheer, in tensest pace, heightened by a subtle sound of occasional clattering hoof, comes a new tripping pace of the old hymn, first in wordless tones of whispering band. In its refrain solo tenor joins the flight with a stirring verse:

183

singing the hymn or agreeing countertheme as he sweetly lists, adding, not doubling, a new swing of independent phrase, not bound to the slavish trip of wordless voices : now a resounding bass, now the tune, now a new melody ; singing to the middle strain the line :

> " Brothers, run your high career ! "

back to the first :

> " Joyous as a hero conqu'ring, "

to which the full chorus of men echo, ending the
verse all together, not without special after-strain.
Whence on double theme, quick and slower,
both from the heart of the main tune:

too close-knit for fettering words, the instrumental
wing of muse soars free to dazzling abandon
of gayest fugal maze, where here the coursing
motive, there the sonorous line of hymn, each in
various crowning phrases, weave their festal woof,
so that eye and ear despair of tracing the threads.

At the thickest, at least six independent melodies are singing at once their sweetly clashing madrigal. As the fray lapses for a breath, we discern for a moment dainty sequence of agreeing strides returning to the strife, ending in big stentorian unison calls to the mighty rhythm. Distant strains of the simple hymn approach and lead to chorus on the original verse:

"Joy, thou spark of Heaven descended."

But the lowest bass cannot be restrained and goes coursing in precipitous career to the fervent song of noble hymn. At once is poise of meaning and purpose, and exalted, headlong drive of resistless action "in drunken ecstasy,"—simply, with a refrain of parting line of first verse. The tumultuous march is over.

Andante maestoso. In majestic gait, too fervent for rhythmic utterance, the basses, sustained by the brass, shout solemn tones of new chorale of final call:

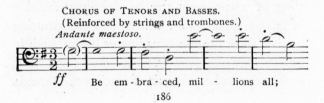

CHORUS OF TENORS AND BASSES.
(Reinforced by strings and trombones.)
Andante maestoso.

ff   Be em - bra - ced, mil - lions all;

BEETHOVEN'S NINTH SYMPHONY

(Male chorus, reinforced by trombones.)

Broth - ers,   o'er the star - ry tent

answered by full chorus, universal, men and women, backed by all the band of woodwind and lower brass, while the quick motive and melodic reminder of the old air sound in statelier strum of strings, rearing a climax on the second line:

"This kiss for the world is meant!"

Again the solemn, simple strain of men and of brass sounds the next lines:

"Brothers, o'er the starry tent
Is a Father's kindly thrall."

On the same plan the chorus of singers and instruments affirm the great appeal; nothing but tripping strain reminds us of original air,—mere solemn fervent chant.

Suddenly we turn into still more pious mood, *adagio ma non troppo*, *ma divoto*, in all but slowest pace of prayerful song, where melodic quick beat has vanished, but the stern chanting tones

have more of devout beauty.   As the woodwind
and low strings lead and guide the hymn, the
full chorus sound the solemn ending line of the
Ode:

(Mixed chorus, reinforced by woodwind and low strings.)
Adagio ma non troppo, ma divoto.

In the third line:

"... o'er the starry tent,"

trombones add their blast; in the last:

"Is a loving Father's thrall,"

high strings and all the basses join in tensest
whispering chorus.   Just as all sense of tune has
gone, the lay of original hymn dances into the
midst, *allegro energico sempre ben marcato*, in
clearest accent, though ever in liveliest, springing
tread, and the singers, led by women, break without prelude into the original joyous verse:

"Joy, thou spark of Heaven descended."

Acme of glee is added by nervous, quickest coursing, first of violins, then of basses of wood and strings; later by both groups.

The full instrumental freedom of the previous chorus might, after all, point to a combined form, where voices are but trumpet tones of legend, appearing here and there, the instruments being allowed a full formal career. The only weakness, then, is the limiting significance of words, which may, after all, be no more than Schumann's title, —*i.e.*, when they can be found exactly to fit the original mood, heightening and not weakening the pure musical meaning. They may then not dominate, but take their place in the ranks, though in simplest lines merely, carefully hedged from leadership and interference. Thus such a highest form would be, if not reached, yet suggested in the previous chorus.

But this is merely a half. Through the midst of joyous dance and high voices, and long tones of altos, sustained by clarinets and brass, sounds the solemn greeting:

" Be embraced, millions all;"

so that the whole, neither dance nor chant, is a completed pæan of universal profound joy, uniting all of individual Ecstasy and Love, acme of the ideal state of art, when highest personal bliss joins in strongest humanity, crowned to perfect state of outer beauty and of inner detail, Greek ideal meeting Christian in simple spontaneous joy.

All through the two completing chants, the pagan bliss, the Christian kiss, are closely bound, interchanging voices and places. The basses now sing the blissful dance, tenor and alto hold the chant, interspersed horns and other voices ring out short invocations, while, all about, the rushing phrase, which first appeared at intervals, ever accompanies the hymnal melody, spurring and stirring the bacchanalian pace. One voice ends the phrase of greeting and another instantly catches it on lower or higher plane, or two chant it in duet, while the other two sing the dance of joy in canon ; now double canon is sounding on both melodies, ranging the speechless armies, each in their lines. After final, united burst, low basses sing hushed, to dim strumming of lower wood, the after-strain :

" Ye lie prostrate, myriads all,"

all changed in rhythm, tune, design. Single-toned, to vaguest strums, each separate voice sings the question in turn; all answer together in unison, joining in sweet accord on the last phrase:

" Brothers, o'er the starry tent,"

which ends the chorus in gentle harmony of calm faith.

Final Chorus. A new swing,—the chant is gone, the dross of monkish hymn is dropped, all is on buoyant wing, in highest poetic note, as solo tenor and bass sing the new strain:

(Quartet, with harmony in wood and horns.)

to the first rolling verse, the verbal motto of the Symphony, while strings carry on the cheering trip which they have first played alone as prelude:

chiming softly against the singers in rhythmic and melodic clash of oboe, that sweetly grows in harmony. Treading on their heels, the higher solos try the same tune with their own friendly opposing flute. In the same pinching way, lower woodwind and flute continue the song, and now, without words between the verses, the prelude phrase is ever tripping along in contrary lines. The whole is a merry, exalted madrigal, where voices and instruments take equal part. Now they slide gently into the second phrase in purer, simpler song:

where bass takes up the air of soprano, which finds another tune above. Indeed, each of the four solo voices has entered in its separate turn on the tune, and each follows the chorus of the first, all singing away as in busy hive the sunny magic of healing Joy, while the song circles about in dizzy maze. Presently, when solo voices and instruments are thus started on the merry round, the chorus steal in, whispering the tune in unison single phrase of the "magic charm," where all voices and band shout forth the line:

> "Despot Fashion's cruel pain,"

in ascending figure, entering, in loud climax:

> "All mankind are clasped,"

ending the verse in slow, gently winding cadence:

> "Under thy bewitching reign."

Again the gentle ascent and strong burst of song; in closing, the solo voices light on a new pitch of tune and carol the ending line in freer course of trilling cadence.

Now the voices veer to the original tone; a newer, vaster gathering pace is struck, hurrying with increasing power into loudest chorus in fastest motion, a final cosmic appeal:

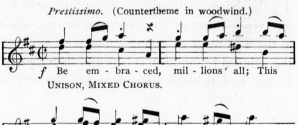

Prestissimo. (Countertheme in woodwind.)

f Be em - bra - ced, mil - lions' all; This
UNISON, MIXED CHORUS.

kiss . . . . for the world is meant!

where the literal air, but not the mood or spirit, is new, with complete phrase in instruments; the answer is pure glee,—song of rejoicing, struck again and again by instruments:

(Tutti, in four octaves.)

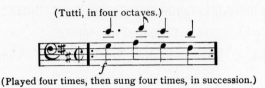

(Played four times, then sung four times, in succession.)

finally reaching the singers on the line:

"Is a loving Father's thrall."

The mighty climax is in slower notes of suppressed emotion:

"This kiss for the world is meant!"

To the dying peals, still in highest climax, the first verse, chant of the Goddess, returns, while in the wild maze of raging tones the motive of the original hymn gleams here and there, simply at first and redoubled in speed, all together in careless abandon of celebration.

VIII

SCHUMANN

FIRST SYMPHONY, IN B FLAT*

AT rough glance this first of Schumann's symphonies seems to begin in a way frequent with older masters: the premise of a motto, a basic theme of the whole. Such appears the beginning phrase, in horns and trumpets:

Andante un poco maestoso.

in slow, heavily measured stride, acclaimed by echoing chorus. Gradually the *tempo* quickens in the same figure, with ever growing sound, until from majestic march we have dashed into liveliest gayety. Now the theme is here in the same movement, though transformed in rate:

---

* Op. 38, composed in 1841.

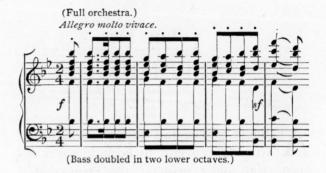

(Full orchestra.)
Allegro molto vivace.

(Bass doubled in two lower octaves.)

We might very well presume the basic quality of our original strain. But we must be chary in this kind of reading. It is best not to fasten a prejudice of meaning too early in a work. Let the poet develop it to our unbiassed ear. Perhaps the prelude is merely like one of those *Adagio* beginnings of Haydn, which in their restraint of emotion but whet our wish for the dance. The whole symphony has no deep, philosophic quality. It is simply unpremeditated joy,—written at the climax of the poet's happiness. We ourselves will enjoy it the more without too anxious searching for latent currents.

This *Allegro* theme begins with the most infectious spirit in the full band, answered saucily in a running phrase from violins:

(Violins, doubled in lower 8ves.)

STRINGS AND FAGOTS.

The jolly repartee continues until, in the second melody, there is an outward droop of mood. At least from the electric sprightliness of the main tune and its setting there is a sudden change to a naïve, personal vein.

On the wing of the little accompanying strain, moving ever higher and higher, we are borne back to the plane of the first melody.

Now, after the repeated sketching of characters, comes the telling of the story. See how spins the yarn of old ballad, literally from the

CLARINETS AND FAGOTS.

VIOLAS.

(See page 197, line 5.)

thread of the quick main melody. The low
strings make a basic plot of ominous bustle,
while aloft in the wood sings a clear idyl of delicate fancy, of a sentiment not free from a sombre
hue :

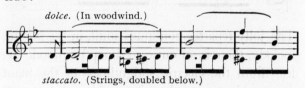

dolce. (In woodwind.)

staccato. (Strings, doubled below.)

It is all most poetical. To be sure, there is a
constant drift back to the gay dance of the first
subject. But Schumann has the real story-telling
instinct. Before you are aware, he has spun another thread into a sequence of narrative,—one
that first appeared in closing the statement of
subjects :

SCHUMANN

(Themes in woodwind, each doubled in 8ves.)

(Full accompaniment of strings in triplet figure.)

By natural flow in answering voices there is
gradually massed an overpowering climax, where,
as the woodwind hold the long chords, and the
strings are running in doubly quickened figure,
the brass sound the original big legend with
greater solemnity than ever, ending in a long
pause. Then back to the swing of the *Allegro*,
with both melodies, now ending in a rollicking
gale on the trip of the main subject, when suddenly—here is one of those puzzling touches of
Schumann. New it is in melody, but integral
part of the whole poem, like a figure that has
long been in the background. It is that kind of
secular hymn in which Schumann, towards the
close, before the final burst, will give a special,
poetic, conclusive confidence. Here it is first
given in the strings, then it is published farther,
with fuller voice in larger chorus. After its close
the motto is sounded in fine conflict of brass and
woodwind, followed by a spirited ending.

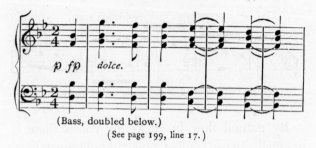

(Bass, doubled below.)

(See page 199, line 17.)

The *Larghetto* is one simple, sincere song, a stay of merriment; but there is no sadness, rather a settled, deep content:

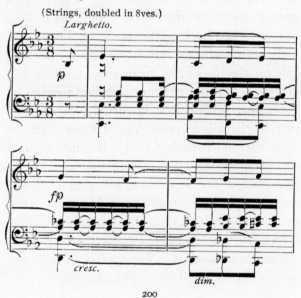

(Strings, doubled in 8ves.)

Larghetto.

SCHUMANN

There is none of the strife of discussion, nor the thread of story; but there is the clear, steady out-pouring of melody. Both subjects are sung clearly, almost beyond the need of quoting. The second is a mere episodal foil to the mood and flow of the first:

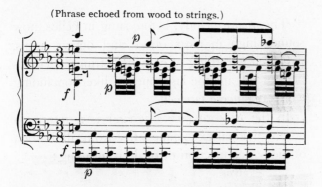

(Phrase echoed from wood to strings.)

But what would, in epic Allegro, be discussion, is here, in lyric Andante, a kind of tonal musing on a strain

gotten somehow from the close of the main theme, cast about in voices of wood and strings, while cellos and violas are at the same time discussing another:

cresc.

The main melody, before sung in cellos, now sounds high in clear oboes and octave horns, with rich wreathing of entwined strings. Perhaps best of all are the last touches, like concluding words of sincere farewell.

In the *Scherzo* (*molto vivace*) is a return to pure individual exuberance, free from all burden of hidden connection or of deep meaning:

STRINGS.
Scherzo. Molto vivace.

There is no mistaking the clear succession of melodies. The minor key adds no sombre tinge, though it may give a certain boisterous air. By contrast, the first *Trio* has the daintiest, most intimate naïveté in all music, though it is almost too quickly said to catch :

TRIO. *Molto piu vivace.*

(Alternations of string and woodwind.)

There is an air (or a trick) of leaving much unsaid, a sort of " you know" in tones, wherein lies the effect of this special confidence. Musically, it consists in omitting the transition from one chord to another, leaving it to the hearer,— also by the light suggestiveness of rhythm, hopping from a question on high to its answer far below. This responsiveness lends itself to much playful halting and coquetry.

The second *Trio* is rather the reflective stage ; there are no new sensations or emotions.

The end is full of lightest poetry. The *Coda* is a last conclusive strain from the second melody

TRIO II.

(Strings, with rhythmic chords in the wood.)

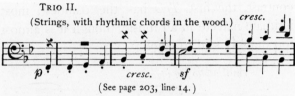

(See page 203, line 14.)

of the first Trio. Then, again, in discourse of wood and strings, the first melody of the latter breaks into articulate pleading, with a final confident, serene answer, where the chords of strings are quaintly followed, step by step, by echoing woodwind. The last note is a joint whisper.

Allegro animato e grazioso. The *Finale* seems to have the gayety of the ballroom. There may be darker figures here and there, but they only prove to be in masquerade, with an air almost of flippant frivolity.

The very beginning, to be sure, is a broader strain:

(Full orchestra.)

But it seems mere introduction, a more contained utterance of the joyous feeling, ending with a burst of childlike simplicity.

The main tune has the infectious gait of the dance :

The second melody has a legendary tinge that is belied by its lightness

and by the comic interruption of a rough
unison phrase, which has a decided mock seriousness. Not until it has ended do we suspect
that it is, after all, the same as our supposed
introduction.

Presently it breaks in with full chorus, and
now, though in soft wood, it spins a whole
melody out of the brief phrase. When this is
echoed in loudest acclaim and ends in triumphant,
lengthy cadence, we are bewildered with the
dignity of the brief strain that seemed mere prelude or *fanfare*. We are beginning to feel that
it is the pivotal phrase of all. It seems here,
indeed, to fill a special part, quite new in music,
that Schumann himself discovered. It is like the
last of the children's "scenes," where "the poet
speaks."* For here we have, besides the objective
melodies of official rank, another of more intimate utterance of the poet's own thought, hovering about the other two. It is exactly the free
preface of the story-teller, his recurring asides and
humorous sallies.

But the conclusion of the statement dispels
flippancy and restores sincerity. At the outset

---

* Schumann, op. 15.

of the discussion we begin with the most serious
end of our subjective strain :

in a sombre guise of minor, interrupted ever by
the major chant high in the woodwind.   And
now comes the psychological phase, the brown
color needed of a fine fugal rumination on a
solid theme suggested from the earlier comic
interruption :

But here it is in sober earnest,—there is no
pretence.   It is very serious and all in the

thoughtful strings. Soon the theme extends, with the delicious duality and discussion which means progress to the thinking musician :

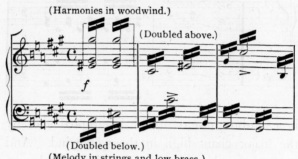

(Harmonies in woodwind.)

(Doubled above.)

f

(Doubled below.)
(Melody in strings and low brass.)

Now, as the strings subside into a mere humming background, the lighter woodwind take up the argument. But they are too friendly for serious dispute, and they soon fall into mere sweet responsive song ending in a lyric cadence in solo flute. After all, in the strings lies the quality of musing thought.

From the cadence we are back in the dancing main melody. And we have the full allowance of all the original tunes again. But, mark well instead of ending, here comes once again the discussion,—not quite as before: less darkly musing; broader; bringing a big, deep con-

clusion from the full chorus. We seem even to
hear the motto suggested in the brass. The
"bone" of discussion, if not of contention, develops at the end into firm responsive strains
between mixed groups of brass, wood, and
strings,—equal factions of the whole band:

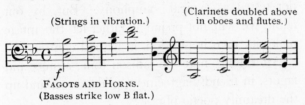

(Strings in vibration.)   (Clarinets doubled above in oboes and flutes.)

f   FAGOTS AND HORNS.
(Basses strike low B flat.)

We have hardly noticed that the reflection
was all on the initial strain of the poet's thought.
The nominal themes have, somehow, vanished
to hazier distance. Then, by a last added word
of rumination, the personal message is brought
home more closely. Thus does the formal freedom of our master utter a certain reality of
message. In the growing dominance of the
poetic phrase, especially in the glad ending, we
are borne back to the joyousness of the beginning
of the symphony. There is, indeed, a clear kinship of these basic themes, of first word and last.
In the freedom of the latest, with all its breadth,
there is a new gain of intimate vein.

SCHUMANN

FOURTH SYMPHONY, IN D MINOR*

INTRODUCTION ; *Allegro*, *Romanze*, *Scherzo*, and *Finale* "in einem Satze,"—runs the title,—all in one. This means much more than mere absence of stop. It is a new kind of plan, and. in truth, makes a new sort of work. It must not be taken nor tested as typical symphony. But, by our habit, we will not prejudge, rather let the music make its own impression, in natural course.

After long note on unison tone, strings and fagots, in friendly agreement, glide down and up the dreamily poetic phrase :

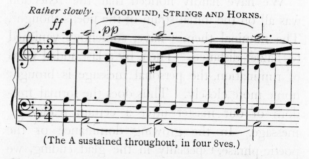

Rather slowly. WOODWIND, STRINGS AND HORNS.

(The A sustained throughout, in four 8ves.)

Clarinets then join the pleasant ramble, that has the magic of unending promise, dotted anon by assured rest in new tonal quarter, where the origi-

---

* Op 120, composed in 1841, rewritten in 1851.

nal note, long sustained, points the cadence with
sense of lesser melody. Still more voices are
now gliding hand in hand, with much freer path,
too. Though the placid pace is never broken,
there is yet an almost exultant, swelling tone and
movement,—and we have said nothing of the
richness of contrary figures swaying in opposite
ways, and meeting all in glorious harmony of
large agreement. At the height of the ascent,
all burst uncontrolled into big conclusive strain,
that dies down to mere soft tread of basses. A
new, quicker figure here enters timidly, singing

in ever rising curves, and spurring the older glide,
until it bursts in full bloom of melody in spirited
chorus:

But the heart of the *Allegro* is ever the former
timid phrase; after the clear and definite cadence
in home tone, it steals and twines with intimate
charm its playful way in close, though gentle
chase of voices,—like constant spray of brilliant
fountain:

Soon, as the phrases are still rising from below,
an answer sings from above with cadence of sweet
assurance in neighboring tone:

The same pleasant close is rung in the first tone,
and in another, yonder. Now, accompanying

the *Allegro* theme, a running duet comes tripping down in strings and wood, answered fitly in
lower voices of each group. Another ascent,
with something of strain, still on the quicker
phrase, brings first a noisy descent, and then the
merriest sort of close with abrupt stop, in which
the melodious motive is ever eminent, clear
though elusive. Thence the whole of this lively
phrase is repeated.

The thoughtful phase must, of course, begin
in playful chase of rising voices on the first quick
motive ; but it is all in far distant scene. For,
a sudden bolt from the clear sky (one loud unison
tone of descent) has shifted the whole plane of
action, as if by magic. We are far away in the
shade of some woods, without the least of
familiar moorings. The chase of fairy strains
has a more sombre sound. Now the first full
phrase sings aloud, as at the beginning, in distant
minor tone, followed by hushed, mysterious
soughing of low strings and almost moaning of
wood. Oft repeated, in ever new shifting tone,
sings the strange plaint. Now a more peaceful
sense steals in, and then in glad major the phrase
rings out a last joyous verse, to start into being a
new song, clear and bright of tune and mood, all

in simple, stirring chords as of war-song, in plain-
est rhythm (all changed from mystic rambling),
that now holds its active course in lower voices,
churning the current of rhythm in the pauses of
the new song:

(All doubled in lower 8ves.)

The two are perfectly wedded, the running phrase
ever in clear, insistent response, phrase for phrase,
having the wonderful virtue of indefinite thread,
as they wander and fly along through new lights
of tone. At the last edge of the journey a third
figure enters the scene, perhaps chief of all in
beauty.

In quiet innocence or contained wealth of
rhythm, it sings as it seems the consummation of
all the story. It comes at the nick of the plot,
as if all else had prepared for the full effect of its
beauty. And it has the Schumann way of a
tune speaking as if in words, and saying its message again and again, ever new and ever welcome.
The strange part of it is that neither of these two

SCHUMANN

Wood, Strings and Horns.

(See page 214, line 12.)

principal tunes has any official business with the
design. They simply complete the others, are
uttered of their own necessity, not for, but
against formal reason. The final melody simply
blossoms out of the discussion and crowns the
whole.

The first *Allegro* theme intrudes its say as if
jealous, but yields instantly to the quiet power of
the new melody, returns again to the attack, and

now brings a bit of the martial song in its wake. Again follows the sombre verse in minor, with plaintive answer of wood and strings. Then sings the triumphant duet of first motive and joyous war-song, two songs woven in one, blended or wedded by force of their difference and contrast. To be sure, the sharp accents of the warrior tune hold higher sway over the phrases of theme, which merely fill the gaps, and it winds its full course unhindered, repeating or halting, as it lists.

And yet the companion seems ever in perfect place, almost part of the other. A true journey it is, of two; for, most clearly they appear before our eyes always in some new quarter (of tone), where they sing their gay story. At the top of the climb they both pause for a long breath. Then, as before, the latest melody steps on the scene, somehow solving all questions with the magic of its beauty, like fairy in old story.

But, of course, the formal hero is the first theme, that breaks for a moment into the latest, gentle melody, appears again with his martial companion, and finally sings the whole original refrain as at the beginning. Instead of the former airy chase of sprites (of the motive), there is now a much more serious discussion. The whole first phrase sings and dins its say on rising scale of pitch, each tone clashing roughly against the last, with academic zeal. Suddenly it ceases,—as if the final triumph were not a matter of mere argument. Instead, a vague trembling of voices leads on simplest phrase, with broad swelling volume, suddenly to bright pace of war-song, followed ever by loyal phrase of theme. It is briefer than before, rises to higher scene before singing a full line. There is, indeed, a pent, electric state all about. Suddenly into the midst sings the fairy tune, like final essence or spirit of all the strife, and with a freer, bolder, and even more joyous wing of melody, stronger, too, of tone, and lastly, with actual martial force and spirit, so that we hardly know our gentle figure in the full equipment of *Pallas Athene*, taking sovereign possession, not merely entering gently as visiting spirit,—striding about with awing majesty. Though our first main theme returns, it is no longer as principal. There is no more to say. The rest is a mere general good-by, said noisily and frequently. The real last word has been spoken, and not by the "hero,"—by none of the principals,—by this

figure that entered with least importance, and
by purest natural right took the lead of all.

The significant link of suspended chord carries
us over from the *Allegro* to the *Romanze* without
the usual formal gulf. All the air and fragrance
of ancient (German) ballad breathes here. Words
are not needed. The essence is there. That is
the great truth about music, the directness of its
power and beauty. In simple swing of minor
strain lies a clear verse of ancient legend:

(Solo oboe, doubled below in cello.)
Romanze, rather slowly.

After a cadence flows the dreamy glide of friendly
voices of the beginning, It seems now to find
its true place and beauty. A special magic lies
in the subjective touch of the original phrase of
introduction, that comes after the line of ballad,—
exactly as if the poet, after a verse of classic
story, has another of his own modern thought

and say.   With swelling chorus, really in big
double movement, one group rising as the other
descends,   the   broad   conclusive   strain   comes
sweeping down, and ends—most quaintly in a
line of the ballad.

There comes a verse that makes us sigh for a
mint of new words, to give sense of a more intimate poetry, a more delicate fragrance of special
message than music seems ever to have borne.
The former even glide is topped in high strings
with accompanying gentle ripple of melodious
flow :

STRINGS AND HORNS.

p dolce.

pizz.
(Basses 8ve lower.)

It is all, one sees instantly, the subjective vein,
not the legend, and it ends in a peculiar burst of
confidence.   This seems to prompt a melodic
observation that, with perfect sequence of inner
meaning, is outwardly all new :

219

STRINGS, HORNS AND FAGOTS.

and returns to the preceding vein of gliding phrase, again with the gentle ripple of high strings, and the appealing burst at the close. The latter phrase is repeated, and leads to a concluding verse of the ballad.

In lively, speedy humor the *Scherzo* dances noisily upon the scene. He comes in "like a lion," shaking his blustering locks. There is a whirling dance, of heavy trip but rushing pace, where every phrase is echoed below almost in comedy:

(Tutti, with reinforced harmonies.) (In 8ves.)

and the answer of main tune is a chain of halting, jolting thuds, singing in irregular beat,—like a line of stone-hewers steadily striking out of time :

STRINGS, WOOD AND HORNS.

This is all repeated, and the dance goes discoursing freely on main theme, soon simmering down more timidly, but with the constant play of mocking echo. It has fallen from the first fierce vehemence, but soon rushes to the original dance with stamping thud of main phrase and jolting strokes of answer. All this second phrase is repeated, too.

Schumann's Trios (of symphony) are his special spot for a quiet lyric, almost more than the Andantes. He confessed his own poet nature, as stormy "Florestan" and gentle "Eusebius." Nowhere is this clearer than in his Scherzos and Trios.

In many ways the Trio is like the indescribable first strain of *Allegro*, ever in outward line of waving strings; and this, we know, was but a

(See page 221, line 17.)

phrase of the introduction. Here, in the common kinship of themes, as well as in its unbroken flow, this work is unlike other symphonies; an air of quiet intimacy pervades,— a waiving of ceremony, that hardly fits with the big pomp of full-accoutred symphony, playing in loudest chorus to universal audience. In a way this poem is like certain plays that are meant for quiet reading rather than visible action.

The flowing curve of higher strings is like an earlier verse of *Allegro*. The melody itself descends most simply and rises again by single steps. But there is, between the voices, in each accent a special pinch of dainty harmony, that gives the whole the subtlest fragrance. Indeed, it seems too delicate for profaning words. The very rhythm is implied; the main strokes are merely understood; and so there is no final beat. But, after rehearsing, the light, downy phrase is pregnant theme for free discoursing, and there is ever that gentle, magic turn of farthest harmony; and a broad conclusion is not wanting, leading back to discussion.

Of course, the noisy first dance of Scherzo returns, and it ought to end in tempest of romping frolic. But it doesn't. Without the least right in the world, the gentle Trio steals in again with all its special message and finally whispers the last word, not just haltingly nor timidly, but as if to single friend in softest tone. Thus "like a lamb" goes out our *Scherzo*. And without even a pause, the poet brings us in the same whisper, 'mid trembling strings, to a strain familiar as the theme of Allegro, but all in slow pace, long drawn out; the gay phrase almost loses its sparkle.

As the theme repeats, the basses moving dimly through changing depths, suddenly out from the brass starts a clear-marked chant, merely three tones. But they hark back, somewhere in the symphony; we know it is part of the fibre, though we cannot point precisely, until with utmost strain we urge reluctant memory to cadence of martial song in distant *Allegro*,—where it rang in gladdest, quickest song. Yet here it is, the same motto, in solemn tones of ancient brass.

And, while the quicker motive is almost lost in the increasing din, they sound forth in fuller legend, marking again the firm conclusion. Thence the whole phrase soon recovers its own gayer motion, and all the voices rise in swelling sound and speed to loud and long pause,— whence bursts the full flood of merriment.

Even here see the close knitting of common ties. Who ever heard before of the theme of first *Allegro* thus running most fitly in the fibre of the subject of the last? And more still, the answering phrase is the same as the late motto of brass and the early war-song:

Nay, the whole melody is, after all, nothing but our old triumphant duet of first theme and martial strain. Of difference there is really none. Only, now the answer is given a full say, spinning on its phrase really a new melody, with its own special answer. On it flows, seeming to start a fugal argument, when a new answer sings out in rollicking strings :

Here is the first real romp of the symphony, breaking at last through the gentle bonds of gauzy poetry, with soaring swing of the tune, scampering of lower strings, and, withal, a magnificent motion, as of galloping chargers. And they ride magnificently, too, ever into new scenes, up hill and down, 'neath sun and clouds, now in soft distance, now in loudest approach.

The gait suddenly changes. Smoother it is, and gentler in accent and movement ; but steadily onward it flows. The speed all remains. A new song sounds above, in high wood and strings, as gay as the last, but with a more appealing note :

(Strings and wood, higher 8ve in flutes.)

Soon its dulcet phrase is sung in close, eager madrigal, though always clear of contention.

Indeed, the greatest charm comes just in these sweet rejoinders, all in succession down the carolling line. As the jolly refrain of themes nears the end, there are some skipping after-phrases: one borrowed from the ruling trip, which we might call the motto without peril of special meaning. Later there is, to be sure, some spirit of argument, as a fugal theme starts with running scale, and each voice treads rudely on the other's heels. But soon they fling into the old dancing gait, and return to the whole song of the themes.

The discussion is real, in spite of all the merriment. First there is a firm, almost harsh descent into a new tone, as if "play must cease; this is real earnest." The deep tone is answered twice by loud twang. It means clearly and plainly nothing whatever but "Silence; room for the disputants!" There is something here of the academic flavor we caught in the Rhine symphony,—each party beginning in clear opposition, the audience applauding, not too often. The theme can be no other than the motto, the old phrase of war-song, now built to full, logical proportion :

CELLOS AND FAGOTS.

A discussion, to be real and worth its while, must lead somewhere. So, though we get into technicalities, and we have some narrow brushes, there is a true sequence that leads to satisfying harmony in all its senses. Soon the disputing voices themselves join in agreeing shouts of acclaim. Still, it is ever hardest for our Romanticist to give up the moment of meditation. Once again he returns to the maze, revolving all the related bits of thought in one, for final conclusion. Mysterious phrases sound about,—the first in horns and violas, below the theme of violins; a broader one in lower strings :

(Strings and wood, doubled above.)   (Added harmony in wood.)

VIOLAS AND HORNS. *marcato.*   BASSES.

later, one of most solemn stride in united band. We can just discern in all a dim relation to the main fugal theme, in varying pace, each in slower imitation of the other,—getting finally down to real fundamentals, closed with pausing chord, whence, of a sudden, we are allowed to break into the old romp, halted playfully again and again by the pausing chord. The frolic runs here and there into changing lights and in wilder maze, and suddenly drops into the gentler scamper, with smoother motion and no less joyous humor. The short dispute on fugal theme of scale ends, as at first, in glad cadence and long pausing descent, with twang of chord. But, instead of the previous discussion, here is a new melody, though closest akin to the others. But it has the quality of Schumann of summing all the essence of the stirring poetry and thought into the honey of its melody. It is a kind of *summa summarum* of all the foregoing.

The rest, dispute though it seems, is mere pre-

SCHUMANN

tence, mere fun,—breaking out more openly in
the next "quicker" phrase, where, as in Beethoven of old, bass and air change places, with
equal completeness, then scamper in purest frolic
to—a pause.   Here, *Presto*, begins a mad fugue,
literally a chase of voices one after the other in
new coursing theme :

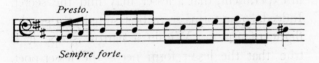

up to the final height, whence, after one more
exchange of bass and treble, the end comes in
melodious acclaim of all the voices.

IX

MENDELSSOHN AND RAFF
PROGRAMME MUSIC

IN various guises we see the symphony limited
by labels. In Beethoven's "Pastoral" is a
frank realism; actual nature-sounds are a part of
the scheme. On the other hand, in Schumann's
"Rhine" Symphony, the title is merely suggested. It is little more than an emblem of the
spirit of Teuton Romanticism that pervades most
of the German music of the century.

It is quite possible, where the greatest may fail
in experiment, that a lesser may find the secret.
Indeed, some forms seem best suited to a gentler
flight of muse. Within a narrow scope it is
true that the lesser form needs the lesser poet.
Versatility is not a symptom of highest genius.
Thus in the strange career of the symphony does
it come about that in the limited field, where the
feeling is narrowed to the sphere of some familiar
idea, a Raff succeeded though a Beethoven failed.

There is no doubt that the true symphony is
a very different poetry from the entitled, which

makes much of its appeal by the mere trick of
association. The former must stand or fall purely
on the strength of its own content. Where pure
music is the direct message, the other is diluted.
The lesser is far the easier, leaning, as on a crutch,
on the constant suggestion of the subject, as opera
on its text. Yet there is no ground for its disparaging. There is no reason why music should
not, in lower flight, hover about the special
themes of folk-lore, with narrower, more defined
scope of feeling.

The "Scotch" Symphony. That Mendelssohn
should not have hit nearer the mark of his symphonies is a problem of its own. The elements
of equipment seemed present in his art,—above
all, a sense of exquisite tonal utterance of the
poetry of outside objects,—that he shows in his
overtures. A want of subjective power may have
barred him from the pure symphonic utterance.
Yet, in a way, he did not descend to Raff's use of
the symphony, with the trick of more definite
association. He strove for a more purely poetic
unity, that he almost attained in the "Italian"
Symphony. Thus one might say, there was as
much distinction in his failure as in Raff's success.

It seems that for the sense of objective charm

that lies in place or story, the overture is a most happy expression, the symphony is not. Right here begins the difference of the two.

The form of the symphony, in four contrasted moods of intimate connection, grew from a spontaneous desire for self-expression. It must ever demand a basic purpose that binds the whole. A national cast is not enough, though reinforced with a title. That is just the wrong kind of unity that is merely external. But there may be all possible difference between this plan and the utterance of a poetic idea of a foreign land in several phases, such as was clearly conceived in the first two movements of the " Italian" Symphony. Though a similar vein may exist in the " Scotch," it is not palpable to the point of assurance.

All this does not prevent a glorious beauty. The well or ill choosing of a name cannot damn a work. We are concerned here with the question of the symphony, its typical idea. The truth is, music like this of Mendelssohn gives new enjoyment to the listener who casts off the puzzling mystery of the title. If, instead of symphony, it be frankly called " Impressions of Scotland," the mind would be far more open to its enrapturing beauty. A title ought ever to be an under- rather than an overstatement of the aim. Its true function is a suggestion of the expressed intention, not a shadowy ideal which the poet vainly seeks. Indeed, the separate parts of the " Scotch" Symphony disclose a wonderful wealth of fine thought and of melodic beauty. It seems as though in their glorious workmanship they make up for a lack of organic poetic purpose. Fine touches abound of most delicate architecture. A clear, sincere process pervades. Yet, it seems, the profound idea is wanting that binds the whole in a convincing epic. With all its beauty, the work shows very well what is not a real symphony. The unity is external,—a national quality of tune. This unity might exist equally in four other Scotch tunes of varying pace and related tone.

But, to waive a subtle point of musical æsthetics, from a lower point of view the " Scotch" Symphony, if it be descriptive, is so in the deepest and broadest sense. It is born of the same thought as the Hebrides Overture, of the mind that reflects with new beauty outer impressions. After all, pictures need no illustrating. There is no subtle plan to search for.

Here they are, all charming melodies in the Scotch humor.

Beginning quietly thoughtful in the introduction, gradually gathering motion, rising to some bold height and descending again gently, here is a little overture of the national drama. In the solemn flow of the introductory melody

WOODWIND, HORNS AND VIOLAS.
Andante con moto.

there is a foreshadowing of the sprightly *Allegro* theme. It has the sombre merriment of the North. Treated with Mendelssohn's own grace and power of light touches, it rushes into a dramatic, stormy episode.

So the romantic and warlike elements are contrasted. But the statement of themes is so little of the work of Mendelssohn; it is the mere suggestion of what he is to sing of. You must listen to the tune in the bass; in thirds; or to the answer, singing at the same time in responsive alternation. We are always in the strife and structure of many voices. Accompanied tune is not enough.

From the storm of this episode comes the lull of first theme in minor, beautifully answered

STRINGS. (Melody doubled below in clarinets.)

Allegro un poco agitato.

(See page 234, line 9.)

above, as it still flows along, making one continuous duet between viola and clarinet, working on to still newer melody in the major. Then the song is taken up in other instruments. With all the complexity of the climax there is perfect clearness if the themes are heard. They are simple as any folk-song. Indeed, they are pure Scottish tunes, though made by a German. In Mendelssohn there is none of modern lack of

(Full orchestra, with higher 8ves.)
Assai animato.

(See page 234, line 12.)

clear melody nor of turgid vehemence of treatment.

There is a kinship between German fancy and Scotch. Some Scotch stories are best told by Germans.* Both nations have a feeling for the

---

* See Hauff's " Märchen."

romance of rough scene and dread danger. There
is a sign of it in the hollow fifths of the wood,
which begin the story of the Allegro, after the
tune-rôles have appeared. They are held while
the little motive

goes on its stormy course, rising oft to higher
tempest, quieting suddenly into the phase of pure
song, but a song of many, grouped as by painter
in fore- and background,—figures that seem independent in their harmony. We have the main
tune in the cellos, little phrases in the first violins,
and a flowing answer in the woodwind. Then
they exchange parts. All this discussion is one
glorious trio, crowned by a fervid burst of wild
passion. It is Scotch in a profound and complete sense : in this savage vehemence, in the lyric
quaintness, in the feeling of stern old ballad.
This latter strikes us most in a long strain, low
in the cellos. And thus we return to the original order of themes, with newer complexity of
all the clans piping together, now with clash of
furious storm, long continued, then gliding gently
through the original *Andante* melody directly into

the *Vivace*, a real *Scherzo*. This is clearest of all, evidently a romping clog, with pipe and bag. It is the most Scottish, too:

Vivace non troppo.

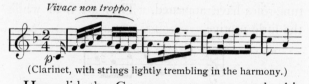

(Clarinet, with strings lightly trembling in the harmony.)

How did the German poet ever catch this broad Celtic fun? There is a big to do and a maze of singing parts. But all is a jolly revel; the frowns are melted into a broad smile. One dainty verse is in brightest contrast. As the strings skip in lightest step:

238

the wood are chirping a little answering rondel of their own. At times there is mere dance-rhythm without tune. But there is a full discussion of the humorous strains, with all their ins and outs. The perfect reflection of Celtic and English humor, now in its lightness, now in its very plainness, is itself a touch of genius. There are many narrow escapes from a broad, German, conclusive strain.

There is none, however, in the main melody of the *Adagio.* We can simply see that it is beautifully pathetic and large enough to include Celt and Teuton alike. But the second strain, in funeral march rhythm, has much of the grim terror of the North. The treatment is purely lyric, a song in varying verses.

The *Finale, allegro vivacissimo,* is a broad, joyous chant, tempered with a minor tinge. The first melody, in triumphant march, is a sort of new

(Melody in strings.)
Allegro vivacissimo.

" The Campbells are Coming." Always firm in this feeling, it is never tempestuous. There is a strong contrasting theme, in full orchestra,

(Greatly reinforced in the whole orchestra.)

lacking the trip of the first. But ever comes the tread of nearing armies. Suddenly there is a bit of Celtic pathos that has outwardly no place in a patriotic piece :

240

Breaking in as it does, it is just the mark of unconscious poet, and a type of the unconscious strength of music. In a wonderful way it strengthens the spirit of the national march. Though there is much of fugal depth, the simplicity of melodies, together with the power of Mendelssohn, rare nowadays, of refined thoroughness of detail, makes a clear picture of the whole. The conclusion breaks from the pervading key into benigner major, like the fugues of Bach, with the feeling of assured serenity. It has a clear trace of a subjective strain, of a wider poetic view.

RAFF'S SYMPHONY "IM WALDE"

WE have shown how Raff's genius lies happily within the extremes of programme music; how he may be said to have solved its problems successfully as to symphonies, achieving here what Mendelssohn reached only in the overture. Indeed, without the symphonies of Raff, it might be held, for lack of supporting examples, that the true symphony cannot be burdened with a special title. More happily than Beethoven in his Sixth Symphony, Raff found the right relation of subject and utterance in the main by a predominance of the mood over mere description. The graphic aim was not pre-eminent, merely the suggestive. The two may approach each other so near as to be well-nigh indistinguishable. But the right attitude of the composer is clear, can never be actual de-lineation, but merely an utterance of the feelings aroused by the subject, whatever it be. As in negative and positive of a picture, there may be the closest correspondence of mood and of event, even in detail. And yet a true musi-cal poem is never more than an utterance of feeling.

The division of the symphony is novel ; there are three parts, of which the first, in Allegro, is entitled " Daytime, Thoughts and Impressions ;" the second, " At Dusk," comprises first a " Rev-ery," second, " Dance of the Dryads ;" the third, all in one movement, is headed " At Night. Quiet Reign of Night in the Forest. Coming and Going of the Wild Hunt with Frau Holle (Hulda) and Wotan. Break of Day."

The poetic design fits perfectly with the

traditional order of symphonic movement and rhythm, and this harmony is a symbol of the fine touch with which Raff uttered his special sense of nature, of the great outer elements of life. His tonal schemes, with all their novel warmth of color and harmony and their objective realism, do not fail of a masterly grasp of the art in its highest reaches, of profound polyphony and of complete breadth of formal design. Indeed, there is no doubt that some of the melodic, harmonic, and chromatic manner that is all attributed to Wagner is quite distinctively Raff's own; that with him it is allied with a true mastery of the art, independent of dramatic illustration; that it is the sensational quality of Wagner's style, his constant reiteration of the same idea on the largest dramatic scale (lacking the economy of highest art), helped, too, by the attraction of visible story, that has stamped his name unduly upon much of modern musical discovery, of which he was not the only pioneer. This symphony of Raff was finished seven years before the first hearing of the Nibelungen Cycle.

Daytime is, after all, the prelude of the real life of the forest. The climax is night, of which the day is the mere dusk.

The first notes of the forest are a deep, sombre humming of low basses (in wood and strings), through which, at intervals, resounds the cry of the horn :

one of the chief elements of this bit of complex beauty. Presently appears the second, where the basses find a tune in their dim groping :

And then, third, the moving answer of higher strings, the motto of the forest :

In lighter pace the high woodwind join, the phrase of the basses grows to a fuller melody,

into which all the woodwind and horns enter in
chorus. The low brass are first heard, on a
sudden hush, in a new harmonic light, preceding
another burst of the melody of the basses. In the
silence of the rest, the strings sing softly and tenderly their former strain, in lower key, so that all
the first seemed but a prelude to this, the heart of
the movement, the sighing legend of the woods.
The song is extended by a new verse sung in close
rejoinder, the woodwind taking part. Presently
the horns, sacred to the forest, take up the song,
joined by the higher strings. The cadence has
sudden brighter gleams of cheer as the last of the
themal elements sounds in this epic of day in
the forest. At the very close it steals in (among
bassoons) so subtly as to be easily lost:

It stands a lighter symbol of the sparkling joy,
the sunlight of the forest, clear of the dread
and danger, and quaintly lifts the whole mood
at the very end of the beautifully sad song,
which is the principal theme of the woods.
Though a mere phrase in a close, it flows along

in the constant cycle of its return, new voices ever joining,—growing to a whole song of praise into which the full band have at last been enticed. The motive has extended here and there, and now has almost the symmetry of full-blown melody. But the source, the tissue, is always the simple, sprightly, rollicking phrase. In its very last note, as it has simmered down to bassoons and lowest strings, is an interval of the fourth by pure chance, the first cry that we heard from the horns. Innocently the bassoon has awakened the sombrer horn to its old motto, which it now sounds again and again, while lowest basses are rumbling away through most solemn changes, at each step, of tonal hue, like huge kaleidoscope of deepest colors. The depth, the changing shades, the dim uncertainty of the forest are there.

For a moment lighter sprites interrupt with a tune that seems new, but is merely a friendlier verse of the old theme of the basses,—singing for cheer, while the dragons growl almost within sound.

And now we have the whole life of the forest, ever in blending of these moods, where dim dread is never quite absent. A lighter motion soon begins and pervades until near the end. But it is the motion, not of birds and humming bees, rather of gnomes and fearsome elves. Much of their doing is of a strain of the song of the basses :

(Strings and wood with *pizz.* Basses and Violas.)

with a dancing kind of step or skip in the high wind. Presently comes a wailing cry from on high, which we hardly know as the beautiful legend of the strings, so distorted is the expression, so changed to a touch of anguish.

But now, with all the light dancing figures about, sounds a comforting bit of the rollicking strain, though it is not enough for the old joviality. All through flit shadowy figures of lightest motion, but uncertain of mood; a kind of secret hovering between the beauty and the terror. Nothing is quite clear; all the former melodies, of quiet beauty and cheer, are perverted; now two are singing together, distorted in form and feeling. Wilder grows the mad whirl, louder the chorus of all, when at the very top of the climax sounds the friendly song of the basses, now noisy with glad acclaim, where all are singing not in unison, but each with a different end of the tune,—later joining in a simpler, united hymn of a kind of deliverance.

Here we are in the same chorus which the basses had first enticed on their original melody, and now follows the same career of lesser strains, of the principal legend, of the rollicking phrase with its climax. Again comes the changing hue of low bass sounds, with the horn call above. There is still a lesser phase of uncertain humor ; but the distorted melodies are absent. There is a sense of coming cheer, and soon the song of the basses bursts forth with utmost brightness in final climax of the rollicking phrase. At the very end is once again the solemn call of the horn through the changing choir of lowest sounds.

At Dusk. Revery. In the cool air of evening, in uncertain light, the strings grope through searching tones, the clarinet trills a strain seeking a clear utterance. Presently the strings (aided

by bassoons) fall into a melody of great beauty
and pathos:

STRINGS AND BASSOON.

which is really the burden of the whole, in pure
lyric vein.   Between the verses the clarinet sends
forth its vaguer rhapsodies, much as a bird,
stirred to carolling by song, vainly tries to echo
the melody.   Other voices, flute and oboe, join in
answering snatches.   And now the horns send out
the golden notes of the tune, while the flute,
instead of listening, continues its carolling in
sweet accord.

In the midst is a madrigal of forest voices,
started by the first strain of the main melody.
But in the graceful interweaving (with new color
of tonal hue) there is missing the human note
which comes with new force in the final verses
of the melody.

The Dance of the Dryads, still in the twilight,

tells its own story, unless we refuse to take the
title with literal fidelity. The dryads cannot be
a very distant kin to the fairies, who seem more
at home in the northern forest. They are crea-
tures of the same kind of humor; indeed, their
humor is the best of them. But these dryads or
elves have a way of varying their guise in the
midst of the dance. The fairies of the first
tune are more impish:

in the slower second they are almost human.
At the end the poet has the lyric mood of the

revery blended with the humor of the fairies, whose dance hovers about the song of the *Largo* in the strings.

The Wild Hunt of the raging host — *das*

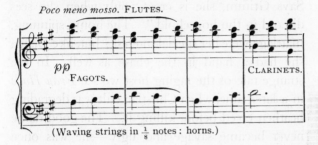

Poco meno mosso. FLUTES.

pp

FAGOTS.

CLARINETS.

(Waving strings in ⅛ notes : horns.)

(See page 250, line 10.)

Wütende Heer—of *Wotan* and *Frau Holle* belongs to the ruder world of German folk-tales rather than to storied legend. In oldest saying *Frau Holle* lived in high mountains, in lakes or in the sky, and was good to mortals, as her name *Hulda* shows.

Indeed, she probably had a mistier past as *Erda*, or Mother Earth herself. She was even later ever a motherly sort of goddess. She certainly made the snow when she shook the feathers of her bed. Says Grimm, she is cross " only when she sees discord in the household." The home, spinning, marriage were her special interest; but, like Diana, she had a hand in the chase as well. In the strange tale of the raging host we see *Frau Holle* in a later time, when Christian cult was degrading heathen creed before killing it. The good dame never became savage and ugly—she was once white and fair—until the Christians came and displaced her with Mary. It was the natural way that the very kindest of the gods—strongest in the people's heart—must be specially attacked. So gradually *Wotan* and *Hulda* sank to a sort of devil and his grandmother. They had a quaint kind of place, too, in the Christian world. The gods die hard; they do not vanish in a day. For a time they are doomed, like a conquered race, to a nether sphere of evil spirits; and they were, in a way, not without their use. To *Wotan* were sent the spirits of men who had died of violence, and *Frau Holle* was given charge of the babes that died unbaptized. And thus the mighty march of worthy gods and heroes became the wild hunt of the wasting host of lost souls and devils.

A whole of the three divisions is of Night, the real element of the forest; or perhaps the forest is her home. Day, after all, the clear sun, never really reaches it. The darker the night the deeper the forest,—which is equally true reversed; and so the darkest depth of the forest must be at midnight.

In the "*Stilles Weben*" of the title is a clue that seems obstinately to refuse utterance other than in its native figure. It means a fulness of life and motion with the least of sound. And so Raff takes a theme from his magic bag of tunes, that fits this humming woof of night in the forest, tingling with the pulsing throb that is busiest when most still:

CELLOS AND BASSES.

Raff's fugal themes are rare, almost unique in being melodies. And so the course of these gently murmuring voices on one tuneful motive is a most poetical utterance of the busy sway of night in the woods, as true whether we read as child or naturalist. Above the strings presently sings the horn (the new voice stealing in ever before it is expected), and, too, the bassoon in softest humming.

Then a new throb is felt in steady ascent, while horns are sounding a distant rhythmic call. Now the approach of the wild hunt of the gods is clear with the new pace of galloping steeds:

STRINGS, CLARINETS AND WOOD.

rising higher and louder as it nears. Suddenly the band is upon us, the thud of the hoofs ringing all about. And now a more measured hunting chorus breaks out in the strings with supporting brass, only to return, later, to ruder clangor alternating with the hunting chorus song.

Now comes the maddest whirl of clash and din, where the one thing clear is the unceasing thud of clattering hoofs, though, at times, strains of the (second) hunting chorus are heard. But presently even that is distorted out of all guise.

(Full brass and strings.)

(See page 254, line 13.)

The answering cries of the horns ring ever

(Reinforced with full harmony of whole orchestra.

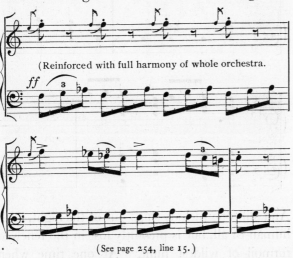

(See page 254, line 15.)

higher; but all is disorder, with no sign of

common (tonal) plan. A vague sort of march time seems patched from shadowy snatches of the hunting songs. Suddenly out of the worst of the din a clear strain pours forth, joyous and festive, without the terror, the brute noise, sweetened and lightened, without loss of pace or freedom :

And still one melody sings out of the night, most human of all, but is presently lost in the renewed turmoil of wildest hunt. At one time when the sounds, uncertain still, have hushed for the moment, the first motto of the night can be heard dimly struggling through the incongruous elements. Through the cycle of all the strains the wild course continues, but reversed, so that when

(Woodwind with *tremolo* strings.)
(See page 256, line 9.)

the last hoof has died away, the *Waldesweben* is heard in its original stillness. At the end, in climax of the whole symphony, the united chorus returns, with break of day, to the legend of the first movement.

THE "*LENORE*" SYMPHONY

The complete title-page is:

FIRST PART . . . . . THE JOY OF LOVE.

Allegro ; Andante quasi Larghetto.

MENDELSSOHN AND RAFF

SECOND PART . . . . SEPARATION.

March; Agitato.

THIRD PART . . . . REUNION IN DEATH.

Introduction and Ballad (after Bürger's "Lenore").

Allegro.

One of the greatest flowers of the species " programme music,"—so ingeniously misunderstood,—the " Lenore" Symphony needs, for intelligent enjoyment, a knowledge of the romantic legend of Bürger's poem and of the divisions of the composer's plan.

But " programme music" is like dangerous medicine. There ought always to be an accompanying warning, much like Beethoven's in the Pastoral Symphony—"rather an expression of feeling than a painting." So, to the " Lenore" listener we would say: Don't find the literal touches of the ghostly ride of the bride and spectral groom. Don't find the

> "Tramp ! tramp ! along the land they rode,
> Splash ! splash ! along the sea,"

nor seek the " coffin'd guest," bidden to swell the nuptial song,—when " the shrouded corpse arose,"

"And hurry! hurry! all the train
   The thundering steed pursues,"—

nor where the felon

"Swings 'mid whistling rain,—
   The wasted form descends—
   The wild career attends."

Nothing is clearer than the composer's intention: to express the feelings kindled in the story in the free manner proper to the tonal art, unhampered by the detail of narrative. The simplest way to enjoy the symphony is to read Bürger's poem or Scott's version; then to resign oneself untrammelled to the musical treatment.

Three of the four movements are mere prelude to the story of the poem, but they are far the most important part of the symphony. The lovers' early happiness shines in the opening theme:

(Bass an 8ve lower.)

(Added woodwind and horns.)

bubbling with joy, breaking into the placid pure delight of the answering melody:

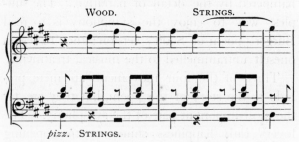

The shadow of a sigh in the strings

is hushed by a laugh in the wood:

(Accompanying strings *ppp;* bass an 8ve lower.)

Thus passes the opening *Allegro*, while the

261

Andante seems but a more complete deepening of a perfect bliss:

Indeed, there is nowhere out of the range of songs, in pure tones, so loftily poetic an utterance of love's happiness.

It is Raff's freedom from an over-sensuous taint, of " emotional" fury (where feeling is falsely measured by the mere violence of passion), that has for the time obscured his music; it is the same trait that will bring it the more lasting place.

In the flow of melodies, with their general whim of interference and interruption, the first is full of a quiet, almost fearful ecstasy that slowly plays into the strong assurance, in the second, of absolute content.

Separation comes first restrained by a patriotic,

warlike mood. Nothing betokens sadness, unless it be the grave cast of the whole march.

(Strings, with clarinets and flutes.)

Cantabile con espressione.

(See page 262, line 16.)

But suddenly, out of the close ranks, the spirit
breaks into tumultuous rebellion, from which,
after a sombre calm, it rejoins the war-march.

While hitherto all is of the clearest, the *Finale*
is, by the nature of its text, restless, undefined,

uncertain. There is no distinct melody or

(See page 263, line 2.)

Agitato, espressivo assai.

STRINGS (the harmony slightly reinforced in the wind).

(See page 263, line 4.)

thought, save reminiscences of former ones, and
these are all distorted into a hopeless wail. The

wild pace of the basses knows no rest until, at last,

> " Her soul is from her body reft ;
> Her spirit be forgiven."

The soothing chorale ends the poem.

It is, perhaps, just to say that other interpretations have been current and even dominant. Many insist on finding in the third movement an approach of the army ; in the *Agitato* a duet of the lovers (in the violins and cellos), Lenore pleading, Wilhelm resisting and finally joining the soldiers.

It must be admitted that the temptation is of the strongest, in the last movement, to find the actual incidents of the ride, funereal and nuptial in one. Nor is it well to cling blindly even to the best theory. At times it seems most clear to hear the whole story from the moment when to Lenore, despairing of her lover's return from the war,

> " —— slowly on the winding stair
> A heavy footstep sounded ;"

how he bids her ride with him

> " O'er stock and stile, a hundred miles—
> Before the matin bells ;

then the events of the furious ride, as the spectral
guests join the nuptial throng, until

> " Sudden at an open grave
>   He checked the wondrous course.

> " The falling gauntlet quits the rein,
>   Down drops the casque of steel,
> The cuirass leaves his shrinking side,
>   The spur his gory heel.

> " The eyes desert the naked skull,
>   The mould'ring flesh the bone ;
> Lenore's lily arms entwine
>   A ghastly skeleton.

> " The furious barb snorts fire and foam
>   And, with a fearful bound,
> Dissolves at once in empty air
>   And leaves her on the ground."

The strongest reason for the descriptive interpretation lies in the whole cast of the *Finale ;* the
reckless, ruthless discord of shrieking wood and
clanging brass. In lieu of a musical reason it
does seem natural to turn to a dramatic one.

The truth is that in a special subject like
" Lenore," with its rapid chase of startling events,
the line must be narrow between objective description and subjective utterance. Raff may
have crossed it in momentary violence to artistic

possibilities. When feeling is thus at the mercy of legend, emotional expression must bear strong resemblance to actual description; it will be a kind of negative of the picture.

But where there are two possible interpretations, the true lover of music will choose the one which lies within the natural sphere of the art.

RAFF'S "WINTER" SYMPHONY

ALLEGRO. "*The First Snow.*" Convincing, and it seems classic pieces of programme music are Raff's symphonies. It may be set down as generally admitted that they are not descriptive. They help in their own way to settle the nice boundaries of entitled music. What Raff himself intended (or thought he intended) is hardly relevant; it is certainly not conclusive. For if we agree that the power of music comes from its utterance of the unconscious intent, the deliberate purpose of the composer is just what we do not care to know. When we consider that all our perceptions are subjective, surely art, in its permanent expression of them, ought to have that attitude,—above all, that particular art whose medium is invisible.

The first division of our symphony is fragrant with the breath of early winter, with its blended tremor and delight. If we cannot see in every phrase a definite symbol, or even a relevance to the subject, we can always be content with the abounding beauty itself. We cannot quite believe that an interlinear interpretation is, somehow, really essential to the true enjoyment. The feeling of winter is there throughout, however indefinable in words.

Against hollow octaves of oboes sounds the frigid, unhoused theme of the fagots:

answered by a shrinking murmur of strings. This duet introduces the prettily dreary song of the main melody, first in the flutes, with graceful trip of accompanying strings:

Though lightly tinged with sadness, it has a strongly human, almost domestic quality, which is rudely shocked by the interrupting strains of the first phrase, figures of hostile nature without, ever answered by the fearful cry of strings, succeeded again by the placid song. Other graphic touches of the unfriendly season are ever break-

ing into fragments of the melody, chiefly a running phrase in the clarinet, with picking strings
and chirping flutes. During one of the strains of
the main subject there sound, deep in the basses,
rough, hammering blows, rasping against the
other harmony, growing louder and fiercer:

Presently, with unlessened noise, they somehow merge into lines of agreement, and then,
with full chorus of each lusty voice, rings out
from the very din of the blows a glorious, fervid
song that draws all man and nature into its ranks.

If we had to say something wise about meaning (which in music is as bad as the moral of
stories), we should guess, say, this. First come
rough blasts of the storm, driving man and beast
in terror to their lairs. Then, presently, man is

seized by the very spirit of the winter; dauntless he revels in the snow; fear itself is turned to fun and frolic. But the stirring song, like day, must end. The frosty first theme comes moaning again, and the strings hum in sad harmony. We must never tie ourselves to any story which links our labels of successive phrases. Otherwise we

(*Tutti* with drums.)

(See page 270, line 11.)

quickly lose the guiding hand of the poet, blinded by our own sense of a preconceived path.

A gloomier hue is cast, of darkening shadows. Night is added to winter. And now the first melody becomes a pious chant in proper fugue, and loses the human note. But the mood grows lighter and brighter. There is more energy in the surrounding figures. Soon the song sounds in all its first fulness of human feeling and of earthly color. Again it ends with the chill strains of the woodwind. Then among symbolic sounds of winter is a new figure in the wood, with humming strings. This is presently doubled in pace, whence it grows cheerily playful, throwing off the cold reserve:

OBOES AND CLARINET. (Doubling flutes.)

(With accompanying strings, Violas in running obligato.)

And the earlier running phrase joins in the gambol, growing more boisterous, when suddenly a theme of mysterious meaning sounds in the basses. As it steals nearer, we greet it as the herald of the joyous song. More and more the spirit infects the ranks; all are summoned, and then out bursts again from full throats and hearts the great chanting praise of winter. And now, though all the blasts blow fierce and cold, they but add to the joy of the glad tune. The true climax of all this first act (of the season's drama) is surely where the first melody turns its sad minor to glad major, and, the fierce winds in captive background, crowns all the strife with triumphant joy.

Allegretto. The second movement is the most mysterious, if we must seek for something more definite than the mere "Allegretto," which the poet has written. The want of a title does seem purposed ; and so it is almost impertinent to insist on finding it in spite of the poet's intent. But it must be yielded that the provision of title for the whole and for each of the other scenes leaves a natural craving for some enlightenment here.

Surely there is here a lyric episode. That is, after the strife and energy must come a phase of quiet thought. The dramatic element has now subsided. Nothing happens, or very little. Nothing is done. The lyric is definite enough ; but it is itself,—not translatable. A quaint song is here for winter evenings, perhaps a ballad, a household glee ; for the voices move all together in four even parts, with marked time, clear tune, and sharp cadence. This is evidently the beginning. We might imagine some old *Minnesong* set to the notes. The tune is rehearsed with dainty interplay of two groups of woodwind. The melody is varied with much delicacy, so that when, later, the simple tune reappears, it seems new.

(See page 273, line 21.)

There is in the middle a swelling glide of strings and a whistling of flutes that is very like the howling of the wind without,—even if we must defy the critics. An ominous theme sounds once in the bass:

274

Then the ballad sings in the minor, with changed surroundings,—no longer a simple glee, but a single voice with trembling strings, while others break in with excited refrain. The wind moans and whistles most clearly. The song descends into unearthly scenes of tone and of tale ; that warning phrase sounds again and again on high, and in a lull of the storm (in major hue of the latest strain, freed of its tragic dross) a hymn is blown in the clear tones of the trumpets. Very earthly the first song now sounds, as it timidly reappears. But the pious air of the hymn prevails. A ballad we are sure it is, with cheerful beginning and terrible haps, ending somehow in heaven.

Larghetto. "*Am Camin.*" "At the fireside" saves us much thinking. But we must have guessed it. How like members of the family the voices steal into the deeply enchanting melody, each appearing somehow after joining unobserved in the circle ! Each entrance of new voice has this quiet way of taking us by surprise. Raff's melodies have a strongly human quality, fragrant of folk or legend poetry, and this is one of the most glorious of them all. The whole symphony was worth writing alone for this tune. The rest of the movement is clear in the intent of the music and of

275

(See page 275, line 19.)

the meaning. What might strictly stand for a second theme is a light, mirthful phrase in the wood answered more thoughtfully in the strings.

But the whole middle phrase has surely a placid, chatty feeling: *häuslich* they would call it in German,—a sort of domestic idyl, without strongly romantic heights. When the first song of the hearth re-enters, the setting is in a way reversed. Before, the fagot played to the strain of the strings. Now, woodwind and horns give a bright color of background, whence the cellos emerge in solo song, followed again in the surprising way of the beginning by violas, second and first violins. Through a stormy burst we wander again into the lighter mood of sprightly laughter and friendly chat, which turns by natural path of thought into the last verse of the serious tune.

Allegro. *"Carnival."* There are many frolics in the classics of music. Indeed, most of its

(See page 276, line 3.)

poetry might be called a simple utterance of pure exuberance of spirit. And it is curious how in such phases of the masters the greatest art is some-how called into service to express the very simplest feeling. Indeed, highest art seems closest akin to primeval emotion.

Of that kind is the *Carnival* of Raff. But it has a way of its own that specially fits the name : something of the unending spinning of the top, the ceaseless buzz of Mayfair, that adds to the subjective feeling the graphic touch of the scene. At first, figures are romping about, more and more frequent, to a figure capable of a most wonderful momentum :

Presently the wood adds a frivolous air that fits the other at almost any point ; and so we are dancing away without fear or care of clash. The dance does seem to sink for a while into song, but not for long. When the second tune comes in :

stacc. STRINGS AND CLARINET.

the general din and vague bustle seek the more regular lines of a round dance,—that is, each is dancing the figure his neighbor had a moment ago, and there is a general maze of successive steps. (It makes us wonder why a dance could not be devised to such counterpoint, the steps answering to the interdependent voices, on the principle of "three blind mice.") Finally the dizzy medley ends in a common burst of general chorus. But a few are caught stealthily dancing away to the first strain, and the rest are gradually infected just as before. Now it must stop, with reluctant skip; and there comes a song that with all possible grace and lightness has a certain speaking way :

In the return of principal theme things are somehow reversed, as in Alice's Wonderland. At first the heavier figures began, the low voices rousing the higher. Now the lighter trebles lead off and are joined each by a bigger neighbor.

Finally the frivolous air is sung below the dance figure by clumsy basses of strings. There is the same maze as before, and the round dance of the second tune. But now the episode is new. Here we break away from all the general impersonal din and mob. This is the best of it all, without a doubt,—a moment of personal confidence, sincere, yet tinged with the lightness of the scene and of the dance's rhythm which holds our talk in its sway:

And mocking voices are spying and laughing

about. It is a *tête-à-tête* snatched from the festival's whirl. Somehow we are loth when it ends, and we are hurried back to the general dance which begins once again. And now the mad frolic rages in real earnest. The former maze was real child's play. Four separate groups at least we can see dancing the figure, each at a different point, all in perfect agreement of motion. For some reason the brass are sounding a big signal blast in the midst. And now, in purest fun, they dance the step just twice as slow, the big basses leading off. At last, with much more diminished speed, all sing the strain together, ending, of course, with maddest clog of all.

X

BRAHMS' FIRST SYMPHONY

THE first symphony has its own interest, like the maiden speech, and in highest degree when it is written in our time. It is like the philosophy of a new teacher. The man's spirit, his personal tone, is specially stamped therein. And in the first there is the added charm of novelty.

To be sure, with many, with most masters it is but tentative,—is, after all, a mere academic essay. No one thinks of Haydn or Mozart's first symphony. Beethoven's had little of his musical individuality. It did not emerge from the shadow of his elders.

It is interesting to count, and to find merely two, Schumann and Brahms, who in the first symphonic work gave an important message. It is somewhat a matter of age. Brahms had waited longest. It is not strange, therefore, that his first word is far the boldest of all. One can imagine none of the earlier masters hearing it without wonder, not even Schumann, who knew Brahms in the piano sonata.

To be sure, this radical trait does not, itself, insure greatness. The past century has been marked with no other quality more than this of novelty, until it has proven its own refutation. Originality has a bigger meaning than strangeness. The conscious striving for *bizarre* effect is a fatal symptom of poetic weakness. The true poet must begin in full sympathy with the best that has gone before him. True individuality must be an unconscious trait of expression. It is not by rejecting, but by crowning the preceding art that a new poet earns high place.

At once an austerity and a mature, fully developed originality appear with the first note. The muse of Brahms seems truly Pegasean, seems to have grown out of the regular course. You do not see the paling lines of older masters' influence. From the beginning he seems to have his God-given manner, like a later Zeus-born hero of song. The whole process, the fragrance of melody, the lesser figures, the very orchestration are his own to a degree almost beyond belief.

There is, in truth, a sense of harking back, with other poets of the age, to elemental things, through myths and legends. In Brahms this primal fragrance of motives is ever fresh in the pure crystal of spontaneous form, that is like organic growth. His scheme of colors is, above all, clear,—not sensuous, for its own sake.

As we read of the young Beethoven coming to Vienna " all for the grand," * so Brahms was filled with true heroic temper, not lacking in most expressive melody.

It is good to have lived in the time of such a man, a great gift of the gods to know him when he comes, a sad fate to fail to see the mark of a great spirit. The truth, after all, is, the people are not the test; on the contrary, the certain test is just the other way. The true audience for living genius must always be those who see far ahead. It may be said, as a rule, that never have the people instantly hailed a true genius; when they have praised an early utterance, the poet has never proven a classic.

Amidst the maze of lesser evidence is one very simple sign of great tonal poetry: an *Andante* melody. Smaller men may roar themselves into a bacchanale of sound and fury, but they cannot think the quiet, measured melody of

---

* Grove's " Dictionary of Music," Vol. I. p. 166 ; Thayer, *Leben*, Vol. I. p. 237.

sober pace. Here alone is a sure proof for Brahms in all his symphonies, not least in the first. Not since Schumann have there appeared such melodies to hold the ear and comfort the soul; nor do we find them in the works of any others living in the time of Brahms.

Reading this prologue of *Sostenuto*, we are struck with the solemnity of message. No bubbling spirits break forth, as in Schumann's first symphony, which, in the new light, seems a little like Haydn. Gathering masses move slowly down (in the wind) in doubled thirds, against a rising phrase of strings:

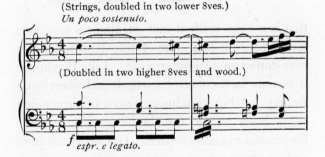

Slowly the double pulse rouses the rhythmic motion, ending in trilling cadence. Now hollow picking of strings

(*Pizz.* strings in 8ves reinforced in four 8ves of wood.)

and piping of wind—of strange token—are answered with the first fervent strain of human appeal

(Strings, doubled in fagots and higher flutes.)

that is a most marked trait of Brahms as a later Eusebius,—his own note of rare tenderness that ever comes after vague striving. Like Beethoven it is, only in the fervent strength and sincerity of feeling. A big conclusive sweep of descending tones leads to the first budding sign of main theme, still in *sostenuto* pace. Gradually it hurries and confuses its arpeggic gait, then turns back for one more splendid march of the first heavy figures. A new answer here glides in, in softest chase of wood and cellos, the very essence of

delicate poesy, most fragrant as it steals its gentle
path upward and down, in rounding phrase

daintily clear as spoken words,—to the sudden
force and motion of *Allegro* theme:

(Basic theme, in strings and fagots.)

Yet—such is the maze of interrelating motives—
this new strain is hardly more than countertheme

to another, a brief, quicker form of our first
phrase of slow moving harmonies. For, with
new vigor of motion, these surging chords, closing
with electric run, are the real theme of *Allegro*,
as of *Sostenuto*, and even of later phase. The new
motive is now, to be sure, the more eminent; but
the older phrase is pressing on in a steady flow of
answering canon. The newer has the apparent
dominance; but the other is really basic. Thus the
sense of pressing onward, groping and struggling
through heavy masses, first dimly, in the *Sostenuto*,
then with joyous hope, is the clear fundamental idea.

Of the especial *Allegro* theme, we must see
first that the quality is less of fullest melody, in
older sense, than of spring of motion and promise
of coming achievement. Yet in its bold wing on
high it has presently rounded a tune. And now
the answer is of phrases of the prologue, of
picking strings and intimate response:

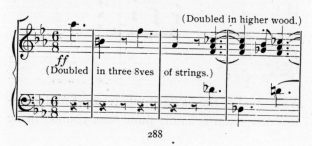

Only they are both transformed in brilliant strength and masterful stride. The note of sympathy yields to the very opposite, of heavily clanging chord and clashing rhythm, yet rising hopefully to bright climax and returning theme.

Here is the splendor of deeds and motion of former promise. Through bold light, the mobile theme darts to new tone, still of minor. Brahms dwells in the sober realm of contained, almost fearful joy. But the melody itself wings in freest career, losing all but semblance of its rhythmic gait,—now in three voices, one on high, two singing below in opposing motion, until they meet in united fall of crashing chords. Even then the motion cannot stop,—the momentum is too great. So in the mere shadowy phrase of close, the big chords tumble along in constant mutual chase, rising to altogether new scene:

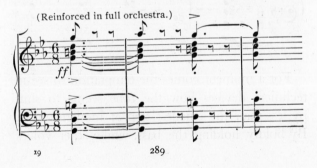

(Reinforced in full orchestra.)

The chase is pursued in lighter steps of lesser phrases. But, before we go farther, we must note two things,—the fulness of thought of our invocation, holding indeed all the germs of *Allegro* song; second, the mastering movement of it all. The sense of Titan stride is the pervading element.

In the run of light figure the chase is more flitting, as of pairs of butterflies, answered, in moments, by curving cadence, where the first theme sounds from below. The chase seems by nature endless, in the change of flickering shades of tone.

(*Pizz.* strings, supported by horns and clarinets.)

For a moment comes the temptation to see in technical devices how the tone seems to shift by less than the smallest step of modern music. By boldly holding the bass, while other voices move through least of steps, a strange intermediate tone somehow shimmers through, with magic sense of new discovered tonal prism, as of an insect world.

The symphony is full of Olympian moments of a certain quiet beatitude, that carry us to the isles of the blest,—a vein out of the nervous humor of the times. So the swing of a placid cadence is reached; the horn begins a friendly call, echoed by the wood. The whole movement is on so great a scale that the structure refuses to betray its lines, though ever giving convincing evidence of its big perfection. It is like the dazzling view of cathedral, where you cannot pierce the maze by clear sight of balancing figures, and yet you feel the overpowering completeness. Here is just such a bewildering wealth of lesser melodies. But there is no doubt at all of the ruling idea of *Allegro*, which now reappears in the double figure of main theme.

And so, here it is again, starting from basses and spurring to friendliest conclusion of wood and strings. A new expressive answer of oboe ends in cooing duet on the simple call. The voices have stolen into the dim shade of new

WOOD AND STRINGS.

Sempre molto piano e dolce.

region, where the call is sounded softly by horns:

(Repeated more than once.)

espress.

as of answering night-doves in the forest. Still darker grows the scene,—then a sudden energy starts the strings:

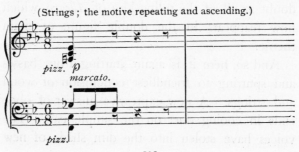

(Strings; the motive repeating and ascending.)

pizz. p
marcato.
pizz.

292

and though it grows to full, vigorous strain of its own, we feel the main theme coursing in the bass. Presently, in inversion, we are merely in the climax of the rehearsed sounding of themes.

The next phase has the galloping motive in full chorus, in various voices, like unruly horses that run amuck. But it is a mere brief vent of spirits before the figure goes gently browsing in slowest pace through strangest pastures, resting a moment in new tonal spot, and wandering on. Suddenly the nervous throb starts in the strings, and, ascending in strange sequence, bursts into a loud hymnal phrase

(Strings, with rhythmic horns.)

8ve lower. . . . . .

that seems to have grown, in thought, out of an earlier bit, where, after the first verse of *Allegro* theme ended in cadence of tumbling chords, the chase of harmonies keeps on. It is here a more articulate and extended strain. Together with the nervous motion, it sounds again in higher

scene; then the shorter phrase of hymnal
chords, as in brilliant chase, soars along in canon
of briefest theme, through glinting light.

As this has come to resounding close, with
gentle echo, we see the mystic enigma of the
close knitting of all this thought, without the
plain themal lines of older symphony. For here,
in softest passing of hazy chords against higher
phrase, is again the gentlest, steady journey of
fleecy clouds that hold the eye in trance of rapt
absorption:

(Strings, brass and wood, doubled in higher 8ve.)

(Drums and basses an 8ve lower.)

and this very bit of musical thought that seems
exactly in its place is the first line of original
Sostenuto. But the mystic trait of these harmonies is the wonder of this first word of latest
symphonist, as they speak a primordial truth from
gravest ages,—before man had lost a higher sense
of deep wondering in the nervous bustle of small
concerns. This vein we see throughout Brahms,
confirmed in different way in each symphony.

It might be all unwitting to the poet (and this is really all beside the mark), save that here and there, in lesser works, he has noted a line of verbal verse as index of his thought.* There seems no doubt that our master uttered a profound sense of elemental beauty, in the hue of ancient legend.

Just how music will give this sense without the titling word, though it can be clearly shown, is not here our special field. By a close glance at the elements, of rhythm, harmony, even the *timbre* of instrument, the subtle association could be surely established.

A certain trait of all this new breath of poetry is an elemental ease of movement, a leisurely lounging along, beyond the touch of hustling time, as if the ages were before us,—a greater reach, a bigger view than the muse has taken through all this century of tense Romanticism.

The drive through stress of shifting masses, that comes as the first vision of the symphony, pervades the whole, independent of first phrase. There is no doubt the discussion is largely on slower motive of main theme, augmented at a rate Beethoven would never have dreamt of. The

---

* See Brahms' Ballads and the *Andante* of Sonata in C.

hymnal strain grows, as do the best melodies in Schumann's symphonies, after and out of the principal themes. When the whole cycle has sung, the elemental groping through moving masses returns, tinged with a sense of prismatic wandering. We must not fail to see that the nervous motion is associated in the *Sostenuto* with the main theme. Indeed, all this thought can be seen in the germ in the first prologue.

The dim journey of browsing meditation has reached the lowest point of descent, and now turns slowly upward.

We might well say that the detail of small phrases and their connection ought to be ignored ; that the true intent is the total impression, from an unstudied view ; that in the close search much is lost of the whole conception. In most masters we have the landmarks of larger themal melodies. With Brahms, in their frequent absence, the smaller motives seem to get a certain symbolic value. Then, the vague sense of former origin may be all we need. Yet the actual and exact discovery is a most pleasant confirmation of our own perception and of the poet's art.

As the thoughtful wandering mounts towards the light, the quicker phrase, without the nervous

strum, plays above. At the height, instead of
the hymnal strain of yore, comes a broad conclusion, descending in irresistible sequence, in
clashing duet of the brief motive and of the
quick phrase that first preceded the main theme:

(Full orchestra, every phrase doubled in 8ves.)

Continued in sequence.

that was indeed its origin. This soon glides into
the slow chromatic chase, the oldest and the all-
pervading figure. Thence by natural though overpowering climax the cycle of themes is reached.

In one way we must keep our view off the small themes, or we shall lose the big sense. The consummate art, in its correspondence of phrases, is here tempting against its own best reception.

The *reprise* is like the original statement, but for the second strain of first theme, with climax of tumbling chords. So the germ and, of course, all trace of the hymnal song are wanting. The whole expressive phrase out of which springs the cooing duet of dove-calls is there in full length. Still, we are held more and more by the predominance of the one idea, to which the others are foil, and with the clear prophetic sway of the *Sostenuto*.

The big ending of the first refrain of themes is lengthened and strengthened to the liveliest accent of the old, driving iambic gait :

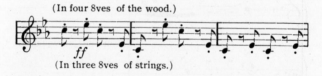

(In four 8ves of the wood.)

(In three 8ves of strings.)

Towards the last line, the slow-shifting cloud masses (of first beginning) return on the lively step of the theme, and end in broad cadence of serene assurance, gliding into one more phase of the *Sostenuto*, in solemn and transfigured mood.

The first link with earlier thought is in the *Andante*, that is certainly German folk-song in fibre; yet there can be no denying the abounding color of a new personality. The vein of true Andante had not been struck for a long

Andante sostenuto.

STRINGS AND FAGOTS.

HORNS.

time, not since Schumann; and there, while gaining a certain intimate charm, it may lose something of broad, world-wide sympathy. In the Rhine Symphony we have rather a folk-idyl than a note of big plaint. It is a dangerous ground, this, searching for elements of such a quality as sympathy. On the other hand, it may be said to vary with each poet, so that with one it has lost all sound message, is a mere weak, personal lament. We have distinguished the fanciful, eerie strain of Schubert and of Mendelssohn from the human of Beethoven. Any kind of feeling may be eminent: legendary, say, idyllic, or intimate. Rough though these labels be, there is a certain kind of tune and of poetic mood where a broad sympathy mainly pervades. This is most clear in the first of our latest master's symphonies. The feeling seems to crop out at special points, as at the beginning, or in the answer. It will

(In woodwind and horns,—repeated.)

yield before the spark of Promethean boldness, to return with new assurance in the cadence :

above all, in its firm second assertion.

And then the best often comes in the after-phrase, as here of cadence, and in the great wide-hearted sweep of concluding strain.

All this seems the full enjoyment of a simple tune, until we stand in a certain novel amaze-ment, when, perhaps on second hearing, we catch down in the bass of conclusion the whole theme over again. It is here that the art and genius of Brahms take on something of the marvellous,—that prompts the use of strange words in superlative. There is in such a dis-covery a sense of delighted wonder, as when, with the aid of lens, we find the hidden beauties of a snowdrop. With such a master one can never reach a state of high disdain ; for the lofty critic can never be sure he has not missed some secret treasure in the vanity of his easy survey. There is never room for the satiety of listener ; one can never feel that one knows Brahms " by heart." There is ever a danger of an entirely new view and tonal purpose that has altogether escaped. There is a bit of the delight of a child's game of hide-and-seek : one may ever be on the invisible heels of the quarry.

Again, we cannot resist a wonder at the strange harmonies in mere cadence, in this first

symphonic word, and finally in the new way—
privilege of highest genius—of saying simplest
thought.

We might speak now of the art of the following strain (really a part of the original answer):

(Strings, with fagots and horns.)

dolce.

(Second voice
of canon.)

with its thread of melody above the canon.
But the spirit and feeling must never be lost in
this smaller view. And so, canon and closer
imitative woof are all lesser in the fervent after-
verse, all still in tone and vein of the first. But

it prepares gently and perfectly for the flowing second subject:

that pours a free carolling song from the oboe. To be sure, in its midst another voice from the wood, in ideal mirror of nature, is roused to the same strain,—not waiting for the leader to end, though it does have a new sense of answer in the varying tune. With the same abandon a third breaks forth in lowest bass. Before we are aware, all this carolling is joined to the human strain of first cadence. With wondrous beauty, as the third voice begins, deep in bass, the second breaks with sudden upward curve, all with spontaneous fervor, though unlooked for, into the noble melody of the beginning. And yet the new carolling song keeps on, and the whole is richest blending of both strains.

There is something in the complete contrast
of these two melodies that gives their union a
sense of special delight of big truth. For this new
running bird-call is the most careless of bucolics,
recking nothing of note of pathos, not even of
melodious outline, finding its charm somehow in
this very tuneless freedom, in the rare clash of its
elusive course against the dainty harmonies in
strings, and other forest notes. So when the
second ingenuous bird-throat strikes the lay, the
whole is enchanting idyl of nature's polyphony.
It is all completed by the resonant voice far in
the bass, in deeper vein, while at the same time
the main theme is sweetly insinuated in freer
phrase of clarinet, in crowning cadence of the
whole. Ever the main subject stands against the
former abandon, for a world-wide sympathy.
The wonder is, how perfectly they join in the
fervent close, how the lighter phrase becomes
aglow by contact with the main theme.

The two are constantly playing each against
the other; and so the feeling of one heightens
the other. The fervent main subject, or its
phrases, will come as foil to the impersonal elusive fancy of the other. To be sure, the first is
main theme, and so it soon holds sole sway,

heralded by most expressive duet (between strings and wood) of two of its appealing phrases. As now the main theme sings, to a gentle triplet tread of bass, a new melodious air is woven about, in high strings, that has just blossomed from the heralding duet:

The full course of the song is more moving even than at first. The homeward journey gives the harmonies a new fervor. The phrases have a more varied guise, and thus, in their union, a richer choral flow. At the end, the big conclusion, with theme in bass, sings its hearty farewell again and again; the after-phrase, on canon theme, closes with repeated strain.

The humor of Brahms is curious, like all higher forms of humor, which is a matter mankind differ about as much as possible. All men laugh; but all men will not laugh for the same cause. So, when it comes to humor, who has the right to speak save of his own special sense? Who may deny another's gift because it is not of the same strain as his own? When two strange nations laugh each at the other's lack of humor, the true jest is for a third.

Brahms' humor does seem new in kind. In other moods he has been charged with striving in the path of Beethoven, for no better reason than a like heroic mould. In their Scherzos the masters have nothing in common. For one point, with Brahms the pace is less than of the first Allegro, instead of the greater of Beethoven. And so the humor is more delicate:

It does make its insidious appeal here, in

quaint, rollicking phrase of clarinets, extending against all law just one measure, with the dulcet countertheme of horn. The answer is conclusive in every way, not failing in the stolen measure. Now the lightest sort of phrase dances down in double notes from high wood on buoyant wing of arpeggic strings, ending in playful cadence:

(Doubled in woodwind.)

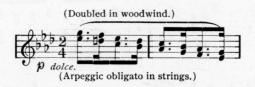

p dolce.
(Arpeggic obligato in strings.)

So now the slower, staid song of clarinet returns, the humor is far clearer,—a quaint mock dignity, of short stride, fearfully balanced between hurry and halting. The novelty, the delicacy and boldness withal cannot be denied, and, too, in a first symphony. The vein of reposeful humor, reflective,—that corresponds to the dry wit of words,—is Brahms' own. Humor with him did not mean high excitement, big rushing movement. It lay rather in the strange taste of a tune, the slow jogging gait, the subtle touch of elfish phrase.

In the second melody, though it begins gently:

CLARINETS.

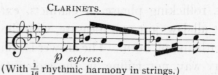

(With $\frac{1}{16}$ rhythmic harmony in strings.)

we have presently a moment of pure, exuberant, joyous motion, playing hide-and-seek with the

(Doubled in 8ves and wood.)

(Accented in strings.)

repressive strain. There is, to be sure, a difference between joy and humor.

What would formerly have been called *Trio* is a new scene in the midst of the Scherzo,— new in color and region of tone, and new in the manner of motion,—a slow swing of two paces, of which each has three lesser steps, well designed for big gathering mass on simplest motive. Contrast is a basic element of humor. It is in the quick conjuring of tonal opposites that Brahms is behind no other poet.

This Trio, in its natural, swinging trip, after the quaint gait of Scherzo, is again a pure buoyant

utterance of high delight. The relapse to the weird tread of the first melody completes the humorous cycle. Yet we must beware of our own terms and symbols. They are, after all, mere images that we have conjured to give shape to the sense that we feel. So there is a touch of exquisite refreshment in the last run of main melody, when the tune extends to charming after-phrase with freer rhythmic utterance, leaving the staid rut of clownish clog. But there is a new touch of friendly meaning; again "the poet speaks," breaking through the guise of his puppet figures. With a like transformed song of all the strains, the movement ends.

Adagio begins a dim passing of chords like clouds across the tonal horizon, all in the spirit of the first thought of the symphony. But now the harmonies of the woodwind are topped by a clear melodic idea in high strings:

Adagio. (Doubled in strings.)

(Doubled in wood.)

that marks a new token. No reminiscent phrase is here that harks back to earlier prophecy; the outcome is at hand, the bright result and reward of the groping and striving. As yet it is shadowy

and infrequent. Scarce is the stately pace defined, when in breaks an opposite, fragmental,
halting gait, of shortest motive :

(Doubled in two lower 8ves.)
Pizz. STRINGS.

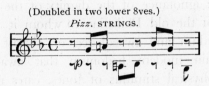

that soon hurries nervously to big height of
sound, whence returns the first placid song.

But, although the main idea of the *Finale* is
new and crowning, yet we must not fail to see
the common woof of lesser figures here and in
earliest beginning. And we must yield a point
that may almost seem the whole. It is not
needful for the listener consciously to know all
the detail, to catch the true ring and purport of
the whole. It may even be possible to lose
oneself in the mass and maze of this under-
growth,—to miss the whole wood for the trees.
The big result is—we have found long ago—the
personal tone that is transmitted through all these
subtle feats of highest art. The true answer,
again to sum in former words, is the balance of
clear view and tense enjoyment. Though there
may be too close a gaze at the visible notes, yet

this danger, in truth, exists, at most, for the single student. In the great world of listeners the lack of balance is all the other way; the fault is a basic ignorance of the dignity of the art, the spirit of the old Philistine to whom it was all tweedledum and tweedledee, or, almost worse, a certain modern hedonism that awaits the mere physical stimulus of tones, cares nothing for a spiritual message.

To feel this common background in first movement and in last is the important need. It is best pointed and confirmed in the concrete phrase. In the very first line was a waving motive of three neighboring notes:

In the second expressive strain is a slight change of outline:

The third is much like the second:

Such phrases abound in the background of the *Adagio* that begins the *Finale*, and bring with them the groping mood that does at last strike sweetness and light. Nor does it spoil this sense of the poet's meaning that the very theme of the Finale itself, symbol of the new joy and truth, has grown out of the old.

If we compare here the basic motive of Brahms' Second Symphony, we see the master's tendency to find a motto, in smallest atom of tonal figure, for the work of greatest depth and reach and breadth.* Nor can we miss the close likeness in the two *sostenuto* preludes of first and last movements. The second halting passage is foil to the groping chords, as a like phrase was in the beginning.

After rehearsing of both strains, a new pulse of nervous hope stirs first in low strings, while the old symbol of dim search is singing faintly above in the wood. Then the expectant mood possesses all the voices, rising on the line of the halting second phrase.

Finally come mere pelting accents (still of an ancient motive)

---

* Vol I. Chap. XIII.

against basses marching steadily up the chromatic line. There is an overpowering mass of heaped and strained expectation. As the answer

sings 'mid softest hum of light wood and lowest

brass and strings, in clear and passionate notes of the horn, here is one of the most overwhelming moments of sublime beauty in all poetry.

We do not care that even here we can trace the theme in small origin; for the mass of intricate striving and groping is all of the past. A transfigured melody here sings in all clearness and with freest reach. And all other sounds have ceased save the restrained hum and harmony of trembling strings and sustaining basses.

There is a ring, here, like no other song in music. Something there seems to be of the tones of Pythian oracle, of celestial message, in the clearness, 'mid the sacred hush. Nor is the song of one voice alone. Slowly a madrigal of responsive voices is reared. In the midst is a single strain of pure hymn, in low brass and wood, in strict choral steps,—a passing touch, in

FAGOTS, HORNS AND TROMBONES.

p dolce.

still higher empyrean, as of pure religious truth. Even the hum of strings has ceased. There is somehow a more human ring as the clarion message bursts out again, more joyously, with new echo in companion horn. The pace, though faster than the first *Adagio*, is still a serenely slow Andante swing. As it moves, now with almost feverish glow, we feel dimly that it is itself mere herald for the new song that breaks forth in firm array of martial tones and step:

Allegro non troppo, ma con brio.

poco. f

STRINGS AND HORNS.

It is, to come to a quick point, the symbol of clear achievement, undisturbed by the very pangs of joy,—a true song of the happy hunting-ground.

In its own way, the herald figure yields nothing in beauty to its proud successor; so that the high point of the symphony seems to lie just in this entrancing moment of breaking light, like the first red ray of dawn. Indeed, it is possible to lay too much stress on the formal eminence of one theme over another.

The marching song is the final distilled flower of the idea that began the Adagio, when higher phrase of strings topped the dim moving chords in the wood. It is the realization of all the lesser motives into a tune of firm serenity. Another answer is this to the charge of imitation. The tune cannot be another's; for we have seen it grow from smallest seed.

The tune swings along in leisurely sequence, and, after full-rounded close, is taken up with added choir of wood. Lastly the brass joins in loudest chorus. Now a new stir and strum of rhythm appear. The repose of steady march is lost; a new answer to the first strain of the tune sounds in quick notes of ancient motive. A new, broad, arpeggic stride is in the violins, above tumbling violas, crossed by another in the basses; then a nervous hurrying of voices in quick coursing phrase,—all in tempest of tonal torrents, ending at last on high, where, with the old solemn clearness, the prophetic figure sings in highest flute, echoed by magic note of the horn, the sacred song in intertwined strains.

In such a moment it seems that the world has,

as yet, no approaching idea of the greatness of
Brahms, as he looms up more heroic than ever
in all dimensions of his art, in every mood of
poetry. For, after this brilliant glimpse of glinting beauty, of ecstatic joy, here is our second
melody (of the Allegro), in serene reserve and
sustained humor of contented pace. Wonderful
is this sudden descent from Gothic passion and
sweetness to Olympian calm. It is alone a
mark of the widest reach of human conception:

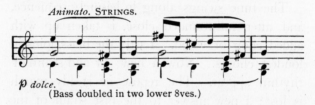

(Bass doubled in two lower 8ves.)

This second melody (of Allegro) but stresses
the true quality, and in its line of newest melody
confirms the intrinsic novelty of the first. There
is not the usual contrast of themes; for both
melodies, instead, stand opposed in quiet, assured,
triumphant stride to the toil and throes that
precede the magic song of the Pythian strain.

More than the first has this second Allegro
tune the comfortable charm of endless delight.
The golden vein seems to lead us in boundless,

pleasant quest. But the gentle motion does end
with a new nervous stir and jolting pace. Yet,
though the quiet is gone, the joy is not. Rather
is there a faster pulsing of rising delight that
must have a more tumultuous utterance. For a
while we relapse into serene glide on a responding phrase of our tune :

Soon, as this is taken up in doubled time and
ragged beat of strings, we are whirled into the
midst of half-unison pæan, in fullest chorus :

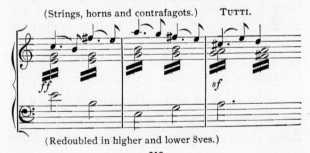

(Strings, horns and contrafagots.) TUTTI.

(Redoubled in higher and lower 8ves.)

319

If we have caught the clinging habit of tracing themes in their mystic course, we see that, from the beginning, of movement and even of symphony, there was contrast between the even flow and eccentric pace. The former was, we have seen, first a dim groping, then an approach of light, last a confident serenity. In the intervals, the ragged rhythm uttered the uncertain mood, the increasing stress that ends in triumph.

Against a line of it a new motive now appears, in petty conflict of its rolling figure :

Quickly it envelops all the previous song and crowns it with a new touch of glee. It may be quite needless to search for a dark origin ; but there is no doubt of the identity of one of our ancient motives, that is here recalled in changed spirit of gladness. After a moment of subdued mood, there is a sudden burst in loud chorus, in duet of the rolling motion on high, and a masterful stride of march that has grown out of the eccentric song. The climax is the joyous flood-tide of the symphony, as the rolling phrase and the stride, now in even pace of triumph, play about in confusion of delight, first one, then the other above, the march carrying the main song, but the merry motive adding the final sparkle.

Now, after a half-pause, re-enters the stately tune of main march with a more festive brilliancy, a prouder ring. The earlier song of Allegro melodies returns with little change, save that new scenes are touched in homeward path. All the joyous episode of stress returns and leads to the magic of the prophetic call, and then to the serene humor of the Olympian melody. So follows, too, once -more the big climax, with the ancient motive entwined about the second melody.

Here the old refrain ceases. Instead of a final verse of main march is here a mystic spot with solemn echo of earliest phrase in high wood against dim figures below, while the strings are running their former quickened, nervous strain. But the tonal light gives the strange hue of sombre mood, with grim sense of barbaric lore, that slowly presses towards the light, in symbolic style of responsive voices of the canon, which at the full flood plunges with utmost joy and speed to the final *fanfare*. First there is mere noisy whir of strings against blast of wind. Slowly the exuberance finds a melodic utterance in the old pace of serene triumph. Just one phrase is chanted to and fro, as by delighted children,

in ever higher tone.

At the top is the mere beat of glad foot, until of a sudden is poured forth from loudest brass and strings the hymnal line that sounded gently once before in earlier *Adagio*, that gives once more the seal of religious truth to the plot of mortal stress and triumph.

In the last line of mad revel the voices start a half-articulate glee, where the vague theme strongly recalls one of the elemental motives.

In structure, as in poetic sense, it is clear that the first pervading struggle through slow-moving masses, the basic figure of the first Allegro, returns in the last for final solace and overpowering triumph.

BRAHMS' THIRD SYMPHONY

THE intense ethical or moral element of Beethoven, the human, the fraternal, is less in Brahms. But his is not the animal materialism of much modern art; it is too sanely balanced, it has too high a stand and standard. There is in Brahms the consummate patience, both of big design and of least detail, that assures a sound poetic message. This is, indeed, the one test of high art. In humor it is a recoil from the tension of Romanticism. As we have said, the high perfection insures a high tone; but the calmness, as of Mozart, leaves the message less tensely clear than of Beethoven and of Schumann. A broader, freer, clearer outlook is Brahms', oceanic in a way, if not quite cosmic. Strange how the view onward is made clearer by a big harking back to earliest ages,—a correction of too straight and strict religious sense by the more primitive significance and feeling of pagan cult. A bad time is this for dogma. It is too definite and is doomed. One might say that nothing that can be defined or formulated in human speech can possibly be permanent. Truth is too big for that jargon of small things. Dogma must go, and, with it, the cult and creed of narrow religion or philosophy. Christianity in its small sense has too long overshadowed the world. Music is the first to proclaim the new message, though elsewhere the legendary element is also prominent.

The harking back to the sense of old lore is important, not for itself as for this recoil from narrow view, to teach the world that all truth does not date from the last two thousand years, that great poetic divination was felt elsewhere than in Oriental lands,—in ancient times, when truth was uttered, if not in individual verse, in legend and belief. This is in common between the two opposing champions of latest music. The one chose, in a literal way, to turn to old legends with full drama of personal god; the other sought the freer, less limiting way of pure art, whose breath, without label of words, somehow stirs man's spirit much as does the air of woods and meadows, calling him from the narrow thrall of dank cloister. There is also a mixture of frugal simplicity with high complexity, that profoundly kindles our sense of ancient truth. To be sure, a special legendary subject cannot be read into any symphony; it lies in the neo-ancient quality of melodies and color of harmony and instruments. Brahms did not mar his message by perverted tales of ancient lore, redolent of animalism and fatalism that must die for lack of buoyant truth. He appeals to the pure musical intuition, and has no outward indices save where, as in the Ballads, an actual verse from Ossian points the mood.

We can never neglect the very beginning in Brahms. In many greatest works it is often purest introduction, preface, not integral; in Haydn it is often irrelevant, nay, literally impertinent; at best, like grace at table. In Brahms, push it aside as we will, it reappears ever with haunting meaning, seems ever like overshadowing motto. Here it is two chords, loud and long; one in the clear bright light of day, the second dark and sombre; we are between clouds and sunshine. In this April light we proceed. In a way, Brahms seems to have the symphonic point of view more than any one,—that is, the element of big design. The perfect placidity of his poise helps here; he is the sanest, perhaps, of all secular

masters (where Bach is absent); at least, he has
least frenzy of poet. Beethoven would begin
with that wonderful reversible way of his: melody
of bass and treble which can be inverted with
equal effect. Think of the mastery for that unconscious art! Somewhat similarly we catch in
Brahms a special profundity of design which

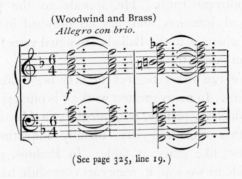

(Woodwind and Brass)
Allegro con brio.

(See page 325, line 19.)

does not lie on the surface, so that you can
never study him in a hurry.

Here in the symphony one can easily neglect
the fact that the motto of the first three bars is
instantly the bass of the next in contrafagottos
and strings, the ominous motive at the foundation of all. The main theme, which here
begins, sweeps down the simple lines of tonic
chord, too free for modern melody. Strange

how there is here a blending of the new and very old! As always, the greatest truth is most simple. The simplicity is all in the general spirit; for, looking at the parts, here is at the very beginning a double rhythm, the main one of basses fighting the swing of the tune:

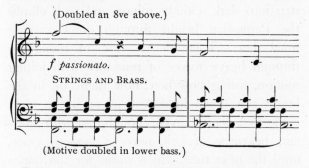

But, through the melodious woof, on goes the actual fugue of the motive of the first three bars. For immediately, in the midst of the tune, the motto answers its last entrance in the bass with another, redoubled in time, in neighboring key of low wood, straightway followed in the original tone on high. Subtly pervasive is this underlying legend, but so subtle that, while feeling, it is almost impossible to see it with conscious eyes. To be sure, it now ceases during the lesser tunes and second theme, but this pro-

found view-point is the rare symphonic quality,
wider, bigger, saner than much of romantic
rhapsody.

Equally with the jolting rhythm is the rude jar
of sudden harmonic change ; beginning in clearest white light of major tone, it plunges the next
step into dark, cloudy minor, and so it climbs
the Parnassian height through quick varying
tonal hue. There is a sense of ploughing
through heavy waves of resistance with jolting
motion, listing now here, now there, up in the
bright sun, down in dark depths ; but it does
come to a gentle haven, though ever with a certain heaviness of gait, never a smooth grace,
until the next tune, which hums for the nonce
like lullaby :

(Melody in strings.)

Quickly, however, rushing to a climax, it changes
the tonal light, and sings again from a new
quarter. There is no return to boisterous theme,

—a line or so of sighing strings with soothing wood, and then, still in remote tonal scene, here is the real second theme, a song most sweetly quaint and appealing, almost plaintive :

(Melody in clarinet and bassoons.)

p grazioso.

(Rhythm in strings.)

with a swing (of $\frac{9}{4}$) that is not dainty nor awkward, but seems in one moment the one, in the next the other; is certainly naïve,—novel yet natural; on the whole, gives the spontaneous song a tinge of slow dance. The rare charm of the song is blended of limping basses of strings and of a high note of flute piping in at oddest moments.

The verse is repeated with some change of parts in the voices and with the same gay overflowing of cadence. Now the inverted first strain of the verse is sung through succeeding hues of tonal light, straying far away and suddenly coming home again into the original tone, where above the lower melody is a pretty bit of phrase, descending to meet the rising tune :

Here is a sudden ominous halt of placid pace. In sombre tones the motto intrudes its dread message, followed by a phase of light flitting figures above and below that are most mysterious :

(Quickened motto in basses of strings and fagots.)

All of Brahms is much more detailed, minute,
than any other master. Broad lines there are
and pervading; but they pervade as arabesque
figures entwined in obscure plan. Are they more
in artisan or workman than in poet phase?
However, the fact that they are not reducible to
language is no reason against or for their greatness. But it is strange how, after Mozart, symphonies rushed to a more defined stage of intense
content and romantic message, and then reacted
completely. The reaction of Brahms is not
merely from Schumann or Schubert; it is the
reaction even from Beethoven. Thus, to show
the minute process: in this difficult phase of the
symphony, before repetition of themes, the sense
of arpeggio figure, of harp-like descending
chords, haunts us with a dim sense of relevance
which is most difficult to realize. To be sure,
in one sense an arpeggio chord is always relevant
(like an adjournment), especially in mere pointing
of the harmony. But it must be more than this
in a melodic voice. Our first search gropes to
the second theme, whose cadence breaks into
falling tones of a chord. But this cannot be the
source. We feel with the sudden change of
hue (and the ominous motto) a total break from

the chain of melody; we must go further back for the trace.

Arpeggio, the harp-like ripple of chord, is itself a sign or touch of the primeval. It is one of the unconscious traits of Brahms in all his music. Throughout lesser figures we see it—too humble for mention. If we go to the theme itself, the main subject, what is it but an arpeggio? Remembering now Brahms' way of doubling and redoubling the pace of his ideas, augmenting and diminishing, every arpeggio gains a new meaning, a special relation to the subject to which it is akin, so that our phase with motto (redoubled) below and arpeggio above is all part of the fibre of the central idea. The phrase here seems to get an added fitness as a guise in quicker notes, still of the shortened motto, that is moving below and about. Even when all resemblance of outline is gone, the quick change of harmony at each big step breathes the same air of ominous harmonic suspense of the first two bars.

We understand now better the meaning of the interruption of second theme,—as a return to the motto, of which, we remark, the full phrase has four notes:

so that the first sounds of the symphony are not the whole, but a motto of the motto, a spirit of the essence.

It is the melodious texture, the perfection of big design and small, that make the art of Brahms sublime. Such absolute honesty of fulfilment can come only from great thought. The world cannot withstand the insistent evidence of this workmanship. One feels as if the sacred verse, " He that is faithful in a very little . . . ," were meant specially for art. It is the perfection and correlation of the smallest details that make the greatest art. Of course, it is not done as toil —that must not be forgotten ; the spontaneous thought alone brings on exultant flow the perfect utterance. But the patient toil has gone before in student years, and by slow labor has tested the right spirit, the spirit that learns all thoroughly before it teaches.

The quicker figure is pulsing down in high wood, while from below slower notes stride upward. There is a long discussion, misty, until we see quicker forms of the motto rising like spirits of the legend all about, while against them are gentle cascades of harp-like tones in the wood, interlacing the whole. Still, as the shadowy discussion continues through cadences that are ever nearing the first tone,* while the motto is rising here and there in vapory figures, the quicker descending phrase has become more definite. The gentle cascades which come trickling down in the wood, above the phantoms of the motto, are seen to be of the closing phrase of second theme. So, in a way, are united the ominous hue of motto with gentler grace of second melody. The whole statement ends in triumphant coursing of final phrase in overwhelming climax, not only of first theme, but of the whole integral texture of the vital thought of the movement.

After the repeat, the shorter motto first still strides noisily about, descending as well as ascend-

---

* *Tone* is here used in its true, complete sense, embracing with a note or sound its whole tonality. It is, too, historically, the original conception, when there were no chords of simultaneous sounds to reinforce tonality. It is a conception harder to realize as we are removed from the old epoch of single-toned music ; but it makes for the true meaning of "Gregorian tones" and Church modes.

ing through rough changes of tone, until, in a remote minor, a changed form of the second theme appears.

(Upper figure in four 8ves of woodwind, the next lower in two 8ves of strings.)

(Repeated with new ending.)

(Lowest figure doubled in basses of strings.)
(See page 334, line 15.)

We must be prepared in our latest master for a disguise of themes more occult by far even than the subtleties of Mozart's " Jupiter" Symphony. Inverted, augmented, or diminished in pace, changed in harmony, the same virtual idea somehow resides, brought out the more by variation and wrought out to higher meaning and conclusion by the life of the discussion.

So we plunge through a clash of guises of the motto into a new phase of second theme,— no longer sweet-humored,—in sombre, almost gloomy minor of low basses, the old quaint step gone—instead, a pace of anxious, eager striving, with here and now a gleam of delusive, ephemeral sweetness of major. Now eager strings take up the agitated song. All trace of the old quality is gone; but outwardly it is the same figure, and it ends, as before, with chain of cadences seeking a familiar tonal home. But the solace of sweet close is not there. Instead, by timid, halting steps we meet—a surprise: to smooth humming motion of strings the horns sound the motto in a new form of beauty:

(Theme in horns, *espress.*)

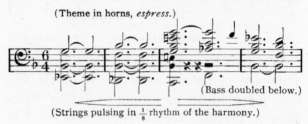

(Bass doubled below.)

(Strings pulsing in $\frac{1}{8}$ rhythm of the harmony.)

with new swing, with moving tenderness. It is as if the melodies had exchanged humors. The sweetly quaint second, in sad distress, is consoled by a new soothing strength of the erst ominous motto, and is followed with the same cheer of oboes.

Through untroubled cadence we come to a mysterious strain of first theme, soon darkening in hue of minor, in various figures gliding down in shadowy chase, suddenly broken by the motto, as at first, heralding the main theme in full force and stirring freshness, and yet ever entwined with the dim sombre motive sounding below or hovering above, which it throws off in the clearer cadence.   Then, as before, to more human, appealing, lesser melody, to distant tonal scene; again the sigh of wood echoed by low strings; now the full former grace and quaint charm of second theme with strange halting dance.   Once more the chain of cadent phrases, through prism of colors, and finally home again to sweetly concluding strain in reversed melody.   In breaks the motto, as before, and the dual phrases of themal fragments, so dim of origin, the quicker theme ascending, the arpeggios trickling down to meet the theme and crossing each other.   For a time the latter gain the mastery; but the true climax is again reached with motto figures rising from the depth of strings while the harp phrase extends to more definite theme, which seems to have a dim relation to all others, and a clear one to none, though, mainly, it is of the text of the motto.   In final verse comes the main theme in bright array, motto and all.   Losing the gloomy sense of change, of human vicissitude, it is transfigured to one of steadily coursing joy.

The stress on a former brief figure of the subject

is now all brilliant with victory. The ending phrase, also from the first verse of main melody:

comes in fervent climax, with a new conclusive breadth and relevance, subtly sealing all former doubts. There is, too, a new turn at the end of intimate strain, in cradling swing,—a human touch before the last lay of fateful legend.

The *Andante* is in the simple classic vein hallowed by rare masters, that fearlessly begins in full tonic chord: stable, absolute, not wavering nor yearning; not at all romantic; settled, assured in placid repose; childlike and ingenuous. Beauty is foremost,—spontaneity is evident rather than intensity of message. And there is ever a sweet echoing cadence in deep brown of low strings:

339

Everywhere is the frugal economy of highest art and soundest, purest thought.

In placid assurance of beauty the melody runs on with ever echoed cadence from resonant depths of the basses. With the finite quality of a tune, it yet spins along as in easy narrative, coming soon to climax of spontaneous though well-restrained fervor, an utterance that betrays as high a state of serene bliss as is known to mortal. The first strain of the lyric dwells and ends in the home tone, neighbor to that of the first *Allegro*. The second gently glides into the abutting key, the nearest resting-place. Thence it roams ever to farther limits, but suddenly swings through moving climax home again. Now the tune turns towards the region on the farther side with inverted answer, but quickly takes refuge once more in the main tone.

The melody now puts on a graceful ornament that enriches, but not disguises her individual beauty. To be sure, it is a mere phrase, a special glimpse of the first friendly strain that we catch here and there; then another, its answer, that looms up through the shifting tonal light in dim minor. The two strains, indeed, sing a duet of gloom and cheer until the former vanishes,

and the sombre call is heard far down in basses,
ever descending in darker depth. Whence
emerges a song of the same fibre in clarinet and
fagot, in plaintive appeal, taken up by horn and

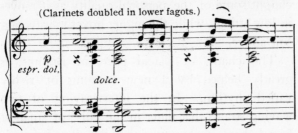

(Clarinets doubled in lower fagots.)

flute. As they end in mournful cadence, the
neglected strings enter with new human note of
soothing appeal:

With no outer relation, it is the meaning of
essential, intrinsic contrast of answering solace.
Taken up by wood, and carried on by strings
with further answer in the wood, the whole is a

melodic poem of its own, with just the quality
lacking in the main verse, a touch of intimate
romance gliding in hushed groping through dim
changing tones to the first theme. But this has
caught some of the personal quality as it moves
in low strings, while the higher hover in wavering
suit above.

The charm of placid pace, in Brahms, is
greatly helped by a new cunning of richly
varied rhythm. In the interweaving of two
waving strains that differ in the pulse of smallest
beat (where one has two, the other three) there is
a gentle clash, a wealth of trembling motion,
with all serenity of separate voices. The melody,
too, is more of song; leaves the staid periods
and soars freely through urgent, even passionate,
sequence of the first phrase, losing in its romantic
guise most of the earlier semblance; and so
through fresh tonal scene:

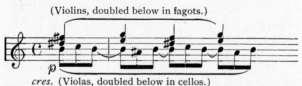

(Violins, doubled below in fagots.)

cres. (Violas, doubled below in cellos.)

But soon the answering motive appears as before and rears a strong climax, and brings us

gradually to the impersonal humor of the first melody.

In the free play of initial motive, we notice the kinship even of this phrase with the former answer,* until it seems that Brahms is all built on the atomic plan, where the whole can be dissected to one bit or motive of central thought. This is wonderfully true of his Second Symphony.

Here the last-quoted phrase in its rhythmic and harmonic variations betrays this basic unity, —finally strikes the first melody, in whimsical rhythmic change of original motive:

(Woodwind, doubled above and below.)

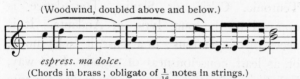

espress. ma dolce.

(Chords in brass; obligato of $\frac{1}{16}$ notes in strings.)

Again the glorious classic grace of Melian Venus. Instead of the old echoes of low strings, the clarinets answer in spirited strain. Indeed, the whole has now a more glowing air of transfigured beauty and more fervent freedom of utterance. At the end of the tune comes the epilogue,—if that can come before the last verse or last act. Freed from staid pace, swinging aloft

---

* See page 339.

on the last bit of cadence to bold Gothic heights,
it seems to translate the cold classic grace to our
warmer Teuton sense, and then commend to us a
final verse of the poem.

Third Movement. The second movement is
certainly the reflective,—that is, it has least of the
dance. In this sense the second and the third are
directly opposed. The third has a distinct dance
swing,—not merely the rhythm of all music.

But what does this mean to us, if it is not
merely a technical matter? It is this: all dances
are national,—of here or there: Hungarian,
Teutonic, Celtic, or Slavic. The dance is
opposed to the pure lyric of Andante. It is
necessarily ingenuous; in a sense, it lacks mood,
or, at least, consciousness of mood. In a way,
it has not the element of individuality for true
mood,—the national sense prevents.

This element is a function of the third movement more than any other. It is naturally the
usual channel of humor; but it need not be. A
dance need not be merry. The sarabande is a
type almost of pathos; the minuet, of stately
grace. The most tender vein may steal into the
Trio of dance, old or new, as of a Bach ga-
votte. A certain barcarolle feeling has here a

special place.   It must be unreflective, of folk or national rather than of individual hue.

If the third movement is looked to for humor, it is certainly not found here, in spite of the *tempo poco allegretto*.   In this respect, of strict category of mood each in place, this symphony is out of the reckoning.   It is possible we may find a humor elsewhere, and thus make good the apparent lack.   We must not forget that the third movement was of old a dance, that the dance became the national channel for pure merriment or profounder mirth.   Technically, the dance is ever in place.

It is possible that the scherzo is too rigidly an element of symphony.   We have seen Mendelssohn miss a footing here.   The scherzo was Beethoven's own typical creation.   It suited his special humor far more than Schubert's.   Indeed, there is no subjective humor of musician to compare with Beethoven's, save Schumann's, and even with the latter the profound sardonic element is wanting.

There is no doubt that, from the traditional point, humor is wanting in this symphony of Brahms, and not merely negatively.   All but the Andante are overcast with sombre clouds. Serenity is confined to the second movement.

Here in the *Allegretto*, with all lagging motion, the step of slow dance is somewhat strongly marked with a beat of the foot that has something of the German *Ländler*, again something of Slavonic in the late deferred accent:

(Strings, aided lightly by flutes and fagots.)

But the gloom is thick overhead, and leaves but a shadow of the dance; even in the second melody, where for a moment we hope for a sunnier light, we have at most the odd shifting mood of first Allegro:

(With waving strings and sustaining woodwind.)

To be sure, after the friendly sequence there is suddenly a cheerful intimate descent in neighboring key of major, merely to be hurried again into the fatalism of first theme, now sung with more poignant feeling by all the treble voices. But in the third is a change of mood. Still in the old uncertain humor, there is much more of joy and trust, though of a timid kind, in the melody with its delicate hesitancy, with just a faint reminder of dance in the pace:

347

This vanishes completely in a kind of postscript of the tune, where all formality of swaying dance is dropped in direct tender appeal, crowned with fervent climax of trustfulness. To be sure, in the rehearsing it is all hushed by the nearing gloom of the first tune. We have heard of a Death's dance. Though there is nothing of the kind here, there is yet a clear tinge of doom, of dim Fate, about the main melody. Once more followed by the second, of uncertain hue, the subject ends in an extended appeal of moving pathos, like a last burst for deliverance, with a final resignation.

Last Movement. Our symphony is thus so burdened with stern gloom that we shall need a strong balance of cheer. Humor seems banished, dethroned from its abode. The only refuge is the *Andante*,—to be sure, of calm serene beauty and assurance. Even there we saw a stress of the one mournful bit of the main tune, and out of it grew the sad second. Though wavering long, it surely settled into sweet contentment. We are used to thinking of the Andante as the true key, its humor as the final mood, leaving to the Allegros a more tempestuous utterance, the first in achieving, the last in the triumph.

We must not forget, however, that in our first movement uncertain fitfulness was really conquered by a clear spirit; the minor yielded at last to the major. We must note, too, the meaning of the alternation in mood of the movements themselves, sombre *allegretto* succeeding serene *andante*.

What, then, shall we make of this barbarous war-tune, ruthless in rough minor, that is softly growling in low violins and bassoons with firm, rapid step :

(Unison theme, doubled in two lower 8ves.)
STRINGS AND FAGOTS.
Allegro.

p e sotto voce.

answered in equally harsh mode and grim, halting pace?

It is certainly all o'ercast, ill-boding for final
cheer. As the melody soars along in higher
flight, among the woodwind, it wings a freer
course, with chance pauses that give new and
bolder rhythm,—again answered haltingly. Now
follows, in strings and lower wood, a phrase in
darkest hues of minor-major, with still a tinge of
war-call as it is heralded and backed by hollow
notes of low brass:

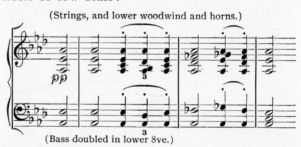

Full of temper as it is, it seems no integral
element, a mere chance strain between verses of

the theme, a certain disputation on the first, mainly on the second motive. Here, by a fine reversing of the answer, is reared upon the modest bass a powerful climax, where, to the halting but insistent inquiry, a broad conclusive response comes marching down in double file from the heights :

(Full orchestra, doubling above and below.)

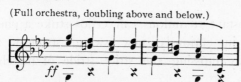

(Continued in inverted bass and treble.)

And here is the heart of the movement, the spot where, conscious striving escaped, a direct thought brings best melody of utterance. Still as the march is kept in striding basses, and violins sound lightly

(Theme in strings, wood and horns doubled below.)

(Rhythmic pace in strings.)

a constant tremulous call, cellos strike a cheery tune in curiously new swing, strongly and broadly crossing the strict stride of marching basses.

All in bright major it sings, and with no trace of sombre shadow. As the air now reaches high wood and strings, it is like brilliant sun glittering

(Strings, reinforced by chords of wood and brass.)

(See page 353, line 6.)

on marching helmets and waving plumes, the

352

vibrant call of trumpets still distantly blended in the war-song.

And the tune has a way of winding through indefinite turns, like constant thread of story or unending line of warriors. Presently a longer curve of cadence appears, and, recurring, soon presses all the verses into its unison strain in full acclaim, leading into a second big climax with similar hammer-thuds :

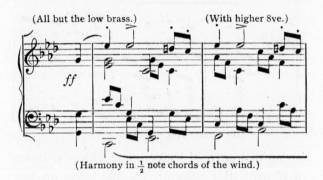

(All but the low brass.)   (With higher 8ve.)

ff

(Harmony in ½ note chords of the wind.)

that grew in earlier crisis out of the answer of main theme. Indeed, throughout, the first motive of the theme gives melodic fibre; the second or answer is bone of contention, meat of discussion. But in the last climax we seem to see the new-gotten phrase stealing over the bass in big broad notes. There is, to be sure, a new thud of accent on the second beat, 'mid richer

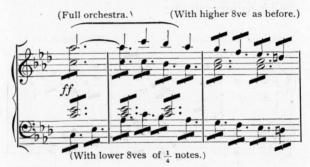

(Full orchestra.)   (With higher 8ve as before.)

(With lower 8ves of $\frac{1}{4}$ notes.)

setting of low tonal background, with new swing of blows. But presently the old stress on first and third re-enters in response. At the height of battle a quick phrase of former bits, doubled in speed, relieves the strain.

Once again the battle rages to the inspiring height, and again, on quicker phrases, tempers down to a semblance of first theme in distant tonal quarter,—but merely for a moment, mingled with other war-cries. Here, again, is a rough snatch of it; there, high in woodwind, a lengthened call of its first notes. At last the strife simmers down to the original tune in the wood, all in the hush of twilight; and now beautiful is the answer, transformed in gait, in speed, and in mood. Almost prayer-like the former trip now sounds in solemn choral notes with hopeful calls:

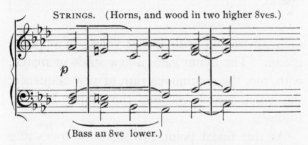

And the main tune goes playfully whispering on, with varying tricks of accompanying figures, that somehow take away the old sting and gloom. Again the solemn cheer of answer; now the latter sings as new song high in the wood, while low violins, like fire-flies, are darting here and there with chance snatches of the subject. The light is mysterious, flickering 'twixt gloom and cheer. Suddenly high strings loudly

sound the solemn strain, and high wood ring out
the quicker snatches:

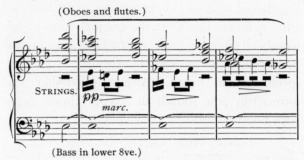

each alternating with lowest voices of opposite
group. The hymn gains a new stride of march,
with, too, the continuous turn of new sequence;
the quick snatch becomes threatening blast of
trumpet.

At this nodal point two sustained tones ring
out alone of the hymn, dimly familiar, while,
below, strings are coursing

on a figure that seems a quick mockery of an earlier slower one. Then, broadly across the quick woof of their motion, here is the solemn second theme, which we thought to have dismissed. It is all a new poetic guise of ancient round of tunes.

Of significant charm is the comfortable conflict of these two paces, the quick triplet playing about the big broad skip of second tune, like a great mountain seen through the laced veil of fleeting mists. So slowly ponderous is the quaint jog of the tune that we do not at first feel the outline, which all recurs as long before, save more freely extended in rhythm and in sequence of tonal scenes, all brighter than before, finally transfigured with blazing halo of dazzling scene and crowned with all-cheering close.

Here is the same rearing of climax on the insistent inquiry of halting fragment, again with the broad conclusive response marching down in double file. Only it is all more assured and exulting. The main theme no longer steals softly into the midst, but boldly rings out on eminent heights. Besides, there is the reversing of tonal scenes, the clear return homeward towards the original regions. This is best marked by the swinging, brilliant war-song, which again comes marching past with the old glittering maze of movement and ever surer air of victory. It ends, as before, with a long curve of cadence, and leads again to the climax of hammer-blows. The whole battle is fought once more, and again, on reaching the heights with a fragment, simmers down to the whole of main melody in mysterious light, and, strangely, in the quaint jog of third tune. Soon it reaches a more familiar spot, and here, amid the same richer setting of background, is that freer flight of the melody, pausing at chance will, as of old.

But the setting is infinitely richer, of deep beauty of wood-sounds, and there is a sense, in the melodic flight, of work done and reward well earned. The strife is all o'er. From this point the whole mood is changed; the feeling is strong of fulfilment, of transfigured purpose. Quicker phrases are merely the placid, subdued company of nature-sounds attending the final conclusive refrain and assertion of theme, now past contention.

So the main melody now enters, losing its old

speed, like chorale hymn, with soft tenderness, ending with a higher strain of new, serene confidence. As the theme mutters again in low bass, —now a little faster,—echoed in high wood, a strain of ancient melody

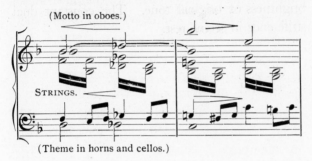

(Motto in oboes.)

STRINGS.

(Theme in horns and cellos.)

gives sweetly comforting answer. It is the motto of the big beginning of the symphony, cleared of turbid gloom, in simple soothing conclusion. The rest seems a mere dying away of the trembling nature-sounds, though there are pauses of solemn chords, and here is a strain in slow trip that soars aloft with strong appeal. We had not thought there was in our second melody of darkest hues such a potency of sweetness and light. Still the pausing chords come. And now the same strain descends from its lofty perch. Though full of solace, it somehow has in the very end a clear tinge of the same flickering mood we saw at the beginning of the whole work, and the same oscillation of light is kept as the basses still mutter the theme through the whispering branches, until all dies away in the clear brightness of original tone. The constant dual strife ends in serene rest.

BRAHMS' FOURTH SYM-PHONY

THE fourth of Brahms' symphonies stands opposed to the others. It has less of the subtle interweaving of basic motive. It seems more of a return to romanticism, freer in scheme and spirit; motion is an element more than intricate design. The harmony, or organic character, is less of visible figures, however obscure. After all, the reappearance of actual motto is not the only test of unity, however minute the phrase may be. There may be most intimate harmony by reason of the relation or contrast purely of the moods of the movement. In a way it is like chemical and mechanical structure. You may start any mechanical separation and approach the chemical solution in the sense of smallest particles; but you will never reach the final constituents. So it may be the best symphonic connection is an invisible one, an inner relation of mood-purpose.

We are struck with the pre-eminent motion

of the first *Allegro* (*non troppo*). It is like getting into a vehicle that instantly is going its delightful pace of speedy journey. The actual tune is secondary :

(Theme doubled in lower 8ves.)

(STRINGS, WOOD AND HORNS.

In fact, the tune lacks rhythmic variation, and leaves the motion supreme with mere tinge of air. It is, indeed, less tune than motion, a thread of movement that becomes more melodic as it proceeds, works itself into song,—a musical story with special episodes.

After the first period, the last cadence suggests the variation of theme in the second, with more fluent note throughout. Towards the end, a jerk of notes, from close of main tune, has much sway :

gets into the bass, goes jolting through the whole chorus, is softened by prettily rustling lower figure.

A firm, assuring conclusion :

moving in its fervor, leads suddenly to the start-ling second melody, of bold, broad, rhythmic curve, that we have a way of finding in Brahms :

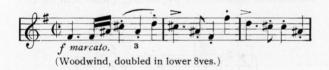

(Woodwind, doubled in lower 8ves.)

A breezy air of resolution is here, not the usual episode of feminine grace that is almost traditional in the second subject of *Allegro*, so that the beginning is but a setting in motion to-wards the more incisive theme. Again there is a sharp jerking motive, which goes driving along between the lines of the smoother, sustained an-

swer, that first sounds in cellos, then climbs to the
heights and holds sway in treble violins:

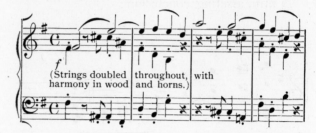

(Strings doubled   throughout,   with
harmony in wood   and horns.)

while the bouncing motive stirs the foam of the
stream of song and returns to the bold swing of
second melody, knocking its uncouth rhythm
against the regular beat, and crashing its relentless
harmonies against the prevailing basic scheme:

(Bass doubled below.)

all an utterance of resistless stress, seeking and
needing obstacles for true progress.

The hostile tide exhausted, the stream runs pelting on in the current of the evener pace (answered between the choirs) :

(Strings, wood; in constant alternation.)

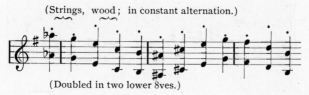

(Doubled in two lower 8ves.)

which takes us back with strange reminder to the very beginning of the first tune, and knits all together in onward drive of action. Again, all is concluded in freer singing strain (built still on the jerking motion) :

(Strings, wood and horns; tune and harmony in 8ves.)

(Bass an 8ve lower.)

but standing on the broad swinging rhythm in triple time that marks the boldness of second theme. It is answered by a strain of softer, more appealing hue of all, in more mincing

(Clar., doubled above in oboe, and below in horns.)

(Strings, *p legg.* sustained by fagots.)

pace ; but, broken only for a moment, it resumes and leads to modest, idyllic bit of tune,
like violet that is the hidden gem of the woods :

WOOD AND HORNS.

STRINGS.

366

somehow with more sweetness than all the prouder blossoms of song, introduced merely by solemn lull of wind, dim call of trumpets, and mystic swirl of strings. After the same ceremony it sings again bold and loud, now echoed by firm call of brass. Apart from our simile it has a flavor of woods in its haunting notes.

Now it rears overpowering climax, tune and call all sounding together, and in the bass the constant stride of even march, until, breaking again into the jerking pace, we return through gradually familiar sounds to main theme as at first. The woodland call has a beautiful way of coming nearer, stronger, and clearer at each new verse, and each time in a new light.

Now the first close (of main melody) has a peculiar charm as it refuses to stray again to strange scene, nestling intimately about the home tone :

(Strings, with sustaining chords in horns and clarinets.)

dolce.

(Doubled below in basses.)

Pretty variations of the subject sing on, which now gambol about and play together.

All the smaller derived phrases show more and more a likeness to original theme, which it were dry to point in detail, varying in speed or changed in outline. Again the sweet nestling in the bosom of the cadence, to be sure, of remoter tone.

The main theme now assumes the guise of first conclusive strain * in sombre minor, and presently rings out in hammer-blows the varied phrase (of main theme), all changed from mild grace to rude quarrel with lower voices in strings, that

---

* See page 363.

come up in contrary figures, all of brilliant
countermarching manœuvre, hostile though ordered, while the jerking motive breaks in from
above in high wood in rough contempt of other
measure :

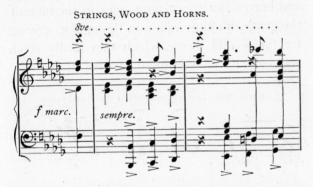

STRINGS, WOOD AND HORNS.

Now the parties in the strings exchange retorts.
All the while the middle voices of violas, allied
with fagots, have echoed on the heels of the
theme, wherever they heard it. So the great
altercation goes on, ever with new alignment of
forces.

Suddenly a hushed semblance of second theme
is whispered in strings, a mere playful phase, the
voices in low strings fleeing in fugual chase across
the scene. Others in high wood pass in similar
view, now against deep background of swirling

strings with the former solemn pauses; vague
bits of the subject are dropped in the wood,
answering in new tonal scene. Again the playful hushed chase in the wood of strains of the
second theme. Now, loud and fierce, strings
and brass shout threatening cries in the tune of
the gentle hunting call, but, through it, striving
for the second theme, which they finally reach
and answer now with more effective strain:

(In woodwind and horns, doubled above and below.)

(In strings, doubled above and below.)

with the broad freedom of triplet pace which is
carried along in other voices and holds its rough
course in spite of main subject, singing in obscure guise in even rhythm. The answer, with
the quicker figure, is a series of tonal perches,
alighting ever in a new quarter with the same
hushed motive:

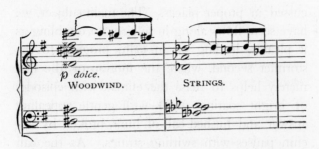

Reaching home at last, the little motive is lengthened and the main theme is heralded in long notes as of motto, interrupted again by long pauses of chords and rich swirling strings.

Brahms has a tendency to make us see bits of the theme even where it is not, like seeing the sun with closed eyes; you hardly know where to stop deriving.

The whole song of the themes begins now, as at first, save at the very beginning, where the first motives are clearly reversed,—as if to show again that the meat is in the movement, not in the tune. Conclusive strain comes as before, but of course the tonal journey is homewards, not afield. This must always be the difference of the first and last parts of the *Allegro*.

The design of the whole is new; we have lost our old order of themes restated and discussed in proper places. The main subject, we have seen, flows along in full course, doubling as it pleases, leading on in calm progress to the stormier second, where the motion of the first merely helps to mass the climax with episodes of bright soaring strain, with gentle appealing answer and hushed call of hunt, broken by solemn pauses with swirling strings. As the call sounds in strong blast, the main crisis is reached on the text of the virile second theme. As the first returns, its own special crisis now arrives on its own motives, followed by a lesser on the second. Hence a short blending of both subjects leads to the last statement, where the full climax of second melody is not allowed.

We cannot but note the difference between the Schumann method of broad, romantic lines, mere connection by contrast and intrinsic relation, and Brahms' minute but concrete kinship of contrapuntal fragments of one pattern. This seems like a new plan for a bigger design, of which, maybe, the poet is to come later.

The whole discussion is not formal, with duly repeated subjects. Rather it seethes in the wake of each, rising to a climax on one and then on the other. The first, instead of leader, is often rather herald; or it forms placid lulls between the storms of the second, though to be sure it has its determined and overpowering triumph.

At the end, indeed, it rises after lesser crisis of second to a last word of magnetic virility and convincing power. But, before, the new answer of second melody* (the first has lost its function in the later stress) has a moment of absolute unanswerable sway.

The main melody then asserts dominance in lordly, stentorian bass. No greater musical symbol is there of complete conquest than melodic possession of bass. In the second line it breaks into uneven pace in insolent defiance. A new height is reached on the short jerk of motive. Twice the fine old conclusion tries its *envoi*. But still echoes and hallooes the first motive of main theme in a frenzy of assertion, and the battle is won.

Ever in kind of rondo fashion returns the first melody; never, as in sonata, is there a good cadence on the second. There is not the duality of the sonata. It is the monarchy of song or

---

* See page 370.

rondo, one prevailing idea,—εἰς χοῦρανος. The second theme, however powerful, is never enduring, has not even a foothold or close of its own, but falls back to the firmer footing of first; the stress of the former is ever resolved in the resistless, placid motion of the latter.

Second Movement. It is a frequent way of Brahms to come through gloom and desert to light and cheer. The best must come last; we must begin with the night to know the day; to fly the highest you must start the lowest. Here, in *andante moderato*, the strangest sense comes o'er us with the strain of horns:

enforced by woodwind. They take us back to darkest edge of doom-tempered world.

As curious fact the tones are of ancient mode, not merely of oldest church or catacomb, but of Stoic Greek song, Phrygian, or Doric.

When enter the clarinets, the gulf is suddenly bridged, the gentle strings sing the same tune, on the same bass, to be sure:

(Melody in clarinets and *pizz.* strings.)

but with all the human sweetness that since those ancient days mankind has learned to feel, and to utter mainly in obedient tones.

But ever the stern color steals across the harmonic scene. The answer, however, has all of the warmer glow of Teuton folk-song:

Suddenly the old tones ring out in the woodwind, somehow less dismal, bolder, ascending in brighter tonal flight. From the height, descending uncertainly, the same sudden warmth of modern cheer is felt again, as the strings again sing the true theme with a new, firmer touch. The answer now comes with more speaking appeal, with more intimate contrast, ending with complete assurance. The second verse is but a freer phase of the first, simple and childlike of humor:

(Strings, with more sustained figure in woodwind; horns.)

buoyant as it gently soars on waving motive in joyous wind, alighting soon with firm tread of sure content in exultant burst of all voices. An answer sings in piping wood:

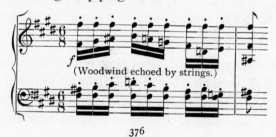

(Woodwind echoed by strings.)

in quaint, quick trip of tones, in shifting prism
of colors, with something of brilliant triumph,
almost of savage glee. It is echoed in strings
and carried higher and stronger, but descends in
solemn strides to the true second subject, all
changed of mood, almost of simple pleading:

(Strings and fagot, with obligato in $\frac{1}{16}$ notes in high violins.)

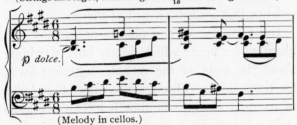

(Melody in cellos.)

which sounds in simplest lines in cellos.

But the accompanying strings lend the special
touch, the high violins of gliding figure, the
seconds of responsive and subordinate strain, all
of richly changing harmonic color. The melody seems to have the Schumann trait of threading story, woven mainly in responsive voices,
when the fagots enter as leaders. Strange how
opposite the feeling in these succeeding themes,
though really of the same fibre.

A speaking force has this latest theme, now
in fagots and strings. At the close an expressive

phrase is handed from voice to voice midst the steps of the tune. But the brief motive soon expands and takes full possession, in echoing and answering voices of the leisurely dulcet cadence that leads back to first theme.

But now, out of the phrases of cadence, has blossomed a figure which lightly hovers, twining about the song of the melody, softening away the harsh lines. Through this contact, and also of its own change, the tune has thawed out its chillier harmonies in serener sunshine of modern experience, and glows with true Gothic love of kind. Striking how music in its modes and harmonies, ancient and recent, thus shows the increasing humanity, the diminishing spirit of destruction, so that the Hercules of to-day must exert his strenuous power all in work of greater blessing to the race, so that a Napoleon ideal of rise and power by destroying action is all fading out of fashion's glamour.

The wonderful magic of music is to reflect this, so that we feel instantly the change of spirit in the change of modes, and know in a flash the inevitable intent of the poet.* Here the transition is absolutely convincing—from stern ancient gloom to modern genial sense of kind—in the poet's varying chords. True, later there is a return to some of the uncertainty, and here rings out the original rough blast of theme. Somehow it has less of chill gloom. It is all in the clear sunny atmosphere of high wood, and there is an electric pulse of accompanying motion above and below. So the sense is bold but hopeful, and soon the theme threads its sequence to clearer tonal light.

And now ring out the sharp clashes of eccentric figure on the quick jerk of the motive, now higher and ever bolder, in keener blasts of the rude theme and ever in brighter flashes of glinting light. The savagery is gone, but the vigor is all there and transfigured. And, finally, the former quaintly clattering phrase raises its warshout once more at the loudest and brightest, suddenly hushing to most expressive verse of the second theme of appealing beauty. It sings first in rich timbre of sentient strings, answered then

---

* If scientific proof is needed, it is at hand in the recent confirmation of modern harmonies by their conformity to newly discovered laws, such as those of Helmholtz.

in full chorus with big sonorous double stride, the air ever a step behind the bass. Once more the strings sing it simply, and the wood answer in touching response from the first strain of main theme, and the clarinets send a sigh from the very heart of it, to which the close (of main subject) comes as truest and surest solace.

In the last word the theme once more sings out in full, as at first; the bitterness is cured in a new way, not softened to modern sense and rounded off, but in its ancient lines transfigured in a true light and verified as a true whole. For the old tones stand as before, but a new base is found for them, and thence a pervading (tonal) light, that justifies and harmonizes all.

Third Movement. A tinge of the old stern mode is in the breezy dash of scherzo song that bursts in big array of voices:

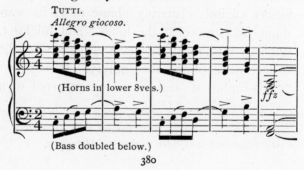

BRAHMS' FOURTH SYMPHONY

It is all vigor typified, idealized, the full sense of freedom, strong and withal a bubbling spring of quick action. In the very beginning there is a type of rock-like power, that gets its secret somehow in a turn of chord that again takes us back for the nonce to grim ancient mode, to the old plagal close, as the schoolmen have it, of the stern Amen, avoiding the soft cadence of modern dominant that slides easily and comfortably to the main tune. Nothing can exceed the bold contempt for all modern smooth trick of chord in the sweep of these primeval harmonies. Heavy fall the blocks of chords in the first phrase of theme, plunging sheer into the resounding deep. Light of spring the answer dances off in chords of curious ponderous grace, where one playful motive is eminent:

(Bass doubled below.)

On sweeps the song with surging figure of after-phrase, in bass:

(Greatly reinforced in full orchestra.)

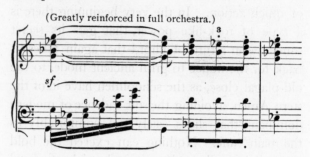

then united in all; repeated with some basic change. In childlike sport the answer now glides along with no heavy chords, mere skipping steps of strings. Another jolly retort is rung between low strings and higher, on simplest phrase from text of main theme, while highest violins are singing merrily on in a skipping answer, and finally draw all the strings in a scampering run back to the main theme, but reversed.

Topsy-turvy it is, basses have the air, the old tune is bass, and it sounds as fine, even merrier. The answer, too, is jolly, upside down. The outer line of tune has, after all, less to do with it; somewhere between the rhythm and harmony lies the magic of the melody. On the answer trips softly now through shades, halting

(See page 382, line 10.)

and groping, when in bursts the cheery song of second theme:

like an old dance or *rigaudon*, where, by way of answer, the wood run mockingly off the scene. The glee goes unbroken; the wood come run-

ning back with the same silly laughter. Then
the dance changes step in mincing pace, de-
murely hushing and slowing with eccentric skip.
Very prettily it is softened down to solemn glide
of pious suppliant, and the tune is hymn .

soon even stern chant, suddenly clashing, vigorous main theme again; but with a new sting
and fire in the dancing retort, finally rollicking
off with a magnificent mocking stride of first
theme in the bass :

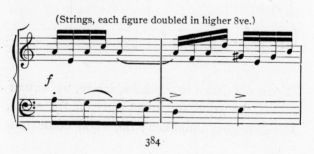

But the answer holds the main flow with slight departure in pace and tonal mood. Indeed, the rollicking motive

saucily rises to learned fugue with real stirring effect, but soon dances off on empty trip.

In bursts on high the first theme, reversed, in full blast, with strange turn of tune and bass; it is answered in loudest strings, all in hollow themal tones. After all, it is mere pranks, playing with the idea of the tune in many phases, fast and slow, and both together; and a little of the answer returns with inverted figure and the bass striding mockingly as before, hushing to softest whisper.

There is ever, even here, that magnificent relevance of all detail, the wonderful logic peculiar to Brahms.

High in woodwind the main theme now pipes timidly as in choir-loft of cathedral; follow the solemn lulls of chords oft repeated. Out of them emerges what seems a new tune of soothing air in simplest lines, ascending and descending:

It has, to be sure, a sense of harking back, but it has all a verse here of its own, a new color of mood. And the further thread is, perhaps, the best as the melody glides simply, far down in murmuring strings,—singing drowsily its answer on high, descending in the wood. So the plan of question and solacing answers continues the discourse, when, on rude blast, breaks in the old after-phrase,* roughly showing kinship with this new strain, the very same tune with some slight changes of pace. Triumphantly it moves out of the moment of confidence and lightly back to the merry tripping of the answer, again with the retorts between high strings and low, on text of theme with all the old scampering back to the full main tune. But this is now inverted, nay, much extended before the answer comes merrily

---

* See page 382.

tumbling with quivering, prancing step, in full, heavy cohorts.

Just as before it hushes again to a lull and again the gay old dance of second theme sings its saucy tune. Instead of pious hymn, however, we are soon lashed (on the figure of a former retort*) into a sort of war-cry, which, mounting in its frenzy, does, at the very top, take on something of the former festive solemnity.

There is the most real simulation in music of actual dispute or discussion. It is, to be sure, reached only in symphony or sonata; and it seems to have been conceived mainly by the German mind. It is one of the highest touches in the art for power, not so much in itself alone as for accumulation and architecture. A real debate goes on here between motion of first theme in bass and a second on high, soon exchanging, of course. It seems to have the seed of unceasing flow. Indeed, it is in the nature of all debate that it must be stopped by force.

A new and firmer assurance is struck when horns take a hand; the tone is friendlier, too, though ever growing in strength. Presently this

---

* See page 385.

works into a hurly-burly on the quick motive, while, above, the wood slowly and definitely affirm the main theme of debate.

And at least one more festive refrain of all the first melody,—big swelling after-phrase, too, all freer now than ever, extending and varying without bondage of mere restatement, ending with conclusive strain of first phrase of main theme.

Finale. A wonderful drive, impetus, has this *passacaglia,** a close thread of connection; everything of beauty is there; the one question still lingers: is it symphonic, at one with the rest? The fragmental working up in short-breathed spurts, almost gasps, like a doomed demon, a Sisyphus, is unlike the symphonic spirit so far as it leads nowhere, to no big climax, cannot in the nature of things, is, in a way, asthmatic, cannot accumulate energy, comes to a height too soon. The whole, indeed, is Titanic; Brahms is ever a Titan. Still, we begin to have glimpses of a form within a form.

It is not the slavish succession of theme or

---

* An ancient contrapuntal form, originally a dance, where the theme recurs in unbroken iteration.

bass that we must keep our curious eyes upon; it is rather the same drive that must come ever in different ways, like the historic attempt of the persistent Scot. To enjoy, you must get away from the idea of ground-bass.

The difference of *passacaglia* and mere variations lies here: in the latter there is no form but constant repetition; in the other there is room for a larger form, within which the lesser can ply its unceasing round. In a sense, the whole is in the first eight bars:

Allegro energico e passionato.

(All the wind.)

(Bass doubled below.)

But, again, you must look as much at the bass as at the melody; if you had to choose, the former is the more typical. Strangely, the theme is really no tune. Successions of notes are not all tunes. There is nothing of symmetry, or responsive balance. It is a mere series of blasts,

all in the wind, too ; more an invocation, a kind
of " Hear, O Israel !", a herald figure of more to
come : " The Lord your God . . ." But see
what happens. In sharp double thuds, this is,
after all, the same strain, though more vehement,
with the strings in strange, slamming, tardy ascent,
on the heels of sturdy calls of the horns on the
same note, clashing with the chords of the theme.

At last something like natural melody seems
to flow in answer :

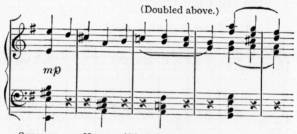

STRINGS AND HORNS. (Theme marcato.)

But it is curiously like fugal theme, repeated before it might blossom into a tune, coming to a
certain climax, too, which, though brief, is fitting.
Before its close, our sense is awake to a dim din
from below. We feel rather than hear the
actual course of the tune in steadily unsteady,
eccentric pace, through all the new fabric above.

Then, in full band, sounds the unmistakable line of the theme high in treble of all the choirs, brass, wood, and strings.

So far is a clear alternation of subject in bass and treble. Now a livelier figure with vigorous, jolting gait sings above the tenor of the theme:

(The theme strengthened by fagots.)

and now a smooth one, very like the last, varied. As the strings surge upward, marking the latest phrase, the wood flow downward, some prettily breaking the even stream with smaller ripples. The persistent bass sings away on the old sonorous text, and still a new motive starts from the last word of cadence, but holds the same flowing pace.

So, on goes this strange progress. Like a stream it is, incessant, unexhausted, unchanging and ever-changing, ever and never the same, gaining, too, and growing in its rough vigor. Only, it has one trait of the sea, as it rises in the climax

(Strings, with touches of the wood.)

espress. cresc.

(Theme in basses, doubled below.)

(See page 391, line 14.)

of each periodic pulse, like the waves advancing in groups.

As each wave has its crest, so there is a slow surging and massing through the series to a fierce height, and soon a lull, where low chords in strings are answered high in the hushed wood:

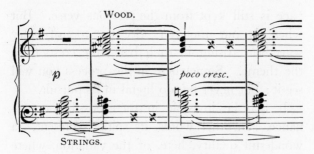

And still, with all disguise, the same essence of tonal idea, rising to its own climax.

After minor strains of gentle plaint and of playful longing, the *dolce* major has a great

(Melody *espressivo* in clarinets, then oboes.)

soothing charm. The melody plays daintily in snatches, tossed back and forth in pretty response between clarinet and oboe, while the viola has started with the foregoing phrase ; the waving of low strings is important part, and the pace is still kept from the previous verse. But where is our motive? See the top of every wave-beat (rising in each bar); the crests form the theme. Somewhere in the process you will see it; but never be too literal in its pursuit.

It may lie invisible in mere possible consonance. In other words, its spirit is present,—a wonderful quality, here, of the variation, where room is left as for invisible, sacred guest, as in ancient custom. You feel the presence in the air largely because you have made room for it. And in so far it is present, too, in your thought, which is all that counts.

Here comes the golden spot, as rich horns sound a deep-toned legend still in quaint halting pace:

(Trombones and fagots with arpeggio figure in low strings.)

The pace throughout changes but in infinitesimal step; the sense of high solemnity forbids. But the melody is warm and full of sympathy. There is still the tinge of the theme in the bass and broken waves in low strings. Again the same melody sings; but more voices enter; all the brass sound the legend, topped by the woodwind, and the melody has greater sweetness and even passion.

Now the first stern chant sounds as at the beginning in full wind; but in the midst a more articulate phrase comes coursing down from high strings as if to give its own terser conclusion.

There is now a new nervous force in the strings trembling with action, as cellos hold the *cantus*, while aloft the woodwind play a melodious countertheme, rising ever more anxiously on ragged, eccentric rhythm, nearer the sun.

Now in lowest basses a new quarrel begins between low strings and high wood. This is the question:

(Strings, wood and brass, doubled above and below.)

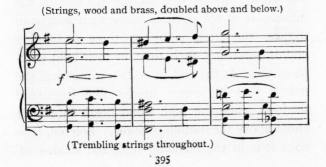

(Trembling strings throughout.)

It is so interesting, vital, mastering, that we do not care to look for the undercurrent motive, though it must be somewhere in low violas. That matter settled, comes a further playful retort between the same groups. You would not guess in this game of hide-and-seek that the theme was staring at you in the first notes of every phrase; but it surely is not good to look too closely for this one literal element—you lose the whole scene. Disputation now merges in the vigorous onward drive, mainly of strings, in nervous triple action, where the wood merely give a clearer tinge to the outer line of theme. The motive is all implied.

Now the motion becomes the most rapid possible under sure control. In coursing streaks, strings and flutes tear up the scale, and the motive clearly stands out on the tip end of the figure. It is not possible more than faintly to suggest the fresh vigor of these succeeding chords, surprising, each time, in their bold completeness. At the end, in sudden whispering, the strings dart in lowest depths like frightened shadows, while the high wood break into clear chord above the rumbling below. Solemn, ominous it is in the blending light and shadow of high pitch of choir of wood, singing in strange odd bits of rhythm against the steady wave of rumbling bass. But the two groups approach; at the end they exchange places and figures.

After the lull, of course, the storm breaks loose the more. Contrary figures start together from the midst of strings, the upper accenting the cantus. High in wood the waving motion continues. Great is the force of these figures, starting their impetus in phrases of two bars, each in magnificent clash, too, of differing rhythm, like companies of horse and foot, countermarching to one big tune or swing. At the end of the verse the motion is more tumultuous, the triplet canter dominates. Here is the phrase which has a familiar sound and surely carries us back to first verse after original statement, with its steady calls of trumpets answered in eccentric notes of theme. Only here the whole force of the band is in action, and the answering notes quiver in nervous triple rhythm.

And still the next verse comes as before, but with much greater force and power of motion. As before, there is a new melody above, answered fugally, and fitting to the lower cantus. We recognize the former course of tunes and phases;

but there is ever newer beauty, richer and fuller grace of motion, the lines of melody are more rounded, the harmonic color is warmer. Indeed, the added wealth of melody so prevails that you cannot swear it is the same verse recurring. The former sequence now grows shadowy. Here, in a beautiful duet in the tree-tops of the wood, seems an inversion of the first hushed verse,* in slow melodious answering calls, while below a former tuneful figure is flowing in the strings. And then this very duet is extended in mellow, speaking song of pervading beauty:

(Wood doubled above and below.)

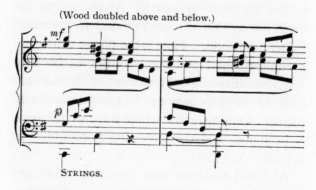

STRINGS.

Follows a gentle verse of new naïve turn in short phrases, each sounding before it seems due,

* See page 392.

while strings stride softly downward in intervening beats :

(Woodwind, strengthened below.)

(*Pizz.* strings doubled above and below.)

In the next the striding strings, in loudest unison, take the lead in time and dignity, and are followed on their heels in canon fashion, while ringing groups shout the chords in the ragged intervals.

The storm has one more verse and breaks out at wildest in overwhelming chords of the brass, shouting the notes of the theme to the heavens, while the strings are coursing down the range of their harmonies like torrents from ever higher leaps. Soon even the waves meet from above and below in the stirred and flooded depths.

And we have said nothing of the Titanic force of these natural harmonies. At the height, for once, we halt in the basic course of theme,—at

the highest note but one; we halt like a brave
horse pausing to leap into the abyss.   Then instead of final descent comes still a new fugal
chase on the last four notes of the theme, ever
rising higher, reckless now of regular rut.   Clashing on the heels of ascending treble comes the
bass furiously pursuing in blind loyalty.   The
strings are ever coursing as before, and the big
harmonies make the heavens ring.   The ambitious climb of Titans heavenward must stop, in
broken chords.

Suddenly in comes an old phrase of the
Scherzo, of retorts on bits of its theme, moving
with perfect fitness in the course of the motive,
and so binding the two cantos together in letter
and spirit.   The end is in final firm song of
theme, though in proud contempt of the strict
rhythm, closing in revel of dance on the quickened trip of the cadence.

LISZT, TSCHAIKOWSKY, STRAUSS

THERE is a danger of impertinence in a survey of contemporary art, in an assured acclaim of the coming classic. So often have the favorites of their day vanished from the lists that it almost seems the master is never hailed in his time. Ever more eminent stands the art of the man whose masterpiece, his great completed symphony, lay buried unknown for ten years after his death. So to-day it were idlest vanity to find in the newly applauded name the latest of the immortals. We cannot know that the work of a modest poet who is now singing, or of one whose song is hushed, may not loom in great dimensions through the sobering years.

All we can do is to note the signs and tendencies and to wonder at the outcome. In the realm of instrumental art a wealth of new traditions must come into the reckoning. Their effect on the symphony (taken as rough type) falls indirectly from another field, of the musical

drama. A history of all music would take cognizance of this school. Side by side the new
tradition has run with the purer art of absolute
tones. The sharp contrast in outer form has delayed a mutual merging of the lines. So in the
days of Bach was the riotous revel of Italian
monody out of all plane with the sublime architecture of the Church school. Almost never have
the symphony and the musical drama had points
of contact in later centuries. Indeed, the *Lied*
is more closely akin to the former. With one
great exception, the composers of the drama and
those who wrote for instruments alone worked
and thought in separate lines, as of different arts.

Of the opera there is here no room for basic
discussion. But we cannot ignore the new
growth that has flowered on the field of the music
drama.

In the middle of the past century came a
wave of recoil, not from the mere spirit,—from
the very foundations of classical masters. A
group of radicals, in various lines of the art, made
common cause of a general revolt from the traditions that stood, broadly, for order or sequence,
—in the creation of rhythmic melody, in the
achievement of genuine harmony, in the cohe-

rent process that fashions a perfect whole. They were impatient artisans in eager pursuit of striking effect. They craved a sensational element in their emotion. They lost heed of the utterance of truest feeling in the quieter process, the " still small voice" of purest art. Yet in their irregular course they lit on sporadic ideas of alluring beauty; they took the world by a storm that almost overthrew a saner balance.

Outer traits of their iconoclasm might be numbered. Melody was sung in fragments; the very name was abolished with the true type. Harmony was largely exploited in bold splurges of strange and sudden group of tones,—harmony that before was viewed as the achieved result of the independent paths of concerted voices. Thus the harmony of Bach was no aim in itself, was ever an incident of a greater polyphony; yet it had an infinite variety that flowed from the vital process of infinite change in the separate movement of voices. Here lies the secret of the inexhaustible harmony of Bach.

A result of the conscious striving for har·monic effect was a certain trait of stereotype, a special almost mechanical mode in the fashioning. Fads and devices have been many in the history

of music, and probably of most art. In oldest
days was the discovered cipher for setting all
words in tones. Later the scheme of false bass,
the parallel motion of voices, started in a certain
way, relieved the composer of all need of harmonic toil, until the Church stemmed its riotous
course by special decree.

Of like nature is the modern use of the extended grace note.* Delay the integral sound
by a neighboring whole tone or half, from above
or from below, and you may give the simplest
chord a new sense of romantic desire. Write it
in more of the voices, and you have transformed
a primitive chord to strangest harmony. There
is no doubt of the real beauty. The harm to
art lies merely in the overdoing. So it is, too,
with the trick of false bass.† And then, to be
sure, the first discoverer has special credit; so it
is, too, with the *faux bourdon*.

Striking is the number of modern motives
where the whole point lies just in this stress of
deferring tone.‡ No doubt, the greater poets de-

---

* The *appoggiatura*.

† Beethoven uses it in the main subject of the Finale of his
Piano Sonata, op. 2 No. 3,

‡ Most of the motives, including the expressive main theme

pended least on the artifice. Many of Wagner's themes are free from it. Brahms disdained its use.

The brevity of the new *motif*, displacing the full cycle of the older melody, gave a tempting scope to this new harmonic manner. Indeed, it may be said, the smaller the separate effect, independent of its place in the whole, the more danger is there of mechanical means. So Monteverde produced a marvellous *furore* with his new *tremolo* and *pizzicato* of strings; and they have remained, though the works have departed.

It was in the lyric drama of Richard Wagner that some of the elements of an ultra-romantic music had their rise; to its exigencies they are expressly fitted. This drama has no place here, save in its bearing upon symphonic writing. Whatever be its outline, from the dramatic point, —of pure musical structure or form there is none beyond the limits of the separate lyrics. And here is involved another of these special traits of this spirit of recoil, that is far the subtlest to perceive.

---

of Wagner's "Tristan and Isolde," are examples; and almost all the themes of Liszt's "Faust" Symphony and of Tschaikowsky's *Pathétique*. See *infra*.

The freedom from form, from the strict coherence of thought in absolute tones, gave the
strongest vent for a newer polyphony, a so-called
counterpoint, much vaunted as the redeeming
symptom of profoundest art,—a thickest mazing
of concerted themes.* This is in the natural
course. The supreme element of high art, with
the frigid name of form, whereby the tonal ideas
grow and merge to significant whole, so that in
the form of music lies its true meaning, acts as
a fetter of other elements. The theme of pure
music cannot have the freedom of the song. It
must be fitted to the stress of discussion and
structural growth, just as the fugal subject is not
a tune. The mystic quality of counterpoint, of
true polyphony, is in its real condition obedient
to the sway of this 'other highest trait of organic wholeness. When that is withdrawn, the
ease of such a massing of simultaneous strains
is infinitely increased. If you may wander end-
lessly, and may stop when you list, you can add
another line of tune above, below, in the middle,

---

* It was reinforced by boldest exploits of the limits of
dissonance, based mainly on the extended license of *appoggiatura* This is seen most strikingly in Richard Strauss's
"Heldenleben." See *infra*.

and so write your "counterpoint" by the yard. But when you must round all in a true cycle of crystal growth and cogent sequence, reaffirmed by the united agreement of all the ideas, you have the testing conditions for true polyphony. Thus it is that the so-called counterpoint of Wagner has so very different a taste from that of Bach or of Beethoven.

Again, we must not forget that these terms *counterpoint* and *form* are not concrete things that you can point to and label by the page; they are qualities that constitute true poetry. There is no guarantee of true form in the outline of sonata or rondo. These are merely types that have served to utter the profound sense of this quality of tonal coherence. It is no mystery. A child will understand whether the parts of a story hang together. The idea is familiar in architecture. Music, that has no directing words nor familiar figures like other arts, needs the test of this pervading sequence of organic structure. There the tonal art reaches its highest. Elsewhere it delights, thrills, startles; there, in the overwhelming consent from all the corners of the document, it tells its resistless message, as of sacred oracle.

It goes without saying that you cannot see form in individual spots. It must come in glinting glimpses of the whole. No matter how beautiful the separate touches, they do not affect the real beauty and meaning of the whole.

Still following our original plan, we will take a direct view of certain works that show the new spirit each in their way, beginning with one of the earliest, Liszt's "Faust" Symphony.

The only clue to a composer's intent, aside from the notes themselves, lies in the title. In this work, accounted by many the greatest that Liszt wrote, the exact title-page is most to the point. For it is all there is of verbal titulation, where, yet, the temptation is constant to find precise correspondence and label of musical phrase,—where, too, it seems that the composer himself must have felt a special meaning in certain motives that recur throughout.

"A Faust Symphony," runs the title (in German), "in three pictures,—in the spirit of Goethe. I, Faust. II, Margarete. III, Mephistopheles, and Final Chorus 'All of earth is but symbol'; for full orchestra and male chorus."

The chorus is not an indispensable part; for, before its beginning, there is an alternate ending of twelve closing bars, in case the chorus is omitted.

Throughout the work certain brief motives form the common text of all the movements. Thus, one is tempted to think of three psychological phases rather than of individual rôles. The German is "*in drei Charakterbildern.*" The meaning of the word *Charakter* is so broad that the title certainly does not forbid our construction. Indeed, it seems very clear, that in *Charakterbild* the stress is laid on the psychological view, as against the mere picture, or *tableau*, as some have translated.

The best test is the music itself. It is evident, however, that we are here in a new kind of writing, with the discursive freedom of opera in pure instrumental music; with the symbolic motive, in place of full-fledged melody; with vehement massive strokes of bold harmonies, instead of the blended song of many voices, of classic art. Without regard to the merits of the newer plan, there is no doubt that Liszt's orchestral works are startling in their likeness to much later music that makes greater pretence of original thought. There is no doubt that Liszt, with all the brilliancy of his *virtuoso* life, is very late in finding

recognition for his composition. There are increasing signs that Liszt was the true author of
much of modern vein that has been ascribed to
others who merely followed in his wake. To-
day, a performance of the "Faust" Symphony,
so rarely heard, must, by the intrinsic music as
well as the impetuous spontaneity, bring striking
proof of a certain prophetic quality.

Where brief motives recur throughout, in opera
or in unsung music, it is impossible not to ascribe
a definite intent of meaning. Where a strain from
a remote movement enters later, here and there,
instead of any other chance phrase, there must
be intended the association of a certain idea that
becomes an intimate element of the poetic content. Once for all,—not to discuss the underlying principle,—the idea of the *motif* is bound
up with that of programme music. Liszt chose
to give no verbal clues. It may seem impertinent to attempt to suggest them. The answer
is that a chance name that may be given to a
symbol may serve no more than as designation, for better study of the music itself. There
need be no intent definitely to translate the
themes.

It is, however, surely urgent for the listener to

mark well these integral elements on which the whole is joined in poetic significance. Their recurrence here must convince us of the subjective nature of the work,—must refute the notion of three objective "pictures," such as the title might seem to mean.

The first of the motives begins the "Faust" movement, *lento assai*:

(Violas and cellos muted.)

It seems to utter the mood of the restless scholar (as we read in Goethe), wondering and dreaming of the true life without the limits of his cloistered cell,—the life that his own narrow quest has all but closed to his view.

Immediately after the motive of wondering follows a second that has the more human impulse of *longing*:

The two alternate, with clear significance, the first growing more restless, the second ever calming with a sense of answered question. The halting sadness is broken by a quicker, active pulse, *allegro impetuoso*, on lesser phrases that are no part of symbolic plan. Rushing to big climax, it is vented in the irresistible drive of first motive. But the following tempest breaks off, sheer, in sudden pause. In the original *lento assai*, the second theme (of longing) appears, for a single strain, to burst with passionate rage into a third motive, *allegro agitato ed appassionato*,—one of those phrases of vehement desire that mark the sadness of latest Russian symphony:

3. *Allegro agitato, ed appassionato assai, molto piu forzando.*

It drives along, in much freer and more extended course than the others, to a height of brilliant joy, where all gloomy tinge is dissolved. But presently, in changed hue of tonal light, above trembling strings, sings our fourth symbol, the most sustained *motif* of all we have so far heard, *espressivo ed appassionato molto.*

It has not quite the serenity of true andante. But there is a trace of contentment,—rather of

achievement.   In the second part is still the sense of longing.   Voice after voice follows as in relentless fugue, and soon the furious (*agitato*) theme is mingled in its career.   Now an entirely new scene moves before us.   *Meno mosso, misterioso e molto tranquillo*, are heard soothing sounds of strings very like the forest notes of the *Waldweben*.   Under their shelter, in mellow mood, the first symbol of longing sings, all transformed to clear happiness of major, winding along in entrancing voyage of tonal light, though it never shifts to the dim gloom of its original mood. Soon comes another joyous phase of older theme, when our second symbol sounds in glad major, *affettuoso*, *poco andante*, in chorus and lower wood-wind, ever answered by delicate strain of strings, *dolce con grazia*. The heart of the movement is here, the true *andante* note is reached of contained bliss, and a little further, a triumphant height, *allegro con fuoco*, that is affirmed with conclusive finality in the big march, *grandioso* (*poco meno mosso*), where the theme is wonderfully changed to an opposite mood of assurance:

(Motive in brass greatly reinforced in wood and strings.)

The first two symbols now sound in responsive duet with martial vigor, crowned with re-entrance of the march. The various motives are woven in rich blending of a canon on the first in the brass, and of the fourth in strings. The masterful pace soon dies down to a lull, when the fourth motive breaks out as at first with the old passionate agitation. This leads to the mood of the beginning, with the themes in their original guise. But, here in the *reprise*, there is more of wealth of interwoven phrase, there is less of anxious gloom in the strife that once again reaches the height of triumphant march.

The close, where the first four motives prevail, begins *andante maestoso assai*, the woodwind and brass singing the first theme over trembling of low strings. Indeed, this very figure of accompaniment seems to mark the return of the old mood of uncertain striving. The theme quickly hurries in pace and darkens in discordant tone, the second hovering about with ominous answer. The serenity is gone, though the strife still rises to big height. The end has the dim feeling of the beginning.

In the second picture, " *Gretchen*," a prelude of melodic duet between flute and clarinet leads to the central theme of the work announced in strings : the unmistakable symbol of the Eternal Feminine, of the words of the closing chorus.

For some kind of understanding of this difficult conception, we must remember several things. For one, this central and crowning melody does not appear in the " Faust" picture, has no part therein. Clearly, then, that canto of the poem (so to speak) is not final; it stops, at

the very least, within the first part of Goethe's drama. Again, the "Gretchen" music seems clearly, like the "Mephistopheles," after all, a mere succeeding phase of *Faust* himself. There is nothing of individual characterization; it is all a subjective drama of a single hero. Thus, there is no trace, in Liszt's setting, of the famous song of Margarete's "*Meine Ruh' ist hin,*" that Schubert has made musically familiar. With Liszt,

we do not think of "Gretchen" individually.
The whole is a beautiful idyl in two veins. But
in the first, with its supreme symbolic theme,
there is interwoven the third of the motives of
the first movement, which had the first sense
of contentment. The second verse of the
"Gretchen" idyl begins with a new melody
dolce amoroso, in strings,—that does not recur as
symbolic motive,—that seems sufficient in the
meaning of its own beauty:

But in the midst of the movement is a dramatic moment, in heightened pace, where the
play of early motives must be of highest significance for the perception of the composer's intent.
And here is the final point that must not be forgotten: all the motives recur here save the first

of all. Thus clearly is that theme confirmed as the restless stirring and vague wondering that is free of the thought of woman.

The second motive—of longing—does play a striking rôle, sounded in brass, against ominous quivering of strings and of harp. Our third symbol—with its more contained sense of hope —now enters in soothing response, *espressivo con intimo sentimento*, in cellos, below muted violins and lightly dropping chords of flutes. Lastly, the fourth passionate symbol sounds in softest strings, *soave con amore*. The interplay of these three themes is ended by the final song of the two verses of the movement, with lesser interweaving of casual motive.

In the third picture, " *Mephistopheles*," after prelude of demonic phrases, the first motive appears in constantly spurring *allegro*. Soon the fourth symbol sounds in new step of dance that has a touch of Satanic mirth.

The second appears, distorted, too, in sardonic trip. But the fourth seems to hold the main sway. It has, too, a more joyous air, and runs to the same triumphant climax as in the first movement, where the " common" time alternates with the dance of six-eighths.

The second symbol has another stranger
disguise, in united hurried pace, where all of
the original longing seems to have vanished.
Indeed, the whole masquerade of motives is
most bewildering, and can be caught only
by a tense concentration. Throughout, there
is a grim playfulness of perversion. It is to
be well noted that all four of the symbolic
themes recur, and another new melody appears. A most spirited verse of the former
march returns, too, where the new figure, of
high wood and strings, is marked *fortissimo
giocoso*.

In the midst of the whirl suddenly sounds the
"Gretchen" melody, symbol of the "Eternal
Feminine." Though the stormy strife breaks
loose again, the demon element has vanished,—
as before a sacred symbol. Once more the
original cycle of themes leads to triumphant
march, and the end comes with unbroken ring
of joy,—the end, that is, of instrumental symphony. But this is, after all, a mere substitute
for the bigger ending with male chorus, who
sing, *Andante mistico*, to the accompanying
"Gretchen" motto, the closing verse of Goethe's
"Faust":

LISZT, TSCHAIKOWSKY, STRAUSS

> " All passing things
> Are symbols sent :
> Here the Inadequate
> Grows to event.
> The Indescribable,
> Here 'tis done,
> Th' Eternal Feminine
> Leads us on.''

Thus we see that in Liszt the close coherence and sequence of musical ideas, and the resulting structure and form, give way to a highly thoughtful play of brief symbolic motives, in a plot of external conception. The whole work becomes a tonal drama, lacking only words and the visible scene.

It is perhaps curious that among classic symphonies—the highest form of music, that may correspond to the drama in poetry, and that may be said to present a kind of view of life of the composer—there are no tragedies. In poetry the tragic seems the native element for the boldest flights and the deepest questions. Now either there is no such analogy between music and poetry, or composers have been strangely conventional. One difference in the art is this:

dramas, like "Hamlet," even "Œdipus," are tragedies in outer event. Music has none of these,—
that is, pure music. It deals only with the moral
state, the sentient, or emotional condition; in
other words, it is purely subjective (though there
are varying degrees of objective association).
Now music in this sense cannot afford to be
tragic, though in a wider view the word might
be applied. The Fifth Symphony is quite as
tragic as the Book of Job, and very like it in
intrinsic content. Here, as in almost all the
great tragedies, there is a moral recoil from the
" arrows of outrageous fortune." This, in the
symphony, is typified in the triumphant *finale*.
In the tragic drama the worst physical ill that can
befall is not the real end, after all. Death, not
even fate, can touch a man's soul. A symphony
that ended in the tragic note would be darker
than any plot of poets. So of this kind of
tragedy that mean complete surrender to despair,
there are in art few, if any,—none among the
classics. Goethe's "Faust," in the first part, is perhaps the nearest approach. *Macbeth* suggests it.
But the hero of the drama is, after all, not the
real *ego* of the poet; the view is never purely
subjective, certainly not in the same degree as in

the pure lyric, or as in music. The tragedy of the drama, once more, is largely external, not moral. But in music, where there are no events, the hopeless tragic note means a surrender, and, in so far, it is, in a certain sense, immoral. Even the Sonata Pathétique ends in a frolic. All the classic symphonies end merrily. There is ever a scherzo after the funeral march in sonata and symphony. It is, therefore, not strange, after all, that there has never been a tragic ending before Tschaikowsky's *Symphonie Pathétique*.

It is significant, not merely as a philosophy in itself, but as the burden of art. The emotional content of art is limited to the feelings which make for a better state. Murder cannot be the theme. There are no patriotic songs save of self-defence. " *Böse Menschen*," say the Germans, " *haben keine Lieder*." So the gospel of despair is surely very near the limit of the musical realm of subjects. Still, truth is the highest object of all, so Tschaikowsky would certainly answer.

There is a consistent sadness blended with tense passion throughout the symphony. In Adagio the bassoons begin an expressive characteristic motive:

against a hollow chord of the basses. Later in a chord of low strings, *Allegro non troppo*, echoed by woodwind, it has not lost its sadness; it returns in various haunting guises. An episode follows in light flitting figures, catching each other in alternate chase in a kind of strained gayety, dropping, after a climax, by vanishing steps into *Andante* song of speaking pathos:

The first motive, repeated, is answered by a phrase highly typical of the new spirit in its passionate quality.

(Air in cellos, doubled above in violins.)

(Strings, with harmony in brass.)

There is no mistaking the blended beauty and desire. This leads into a responsive duet between flute and bassoon, on a new motive:

with a *saltando* rhythm in the strings, other voices joining with more sustained answering figure, suggesting the song into which they lead, again in *Andante*, now with enriched quiver of rhythmic setting. The song, too, comes to a climax in the pure lyric manner. Indeed, the drama is, as it were, full of monologue. The action halts, the other characters disappear, leaving the hero ever alone to pour out his griefs (all in the *Allegro* chapter, too); anon the drama is forced into renewed action. After one of these climaxes the melancholy motive of the introduction enters in *Allegro* on the **G** string of the violin with a fierce obligato (*feroce*) of violas, working up with great animation, though always in sombre mood in the quicker extension of theme sustained in tempestuous sequence :

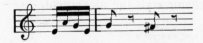

In the midst of the storm, redoubled voices in high wood and brass peal forth a mournful blast, a varied line of the passionate answer of second theme. When the paroxysm has abated, a solemn fateful chorale sounds in the brass that soon rises into a new tempest of lament, that dies away in the wail of first theme. In this final song of main theme is none of the lesser motive.

Instead, insistent reiteration of the motto alternates with the broad fateful strain, descending in

(Full orchestra, theme redoubled in 8ves.)
(See page 425, line 18.)

the brass. The two meet in a blended song of
deep tragedy. A purely lyric plaint of the
second theme ends the movement.

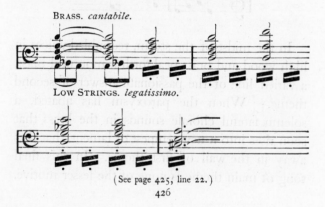

BRASS. *cantabile.*

LOW STRINGS. *legatissimo.*

(See page 425, line 22.)

The second movement, *Allegro con grazia*, is on a dance-like theme of whimsical rhythm in 5-4 time:

Allegro con grazia.

mf

(Cello theme with chords of *pizz.* strings, horns and wood.)

introduced by cellos and taken up by chorus of woodwind. The second melody is but a counterpart of the first, all in simple song form:

The middle verse—*con dolcezza e flebile*—is a quaint blending of the strange dance with a tearful strain.

The third movement is most spirited, almost feverish in the tonal scene that first greets us. To a fitful, elfish play (of alternate strings and woods) —like will-o'-the-wisp in indistinct laughter and *con dolcezza e flebile.*

(STRINGS, WOOD AND HORNS.)

(See page 427, line 9.)

mockery—there is presently added a call as of a bugle, in simplest outline, but ending in a strange barbaric turn, new to us of western culture, of mingled defiance and fatalism :

With all the wildness there is no note of joy. At first it sounds more hopeless than frank lamentation,—a kind of sardonic laugh at personal damnation. The first approach to relief, to a sense of *terra firma*, is where related melody works its way to the major, followed by brilliant flashes of modulating chords. Though wild to savagery, they have lost the uncertain, unsane feeling. They come near to exultation and seem

(Strings, the theme doubled above.)

(See page 428, line 9.)

the true (though not the intended) high point of the symphony. And, strikingly, on its return the first flickering play has a more hopeful tone.

Bright melodic snatches now spring up and illumine the purpose, all to the original murmuring background, though now with lighter hue. And rougher, ruder strokes come in brutal unison, and yet they are looking towards the

light with fine glimpses of it. We are tense as
to the outcome. Through hushed murmuring
of woodnotes comes to the ears gradually the
old call, and still the turn at the end is terrible
and barbaric, though with much softened surroundings, which soon affect the whole. Above
all chime high solemn tones of the wood, and
all rises to a big climax—not of despair. And
now comes the fruit of it. The strange ominous
turn of the call has blossomed into a graceful,
human melody:

CLARINETS AND HORNS.

(Strings, doubled above.)

And so all is well with the world as yet. Presently, after a stern call in united chords, comes an answer of light witchery, from playful siren figures in the woodwind against low droning of strings. We must beware of the too sensuously beautiful, which is always closely akin to fatalism and despair.

Thence we return to the melody which has developed from the trumpet call. Now the figures re-enter, as at first (by good old sonata rule); but the herald call has lost much of its ominous sting, for we know where it led to; we cannot be frightened again by the cry of wolf. At the end, through all its hues and shades, we fall into a clashing strife, as the call, in its worst phase, is hurled from all sides in hardest clangor. If it is not demonic, it is certainly barbaric. What is joyous to one, shocks and frights another. Barbaric it is; for presently it leads to a triumphant pæan on the full-blown melody with all the accoutrement of victory.

To some it may seem, for inherent elements of highest purpose, that the composer ought to have stopped here, or at least to have closed with this as final word.

Adagio lamentoso is the mood of the last movement. It is all a recurrence to one cry of grief, in the strings, followed by a dull note in the wind:

Adagio lamentoso.

STRINGS.

There are extensions of this theme (especially one, where the last note is delayed from above), and other melodies, all of great beauty, especially one in *Andante* (in strings), ever closely echoed below in the basses:

STRINGS, WOOD AND HORNS.

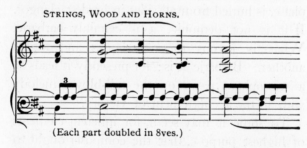

(Each part doubled in 8ves.)

while the horns throb in constant time and tone. And yet it is a mere foil to the other. Nothing can exceed the terrible beauty of its anguish of regret, which grows fiercer at each refrain. We can now see why it must come last, for its own fullest self-expression. It could not be consoled nor tempered ; the tears would not run into smiles.

A reason there must be for a choice, for final word, of a work that is not a symphony. The music of Richard Strauss, so richly charged with the influence of the school of Wagner and Liszt, offers too tempting a significance to resist. The manner and process are here that must sooner or later enter the symphony in its broad sense. Even if Strauss himself does not fulfil an obvious promise to advance to an instrumental work of poetic breadth and profound art, his striking exploits must affect every coming work of value. Moreover, his peculiar merit, as we shall see, is that Strauss is clearly leading towards a reconciliation of warring tendencies. As Brahms, by the temper of his inevitable attitude, firmly eschewed all contact with a contemporary school, his work is in separate lines,—which will in no wise disparage its greatness. The younger writer shoulders all Wagner traditions that may be digested in the art of absolute music, and cheerfully sets himself the task of forging the fitting mould, of fashioning bottles to hold the newer wine.

All the overtures and other orchestral tone-poems of Strauss may justly and broadly be viewed as essays in the wider plan of form and structure. How great is the need of such change does not belong to the present book to discuss. It must depend on the proven worth of these newer elements: in the main, of the brief motif-symbol; of a certain luxuriance of massed themes; of a special device of harmonic and melodic effect. They have been already discussed; they must vary in value; some are clearly ephemeral. Least of all doubt there will be of the permanence of Wagner's masterful strokes of orchestral color. One thing is absolute. True coherence of the tonal thought, a pervading sequence, that make the complete structure, will never be lost so long as there is a vital art of instrumental music.

It will be well, then, to take a glance at the last work of the most radical composer of the day, who, whatever be his merit, has somehow centred the expectation of much of the musical world for the latest idea in tones. Our simple plan will be at once the most direct approach and at the same time its own severest test. For all is new, the very **A B C**; the nature of themes; the process of their treatment; a vast field of undreamt clashes of tones; so that, at first, pure cacophony seems to be an equal means with true harmony. There need be no prejudice towards a final verdict; for opinions are bitterly divided, and, moreover, the startled world can have as yet no estimate of so youthful a living poet.

"A Hero's Life" is the title,—tone-poem for full orchestra. The word *symphonic* is not used. Forthwith, in lively swing, the heroic theme is announced in free declamation, with a mere stray strum of chord, as of old troubadour:

(In stirring motion.)

LOW STRINGS AND HORNS.

It is all rhapsody more than melody, where three parts are striking: the first for a broad, graceful sweep; the second for a most bizarre, quick turn of notes, where the lack of smooth sequence jars the ear; the third, where from on high the motive descends big-stressed in whole steps, reckless of the natural tone. When the final height is reached, we seem to see the second phrase, of strange run, in constant sequence, with response, to triumphant end:

Scarce has the theme started anew with resounding suit of rhythmic vassals, when a new scene sweeps all heroics aside in a trice, and amid rich languor of soft murmurs of whispering harps and strings the high voices sing a dulcet plaint of vague phrase, while lower voices start the more fervent song of second theme. Quickly even this light has changed to another hue, as a third melody, of brighter spring, rises like answer to its forerunner.

The woof of languishing song winds its sweet tenor, ever with new flashes of tonal light.

STRINGS.

(Reinforced and accompanied in wood and harps.)

(3d theme, with added horns.)

(See page 436, line 15.)

Here is one difference from older poetry. You do not wander into slow changes; they come upon you as by sudden shift of total scene. There seems here less of infinite art, more of the rut of recurring device.

As all but the fervent theme remains, there is almost the strife of fugue, the voices rising in higher curves towards a bright empyrean, where the heroic theme now rings a blast. But again the later melodies interfere, first the brighter answer that seems to fit either mood. Here is a clear struggle of languorous beauty with heroic resolve; unmistakable is the quick chase of expressive strain and the spring of action. When the former has almost conquered, the heroic drive, that was lulled, breaks into lusty strife with the siren song, that seems itself to grow fierce in the fight. We feel the growing triumph of the virile theme, in succeeding burst of great beauty. And yet at the height is not the original type of pure vigor ; it is the bright answer of later tune, that seems the tonal idea of joy against the earlier action,—Apollo or Balder against Mars or Wotan. The lesser figures play about in a verse of exquisite delight, that has merely deferred the full course of first motive, ending on high in trembling pause of chord that strongly leads towards the main tone.

Here is one of the main surprises of this youngest music, where mere boldness seems alone to capture our approval. It is really, for all purposes of first hearing, a rough and scraping war of noises ; nothing like it has ever been called music. Indeed, the very directions for the players show the intent, borrowed as they are from hostile sounds of nature. And yet we cannot condemn. After the first rebellion we do feel the subtle *rationale;* it is like a demon mockery of playful harmonies, grim spectres of sweet gambols. Clearly the intent is symbolic, by a certain objective figure. It is not the mere wail of despair. The figures are a mere foil.

It is not the idea of such cacophony that is new, as its actual and abundant use. In earlier days Scarlatti wrote a "cat's fugue" on the theme of scampering chase across the keys. Theory sets no limits to the tones of a phrase to safe-guard the beauty. It is again from a subtle point that form is seen to do this, to hold the right balance. Any theme will do ; and in combina-tion the laws are few and negative ; even they are shaking on their ancient base. In contrary motion of clashing strains there is no rule that one need fear. But, of course, there may be no gain of beauty. The mere freedom from theoretic fault insures no progress. Complaint will all come from an absence of beauty, not from trespass of rule. Art cannot be mastered by a criminal code.

The sense of beauty is so much in the intent, the hidden sequence of idea, that in apparent chaos lie the greatest resources for novel strokes, where the final solution of harmony proves the aim and the striving. All the progress of the art has been gained by such raids on hostile sound. Order and reason have redeemed the wilderness.

It is not that the end justifies the means; but the dissonance, type of evil, is seen as a mere temporary departure from the harmony, type of good, to which it ever tends.

In so far as cacophony slowly gains the hue of tonal color, does it find a basis of beauty. Is there such an intent here? The desert runs on for long stretches of wildest waste. The only reason, it almost seems, can be such as is found in the drama, where music is often used as external, mechanical means. Demoniacal humor shines in the grisly perversion of that strange run in original theme.

One thing is certain. It would not be fair or true art to have a whole scene of chaos and ugliness as a foil to a following scene of beauty. Such an end of cacophony does not count. But there is here, it must be admitted, a slow-growing undertone of clear color. The more we hear, the less we rebel,—a strong redeeming sign. And so the sense of boldness takes captive our remaining remonstrance.

The resulting peace sounds in the expressive flow, instead of heroic drive, in minor of main theme, blended with a varied phrase of yearning song of the second, poised over harmonies of gorgeous, languorous beauty. A phase of the quick motive comes to give a new spring and a fervid crisis with cadence of pathos. The demon perversion of heroic idea returns for a brief shadow. Then the first theme slowly lifts itself from the passive glamour, and throws off the languor and the demon pursuit in desperate bursts of the strange run of quick notes.

Suddenly a little tune of childlike joy (that gets its cheery jingle from the end of third theme) rings out, clear of all strange humors and modern hues.

(Redoubled in full orchestra.)

From this point is a long reign of fantastic monody. There is a sharp succession (in unaccompanied solo violin) of short melodic outbursts, in all kinds of swiftly changing humors. They seem like whims, or shadows of moods, that come as tempting visitations, and so stand out from the main text of subjective emotion. Again, the mere directions help to enlighten the place. The lively joy we last saw, is followed by a sentimental phrase *much quieter*, that later turns

to one of *hypocritical yearning*, then glides into a jolly fling. Ever and again in the midst of these fleeting visions sounds a motive as of peace and solace in full choir of hushed chorus, that slowly

unfolds a growing sequence of lyric song, in various ways. One of these impish phrases was *flippant;* then after the reassuring word comes a strain, *tender, somewhat sentimental,* then an *insolent* turn. So, with the quieting phrase between, they run a rich gamut of humors, *sedate, playful, amiable, jolly again, faster and more raging, suddenly quieter and full of feeling, insistent* and *soothing, angry, scolding, tenderly expressive.* The quieter motive hovers throughout and finally ends the strange chase of elfish moods in full harmony of trembling strings and harps that softly glide or boldly twang. The song has grown to the full length almost of traditional tune. The monodic strains were not all different, some recurring. Of these, several are now treated with much fulness. You might safely say, in the rough, that it is all the heroic spirit proving itself through a chain of experience.

The languishing motive (last quoted) now in turn grows to enchanting bloom of melody, and still the soothing strain plays about. The episode ends in the passive phase of heroic theme, again in minor, again followed by the brief demon play of mocking sprites, with an expressive farewell.

A new figure enters, a fanfare of treble trumpets, in rough and vague harmonic call, that seems very slowly to waken the sleep of the hero. In a long struggle, various of the older chance strains are flitting in teasing chase, in uncertain light. Roughly the martial mood breaks on the sentimental,—at each big rhythmic beat, relentless. Neither can be said to prevail; but the mere strife is a triumph of the martial idea. The languor has vanished.

Still a new phase, heralded by strum of low basses, following the roll of drum, in firm step and liveliest pace. There is no missing the demon theme. But the old bedlam is not here. The theme has the order of rhythmic pace. The sounds are drawn out in the semblance of tune. There is no chorus of imps, each to out-din the other. Though the sense of unearthly tones remains, there is an agreeing harmony, but for one terrible blank at the height of the tempest. Here in a quick chase of chords the pursuer (in the woodwind) has caught his lingering foe (in the strings), in a horrid clash, where the beauty and reason of each is all destroyed. On goes the rough ride of eerie phrase, ever haunting the border of strained sense.

What is this mystic symbol, of shrill and ominous mirth? Whatever be the meaning of the poet, we know that there is here a certain rescue from chaos, a redemption from the furies. Elsewhere in Strauss is the haunting of this goblin humor. The line is here crossed from mania, however wild the riot. There is in latest music, markedly in Strauss, ever this element.

It is a modern vein of Scherzo. A rough line of descent is here from the sardonic fancy of Beethoven. In his Fifth Symphony was a like mood in its place in the general plot.*

The gnome-like phrase has given the main theme a new fillip, though still coursing in sombre minor. When the mocking phrase stops, the wild strain of treble trumpets enter the din. Suddenly all is resolved in the sweet song of the languishing tune, that now soars on new and prouder wing. Recurs the chase of grim sprite and conquering beauty, while the main theme is master in the bass.

With all the joyous spring, the strife is not over. Indeed, in this, the glory of heroic idea, the phase of stress must be present, the very native breath.

The earlier discord of treble trumpets seems somehow more grateful with the sense of brightening triumph; even the mocking phrase grows less inharmonious. That third motive of principal theme, in steady masterful stride of even whole tones, is now eminent, in antiphonal chorus of horns and of lowest brass. But the hero

---

* See Vol. I., 3d ed., pp. 166–169, 226.

gains no easy dominance. Once more the demon
plays his impish gambols, now in canon of several
voices, while still the struggle continues of masterful stride, and of the first heroic strain ; ever
the graceful theme comes to shed the peace of
its beauty.

Once again that jolly jingle breaks in, close
woven with an extended line of the graceful
phrase, and is answered with irresistible power by
the return of soothing legend,—wonder of wonders—in simplest cadence of original tone. Indeed, the eternal maze of motives, without clear
tone or rhythm, gives a new sanction of contented delight to the firm ring of clear chord. It
seems a type, this refreshing return to order, of a
like triumph in the whole art, in tune, tone, and
rhythm.

A sharp line is thus drawn to the long conflict ;
a new turn is marked. We are sure of the sur-
vival of heroic phrase, as it now sounds out in
full career. When we await a like return of the
second melody, we are met by the beauty of a
new idea,—new, yet most fitting. A greater
relevance may thus lie in a strange figure. We
have seen in Schumann the *envoi* of melody that
sums the foregoing in new beauty. Recurrence

(Very expressive.)

(Part of 2d theme, out of a mass of combined motives.)
(See page 446, line 23.)

of themes is not the only means. Indeed, it is in the nature of true coherence that it can never be said to lie in this prescription or that. Its subtle magic is never assured by mere conventions.

The whole texture is woven with crossing skeins of this expressive phrase in a song of moving fervor, closed by a verse of main theme. At this late point a mazing wealth of new melody keeps rising to baffle the quest of themal plan and meaning. One new pathetic strain grows out of another, as if eager of a single hearing before the end.

We seem to see in Strauss, to be just, a vein whereby melodies are developed in separate phases, out of mere earlier germs. The beautiful line that begins the farewell, is a striking type. There seems here a thought of a new plan of inner coherence, with its chain of blossoming tunes, each growing out of the other.

STRINGS. (Slowly.)

Molto espressivo.

(Harmony in horns and trombones.)

(See page 447, line 16.)

Again there seems less stress on actual theme than on a whole group, singing together or in close suit. So the old theme of joy is surrounded by a thick clustering bevy of newest song. Later, in closest twining, of old and strange phrases, we seem to have but a richer vein of the second phase, that before was cut off. And there is still a return to a mad fury, revelling in the thickest fray and fugue of the harsh run (of

448

main theme), where one turn of chord is like the last drop of bitterness.

Final peace comes in a purified mood of heroic idea, in soft pastoral guise. The soothing and the languishing motives sing once more before the last word, of profound pathos.

We have seen that Liszt yielded to the full sway of the fragmental theme. Tschaikowsky, too, made here a strong though not a complete concession. We shall see how Strauss wonderfully links the new and the old idea, and by the plan of melodic growing from germs points a way back to normal art. Of all three, however, the Russian shows in these motives the highest creative power.

The lack of strong-knit musical structure in Liszt (as well as in Strauss) is explained, it cannot be justified, by the special title or purport. All three poets are essentially lyric, though in the symphony the profoundest temper ought to come in play. Series of scenes flash upon us,—lyric plaints, with intervening tempests on themes that have often nothing to do with the plot. Of all three, Tschaikowsky has most sense of outer form. But of close cogency he has almost none;

a sensational riot of passion forbids. With him
fluency takes the place of coherence. But mere
fluency is no surety of clear structure. The
Russian symphony is really an impassioned, impetuous rhapsody. Only there is so easy an
abuse of words. For, the ferocity of passion is
not a measure of depth of true feeling, of a real
intensity. That is a truth the age needs most to
learn. The frenzy can come as well with shallower themes as with the great,—it will come in
improvisation as soon as in the quiet retreat.
We must not seek in unpremeditated art the
supreme mood or mode. Rather is meditation
the surer channel of lofty and lasting truth.

Perhaps the most eminent trait of Strauss is a
freest use of discordant sound, so that he might
almost be dubbed the Poet of Dissonance.*
In the boldness of harmonic touches, whether in
the single motive † or in the group of themes,
he carries the use of delayed note to an undreamt degree; yet both he and Wagner are

---

* We have spoken above, in the course of the *Heldenlied*,
of a rational view of dissonant tones.

† A good example is the languishing motive of the monody,
quoted on page 442 The delay is by double note, that
gives an eerie clash of dual harmony.

here free from mere slavish dependence. In varied flashes of rich harmony Wagner must stand alone of all his school. In his noblest moments of polyphonic climax Strauss completely recalls, if he does not surpass, the older poet.

Indeed, the more the harmony is earned, the less it comes by sensational (and often mechanical) flashes, the truer the art and the beauty. To speak boldly, harmony is not a primary aim; it is the mere dress of a tune, or the single vertical view of the polyphonic woof. It is, in truth, impertinent to make of harmony the chief display. We have spoken above of a rational view of dissonant tunes. Strauss may be said to have carried the harmonic manner of his school to the limits of entrancing beauty and of harshest bedlam. Yet, in all truth, we must instantly add,—a mere figure of speech and the kind of figure that easily lies. For bedlam is just what these clashes are not. It is not a mob of fortuitous sound. An harmonic basis is ever present, however faint. There is hardly need of saying that Strauss has never crossed the bounds of ordered sound.

The boldness of Strauss here lies in the strained extension of older harmonic idea. Yet it is this the path of each new tonal conception. There is no chord that has not a reason rooted in purest science. But the poet dreams the chord first; the reason is afterwards seen. It is in the lines of adornment, delay (of true note), elision, and even subtler feat that the future field is without limit.* Each newer idea begets a fresh group. So Strauss has found his own vein of the romance and humor of a quasi-cacophonous sound. The one danger of the question with Strauss, from a broad view of art, is how far he may lose the whole beauty and meaning in a conscious stress on special effect.

Of high promise is Strauss's own way of

---

* This, to be sure, is to speak of mere harmonic tinkering. For, the infinite ideal lies rather by the true polyphony, that needs no special device. In the boundless crossings of many concerted voices, it finds a natural path of endless new delights. Purest algebra will show that where all the voices sing in independent lines, the harmonic permutations must vary far more rapidly than where one voice holds the melody and all the rest move in a single mass. As elsewhere in the world, the conscious pursuit is barren. In counterpoint the abundant harmony comes of itself, unsought. So counterpoint has ever found the chords ; harmony has merely recorded and repeated them.

having the motives grow, in separate phases, to slowly extended melody. Here he not only transcends the limitations of his school, but he points an original line in the growth of pure musical form. We must never forget that true form is a quality, not a prescription. It is not at all needful to write like Mozart or Schumann. The special value of Strauss is here a true and original sense of intrinsic musical structure. If he would go a step farther, would extend his budding themes in pervading sequence, would restrain an enamoured delight in single sporadic flashes, would eschew the extravagant massing of motives that are not thematic, he would utter a true poetic meaning, in clear homogeneous beauty.

The genius and temper of this radical group all inclined to single effects. Where these are fragmental and often mechanical, the danger is that they will live without the works themselves, like the tremolo of Monteverde, and so the poet be cheated of his immortality. And there is, somehow, no patent of smaller exploits. Even Wagner's harmonies he did not really invent; they are all to be found in Bach. But he did combine them with wonderful lyric touch in fragmental strains of exquisite beauty. This harmonic process Strauss has even extended. But alas! the jumble of pretty effects is like the display of toys in the window.

We have spoken before of the wild error: that sounds might be massed in irrational chaos. But the principle holds quite as true of the rearing of phrase in the whole. It is all the same need of irresistible sequence. Once for all we must never yield to the rough cry for unbridled license to please the mob. There is always a mutinous band in art that mutter for the abandon of all law,—that want the sweetness without the light. There art suddenly tumbles from highest worship to lowest orgy,—a farther fall than Satan's; from light to darkness; from clear vision to chaos; from reason to madness; from true feeling to bestial passion. One who could thus profane the highest temple were a traitor to art.

It is here that our modern world suffers the lack of courage of critic, who has ever an eye for the time of surrender. It is here there is need of true watch-dog, who will boldly assail the false prophet,—who knows the weakness of his own people. Even if they scoff, he must stand his ground. One great German figure still towers to show the reality of type.

Finally in the broad view there is no room for complaint. Art will run its zigzag course, of new experiment. Genius is not a matter of schools. It will break out in varying utterance. There is no need to disparage the individual poet, in pointing mistaken directions. We saw, before the beginning of secular tonal art, how a new plane had to be started. The ground was broken with artisan toil and rude trial. A great descent there was from the high style of Bach to his son's graceful pieces of *salon*. We can hardly imagine the exploits of the modern school embodied in the sonata. As, of old, the pure traditions were never lost, were carried on in concurrent lines, so the ideals of form and cogent sequence were preserved in the later phase by a Schumann and Brahms. Thus we may view the Radicals of our own day as a group who have widely enlarged the resources to be embodied in future works of art.

APPENDIX

BERLIOZ'S FANTASTIC SYMPHONY

A N account of the programme idea, alone in the field of the symphony, would begin with Beethoven's Pastoral. Next in time, and very like in plan is Berlioz's Fantastic Symphony. The whole design, in both these works, appears most clearly in the light of those graphic touches, of thunder and rain, of shepherd notes and funeral march, besides the full list of titles for each scene. By the side-path of such association, the mimicry of nature-sounds and other chance convention, Beethoven led and Berlioz followed to a lower level, that does not lack its lyric beauties, though they do not make the beauty of the whole. If the true base of symphony is of pure tonal meaning, there is no avoiding a surrender in the resort to nature-sounds.

A very different, indeed the highest kind of programmatic art we have seen in the works of Raff, where, with less pretence, a simple poetic subject is treated with main stress on the feeling.* And so in Mendelssohn's symphonies there is an aim to utter a national idea by purely musical means.

The "Faust" symphony of Liszt has the new device of brief motif. To discuss its value as pure tonal symbol would lead us far astray into the whole question of modern music-drama But, granting the full symbolic power of the motif,

---

* See chapter on Raff and Mendelssohn.

APPENDIX

without a kind of special courtesy of agreement, we have seen an inevitable clash of basic plan, as the play of motives bars the true inner structure. The real meaning of music lies in its form by natural growth ; the dramatic play of symbolic fragments, telling the tale in the literal sense of the ideas for which they stand, cannot agree with the former plan. It were like telling an epic in two languages at once.

The Berlioz Symphony, in some ways, to be sure, the forerunner of the later Radical school, does not use the strict *leitmotif*, though it has the leading melody of special association.

Interesting, of course, is the preface, with the titles :

1. REVERIES; PASSIONS. (*Largo; Allegro agitato ed appassionato assai.*)
2. A BALL. (VALSE. *Allegro, non troppo.*)
3. IN THE COUNTRY. (*Adagio.*)
4. MARCH TO THE SCAFFOLD. (*Allegretto non troppo.*)
5. WITCHES' SABBATH. DIES IRÆ ; WITCHES' ROUND DANCE. (*Larghetto ; Allegro assai ; Allegro.*)

Most significant is the foreword that precedes a full account of *An Episode in the Life of an Artist,* which is the burden of the symphony :

"The following programme must be distributed whenever the symphony is performed dramatically, and followed by the monodrama 'Lelio,' that ends and completes the story. In this case the whole orchestra is disposed on the stage behind the lowered curtain.

"If the symphony alone is played, this arrangement is not needed ; in fact, the programme may even be dispensed with, the titles of the five movements alone being retained. The author hopes that the symphony may offer in itself a musical interest independent of all dramatic intent."

The composer shows here exactly the right perception. In so far as his symphony tells its own story, in pure musical

458

process, it stands on a higher plane than Beethoven's "Pastoral." But again we must not forget that genius is not a mere matter of school or method. Even with a stray lapse in general plan, smaller lyric beauties of the greater poet may transcend the pervading process of the lesser.

To test the Berlioz symphony in this high purpose, we must, in hearing the work, ask the one question : Does the music tell the story, or merely heighten the effect ? Therefore, the full account of small incident, in our "episode," must fairly be reserved to the end, there to test the message of the music.

A dreamy melody begins, *Largo,* followed by more feverish strains, and a more fervent burst of the first tune, in full melodic career, with free play of lesser phrases. The whispered close is broken by bright chords, *Allegro agitato appassionato assai,* that heralds a song of sweeping beauty. It is not a mere theme, though its essence is most centred in the first phrase. The middle verse stresses the passion ; the

Allegro agitato e appassionato assai.

FLUTES AND VIOLINS.

whole needs no words for the clear stamp of a lyric of love. On the first phrase in low strings rises a fiery dialogue of profound beauty, against a new answer in high wood. Then the sovereign beauty of the song reigns alone. Later a second climax is reared in fevered response of lower strains of first phrase, topped by a higher course of the passionate motive, ending in crowning verse of the pure melody. The close comes *religiosamente* in softest solemn strokes of united chords. The first strain has not recurred.

Sounds of glad expectancy soon usher the clear notes of expressive waltz, that flows in its repeated course, with intermittent vaguer play. But in the midst the love-lyric sings a verse right through the gayety of dance,—and once more, before the bright close, alone in softest confidence.

Bucolic reeds betray the scene, of mournful (English) horn and cheering oboe, echoing a chance tune in lonely duet. The quaint simplicity, the impromptu song of the *Ranz des vaches*, all mark the rustic spot. The oboe, too, has moved his distant notes to clearer foreground. And now, in gathering of all the accompanying sounds, low strings sing the main rustic theme. But it is not all a placid pastoral. A tremulous pulse pervades. A passionate phrase now strikes in romantic depths of strings. Suddenly answers on high—the soothing love-song. The bitter, jealous theme wars with its own solace. Peace comes with a return of the first idyl.

The march to the scaffold hardly needs the title, with the solemn doom of funeral tramp, the fatal ring of death-song, with the sad terror of overwhelming chorus, that gives a more poignant sense to the single gentlest strain of impassioned love, just before the end that has somehow a sudden rift of hope.

APPENDIX

The last scene is, once more, clearly pointed by the title Witches' Sabbath, that begins a stormy revel in mad medley of restless discord and vague cries. First of defined strains is the old love-motive, now piping dimly distant in merry mockery, over the dull dance of low drums. Now bursts a tempest of warring cries. Then the full course of love-song dances as before, where the cheer is blighted by uncanny trip of basses and the nearing rage of mad cries. Symbols of doom abound in the clang of bells and ring of fateful *Dies Iræ*, that is itself distorted in mocking rhythm. The Witches' Round Dance starts a grim orgy ; later the pitiless chant mingles with the dance to crown the hopeless terror that ends the dream.

For, a dream it is, and we have little need to read the story of young artist, whose ineffectual draught brings, not death, but strangest visions of desires, of his love in varying scenes. He kills her and is condemned, and dreams the full cup of last agonies.

Most of the tragic tale is told without the words of pro-gramme. So far we must yield. But first are the titles that give, themselves, a strongest clue. Finally, to waive the old question of former pages,* and even the need of these verbal hints, the mystery soon vanishes of this magic of musical narrative. Though we bar all telltale names that the poet offers, and though we grant the graphic touch of main line of picture, the means are not pure musical resources. A con-fusion is here that is rarely solved. In the art of the master there is no room for nature-sounds and like conventions.

---

* See the chapters on Schumann in Vol. I., and on the Pastoral Symphony, on Raff, on Liszt, in Vol. II.

APPENDIX

Even with lowest minstrel, the shepherd's reed pipes of rustic scene,—the waltz is ever its own symbol of light gayety ; a funeral march needs no master hand to make its meaning clear. The pure beauty of the melodies, in the hue and contrast of their humors, may justly spin their thread of epic sentiment.* And here the main recurring song is a true symbol in the story. Again, as in the "Pastoral" of Beethoven, and in the "Faust" of Liszt, the intrusion of extraneous signs, of tempest, of the chance clang of bells, even of the song for mere dramatic, for no musical reason, must break the pure woof of tunes.

The true meaning of music lies still in the play of mere tonal thoughts in the vital essence of their growth to fulness of organic art.

---

* Schumann's *Noveletten*, for the piano, have a striking sense and fragrance of narrative, without the least aid of words.

GADE'S SYMPHONY No. 4, IN B FLAT

Andantino. Allegro vivace é gracioso.
Andante con moto.
Scherzo. Allegro ma non troppo é tranquillamente.
Finale. Allegro molto vivace.

GADE has been likened to a landscape-painter. The simile is true in so far as his melodic figures do not stand out in sharp relief. Instead, by a true artistic process, by close continuity of treatment, by intuitive grasp of form, by a fine sense of orchestral color, he gives the whole a poetic tone, where it is difficult to choose salient phrases. Of course, this is equivalent to saying that Gade has genuine mastery, without the periodic strain and labored method of composers of higher lyric power. So he must stand as a true tonal poet, though of a lesser message. Gade seems to have the trait of naïve unconsciousness which strives for no special effects, does not seek to astonish by clever originality ; and so the inner feeling is most perfectly expressed. He has been called a composer for musicians ; rather he is for the true music lover, who feels sincerity of sentiment. Then Gade's temper is one of quiet, unpretending contentment, a certain repose that is strange to us Americans ; but, once caught, it is the more keenly welcome. The only way to understand Gade, however, is to take his works each as a whole, consecutively, not in melodic snatches. Hence, in suggest-

APPENDIX

ing his musical thought, the mere quoting of "themes," of itself, is of slight use. Where we are accustomed to look for melodic subjects, we find a disappointing simplicity until we see that the essence of the theme lies in some harmonic or rhythmic trait of the setting ; or, again, the true beauty does not appear until the discussion of one theme with another. Gade seems to drift along into his episodes in utter disregard of the approved way of ceremonious introduction. The only help is to listen sharply for the whole story as it develops.

Throughout the Fourth Symphony there is the simple, clear mood of joy, in different phases, now noisy, now quiet, exultant or reflective, here in lightest fancy, there in quaintest utterance.

The first movement begins with the *sostenuto* introduction, which is not part of the principal melody. Even on entering the *Allegro*, the *sostenuto* feeling lingers before it bursts into the leading theme

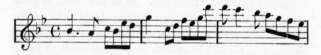

in woodwind and strings, repeated by the full orchestra. This is followed closely by a sweeping, soothing phrase :

first in the cellos, gradually pervading all the strings and the woodwind. The second melody is a flight from the noisy shout into the realm of lightest fancy, all in the strings. The subject

depends for its effect on the dancing rhythm and full harmony of the lower strings. Most beautiful of all is the binding together of the two melodies before the *reprise*, where the real feeling, elusive as a fire-fly, is often expressed independent of actual subjects, in a responsive and harmonic play of them all, or in motives that subtly and almost invisibly grow out of the principal themes. After the repetition appears an inversion of the second melody, leading into a brilliantly fanciful development, out of which the first theme steals with surprising stillness, again re-echoed by the whole orchestra. Again follows the second melody with the same beautiful passage as before. At the end there is another lull in the strings before the principal subject is sung in triumphant canonic stretto.

The *Andante* begins in a characteristic idyl. Throughout there is an unbroken stream of melody, yet not reiterated nor diluted. The first theme seems almost ended when it leads into one of such beauty that the former sounds like introduction. The melodic texture is so close that it is difficult to separate first from second theme ; nor does it matter where all is melody. There is no purpose in quoting each distinct from the beautiful intertwining of all, nor in whole, nor in part.

The *Scherzo* returns to the vein of light fancy of the second tune of *Allegro*. It lies, of course, largely in the strings. The subject

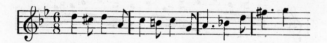

again depends for its beauty upon the rhythm and harmony of the accompaniment. The first Trio is in sharp contrast, with its simple diatonic theme, though still in dancing rhythm :

The second, equally poetic, abandons the dance. Simplicity itself, the melody is sung in strict *legato* by the violins :

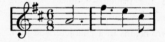

while the violas sway in graceful rhythm.

The *Finale* is the climax : one continuous, infectious frolic. The opening melody, less impressive in its first

APPENDIX

statement, gradually carries all before it by an insistent swing and spirit ; the second has a more quiet, contained happiness.

The whole is complete sonata-form without the repetition.

GOETZ'S SYMPHONY IN F MAJOR

BETWEEN title-page and score is given a motto :

" In des Herzens stille Räume
Musst du fliehen aus des Lebens Drang."

SCHILLER.

Into the quiet chambers of the soul
Flee for refuge from the stress of life.

Hermann Goetz has something of the strange charm that clings to the figure of Chatterton, though it lies not in the precocity of his work, but in the keen regret for the loss to music from his untimely death. Somehow this feeling is almost greater than in the cases of Mozart and Schubert, whose work seemed to grow in natural career to complete fulfilment. That of Goetz, it is clear, had merely begun. His was not the early day of rapid outpouring of melody. The romantic message, of German folk-song, of rebellion against classic formalism, had been uttered. Goetz was born to the later time when the better vein of tonal poetry sought the blending of classic art with modern feeling, the quality of form, rather than the barren stereotype.

A near contemporary of Brahms, Goetz would, in almost certain probability, have joined that master in the neo-classic period of German symphony. They might have been the Mozart and Beethoven or the Mendelssohn and Schumann of the latest age of masters.

468

APPENDIX

The symphony of Goetz is scored quite simply, with four horns, two trumpets, and three trombones.

Through chords of horns and clarinets, and waving strings, the theme of *Allegro* steals in, in lowest basses and cellos

topped with melodious answer of violins and wood. The melody has the secret of endless thread, though of its own special strain. An embodiment there seems here, in clearest crystal of pure tones, of a spirit that found other utterance in a setting of actual legend and drama. A most spirited climax breaks sheer before the expressive motive, the true second subject :

an idyl in the heart of the fervent song of the main text, whence it soon gains a new spring that leads to a concluding phrase, that sums the joyous sense of the whole :

APPENDIX

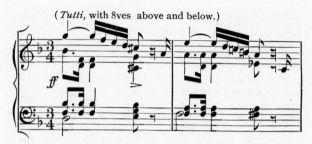

(*Tutti*, with 8ves above and below.)

Very beautifully the first melody comes coursing into the bass of the end of the third, pursued in turn by another entrance in high treble. Before the repeat, this free canon on main theme dies to a sombre lull.

The discussion begins much like the prelude, then it is given o'er to a placid, dulcet guise of the first strain, where a most expressive countertheme is more and more eminent, at first below in cellos, later in high solo flute. In the discussion no theme enters but the fervent flow of the dominant song. And so, the idyllic episode recurs at the end, just as in the beginning, though there is a last special verse on the thread of main melody.

The brief themes of the *Intermezzo* do not, in themselves, seem the full text. It is in their commingling and interplay that the true purpose appears and the humor of the whole is shown. The first, a mere call of horns :

HORNS.
Allegretto.

470

is answered almost jestingly by high wood.   Soon the second runs right on the heels of the first :

and thus the relevant beauty of both is most clear, though there are verses of the separate tunes.   An entirely new color comes with a third one, in minor strings :

sombrely playful, stealing anon into sunnier light (of major),— finding its own thread of weaving song without the need of other text, until far on, where the first sings anew in horns, and, somehow, a kinship of tune now appears. Then, again, the third makes playful answer, much like the former second. One more verse follows of the third alone.

The ending is altogether naïve. The minor hue of the third is broken by a new hymnal tune,—*un poco meno moto :*

in strings, with sustaining notes of wood and horns. Its solemnity leads most temptingly to the merriness of the second melody, that now gambols about in all kinds of light, with answering strain now and then from the first theme. After a big, coursing climax, a new response comes to the purling song of second theme,—building a new, expressive tune on the simple call of the first, growing finally to full melody, out of all the original lines. The very end is in duet of the first call, and of a simple, major strain of third theme.

The slow movement of symphony is probably the final test of the composer. No pomp or tricks of scoring can fill the want. Pure melody there must be, in quiet, contained flow, without the nervous throb, the quick rising storms of the *Allegro.* So the slow movement is the final essence of the

APPENDIX

poet's thought ; its utterance is the end of all the earlier stress.

By this high test, Goetz is not wanting. Beginning in low strings, the noble song winds a graceful curve of solemn beauty :

There is, again, a striking quality here that marks a difference from the style of the great romantic masters and from any of their successors. A certain lyric strain, of modern sense and feeling, here was finding highest expression in the symphony. With the death of the poet, the spring seems to have dried ; or it may have found a less pure channel in other forms. In certain ways, Goetz reminds us of Gade, mainly in weaving small themes of lesser import to a beautiful tonal scene. Gade has been called the landscape-painter of music. The *Intermezzo*, here, shows some of this art and method. But the *Adagio* is, all, spontaneous flowing song. In the midst, in complete change of tone, is an episode of simpler lines of tune and of quieter humor. The mode, too, is in serene major, leaving tne romantic color of the first.

APPENDIX

(Horns, with obligato strings.)

dolce.

Cellos and Basses.

With the art of a master, the horns, that first sing the theme, are answered, in unguarded moments, by clarinets, with exquisite touch of dissonance. A speaking climax leads to a varied verse of first melody, *un poco piu largo*,—really a free song of first violins, with *pizzicato* of lower strings. Soon the cellos are drawn into the melody. Then, above the later, flowing course of all the strings breaks the chorus of wood in the original melody, *tempo primo*.

The second theme returns briefly, and is followed by a still bolder verse of main tune, *molto agitato*, where tumultuous waves of responsive phrase play in eager canon. The final verse has the theme transfigured in placid song of serene major without the dross of the earlier passion.

In the *Finale, Allegro con fuoco*, joyousness is clearly stamped on the swing and line of the theme. Again the sense of ever-winding thread is there, as of unending dance. The bright motive that begins, plays a large part in the digressions between the verses of tune. In the simple phrases of second subject, woven in canon of three voices, in strings and wood, we seem to see again the art that paints in minute touches,—that can rear a great work on small figures. With

474

APPENDIX

Allegro con fuoco.

ƒƒ

(Tutti, reinforced in 8ves.)

(See page 469, line 14.)

all the melodious beauty there is a festive interplay of phrase
(where, too, the answers of themes have no small share)
that gives a richness of polyphonic life and harmony, and
makes, perhaps, the main charm. The lyric beauty of the
second theme is clearer in a later appearance:

p

where the melodic flow is freer than in the first fugual statement. With all the wealth of contrapuntal art, there is a

gay freedom in the informal entrance of voices in unexpected response, and a blithe discourse of lesser strains, where, anon, the main theme strikes in with the highest note of festal glee. In the midst is quite a disputation, as phrases, from second theme and its answer, meet from above and below,—all sustained in long sequence. At each meeting they reach a final concord by narrowest pinch of dissonance. Then the controversy is repeated with changed positions of the parties.

In the final return to the first array of disputant strains, a high point is reached of dramatic feeling,—though the word seems a mockery of the real beauty.

From here the pure note of high delight reigns, first in the mere dancing swing of main theme, then in the full play of both subjects. There is a fine ring in the joyous pranks that end the symphony.

GILCHRIST'S SYMPHONY IN
C MAJOR

THE symphony begins with a spirited unison attack on the motive :

Vivace impetuoso.

ff

(In unison of full orchestra.)

presently falling into soft, sliding chords in united band, and broken whispers of sighing melody before the entrance, *molto allegro*, in strings, of the main theme, in strong, swinging rhythm :

Allegro molto.

(In strings, an octave lower.)

followed by a vigorous answer. The theme presently varies its song in saucy humor and dashes into a *ff* cadence, whence emerges the gentle second melody, mostly in woodwind, of which the answer glides into a flow of tender song, one of those phrases which with the composer we feel we cannot have without rehearing and rehearsing. The second theme now re-enters in more heroic guise, in full orchestra, with added noisy coursing of violins.

APPENDIX

(In wood and *pizz.* strings.)

(See page 477, line 8.)

After a triumphant climax and cadence the discussion
begins, briskly, on odd ends of the second theme. Through
misty changes of color echoes a more subdued strain, in playful duet of strings and wood, from the old, repeated phrase.
Out of it emerges, very simply, a new song, in strings and
clarinet :

(In clarinet and strings.)

This, with the preceding strain, is led through fresh and
moving changes of tonal scene, with answering bits rising
anon to a climax, so that the whole discussion is a woof of
clear, running melody rather than a mass of complex tones.

APPENDIX

At the end of this idyllic dialogue, the spirited attack of the second theme breaks the spell and rushes in noisy ascent into the introduction, whence, through the whole of its varied course, we enter again on the simple, joyful song of the first melody, followed by the second, with the strain which we like to repeat, ending in triumphant blast of second theme.

The *Adagio*, in prelude, foreshadows the main tune in sombre, descending chords and chanting clarinet. Here, where all is lyric song, we do not know whether most to enjoy the first melody, sung by solo clarinet in naïve rhythm and a sort of Phrygian mode, softened by the murmuring hum of strings :

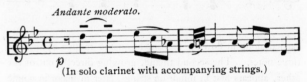

Andante moderato.

(In solo clarinet with accompanying strings.)

or the more speaking later theme in low cellos, with rhythmic woodwind :

Con espress.

(In cellos with accompanying woodwind.)

But it is not quite all lyric song. Out of the second melody grows a phrase that proves the bone of contention, with a distinct sense of altercation between basses and trebles, in pure counterpoint, after which the main melody, with a new breath of pastoral freshness, returns to close.

APPENDIX

The *Scherzo Bacchanale* is perhaps truest of all to its own humor. There is no escaping the rollicking dash of the theme, in violins :

(In violins with *pizz.* strings.)

carried along in flowing merriment on the motive of the first three notes. The second theme, growing directly out of the other, appears first in minor on strings, later in major in comic cellos, with a special abandon of drollery :

mocked lightly by the high woodwind.

APPENDIX

But most of all has the *Trio* the Bacchanale flavor, as the strings, in clumsy gait, stumble along, falling and picking themselves up :

A brilliant extension of the dance, with contrary figures joining in, leads through the repeated Trio back to the original Scherzo.

The *Finale* is based on two very opposite themes, one a true *fanfare*, in spirit and in function, with its electric motive :

(Doubled above and below in full orchestra.)

the bass descending in diatonic steps, followed in sequence. The second, in spite of a quicker pace, has distinctly more sentiment, and is marked *legato espressivo :*

(Mainly in strings.)

Singing mainly in strings, it draws on most of the band, though seldom in *tutti,* working in profuse polyphony on its smallest motives. Though the movement is rather rondo than sonata, it has more of discussion than any of the others, ever on the second melody, and, in mood, hovering between sparkling fun and gentler feeling, until an answering kind of melody is suddenly evolved, like the wings of a chrysalis :

(Melody in clarinets and flutes.)

in clear retort to the original (second) tune, and the more welcome and relevant for the waiting.

Here follows the greatest polyphonic revel of all, around the (second) melody, part and whole, in changing tonal settings, with a new and quicker counter-phrase in strings : the kind of passage where, in the glow of the story, a composer will do all the feats of counterpoint without knowing it—the only true way. But we must hold fast to the outline of the theme, even in small fragments, else we lose all bearings in the dizzy whirl, though here and there the new-fledged tune does appear clear in a placid calm. The whole shows how a lesser melody (in official rank) will assume control, and from its small compass give full resources for varied and spirited discussion, leaving to the principal theme little more than the formality of introduction and finally of a triumphant ending.

GOLDMARK'S LÄNDLICHE HOCHZEIT (COUNTRY WEDDING) SYMPHONY

THE title ought not to suggest a peasant wedding, This would surely have been called *Bauernhochzeit*, —a well-known term and a most characteristic event of German village life. This is evidently not what the composer meant. The title means the typical wedding, which must, of course, have the simple surroundings of the country for full course of festivity. The fourth number, "Im Garten," is clearest proof. For the peasant has no garden ; that is quite a special mark of social difference. A peasant wedding is a most picturesque festival, expressive of true folk tradition. No one, if he were in the neighborhood, would miss a sight of the highly-colored costumes, richly worked, nor the jolly scenes at the tavern. And a peasant wedding were unmistakable in music. We should not fail to find the rollicking Ländler, the peasant waltz, towards the end.

The country wedding of Goldmark is altogether another sort of celebration. The difference were not worth noting, save that it has so sharp a meaning in Germany itself, the land of the composer, and, therefore, in his mind.

The symphony is all written in simple lyric manner, is "symphony" merely in a very general sense. It were a mistake to read into it too many scenes and situations, too much detailed meaning, however tempting this may be. For, it is the sentiment that finds fullest play, with no more of special labelling than the titles themselves of the five parts :

APPENDIX

1. Wedding March (Variations).   2. Bridal Song (*Intermezzo*).   3. Serenade (*Scherzo*).   4. In the Garden (*Andante*).   5. Dance (*Finale*).

Under the big name of "March" in the variations, a sense of expectancy in different phases is poetically uttered. First, the pretty rollicking theme alone :

Moderato molto.

then contrasted moods, where the melody is woven in subtle beauty, seeking often to elude all sense of march, while keeping the essence of festive idea ever prominent.   Thus, after first simple accent of march comes a dreamily flowing canon of strings, *poco animato*, that plays into a suggestion of the melody ; then the march breaks in full tread in basses, with acclaim of all the band.   Third is a gently swinging, almost sad *Andante con moto*, beginning in strings, horns, and fagots,—restless often in seeking new tones, reaching the tune in clear light, or ending in quaint cadence.   The flowing *obligato* of lower strings is strengthened in fagots ; the chorus in swing of slow dance just escapes the sense of dragging ; then a smart trip,—*Allegro scherzando*,—the violins leading the motion, the solo horn holding the tune.   In delicate confidence flute and violin start the duet, *Allegretto poco andantino*, where only cellos guard a reminder of the theme. *Molto vivace* breaks in a most charming verse of the tune, in

APPENDIX

three time. Before the final refrain of the simple march is a very extended verse, beginning, we are sure, in church, as the solemn organ tones (of the wood) drone out a fugal play about the simple *chorale* that is first given out by oboes:

Later the flutes and clarinets join in the hymnal song. Between its lines an intimate strain is played in soft trio of solo violins and viola,—that reminds us of *Walther* behind the church pillar, in the *Meistersinger*. The sacred and secular strains are richly blended in the close.

The *Bridal Song* stands out in the clear beauty of sense and song, throughout all the verse, and has no need of cumbering words.

The *Serenade* is like dainty madrigal in several verses. The themes, to be sure, have with all lightness a serious grace and feeling. But between them are flashes of fine humor in lesser phrase and in tne interplay of motive. So the whole is beautifully blended of bubbling humor and tender sentiment,

APPENDIX

where each runs into the other, and each is pressing for main
utterance. The first verse is on the pretty vein of main
theme, whose mirth and lightness is not free from sentiment.
In the second there is a new tinge of pathos in the graceful
melody :

But its own answer has a true humor of well-marked
primitive bass, as of bagpipe. Before the last rehearsing of
verses is the full interweaving in big polyphonic climax, all in
the ancient manner of stately madrigal.

The scene " In the Garden" has the most intimate shade
of beauty, where the clarinet tenderly and dreamily begins its
appealing song in rarest harmonies of wood and lower strings.
Later it is heard in high violins.

Two distinct melodic elements there are in this romance.
Against the rare delicacy of the first is the ardent tone of the
second, in cellos echoed by violins.

Though beginning *poco piu lento*, there is ever a rising to
passionate climax, where question of lower voices spurs the
answer of higher,—and then a subsiding to the timid first
phrase. As the *Andante* may be called the epitome of a
symphony, so this idyl is clearly the heart of the work.

APPENDIX

Poco piu lento.   *tenderly.*

STRINGS. *pp*

p cantabile.

(See page 486, line 16.)

The *Dance Allegro molto*, is all on big scale. In polyphonic design, it is profoundest of all the movements. For after a brief *fanfare*, violins lead off a fugue in four voices, on the dance of theme.

(Dance theme.)

f (Later counter-theme.)

487

APPENDIX

Later, as the woodwind take up the tune, a jolly counter-theme runs in cellos and fagots, that adds a jogging pace, so that the whole gets a rich charm of cheery bustle. The fugue, somehow, has not the least smell of the lamp. The more complete it is the more we think of a gay reel, with varying figures and freedom of individual motion. Soon the polyphonic maze gives way to a second tune of united simple dance :

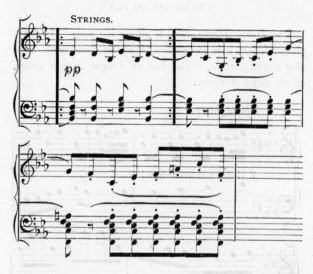

started gently in strings, waxing lustier with added woodwind, finally bursting into big march-like fling in loudest chorus. Whimsically the soft tread and the heavy stamp of jig alternate, and there are sudden lulls broken by frightening volume. Then back to the comfortable swing of first round dance.

APPENDIX

For a moment we steal out of doors, and are again lost in the rare strain of the garden scene. Of surprising beauty is the epilogue, where the simple second tune (of dance) broadens into true, moving song, like festive hymn, rising to height of fervent appeal, that is too intimate for mere trip of foot. As the original swing steals into the midst, the end is in climax that is much more than frolic of dance.

INDEX

Ambros, von, 13

American symphony, an, 477–482

Andante : Melody, 42, 69, 284, 299 ; movement, 84, 99, 111, 262–3, 344, 472 (see Lyric); in Mozart and Beethoven, 22 *et seq.*, 46, 49, 69; of G minor symphony, 45, 49

Aristophanes, 101

Art, 160, 175, 323, 455 (see Preface); and nature, 141

Arts, basic purpose of the various, 137 *et seq.*, 324, 421 *et seq.*

Bach, 40, 241, 326, 403, 407, 453, 455

Ballad, 218   (See Folk-Song ; " Lenore.")

Beauty in art, 144, 439   (See Art.)

Beethoven, 13–14, 16, 18, 22, 24, 31, 34–194, 230, 247, 282, 284, 286, 295, 299, 326, 331, 407, 457 ; disciple of Mozart and Haydn, 53–58, 69 *et seq.*, 79 ; humor of, 49 *et seq.*, 76–7, 97 *et seq.*, 305–6; poet of fraternity, 98–101, 323, 378 ; of humor, 101–3, 111 *et seq.* ; first symphony, 34–58 ; second symphony, 59–86; third symphony, 41, 113; fourth symphony, 87–110; fifth symphony, 37, 39, 97, 111, 113, 149, 445; sixth (pastoral) symphony, 111, 133–152, 230, 242, 457; seventh symphony, 111, 113; eighth symphony, 111–132; ninth (choral) symphony, 99, 153–194

INDEX

Berlioz, Fantastic Symphony, 457–462

Brahms, 282–400, 405, 433, 455, 468; first symphony,
282–322; second symphony, 313; third symphony,
323–360; fourth symphony, 361–400; humor of, 305–
10; greatness, 318; and Beethoven compared, 323

Bürger, "Lenore" ballad translated by Scott, 257–267

Cacophony, 141, 143–4, 435 *et seq.*, 438 *et seq.*, 451–2

Canon, 25, 190

Chadwick. (See Preface.)

Chorale, 485 (See Hymn.)

Cimarosa, 17

Coherence in music. (See Sequence, Form.)

Content, emotional, in pure art, 13 *et seq.*, 263 (See
Feeling.)

Counterpoint (see Polyphony), 279, 406–7, 451–2

Criticism, 178–9, 454–5

Dance, 344 *et seq.*, 346 (See Scherzo.)

Definite utterance in music, 153, 171, 189; in art, 324

Depiction. (See Descriptive, Programme.)

Descriptive music, 136–140, 145 *et seq.*, 148–9, 230–1,
241–3, 267 *et seq.*, 408, 457 *et seq.*, 461 *et seq.*
(See, generally, Chaps. VI. and IX.)

Development, themal, 315 *et seq.*, 317, 320, 361, 464
(see Discussion), 371, 372 *et seq.*, 447–8

Discussion, themal, 84, 135, 160, 171–2, 180–1, 208–9,
217, 223, 226–7, 335, 386, 387, 406, 464

Disputation. (See Discussion.)

Dogma, 323

492

INDEX

INDEX

494

INDEX

INDEX

INDEX

INDEX

THE END

MODERN SYMPHONIES

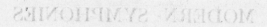

GREAT WORKS
OF
MUSIC

Volume Three

MODERN SYMPHONIES

PREFACE

CRITICISM of contemporary art is really a kind
of prophecy. For the appreciation of the classical
past is an act of present perception, not a mere
memory of popular verdicts. The classics live only
because they still express the vital feeling of to-day.
The new art must do more,—must speak for the
morrow. And as the poet is a kind of seer, the true
critic is his prophetic herald.

It is with due humility that we approach a view
of the work of our own time, with a dim feeling that
our best will be a mere conjecture. But we shall
the more cheerfully return to our resolution that our
chief business is a positive appreciation. Where we
cannot praise, we can generally be silent. Certain
truths concerning contemporary art seem firmly
grounded in the recorded past. The new Messiah
never came with instant wide acclaim. Many false
prophets flashed brilliantly on the horizon to fall
as suddenly as they rose. In a refracted view we see
the figures of the great projected in too large dimension upon their day. And precisely opposite we fail
to glimpse the ephemeral lights obscuring the truly
great. The lesson seems never to be learned; indeed
it can, of course, never be learned. For that would
imply an eternal paradox that the present generation
must always distrust its own judgment.

1

Who could possibly imagine in Schubert's time the sway he holds to-day. Our minds reel to think that by a mere accident were recovered the Passion of Bach and the symphonies of Schubert. Or must we prayerfully believe that a Providence will make the best prevail? And, by the way, the serious nature of this appreciation appears when we see how it was ever by the greatest of his time that the future master was heralded.

The symphony of the present age has perhaps fallen somewhat in estate. It was natural that it should rush to a high perfection in the halcyon days of its growth. It is easy to make mournful predictions of decadence. The truth is the symphony is a great form of art, like a temple or a tragedy. Like them it has had, it will have its special eras of great expression. Like them it will stay as a mode of utterance for new communities and epochs with varying nationality, or better still, with vanishing nationalism.

The tragedy was not exhausted with Sophocles, nor with Shakespeare nor with Goethe. So the symphony has its fallow periods and it may have a new resurgence under new climes. We are ever impatient to shelve a great form, like vain women afraid of the fashion. It is part of our constant rage for novelty. The shallower artist ever tinkered with new devices,—to some effects, in truth. Such is the empiric course of art that what is born of vanity may be crowned with highest inspiration.

The national element will fill a large part of our

survey. It marks a strange trait of our own age
that this revival of the national idea falls in the
very time when other barriers are broken. Ancient
folk-song grew like the flower on the battle-field of
races. But here is an anxious striving for a special
dialect in music. Each nation must have its proper
school; composers are strictly labelled, each one
obedient to his national manner. This state of
art can be but of the day. Indeed, the fairest promise
of a greater future lies in the morrow's blending
of these various elements in the land where each
citizen has a mixed inheritance from the older
nations.

In the bewildering midst of active spirits comes
the irresistible impulse to a somewhat partisan
warfare. The critic, if he could view himself from
some empyræan perch, remote in time and place,
might smile at his own vehemence. In the clash of
aims he must, after all, take sides, for it is the
tendency that is momentous; and he will be excited
to greater heat the stronger the prophet that he
deems false. When the strife is over, when currents
are finally settled, we may take a more contented
joy in the impersonal art that remains.

The choice from the mass of brilliant vital
endeavor is a new burden and a source almost of
dismay. Why should we omit so melodious a work
as Moskowski's *Jeanne d'Arc*,—full of perhaps too
facile charm? It was, of course, impossible to treat
all the wonderful music of the Glazounows and the
Kallinikows. And there is the limpid beauty of the

PREFACE

Bohemian *Suk,* or the heroic vigor of a *Volbach.*
We should like to have mentioned *Robert Volkmann*
as a later Romanticist; and *Gade* has ever seemed
a true poet of the Scandinavian symphony.

Of the modern French we are loth to omit the
symphonies of *Chausson* and of *Dukas.* In our own
America it is a still harder problem. There is the
masterly writing of a *Foote;* the older *Paine* has
never been fully valued in the mad race for novelty.
It would have been a joy to include a symphony of
rare charm by *Martinus van Gelder.*

A critical work on modern art cannot hope to
bestow a crown of laurels among living masters; it
must be content with a view of active tendencies.
The greatest classic has often come into the world
amid least expectation. A critic in the year 1850
must need have omitted the Unfinished Symphony,
which was then buried in a long oblivion.

The present author prefers to treat the main
modern lines, considering the special work mainly
as example. After all, throughout the realm of art
the idea is greater than the poet, the whole art more
than the artist,—though the particular enshrine-
ment in enduring design may reflect a rare
personality.

Philip H. Goepp.

Note: Especial thanks are owed to the Philadelphia
Orchestra for a free use of its library, and to Messrs. G.
Schirmer Company for a like courtesy.—P. H. G.

MODERN SYMPHONIES

CHAPTER I

THE SYMPHONY DURING THE NINE-TEENTH CENTURY

AFTER the long dominance of German masters of the musical art, a reaction could not fail to come with the restless tendencies of other nations, who, having learned the lesson, were yet jealous of foreign models and eager to utter their own message. The later nineteenth century was thus the age of refraction of the classic tradition among the various racial groups that sprang up with the rise of the national idea. We can see a kind of beginning in the Napoleonic destruction of feudal dynasties. German authority in music at the beginning of the century was as absolute as Roman rule in the age of Augustus. But the seed was carried by teachers to the various centres of Europe. And, with all the joy we have in the new burst of a nation's song, there is no doubt that it is ever best uttered when it is grounded on the lines of classic art. Here is a paramount reason for the strength of the modern Russian school. With this semi-political cause in mind it is less difficult

7

to grasp the paradox that with all the growth of inter-communication the music of Europe moves in more detached grooves to-day than two centuries ago. The suite in the time of Bach is a special type and proof of a blended breadth and unity of musical thought in the various nations of Europe of the seventeenth century. In the quaint series of dances of the different peoples, with a certain international quality, one sees a direct effect of the Thirty Years' War,—the beneficent side of those ill winds and cruel blasts, when all kinds of nations were jostling on a common battle-ground. And as the folk-dances sprang from the various corners of Europe, so different nations nursed the artistic growth of the form. Each would treat the dances of the other in its own way, and here is the significance of Bach's separate suites,—English, French and German.

Nationalism seems thus a prevailing element in the music of to-day, and we may perceive two kinds, one spontaneous and full of charm, the other a result of conscious effort, sophisticated in spirit and in detail. It may as well be said that there was no compelling call for a separate French school in the nineteenth century as a national utterance. It sprang from a political rather than an artistic motive; it was the itch of jealous pride that sharply stressed the difference of musical style on the two sides of the Rhine. The very influence of German music was needed by the French rather than a bizarre invention of national traits. The broader art of a Saint-Saëns here shines in contrast with the brilliant conceits of his younger compatriots, though it cannot be denied that the latter are grounded in classic counterpoint. With other nations the impulse was more natural: the racial song of the Scandinavians, Czechs and other Slavs craved a deliverance as much as the German in the time of Schubert. In France, where music had long flourished, there was no stream of suppressed folk-song.

But the symphony must in the natural course have suffered from the very fulness of its own triumph. We know the Romantic reaction of Schumann, uttered in smaller cyclic forms; in Berlioz is almost a complete abandonment of pure music, devoid of special description. Liszt was one of the mighty figures of the century, with all the external qualities of a master-genius, shaking the stage of Europe with the weight of his personality, and, besides, endowed with a creative power that was not understood in his day. With him the restless tendency resulted in a new form intended to displace the symphony: the symphonic poem, in a single, varied movement, and always on a definite poetic subject. Here was at once a relief and a recess from the classic rigor. Away with sonata form and all the odious code of rules! In the story of the title will lie all the outline of the music.

Yet in this rebellious age—and here is the significance of the form—the symphony did not languish, but blossomed to new and varied flower. Liszt turned back to the symphony from his new-fangled device for his two greatest works. It has, indeed, been charged that the symphony was accepted by the Romantic masters in the spirit of a challenge. Mendelssohn and even Schumann are not entirely free from such a suspicion. Nevertheless it remains true that all of them confided to the symphony their fairest inspiration. About the middle of the century, at the high point of anti-classical revolt, a wonderful group of symphonies, by Berlioz, Mendelssohn, Schumann, and Liszt, were presented to the world. With the younger Brahms on a returning wave of neo-classicism the form became again distinctively a personal choice. Finally, in the spontaneous utterance of a national spirit on broad lines, as in the later Russian and Finnish examples, with the various phases of surging resolution, of lyric contemplation and of rollicking humor, the symphony has its best sanction in modern times.

To return to the historical view, the course of the symphony during the century cannot be adequately scanned without a glance at the music-drama of Richard Wagner. Until the middle of the century, symphony and opera had moved entirely in separate channels. At most the overture was affected, in temper and detail, by the career of the nobler form.

The restless iconoclasm of a Liszt was now united, in a close personal and poetic league, with the new ideas of Wagner's later drama. Both men adopted the symbolic motif as their main melodic means;

10

with both mere iteration took the place of development; a brilliant and lurid color-scheme (of orchestration) served to hide the weakness of intrinsic content; a vehement and hysteric manner cast into temporary shade the classic mood of tranquil depth in
which alone man's greatest thought is born.

But a still larger view of the whole temper of art
in Europe of the later century is needed. We wander
here beyond the fine distinctions of musical forms. A
new wave of feeling had come over the world that
violently affected all processes of thought. And
strangely, it was strongest in the land where the
great heights of poetry and music had just been
reached. Where the high aim of a Beethoven and a
Goethe had been proclaimed, arose a Wagner to
preach the gospel of brute fate and nature, where love
was the involuntary sequence of mechanical device
and ended in inevitable death, all overthrowing the
heroic idea that teems throughout the classic scores,
crowned in a greatest symphony in praise of " Joy."

Such was the intrinsic content of a " Tristan and
Isolde " and the whole " Nibelungen-Ring," and it
was uttered with . sensuous wealth of sound and a
passionate strain of melody that (without special
greatness of its own) dazzled and charmed the world
in the dramatic setting of mediæval legend. The new
harmonic style of Wagner, there is good reason to
suppose, was in reality first conceived by Liszt, whose
larger works, written about the middle of the cen-

11

tury, have but lately come to light.* In correspondence with this moral mutiny was the complete revolt from classic art—tradition: melody (at least in theory), the vital quality of musical form and the true process of a coherent thread, were cast to the winds with earlier poetic ideals.

If it were ever true that a single personality could change an opposite course of thought, it must be held that Richard Wagner, in his own striking and decadent career, comes nearest to such a type. But he was clearly prompted and reinforced in his philosophy by other men and tendencies of his time. The realism of a Schopenhauer, which Wagner frankly adopted without its full significance (where primal will finds a redemption in euthanasia), led by a natural course of thought to Nietzsche's dreams of an overman, who tramples on his kind.

In itself this philosophy had been more of a passing phase (even as Schopenhauer is lost in the chain of ethical sages) but for its strange coincidence with the Wagnerian music. The accident of this alliance gave it an overwhelming power in Germany, where it soon threatened to corrupt all the arts, banishing idealism

---

* The " Dante " Symphony of Liszt was written between 1847 and 1855; the " Faust " Symphony between 1854 and 1857. Wagner finished the text of *Tristan und Isolde* in 1857; the music was not completed until 1859. In 1863 was published the libretto of the *Nibelungen-Ring*. In 1864 Wagner was invited by King Ludwig of Bavaria to complete the work in Munich.

from the land of its special haunts.* The ultimate weakness of the Wagnerian philosophy is that it finds in fatalism an excuse for the surrender of heroic virtue,—not in the spirit of a tragic truth, but in a glorification of the senses; just as in Wagner's final work, the ascetic, sinless type becomes a figure almost of ridicule, devoid of human reality. It is significant that with the revival of a sound art, fraught with resolute aspiration, is imminent a return to an idealistic system of philosophy.

In the musical art even of Germany the triumph was never complete. The famous feud of Brahms and Wagner partisans marked the alignment of the classical and radical traditions. Throughout the second half of the century the banner of a true musical process was upheld; the personal meeting of the youthful Brahms with the declining Schumann is wonderfully significant, viewed as a symbol of this passing of the classic mantle. And the symphonies of Gustav Mahler seem an assurance of present tendencies. The influence of Bach, revived early in the century, grew steadily as a latent leaven.

Nevertheless in the prevailing taste and temper

---

* In literature this movement is most marked, as may be seen by contrasting the tone of Goethe with that of Sudermann; by noting the decadence from the stories of a Chamisseau and Immermann to those of a Gottfried Keller; from the novels of Freytag to the latest of Frenssen and Arthur Schnitzler; from the poems of Heine to those of Hoffmansthal, author of the text of Strauss' later operas.

Or, contrast merely the two typical dramas of love, Goethe's "Faust" and Wagner's "Tristan and Isolde."

of present German music, in the spirit of the most popular works, as those of Richard Strauss (who seems to have sold his poetic birthright), the aftermath of this wave is felt, and not least in the acclaim of the barren symphonies of a Bruckner. It is well known that Bruckner, who paid a personal homage to Wagner, became a political figure in the partisan dispute, when he was put forth as the antagonist of Brahms in the symphony. His present vogue is due to this association and to his frank adoption of Wagner idiom in his later works, as well as, more generally, to the lowered taste in Germany.

In all this division of musical dialect, in the shattering of the classic tower among the diverse tongues of many peoples, what is to be the harvest? The full symbol of a Babel does not hold for the tonal art. Music is, in its nature, a single language for the world, as its alphabet rests on ideal elements. It has no national limits, like prose or poetry; its home is the whole world; its idiom the blended song of all nations.

In such a view there is less hope in the older than in the newer world. No single, limited song of one nation can in the future achieve a second climax of the art. It is by the actual mingling of them all that the fairest flower and fruit must come. The very absence of one prevailing native song, held a reproach to America, is in reality her strength; for hers is the common heritage of all strains of song. And it may be her destiny to lead in the glorious merging of them all.

14

CHAPTER II

BERLIOZ AND LISZT

THE path of progress of an art has little to do with mere chronology. For here in early days are bold spirits whose influence is not felt until a whole generation has passed of a former tradition. Nor are these patient pioneers always the best-inspired prophets; the mere fate of slow recognition does not imply a highest genius. A radical innovation may provoke a just and natural resistance. Again, a gradual yielding is not always due to the pure force of truth. Strange and oblique ideas may slowly win a triumph that is not wholly merited and may not prove enduring.

To fully grapple with this mystery, we may still hold to the faith that final victory comes only to pure truth, and yet we may find that imperfect truth will often achieve a slow and late acceptance. The victory may then be viewed in either of two ways: the whole spirit of the age yields to the brilliant allurement, or there is an overweighing balance of true beauty that deserves the prize of permanence. Of such a kind were two principal composers of the symphony: Franz Liszt and Hector Berlioz. Long after they had wrought their greatest works, others had come and

15

gone in truer line with the first masters, until it seemed these radical spirits had been quite rejected.

Besides the masters of their own day, Schumann and Mendelssohn, a group of minor poets, like Raff and Goetz, appeared, and at last Brahms, the latest great builder of the symphony, all following and crowning the classical tradition.

The slow reception of the larger works of Liszt strangely agrees with the startling resemblance of their manner to the Russian style that captivated a much later age. It seemed as if the spirit of the Hungarian was suddenly revived in a new national group. His humor wonderfully suited the restless and sensational temper of an age that began after his death.

The very harmonies and passionate manner that influence modern audiences evoked a dull indifference in their own day.* They roused the first acclaim when presented in the more popular form of the music-drama. It may well be questioned whether Liszt was not the fountain source of the characteristic harmonies of Wagner's later opera.

Historically considered, that is in their relation to other music preceding and following them, the symphonies of Liszt have striking interest. They are in boldest departure from all other symphonies, save possibly those of Berlioz, and they were prophetic in

---

* Compare the similarity of the themes of the Faust Symphony of Liszt and of the *Pathétique* of Tschaikowsky in the last chapter of vol. ii, " Symphonies and Their Meaning."

a degree only apparent a half-century later. If the quality of being ahead of his time be proof, instead of a symptom, of genius, then Liszt was in the first rank of masters. The use of significant motif is in both of his symphonies. But almost all the traits that startled and moved the world in Tschaikowsky's symphonies are revealed in this far earlier music: the tempestuous rage of what might be called an hysterical school, and the same poignant beauty of the lyric episodes; the sheer contrast, half trick, half natural, of fierce clangor and dulcet harmonies, all painted with the broad strokes of the orchestral palette. Doubly striking it is how Liszt foreshadowed his later followers and how he has really overshadowed them; not one, down to the most modern tone-painters, has equalled him in depth and breadth of design, in the original power of his tonal symbols. It seems that Liszt will endure as the master-spirit in this reactionary phase of the symphony.

Berlioz is another figure of a bold innovator, whose career seemed a series of failures, yet whose music will not down. His art was centred less upon the old essentials, of characteristic melody and soul-stirring harmonies, than upon the magic strokes of new instrumental grouping,—a graphic rather than a pure musical purpose. And so he is the father not only of the modern orchestra, but of the fashion of the day that revels in new sensations of startling effects, that are spent in portraying the events of a story.

Berlioz was the first of a line of *virtuosi* of the

orchestra, a pioneer in the art of weaving significant strains,—significant, that is, apart from the music. He was seized with the passion of making a pictured design with his orchestral colors. Music, it seems, did not exist for Berlioz except for the telling of a story. His symphony is often rather opera. A symphony, he forgot, is not a musical drama without the scenery. This is just what is not a symphony. It is not the literal story, but the pure musical utterance. Thus Berlioz's " Romeo and Juliet " symphony is in its design more the literal story than is Shakespeare's play. And yet there is ever a serious nobility, a heroic reach in the art of Berlioz, where he stands almost alone among the composers of his race. Here, probably, more than in his pictured stories, lies the secret of his endurance. He was, other than his followers, ever an idealist. And so, when we are on the point of condemning him as a scene-painter, we suddenly come upon a stretch of pure musical beauty, that flowed from the unconscious rapture of true poet. As the bee sucks, so may we cull the stray beauty and the more intimate meaning, despite and aside from this outer intent.

CHAPTER III
BERLIOZ. "ROMEO AND JULIET."

DRAMATIC SYMPHONY

IN the sub-title we see the growing impulse towards graphic music. A "dramatic symphony" is not promising. For, if music is the most subjective expression of the arts, why should its highest form be used to dramatize a drama? Without the aid of scene and actors, that were needed by the original poet, the artisan in absolute tones attempts his own theatric rendering. Clearly this symphony is one of those works of art which within an incongruous form (like certain ancient pictures) affords episodes of imperishable beauty.

Passing by the dramatic episodes that are strung on the thread of the story, we dwell, according to our wont, on the stretches where a pure musical utterance rises to a lofty height of pathos or of rarest fantasy.

In the first scene of the Second Part is the clear intent of a direct tonal expression, and there is a sustained thread of sincere sentiment. The passion of Romeo shines in the purity rather than in the intensity of feeling. The scene has a delicate series of moods, with subtle melodic touches and dramatic surprises of chord and color. The whole seems a reflection of Romeo's humor, the personal (*Allegro*)

19

theme being the symbol as it roams throughout the
various phases,—the sadness of solitude, the feverish
thrill of the ball. Into the first phrase of straying
violins wanders the personal motive, sadly meditative.

(Choir of wood, with
sustained chords of strings)

Sweeter dreams now woo the muser, warming into
passion, pulsing with a more eager throb of desire,
in changed tone and pace. Suddenly in a new quarter amid a quick strum of dance the main motive
hurries along. The gay sounds vanish, ominous
almost in the distance. The sadness of the lover
now sings unrestrained in expressive melody (of
oboe), in long swinging pace, while far away rumbles
the beat of festive drum.

The song rises in surging curves, but dies away

20

among the quick festal sounds, where the personal
motive is still supreme, chasing its own ardent antics,
and plunges headlong into the swirl of dance.

Il Penseroso (in his personal rôle) has glided into
a buoyant, rollicking Allegro with joyous answer.
Anon the outer revel breaks in with shock almost of
terror. And now in climax of joy, through the festal
strum across the never-ceasing thread of transformed
meditation resound in slowest, broadest swing the

(Ob. with fl. and cl.
and arpeggic cellos)

warm tones of the love-song in triumph of bliss.*
As the song dies away, the festal sounds fade. Grim
meditation returns in double figure,—the slower,
heavier pace below. Its shadows are all about as in
a fugue of fears, flitting still to the tune of the dance
and anon yielding before the gaiety. But through the
returning festal ring the fateful motive is still straying in the bass. In the concluding revel the hue of
meditation is not entirely banned.

The Shakespearian love-drama thus far seems to be
celebrated in the manner of a French romance. After
all, the treatment remains scenic in the main; the

---

* In unison of the wind. Berlioz has here noted in the
score " *Réunion des deux Thémes, du Larghetto et de
L'Allegro*," the second and first of our cited phrases.

feeling is diluted, as it were, not intensified by the
music.

The stillness of night and the shimmering moonlight are in the delicate harmonies of (*Allegretto*)
strings. A lusty song of departing revellers breaks
upon the scene. The former distant sounds of feast
are now near and clear in actual words.

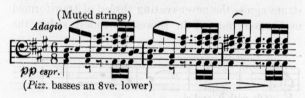

There is an intimate charm, a true glamor of love-
idyll about the Adagio. On more eager pulse rises
a languorous strain of horn and cellos. The flow

of its passionate phrase reaches the climax of prologue where, the type and essence of the story, it
plays about the lovers' first meeting. As lower
strings hum the burden of desire, higher wood add
touches of ecstasy, the melting violins sing the wooing song, and all break into an overwhelming rapture,

as though transfigured in the brightness of its own vehemence, in midst of a trembling mystery.

The restless spirit starts (*allegro agitato*) in fearsome agitation on quick nervous throb of melody; below, violas sing a soothing answer; there is a clear dialogue of wistful lovers.

Instead of the classic form of several verses led by one dominant melody to varied paths and views, here almost in reverse we seem to fall from a broader lyric mood to a single note of sad yearning that

(Fl. with Eng. horn an 8ve. below)

(Muted violins with sustained lower *p espress.* strings)

grows out of the several strains. Upon such a motive a new melody sings. The delicate bliss of early love is all about, and in the lingering close the timid ecstasies of wooing phrase. But this is a mere prelude to the more highly stressed, vehement song of love that follows on the same yearning motive. Here is the crowning, summing phase of the whole poem, without a return to earlier melody save that, by significant touch, it ends in the same expressive turn as the former languorous song.

The first melody does not reappear, is thus a kind

of background of the scene. The whole is a dramatic lyric that moves from broader tune to a reiterated note of sad desire, driven to a splendid height of crowned bliss. The turbulence of early love is there; pure ardor in flaming tongues of ecstasy; the quick turn of mood and the note of omen of the original poem: the violence of early love and the fate that hangs over.

Berlioz has drawn the subject of his Scherzo from Mercutio's speech in Scene 4 of the First Act of Shakespeare's tragedy. He has entitled it "Queen Mab, or the Fairy of Dreams," and clearly intends to portray the airy flight of Mab and her fairies. But we must doubt whether this, the musical gem of the symphony, has a plan that is purely graphic,— rather does it seem to soar beyond those concrete limits to an utterance of the sense of dreams themselves in the spirit of Mercutio's conclusion:

> " . . . I talk of dreams
> Which are the children of an idle brain,
> Begot of nothing but vain fantasy;
> Which is as thin of substance as the air; "

And we may add, as elusive for the enchanted mind to hold are these pranks and brilliant parade of tonal sprites. It stands one of the masterpieces of program-music, in equal balance of pure beauty with the graphic plan.

Imps they are, these flitting figures, almost insects with a personality. In pace there is a division,

24

where the first dazzling speed is simply the fairy
rhythm (halted anon by speaking pauses or silences),
and the second, a kind of idyll or romance in miniature. It is all a drama of fairy actors, in a dream-
land of softest tone. The main figure leads its
troop on gossamer thread of varied journey.

Almost frightening in the quickest, pulsing motion
is the sudden stillness, as the weird poising of trembling sprites. Best of all is the resonant beauty of
the second melody in enchanting surprise of tone.

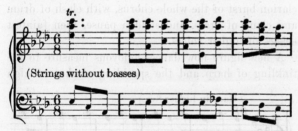

Anon, as in a varied dance, the skipping, mincing
step is followed by a gentle swaying; or the figures
all run together down the line to start the first dance
again, or the divided groups have different motions,
or one shouts a sudden answer to the other.

Much slower now is the main song (in flute and

25

English horn) beneath an ariel harmony (of overtones), while a quicker trip begins below of the same
figure. And in the midst is a strange concert of low
dancing strings with highest tones of harp,—strange
mating of flitting sprites.

We are suddenly back in the first, skipping dance,
ever faster and brighter in dazzling group of lesser
figures. And here is the golden note of fairy-land,—
the horn in soft cheery hunter's lay, answered by echoing voices. For a moment the call is tipped with
touch of sadness, then rings out brightly in a new
quarter. Beautiful it sings between the quick
phrases, with a certain shock of change, and there
is the terror of a sudden low rumbling and the thrill
of new murmuring sounds with soft beat of drum
that hails the gathering fairies. There is a sudden
clarion burst of the whole chorus, with clash of drum
and clang of brass, and sudden pause, then faintest
echoes of higher voices.

A new figure now dances a joyous measure to the
tinkling of harp and the sparkling strokes of high

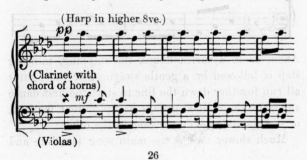

cymbals and long blown tone of horns. The very essence it is of fairy life. And so the joy is not unmixed with just a touch of awe. Amidst the whole tintinnabulation is a soft resonant echo of horns below, like an image in a lake. The air hangs heavy with dim romance until the sudden return to first fairy verse in sounds almost human. Once more come the frightening pauses.

The end is in a great crash of sweet sound—a glad awakening to day and to reality.

CHAPTER IV

A SYMPHONY TO DANTE'S "DIVINA COMMEDIA"

FOR ORCHESTRA AND CHORUS OF SOPRANOS AND ALTOS

THE " Divina Commedia " may be said in a broad view to belong to the great design by which Christian teaching was brought into relation with earlier pagan lore. The subject commands all the interest of the epics of Virgil and of Milton. It must be called the greatest Christian poem of all times, and the breadth of its appeal and of its art specially attest the age in which it was written, when classic pagan poetry broke upon the world like a great treasure-trove.

The subject was an ideal one in Dante's time,— a theme convincing and contenting to all the world, and, besides, akin to the essence of pagan poetry. The poet was needed to celebrate all the phases of its meaning and beauty. This is true of all flashes of evolutionary truth. As in the ancient epics, an idea once real to the world may be enshrined in a design of immortal art.

To-day we are perhaps in too agnostic a state to be absorbed by such a contemplation. The subject in a narrower sense is true at most to those who will to cherish the solace of a salvation which they have not fully apprehended. And so the Liszt symphony of the nineteenth century is not a complete reflection of the Dante poem of the fourteenth. It becomes for the devout believer almost a kind of church-liturgy,—a Mass by the Abbé Liszt.

Rare qualities there undoubtedly are in the music: a reality of passion; a certain simplicity of plan; the sensuous beauty of melodic and harmonic touches. But a greatness in the whole musical expression that may approach the grandeur of the poem, could only come in a suggestion of symbolic truth; and here the composer seems to fail by a too close clinging to ecclesiastic ritual. Yet in the agony of remorse, rising from hopeless woe to a chastened worship of the light, is a strain of inner truth that will leave the work for a long time a hold on human interest.

Novel is the writing of words in the score, as if they are to be sung by the instruments,—all sheer aside from the original purpose of the form. Page after page has its precise text; we hear the shrieks of the damned, the dread inscription of the infernal portals; the sad lament of lovers; the final song of praise of the redeemed. A kind of picture-book music has our symphony become. The *leit-motif* has crept into the high form of absolute tones to make it as definite and dramatic as any opera.

I. INFERNO

The legend of the portal is proclaimed at the outset in a rising phrase (of the low brass and strings)

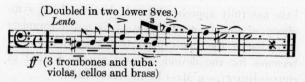

(Doubled in two lower 8ves.)

Lento

ff (3 trombones and tuba:
violas, cellos and brass)

Per me si va nella cit-ta do-lente;
Per me si va nell' eterno dolore;

and in still higher chant—

Per me si va tra la perduta gente.

Then, in antiphonal blast of horns and trumpets
sounds the fatal doom in grim monotone (in descending harmony of trembling strings):

(Chant in octaves of trumpets and horns)

ff La scia- te ogni spe - ran - - za.

(Brass, wood and *tremolo* strings)

Lasciate ogni speranza mi ch' entrate! *

A tumult on a sigh (from the first phrase) rises
again and again in gusts. In a violent paroxysm
we hear the doom of the monotone in lowest horns.

* " Through me the way is to the city dolent;
Through me the way is to eternal dole;
Through me the way among the people lost.
All hope abandon, ye who enter in! "

—From Longfellow's translation.

The fateful phrases are ringing about, while pervading all is the hope-destroying blast of the brass. But the storm-centre is the sighing motive which now enters on a quicker spur of passionate stride (*Allegro frenetico, quasi doppio movimento*). In its winding

(Woodwind and violas)

sequences it sings a new song in more regular pace. The tempest grows wilder and more masterful, still following the lines of the song, rising to towering height. And now in the strains, slow and faster, sounds the sigh above and below, all in a madrigal of woe. The whole is surmounted by a big descending phrase, articulate almost in its grim dogma, as it runs into the line of the first legend in full tumult of gloom. It is followed by the doom slowly proclaimed in thundering tones of the brass, in midst of a tempest of surging harmonies. Only it is all more fully and poignantly stressed than before, with long, resonant echoes of the stentorian tones of lowest brass.

Suddenly we are in the dulcet mood (*Quasi Andante, ma sempre un poco mosso*) 'mid light waving strings and rich swirling harp, and soothing tones

31

of flutes and muted horns. Then, as all other voices are hushed, the clarinet sings a strain that ends in lowest notes of expressive grief (*Recit., expressivo dolente*)—where we can almost hear the words. It is answered by a sweet plaint of other wood, in

(Clarinets and bassoons)

questioning accents, followed by the returning waves of strings and harp, and another phrase of the lament; and now to the pulsing chords of the harp the mellow English horn does sing (at least in the score) the words,—the central text of all:

* "There is no greater sorrow than to be mindful of the happy time in misery."—*From Longfellow's translation.*

Other voices join the leader. As the lower reed start the refrain, the higher enter in pursuit, and then the two groups sing a melodic chase. But the whole phrase is a mere foil to the pure melody of the former plaint that now returns in lower strings. And all so far is as a herald to the passage of intimate sentiment (*Andante amoroso*) that lies a lyric gem in the heart of the symphony. The melting strain is stressed in tenderness by the languor of harmonies, the delicate design of elusive rhythm and the appealing whisper of harp and two violins,—tipped by the touch of mellow wood.

Andante amoroso. (*Tempo rubato*)
dolce con intimo sentimento

(Melody in first violins; arpeggios of harp and violas; lower woodwind and strings)

With the rising passion, as the refrain spreads in wider sequences, the choirs of wood and strings are drawn into the song, one group answering the other in a true love duet.

The last cadence falls into the old sigh as the dread oracle sounds once more the knell of hope. Swirling strings bring us to a new scene of the world of shades. In the furious, frenetic pace of yore (*Tempo primo,*

Allegro, alla breve) there is a new sullen note, a dull martial trip of drums with demonic growls (in the lowest wood). The sigh is there, but perverted in humor. A chorus of blasphemous mockery is stressed by strident accents of lower wood and strings.*

Gradually we fall into the former frenzied song, amid the demon cacchinations, until we have plunged back into the nightmare of groans. Instead of the big descending phrase we sink into lower depths of gloom, wilder than ever, on the first tripping motive. As the sighing strain resounds below in the midst of a chorus of demon shrieks, there enters the chant of inexorable fate. Mockery yields to a tinge of pathos, a sense almost of majestic resignation, an apotheosis of grief.

II. PURGATORIO

A state of tranquillity, almost of bliss, is in the opening primal harmonies (of harp and strings and

Andante con moto quasi Allegretto.   *Tranquillo assai*
(Oboe *molto espressivo*)

Sempre piano é legato
(Full arpeggic harp and muted strings)

* We are again assisted by the interpreting words in the score.

34

soft horns). Indeed, what else could be the mood of relief from the horrors of hell? And lo! the reed strikes a pure limpid song echoed in turn by other voices, beneath a rich spray of heavenly harmonies.

This all recurs in higher shift of tone. A wistful phrase (*piu lento,* in low strings) seems to breathe

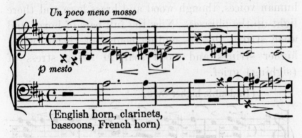

Un poco meno mosso

p mesto

(English horn, clarinets, bassoons, French horn)

a spoken sob. Then, as in voices of a hymn, chants a more formal liturgy of plaint where the phrase is almost lost in the lowest voice. It is all but articulate, with a sense of the old sigh; but it is in a calmer spirit, though anon bursting with passionate grief (*lagrimoso*).

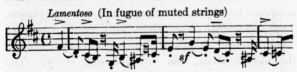

Lamentoso (In fugue of muted strings)

And now in the same vein, of the same fibre, a fugue begins of lament, first in muted strings.

It is the line of sad expressive recitative that heralded the plaint and the love-scene. There is here the full charm of fugue: a rhythmic quality of single theme, the choir of concerted dirge in independent and interdependent paths, and with every note of integral melody. There is the beauty of pure tonal architecture blended with the personal significance of the human (and divine) tragedy.

The fugue begins in muted strings, like plaintive human voices, though wood and brass here and there light up the phrases. Now the full bass of horns and wood strikes the descending course of theme, while higher strings and wood soar in rising stress of (sighing) grief.

(In double higher 8ves.)

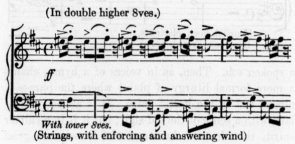

With lower 8ves.
(Strings, with enforcing and answering wind)

A hymnal verse of the theme enters in the wood answered by impetuous strings on a coursing phrase. The antiphonal song rises with eager stress of themal attack. A quieter elegy leads to another burst, the motive above, the insistent sigh below. The climax of fugue returns to the heroic main plaint below, with sighing answers above, all the voices of wood and brass enforcing the strings.

Then the fugue turns to a transfigured phase; the theme rings triumphant retorts in golden horns and

in a masterful unison of the wood; the wild answer
runs joyfully in lower strings, while the higher are
strumming like celestial harps. The whole is transformed to a big song of praise ever in higher harmonies. The theme flows on in ever varying thread,
amidst the acclaiming tumult.

But the heavenly heights are not reached by a
single leap. Once more we sink to sombre depths
not of the old rejection, but of a chastened, wistful
wonderment. The former plaintive chant returns, in
slower, contained pace, broken by phrases of mourning recitative, with the old sigh. And a former brief
strain of simple aspiration is supported by angelic
harps. In gentle ascent we are wafted to the acclaim
of heavenly (treble) voices in the *Magnificat*. A
wonderful utterance, throughout the scene of Purga-
tory, there is of a chastened, almost spiritual grief
for the sin that cannot be undone, though it is not
past pardon.

The bold design of the final Praise of the Almighty
was evidently conceived in the main as a service. An
actual depiction, or a direct expression (such as is
attempted in the prologue of Boito's Mefistofele) was
thereby avoided. The Holy of Holies is screened
from view by a priestly ceremony,—by the mask of
conventional religion. Else we must take the composer's personal conception of such a climax as that
of an orthodox Churchman. And then the whole
work, with all its pathos and humanity, falls to the
level of liturgy.

The words of invisible angel-chorus are those of the blessed maid trusting in God her savior, on a theme for which we are prepared by preluding choirs of harps, wood and strings. It is sung on an ancient Church tone that in its height approaches the mode of secular song. With all the power of broad rhythm, and fulness of harmony and volume, the feeling is of conventional worship. With all the purity of shimmering harmonies the form is ecclesiastical in its main lines and depends upon liturgic symbols for its effect and upon the faith of the listener for its appeal.

At the end of the hymn, on the entering *Hosanna!* and *Hallelujah!* we catch the sacred symbol (of seven tones) in the path of the two vocal parts, the lower descending, the higher ascending as on heavenly scale. In the second, optional ending the figure is completed, as the bass descends through the seven whole tones and the treble (of voices and instruments) rises as before to end in overpowering *Hallelujah!* The style is close knit with the earlier music. A pervading motive is the former brief phrase of aspiration; upon it the angelic groups seem to wing their flight between verses of praise. By a wonderful touch the sigh, that appeared inverted in the plaintive chant of the *Purgatorio,* is finally glorified as the motive of the bass to the words of exultation.

CHAPTER V

THE SYMPHONIC POEMS OF LISZT

LISZT was clearly a follower of Berlioz in the abandon to a pictorial aim, in the revolt from pure musical form, and in the mastery of orchestral color. If we feel in almost all his works a charming translation of story in the tones, we also miss the higher empyræan of pure fancy, unlimited by halting labels. It is a descent into pleasant, rich pastures from the cosmic view of the lofty mountain. Yet it must be yielded that Liszt's program-music was of the higher kind that dwells in symbols rather than in concrete details. It was a graphic plan of symbolization that led Liszt to choose the subjects of his symphonic poems (such as the " Préludes " and the " Ideals ") and to prefer the poetic scheme of Hugo's " Mazeppa " to the finer verse of a Byron. Though not without literal touches, Liszt perceived that his subjects must have a symbolic quality.

Nevertheless this pictorial style led to a revolution in the very nature of musical creation and to a new form which was seemingly intended to usurp the place of the symphony. It is clear that the symphonic poem is in very essence opposed to the symphony. The genius of the symphony lies in the overwhelming breadth and intensity of its expression

39

without the aid of words. Vainly decried by a later age of shallower perception, it achieved this Promethean stroke by the very magic of the design. At one bound thus arose in the youngest art a form higher than any other of human device,—higher than the epic, the drama, or the cathedral.

Bowing to an impatient demand for verbal meaning, Liszt invented the Symphonic Poem, in which the classic cogency yielded to the loose thread of a musical sketch in one movement, slavishly following the sequence of some literary subject. He abandoned sheer tonal fancy, surrendering the magic potency of pure music, fully expressive within its own design far beyond the literal scheme.*

The symphonic poems of Liszt, in so far as his intent was in destructive reaction to the classic process, were precisely in line with the drama of Wagner. The common revolt completely failed. The higher, the real music is ever of that pure tonal design where the fancy is not leashed to some external scheme. Liszt himself grew to perceive the inadequacy of the new device when he returned to the symphony for his greatest orchestral expression, though even here he never escaped from the thrall of a literal subject.

And strangely, in point of actual music, we cannot fail to find an emptier, a more grandiose manner in all these symphonic poems than in the two sym-

---

* Mendelssohn with perfect insight once declared,— " Notes have as definite a meaning as words, perhaps even a more definite one."

phonies. It seems as if an unconscious sense of the greater nobility of the classic medium drove Liszt to a far higher inspiration in his melodic themes.

Yet we cannot deny the brilliant, dazzling strokes, and the luscious harmonies. It was all a new manner, and alone the novelty is welcome, not to speak of the broad sweep of facile melody, and the sparkling thrills.

LES PRÉLUDES

This work has a preface by the composer, who refers in a footnote to the "*Méditations poétiques*" of Lamartine.

"What else is our life than a series of preludes to that unknown song of which the first solemn note is struck by death? Love is the morning glow of every heart; but in what human career have not the first ecstasies of bliss been broken by the storm, whose cruel breath destroys fond illusions, and blasts the sacred shrine with the bolt of lightning. And what soul, sorely wounded, does not, emerging from the tempest, seek to indulge its memories in the calm of country life? Nevertheless, man will not resign himself for long to the soothing charm of quiet nature, and when the trumpet sounds the signal of alarm, he runs to the perilous post, whatever be the cause that calls him to the ranks of war,—that he may find in combat the full consciousness of himself and the command of all his powers."

How far is the music literally graphic? We cannot look for the "unknown song" in definite sounds. That would defeat, not describe, its character. But the first solemn notes, are not these the solemn rising phrase that reappears in varying rhythm and pace all about the beginning and, indeed, the whole course

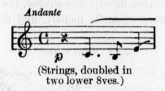

Andante

(Strings, doubled in
two lower 8ves.)

of the music. Just these three notes abound in the mystic first "prelude," and they are the core of the great swinging tune of the Andante maestoso, the beginning and main pulse of the unknown song.

Andante maestoso

(Basses of strings, wood and brass, doubled below; arpeggic harmonies in upper strings; sustained higher wood)

Now (*dolce cantando*) is a softer guise of the phrase. For death and birth, the two portals, are like

(Strings, with arpeggic violins)

dolce cantando

(*Pizz.* basses)

42

elements. Even here the former separate motive sounds, and so in the further turn of the song (*expressivo dolente*) on new thread.

The melody that sings (*expressivo ma tranquillo*) may well stand for "love, the glow of dawn in every heart." Before the storm, both great motives (of love and death) sound together very beautifully, as in

(Horns and lower strings, with
arpeggic harp and violins)

Tennyson's poem. The storm that blasts the romance begins with the same fateful phrase. It is all about, even inverted, and at the crisis it sings with the fervor of full-blown song. At the lull the soft guise reappears, faintly, like a sweet memory.

The Allegretto pastorale is clear from the preface. After we are lulled, soothed, caressed and all but entranced by these new impersonal sounds, then, as if the sovereign for whom all else were preparing, the song of love seeks its recapitulated verse. Indeed here is the real full song. Is it that in the memory lies the reality, or at least the realization?

Out of the dream of love rouses the sudden alarm of brass (*Allegro marziale animato*), with a new war-tune fashioned of the former soft disguised motive. The air of fate still hangs heavy over all. In spirited retorts the martial madrigal proceeds, but it is not all mere war and courage. Through the clash of strife break in the former songs, the love-theme in triumph and the first expressive strain in tempestuous joy. Last of all the fateful original motto rings once more in serene, contained majesty.

On the whole, even with so well-defined a program, and with a full play of memory, we cannot be quite sure of a fixed association of the motive. It is better to view the melodic episodes as subjective phases, arising from the tenor of the poem.

TASSO

Liszt's "Tasso" is probably the earliest celebration, in pure tonal form, of the plot of man's suffering and redemption, that has been so much followed that it may be called the type of the modern symphony.* In this direct influence the "Tasso" poem has been the most striking of all of Liszt's creations.

---

* We may mention such other works of Liszt as "Mazeppa" and the "Faust" Symphony; the third symphony of Saint-Saëns; Strauss' tone poem "Death and Transfiguration"; Volbach's symphony, besides other symphonies such as a work by Carl Pohlig. We may count here, too, the Heldenlied by Dvôrák, and Strauss' Heldenleben (see Vol. II).

THE SYMPHONIC POEMS OF LISZT

The following preface of the composer accompanies the score:

"In the year 1849 the one hundredth anniversary of Goethe's birth was celebrated throughout Germany; the theatre in Weimar, where we were at the time, marked the 28th of August by a performance of 'Tasso.'

"The tragic fate of the unfortunate bard served as a text for the two greatest poets produced by Germany and England in the last century: Goethe and Byron. Upon Goethe was bestowed the most brilliant of mortal careers; while Byron's advantages of birth and of fortune were balanced by keenest suffering. We must confess that when bidden, in 1849, to write an overture for Goethe's drama, we were more immediately inspired by Byron's reverential pity for the shades of the great man, which he invoked, than by the work of the German poet. Nevertheless Byron, in his picture of Tasso in prison, was unable to add to the remembrance of his poignant grief, so nobly and eloquently uttered in his 'Lament,' the thought of the 'Triumph' that a tardy justice gave to the chivalrous author of 'Jerusalem Delivered.' We have sought to mark this dual idea in the very title of our work, and we should be glad to have succeeded in pointing this great contrast,—the genius who was misjudged during his life, surrounded, after death, with a halo that destroyed his enemies. Tasso loved and suffered at Ferrara; he was avenged at Rome; his glory still lives in the folk-songs of Venice. These three elements are inseparable from his immortal memory. To represent them in music, we first called up his august spirit as he still haunts the waters of Venice. Then we beheld his proud and melancholy figure as he passed through the festivals of Ferrara where he had produced his master-works. Finally we followed him to Rome, the eternal city, that offered him the crown and glorified in him the martyr and the poet.

45

"*Lamento e Trionfo:* Such are the opposite poles of the destiny of poets, of whom it has been justly said that if their lives are sometimes burdened with a curse, a blessing is never wanting over their grave. For the sake not merely of authority, but the distinction of historical truth, we put our idea into realistic form in taking for the theme of our musical poem the motive with which we have heard the gondoliers of Venice sing over the waters the lines of Tasso, and utter them three centuries after the poet:

" ' Canto l'armi pietose e'l Capitano
Che'l gran Sepolcro liberò di Christo! '

" The motive is in itself plaintive; it has a sustained sigh, a monotone of grief. But the gondoliers give it a special quality by prolonging certain tones—as when distant rays of brilliant light are reflected on the waves. This song had deeply impressed us long ago. It was impossible to treat of Tasso without taking, as it were, as text for our thoughts, this homage rendered by the nation to the genius whose love and loyalty were ill merited by the court of Ferrara. The Venetian melody breathes so sharp a melancholy, such hopeless sadness, that it suffices in itself to reveal the secret of Tasso's grief. It lent itself, like the poet's imagination, to the world's brilliant illusions, to the smooth and false coquetry of those smiles that brought the dreadful catastrophe in their train, for which there seemed to be no compensation in this world. And yet upon the Capitol the poet was clothed with a mantle of purer and more brilliant purple than that of Alphonse."

With the help of the composer's plot, the intent of the music becomes clear, to the dot almost of the note. The whole poem is an exposition of the one sovereign melody, where we may feel a kindred trait of Hungarian song, above all in the cadences, that

must have stirred Liszt's patriot heart. Nay,—
beginning as it does with melancholy stress of the
phrase of cadence and the straying into full rhyth-
mitic exultation, it seems (in strange guise) another

of Liszt's Hungarian rhapsodies,—that were, perhaps,
the greatest of all he achieved, where his unpremeditated frenzy revelled in purest folk-rhythm and
tune. The natural division of the Hungarian dance,
with the sad *Lassu* and the glad *Friss,* is here clear in

order and recurrence. The Magyar seems to the manner born in both parts of the melody.*

In the accents of the motive of cadence (*Lento*) we feel the secret grief of the hero, that turns *Allegro strepitoso,* in quicker pace to fierce revolt.

In full tragic majesty the noble theme enters, in panoply of woe. In the further flow, as in the beginning, is a brief chromatic strain and a sigh of descending tone that do not lie in the obvious song, that are drawn by the subjective poet from the latent fibre. Here is the modern Liszt, of rapture and anguish, in manner and in mood that proved so potent a model with a later generation.†

The verse ends in a prolonged threnody, then turns to a firm, serenely grave burst of the song in major, *Meno Adagio,* with just a hint of martial grandeur. For once, or the nonce, we seem to see the hero-poet acclaimed. In a middle episode the motive of the cadence sings expressively with delicate harmonies, rising to full-blown exaltation. We may see here an actual brief celebration, such as Tasso did receive on entering Ferrara.

And here is a sudden fanciful turn. A festive dance strikes a tuneful trip,—a menuet it surely is, with all the ancient festal charm, vibrant with tune and spring, though still we do not escape the source

---

* A common Oriental element in Hungarian and Venetian music has been observed. See Kretschmar's note to Liszt's " Tasso " (Breitkopf & Haertel).

† See note in the final chapter of Volume II.

of the first pervading theme. Out of the midst of the dance sings slyly an enchanting phrase, much like a secret love-romance. Now to the light continuing dance is joined a strange companion,—the heroic melody in its earlier majestic pace. Is it the poet in serious meditation at the feast apart from the joyous abandon, or do we see him laurel-crowned, a centre of the festival, while the gay dancers flit about him in homage?

More and more brilliant grows the scene, though ever with the dominant grave figure. With sudden stroke as of fatal blast returns the earlier fierce burst of revolt, rising to agitation of the former lament, blending both moods and motives, and ending with a broader stress of the first tragic motto.

Now, *Allegro con brio,* with herald calls of the brass and fanfare of running strings (drawn from the personal theme), in bright major the whole song bursts forth in brilliant gladness. At the height the exaltation finds vent in a peal of simple melody. The "triumph" follows in broadest, royal pace of the main song in the wind, while the strings are madly coursing and the basses reiterate the transformed motive of the cadence. The end is a revel of jubilation.

MAZEPPA

The Mazeppa music is based upon Victor Hugo's poem, in turn founded upon Byron's verse, with an added stirring touch of allegory.

4 49

The verses of Hugo first tell how the victim is tied to the fiery steed, how—

" He turns in the toils like a serpent in madness,
   And . . . his tormentors have feasted in gladness
      Upon his despair.

. . . .

They fly.—Empty space is behind and before them

. . . .

The horse, neither bridle nor bit on him feeling,
Flies ever; red drops o'er the victim are stealing:
      His whole body bleeds.
Alas! to the wild horses foaming and champing
That followed with mane erect, neighing and stamping,
      A crow-flight succeeds.
The raven, the horn'd owl with eyes round and hollow,
The osprey and eagle from battle-field follow,
      Though daylight alarm.

. . . .

Then after three days of this course wild and frantic,
Through rivers of ice, plains and forests gigantic,
      The horse sinks and dies;

. . . .

Yet mark! That poor sufferer, gasping and moaning,
To-morrow the Cossacks of Ukraine atoning,
      Will hail as their King;

. . . .

To royal Mazeppa the hordes Asiatic
Will show their devotion in fervor ecstatic,
      And low to earth bow."

In his splendid epilogue the poet likens the hero to the mortal on whom the god has set his mark. He sees himself bound living to the fatal course of genius, the fiery steed.

50

" Away from the world—from all real existence
He is borne upwards, despite his resistance
    On feet of steel.
He is taken o'er deserts, o'er mountains in legions,
Grey-hoary, thro' oceans, and into the regions
    Far over the clouds;
A thousand base spirits his progress unshaken
Arouses, press round him and stare as they waken,
    In insolent crowds

.   .   .   .

He cries out with terror, in agony grasping,
Yet ever the name of his Pegasus clasping,
    They heavenward spring;
Each leap that he takes with fresh woe is attended;
He totters—falls lifeless—the struggle is ended—
    And rises as King! *

The original *Allegro agitato* in broad 6/4 time
(aptly suggestive of the unbridled motion) grows

(In brass and strings with lower 8ve.)

ff sempre
**(With constant clattering higher strings and
chord of low wind on the middle beat)**

more rapid into an *alla breve* pace (in two beats),
with dazzling maze of lesser rhythms. Throughout
the work a song of primeval strain prevails. Here
and there a tinge of foreshadowing pain appears, as
the song sounds on high, *espressivo dolente*. But the

---

* The English verses are taken for the most part from
the translation of F. Corder.

fervor and fury of movement is undiminished. The brief touch of pathos soon merges in the general heroic mood. Later, the whole motion ceases, "the horse sinks and dies," and now an interlude sings a pure plaint (in the strain of the main motive). Then, *Allegro,* the martial note clangs in stirring trumpet and breaks into formal song of war, *Allegro marziale.*

In the wake of this song, with a relentless trip and tramp of warrior hordes, is the real clash and jingle of the battle, where the sparkling thrill of strings and the saucy counter theme are strong elements in the stirring beauty.

There is a touch here of the old Goth, or rather the Hun, nearer akin to the composer's race.

At the height rings out the main tune of yore, transformed in triumphant majesty.

The musical design embraces various phases. First is the clear rhythmic sense of the ride. We think of other instances like Schubert's "Erl-King" or the ghostly ride in Raff's "Lenore" Symphony.

The degree of vivid description must vary, not

only with the composer, but with the hearer. The greatest masters have yielded to the variety of the actual graphic touch. And, too, there are always interpreters who find it, even if it was never intended. Thus it is common to hear at the very beginning of the " Mazeppa " music the cry that goes up as starts the flight.

We are of course entitled, if we prefer, to feel the poetry rather than the picture. Finally it is probably true that such a poetic design is not marred merely because there is here or there a trick of onomatopœia; if it is permitted in poetry, why not in music? It may be no more than a spur to the fancy, a quick conjuring of the association.

HUNNENSCHLACHT—" THE BATTLE OF THE HUNS "

Liszt's symphonic poem, " Hunnenschlacht," one of the last of his works in this form, completed in 1857, was directly inspired by the picture of the German painter, Wilhelm Kaulbach, which represents the legend of the aerial battle between the spirits of the Romans and Huns who had fallen outside of the walls of Rome.*

---

* A description of the picture is cited by Lawrence Gilman in his book, " Stories of Symphonic Music," as follows:

" According to a legend, the combatants were so exasperated that the slain rose during the night and fought in the air. Rome, which is seen in the background, is said to have been the scene of this event. Above, borne on a shield,

The evidence of the composer's intent is embodied in a letter written in 1857 to the wife of the painter, which accompanied the manuscript of an arrangement of the music for two pianos. In the letter Liszt speaks of "the meteoric and solar light which I have borrowed from the painting, and which at the Finale I have formed into one whole by the gradual working up of the Catholic *choral* 'Crux fidelis,' and the meteoric sparks blended therewith." He continues: "As I have already intimated to Kaulbach, in Munich, I was led by the musical demands of the material to give proportionately more place to the solar light of Christianity, personified in the Catholic *choral* . . . than appears to be the case in the glorious painting, in order to win and pregnantly represent the conclusion of the Victory of the Cross, with which I both as a Catholic and as a man could not dispense."

The work begins *tempestuoso* (*allegro non troppo*), with a nervous theme over soft rolling drums and

Tempestuoso. Allegro non troppo

mf (Bassoons with *tremolo* cellos and roll of kettle-drums)

is Attila, with a scourge in his hand; opposite him Theodoric, King of the Visigoths. The foreground is a battlefield, strewn with corpses, which are seen to be gradually reviving, rising up and rallying, while among them wander wailing and lamenting women."

trembling low strings, that is taken up as in fugue
by successive groups and carried to a height where
enters a fierce call of the horns. The cries of battle
spread with increasing din and gathering speed. At
the first climax the whole motion has a new energy,
as the strings in feverish chase attack the quickened
motive with violent stress. Later, though the motion
has not lessened, the theme has returned to a semblance of its former pace, and again the cries of battle
(in brass and wood) sound across its path.

In the hush of the storm the full-blown call to
arms is heard in lowest, funereal tones. Of a sudden, though the speed is the same, the pace changes
with a certain terror as of a cavalry attack. Presently
amid the clattering tramp sounds the big hymn,—in
the ancient rhythm that moves strangely out of the
rut of even time.*

A single line of the hymn is followed by a refrain
of the battle-call, and by the charge of horse that

---

* Quoted on the following page.

brings back the hymn, in high pitch of trumpets.
And so recur the former phases of battle,—really
of threat and preparation. For now begins the
serious fray in one long gathering of speed and power.
The first theme here grows to full melodic song, with
extended answer, led by strepitous band of lower
reed over a heavy clatter of strings. We are in a

(Trombones with lower 8ve)

mp Marcato

maze of furious charges and cries, till the shrill
trumpet and the stentorian trombone strike the full
call in antiphonal song. The tempest increases with
a renewed charge of the strings, and now the more
distant calls have a slower sweep. Later the battle
song is in the basses,—again in clashing basses and
trebles; nearer strike the broad sweeping calls.

Suddenly over the hushed motion in soothing harmonies sings the hymn in pious choir of all the brass.
Then the gathering speed and volume is merged in a
majestic tread as of ordered array (*Maestoso assai;
Andante*) ; a brief spirited prelude of martial motives
is answered by the soft religious strains of the organ
on the line of the hymn:

" Crux fidelis, inter omnes
  Arbor una nobilis,
  Nulla silva talem profert
  Fronde, flore, germine.
  Dulce lignum, dulces clavos,
  Dulce pondus sustinet." *

As in solemn liturgy come the answering phrases
of the organ and the big chorus in martial tread.
As the hymn winds its further course, violins entwine
about the harmonies. The last line ends in expressive
strain and warm line of new major tone,—echoed in
interluding organ and violins.

Suddenly a strict, solemn tread, with sharp stress
of violins, brings a new song of the *choral*. Strings
alone play here " with pious expression "; gradually
reeds add support and ornament. A lingering phrase
ascends on celestial harmonies. With a stern shock
the plain hymn strikes in the reed, against a rapid
course of strings, with fateful tread. In interlude
sound the battle-cries of yore. Again the hymn ends
in the expressive cadence, though now it grows to a
height of power.

Here a former figure (the first motive of the battle)

---

* Faithful cross, among the trees
  Thou the noblest of them all!
  Forest ne'er doth grow a like
  In leaf, in flower or in seed.
  Blessed wood and blessed nails,
  Blessed burden that it bears!

reappears in a new guise of bright major,* in full, spirited stride, and leads once more to a blast of the hymn, with organ and all, the air in unison of trumpets and all the wood. The expressive cadence merges into a last fanfare of battle, followed by a strain of hymns and with reverberating Amens, where the organ predominates and holds long after all other sounds have ceased.

---

* In the whole tonality we may see the "meteoric and solar light" of which the composer speaks in the letter quoted above.

CHAPTER VI

THE SYMPHONIC POEMS OF SAINT-SAËNS

THERE is something charming and even ideal in a complete versatility, quite apart from the depth of the separate poems, where there is a never-failing touch of grace and of distinction. The Philip Sydneys are quite as important as the Miltons, perhaps they are as great. Some poets seem to achieve an expression in a certain cyclic or sporadic career of their fancy, touching on this or that form, illuminating with an elusive light the various corners of the garden. Their individual expression lies in the *ensemble* of these touches, rather than in a single profound revelation.

A symptom of the eminence of Saint-Saëns in the history of French music lies in his attitude towards the art as a whole, especially of the German masters, —the absence of national bias in his perceptions. He was foremost in revealing to his countrymen the greatness of Bach, Beethoven and Schumann. Without their influence the present high state of French music can hardly be conceived.

It is part of a broad and versatile mastery that it is difficult to analyze. Thus it is not easy to find salient traits in the art of M. Saint-Saëns. We are apt to think mainly of the distinguished beauty of his harmonies, until we remember his subtle counterpoint, or in turn the brilliancy of his orchestration. The one trait that he has above his contemporaries is an inbred refinement and restraint,—a thoroughgoing workmanship. If he does not share a certain overwrought emotionalism that is much affected nowadays, there is here no limitation—rather a distinction. Aside from the general charm of his art, Saint-Saëns found in the symphonic poem his one special form, so that it seemed Liszt had created it less for himself than for his French successor. A fine reserve of poetic temper saved him from hysterical excess. He never lost the music in the story, disdaining the mere rude graphic stroke; in his dramatic symbols a musical charm is ever commingled. And a like poise helped him to a right plot and point in his descriptions. So his symphonic poems must ever be enjoyed mainly for the music, with perhaps a revery upon the poetic story. With a less brilliant vein of melody, though they are not so Promethean in reach as those of Liszt, they are more complete in the musical and in the narrative effect.

DANSE MACABRE

Challenged for a choice among the works of the versatile composer, we should hit upon the *Danse Macabre* as the most original, profound and essentially beautiful of all. It is free from certain lacks that one feels in other works, with all their

60

charm,—a shallowness and almost frivolity; a facility of theme approaching the commonplace.

There is here an eccentric quality of humor, a dæmonic conceit that reach the height of other classic expression of the supernatural.

The music is founded upon certain lines of a poem of *Henri Calais* (under a like title), that may be given as follows:

> Zig-a-zig, zig-a-zig-a-zig,
> Death knocks on the tomb with rhythmic heel.
> Zig-a-zig, zig-a-zig-zig,
> Death fiddles at midnight a ghostly reel.
>
> The winter wind whistles, dark is the night;
> Dull groans behind the lindens grow loud;
> Back and forth fly the skeletons white,
> Running and leaping each under his shroud.
> Zig-a-zig-a-zig, how it makes you quake,
> As you hear the bones of the dancers shake.
>
> .   .   .   .
>
> But hist! all at once they vanish away,
> The cock has hailed the dawn of day.

The magic midnight strokes sound clear and sharp. In eager chords of tuned pitch the fiddling ghost summons the dancing groups, where the single fife is soon followed by demon violins.

Broadly sings now the descending tune half-way between a wail and a laugh. And ever in interlude is the skipping, mincing step,—here of reeds answered by solo violin with a light clank of cymbals. Answering the summoning fifes, the unison troop of fiddlers

dance the main step to bright strokes of triangle, then
the main ghostly violin trips in with choir of wind.
And broadly again sweeps the song between tears and

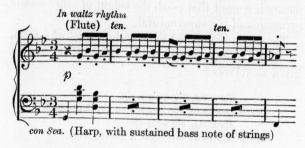

con 8va. (Harp, with sustained bass note of strings)

smiles. Or Death fiddles the first strain of reel for
the tumultuous answer of chorus.

Now they build a busy, bustling fugue (of the
descending song) and at the serious moment sud-

denly they skip away in new frolicsome, all but joyous,
tune: a shadowy counterfeit of gladness, where the
sob hangs on the edge of the smile. As if it could no
longer be contained, now pours the full passionate
grief of the broad descending strain. Death fiddles

his mournful chant to echoing, expressive wind. On
the abandon of grief follows the revel of grim humor
in pranks of mocking demons. All the strains are
mingled in the ghostly bacchanale. The descending song is answered in opposite melody. A
chorus of laughter follows the tripping dance. The
summoning chords, acclaimed by chorus, grow to
appealing song in a brief lull. At the height, to the
united skipping dance of overpowering chorus the
brass blows the full verse of descending song. The
rest is a mad storm of carousing till . . . out of
the whirling darkness sudden starts the sharp, sheer
call of prosaic day, in high, shrill reed. On a minish-
ing sound of rolling drum and trembling strings,
sings a brief line of wistful rhapsody of the departing
spirit before the last whisking steps.

PHÆTON

On a separate page between title and score is a
"*Notice*,"—an epitome of the story of Phæton,
as follows:

"Phæton has been permitted to drive the chariot
of the Sun, his father, through the heavens. But his
unskilful hands frighten the steeds. The flaming
chariot, thrown out of its course, approaches the ter-
restrial regions. The whole universe is on the verge
of ruin when Jupiter strikes the imprudent Phæton
with his thunderbolt."

There is a solemn sense at first (*Maestoso*), a mid-

air poise of the harmony, a quick spring of resolution and—on through the heavens. At the outset
and always is the pervading musical charm. In
the beginning is the enchantment of mere motion in
lightest prancing strings and harp with slowly ascending curve. In farther journey comes a spring of the
higher wood and soon a firm note of horns and a blast
of trumpets on a chirruping call, till the whole panoply of solar brilliance is shimmering. Now with the
continuing pulse (of saltant strings) rings a buoyant,

regnant air in the brass. A (canon) chase of echoing
voices merely adds an entrancing bewilderment, then
yields to other symbols and visions.

Still rises the thread of pulsing strings to higher
empyræan and then floats forth in golden horns, as
we hang in the heavens, a melody tenderly solemn,
as of pent delight, or perhaps of a more fatal hue,
with the solar orb encircled by his satellites.

Still on to a higher pole spins the dizzy path; then
at the top of the song, it turns in slow descending
curve. Almost to Avernus seems the gliding fall when
the first melody rings anew. But there is now an
anxious sense that dims the joy of motion and in the

returning first motive jars the buoyant spring.
Through the maze of fugue with tinge of terror
presses the fatuous chase, when—crash comes the
shock of higher power. There is a pause of motion
in the din and a downward flight as of lifeless figure.

Now seems the soul of the sweet melody to sing,
in purest dirge, without the shimmer of attendant
motion save a ghostly shadow of the joyous symbol.

THE YOUTH OF HERCULES

The "Legend" is printed in the score as follows:
"Fable tells us that upon entering into life Hercules saw the two paths open before him: of pleasure
and of virtue.

"Insensible to the seductions of Nymphs and Bac-
chantes, the hero devotes himself to the career of
struggle and combat, at the end of which he glimpses
across the flames of the funeral pyre the reward of
immortality."

We can let our fancy play about the score and
wonderfully hit an intention of the poet. Yet that is

often rather a self-flattery than a real perception.
In the small touches we may lose the greater beauty.
Here, after all, is the justification of the music. If
the graphic picture is added, a little, only, is gained.
The main virtue of it lies in our better grasp of the
musical design.

In the muted strings, straying dreamily in pairs, is
a vague line of the motto,—a foreshadowing of the
heroic idea, as are the soft calls of the wind with
wooing harp a first vision of delight.

Now begins the main song in sturdy course of unmuted strings. The wood soon join in the rehearsing.
But it is not all easy deciphering. The song wanders
in gently agitated strings while the horns hold a solemn phrase that but faintly resembles the motto.*

---

* It is well to resist the vain search for a transnotation
of the story. And here we see a virtue of Saint-Saëns himself, a national trait of poise that saved him from losing
the music in the picture. His symphonic poems must be
enjoyed in a kind of musical revery upon the poetic subject.
He disdained the rude graphic stroke, and used dramatic
means only where a musical charm was commingled.

Lesser phrases play about the bigger in rising flight of aspiration, crowned at the height with a ray of glad light.

As the dream sinks slowly away, the stern motto is buried in quick flashes of the tempting call. These are mere visions; now comes the scene itself of temptation.

To ripples of harp the reed sings enchantingly in swaying rhythm; other groups in new surprise of

scene usurp the melody with the languishing answer, until one Siren breaks into an impassioned burst, while her sisters hold the dance.

Straight upon her vanished echoes shrieks the shrill pipe of war, with trembling drum. We hear a yearning sigh of the Siren strain before it is swept away in the tide and tumult of strife. Beneath the whirl and motion, the flash and crash of arms, we have glimpses of the heroic figure.

Here is a strange lay in the fierce chorus of battle-cries: the Siren song in bright insistence, changed to the rushing pace of war.

The scene ends in a crash. Loud sings a solemn phrase; do we catch an edge of wistful regret? Now returns the sturdy course of the main heroic melody; only it is slower (*Andante sostenuto*), and the high stress of cadence is solemnly impassioned.

As if to atone for the slower pace, the theme strikes into a lively fugue, with trembling strings (*Allegro animato*).

There is an air of achievement in the relentless progress and the insistent recurrence of the masterful motive. An episode there is of mere striving and straining, before the theme resumes its vehement attack, followed by lusty echoes all about as of an army of heroes. There is the breath of battle in the rumbling basses and the shaking, quivering brass.

At last the plain song resounds in simple lines of ringing brass, led by the high bugle.*

Yet the struggle, the inner combat, is not over. At the very moment of triumph sings on high over purling harp the mastering strain of Sirens, is buried beneath martial clash and emerges with its enchantment. But here the virile mood and motive gains the victory and strides on to final scene.

We remember how Hercules built and ascended his own funeral pyre. In midst of quivering strings, with dashing harp and shrieking wood, a roll of drum and a clang of brass sounds the solemn chant of the trombone, descending in relentless steps. As the lowest is reached, there comes a spring of freedom in the

---

* Saint-Saëns employs besides the usual 4 horns, 2 trumpets, 3 trombones and tuba, a small bugle (in B-flat) and 2 cornets.

pulsing figures, like the winging of a spirit, and a final acclaim in a brief line of the legend.

OMPHALE'S SPINNING WHEEL

Between title and score is this *Notice:*

"The subject of this symphonic poem is feminine witchery, the triumphant struggle of weakness. The spinning wheel is a mere pretext, chosen from the point of view of rhythm and the general atmosphere of the piece.

"Those persons who might be interested in a study of the details of the picture, will see . . . the hero groaning in the toils which he cannot break, and . . . Omphale mocking the vain efforts of Hercules."

The versions of the story differ slightly. After the fulfilment of his twelve labors Hercules is ordered by the oracle to a period of three years' service to expiate the killing of the son of King Eurytus in a fit of madness. Hermes placed him in the household of Omphale, queen of Lydia, widow of Tmolus. Hercules is degraded to female drudgery, is clothed in soft raiment and set to spin wool, while the queen assumes the lion skin and club.

In another version he was sold as slave to Omphale, who restored him to freedom. Their passion was mutual. The story has a likeness to a similar episode of Achilles.

The spinning-wheel begins *Andante* in muted strings alternating with flutes and gradually hurries into a lively motion. Here the horn accents the spinning, while another thread (of higher wood) runs through the graceful woof. A chain of alluring harmonies preludes the ensnaring song, mainly of woodwind above the humming strings, with soft dotting of the harmony by the horns. The violins, to be sure, often enforce the melody.

In the second verse, with fuller chorus, the harp adds its touches to the harmony of the horns, with lightest tap of tonal drum. Later a single note of the trumpet is answered by a silvery laugh in the wood. Between the verses proceeds the luscious chain of harmonies, as with the turning of the wheel.

Now with the heavily expressive tones of low, unmuted strings and the sonorous basses of reed and brass (together with a low roll of drum and soft clash of cymbals) an heroic air sings in low strings and brass, to meet at each period a shower of notes from the harp. The song grows intense with the

(Wood and *trem.* violins doubled above)

(Horns)

p espress. e pesante

(Cellos, basses, bassoons and trombone, doubled below)

added clang of trumpets and roll of drums,—only to succumb to the more eager attack of the siren chorus. At last the full effort of strength battling vainly with weakness reaches a single heroic height and sinks away with dull throbs.

In soothing answer falls the caressing song of the high reed in the phrase of the heroic strain, lightly, quickly and, it seems, mockingly aimed. In gently railing triumph returns the pretty song of the wheel, with a new buoyant spring. Drums and martial brass yield to the laughing flutes, the cooing horns and the soft rippling harp with murmuring strings, to return like captives in the train at the height of the gaiety.

CHAPTER VII

CÉSAR FRANCK

THE new French school of symphony that broke upon the world in the latter part of the nineteenth century had its pioneer and true leader in César Franck.* It was he who gave it a stamp and a tradition.

The novelty of his style, together with the lateness of his acclaim (of which it was the probable cause), have marked him as more modern than others who were born long after him.

The works of Franck, in other lines of oratorio and chamber music, show a clear personality, quite apart from a prevailing modern spirit. A certain charm of settled melancholy seems to inhere in his wonted style. A mystic is Franck in his dominant moods, with a special sense and power for subtle harmonic process, ever groping in a spiritual discontent with defined tonality.

A glance at the detail of his art discloses Franck as one of the main harmonists of his age, with Wagner and Grieg. Only, his harmonic manner was

---

* If language and association, as against the place of birth, may define nationality, we have in César Franck another worthy expression of French art in the symphony. He was born at Liège in 1822; he died in 1890.

blended if not balanced by a stronger, sounder
counterpoint than either of the others. But with all
the originality of his style we cannot escape a sense of
the stereotype, that indeed inheres in all music that
depends mainly on an harmonic process. His harmonic ideas, that often seem inconsequential, in the
main merely surprise rather than move or please.
The enharmonic principle is almost too predominant,
—an element that ought never to be more than occasional. For it is founded not upon ideal, natural
harmony, but upon a conventional compromise, an ex-
pedient compelled by the limitation of instruments.
This over-stress appears far stronger in the music of
Franck's followers, above all in their frequent use
of the whole tone " scale " which can have no other
rationale than a violent extension of the enharmonic
principle.* With a certain quality of kaleidoscope,
there is besides (in the harmonic manner of César
Franck) an infinitesimal kind of progress in smallest steps. It is a dangerous form of ingenuity, to

---

* Absolute harmony would count many more than the
semitones of which our music takes cognizance. For purpose of convenience on the keyboard the semitonal raising
of one note is merged in the lowering of the next higher
degree in the scale. However charming for occasional surprise may be such a substitution, a continuous, pervading
use cannot but destroy the essential beauty of harmony
and the clear sense of tonality; moreover it is mechanical
in process, devoid of poetic fancy, purely chaotic in effect.
There is ever a danger of confusing the novel in art with
new beauty.

which the French are perhaps most prone,—an originality mainly in details.

And yet we must praise in the French master a wonderful workmanship and a profound sincerity of sentiment. He shows probably the highest point to which a style that is mainly harmonic may rise. But when he employs his broader mastery of tonal architecture, he attains a rare height of lofty feeling, with reaches of true dramatic passion.

The effect, to be sure, of his special manner is somewhat to dilute the temper of his art, and to depress the humor. It is thus that the pervading melancholy almost compels the absence of a " slow movement " in his symphony. And so we feel in all his larger works for instruments a suddenness of recoil in the Finale.

One can see in Franck, in analogy with his German contemporaries, an etherealized kind of " Tristan and Isolde,"—a " Paolo and Francesca " in a world of shades. Compared with his followers the quality of stereotype in Franck is merely general; there is no excessive use of one device.

A baffling element in viewing the art of Franck is his remoteness of spirit, the strangeness of his temper. He lacked the joyous spring that is a dominant note in the classic period. Nor on the other hand did his music breathe the pessimism and naturalism that came with the last rebound of Romantic reaction. Rather was his vein one of high spiritual absorption—not so much in recoil, as merely apart from the world in a kind of pious seclusion. Perhaps his main point of view was the church-organ. He seems a religious prophet in a non-religious age. With his immediate disciples he was a leader in the manner of his art, rather than in the temper of his poetry.

SYMPHONY IN D MINOR

The scoring shows a sign of modern feeling in the prominence of the brasses. With all contrast of spirit, the analogy of Franck with the Liszt-Wagner school and manner is frequently suggestive.

The main novelty of outer detail is the plan of merely three movements. Nor is there a return to the original form, without the Scherzo. To judge from the headings, the " slow " movement is absent. In truth, by way of cursory preamble, the chronic vein of César Franck is so ingrainedly reflective that there never can be with him an absence of the meditative phrase. Rather must there be a vehement rousing of his muse from a state of mystic adoration to rhythmic energy and cheer.*

---

* The key of the work is given by the composer as D minor. The first movement alone is in the nominal key. The second (in B flat) is in the submediant, the last in the tonic major. The old manner in church music, that Bach often used, of closing a minor tonality with a major chord, was probably due to a regard for the mood of the congregation. An extension of this tradition is frequent in a long coda in the major. But this is quite different in kind from a plan where all of the last movement is in insistent major. We know that it is quite possible to begin a work

Lento in basses of the strings a strain sounds like a basic motive, answered with harmonies in the wood. In further strings lies the full tenor of quiet reflection, with sombre color of tonal scheme. Motives are less controlling probably in Franck than in any other symphonist,—less so, at any rate, than his one

special mood and manner. Yet nowhere is the strict figural plot more faithful in detail than with César Franck.

The theme has an entirely new ring and answer when it enters Allegro after the Lento prelude. The further course of the tune here is in eccentric, resolute stride in the descending scale. Our new answer is much evident in the bass. The Allegro seems a mere irruption; for the Lento prelude reappears in full solemnity. Indeed, with all the title and pace, this

at some distance from the main key, leading to it by tortuous path of modulation; though there is no reason why we may not question the composer's own inscription, the controlling point is really the whole tonal scheme. Here the key of the second movement is built on a design in minor,—would have less reason in the major. For it rests on a degree that does not exist in the tonic major. To be sure, Beethoven did invent the change to a lowered submediant in a succeeding movement. And, of course, the final turn to the tonic major is virtually as great a license.

seems very like the virtual "slow" movement. A
mood of rapt, almost melancholy absorption prevails,
with rare flashes of joyous utterance, where the
Allegro enters as if to break the thrall of meditation.
A very striking inversion of the theme now appears.
The gradual growth of phrases in melodious instal-
ments is a trait of Franck (as it is of Richard
Strauss). The rough motto at each turn has a new

phase and frequently is transfigured to a fresh tune.
So out of the first chance counterfigures somehow
spring beautiful melodies, where we feel the fitness
and the relevance though we have not heard them
before. It is a quality that Franck shares with
Brahms, so that in a mathematical spirit we might
care to deduce all the figures from the first phrase.
This themal manner is quite analogous to the harmonic style of Franck,—a kaleidoscope of gradual
steps, a slow procession of pale hues of tone that with
strange aptness reflect the dim religious light of
mystic musing.

More and more expressive are the stages of the first

figures until we have a duet *molto cantabile* in the strings. Much of the charm of the movement lies in the balance of the new rhythms, the eccentric and the flowing. By some subtle path there grows a song

in big tones of unison, wood and strings and trumpets, that is the real hymnal refrain of the movement. Between this note almost of exultation and all shades of pious dreaming the mood is constantly shifting.

Another phrase rises also to a triumphant height (the clear reverse of the former tuneful melody) that comes now like a big *envoi* of assuring message.

Though the whole movement is evenly balanced be-tween Allegro and Penseroso (so far as pace is concerned), the mood of reflection really finds full vent; it has no reason for a further special expression.

Simple as the Allegretto appears in its suggestion of halting dance, the intent in the episodes is of the subtlest. The slow trip of strings and harp is soon given a new meaning with the melody of English horn. Throughout we are somehow divided between pure dance and a more thoughtful muse. In the first departure to an episode in major, seems to sing the essence of the former melody in gently murmuring strings, where later the whole chorus are drawn in. The song moves on clear thread and wing right out of the mood of the dance-tune; but the very charm lies in the mere outer change of guise. And so the second episode is still far from all likeness with the first dance beyond a least sense of the old trip that does appear here and there. It is all clearly a true scheme of variations, the main theme disguised beyond outer semblance, yet faithfully present throughout in the essential rhythm and harmony.

In the Finale, *Allegro non troppo,* we are really clear, at the outset, of the toils of musing melancholy.

79

After big bursts of chords, a tune rolls pleasantly along, *dolce cantabile,* in basses of wood and strings. Expressive after-phrases abound, all in the same jolly mood, until the whole band break boisterously on the simple song, with a new sonorous phrase of basses. Then, in sudden remove, sounds the purest bit of melody of all the symphony, in gentlest tones

Dolce cantabile

(In the brass)

of brass (trumpet, trombone and tuba). But, though in complete recoil from the rhythmic energy of Allegro theme, it is even farther from the re-flective mood than the latter. It shows, in this very contrast, the absence of the true lyric in the meditative vein, frequent with César Franck. The burst of melody blossoms ever fairer. In its later musing the tune browses in the bass. A waving phrase grows in the violins, which continues with strange evenness through the entrance of new song where we are sur-prised by the strange fitness of the Allegretto melody. And the second phase of the latter follows as if it belonged here. So, almost listless, without a hair of rhythmic change (*les temps out toujours la même valeur*), the Finale theme sings again most softly in the strings. It has, to be sure, lost all of its color, without the original throb of accompanying sounds. The phase of the movement is a shadowy procession of former ideas, united in the dreamy haze that enshrouds them. The stir that now begins is not of the first pale hue of thought, rather the vein of big discussion, brewing a storm that breaks finally in full blast on the gentle melody (of the brass) transfigured in ringing triumph, in all the course of the song. Nor is the succeeding phase the mystic habit of our poet; it is a mere farther digestion of the meat of the melody that leads once more to a height of climax whence we return to first course of themes, tuneful afterphrase and all, with the old happy motion. The counterpoint here is the mere joyous ringing of many strains all about.

Against all rules comes a new chorusing pæan on the theme of Allegretto, led by stentorian basses, together with an enchanting after-strain, which we might have remarked before. And still another quarter, long hushed, is heard anew, as a voice sounds a faint reminder of the hymn of the first Allegro. Indeed, the combining strains before the close seem sprung all of one parental idea. The motto of the beginning sings in fittest answer to the latest phrases. The very maze of the concert forbids our turning to their first origin. The end is in joyous chanting of the Finale melody.

CHAPTER VIII

D'INDY AND THE FOLLOWERS OF FRANCK

PERHAPS the noblest essay in symphonic music of the followers of Franck is the second symphony of Vincent D'Indy.* His vein is indeed throughout nearest akin of all the disciples to the serious muse of the master.

Though D'Indy is surpassed in a certain poetic originality by some of his compatriot contemporaries, there is in this symphony a breadth of design and detail, a clear melodic quality and a sustained lofty feeling that seem to mark it the typical French symphony of its time. The strength of the work lies in a unity that is not merely of figure and outline. If we must measure a symphony mainly by the slow movement, we cannot avoid, with all the languorous beauty, a certain conventionality of mood, stressed with an exotic use of the appoggiatura, while in the Scherzo is a refined savagery of modern cacophony.

The directions are all in French; we are reminded of Schumann's departure from the Italian fashion.

Each movement, save the third, has its prelude: a gathering of threads before the new story. The first notes of basses, together with the answer on high, sound a prophetic legend of the whole.

---

* Vincent d'Indy was born in Paris on March 27, 1852.

The harmonic lucubrations are profoundly subtle.
Indeed the very nature of the first phrase is of dim

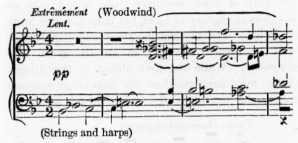

groping; it ends in a climax of the answer and
merges into the main song of the Allegro (*très vif*) in
horns, with rapid trip of strings.

Throughout (from a technical view) is a fine mastery of the device of ornamental notes, and secondary

harmonies; there is also a certain modern sense of chords and their relations. Together with an infinite brilliance of these resources there is not only no weakness in cogency of form, but there is a rare unity of design. The movements are bound together, at least in themal relation, as strictly as in any symphony. While the first phrase of the Allegro theme may hark back to the answer of original motto, the second is the main thread of narra-

(Flutes, oboes and clarinets)

tive. Again and again is the climax rung on the first high note of the theme. Then, in lieu of cadence, out of a bright dissonance the quick notes dance upward in sturdy pace, the answer of the Allegro in sharp disguise. And then from the height descends a refreshing spray of subtlest discords, ending in another masterful burst of new harmony.

The dainty, dazzling play is stopped by a rough thud of basses and a fierce clang of chords. In the sharp blare of brass on the ascending phrase is almost lost the original motto in lowest basses. It is now heard in gradually quickened speed, while the rising phrase runs more timidly. At last the quickened motto sinks gently into lulling motion, *un peu plus modéré.* Above, in strings and horns, the melody haunts us with a dim sense that takes us to the first languishing answer of the original legend. And the whole is strong-knit; for the very Allegro theme began in resolute mood of a like figure. A counterstrain rises to meet the main phrase. The whole episode is an intertwining of song in the vein of the first answer of motto.

The quick rising notes suddenly return with snatches of the main motive, the chain of echoing phrases runs a gamut of moods, fitful, anxious, soothed, until the bright upward trip begins anew, with the enchanting burst of chord and descending harmonies. A climactic height is stressed by a rough meeting of opposing groups, in hostile tone and movement, ending in a trill of flutes and a reëntry of the episode.

In the returning Allegro the thread is still the same, though richer in color and texture. Again there is the plunge into dark abyss, with shriek of harp, and the ominous theme in the depths. The slow ascending phrase here has a full song and sway. The end is in spirited duet of two quick motives.

The second movement, *modérément lent,* begins in revery on the answer of original motive, and the stately pathos of the theme, in horns, clarinets and violas, with rhythmic strings, grows naturally out of the mood.

Plus animé, in subtle change of pace (from ¾ to ⅔), the episode begins with eccentric stride of harps (and added woodwind), that serves as a kind of

Modérément Lent.

(Melody in horns, clarinets
and violas)

(Acc'd in
strings)

accompanying figure and foil for the sweeping song
of the real second melody (in oboe solo, succeeded by
the clarinet).

(Oboe solo)

Très espress.

(Violins)

(Acc't in bassoons, horns, harps and basses)

In the clash of themes and harmonies of the climax,
the very limits of modern license seem to be invoked.
Later the three themes are entwined in a passage
of masterly counterpoint.

There is a touch of ancient harmony in the delicate
tune of third movement, which has the virtue of end-

less weaving. It is sung by solo violin, mainly supported by a choir of lower strings.

A final conclusive line is given by the solo flute. Besides the constant course of varying tune, there is a power of ever changing harmony that seems to lie in some themes.

One can hardly call it all a Scherzo. It is rather an idyll after the pathos of the Andante. Or, from another view, reversing the usual order, we may find the quality of traditional Trio in the first melody and a bacchanale of wild humor in the middle. For, out

of a chance phrase of horns grows of all the symphony the boldest harmonic phrase (repeated through ten bars). Above rings a barbarous cry, in defiance of common time and rhythm.

Suddenly we are surprised by the sound of the martial stride of the second theme of the Andante which moves on the sea of rough harmony as on a native element. One whim follows another. The same motion is all there, but as if in shadow, in softest sound, and without the jar of discord; then comes the fiercest clash of all, and now a gayest dance of the first tune, *assez vif,* in triple rhythm, various figures having their *pas seul.* A second episode returns, brilliant in high pace but purged of the former war of sounds. At the end is the song of the first tune, with new pranks and sallies.

The beginning of the Finale is all in a musing review of past thoughts. The shadow of the last tune lingers, in slower pace; the ominous dirge of first motto sounds below; the soothing melody of the Andante sings a verse. In solemn fugue the original motto is reared from its timid phrase to masterful utterance, with splendid stride. Or

rather the theme is blended of the first two phrases, merging their opposite characters in the new mood of resolution. The strings prepare for the sonorous entrance of woodwind and horns. One of the greatest fugal episodes of symphonies, it is yet

a mere prelude to the real movement, where the light
theme is drawn from a phrase of latest cadence.
And the dim hue of minor which began the symphony, and all overspread the prelude, at last
yields to the clear major. There is something of
the struggle of shadow and light of the great third
symphony of Brahms.

The continuous round of the theme, in its unstable
pace (of ⁵⁄₄), has a strange power of motion, the feel-

ing of old passacaglia. To be sure, it is the mere
herald and companion of the crowning tune, in solo
of the reeds.

From the special view of structure, there is no
symphony, modern or classic, with such an overpowering combination and resolution of integral themes in
one movement. So almost constant is the derivation
of ideas, that one feels they must be all related.
Thus, the late rush of rhythm, in the Finale, is
broken by a quiet verse where with enchanting subtlety we are carried back somewhere to the idyll of
third movement.

89

Above, rises another melody, and from its simple outline grows a fervor and pathos that, aside from the basic themes of the whole work, strike the main feeling of the Finale.

The martial trip from the Andante joins later in the return of the whirling rhythm. At last the motto strikes on high, but the appealing counter-melody is not easily hushed.

It breaks out later in a verse of exalted beauty and passion. The struggle of the two ideas reminds us of the Fifth Symphony. At last the gloom of the fateful motto is relieved by the return of the original answer, and we seem to see a new source of latest ideas, so that we wonder whether all the melodies are but guises of the motto and answer, which now at the close, sing in united tones a hymn of peace and bliss.

CHAPTER IX

DÉBUSSY AND THE INNOVATORS

A T intervals during the course of the art have appeared the innovators and pioneers,—rebels against the accepted manner and idiom. The mystery is that while they seem necessary to progress they seldom create enduring works. The shadowy lines may begin somewhere among the Hucbalds and other early adventurers. One of the most striking figures is Peri, who boldly, almost impiously, abandoned the contrapuntal style, the only one sanctioned by tradition, and set the dramatic parts in informal musical prose with a mere strumming of instruments.

It is not easy to see the precise need of such reaction. The radical cause is probably a kind of inertia in all things human, by which the accepted is thought the only way. Rules spring up that are never wholly true; at best they are shifts to guide the student, inadequate conclusions from past art. The essence of an art can never be put in formulas. Else we should be content with the verbal form. The best excuse for the rule is that it is meant to guard the element of truth in art from meretricious pretence.

And, we must not forget, Art progresses by slow degrees; much that is right in one age could not come in an earlier, before the intervening step.

The masters, when they had won their spurs, were ever restive under rules.* Yet they underwent the strictest discipline, gaining early the secret of expression; for the best purpose of rules is liberation, not restraint. On the other hand they were, in the main, essentially conservative. Sebastian Bach clung to the older manner, disdaining the secular sonata for which his son was breaking the ground.

The master feels the full worth of what has been achieved; else he has not mastered. He merely gives a crowning touch of poetic message, while the lighter mind is busy with tinkering of newer forms. For the highest reaches of an art, the poet must first have grasped all that has gone before. He will not rebel before he knows the spirit of the law, nor spend himself on novelty for its own sake.

The line between the Master and the Radical may often seem vague. For, the former has his Pro-

---

* Some of the chance sayings of Mozart (recently edited by Kerst-Elberfeld) betray much contempt for academic study: "Learning from books is of no account. Here, here, and here (pointing to ear, head, and heart) is your school." On the subject of librettists "with their professional tricks," he says: "If we composers were equally faithful to our own rules (which were good enough when men knew no better), we should turn out just as poor a quality in our music as they in their librettos." Yet, elsewhere, he admits: "No one has spent so much pains on the study of composition as myself. There is hardly a famous master in music whom I have not read through diligently and often."

methean strokes, all unpremeditated, compelled by the inner sequence,—as when Beethoven strikes the prophetic drum in the grim Scherzo of the Fifth Symphony; or in the Eroica when the horn sounds sheer ahead, out of line with the sustaining chorus; or when Bach leaps to his harmonic heights in organ fantasy and toccata; or Mozart sings his exquisite clashes in the G Minor Symphony.

As the true poet begins by absorption of the art that he finds, his early utterance will be imitative. His ultimate goal is not the strikingly new but the eternally true. It is a question less of men than of a point of view.

It seems sometimes that in art as in politics two parties are needed, one balancing the weaknesses of the other. As certain epochs are overburdened by the spirit of a past poet, so others are marred by the opposite excess, by a kind of neo-mania. The latter comes naturally as reaction from the former. Between them the poet holds the balance of clear vision.

When Peri overthrew the trammels of counter-point, in a dream of Hellenic revival of drama, he could not hope to write a master-work. Destructive rebellion cannot be blended with constructive beauty. An antidote is of necessity not nourishment. Others may follow the path-breaker and slowly reclaim the best of old tradition from the new soil. The strange part of this rebellion is that it is always marked by the quality of stereotype which it seeks to avoid. This is an invariable symptom. It cannot be otherwise; for the rejection of existing art leaves too few resources. Moreover, the pioneer has his eye too exclusively upon the mere manner.

A wholesome reaction there may be against excess. When Gluck dared to move the hearts of his hearers instead of tickling their ears, he achieved his purpose by positive beauty, without actual loss. In this sense every work of art is a work of revolution. So Wagner, especially in his earlier dramas,* by sheer sincerity and poetic directness, corrected a frivolous tradition of opera. But when he grew destructive of melody and form, by theory and practice, he sank to the rôle of innovator, with pervading trait of stereotype, in the main merely adding to the lesser resources of the art. His later works, though they contain episodes of overwhelming beauty, cannot have a place among the permanent classics, alone by reason of their excessive reiteration.

One of the most charming instances of this iconoclasm is the music of Claude Débussy.† In a way we are reminded of the first flash of Wagner's later manner: the same vagueness of tonality, though with a different complexion and temper. Like the German, Débussy has his own novel use of instruments. He is also a rebel against episodic melody. Only, with Wagner the stand was more of theory than of prac-

---

* The " Flying Dutchman," " Lohengrin " and " Tannhäuser " seemed destined to survive Wagner's later works.
† Born in 1862.

tice. His lyric inspiration was here too strong; otherwise with Débussy. Each article of rebellion is more highly stressed in the French leader, save as to organic form, where the latter is far the stronger. And finally the element of mannerism cannot be gainsaid in either composer.*

Among the special traits of Débussy's harmonic manner is a mingling with the main chord of the third below. There is a building downward, as it were. The harmony, complete as it stands, seeks a lower foundation so that the plain tower (as it looked at first) is at the end a lofty minaret. It is striking that a classic figure in French music should have stood, in the early eighteenth century, a champion of this idea, to be sure only in the domain of theory. There is a touch of romance in the fate of a pioneer, rejected for his doctrine in one age, taken up in the art of two centuries later.†

---

* Some recurring traits Wagner and Débussy have in common, such as the climactic chord of the ninth. The melodic appoggiatura is as frequent in the earlier German as the augmented chord of the fifth in the later Frenchman.

† Rameau, when the cyclopædic spirit was first stirring and musical art was sounding for a scientific basis, insisted on the element of the third below, implying a tonic chord of 6, 5, 3. Here he was opposed by Fétis, Fux and other theoretic authority; judgment was definitively rendered against him by contemporary opinion and prevailing tradition. It cannot be said that the modern French practice has justified Rameau's theory, since with all the charm of the enriched chord, there is ever a begging of the question of the ultimate root.

A purely scientific basis must be shunned in any direct approach of the art whether critical or creative, —alone for the fatal allurement of a separate research. The truth is that a spirit of fantastic experiment, started by the mystic manner of a César Franck, sought a sanction in the phenomena of acoustics. So it is likely that the enharmonic process of Franck led to the strained use of the whole-tone scale (of which we have spoken above) by a further departure from tonality.*   And yet, in all truth, there can be no doubt of the delight of these flashes of the modern French poet,—a delicate charm as beguiling as the bolder, warmer harmonies of the earlier German.   Instead of the broad exultation of Wagner there is in Débussy the subtle, insinuating dissonance.   Nor is the French composer wanting in audacious strokes.   Once for all he stood the emancipator of the art from the stern rule of individual vocal procedure.   He cut the Gordian knot of harmonic pedagogy by the mere weapon of poetic elision.   He simply omitted the obvious link by a license ancient in poetry and even in prose.   He devised in his harmonies the paradox, that is the essence of art, that the necessary step somehow becomes unnecessary.

---

* As the lower overtones, discovered by a later science, clearly confirm the tonal system of the major scale, slowly evolved in the career of the art,—so the upper overtones are said to justify the whole-tone process. At best this is a case of the devil quoting scripture. The main recurring overtones, which are lower and audible, are all in support of a clear prevailing tonality.

Though Wagner plunges without ceremony into his languorous chords, he carefully resolves their further course. Débussy has them tumbling in headlong descent like sportive leviathans in his sea of sound. Moreover he has broken these fetters of a small punctilio without losing the sense of a true harmonic sequence. Nay, by the very riotous revel of upper harmonies he has stressed the more clearly the path of the fundamental tone. When he enters the higher sanctuary of pure concerted voices, he is fully aware of the fine rigor of its rites. And finally his mischievous abandon never leads him to do violence to the profoundest element of the art, of organic design.*

"THE SEA." THREE SYMPHONIC SKETCHES

I.—*From Dawn to Noon on the Sea.* In awesome quiet of unsoothing sounds we feel, over a dual elemental motion, a quick fillip as of sudden lapping wave, while a shadowy air rises slowly in hollow intervals. Midst trembling whispers descending (like the

---

* In the drama Débussy avoids the question of form by treating the music as mere scenic background. Wagner, in his later works, attempted the impossible of combining a tonal with the dramatic plot. In both composers, to carry on the comparison beyond the technical phase, is a certain reaching for the primeval, in feeling as in tonality. Here they are part of a larger movement of their age. The subjects of their dramas are chosen from the same period of mediæval legend, strongly surcharged in both composers with a spirit of fatalism where tragedy and love are indissolubly blended.

7   97

soughing wind), a strange note, as of distant trumpet, strikes in gentle insistence—out of the other rhythm—and blows a wailing phrase. The trembling whisper has sunk to lowest depths. Still continues the lapping of waves—all sounds of unhuman nature.

(Muted trumpet, with Eng. horns in lower 8ve.)

(Cellos with basses in lower 8ve.)

On quicker spur the shadowy motive flits faster here and there in a slow swelling din of whispering, to the insistent plash of wave. Suddenly the sense of desolation yields to soothing play of waters—a *berceuse* of the sea—and now a song sings softly (in horn), though strangely jarring on the murmuring lullaby. The soothing cheer is anon broken by a shift of new tone. There is a fluctuation of pleasant and

strange sounds; a dulcet air on rapturous harmony
is hushed by unfriendly plash of chord.

Back again in the quieter play of rhythm the
strange, sweet song (of horns) returns.

In a ravishing climax of gentle chorus of quick
plashing waves and swirling breeze the song sings
on and the trumpet blows its line of tune to a ringing
phrase of the clarinet.

When this has died down, the lapping waves, as in
concert, strike in full chord that spreads a hue of
warmth, as of the first peep of sun. It is indeed as
though the waves rose towards the sun with a glow
of welcome.

In the wake of the first stirring shock is a host of
soft cheering sounds of bustling day, like a choir
of birds or bells. The eager madrigal leads to a final
blast (with acclaiming chorus of big rocking waves),
echoed in golden notes of the horns. One slight touch
has heightened the hue to warmest cheer; but once
do we feel the full glow of risen sun.

The chilling shadows return, as the wistful air of hushed trumpet sounds again. We hover between flashes of warming sun, until the waves have abated; in soothing stillness the romantic horn * sings a lay of legend.

Now to friendly purling of playful wavelets, the sea moves in shifting harmonies. In sudden climax the motion of the waves fills all the brass in triumphant pæan, in the gleam of high noon.

II.—*Play of the Waves.* There is a poetic background as for the play of legend. We seem to be watching the sea from a window in the castle of *Pelléas.* For there is a touch of dim romance in a phrase of the clarinet.

The movement of waves is clear, and the unconscious concert of sea-sounds, the deeper pulse of ocean (in the horns), the flowing ripples, the sharp dash of lighter surf (in the Glockenspiel), all with a constant tremor, an instability of element (in trembling strings). We cannot help feeling the illusion of scene in the impersonal play of natural sounds. Anon will come a shock of exquisite sweetness that must have something of human. And then follows a resonant clash with spray of colliding seas.

Here the story of the waves begins, and there are clearly two rôles.

To light lapping and cradling of waters the wood sings the simple lay, while strings discourse in quicker,

* English horn.

higher phrase. The parts are reversed. A shower
of chilling wave (in gliding harps) breaks the thread.

(Highest and lowest figure in strings.
Middle voices in octaves of wood)

Now golden tones (of horns) sound a mystic
tale of one of the former figures. The scene shim-

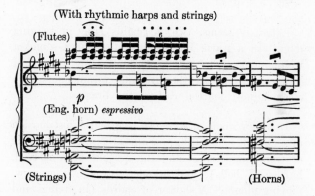

mers in sparkling, glinting waters (with harp and
trilling wood and strings). But against the soothing

101

background the story (of English horn) has a chill, ominous strain.

With the returning main song comes the passionate crisis, and we are back in the mere plash and play of impersonal waves.

On dancing ripples, a nixie is laughing to echoing horns and lures us back to the story.

Later, it seems, two mermaids sing in twining duet. In a warm hue of light the horns sound a weird tale. It is taken up by teasing chorus of lighter voices. In the growing volume sounds a clear, almost martial call of the brass.

In a new shade of scene we recover the lost burden of song; the original figures appear (in the slower air of trembling strings and the quicker play of reed, harp and bells), and wander through ever new, moving phases. A shower of chords (in strings and shaking brass) brings back the ominous melody, amidst a chorus of light chatter, but firmly resting

102

on a warm background of harmony. And the strain
roves on generous path and rises out of all its gloom
to a burst of profound cheer.

(1st violins with lower 8ve.)

(2d violins; percussion
with cellos below)

(Harps with violas)

(Flutes with higher 8ve.)

(See page 104, line 11.)

As in all fairy tales, the scene quickly vanishes. On
dancing rays and ripples is the laughing nixie; but
suddenly breaks the first song of the main figures.
A climactic phrase of trumpets ends with a burst of
all the chorus on stirring harmony, where in diminishing strokes of bells long rings the melodic note.

The teasing motive of the nixie returns while the trumpet sounds a shadowy echo of its phrase, again to dying peal of bells. A chorus of eerie voices sing the mocking air, and again sounds the refrain of trumpet as in rebuke. On a tumult of teasing cries flashes a delivering burst of brilliant light, and we are back in the first scene of the story. Only the main figure is absent. And there is in the eager tension of pace a quivering between joy and doubt. Then, in answer to the lighter phrase of the other, is the returning figure with a new song now of blended longing and content that soars into higher flights until a mighty chorus repeats the strain that rises to triumphant height of joy and transforms the mocking motive to the same mood.

But it is all a play of the waves. And we are left once more to the impersonal scene where yet the fragrance of legend hovers over the dying harmonies.

III.—Dialogue of the Wind and the Sea. Tumultuous is the humor of the beginning; early sounds the stroke of wave of the first hour of the sea. The muted trumpet blows a strain (to trembling strings) that takes us back to the first (quoted) tune of the symphony in the wistful mood of dawn. For a symphony it proves to be in the unity of themes and thought. Now unmuted and unrestrained in conflict of crashing chords, the trumpet blows again the motto of the roving sea. In various figures is the

104

pelagic motion, in continuous coursing strings, in the sweeping phrase of the wood-wind, or in the original wave-motion of the horns, now unmuted.

The main burden is a plaint

(in the wood) against the insistent surge (of strings), on a haunting motive as of farewell or eventide, with much stress of pathos. It is sung in sustained duet against a constant churning figure of the sea, and it is varied by a dulcet strain that grows out of the wave-motive.

Indeed, the whole movement is complementary of the first, the obverse as it were. The themes are of the same text; the hue and mood have changed from the spring of dawn to the sadness of dusk. The symbol of noontide peace reappears with minor tinge, at the hush of eve. The climactic motive of the sea acclaiming the rising sun is there, but reversed.

The sea too has the same tempestuous motion (indeed, the plaintive song is mainly of the wind), unrestrained by the sadder mood. At the passionate climax, where the higher figure sinks toward the rising lower, it is as if the Wind kissed the Sea.

The concluding scene begins as in the first movement, save with greater extension of expressive melody. And the poignant note has a long song against a continuous rippling (of harps).

More elemental figures crowd the scene; the first melody (of trumpet) has a full verse, and the dulcet phrase (of wave-motive).

Toward the end the plaintive song has an ever-growing chorus of acclaiming voices. In the fever of united coursing motion the phrase loses the touch of sadness until in eager, spirited pace, as of galloping steeds, it ends with a shout of victory.

DUKAS. "THE SORCERER'S APPRENTICE"

Chief among the companions of Claude Débussy in his adventures is Paul Dukas.* Though he lags somewhat in bold flights of harmonies, he shows a clearer vein of melody and rhythm, and he has an advantage in a greater freedom from the rut of repeated device.

It is somehow in the smaller forms that the French composer finds the trenchant utterance of his fancy. A Scherzo, after the ballad of Goethe, "The Sorcerer's Apprentice," tells the famous story of the boy who in his master's absence compels the spirit in

* Born in 1865.

the broom to fetch the water; but he cannot say the magic word to stop the flood, although he cleaves the demon-broom in two.

After the title-page of the score is printed a prose version (by Henri Blaze) of Goethe's ballad, "Der Zauberlehrling."

Of several translations the following, by Bowring, seems the best:

THE SORCERER'S APPRENTICE

I am now,—what joy to hear it!—
  Of the old magician rid;
And henceforth shall ev'ry spirit
  Do whate'er by me is bid:
    I have watch'd with rigor
      All he used to do,
    And will now with vigor
      Work my wonders, too.

      Wander, wander
      Onward lightly,
      So that rightly
      Flow the torrent,
    And with teeming waters yonder
    In the bath discharge its current!

And now come, thou well-worn broom,
  And thy wretched form bestir;
Thou hast ever served as groom,
  So fulfil my pleasure, sir!
    On two legs now stand
      With a head on top;
    Water pail in hand,
      Haste and do not stop!

SYMPHONIES AND THEIR MEANING

Wander, wander
Onward lightly,
So that rightly
Flow the torrent,
And with teeming waters yonder
In the bath discharge its current!

See! he's running to the shore,
And has now attain'd the pool,
And with lightning speed once more
Comes here, with his bucket full!
Back he then repairs;
See how swells the tide!
How each pail he bears
Straightway is supplied!

Stop, for lo!
All the measure
Of thy treasure
Now is right!
Ah, I see it! woe, oh, woe!
I forget the word of might.

Ah, the word whose sound can straight
Make him what he was before!
Ah, he runs with nimble gait!
Would thou wert a broom once more!
Streams renew'd forever
Quickly bringeth he;
River after river
Rusheth on poor me!

Now no longer
Can I bear him,
I will snare him,
Knavish sprite!
Ah, my terror waxes stronger!
What a look! what fearful sight!

108

Oh, thou villain child of hell!
  Shall the house through thee be drown'd?
Floods I see that widely swell,
  O'er the threshold gaining ground.
    Wilt thou not obey,
      O thou broom accurs'd!
    Be thou still, I pray,
      As thou wert at first!

        Will enough
        Never please thee?
        I will seize thee,
        Hold thee fast,
      And thy nimble wood so tough
      With my sharp axe split at last.

See, once more he hastens back!
  Now, O Cobold, thou shalt catch it!
I will rush upon his track;
  Crashing on him falls my hatchet.
    Bravely done, indeed!
      See, he's cleft in twain!
    Now from care I'm freed,
      And can breathe again.

        Woe oh, woe!
        Both the parts,
        Quick as darts,
        Stand on end,
      Servants of my dreaded foe!
      O ye gods, protection send!

And they run! and wetter still
  Grow the steps and grows the hall.
  Lord and master, hear me call!
Ever seems the flood to fill.

109

Ah, he's coming! see,
    Great is my dismay!
Spirits raised by me
    Vainly would I lay!

    " To the side
    Of the room
    Hasten, broom,
    As of old!
Spirits I have ne'er untied
Save to act as they are told."

In paragraphs are clearly pointed the episodes: the boy's delight at finding himself alone to conjure the spirits; the invocation to the water, recurring later as refrain (which in the French is not addressed to the spirit); then the insistent summons of the spirit in the broom; the latter's obedient course to the river and his oft-repeated fetching of the water; the boy's call to him to stop,—he has forgotten the formula; his terror over the impending flood; he threatens in his anguish to destroy the broom; he calls once more to stop; the repeated threat; he cleaves the spirit in two and rejoices; he despairs as two spirits are now adding to the flood; he invokes the master who returns; the master dismisses the broom to the corner.

There is the touch of magic in the first harmonics of strings, and the sense of sorcery is always sustained in the strange harmonies.*

---

* The flageolet tones of the strings seem wonderfully designed in their ghostly sound for such an aerial touch. Dukas uses them later in divided violins, violas and cellos, having thus a triad of harmonics doubled in the octave.

The remaining instruments are: Piccolo, 2 flutes, 2 oboes,

After a mystic descent of eerie chords, a melodious cooing phrase begins in higher wood, echoed from one voice to the other, while the spirit-notes are still sounding.

Suddenly dashes a stream of descending spray, met by another ascending; in the midst the first phrase is rapidly sounded (in muted trumpet). As suddenly the first solemn moment has returned, the phrase has grown in melody, while uncanny harmonies prevail. Amidst a new feverish rush a call rings

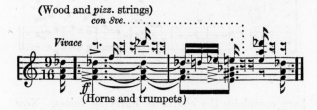

(Wood and *pizz.* strings)
con 8ve.
Vivace
(Horns and trumpets)

loud and oft (in trumpets and horns) ending in an insistent, furious summons. The silence that ensues is as speaking (or in its way as deafening) as were the calls.

After what seems like the grating of ancient joints, set in reluctant motion, the whole tune of the first wooing phrase moves in steady gait, in comic bassoons, to the tripping of strings, further and fuller extended as other voices join. The beginning phrase

2 clarinets, bass-clarinet, 3 bassoons, contra-bassoon (or contra-bass sarrusophon); 4 horns, 2 trumpets (often muted); 2 cornets-à-pistons; 3 trombones; 3 kettle-drums; harp; glockenspiel; big drum, cymbals and triangle.

of chords recurs as answer. Ever the lumbering trip continues, with strange turn of harmony and color, followed ever by the weird answer. A fuller apparition comes with the loud, though muffled tones of the trumpets. The original tune grows in new turns and folds of melody, daintily tipped with the ring of bells over the light tones of the wood. The brilliant

(Acc't in *pizz*. strings)

harp completes the chorus of hurrying voices. Now with full power and swing the main notes ring in sturdy brass, while all around is a rushing and swirling (of harps and bells and wood and strings). And still more furious grows the flight, led by the unison violins.

A mischievous mood of impish frolic gives a new turn of saucy gait. In the jovial answer, chorussed in simple song, seems a revel of all the spirits of rivers and streams.

At the top of a big extended period the trumpet sends a shrill defiant blast.

But it is not merely in power and speed,—more in an infinite variety of color, and whim of tune and rhythmic harmony, that is expressed the full gamut of disporting spirits. Later, at fastest speed of tripping harp and wood, the brass ring out that first, insistent summons, beneath the same eerie harmonies —and the uncanny descending chords answer as before. But alas! the summons will not work the other way. Despite the forbidding command and all the other exorcising the race goes madly on.

And now, if we are intent on the story, we may see the rising rage of the apprentice and at last the fatal stroke that seemingly hems and almost quells the flood. But not quite! Slowly (as at first) the hinges start in motion. And now, new horror! Where there was one, there are now two ghostly figures scurrying to redoubled disaster. Again and again the stern call rings out, answered by the wildest tumult of all. The shouts for the master's aid seem to turn to shrieks of despair. At last a mighty call o'ermasters and stills the storm. Nothing is heard but the first fitful phrases; now they seem mere echoes, instead of forewarnings. We cannot fail to see the fine parallel, how the masterful command is effective as was the similar call at the beginning.

Significantly brief is the ending, at once of the story and of the music. In the brevity lies the point of the plot: in the curt dismissal of the humbled spirit, at the height of his revel, to his place as broom in the corner. Wistful almost is the slow vanishing until the last chords come like the breaking of a fairy trance.

8   113

CHAPTER X

TSCHAIKOWSKY

THE Byron of music is Tschaikowsky for a certain alluring melancholy and an almost uncanny flow and sparkle. His own personal vein deepened the morbid tinge of his national humor.

We cannot ignore the inheritance from Liszt, both spiritual and musical. More and more does the Hungarian loom up as an overmastering influence of his own and a succeeding age. It seems as if Liszt, not Wagner, was the musical prophet who struck the rock of modern pessimism, from which flowed a stream of ravishing art. The national current in Tschaikowsky's music was less potent than with his younger compatriots; or at least it lay farther beneath the surface.

For nationalism in music has two very different bearings. The concrete elements of folk-song, rhythm and scale, as they are more apparent, are far less important. The true significance lies in the motive of an unexpressed national idea that presses irresistibly towards fulfilment. Here is the main secret of the Russian achievement in modern music,— as of other nations like the Finnish. It is the cause that counts. Though Russian song has less striking

114

traits than Hungarian or Spanish, it has blossomed in a far richer harvest of noble works of art.

Facile, fluent, full of color, Tschaikowsky seems equipped less for subjective than for lyric and dramatic utterance, as in his " Romeo and Juliet " overture. In the " Manfred " Symphony we may see the most fitting employment of his talent. Nor is it unlikely that the special correspondence of treatment and subject may cause this symphony to survive the others, may leave it long a rival of Schumann's " Manfred " music.

With Tschaikowsky feeling is always highly stressed, never in a certain natural poise. He quite lacks the noble restraint of the masters who, in their symphonic lyrics, wonderfully suggest the still waters that run deep.

Feeling with Tschaikowsky was frenzy, violent passion, so that with all abandon there is a touch of the mechanical in his method. Emotion as the content of highest art must be of greater depth and more quiet flow. And it is part or a counterpart of an hysterical manner that it reacts to a cold and impassive mood,—such as we feel in the Andante of the Fourth Symphony.

The final quality for symphonic art is, after all, less the chance flash of inspiration than a big view, a broad sympathy, a deep well of feeling that comes only with great character.

Nay, there is a kind of peril in the symphony for the poet of uncertain balance from the betrayal of his own temper despite his formal plan. Through all the triumph of a climax as in the first movement of the Fourth Symphony, we may feel a subliminal sadness that proves how subtle is the expression in music of the subjective mood. There is revealed not the feeling the poet is conscious of, but, below this, his present self, and in the whole series of his works, his own personal mettle. What the poet tries to say is very different from what he does say. In a symphony, as in many a frolic, the tinge of latent melancholy will appear.

SYMPHONY NO. 4

Reverting to a great and fascinating question as to the content of art, we may wonder whether this is not the real tragic symphony of Tschaikowsky, in the true heroic sense, in a view where the highest tragedy is not measured by the wildest lament. There may be a stronger sounding of lower depths with a firmer touch (with less of a conscious kind of abandon),— whence the recoil to serene cheer will be the greater.

There is surely a magnificent aspiration in the first Allegro, a profound knell of destiny and a rare ring of triumph. Underlying all is the legend of trumpets, *Andante sostenuto* (¾), with a dim touch

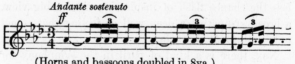

(Horns and bassoons doubled in 8va.)

of tragedy. Opposite in feeling is the descending motive of strings, *Moderato con anima* (⅝). First gently expressive, it soon rises in passion (the original

(Strings and one horn, the melody doubled below)

motto always sounding) to a climax whence an ascending motive, in lowest basses, entering in manner of fugue, holds a significant balance with the former. Each in turn rears a climax for the other's

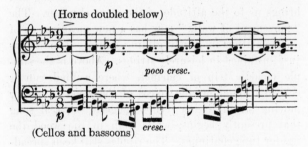

(Cellos and bassoons)

entrance; the first, lamenting, leads to the soothing hope of the second that, in the very passion of its refrain, loses assurance and ends in a tragic burst.

Suddenly a very new kind of solace appears *Dolce*

grazioso, in a phrase of the clarinet that leads to a duet of wood and *cantabile* strings, impersonal almost in the sweetness of its flowing song.

In such an episode we have a new Tschaikowsky,— no longer the subjective poet, but the painter with a certain Oriental luxuriance and grace. It is interesting to study the secret of this effect. The preluding strain lowers the tension of the storm of feeling and brings us to the attitude of the mere observer. The "movement of waltz" now has a new meaning, as of an apparition in gently gliding dance. The step is just sustained in leisurely strings. Above is the simple melodic trip of clarinet, where a final run is echoed throughout the voices of the wood; a slower moving strain in low cellos suggests the real song that presently begins, while high in the wood the lighter tune continues. The ripples still keep spreading throughout the voices, at the end of a line. The tunes then change places, the slower singing above.

With all the beauty, there is the sense of shadowy picture,—a certain complete absence of passion. Now the lower phrase appears in two companion voices (of strings), a hymnal kind of duet,—*ben sostenuto il tempo precedente.* Here, very softly in the same timid pace, enters a chorus, on high, of the old sighing motive. Each melody breaks upon the other and

ceases, with equal abruptness. There is no blending, in the constant alternation, until the earlier (lamenting) motive conquers and rises to a new height where a culminating chorale sounds a big triumph, while the sighing phrase merely spurs a new verse of assurance.

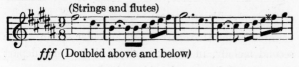

A completing touch lies in the answering phrase of the chorale, where the answer of original motto is transformed into a masterful ring of cheer and confidence.

As is the way with symphonies, it must all be sung and striven over again to make doubly sure. Only there is never the same depth of lament after the triumph. In a later verse is an augmented song of the answer of trumpet legend, in duet of thirds, in slow, serene pace, while the old lament sounds below in tranquil echoes and united strains. Before the end, *molto piu vivace,* the answer rings in new joyous rhythm.

Somewhat the reverse of the first movement, in the second the emotional phase grows slowly from the naïve melody of the beginning. Against the main melody that begins in oboe solo (with *pizzicato* strings), *semplice ma grazioso,* plays later a rising

counter-theme that may recall an older strain. The second melody, in Greek mode, still does not depart

120

from the naïve mood, or lack of mood. A certain modern trait is in this work, when the feeling vents and wastes itself and yields to an impassive recoil, more coldly impersonal than the severest classic.

A sigh at the end of the second theme is a first faint reminder of the original lament. Of it is fashioned the third theme. A succeeding climax strongly

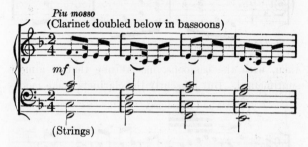

brings back the subjective hue of the earlier symphony. A counter-theme, of the text of the second melody of Allegro,—now one above, now the other— is a final stroke. Even the shaking of the trumpet figure is there at the height, in all the brass. Yet as a whole the first melody prevails, with abundant variation of runs in the wood against the song of the strings.

The Scherzo seems a masterly bit of humor, impish, if you will, yet on the verge always of tenderness. The first part is never-failing in the flash and sparkle of its play, all in *pizzicato* strings, with a wonderful

dæmonic quality of the mere instrumental effect.
Somewhat suddenly the oboe holds a long note and

then, with the bassoons, has a tune that is almost
sentimental. But presently the clarinets make mock-

ing retorts. Here, in striking scene, all the brass
(but the tuba) very softly blow the first melody with
eccentric halts, in just half the old pace except when
they take us by surprise. The clarinet breaks in
with the sentimental tune in faster time while the
brass all the while are playing as before. There are
all kinds of pranks, often at the same time. The pic-

colo, in highest treble, inverts the second melody, in
impertinent drollery. The brass has still newer
surprises. Perhaps the best of the fooling is where
strings below and woodwind above share the melody
between them, each taking two notes at a time.

The first of the Finale is pure fanfare, as if to
let loose the steeds of war; still it recurs as leading
idea. There is a kind of sonorous terror, increased
by the insistent, regular notes of the brass, the
spirited pace of the motive of strings,—the barbaric
ring we often hear in Slav music. At the height

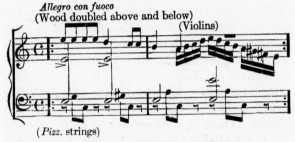

the savage yields to a more human vein of joyousness,
though at the end it rushes the more wildly into a

series of shrieks of trebles with tramping of basses. The real battle begins almost with a lull, the mere sound of the second tune in the reeds with light strum of strings and triangle. As the theme is redoubled (in thirds of the wood), the sweep of strings of the first motive is added, with chords of horns. A rising figure is now opposed to the descent of the second melody, with shaking of woodwind that brings back the old trumpet legend. Here the storm grows apace, with increasing tumult of entering hostile strains, the main song now ringing in low brass.

In various versions and changes we seem to see earlier themes briefly reappearing. Indeed there is a striking kinship of themes throughout, not so much in outline as in the air and mood of the tunes. This seems to be proven by actual outer resemblance when the motives are developed. Here in a quiet spot— though the battle has clearly not ceased—is the answer of old trumpet motto, that pervaded the first Allegro. There is a strong feeling of the Scherzo here in the *pizzicato* answers of strings. The second theme of the Andante is recalled, too, in the strokes of the second of the Finale. In the thick of the fray is a wonderful maze of versions of the theme, diminished and augmented at the same time with the original pace. Yet it is all a clear flow of melody and rich harmony. The four beats of quarter notes, in the lengthened theme, come as high point like the figure of the leader in battle. A later play of changes is like the sport of the Scherzo. This insensibly leads to the figure of the fanfare, whence the earlier song returns with the great joyous march.

The final height of climax is distinguished by a stentorian, fugal blast of the theme in the bass, the higher breaking in on the lower, while other voices are raging on the quicker phrases. It is brought to a dramatic halt by the original prelude of trumpet legend, in all its fulness. Though the march-song recurs, the close is in the ruder humor of the main themes.

THE "MANFRED" SYMPHONY

Schumann and Tschaikowsky are the two most eminent composers who gave tonal utterance to the sombre romance of Byron's dramatic poem.* It is interesting to remember that Byron expressly demanded the assistance of music for the work. If we wish to catch the exact effect that is sought in the original conception, Schumann's setting is the nearest approach. It is still debated whether a scenic representation is more impressive, or a simple reading, reinforced by the music.

Tschaikowsky's setting is a "symphony in four pictures, or scenes (*en quatre tableaux*), after Byron's dramatic poem." In the general design and spirit there is much of the feeling of Berlioz's "Fantastic" Symphony, though the manner of the music shows no resemblance whatever. There is much more like-

---

* Prefixed are the familiar lines:
"There are more things in heaven and earth, Horatio,
Than are dreamt of in your philosophy."

ness to Liszt's "Faust" Symphony, in that the pervading recurrence of themes suggests symbolic labels. Moreover, in the very character of many of the motives, there is here a striking line of descent.

Lento lugubre, the first scene or picture, begins with a theme in basses of reeds:

with later *pizzicato* figure of low strings.

An answering strain is one of the most important of all the melodies:

On these, a bold conflict and climax is reared. If we care to indulge in the bad habit of calling names, we might see "Proud Ambition" in the first motives, intertwined with sounds of sombre discontent. The pace grows *animando,—piu mosso; moderato molto.* Suddenly Andante sings a new, ex-

pressive song, with a dulcet cheer of its own, rising
to passionate periods and a final height whence,
Andante con duolo, a loudest chorus of high wood
and strings, heralded and accompanied by martial
tremolo of low wood, horns, basses, and drums, sound
the fateful chant that concludes the first scene, and,
toward the close of the work, sums the main idea.

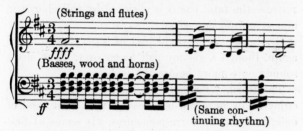

The apparition of the Witch of the Alps is pictured in daintiest, sparkling play of strings and wood,
with constant recurrence of mobile figures above
and below. It seems as if the image of the fountain
is fittest and most tempting for mirroring in music.
Perhaps the most beautiful, the most haunting, of
all the "Manfred" music of Schumann is this same
scene of the Witch of the Alps.

Here, with Tschaikowsky, hardly a single note of
brass intrudes on this *perpetuum mobile* of light,
plashing spray until, later, strains that hark back
to the first scene cloud the clear brilliancy of the
cascade. Now the play of the waters is lost in the
new vision, and a limpid song glides in the violins,
with big rhythmic chords of harps, is taken up in

clarinets, and carried on by violins in new melodic verse, *con tenerezza e molto expressione*. Then the whole chorus sing the tune in gentle volume. As it dies away, the music of the falling waters plash as before. The returning song has phases of varying sadness and passion. At the most vehement height,—and here, if we choose, we may see the stern order to retire,—the fatal chant is shrieked by full chorus in almost unison fierceness.

Gradually the innocent play of the waters is heard again, though a gloomy pall hangs over. The chant sounds once more before the end.

The third, " Pastoral," scene we are most free to enjoy in its pure musical beauty, with least need of definite dramatic correspondences. It seems at first as if no notes of gloom are allowed to intrude, as if the picture of happy simplicity stands as a foil to the tragedy of the solitary dreamer; for an early climax gives a mere sense of the awe of Alpine nature.

Still, as we look and listen closer, we cannot escape so easily, in spite of the descriptive title. Indeed, the whole work seems, in its relation to the poem upon which it is based, a very elusive play in a double kind of symbolism. At first it is all a clear subjective utterance of the hero's woes and hopes and fears, without definite touches of external things. Yet, right in the second scene the torrent is clear almost to the eye, and the events pass before us with sharp distinctness. Tending, then, to look on the third as purest pastoral, we are struck in the midst by an ominous strain from one of the earliest moments of the work, the answer of the first theme of all. Here notes of horns ring a monotone; presently a church-bell adds a higher note. The peaceful pastoral airs then return, like the sun after a fleeting storm.

The whole of this third scene of Tschaikowsky's agrees with no special one in Byron's poem, unless we go back to the second of the first act, where Manfred, in a morning hour, alone upon the cliffs, views the mountains of the Jungfrau before he makes a foiled attempt to spring into the abyss. By a direction of the poet, in the midst of the monologue, " the shepherd's pipe in the distance is heard," and Manfred muses on " the natural music of the mountain reed."

The last scene of the music begins with Byron's fourth of Act II and passes over all the incidents of the third act that precede the hero's death, such as the two interviews with the Abbot and the glorious invocation to the sun.

From Tschaikowsky's title, we must look for the awful gloom of the cavernous hall of Arimanes, Byron's " Prince of Earth and Air." The gray figure from most ancient myth is not less real to us than Mefistofeles in " Faust." At least we clearly feel the human daring that feared not to pry into forbidden mysteries and refused the solace of unthinking faith. And it becomes again a question whether the composer had in mind this subjective

attitude of the hero or the actual figures and abode
of the spirits and their king.   It is hard to escape
the latter view, from the general tenor, the clear-cut
outline of the tunes, of which the principal is like
a stern chant:

The most important of the later answers lies largely
in the basses.

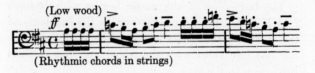

There is, on the whole, rather an effect of gloomy
splendor (the external view) than of meditation; a
sense of visible massing than of passionate crisis,
though there is not wanting a stirring motion and
life in the picture.   This is to speak of the first part,
Allegro con fuoco.

The gloomy dance dies away.   *Lento* is a soft fugal
chant on elemental theme; there is all the solemnity
of cathedral service; after the low-chanted phrase

follows a tremendous blare of the brass. The repeated chant is followed by one of the earliest, characteristic themes of the first scene. And so, if we
care to follow the graphic touch, we may see here the
intrusion of Manfred, at the most solemn moment of
the fearful revel.

As Manfred, in Byron's poem, enters undaunted,
refusing to kneel, the first of the earlier phases rings
out in fierce *fortissimo*. A further conflict appears
later, when the opening theme of the work sounds
with interruptions of the first chant of the spirits.

A dulcet plaint follows, *Adagio,* in muted strings,
answered by a note of horn and a chord of harp.

Adagio
(Muted strings answered by horn and harp)

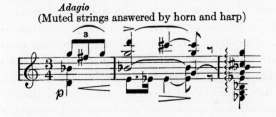

It all harks back to the gentler strains of the first
movement. In the ethereal *glissando* of harps we see
the spirit of Astarte rise to give the fatal message.
The full pathos and passion of the *lento* episode of
first scene is heard in brief, vivid touches, and is
followed by the same ominous blast with ring of horn,
as in the first picture.

A note of deliverance shines clear in the final

phrase of joined orchestra and organ, clearer perhaps than in Manfred's farewell line in the play: "Old man! 'tis not so difficult to die." To be sure, Schumann spreads the same solace o'er the close of his setting, with the Requiem. The sombre splendor of romance is throughout, with just a touch of turgid. In the poignant ecstasy of grief we feel vividly the foreshadowing example of Liszt, in his "Dante" and "Faust" Symphonies.

FIFTH SYMPHONY (*E MINOR*)

With all the unfailing flow of lesser melodies where the charm is often greatest of all, and the main themes of each movement with a chain of derived phrases, one melody prevails and reappears throughout. The fluency is more striking here than elsewhere in Tschaikowsky. All the external sources,—all the glory of material art seem at his command. We are reminded of a certain great temptation to which all men are subject and some fall,—however reluctantly. Throughout there is a vein of dæmonic. The second (Allegro) melody grows to a high point of pathos,—nay, anguish, followed later by buoyant, strepitant, dancing delight, with the melting answer, in the latest melody. The dæmon is half external fate—in the Greek sense, half individual temper. The end is almost sullen; but the charm is never failing; at the last is the ever springing rhythm.

The march rhythm of the opening Andante is carried suddenly into a quick trip, *Allegro con anima* (6/8), where the main theme of the first movement now begins, freely extended as in a full song of verses. New accompanying figures are added, contrasting phrases or counter-melodies, to the theme.

One expressive line plays against the wilder rhythm of the theme, with as full a song in its own mood as the other. A new rhythmic motive, of great

charm, *un pocchetino piu animato,* is answered by
a bit of the theme. Out of it all grows, in a clear

welded chain, another episode, where the old rhythm
is a mere gentle spur to the new plaint,—*molto piu
tranquillo, molto cantabile ed espressivo.*

To be sure, the climax has all of the old pace
and life, and every voice of the chorus at the loudest.
In the answering and echoing of the various phrases,
rhythmic and melodic, is the charm of the discussion
that follows. Later the three melodies come again
in the former order, and the big climax of the plain-

tive episode precedes the end, where the main theme
dies down to a whisper.

Andante cantabile, con alcuna licenza. After preluding chords in lowest strings a solo horn begins a

languishing song, *dolce con molto espressione.* It
is a wonderful elegy, a yearning without hope, a
swan-song of desire, sadder almost than the frank despair of the Finale of the *Pathétique* symphony,—
pulsing with passion, gorgeous with a hectic glow
of expressive beauty, moving too with a noble grace.
Though there is a foil of lighter humor, this is
overwhelmed in the fateful gloom of the returning
main motto.

The abounding beauty with all its allurement
lacks the solace that the masters have led
us to seek in the heart of a symphony. The
clarinet presently twines a phrase about the tune
until a new answer sounds in the oboe, that now
sings in answering and chasing duet with the horn.

The phrase of oboe proves to be the main song, in full extended periods, reaching a climax with all the voices.

Well defined is the middle episode in minor reared on a new theme of the clarinet with an almost fugal polyphony that departs from the main lyric mood.

At the height all the voices fall into a united chorus on the original motto of the symphony. The first melodies of the Andante now return with big sweep and power, and quicker phrases from the episode. The motto reappears in a final climax, in the trombones, before the hushed close.

We must not infer too readily a racial trait from
the temper of the individual composer.   There is here
an error that we fall into frequently in the music
of such men as Grieg and Tschaikowsky.   The prevailing mood of the Pathetic Symphony is in large
measure personal.   Some of the more recent Russian
symphonies are charged with buoyant joyousness.
And, indeed, the burden of sadness clearly distinguishes the last symphony of Tschaikowsky from its
two predecessors, the Fourth and the Fifth.

The tune of the *valse, Allegro moderato,* is first
played by the violins, *dolce con grazia,* with accompanying strings, horns and bassoon.   In the second
part, with some loss of the lilt of dance, is a subtle
design—with a running phrase in *spiccato* strings
against a slower upward glide of bassoons.   The duet
winds on a kind of *crescendo* of modulations.   Later

the themes are inverted, and the second is redoubled
in speed.   The whole merges naturally into the first
waltz, with a richer suite of adorning figures.   The

dance does not end without a soft reminder (in low woodwind) of the original sombre phrase.

Almost for the first time a waltz has entered the shrine of the symphony. And yet perhaps this dance has all the more a place there. It came on impulse (the way to visit a sanctuary), not by ancient custom. But with all its fine variety, it is a simple waltz with all the careless grace,—nothing more, with no hidden or graphic meaning (as in Berlioz's Fantastic Symphony).

The middle episode, though it lacks the dancing trip, is in the one continuing mood,—like a dream of youthful joys with just a dimming hint of grim reality in the returning motto.

In the Finale the main legend of the symphony is transformed and transfigured in a new, serener mood, and is brought to a full melodic bloom. Indeed, here is the idealization of the original motto. *Andante maestoso* it begins in the tonic major. When the theme ceases, the brass blow the rhythm on a monotone, midst an ascending *obligato of strings.*

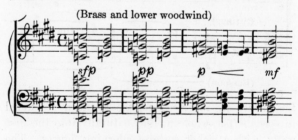

(Brass and lower woodwind)

(See page 139, line 1.)
138

In answer comes a new phrase of chorale. Later the chorale is sounded by the full band, with intermediate beats of rhythmic march.

Once more there is a well-marked episode, with a full share of melodic discussion, of clashing themes, of dramatic struggle. First in the tonic minor a theme rises from the last casual cadence in resonant march, *Allegro vivace*. Then follows a duet, almost

a harsh grating of an eccentric figure above against

the smoother course of the latest Allegro motive. The themes are inverted. Presently out of the din rises a charming canon on the prevailing smoother phrase, that soars to a full sweep of song. A new

hymnal melody comes as a final word. Though the main motto returns in big chorus, in full extension, in redoubled pace and wild abandon, still the latest melody seems to contend for the last say. Or, rather,

(See page 141, line 2.)

it is a foil, in its simple flow, to the revel of the motto, now grown into a sonorous, joyous march. And we seem to see how most of the other melodies, —the minor episode, the expressive duet—have sprung from bits of the main text.

To return for another view,—the Finale begins in a mood that if not joyous, is religious. Out of the cadence of the hymn dances the Allegro tune almost saucily. Nor has this charming trip the ring of gladness, though it grows to great momentum. As a whole there is no doubt of the assurance, after the earlier fitful gloom, and with the resignation an almost militant spirit of piety.

In the dulcet canon, an exquisite gem, bliss and sadness seem intermingled; and then follows the crowning song, broad of pace, blending the smaller rhythms in ecstatic surmounting of gloom. In further verse it doubles its sweet burden in overlapping voices, while far below still moves the rapid trip.

But the motto will return, in major to be sure, and tempered in mercy. And the whole hymn dominates, with mere interludes of tripping motion, breaking at the height into double pace of concluding strain. Before falling back into the thrall of the legend the furious race rushes eagerly into the deepest note of bliss, where in sonorous bass rolls the broad, tranquil song. And though the revel must languish, yet we attend the refrain of all the melodies in crowning rapture. Then at last, in stern minor, sounds the motto, still with the continuing motion, in a loud and long chant.

In blended conclusion of the contending moods comes a final verse of the legend in major, with full accoutrement of sounds and lesser rhythm, in majestic pace. And there is a following frolic with a verse of the serene song. The end is in the first Allegro theme of the symphony, in transfigured major tone.

We must be clear at least of the poet's intent. In the Fifth Symphony Tschaikowsky sang a brave song of struggle with Fate.

CHAPTER XI

THE NEO-RUSSIANS

FOR some mystic reason nowhere in modern music is the symphony so justified as in Russia. Elsewhere it survives by the vitality of its tradition. In France we have seen a series of works distinguished rather by consummate refinement than by strength of intrinsic content. In Germany since the masterpieces of Brahms we glean little besides the learnedly facile scores of a Bruckner, with a maximum of workmanship and a minimum of sturdy feeling,—or a group of " heroic " symphonies all cast in the same plot of final transfiguration. The one hopeful sign is the revival of a true counterpoint in the works of Mahler.

Some national song, like the Bohemian, lends itself awkwardly to the larger forms. The native vein is inadequate to the outer mould, that shrinks and dwindles into formal utterance. It may be a question of the quantity of a racial message and of its intensity after long suppression. Here, if we cared to enlarge in a political disquisition, we might account for the symphony of Russians and Finns, and of its absence in Scandinavia. The material elements, abundant rhythm, rich color, individual and varied folk-song, are only the means by which the national

143

temper is expressed. Secondly, it must be noted as a kind of paradox, the power of the symphony as a national utterance is increased by a mastery of the earlier classics. With all that we hear of the narrow nationalism of the Neo-Russians, we cannot deny them the breadth that comes from a close touch with the masters. Mozart is an element in their music almost as strong as their own folk-song. Here, it may be, the bigger burden of a greater national message unconsciously seeks the larger means of expression. And it becomes clear that the sharper and narrower the national school, the less complete is its utterance, the more it defeats its ultimate purpose.

The broad equipment of the new Russian group is seen at the outset in the works of its founder, Balakirew. And thus the difference between them and Tschaikowsky lay mainly in the formulated aim.*

The national idea, so eminent in modern music, is not everywhere equally justified. And here, as in an object-lesson, we see the true merits of the problem. While one nation spontaneously utters its cry, another, like a cock on the barnyard, starts a movement in mere idle vanity, in sheer self-glorification.

In itself there is nothing divine in a national idea that needs to be enshrined in art. Deliberate segre-

* In the choice of subjects there was a like breadth. Balakirew was inspired by " King Lear," as was Tschaikowsky. And amid a wealth of Slavic legend and of kindred Oriental lore, he would turn to the rhythms of distant Spain for a poetic theme.

gation is equally vain, whether it be national or social.
A true racial celebration must above all be spontaneous. Even then it can have no sanction in art,
unless it utter a primal motive of resistance to suppression, the elemental pulse of life itself. There is
somehow a divine dignity about the lowest in human
rank, whether racial or individual. The oppressed
of a nation stands a universal type, his wrongs are the
wrongs of all, and so his lament has a world-wide
appeal. And in truth from the lowest class rises ever
the rich spring of folk-song of which all the art is
reared, whence comes the paradox that the peasant
furnishes the song for the delight of his oppressors,
while they boast of it as their own. Just in so far as
man is devoid of human sympathy, is he narrow and
barren in his song. Music is mere feeling, the fulness
of human experience, not in the hedonic sense of
modern tendencies, but of pure joys and profound
sorrows that spring from elemental relations, of man
to man, of mate to mate.

Here lies the nobility of the common people and of
its song; the national phase is a mere incident of
political conditions. The war of races is no alembic
for beauty of art. If there were no national lines,
there would still be folk-song,—merely without sharp
distinction. The future of music lies less in the dif-
ferentiation of human song, than in its blending.

Thus we may rejoice in the musical utterance of a
race like the Russian, groaning and struggling
through ages against autocracy for the dignity of man

himself,—and in a less degree for the Bohemian, seeking to hold its heritage against enforced submergence. But we cannot take so seriously the proud self-isolation of other independent nations.

BALAKIREW.* SYMPHONY IN C

The national idea shines throughout, apart from the "Russian Theme" that forms the main text of the Finale. One may see the whole symphony leading up to the national celebration.

As in the opening phrase (in solemn *Largo*) with

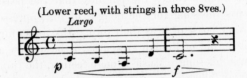

its answer are proclaimed the subjects that presently

appear in rapid pace, so the whole movement must be taken as a big prologue, forecasting rather than realizing. There is a dearth of melodic stress and

---

* Mili Alexeivich Balakirew was born at Nizhni-Novgorod in 1836; he died at St. Petersburg in 1911. He is regarded as the founder of the Neo-Russian School.

balance; so little do the subjects differ that they are in essence merely obverse in outline.

Mystic harmonies and mutations of the motto lead to a quicker guise (*Allegro vivo*). Independently of themes, the rough edge of tonality and the vigorous primitive rhythms are expressive of the Slav feeling. Withal there is a subtlety of harmonic manner that could come only through the grasp of the classics common to all nations. Augmentation and diminution of theme abound, together with the full fugal manner. A warm, racial color is felt in the prodigal use of lower reeds.*

In all the variety of quick and slower melodies a single phrase of five notes, the opening of the symphony, pervades. In all kinds of humor it sings, martial, solemn, soothing, meditative, or sprightly. Poetic in high degree is this subtle metamorphosis, so that the symphony in the first movement seems to prove the art rather than the national spirit of the Neo-Russians.

Of the original answer is wrought all the balance and foil of second theme, and like the first it reaches a climactic height. But the first is the sovereign figure of the story. It enters into the pattern of every new phase, it seems the text of which all the melodies are fashioned, or a sacred symbol that must be all-pervading. In a broader pace (*Alla breve*)

---

* Besides the English horn and four bassoons there are four clarinets,—double the traditional number.

147

is a mystic discussion of the legend, as of dogma, ending in big pontifical blast of the answering theme.

The whole movement is strangely frugal of joyous abandon. Instead of rolling, revelling melody there is stern proclamation, as of oracle, in the solemn pauses. The rhythm is purposely hemmed and broken. Restraint is everywhere. Almost the only continuous thread is of the meditative fugue.

A single dulcet lyric verse (of the motto) is soon

banished by a sudden lively, eccentric phrase that has an air of forced gaiety, with interplay of mystic symbols. At last, on a farther height, comes the first

joyous abandon (in a new mask of the motto), recurring anon as recess from sombre brooding.

Here the second subject has a free song,—in gentle chase of pairs of voices (of woodwind and muted strings and harp) and grows to alluring melody. As

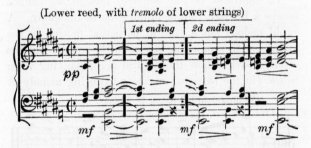

(Lower reed, with *tremolo* of lower strings)

from a dream the eccentric trip awakens us, on ever higher wing. At the top in slower swing of chords horn and reeds chant the antiphonal legend, and in growing rapture, joined by the strings, rush once more into the jubilant revel, the chanting legend still sounding anon in sonorous bass.

The climax of feeling is uttered in a fiery burst of all the brass in the former dulcet refrain from the motto. In full sweep of gathering host it flows in unhindered song. Somehow by a slight turn, the tune is transformed into the alluring melody of the second theme. When the former returns, we feel that both strains are singing as part of a single song and that the two subjects are blended and reconciled in rapture of content.

A new mystic play of the quicker motto, answered by the second theme, leads to an overpowering blast

149

of the motto in slowest notes of brass and reed, ending in a final fanfare.

All lightness is the Scherzo, though we cannot escape a Russian vein of minor even in the dance. A rapid melody has a kind of perpetual motion in the strings, with mimicking echoes in the wood. But the strange part is how the natural accompanying voice below (in the bassoon) makes a haunting melody of

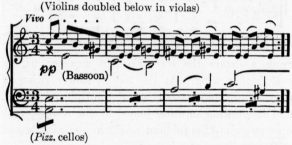

its own,—especially when they fly away to the major. As we suspected, the lower proves really the principal song as it winds on in the languorous English horn or in the higher reed. Still the returning dance has now the whole stage in a long romp with strange peasant thud of the brass on the second beat. Then the song rejoins the dance, just as in answering glee, later in united chorus.

A quieter song (that might have been called the Trio) has still a clinging flavor of the soil,—as of a folk-ballad, that is not lost with the later madrigal nor with the tripping figure that runs along.

Strangely, after the full returning dance, an epi-

(Trio) *Poco meno mosso*

logue of the ballad appears over a drone, as of bag-pipe, through all the harmony of the madrigal. Strangest of all is the playful last refrain in the high piccolo over the constant soft strumming strings.

The Andante, in pure lyric mood, is heavily charged with a certain Oriental languor. The clari-

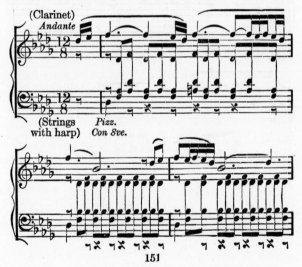

net leads the song, to rich strum of harp and strings, with its note of sensuous melancholy. Other, more external signs there are of Eastern melody, as in the graceful curl of quicker notes. Intermediate strains between the verses seem gently to rouse the slumbering feeling,—still more when they play between the lines of the song. The passion that is lulled in the languor of main melody, is somehow uttered in the later episode,—still more in the dual song of both

melodies,—though it quickly drops before a strange coquetry of other strains. Yet the climax of the main song is reached when the lighter phrase rings fervently in the high brass. Here the lyric beauty is stressed in a richer luxuriance of rhythmic setting. Once more sings the passionate tune; then in midst of the last verse of the main song is a quick alarm of rushing harp. The languorous dream is broken; there is an air of new expectancy. Instead of a close is a mere pause on a passing harmony at the portals of the high festival.

With a clear martial stress the "Russion Theme" is sounded (in low strings), to the full a national

tune of northern race. Enriched with prodigal harmony and play of lesser themes it flows merrily on, yet always with a stern pace, breaking out at last in a blare of warlike brass.

Nor does the martial spirit droop in the second tune, though the melodies are in sheer contrast. In faster rhythm, the second is more festal so that the first returning has a tinge almost of terror. An

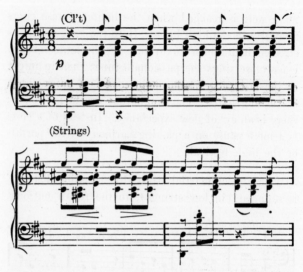

after-strain of the second has a slightest descent to reflective feeling, from which there is a new rebound

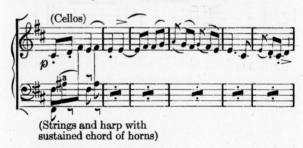

to the buoyant (festal) melody.

Here in grim refrains, in dim depths of basses

(with hollow notes of horns) the national tune has a free fantasy until it is joined by the second in a loud burst in the minor.

Now the latter sings in constant alternation with the answering strain, then descends in turn into the depths of sombre musing. There follows a big, resonant dual climax (the main theme in lower brass), with an edge of grim defiance. In the lull we seem to catch a brief mystic play of the first motto of the symphony (in the horns) before the last joyous song of both melodies,—all with a power of intricate design and a dazzling brilliancy of harmony, in proud national celebration.

A last romp is in polacca step on the tune of the Russian Theme.

RIMSKY-KORSAKOW.* "ANTAR," SYMPHONY

The title-page tells us that "the subject is taken from an Arabian tale of Sennkowsky." Opposite the beginning of the score is a summary of the story, in Russian and in French, as follows:

I.—Awful is the view of the desert of Sham; mighty in their desolation are the ruins of Palmyra, the city razed by the spirits of darkness. But Antar, the man of the desert, braves them, and dwells serenely in the midst of the scenes of destruction. Antar has forever forsaken the company of mankind. He has sworn eternal hatred on account of the evil they returned him for the good which he intended.

Suddenly a charming, graceful gazelle appears. Antar

* Nicholas Rimsky-Korsakow, Russian, 1844–1908.

starts to pursue it. But a great noise seems pulsing through the heavens, and the light of day is veiled by a dense shadow. It is a giant bird that is giving chase to the gazelle.

Antar straightway changes his intent, and attacks the monster, which gives a piercing cry and flies away. The gazelle disappears at the same time, and Antar, left alone in the midst of ruins, soon goes to sleep while meditating on the event that has happened.

He sees himself transported to a splendid palace, where a multitude of slaves hasten to serve him and to charm his ear with their song. It is the abode of the Queen of Palmyra,—the fairy Gul-nazar. The gazelle that he has saved from the talons of the spirit of darkness is none other than the fairy herself. In gratitude Gul-nazar promises Antar the three great joys of life, and, when he assents to the proffered gift, the vision vanishes and he awakes amid the surrounding ruins.

II.—The first joy granted by the Queen of Palmyra to Antar are the delights of vengeance.

III.—The second joy—the delights of power.

IV.—Antar has returned to the fallen remains of Palmyra. The third and last gift granted by the fairy to Antar is the joy of true love. Antar begs the fairy to take away his life as soon as she perceives the least estrangement on his side, and she promises to do his desire.

After a long time of mutual bliss the fairy perceives, one day, that Antar is absent in spirit and is gazing into the distance. Straightway, divining the reason, she passionately embraces him. The fire of her love enflames Antar, and his heart is consumed away.

Their lips meet in a last kiss and Antar dies in the arms of the fairy.

The phases of the story are clear in the chain of musical scenes, of the movements themselves and

within them. In the opening Largo that recurs in
this movement between the visions and happenings,
a melody appears (in violas) that moves in all the

acts of the tragedy. It is clearly the Antar motive,—
here amidst ruin and desolation.

The fairy theme is also unmistakable, that first
plays in the flute, against soft horns, *Allegro giocoso,*

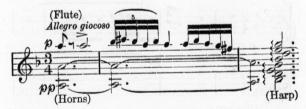

and is lost in the onrushing attack, *furioso,* of a
strain that begins in murmuring of muted strings.

Other phrases are merely graphic or incidental.
But the Antar motive is throughout the central moving figure.

The scene of the desert returns at the end of the
movement.

In the second (*Allegro,* rising to *Molto allegro,*

157

returning *allargando*) the Antar motive is seldom
absent. The ending is in long notes of solo oboe and
first violins. There is no trace of the fairy queen
throughout the movement.

The third movement has phases of mighty action
(as in the beginning, *Allegro risoluto alla Marcia*),
of delicate charm, and even of humor. The Antar
melody plays in the clangor of big climax in sonorous
tones of the low brass, against a quick martial phrase
of trumpets and horns. Again there is in this movement no sign of the fairy queen.

In the fourth movement, after a prelude, *Allegretto
vivace,* with light trip of high flutes, a melody, of
actual Arab origin, sings *Andante amoroso* in the

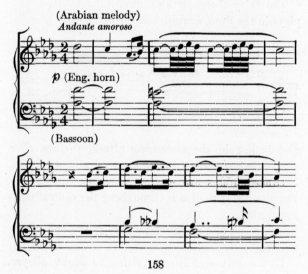

English horn, and continues almost to the end, broken only by the dialogue of the lover themes. At the close a last strain of the Antar melody is followed by the fairy phrase and soft vanishing chord of harp and strings.

"SCHÉRÉZADE," AFTER "A THOUSAND AND ONE NIGHTS." SYMPHONIC SUITE

Prefixed to the score is a " program," in Russian and French: " The Sultan Schahriar, convinced of the infidelity of women, had sworn to put to death each of his wives after the first night. But the Sultana Schérézade saved her life by entertaining him with the stories which she told him during a thousand and one nights. Overcome by curiosity, the Sultan put off from day to day the death of his wife, and at last entirely renounced his bloody vow.

Many wonders were told to Schahriar by the Sultana Schérézade. For the stories the Sultana borrowed the verses of poets and the words of popular romances, and she fitted the tales and adventures one within the other.

I. The Sea and the Vessel of Sindbad.

II. The Tale of the Prince Kalender.

III. The Young Prince and the Young Princess.

IV. Feast at Bagdad. The Sea. The Vessel is Wrecked on a Rock on which is Mounted a Warrior of Brass. Conclusion."

With all the special titles the whole cannot be regarded as close description. It is in no sense narrative music. The titles are not in clear order of events, and, moreover, they are quite vague.

In the first number we have the sea and merely the vessel, not the voyages, of Sindbad. Then the story of the Prince Kalender cannot be distinguished among the three tales of the royal mendicants. The young prince and the young princess,—there are many of them in these Arabian fairy tales, though we can guess at the particular one. Finally, in the last number, the title mentions an event from the story of the third Prince Kalender, where the vessel (not of Sindbad) is wrecked upon a rock surmounted by a warrior of brass. The Feast of Bagdad has no special place in any one of the stories.

The truth is, it is all a mirroring in tones of the charm and essence of these epic gems of the East. It is not like the modern interlinear description, although it might be played during a reading on account of the general agreement of the color and spirit of the music. But there is the sense and feeling of the story, *das Märchen,* and the romance of adventure. The brilliancy of harmony, the eccentricity and gaiety of rhythm seem symbolic and, in a subtle way, descriptive. As in the subject, the stories themselves, there is a luxuriant imagery, but no sign of the element of reflection or even of emotion.

I.—The opening motive, in big, broad rhythm, is clearly the Sea. Some have called it the Sindbad

160

motive. But in essence these are not very different.
The Sea is here the very feeling and type of adventure,—nay, Adventure itself. It is a necessary part
of fairy stories. Here it begins and ends with its
rocking theme, ever moving onward. It comes in
the story of the Prince Kalender.

The second of the main phrases is evidently the
motive of the fairy tale itself, the feeling of "once
upon a time," the idea of story, that leads us to the
events themselves. It is a mere strumming of chords
of the harp, with a vague line, lacking rhythm, as
of musical prose. For rhythm is the type of event,
of happenings, of the adventure itself. So the formless phrase is the introduction, the narrator, *Märchen*
in an Oriental dress as Schérézade.

The first number passes for the most part in a
rocking of the motive of the sea, in various moods
and movements: *Largo e maestoso, Allegro non
troppo,—tranquillo.* At one time even the theme
of the story sings to the swaying of the sea.*

II.—In the tale of the Prince Kalender Schérézade,
of course, begins the story as usual. But the main
thread is in itself another interwoven tale,—*Andantino Capriccioso, quasi recitando,* with a solo in the
bassoon *dolce e espressivo,*—later *poco piu mosso,*

---

* We remember how Sindbad was tempted after each
fortunate escape from terrible dangers to embark once
more, and how he tells the story of the seven voyages on
seven successive days, amid luxury and feasting.

in violins.* There is most of happenings here. A very strident phrase that plays in the brass *Allegro molto,* may be some hobgoblin, or rather an evil jinn, that holds the princess captive and wrecks the hero's vessel. The sea, too, plays a tempestuous part at the same time with the impish mischief of the jinn.

III.—The third number is the idyll,—both of the stories and of the music. Here we are nearest to a touch of sentiment,—apart from the mere drama of haps and mishaps.† But there are all kinds of

---

* In the old version the word " Calender " is used; in the new translation by Lane we read of " The Three Royal Mendicants." In certain ancient editions they are called Karendelees,"—*i.e.,* " miserable beggars." Each of the three had lost an eye in the course of his misfortunes. The story (of the Third Kalender) begins with the wreck of the prince's vessel on the mountain of loadstone and the feat of the prince, who shoots the brazen horseman on top of the mountain and so breaks the charm. But there is a long chain of wonders and of troubles, of evil enchantments and of fateful happenings.

† The story, if any particular one is in the mind of the composer, is probably that of the Prince Kamar-ez-Zemán and the Princess Budoor. In the quality of the romance it approaches the legends of a later age of chivalry. In the main it is the long quest and the final meeting of a prince and a princess, living in distant kingdoms. Through the magic of genii they have seen each other once and have exchanged rings. The rest of the story is a long search one for the other. There are good and evil spirits, long journeys by land and sea, and great perils. It is an Arab story of the proverbial course of true love.

162

special events. There is no prelude of the narrator. The idyll begins straightway, *Andantino quasi allegretto,* winds through all kinds of scenes and storms, then sings again *dolce e cantabile.* Here, at last, the Schérézade phrase is heard on the violin solo, to chords of the harp; but presently it is lost in the concluding strains of the love story.

IV.—The last number begins with the motive of the sea, like the first, but *Allegro molto,* again followed by the phrase of the story teller. The sea returns *Allegro molto e frenetico* in full force, and likewise the vague motive of the story in a cadenza of violin solo. Then *Vivo* comes the dance, the pomp and gaiety of the Festival, with tripping tambourine and strings and the song first in the flutes.* Presently a reminder of the sea intrudes,—*con forza* in lower wood and strings. But other familiar figures flit by, —the evil jinn and the love-idyll. Indeed the latter has a full verse,—in the midst of the carnival.

Right out of the festival, rather in full festal array, we seem to plunge into the broad movement of the surging sea, *Allegro non troppo e maestoso,* straight on to the fateful event. There are no sighs and tears. Placidly the waves play softly about. And *dolce e capriccioso* the siren Schérézade once more reappears to conclude the tale.

* We may think of the revels of Sindbad before the returning thirst for adventure.

RACHMANINOW. SYMPHONY IN E MINOR *

I.—The symphony begins with the sombre temper of modern Russian art; at the outset it seems to throb with inmost feeling, uttered in subtlest design.

The slow solemn prelude (*Largo*) opens with the

chief phrase of the work in lowest strings to ominous chords, and treats it with passionate stress until the main pace of Allegro.

But the germ of prevailing legend lies deeper. The work is one of the few symphonies where the whole is reared on a smallest significant phrase. The first strain (of basses) is indeed the essence of the following melody and in turn of the main Allegro theme. But, to probe still further, we cannot help feeling

---

* Sergei Rachmaninow, born in 1873.

164

an ultimate, briefest motive of single ascending tone against intrinsic obstacle, wonderfully expressed in the harmony, with a mingled sense of resolution and regret. And of like moment is the reverse descending tone. Both of these symbols reappear throughout the symphony, separate or blended in larger melody, as principal or accompanying figures. Aside from this closer view that makes clear the tissue of themal discussion, the first phrase is the main melodic motto, that is instantly echoed in violins with piquant harmony. In the intricate path of deep musing we feel the mantle of a Schumann who had himself a kind of heritage from Bach. And thus we come to see the national spirit best and most articulate through the medium of ancient art.

The main Allegro melody not so much grows out of the Largo prelude, as it is of the same fibre and

identity. The violins sing here against a stately march of harmonies. Such is the fine coherence that the mere heralding rhythm is wrought of the first chords of the Largo, with their descending stress. And the expressive melody is of the same essence as the original sighing motto, save with a shift of accent that gives a new fillip of motion. In this movement at least we see the type of real symphony, that throbs and sings and holds us in the thrall of its spirit and song.

Moments there are here of light and joy, quickly drooping to the darker mood. Following the free flight of main melody is a skein of quicker figures, on aspirant pulse, answered by broad, tragic descent in minor tones.

Milder, more tranquil sings now the second melody, a striking embodiment of the sense of striving ascent. Chanted in higher reeds, it is immediately

followed and accompanied by an expressive answer in the strings. On the wing of this song we rise to a height where begins the path of a brief nervous motive (of the first notes of the symphony) that with the descending tone abounds in various guise. As a bold glance at the sun is punished by a sight of solar figures all about, so we feel throughout the tonal story the presence of these symbols. An epilogue of wistful song leads to the repeated melodies.

The main figure of the plot that follows is the first melody, now in slow, graceful notes, now in feverish pace, though the brief (second) motive moves constantly here and there. A darkest descent follows into an Avernus of deep brooding on the legend, with an ascending path of the brief, nervous phrase and a reverse fall, that finally wears out its own despair and ends in a sombre verse of the prelude, with new shades of melancholy, then plunges into an overwhelming burst on the sighing phrase. Thence the path of brooding begins anew; but it is now ascendant, on the dual pulse of the poignant motto and the brief, nervous motive. The whole current of passion is thus uttered in the prelude strain that at the outset was pregnant with feeling. At the crisis it is answered or rather interwoven with a guise of the second theme, in hurried pace, chanted by stentorian brass and wood in hallooing chorus that reaches a high exultation. To be sure the Russian at his gladdest seems tinged with sense of fate. So from the single burst we droop again. But the gloom is pierced by brilliant shafts,—herald calls (of brass and wood) that raise the mood of the returning main melody, and in their continuous refrain add a buoyant stimulus. And the verse of quicker figures has a new fire and ferment. All absent is the former descent of minor tones. Instead, in solemn hush of tempest, without the poignant touch, the tranquil second melody returns with dulcet answer of strings. A loveliest verse is of this further song where, in a dual chase of tune, the melody moves in contained rapture. In the cadence is a transfigured phase of the ascending tone, mingled with the retiring melody, all woven to a soothing cadence.

But the struggle is not over, nor is redemption near. The dulcet phrases sink once more to sombre depth where there is a final, slow-gathering burst of passion on the motto, with a conclusive ring almost of fierce triumph.

II.—The second movement, *Allegro molto,* is a complete change from introspection and passion to an

abandon as of primitive dance. Strings stir the feet; the horns blow the first motive of the savage tune; the upper wood fall in with a dashing jingle,—like a stroke of cymbals across the hostile harmonies.

Whether a recurring idiom is merely personal or belongs to the special work is difficult to tell. In reality it matters little. Here the strange rising tone is the same as in the former (second) melody. In the rude vigor of harmonies the primitive idea is splendidly stressed.

Right in the answer is a guise of short, nervous phrase, that gets a new touch of bizarre by a leap of the seventh from below. In this figure that moves throughout the symphony we see an outward symbol of an inner connection.—Bells soon lend a festive ring to the main tune.

In quieter pace comes a tranquil song of lower voices with a companion melody above,—all in serene major. Though it grew naturally out of the rude

Molto cantabile

8ve.

dance, the tune has a contrasting charm of idyll and, too, harks back to the former lyric strains that followed the second melody. When the dance returns, there is instead of discussion a mere extension of main motive in full chorus.

But here in the midst the balance is more than restored. From the dance that ceases abruptly we go straight to school or rather cloister. On our recurring nervous phrase a fugue is rung with all pomp and ceremony (*meno mosso*); and of the dance there are mere faint echoing memories, when the

fugal text seems for a moment to weave itself into the first tune.

Instead, comes into the midst of sermon a hymnal chant, blown gently by the brass, while other stray

voices run lightly on the thread of fugue. There is, indeed, a playful suggestion of the dance somehow in the air. A final tempest of the fugue * brings us

---

* It is of the first two notes of the symphony that the fugal theme is made. For though it is longer in the strings, the brief motion is ever accented in the wood. Thus relentless is the themal coherence. If we care to look closer we see how the (following) chant is a slower form of the fugal theme, while the bass is in the line of the dance-tune. In the chant in turn we cannot escape a reminder, if not a likeness, of the second theme of the first movement.

back to the full verse of dance and the following
melodies. But before the end sounds a broad hymnal
line in the brass with a dim thread of the fugue, and
the figures steal away in solemn stillness.

III.—The Adagio has one principal burden, first
borne by violins,—that rises from the germ of earlier

(Strings with added harmony in bassoons and horns)

lyric strains. Then the clarinet joins in a quiet
madrigal of tender phrases. We are tempted to find
here an influence from a western fashion, a taint of
polythemal virtuosity, in this mystic maze of many
strains harking from all corners of the work, without
a gain over an earlier Russian simplicity. Even the
Slavic symphony seems to have fallen into a state
of artificial cunning, where all manners of greater

171

or lesser motives are packed close in a tangled mass.

It cannot be said that a true significance is achieved in proportion to the number of concerting themes. We might dilate on the sheer inability of the hearer to grasp a clear outline in such a multiple plot.

There is somehow a false kind of polyphony, a too great facility of spurious counterpoint, that differs subtly though sharply from the true art where the number entails no loss of individual quality; where the separate melodies move by a divine fitness that measures the perfect conception of the multiple idea; where there is no thought of a later padding to give a shimmer of profound art. It is here that the sym-

172

phony is in danger from an exotic style that had its origin in German music-drama.

From this point the Rachmaninow symphony languishes in the fountain of its fresh inspiration, seems consciously constructed with calculating care.

There is, after all, no virtue in itself in mere themal interrelation,—in particular of lesser phrases. One cogent theme may well prevail as text of the whole. As the recurring motives are multiplied, they must lose individual moment. The listener's grasp becomes more difficult, until there is at best a mystic maze, a sweet chaos, without a clear melodic thought. It cannot be maintained that the perception of the modern audience has kept pace with the complexity of scores. Yet there is no gainsaying an alluring beauty of these waves of sound rising to fervent height in the main melody that is expressive of a modern wistfulness.

But at the close is a fierce outbreak of the first motto, with a defiance of regret, in faster, reckless pace, brief, but suddenly recurring. Exquisite is this

cooing of voices in mournful bits of the motto, with a timid upper phrase in the descending tone.

On we go in the piling of Ossa on Pelion, where the motto and even the Scherzo dance lend their text. Yet all is fraught with sentient beauty as, rising in Titanic climb, it plunges into an overwhelming cry in the Adagio melody. Throughout, the ascending and descending tones, close interwoven, give a blended hue of arduous striving and regret.

After a pause follow a series of refrains of solo voices in the melody, with muted strings, with mingled strains of the motto. In the bass is an undulation that recalls the second theme of former movement. And the clarinet returns with its mystic madrigal of melody; now the Adagio theme enters and gives it point and meaning. In one more burst it sings in big and little in the same alluring harmony, whence it dies down to soothing close in brilliant gamut as of sinking sun.

IV.—Allegro vivace. Throwing aside the clinging

fragments of fugue in the prelude we rush into a gaiety long sustained. Almost strident is the ruthless merriment; we are inclined to fear that the literal coherence of theme is greater than the inner connection of mood. At last the romp hushes to a whisper of drum, with strange patter of former dance. And following and accompanying it is a new hymnal (or is it martial) line, as it were the reverse of the other

(Reeds and horns)

(Strings with the quicker dance phrase of 2d movement)

chant. The gay figures flit timidly back,—a struggle 'twixt pleasure and fate,—but soon regain control.

If we cared to interpret, we might find in the Finale a realized aspiration. The truth is the humors of the themal phrases, as of the movements, jar: they are on varying planes. The coarser vein of the last is no solace to the noble grief of the foregoing.

Again the change or series of moods is not clearly defined. They seem a parade of visions. The hymn may be viewed as a guise of the former chant of the Scherzo, with the dance-trip in lowest bass.

Straight from the rush and romp we plunge anew into a trance of sweet memories. The lyric vein here binds together earlier strains, whose kinship had not appeared. They seemed less significant, hidden as subsidiary ideas. If we care to look back we find a germ of phrase in the first Prelude, and then the answer of the second (Allegro) theme of first movement. There was, too, the sweep of dual melody following the rude dance of Scherzo. Above all is here the essence and spirit of the central Adagio melody of the symphony.

The answering strain is of high beauty, with a melting sense of farewell. From the sad ecstasy is a

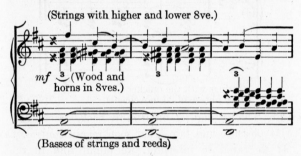

(Strings with higher and lower 8ve.)

mf (Wood and horns in 8ves.)

(Basses of strings and reeds)

descent to mystic musing, where abound the symbols of rising and falling tones. More and more moving is the climactic melody of regret with a blended song in large and little. Most naturally it sinks into a full verse of the Adagio tune—whence instantly is aroused a new battle of moods.

While the dance capers below, above is the sobbing phrase from the heart of the Adagio. The trip falls into the pace of hymnal march. The shadows of many figures return. Here is the big descending scale in tragic minor from the first movement. Large it looms, in bass and treble. Answering it is a figure of sustained thirds that recalls the former second (Allegro) melody. And still the trip of dance goes on.

Sharpest and strongest of all these memories is the big sigh of sombre harmonies from the first Largo prelude, answered by the original legend. And the dance still goes tripping on and the tones rumble in descent.

The dance has vanished; no sound but the drone of dull, falling tones, that multiply like the spirits of the sorcerer apprentice, in large form and small, with the big rumbling in a quick patter as of scurrying mice.

Suddenly a new spirit enters with gathering volume and warmer harmony. As out of a dream we gradually emerge, at the end with a shock of welcome to light and day, as we awake to the returning glad dance. And here is a new entrancing countertune above that crowns the joy.

Once again the skip falls into the ominous descent with the phantom of Scherzo dance in basses. Now returns the strange hymnal line of march and the other anxious hue.

But quickly they are transformed into the tempest of gaiety in full parade. When a new burst is preparing, we see the sighing figure all changed to opposite mood. The grim tune of Scherzo dance enters mysteriously in big and little and slowly takes on a softened hue, losing the savage tinge.

After the returning dance, the farewell melody sings from full throat. Before the ending revel we may feel a glorified guise of the sombre legend of the symphony.

CHAPTER XII

SIBELIUS. A FINNISH SYMPHONY *

WE must expect that the music of newer nations will be national. It goes without saying; for the music comes fresh from the soil; it is not the result of long refined culture. There is the strain and burst of a burden of racial feeling to utter itself in the most pliant and eloquent of all the languages of emotion. It is the first and noblest sentiment of every nation conscious of its own worth, and it has its counterpart in the individual. Before the utterance has been found by a people, before it has felt this sense of its own quality, no other message can come. So the most glorious period in the history of every country (even in the eyes of other nations) is the struggle for independence, whether successful or not.

All on a new plane is this northernmost symphony, with a crooning note almost of savage, and sudden, fitful bursts from languorous to fiery mood. The harmony, the turn of tune have a national quality, delicious and original, though the Oriental tinge

---

* Symphony No. 1, in E minor, by Jan Sibelius, born in 1865.

appears, as in Slav and Magyar music, both in bold
and in melancholy humor. Though full of strange
and warm colors, the harmonic scheme is simple;
rather is the work a tissue of lyric rhapsody than
the close-woven plot of tonal epic. A certain trace
of revery does find a vent in the traditional art of
contrary melodies. But a constant singing in pairs
is less art than ancient folk-manner, like primal
music in the love or dance songs of savages.

The symphony begins with a quiet rhapsody of
solo clarinet in wistful minor, clear without chords,
though there is a straying into major. There is no
accompaniment save a soft roll of drum, and that
soon dies away.

The rhapsody seems too vague for melody; yet
there are motives, one in chief, winding to a pause;
here is a new appealing phrase; the ending is in a

return to the first. Over the whole symphony is cast
the hue of this rhapsody, both in mood and in the
literal tone.

All opposite, with sudden spring of buoyant strings, strikes the Allegro tune ending in a quick, dancing trip. The first voice is immediately pursued by an-

other in similar phase, like a gentler shadow, and soon rises to a passionate chord that is the main idiom of the movement.

A second theme in clear-marked tones of reed and horns, as of stern chant, is taken up in higher wood and grows to graceful melody in flowing strings.

180

There is a series of flights to an ever higher perch of harmony until the first Allegro motive rings out in fullest chorus, again with the companion tune and the cadence of poignant dissonance.

A new episode comes with shimmering of harp and strings, where rare and dainty is the sense of primal

harmony that lends a pervading charm to the symphony. Here the high wood has a song in constant thirds, right from the heart of the rhapsody, all bedecked as melody with a new rhythm and answer. Soon this simple lay is woven in a skein of pairs of voices, meeting or diverging. But quickly we are back in the trance of lyric song, over palpitating strings, with the refrain very like the former companion phrase that somehow leads or grows to a

rhythmic verse of the first strain of the rhapsody. Here begins a long mystic phase of straying voices (of the wood) in the crossing figures of the song, in continuous fantasy that somehow has merged into the line of second Allegro theme, winging towards a brilliant height where the strings ring out the strain amid sharp cries of the brass in startling hues of harmony and electric calls from the first rhapsody.

From out the maze and turmoil the shadowy melody rises in appealing beauty like heavenly vision and lo! is but a guise of the first strain of rhapsody. It rises amid flashes of fiery brass in bewildering blare of main theme, then sinks again to the depth of brooding, though the revery of the appealing phrase has a climactic height of its own, with the strange, palpitating harmonies.

In a new meditation on bits of the first Allegro theme sounds suddenly a fitful burst of the second, that presently emerges in triumphant, sovereign song. Again, on a series of flights the main theme is reached and leaps once more to impassioned height.

But this is followed by a still greater climax of moving pathos whence we descend once more to lyric meditation (over trembling strings). Follows a final tempest and climax of the phrase of second theme.

The movement thus ends, not in joyous exultation, but in a fierce triumph of sombre minor.

The Andante is purest folk-melody, and it is strange how we know this, though we do not know the special theme. We cannot decry the race-element as a rich fount of melody. While older nations strive and strain, it pours forth by some mystery in prodigal flow with less tutored peoples who are singing their first big song to the world. Only, the ultimate goal for each racial inspiration must be a greater universal celebration.

The lyric mood is regnant here, in a melody that, springing from distant soil, speaks straight to every heart, above all with the concluding refrain. It is of the purest vein, of the primal fount, deeper than mere racial turn or trait. Moreover, with a whole coronet of gems of modern harmony, it has a broad swing and curve that gives the soothing sense of fire-

side; it bears a burden of elemental, all-contenting emotion. In the main, the whole movement is one lyric flight. But there come the moods of musing and rhapsodic rapture. In a brief fugal vein is a mystic harking back to the earlier prelude. In these lesser phrases are the foil or counter-figures for the bursts of the melody.

It is the first motive of the main tune that is the refrain in ever higher and more fervent exclamation, or in close pressing chase of voices. Then follows a melting episode,—some golden piece of the melody in plaintive cellos, 'neath tremulous wood or delicate choirs of strings.

But there is a second tune, hardly less moving,

in dulcet group of horns amid shimmering strings
and harp, with a light bucolic answer in playful reed.

And it has a glowing climax, too, with fiery trumpet,
and dashing strings and clashing wood.

Gorgeous in the warm depth of horns sound now
the returning tones of the first noble melody, with
playful trill of the wood, in antiphonal song of trumpets and strings. And there are revels of new turns
of the tune (where the stirring harmony seems the
best of all) that will rise to a frenzy of tintinnabulation. A quicker countertheme lends life and motion
to all this play and plot.

A big, solemn stride of the middle strain (of
main melody) precedes the last returning verse, with
all the tender pathos of the beginning.

The Scherzo is wild race-feeling let loose—national music that has not yet found a melody. Significantly the drums begin the tune, to a dancing strain of *pizzicato* strings. The tune is so elemental that the

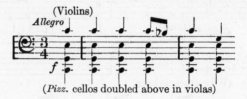

(*Pizz.* cellos doubled above in violas)

drums can really play it; the answer is equally rude, —an arpeggic motive of strings against quick runs of the higher wood. Out of it grows a tinge of tune with a fresh spring of dance,—whence returns the first savage motive. This is suddenly changed to the guise of a fugal theme, with new close, that starts a maze of disputation.

Right from the full fire of the rough dance, sad-stressed chords plunge into a moving plaint with much sweetness of melody and higher counter-melody. Then returns again the original wild rhythm.

In the last movement the composer confesses the "Fantasy" in the title. It begins with a broad sweep of the returning rhapsody, the prologue of the symphony, though without the former conclusion. Now it sings in a strong unison of the strings *largamente ed appassionato,* and with clang of chord in lower brass. The appealing middle phrase is all disguised in strum as of dance. The various strains sing freely in thirds, with sharp punctuating chords. Throughout is a balance of the pungent vigor of harmonies with dulcet melody.

In sudden rapid pace the strumming figure dances in the lower reed, then yields to the play (in the strings) of a lively (almost comic) tune of a strong national tinge,—a kind that seems native to northern countries and is not unlike a strain that crept into

American song. A tempest of pranks is suddenly halted before the entrance of a broad melody, with underlying harmonies of latent passion. The feeling of fantasy is in the further flow, with free singing chords of harp. But ever between the lines creeps in the strumming phrase, from the first prelude, returned to its earlier mood.

187

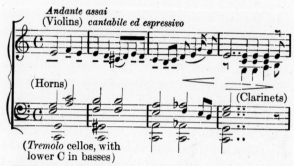

With baffling mystery anon come other appealing phrases from the beginning, that show the whole to be the woof almost of a single figure, or at least to lie within the poetic scope of the prologue. A fugal revel of the comic phrase with the quick strum as counter-theme ends in a new carnival,—here a dashing march, there a mad chase of strident harmonies. Now sings the full romance and passion of the melody through the whole gamut from pathos to rapture. It ends with poignant stress of the essence of the song, with sheerest grating of straining harmonies. In the midst, too, is again the mystic symbol from the heart of the prelude. Then with a springing recoil comes a last jubilation, though still in the prevailing minor, with a final coursing of the quick theme.

The whole is a broad alternation of moods, of wild abandon and of tender feeling,—the natural dual quality of primal music. So, at least in the Finale, this is a Finnish fantasy, on the very lines of other national rhapsody.

CHAPTER XIII

BOHEMIAN SYMPHONIES

IN the music of modern Bohemia is one of the most vital utterances of the folk-spirit. The critic may not force a correspondence of politics and art to support his theory. Yet a cause may here be found as in Russia and Finland. (Poland and Hungary had their earlier song). There is a sincerity, an unpremeditated quality in Bohemian music that is not found among its western neighbors. The spirit is its own best proof, without a conscious stress of a national note. Indeed, Bohemian music is striking, not at all in a separate tonal character, like Hungarian, but rather in a subtle emotional intensity, which again differs from the wild abandon of the Magyars. An expression it must be of a national feeling that has for ages been struggling against absorption. Since ancient times Bohemia has been part of a Teutonic empire. The story of its purely native kings is not much more than legendary. Nor has it shared the harder fate of other small nations; for the Teuton rule at least respected its separate unity.

But the long association with the German people has nearly worn away the racial signs and hall-marks of its folk-song. A Bohemian tune thus has a taste much like the native German. Yet a quality of its

189

own lies in the emotional vitality, shown in a school of national drama and, of late, in symphony. It is not necessary to seek in this modern culmination a correspondence with an impending danger of political suppression. Art does not follow history with so instant a reflection.

The intensity of this national feeling appears when Smetana himself, the minstrel of the people, is charged at home with yielding to the foreign influence. Here again is the hardship of the true national poet who feels that for the best utterance of his message he needs the grounding upon a broader art; here is the narrow Chauvinism that has confined the music of many lands within the primitive forms.

Two types we have in Bohemian music of later times: one, Smetana, of pure national celebration; a second, Dvôrák, who with a profound absorption of the German masters, never escaped the thrall of the folk-element and theme.

SMETANA. SYMPHONIC POEM, "THE MOLDAU RIVER" *

Simplicity is uppermost in these scores; yet the true essence is almost hidden to the mere reader. With all primitive quality they are more difficult than many a classic symphony. The latent charm of

---

* Friedrich Smetana, 1824–1884, foremost among Bohemian dramatic composers, wrote a cycle of symphonic poems under the general title "My Country." Of these the present work is the second.

folk humor and sentiment depends more on tradition and sympathy than on notation.

The naïvely graphic impulse (that we find throughout the choral works of Bach) that merely starts a chance themal line, as here of the first branch of the Moldau, does not disturb the emotional expression. And while the feeling is sustained, the art is there, not to stifle but to utter and set free the native spring of song.

It must be yielded that the design is not profound; it smacks of the village fair rather than of grand tragedy. Song is ever supreme, and with all abundance of contrapuntal art does not become sophisticated. The charm is not of complexity, but of a more child-like, sensuous kind.

It must all be approached in a different way from other symphonic music. The minstrel is not even the peasant in court costume, as Dvôrák once was called. He is the peasant in his own village dress, resplendent with color and proud of his rank.

We cannot enjoy the music with furrowed brow. It is a case where music touches Mother Earth and rejuvenates herself. Like fairy lore and proverbs, its virtue lies in some other element than profound design. For any form of song or verse that enshrines the spirit of a people and is tried in the forge of ages of tradition, lives on more surely than the fairest art of individual poet.

The stream is the great figure, rising from small sources in playful flutes, with light spray of harp and

Allegro commodo non agitato

p lusingando
(Flute with chord of *pizz.* strings)

strings. The first brook is joined by another (in clarinets) from a new direction. Soon grows the number and the rustle of confluent waters. The motion of the strings is wavelike, of a broader flow, though underneath we scan the several lesser currents. Above floats now the simple, happy song, that expands

(Reeds and horns with waving strings and stroke of triangle)

with the stream and at last reaches a glad, sunny major.

Still to the sound of flowing waters comes the forest hunt, with all the sport of trumpets and other brass.

It is descriptive music, tonal painting if you will; but the color is local or national. The strokes are not so much of events or scenes as of a popular humor and character, which we must feel with small stress

192

of each event. The blowing of trumpets, the purling
of streams, the swaying of trees, in primal figures, all
breathe the spirit of Bohemia.

The hunt dies away; emerging from the forest the
jolly sounds greet us of a peasant wedding. The

(Reeds and strings)

parade reaches the church in high festivity and slowly
vanishes to tinkling bells.

Night has fallen; in shifted scene the stream is
sparkling in the moonlight still to the quiet sweet
harmonies. But this is all background for a dance
of nymphs, while a dulcet, sustained song sounds
through the night. At last, to the golden horns a
faintest harmony is added of deeper brass. Still
very softly, the brass strike a quicker phrase and we
seem to hear the hushed chorus of hunt with the call
of trumpets, as the other brass lead in a new verse
that grows lustier with the livelier song and dance,
till—with a flash we are alone with the running
stream with which the dance of nymphs has somehow merged.

On it goes, in happy, ever more masterful course, a symbol of the nation's career, surging in bright major and for a moment quieting before the mighty Rapids of St. Johann. Here the song of the stream is nearly lost in the rush of eddies and the strife of big currents, with the high leaps of dashing spray,— ever recurring like unceasing battle with a towering clash at the height of the tempest. At last all meet in overpowering united torrent, suddenly to hush before the stream, at the broadest, rushes majestically along in hymnal song of exalted harmonies and triumphant melody, with joyous after-strains.

As the pilgrim to his Mecca, so the waters are wafted into the climactic motive of the Hradschin, the chant of the holy citadel. The rest is a long jubila-

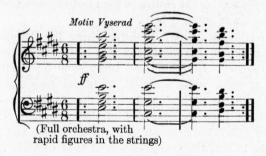

(Full orchestra, with rapid figures in the strings)

tion on quicker beats of the chant, amid the plash of waters and the shaking of martial brass. Strangely, as the other sounds die away, the melody of the stream emerges clear and strong, then vanishes in the distance before the jubilant Amen.

In the general view we must feel a wonderful contrast here with the sophomoric state of the contemporary art in other lands where the folk-song has lost its savor,—where the natural soil is exhausted and elegant castles are built in the air of empty fantasy, or on the sands of a vain national pride.

DVÔRÁK. SYMPHONY, "FROM THE NEW WORLD." *

It is a much-discussed question how far Dvôrák's American symphony is based on characteristic folk-song. Here are included other questions: to what extent the themes are based on an African type, and whether negro music is fairly American folk-song. Many, perhaps most people, will answer with a general negative. But it seems to be true that many of us do not really know the true negro song,—have quite a wrong idea of it.

To be sure, all argument aside, it is a mistake to think that folk-song gets its virtue purely from a distinctive national quality,—because it is Hungarian, Scandinavian, or Slavonic. If all the national modes and rhythms of the world were merged in one republic, there would still be a folk-song of the true type and value. There is a subtle charm and strength in the spontaneous simplicity, all aside from racial color. It is here that, like Antæus, the musician touches Mother Earth and renews his strength. So, when Dvôrák suddenly shifts in the midst of his New World fantasy into a touch of Bohemian song, there is no real loss. It is all relevant in the broad

---

* Anton Dvôrák, 1841–1904.

sense of folk feeling, that does not look too closely at geographical bounds. It is here that music, of all arts, leads to a true state of equal sympathy, regardless of national prejudice. What, therefore, distinguishes Dvôrák's symphony may not be mere negro melody, or even American song, but a genuine folk-feeling, in the widest meaning.

In one way, Dvôrák's work reminds us of Mendelssohn's Scotch Symphony: both exploit foreign national melody in great poetic forms. One could write a Scotch symphony in two ways: one, in Mendelssohn's, the other would be to tell of the outer impression in the terms of your own folk-song. That is clearly the way Mendelssohn wrote most of the Italian Symphony,—which stands on a higher plane than the Scotch. For folk-song is the natural language of its own people. It is interesting to see the exact type that each theme represents; but it is not so important as to catch the distinction, the virtue of folk-song *per se* and the purely natural utterance of one's own. Of course, every one writes always in his folk-tones. On the other hand, one may explore one's own special treasures of native themes, as Dvôrák himself did so splendidly in his Slavic Dances and in his Legends. So one must, after all, take this grateful, fragrant work as an idea of what American composers might do in full earnest. Dvôrák is of all later masters the most eminent folk-musician. He shows greatest sympathy, freedom and delight in revelling among the simple tones and rhythms of popular utterance, rearing on them, all in poetic spontaneity, a structure of high art. Without strain or show, Dvôrák stood perhaps the most genuine of late composers, with a firm foot on the soil of native melody, yet with the balance and restraint and the clear vision of the trained master.*

In a certain view, it would seem that by the fate of servitude the American negro has become the element in our own national life that alone produces true folk-song,—that corresponds to the peasant and serf of Europe, the class that must find in song the refuge and solace for its loss of material joys. So Dvôrák perhaps is right, with a far seeing eye, when he singles the song of the despised race as the national type.

Another consideration fits here. It has been suggested that the imitative sense of the negro has led him to absorb elements of other song. It is very difficult to separate original African elements of song from those that may thus have been borrowed. At any rate, there is no disparagement of the negro's musical genius in this theory. On the contrary, it would be almost impossible to imagine a musical people that would resist the softer tones of surround-

---

* The whole subject of American and negro folk-song is new and unexplored. There are races of the blacks living on the outer reefs and islands of the Carolinas, with not more than thirty whites in a population of six thousand, where " spirituals " and other musical rites are held which none but negroes may attend. The truest African mode and rhythm would seem to be preserved here; to tell the truth, there is great danger of their loss unless they are soon recorded.

ing and intermingling races. We know, to be sure, that Stephen Foster, the author of " The Old Folks at Home," " Massa's in the Cold, Cold Ground," and other famous ballads, was a Northerner, though his mother came from the South. We hear, too, that he studied negro music eagerly. It is not at all inconceivable, however, Foster's song may have been devoid of negro elements, that the colored race absorbed, wittingly or unwittingly, something of the vein into their plaints or lullabies,—that, indeed, Foster's songs may have been a true type that stirred their own imitation. From all points of view,—the condition of slavery, the trait of assimilation and the strong gift of musical expression may have conspired to give the negro a position and equipment which would entitle his tunes to stand as the real folk-song of America.

The eccentric accent seems to have struck the composer strongly. And here is a strange similarity with Hungarian song,—though there is, of course, no kinship of race whatever between Bohemians and Magyars. One might be persuaded to find here simply an ebullition of rhythmic impulse,—the desire for a special fillip that starts and suggests a stronger energy of motion than the usual conventional pace. At any rate, the symphony begins with just such strong, nervous phrases that soon gather big force. Hidden is the germ of the first, undoubtedly the chief theme of the whole work.

It is more and more remarkable how a search will show the true foundation of almost all of Dvôrák's themes. Not that one of them is actually borrowed, or lacks an original, independent reason for being.

Whether by imitation or not, the pentatonic scale of the Scotch is an intimate part of negro song. This avoidance of the seventh or leading tone is seen throughout the symphony as well as in the traditional jubilee tunes. It may be that this trait was merely confirmed in the African by foreign musical influence. For it seems that the leading-note, the urgent need for the ascending half-tone in closing, belongs originally to the minstrelsy of the Teuton and of central Europe, that resisted and conquered the sterner modes of the early Church. Ruder nations here agreed with Catholic ritual in preferring the larger interval of the whole tone. But in the quaint jump of the third the Church had no part, clinging closely to a diatonic process.

The five-toned scale is indeed so widespread that it cannot be fastened on any one race or even family of nations. The Scotch have it; it is characteristic of the Chinese and of the American Indian. But, independently of the basic mode or scale, negro songs show here and there a strange feeling for a savage kind of lowering of this last note. The pentatonic scale simply omits it, as well as the fourth step. But the African will now and then rudely and forcibly lower it by a half-tone. In the minor it is more natural; for it can then be thought of as the fifth of the relative major. Moreover, it is familiar to us in the Church chant. This effect we have in the beginning of the Scherzo. Many of us do not know

the true African manner, here. But in the major it
is much more barbarous. And it is almost a pity that
Dvôrák did not strike it beyond an occasional touch
(as in the second quoted melody). A fine example
is " Roll, Jordan Roll," in E flat (that opens, by
the way, much like Dvôrák's first theme), where the
beginning of the second line rings out on a savage
D flat, out of all key to Caucasian ears.

We soon see stealing out of the beginning *Adagio*
an eccentric pace in motion of the bass, that leads to
the burst of main subject, *Allegro molto,* with a cer-

tain ragged rhythm that we Americans cannot dis-
claim as a nation. The working up is spirited, and
presently out of the answer grows a charming jingle
that somehow strikes home.

ppp (Violins, with harmony in lower strings)

It begins in the minor and has a strange, barbaric
touch of cadence. Many would acknowledge it at
most as a touch of Indian mode. Yet it is another
phase of the lowered seventh. And if we care to
search, we find quite a prototype in a song like
"Didn't My Lord Deliver Daniel." Soon the phrase
has a more familiar ring as it turns into a friendly
major. But the real second theme comes in a solo
tune on the flute, in the major,

(Strings)

with a gait something like the first.* Less and less
we can resist the genuine negro quality of these melo-

---

* Again it is interesting to compare here the jubilee song,
"Oh! Redeemed," in the collection of "Jubilee and Plan-
tation Songs," of the Oliver Ditson Company.

dies, and, at the same time, their beauty and the value of the tonal treasure-house in our midst.

The whole of the first Allegro is thus woven of three melodious and characteristic themes in very clear sonata-form. The second, Largo, movement is a lyric of moving pathos, with a central melody that may not have striking traits of strict African song, and yet belongs to the type closely associated with the negro vein of plaint or love-song. The rhythmic

(English horn solo)

turns that lead to periods of excitement and climaxes of rapid motion, are absent in the main melody. But

(Oboe and clarinets)

pp

(Basses *pizz.* with *tremolo* figures in violins)

202

they appear in the episode that intervenes. Even
here, in the midst, is a new contrast of a minor
lament that has a strong racial trait in the sudden
swing to major and, as quickly, back to the drearier
mode. This is followed by a rhapsody or succession
of rapid, primitive phrases, that leads to a crisis
where, of a sudden, three themes sing at once, the
two of the previous Allegro and the main melody of
the Largo, in distorted pace with full chorus. This
excitement is as suddenly lulled and soothed by the
return of the original moving song.

The Scherzo starts in a quick three-beat strum on
the chord we have pointed to as a true model trait of
negro music, with the lowered leading-note. The

theme, discussed in close stress of imitation, seems
merely to mark the rapid swing in the drone of
strange harmony. But what is really a sort of Trio
(*poco sostenuto*) is another sudden, grateful change
to major, perfectly true to life, so to speak, in this
turn of mode and in the simple lines of the tune.
The lyric mood all but suppresses the dance, the

melody sounding like a new verse of the Largo. The trip has always lingered, but not too much for the delicious change when it returns to carry us off our feet.

The Scherzo now steals in again, quite a piece, it seems, with the Trio. As the rising volume nears a crisis, the earliest theme (from the first Allegro) is heard in the basses. In the hushed discourse of Scherzo theme that follows, the old melody still intrudes. In mockery of one of its turns comes an enchanting bit of tune, as naïve an utterance as any, much like a children's dancing song. And it returns later with still new enchantment of rhythm. But the whole is too full of folk-melody to trace out, yet is, in its very fibre, true to the idea of an epic of the people.

Presently the whole Scherzo and Trio are rehearsed; but now instead of the phase of latest melodies is a close where the oldest theme (of Allegro) is sung in lusty blasts of the horns and wood, with answers of the Scherzo motive.

In the last movement, *Allegro con fuoco,* appears early a new kind of march tune that, without special

Allegro con fuoco

ff (Horns and trumpets with full orchestra)

trick of rhythm, has the harsh note of lowered leading-note (in the minor, to be sure) in very true

keeping with negro song. The march is carried on,
with flowing answer, to a high pitch of varied splendor and tonal power. The second theme is utterly
opposed in a certain pathetic rhapsody. Yet it rises,
at the close, to a fervent burst in rapid motion. We

may expect in the Finale an orgy of folk-tune and
dance, and we are not disappointed. There is, too,
a quick rise and fall of mood, that is a mark of the
negro as well as of the Hungarian. By a sudden
doubling, we are in the midst of a true " hoe-down,"
in jolliest jingle, with that naïve iteration, true to
life; it comes out clearest when the tune of the bass
(that sounds like a rapid " Three Blind Mice ") is

(Strings, wood and brass)

Con 8ve.

(See page 205, line 9.)

put in the treble. A pure idealized negro dance-frolic is here. It is hard to follow all the pranks; lightly as the latest phrase descends in extending melody, a rude blast of the march intrudes in discordant humor. A new jingle of dance comes with a re-doubled pace of bits of the march. As this dies down to dimmest bass, the old song from the Largo rings high in the wood. Strangest of all, in a fierce shout of the whole chorus sounds twice this same pathetic strain. Later comes a redoubled speed of the march in the woodwind, above a slower in low strings. Now the original theme of all has a noisy say. Presently the sad second melody has a full verse. Once more the Largo lullaby sings its strain in the minor. In the close the original Allegro theme has a literal, vigorous dispute with the march-phrase for the last word of all.

The work does less to exploit American music than to show a certain community in all true folk-song. Nor is this to deny a strain peculiar to the new world. It seems a poet of distant land at the same time and in the same tones uttered his longing for his own country and expressed the pathos and the romance of the new. Dvôrák, like all true workers, did more than he thought: he taught Americans not so much the power of a song of their own, as their right of heritage in all folk-music. And this is based not merely on an actual physical inheritance from the various older races.

If the matter, in Dvôrák's symphony, is of American negro-song, the manner is Bohemian. A stranger-poet may light more clearly upon the traits of a foreign lore. But his celebration will be more conscious if he endeavor to cling throughout to the special dialect. A true national expression will come from the particular soil and will be unconscious of its own idiom.

The permanent hold that Dvôrák's symphony has gained is due to an intrinsic merit of art and sincere sentiment; it has little to do with the nominal title or purpose.

CHAPTER XIV

THE EARLIER BRUCKNER *

WHATEVER be the final answer of the mooted question of the greatness of Bruckner's symphonies, there is no doubt that he had his full share of technical profundity, and a striking mastery of the melodious weaving of a maze of concordant strains. The question inevitably arises with Bruckner as to the value of the world's judgments on its contemporary poets. There can be no doubt that the *furore* of the musical public tends to settle on one or two favorites with a concentration of praise that ignores the work of others, though it be of a finer grain. Thus Schubert's greatest— his one completed—symphony was never acclaimed until ten years after his death. Even his songs somehow brought more glory to the singer than to the composer. Bach's oratorios lay buried for a full century. On the other hand, names great in their day are utterly lost from the horizon. It is hard to conceive the *éclat* of a Buononcini or a Monteverde,—whose works were once preëminent. There are elements in art, of special, sensational effect, that make a peculiar appeal in their time, and are incompatible with true and permanent great-

* Anton Bruckner, born at Annsfelden, Austria, 1828; died in Vienna in 1896.

ness. One is tempted to say, the more sudden and vehement the success, the less it will endure. But it would not be true. Such an axiom would condemn an opera like "Don Giovanni," an oratorio like the "Creation," a symphony like Beethoven's Seventh. There is a wonderful difference, an immeasurable gulf between the good and the bad in art; yet the apparent line is of the subtlest. Most street songs may be poor; but some are undoubtedly beautiful in a very high sense. It is a problem of mystic fascination, this question of the value of contemporary art. It makes its appeal to the subjective view of each listener. No rule applies. Every one will perceive in proportion to his capacity, no one beyond it. So, a profound work may easily fail of response, as many works in the various arts have done in the past, because the average calibre of the audience is too shallow, while it may deeply stir an intelligent few. Not the least strange part of it all is the fact that there can, of necessity, be no decision in the lifetime of the poet. Whether it is possible for obscure Miltons never to find their meed of acclaim, is a question that we should all prefer to answer in the negative. There is a certain shudder in thinking of such a chance; it seems a little akin to the danger of being buried alive.

The question of Bruckner's place can hardly be said to be settled, although he has left nine symphonies. He certainly shows a freedom, ease and mastery in the symphonic manner, a limpid flow of melody

14   209

and a sure control in the interweaving of his themes, so that, in the final verdict, the stress may come mainly on the value of the subjects, in themselves. He is fond of dual themes, where the point lies in neither of two motives, but in the interplay of both; we see it somewhat extended in Richard Strauss, who uses it, however, in a very different spirit. The one evident and perhaps fatal lack is of intrinsic beauty of the melodic ideas, and further, an absence of the strain of pathos that sings from the heart of a true symphony. While we are mainly impressed by the workmanship, there is no denying a special charm of constant tuneful flow. At times this complexity is almost marvellous in the clear simplicity of the concerted whole,—in one view, the main trait or trick of symphonic writing. It is easy to pick out the leading themes as they appear in official order. But it is not so clear which of them constitute the true text. The multiplicity of tunes and motives is amazing.

Of the Wagner influence with which Bruckner is said to be charged, little is perceptible in his second symphony. On the contrary, a strong academic tradition pervades. The themes are peculiarly symphonic. Moreover they show so strikingly the dual quality that one might say, as a man may see double, Bruckner sang double. Processes of augmenting and inverting abound, together with the themal song in the bass. Yet there is not the sense of overloaded learning. There is everywhere a clear and melodious polyphony.

But with all masterly architecture, even enchanting changes of harmony and a prodigal play of melody, the vacuity of poetic ideas must preclude a permanent appeal. Bruckner is here the schoolmaster:
his symphony is a splendid skeleton, an object lesson
for the future poet.

In the FOURTH (ROMANTIC) SYMPHONY the main
light plays throughout on the wind. The text is a
call of horns, that begins the work. It is a symphony

of wood-notes, where the forest-horn is sovereign,—
awakening a widening world of echoes, with a murmuring maze of lesser notes. One has again the
feeling that in the quiet interweaving of a tapestry
of strains lies the individual quality of the composer,
—that the *forte* blasts, the stride of big unison figures
are but the interlude.

In the Andante the charm is less of tune than of
the delicate changing shades of the harmony and
of the colors of tone. We are ever surprised in the
gentlest way by a turn of chord or by the mere entrance of a horn among the whispering strings. The

shock of a soft modulation may be as sudden as of the loud, sudden blare. But we cannot somehow be consoled for the want of a heart-felt melody.

The Scherzo is a kind of hunting-piece, full of the sparkle, the color and romance of bugles and horns, —a spirited fanfare broken by hushed phrases of strings or wood, or an elf-like mystic dance on the softened call of trumpets. The Trio sings apart, between the gay revels, in soft voices and slower pace, like a simple ballad.

The Finale is conceived in mystical retrospect, beginning in vein of prologue: over mysterious murmuring strings, long sustained notes of the reed and horn in octave descent are mingled with a soft carillon of horns and trumpets in the call of the Scherzo. In broad swing a free fantasy rises to a loud refrain (in the brass) of the first motive of the symphony.

In slower pace and hush of sound sings a madrigal of tender phrases. A pair of melodies recall like figures of the first Allegro. Indeed, a chain of dulcet strains seems to rise from the past.

The fine themal relevance may be pursued in infinite degree, to no end but sheer bewilderment. The truth is that a modern vanity for subtle connection, a purest pedantry, is here evident, and has become a baneful tradition in the modern symphony. It is an utter confusion of the letter with the spirit. Once for all, a themal coherence of symphony must lie in the main lines, not in a maze of unsignificant figures.

Marked is a sharp alternation of mood, tempestuous and tender, of Florestan and Eusebius. The
lyric phase yields to the former heroic fantasy and
then returns in soothing solace into a prevailing
motive that harks back to the second of the beginning
movement. The fantasy, vague of melody, comes

(in more than one sense) as relief from the small
tracery. It is just to remember a like oscillation
in the first Allegro.

When the prologue recurs, the phrases are in
ascent, instead of descent of octaves. A climactic
verse of the main dulcet melody breaks out in resonant choir of brass and is followed by a soft rhapsody
on the several strains that hark back to the beginning. From the halting pace the lyric episode rises
in flight of continuous song to enchanting lilt. Now
in the big heroic fantasy sing the first slow phrases
as to the manner born and as naturally break into a
pæan of the full motive, mingled with strains of the

213

original legend of the symphony, that flows on to broad hymnal cadence.

In mystic musing we reach a solemn stillness where the prologue phrase is slowly drawn out into a profoundly moving hymn. Here we must feel is Meister Bruckner's true poetic abode rather than in the passion and ecstasy of romance into which he was vainly lured.*

---

* Bruckner's Fifth Symphony (in B flat) is a typical example of closest correlation of themes that are devoid of intrinsic melody.

An introduction supplies in the bass of a hymnal line the main theme of the Allegro by inversion as well as the germ of the first subject of the Adagio. Throughout, as in the Romantic Symphony, the relation between the first and the last movement is subtle. A closing, jagged phrase reappears as the first theme of the Finale.

The Adagio and Scherzo are built upon the same figure of bass. The theme of the Trio is acclaimed by a German annotator as the reverse of the first motive of the symphony.

In the prelude of the Finale, much as in the Ninth of Beethoven, are passed in review the main themes of the earlier movements. Each one is answered by an eccentric phrase that had its origin in the first movement and is now extended to a fugal theme.

The climactic figure is a new hymnal line that moves as central theme of an imposing double fugue.

CHAPTER XV.

THE LATER BRUCKNER

I N Bruckner's later works appears the unique instance of a discipline grounded in the best traditions, united to a deft use of ephemeral devices. The basic cause of modern mannerism, mainly in harmonic effects, lies in a want of formal mastery; an impatience of thorough technic; a craving for quick sensation. With Bruckner it was the opposite weakness of original ideas, an organic lack of poetic individuality. It is this the one charge that cannot be brought home to the earlier German group of reaction against the classic idea.

There is melody, almost abundant, in Wagner and Liszt and their German contemporaries. Indeed it was an age of lyricists. The fault was that they failed to recognize their lyric limitation, lengthening and padding their motives abnormally to fit a form that was too large. Hence the symphony of Liszt, with barren stretches, and the impossible plan of the later music-drama. The truest form of such a period was the song, as it blossomed in the works of a Franz.

Nor has this grandiose tendency even yet spent its course. A saving element was the fashioning of a new form, by Liszt himself,—the Symphonic Poem,

—far inferior to the symphony, but more adequate to the special poetic intent.

Whatever be the truth of personal gossip, there is no doubt that Bruckner lent himself and his art to a championing of the reactionary cause in the form that was intrinsically at odds with its spirit. Hence in later works of Bruckner these strange episodes of borrowed romance, abruptly stopped by a firm counterpoint of excellent quality,—indeed far the best of his writing. For, if a man have little ideas, at least his good workmanship will count for something.

In truth, one of the strangest types is presented in Bruckner,—a pedant who by persistent ingenuity simulates a master-work almost to perfection. By so much as genius is not an infinite capacity for pains, by so much is Bruckner's Ninth not a true symphony. Sometimes, under the glamor of his art, we are half persuaded that mere persistence may transmute pedantry into poetry.

It seems almost as if the Wagnerians chose their champion in the symphony with a kind of suppressed contempt for learning, associating mere intellectuality with true mastery, pointing to an example of greatest skill and least inspiration as if to say: " Here is your symphonist if you must have one." And it is difficult to avoid a suspicion that his very partisans were laughing up their sleeve at their adopted champion.

We might say all these things, and perhaps we have gone too far in suggesting them. After all we have no business with aught but the music of Bruckner, whatever may have been his musical politics, his vanity, his ill judgment, or even his deliberate partisanship against his betters. But the ideas themselves are unsubstantial; on shadowy foundation they give an illusion by modern touches of harmony and rhythm that are not novel in themselves. The melodic idea is usually divided in two, as by a clever juggler. There is really no one thought, but a plenty of small ones to hide the greater absence.

We have merely to compare this artificial manner with the poetic reaches of Brahms to understand the insolence of extreme Wagnerians and the indignation of a Hanslick. As against the pedantry of Bruckner the style of Strauss is almost welcome in its frank pursuit of effects which are at least grateful in themselves. Strauss makes hardly a pretence at having melodic ideas. They serve but as pawns or puppets for his harmonic and orchestral *mise-en-scène*. He is like a play-wright constructing his plot around a scenic design.

Just a little common sense is needed,—an unpremeditated attitude. Thus the familiar grouping, "*Bach, Beethoven* and *Brahms,*" is at least not unnatural. Think of the absurdity of "*Bach, Beethoven* and *Bruckner*"! *

The truth is, the Bruckner cult is a striking symptom of a certain decadence in German music; an

---

* A festival was held in Munich in the summer of 1911, in celebration of "Bach, Beethoven and Bruckner."

incapacity to tell the sincere quality of feeling in the dense, brilliant growth of technical virtuosity. In the worship at the Bayreuth shrine, somehow reinforced by a modern national self-importance, has been lost a heed for all but a certain vein of exotic romanticism, long ago run to riotous seed, a blending of hedonism and fatalism. No other poetic message gets a hearing and the former may be rung in endless repetition and reminiscence, provided, to be sure, it be framed with brilliant cunning of workmanship.

Here we feel driven defiantly to enounce the truth: that the highest art, even in a narrow sense, comes only with a true poetic message. Of this Bruckner is a proof; for, if any man by pure knowledge could make a symphony, it was he. But, with almost superhuman skill, there is something wanting in the inner connection, where the main ideas are weak, forced or borrowed. It is only the true poetic rapture that ensures the continuous absorption that drives in perfect sequence to irresistible conclusion.

SYMPHONY NO. 9

I.—Solenne. Solemn mystery is the mood, amid trembling strings on hollow unison, before the eight

Misterioso

p

(Eight horns with *tremolo* strings on D in three octaves)

218

horns strike a phrase in the minor chord that in
higher echoes breaks into a strange harmony and
descends into a turn of melodic cadence. In answer
is another chain of brief phrases, each beginning

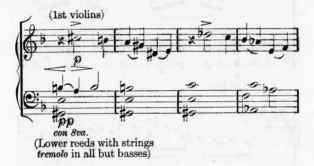

(1st violins)

pp
con 8va.
(Lower reeds with strings
tremolo in all but basses)

with a note above the chord (the common mark and
manner of the later school of harmonists *) and a
new ascent on a literal ladder of subtlest progress,
while hollow intervals are intermingled in the pinch
of close harmonies. The bewildering maze here begins of multitudinous design, enriched with modern
devices.

A clash of all the instruments acclaims the climax
before the unison stroke of fullest chorus on the
solemn note of the beginning. A favorite device of
Bruckner, a measured tread of *pizzicato* strings with
interspersed themal motives, precedes the romantic
episode. Throughout the movement is this alternation of liturgic chorale with tender melody.

---

* See Vol. II, note, page 104.

Bruckner's pristine polyphonic manner ever appears in the double strain of melodies, where each complements, though not completes the other. However multiple the plan, we cannot feel more than the quality of *unusual* in the motives themselves, of some interval of ascent or descent. Yet as the melody grows to larger utterance, the fulness of polyphonic art brings a beauty of tender sentiment, rising to a moving climax, where the horns lead the song in the heart of the madrigal chorus, and the strings alone sing the expressive answer.

220

(Violins doubled in 8ve.)

(Strings, wood and horns)

A third phrase now appears, where lies the main poetry of the movement. Gentle swaying calls of

221

soft horns and wood, echoed and answered in close pursuit, lead to a mood of placid, elemental rhythm, with something of " Rheingold," of " Ossian " ballad, of the lapping waves of Cherubini's " Anacreon." In the midst the horns blow a line of sonorous melody, where the cadence has a breath of primal legend. On the song runs, ever mid the elemental motion, to a resonant height and dies away as before. The intimate, romantic melody now returns, but it is rocked on the continuing pelagic pulse; indeed, we hear anon a faint phrase of the legend, in distant trumpet, till we reach a joint rhapsody of both moods; and in the never resting motion, mid vanishing echoes, we dream of some romance of the sea.

Against descending harmonies return the hollow, sombre phrases of the beginning, with the full cadence of chorale in the brass; and beyond, the whole prelude has a full, extended verse. In the alternation of solemn and sweet episode returns the tender melody, with pretty inversions, rising again to an ardent height. The renewed clash of acclaiming chorus ushers again the awful phrase of unison (now in octave descent), in towering majesty. But now it rises in the ever increasing vehemence where the final blast is lit up with a flash of serene sonority.

This motive, of simple octave call, indeed pervades the earlier symphony in big and little. And now, above a steady, sombre melodic tread of strings it rises in a fray of eager retorts, transfigured in wonderful harmony again and again to a brilliant height,

222

pausing on a ringing refrain, in sombre hue of overpowering blast.

A soft interlude of halting and diminishing strings leads to the romantic melody as it first appeared, where the multiple song again deepens and ennobles the theme. It passes straight into the waving, elemental motion, where again the hallowed horn utters its sibyl phrase, again rising to resonant height. And again merges the intimate song with the continuing pulse of the sea, while the trumpet softly sounds the legend and a still greater height of rhapsody.

Dull brooding chords bring a sombre play of the awing phrase, over a faint rocking motion, clashing in bold harmony, while the horns surge in broader melody. The climactic clash ends in a last verse of the opening phrase, as of primal, religious chant.

II.—Scherzo. In the dazzling pace of bright clashing harmonies, the perfect answers of falling and rising phrases, we are again before the semblance, at

least, of a great poetic idea. To be sure there is a touch of stereotype in the chords and even in the pinch and clash of hostile motives. And there is not the distinctive melody,—final stamp and test of the

shaft of inspiration. Yet in the enchantment of
motion, sound and form, it seems mean-spirited to
cavil at a want of something greater. One stands
bewildered before such art and stunned of all judgment.

A delight of delicate gambols follows the first
brilliant dance of main motive. Amid a rougher
trip of unison sounds the sonorous brass, and to softest jarring murmur of strings a pretty jingle of reed,

with later a slower counter-song, almost a madrigal
of pastoral answers, till we are back in the ruder
original dance. The gay cycle leads to a height of
rough volume (where the mystic brass sound in the
midst) and a revel of echoing chase.

In sudden hush of changed tone on fastest fairy
trip, strings and wood play to magic harmonies. In
calming motion the violins sing a quieter song, ever

echoed by the reed. Though there is no gripping force of themal idea, the melodies are all of grateful charm, and in the perfect round of rhythmic design we may well be content. The original dance recurs with a full fine orgy of hostile euphony.

III.—Adagio. Feierlich,—awesome indeed are these first sounds, and we are struck by the original-

ity of Bruckner's technic. After all we must give the benefit at least of the doubt. And there is after this deeply impressive *introit* a gorgeous Promethean

spring of up-leaping harmonies. The whole has certainly more of concrete beauty than many of the labored attempts of the present day.

The prelude dies down with an exquisite touch of precious dissonance,—whether it came from the heart or from the workshop. The strange and tragic part is that with so much art and talent there should not be the strong individual idea,—the flash of new tonal figure that stands fearless upon its own feet. All this pretty machinery seems wasted upon the framing and presenting, at the moment of expectation, of the shadows of another poet's ideas or of mere platitudes.

In the midst of the broad sweeping theme with a

promise of deep utterance is a phrase of horns with the precise accent and agony of a *Tristan*. The very semblance of whole motives seems to be taken from the warp and woof of Wagnerian drama. And thus the whole symphony is degraded, in its gorgeous capacity, to the reëchoed rhapsody of exotic roman-

ticism. It is all little touches, no big thoughts,—a
mosaic of a symphony.

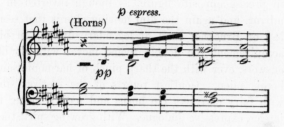

And so the second theme * is almost too heavily
laden with fine detail for its own strength, though

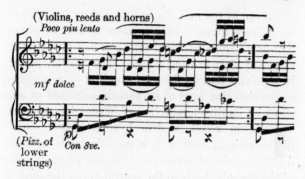

it ends with a gracefully delicate answer. The main
melody soon recurs and sings with a stress of warm
feeling in the cellos, echoed by glowing strains of

---

* We have spoken of a prelude, first and second theme;
they might have been more strictly numbered first, second
and third theme

the horns. Romantic harmonies bring back the solemn air of the prelude with a new counter melody, in precise opposite figure, as though inverted in a mirror, and again the dim moving chords that seem less of Bruckner than of legendary drama. In big accoutrement the double theme moves with double answers, ever with the sharp pinch of harmonies and heroic mien. Gentlest retorts of the motives sing with fairy clearness (in horns and reeds), rising to tender, expressive dialogue. With growing spirit they ascend once more to the triumphant clash of empyræan chords, that may suffice for justifying beauty.

Instead of the first, the second melody follows with its delicate grace. After a pause recurs the phrase that harks from mediæval romance, now in a stirring ascent of close chasing voices. The answer, perfect in its timid halting descent, exquisite in accent and in the changing hues of its periods, is robbed of true effect by its direct reflection of Wagnerian ecstasies.

As if in recoil, a firm hymnal phrase sounds in the strings, ending in a more intimate cadence. Another chain of rarest fairy clashes, on the motive of the prelude, leads to the central verse, the song of the first main melody in the midst of soft treading strings, and again descends the fitting answer of poignant accent.

And now, for once forgetting all origin and clinging sense of reminiscence, we may revel in the rich romance, the fathoms of mystic harmony, as the main

song sings and rings from the depths of dim legend
in lowest brass, amidst a soft humming chorus, in
constant shift of fairy tone.

A flight of ascending chords brings the big exaltation of the first prophetic phrase, ever answered by
exultant ring of trumpet, ending in sudden awing
pause. An eerie train of echoes from the verse of
prelude leads to a loveliest last song of the poignant
answer of main song, over murmuring strings. It

is carried on by the mystic choir of sombre brass in
shifting steps of enchanting harmony and dies away
in tenderest lingering accents.*

---

* In place of the uncompleted Finale, Bruckner is said
to have directed that his " *Te Deum* " be added to the
other movements.

CHAPTER XVI

HUGO WOLFF *

"PENTHESILEA." SYMPHONIC POEM †

AN entirely opposite type of composer, Hugo Wolff, shows the real strength of modern German music in a lyric vein, sincere, direct and fervent. His longest work for instruments has throughout the charm of natural rhythm and melody, with subtle shading of the harmony. Though there is no want of contrapuntal design, the workmanship never obtrudes. It is a model of the right use of symbolic motives in frequent recurrence and subtle variation.

In another instrumental piece, the "Italian Serenade," all kinds of daring suspenses and gentle clashes and surprises of harmonic scene give a fragrance of dissonant euphony, where a clear melody ever rules. "Penthesilea," with a climactic passion and a sheer contrast of tempest and tenderness, uttered with all the mastery of modern devices, has a pervading thrall of pure musical beauty. We are tempted to hail in Wolff a true poet in an age of pedants and false prophets.

---

* Hugo Wolff, born in 1860, died in 1903.

† After the like-named tragedy of Heinrich von Kleist.

HUGO WOLFF

PENTHESILEA—A TRAGEDY BY HEINRICH VON KLEIST.*

As Wolff's work is admittedly modelled on Kleist's tragedy, little known to the English world, it is important to view the main lines of this poem, which has provoked so divergent a criticism in Germany.

On the whole, the tragedy seems to be one of those daring, even profane assaults on elemental questions by ways that are untrodden if not forbidden. It is a wonderful type of Romanticist poetry in the bold choice of subject and in the intense vigor and beauty of the verse. Coming with a shock upon the classic days of German poetry, it met with a stern rebuke from the great Goethe. But a century later we must surely halt in following the lead of so severe a censor. The beauty of diction alone seems a surety of a sound content,—as when Penthesilea exclaims:

" A hero man can be—a Titan—in distress,
But like a god is he when rapt in blessedness."

An almost convincing symbolism has been suggested of the latent meaning of the poem by a modern critic,†—a symbolism that seems wonderfully reflected in Wolff's music. The charge of perverted passion can be based only on certain lines, and these are spoken within the period of madness that has overcome the heroine. This brings us to the final point which may suggest the main basic fault in the poem, considered as art. At least it is certainly a question whether pure madness can ever be a fitting subject in the hero of a tragedy. Ophelia is an episode; Hamlet's madness has never been finally determined. Though the Erinnys hunted Orestes in more than one play,

* German, 1776–1811.

†Kuno Francke. See the notes of Philip Hale in the programme book of the Boston Symphony Orchestra of April 3–4, 1908.

yet no single Fury could, after all, be the heroine of tragedy. Penthesilea became in the crisis a pure Fury, and
though she may find here her own defense, the play may
not benefit by the same plea. On the other hand, the madness is less a reality than an impression of the Amazons
who cannot understand the heroine's conflicting feelings.
There is no one moment in the play when the hearer's sympathy for the heroine is destroyed by a clear sense of her
insanity.

For another word on the point of symbolism, it must be
remembered that the whole plot is one of supernatural
legend where somehow human acts and motives need not
conform to conventional rule, and where symbolic meaning,
as common reality disappears, is mainly eminent. It is in
this same spirit that the leading virtues of the race, of
war or of peace, are typified by feminine figures.

The Tragedy is not divided into acts; it has merely four
and twenty scenes—upon the battlefield of Troy. The
characters are Penthesilea, Queen of the Amazons; her
chief leaders, Prothoe, Meroe and Asteria, and the high
priestess of Diana. Of the Greeks there are Achilles,
Odysseus, Diomede and Antilochus. Much of the fighting
and other action is not seen, but is reported either by
messengers or by present witnesses of a distant scene.

The play begins with the battle raging between Greeks
and Amazons. Penthesilea with her hosts amazes the
Greeks by attacking equally the Trojans, her reputed allies.
She mows down the ranks of the Trojans, and yet refuses
all proffers of the Greeks.

Thus early we have the direct, uncompromising spirit,—
a kind of feminine Prometheus. The first picture of the
heroine is of a Minerva in full array, stony of gaze and
of expression until—she sees Achilles. Here early comes
the conflict of two elemental passions. Penthesilea recoils
from the spell and dashes again into her ambiguous warfare. For once Greeks and Trojans are forced to fight in
common defence.

HUGO WOLFF

" The raging Queen with blows of thunder struck
   As she would cleave the whole race of the Greeks
   Down to its roots. . . .

. . . .

   More of the captives did she take
   Than she did leave us eyes to count the list,
   Or arms to set them free again.

. . . .

   Often it seemed as if a special hate
   Against Achilles did possess her breast.

. . . .

   Yet in a later moment, when
   His life was given straight into her hands,
   Smiling she gave it back, as though a present;
   His headlong course to Hades she did stay."

In midst of the dual battle between Achilles and the
Queen, a Trojan prince comes storming and strikes a treach-
erous blow against the armor of the Greek.

" The Queen is stricken pale; for a brief moment
   Her arms hang helpless by her sides; and then,
   Shaking her locks about her flaming cheeks,
   Dashes her sword like lightning in his throat,
   And sends him rolling to Achilles' feet."

The Greek leaders resolve to retreat from the futile fight
and to call Achilles from the mingled chase of love and
war.

Achilles is now reported taken by the Amazons. The
battle is vividly depicted: Achilles caught on a high ledge
with his war-chariot; the Amazon Queen storming the
height from below. The full scene is witnessed from the
stage,—Penthesilea pursuing almost alone; Achilles suddenly dodges; the Queen as quickly halts and rears her
horse; the Amazons fall in a mingled heap; Achilles
escapes, though wounded. But he refuses to follow his

233

companions to the camp; he swears to bring home the Queen wooed in the bloody strife of her own seeking.

Penthesilea recoils with like vehemence from the entreaties of her maids, intent upon the further battle, resolved to overcome the hero or to die. She forbids the Festival of Roses until she has vanquished Achilles. In her rage she banishes her favorite Prothoe from her presence, but in a quick revulsion takes her back.

In the next scene the high priestess and the little Amazon maids prepare the Feast, which Penthesilea had ordered in her confident attack upon the fleeing Greeks. One of the Rose-maidens recounts the passing scene of the Queen's amazing action. The indignant priestess sends her command to the Queen to return to the celebration. Though all the royal suite fling themselves in her path, Penthesilea advances to the dual battle.*

In a renewal of her personal contest, regardless of the common cause, and in her special quest of a chosen husband, Penthesilea has broken the sacred law.

The flight now follows of the Amazon hosts. When the two combatants meet in the shock of lances, the Queen falls in the dust; her pallor is reflected in Achilles' face. Leaping from his horse, he bends o'er her, calls her by names, and woos life back into her frame. Her faithful maids, whom she has forbidden to harm Achilles, lead her away. And here begins the seeming madness of the Queen when she confesses her love. For a moment she yields to her people's demands, but the sight of the rose-wreaths kindles her rage anew. Prothoe defends her in these lines:

---

* The law of the Amazons commanded them to wage war as told them by the oracle of Mars. The prisoners were brought to the Feast of Roses and wedded by their captors. After a certain time they were sent back to their homes. All male children of the tribe were put to death.

" Of life the highest blessing she attempted.   *
Grazing she almost grasped. Her hands now fail her
For any other lesser goal to reach."

In the last part of the scene the Queen falls more and
deeper into madness. It is only in a too literal spirit that
one will find an oblique meaning,—by too great readiness
to discover it. In reality there seems to be an intense
conflict of opposite emotions in the heroine: the pure
woman's love, without sense of self; and the wild overpowering greed of achievement. Between these grinding
stones she wears her heart away. A false interpretation of
decadent theme comes from regarding the two emotions as
mingled, instead of alternating in a struggle.

Achilles advances, having flung away his armor. Prothoe
persuades him to leave the Queen, when she awakes, in the
delusion that she has conquered and that he is the captive.
Thus when she beholds the hero, she breaks forth into the
supreme moment of exaltation and of frenzied triumph.
The main love scene follows:

Penthesilea tells Achilles the whole story of the Amazons,
the conquest of the original tribe, the rising of the wives
of the murdered warriors against the conquerors; the
destruction of the right breast (*A-mazon*); the dedication
of the " brides of Mars " to war and love in one. In seeking out Achilles the Queen has broken the law. But here
again appears the double symbolic idea: Achilles meant to
the heroine not love alone, but the overwhelming conquest,
the great achievement of her life.

The first feeling of Penthesilea, when disillusioned, is of
revulsive anger at a kind of betrayal. The Amazons recover ground in a wild desire to save their Queen, and they
do rescue her, after a parting scene of the lovers. But
Penthesilea curses the triumph that snatches her away; the
high priestess rebukes her, sets her free of her royal
duties, to follow her love if she will. The Queen is driven

from one mood to another, of devoted love, burning ambition and mortal despair.

Achilles now sends a challenge to Penthesilea, knowing the Amazon conditions. Against all entreaty the Queen accepts, not in her former spirit, but in the frenzy of desperate endeavor, in the reawakened rage of her ambition, spurred and pricked by the words of the priestess.

The full scene of madness follows. She calls for her dogs and elephants, and the full accoutrement of battle. Amidst the terror of her own warriors, the rolling of thunder, she implores the gods' help to crush the Greek. In a final touch of frenzy she aims a dart at her faithful Prothoe.

The battle begins, Achilles in fullest confidence in Penthesilea's love, unfrightened by the wild army of dogs and elephants. The scene, told by the present on-lookers, is heightened by the cries of horror and dismay of the Amazons themselves.

Achilles falls; Penthesilea, a living Fury, dashes upon him with her dogs in an insane orgy of blood. The Queen in the culminating scene is greeted by the curses of the high priestess. Prothoe masters her horror and turns back to soothe the Queen. Penthesilea, unmindful of what has passed, moves once more through the whole gamut of her torturing emotions, and is almost calmed when she spies the bier with the hero's body. The last blow falls when upon her questions she learns the full truth of her deed. The words she utters (that have been cited by the hostile critics) may well be taken as the ravings of hopeless remorse, with a symbolic play of words. She dies, as she proclaims, by the knife of her own anguish.

The last lines of Prothoe are a kind of epilogue:

" She sank because too proud and strong she flourished.
The half-decayéd oak withstands the tempest;
The vigorous tree is headlong dashed to earth
Because the storm has struck into its crown." *

---

* Translations, when not otherwise credited, are by the author.

The opening scene—"Lively, vehement: Departure of the Amazons for Troy"—begins impetuous
and hefty with big strokes of the throbbing motive,

the majestic rhythm coursing below, lashed by a
quicker phrase above. Suddenly trumpets sound,
somewhat more slowly, a clarion call answered by a
choir of other trumpets and horns in enchanting retort of changing harmonies. Ever a fresh color of

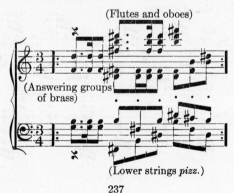

tone sounds in the call of the brass, as if here or yonder on the battle-field. Sometimes it is almost too sweetly chanting for fierce war. But presently it turns to a wilder mood and breaks in galloping pace into a true chorus of song with clear cadence.

The joyful tinge is quickly lost in the sombre hue of another phase of war-song that has a touch of funeral trip (though it is all in ¾ time):

A melody in the minor plays first in a choir of horns and bassoons, later in united strings, accompanied by soft rolls of drums and a touch of the lowest brass. Harp and higher woodwind are added, but the volume is never transcendent save in a single burst when it is quickly hushed to the first ominous whisper. Out of this sombre song flows a romance of tender sentiment, *tranquillo* in strings, followed by the wood. The crossing threads of expressive melody

rise in instant renewal of stress and agitation. The joy of battle has returned, but it seems that the passion of love burns in midst of the glow of battle, each in its separate struggle, and both together in one fatal strife. The sombre melody returns in full career, dying down to a pause.*

---

* In a somewhat literal commentary attributed to Dr. Richard Batka, the Amazons here, "having reached their destination, go into night-encampment—as represented by the subdued roll of the kettle-drums, with which the movement concludes."

Molto sostenuto, in changed rhythm of three slow beats, comes " Penthesilea's Dream of the Feast of Roses." Over a thick cluster of harmonies in harp and strings the higher wood sing a new song in long drawn lyric notes with ravishing turns of tonal color.

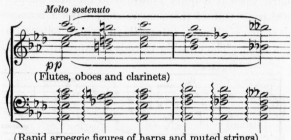

(Flutes, oboes and clarinets)

(Rapid arpeggic figures of harps and muted strings)

—a dual song and in many groups of two. The tranquil current of the dream is gradually disturbed; the main burden is dimmed in hue and in mood. Faster, more fitful is the flow of melody, with hostile intruding motive below; it dashes at last into the tragic phase—Combats; Passions; Madness; Destruction—in very rapid tempo of 2/2 rhythm:

In broad, masterful pace, big contrary figures sweep up and down, cadencing in almost joyous chant, gliding, indeed, into a pure hymn, as of triumph (that harks back to the chorussing song in the beginning).

Throughout the poem the musical symbols as well as the motives of passion are closely intertwined. Thus the identity of the impetuous phrase of the very beginning is clear with the blissful theme of the Dream of the Feast of Roses. Here, at the end of the chorussing verse is a play or a strife of phrases where we cannot escape a symbolic intent. To *tremolo* of violas the cellos hold a tenor of descending melody over a rude rumbling phrase of the basses of wood and strings, while the oboe sings in the treble an expressive answer of ascending notes. A conflict is

evident, of love and ambition, of savage and of gentle passion, of chaos and of beauty. At the height, the lowest brass intrude a brutal note of triumph of the descending theme. To the victory of Pride succeeds a crisis of passionate yearning. But at the very height is a plunge into the fit of madness, the fatal descending phrase (in trombones) is ever followed by furious pelting spurts in the distorted main theme.

At last the paroxysm abates, throbbing ever slower, merging into the tender song of the Dream that now rises to the one great burst of love-passion. But it ends in a wild rage that turns right into the war-song of the beginning. And this is much fuller of incident than before. Violins now ring an hostile motive (the former rumbling phrase of basses) from the midst of the plot against the main theme in trumpets. Instead of the former pageantry, here is the pure frenzy of actual war. The trumpet melodies resound amidst the din of present battle. Instead of the other gentler episodes, here is a more furious raving of the mad Queen (in the hurried main motive), where we seem to see the literal dogs of war let loose and spurred on,—each paroxysm rising to a higher shock.

Great is the vehemence of speed and sound as the dull doom of destruction drones in the basses against a grim perversion of the yearning theme above, that overwhelms the scene with a final shriek.

Slowly the dream of love breathes again, rises to a fervent burst, then yields to the fateful chant and ends in a whisper of farewell.

CHAPTER XVII

MAHLER *

IN Mahler the most significant sign is a return to a true counterpoint, as against a mere overlading of themes, that began in Wagner and still persists in Strauss,—an artificial kind of structure that is never conceived as a whole.

While we see in Mahler much of the duophonic manner of his teacher, Bruckner, in the work of the younger man the barren art is crowned with the true fire of a sentient poet. So, if Bruckner had little to say, he showed the way to others. And Mahler, if he did not quite emerge from the mantle of Beethoven, is a link towards a still greater future. The form and the technic still seem, as with most modern symphonies, too great for the message. It is another phase of orchestral virtuosity, of intellectual strain, but with more of poetic energy than in the symphonies of the French or other Germans.

In other forms we see this happy reaction towards ancient art, as in the organ music of a Reger. But in the Finale of Mahler's Fifth Symphony there is a true serenity, a new phase of symphony, without the climactic stress of traditional triumph, yet none the less joyous in essence.

We cannot help rejoicing that in a sincere and

* Gustav Mahler, 1860–1911.

poetic design of symphony is blended a splendid renaissance of pure counterpoint, that shines clear above the modern spurious pretence. The Finale of Mahler's Fifth Symphony is one of the most inspired conceptions of counterpoint in all music. In it is realized the full dream of a revival of the art in all its glorious estate.

SYMPHONY NO. 5

I.—1. *Funeral March.*
    2. *In stormy motion (with greatest vehemence).*
II.—3. *Scherzo (with vigor,—not too fast).*
III.—4. *Adagietto (very slowly).*
    5. *Rondo-Finale (allegro).*

Mahler's Fifth Symphony, whatever be its intrinsic merit, that can be decided only by time and wear, undoubtedly marks a high point of orchestral splendor, in the regard of length and of the complexity of resources. By the latter is meant not so much the actual list of instruments as the pervading and accumulating use of thematic machinery.*

The plan of movements is very original and in a way, two-fold. There are three great divisions, of

---

* The symphony is probably the longest instrumental work that had appeared at the time of its production in 1904. The list of instruments comprises 4 flutes, 3 oboes, 3 clarinets, 2 bassoons, contra-bassoon, 6 horns, 4 trumpets, 3 trombones, tuba, kettle-drums, cymbals, bass-drum, snare-drum, triangle, glockenspiel, gong, harp and strings.

Compared with D'Indy's Second Symphony, the Fifth of Mahler has a larger body of brass as well as of wood-wind.

which the first comprises a Funeral March, and an untitled Allegro in vehement motion. The second division has merely the single movement, Scherzo. In the third are an Adagietto and a Rondo Finale.

I.—1. Funeral March.—A call of trumpet, of heroic air and tread, is answered by strident chords ending in a sonorous motive of horns that leads to the funeral trip, of low brass. The mournful song of the principal melody appears presently in the strings, then returns to the funeral trip and to the strident chords. The first trumpet motive now sounds with this clanging phrase and soon the original call abounds in other brass. The deep descending notes of the horns recur and the full song of the funeral melody much extended, growing into a duet of cellos and high wood-wind,

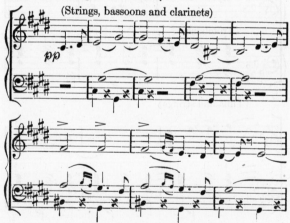
(Strings, bassoons and clarinets)

and further into hymnal song on a new motive.

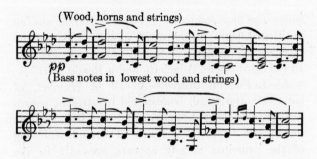

(Wood, horns and strings)

(Bass notes in lowest wood and strings)

So the various melodies recur with new mood and manner. Suddenly, in fierce abandon, a martial tramp of the full band resounds, in gloomy minor,

Suddenly faster. Impassioned
(Rapid descending figure in violins)
(Trumpet)
(Trombones)
(Tuba and strings)

the violins in rapid rage of wailing figure: the trumpet strikes the firm note of heroic plaint.

Wild grief breaks out on all sides, the strings singing in passionate answer to the trumpet, the high wood carrying on the rapid motion. At the height of the storm the woodwind gain control with measured rhythm of choral melody. Or perhaps the real height is the expressive double strain, in gentle pace, of the strings, and the wood descending from on high.

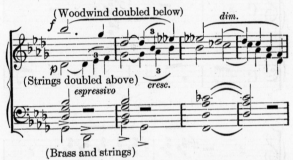

The duet is carried on in wilder mood by most of the voices.

A return to the solemn pace comes by imperceptible change, the softer hues of grief merging with the fiercer cries. Now various strains sound together, —the main funeral melody in the woodwind.

In the close recurs the full flow of funeral song, with the hymnal harmonies. In the refrain of the stormy duet the sting of passion is gone; the whole plaint dies away amid the fading echoes of the trumpet call.

I.—2. The second movement, the real first Allegro, is again clearly in two parts. Only, the relative paces are exactly reversed from the first movement. In tempestuous motion, with greatest vehemence, a rushing motive of the basses is stopped by a chord of brass and strings,—the chord itself reverberating to the lower rhythm.

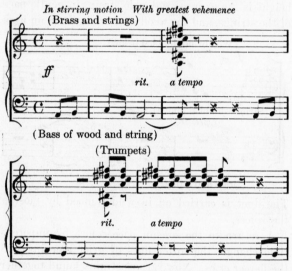

Throughout the whole symphony is the dual theme, each part spurring the other. Here presently are phrases in conflicting motion, countermarching in a stormy maze. It is all, too, like noisy preparation,—a manœuvring of forces before the battle. Three distinct figures there are before a blast of horn in slower notes, answered by shrill call in highest wood. There enters a regular, rhythmic gait and a clearer tune, suggested by the call.

In the brilliant medley there is ever a new figure we had not perceived. So when the tune has been told, trumpets and horns begin with what seems almost the main air, and the former voices sound like mere heralds. Finally the deep trombones and tuba enter with a sonorous call. Yet the first rapid trip of all has the main legend.

As the quicker figures gradually retire, a change of pace appears, to the tramp of funeral. Yet the initial and incident strains are of the former text. Out of it weaves the new, slower melody:

Throughout, the old shrill call sounds in soft lament. Hardly like a tune, a discourse rather, it winds along, growing and changing naïvely ever to a new phrase. And the soft calls about seem part of the melody. An expressive line rising in the clarinet harks back to one of the later strains of the funeral march.

The second melody or answer (in low octaves of

strings) is a scant disguise of the lower tune in the stormy duet of the first movement. Yet all the strains move in the gentle, soothing pace and mood until suddenly awakened to the first vehement rhythm.

Before the slower verse returns is a long plaint of cellos to softest roll of drums. The gentle calls that usher in the melody have a significant turn, upwards instead of down. All the figures of the solemn episode appear more clearly.

On the spur of the hurrying main motive of trumpets the first pace is once more regained.

A surprise of plot is before us. In sudden recurrence of funeral march the hymnal song of the first movement is heard. As suddenly, we are plunged into the first joyful scene of the symphony. Here it is most striking how the call of lament has become triumphant, as it seems without a change of note. And still more wonderful,—the same melody that first uttered a storm of grief, then a gentle sadness, now has a firm exultant ring. To be sure, it is all done with the magic trip of bass,—as a hymn may be a perfect dance.

Before the close we hear the first fanfare of trumpet from the opening symphony, that has the ring of a motto of the whole. At the very end is a transfigured entrance,—very slowly and softly, to a celestial touch of harp, of the first descending figure of the movement.

251

II.—3. *Scherzo.* Jovial in high degree, the Scherzo begins with the thematic complexity of modern fashion. In dance tune of three beats horns lead off with a jolly call; strings strike dancing chords; the lower wind play a rollicking answer, but together with the horns, both strains continuing in dancing duet. Still the saucy call of horns seems the main text, though no single tune reigns alone.

The violins now play above the horns; then the cellos join and there is a three-part song of independent tunes, all in the dance. So far in separate

voices it is now taken up by full chorus, though still
the basses sing one way, trebles another, and the
middle horns a third. And now the high trumpet
strikes a phrase of its own. But they are all in
dancing swing, of the fibre of the first jolly motive.

A new episode is started by a quicker *obligato* of
violins, in neighboring minor, that plays about a
fugue of the woodwind on an incisive theme where
the cadence has a strange taste of bitter sweet harmony in the modern Gallic manner.

Horns and violins now pursue their former duet,
but in the changed hue of minor where the old con-
cords are quaintly perverted. But this is only to give

a merrier ring to the bright madrigal that follows in sweetly clashing higher wood, with the trip still in the violins. Thence the horns and violins break again into the duet in the original key. Here the theme is wittily inverted in the bass, while other strings sing another version above.

So the jolly dance and the quaint fugue alternate; a recurring phrase is carried to a kind of dispute, with opposite directions above and below and much augmented motion in the strings.

In the dance so far, in "three time," is ever the vigorous stamp on the third beat, typical of the German peasant "*Ländler.*'" Here of a sudden is a change as great as possible within the continuing dance of three steps. "More tranquil" in pace, in soft strings, without a trace of the *Ländler* stamp, is a pure waltz in pretty imitation of tuneful theme.

And so the return to the vigorous rough dance is the more refreshing. The merry mood yields to a darker temper. "Wild" the strings rush in angry fugue on their rapid phrase; the quaint theme is torn to shreds, recalling the fierce tempest of earlier symphony.

But the first sad note of the Scherzo is in the recitative of horn, after the lull. A phrase of quiet reflection, with which the horn concludes the episode as with an *"envoi,"* is now constantly rung; it is wrought from the eerie tempest; like refined metal the melody is finally poured; out of its guise is the theme now of mournful dance.

"Shyly" the tune of the waltz answers in softest oboe. In all kinds of verses it is sung, in expressive duet of lower wood, of the brass, then of high reeds; in solo trumpet with countertune of oboe, finally in high flutes. Here we see curiously, as the first themes reappear, a likeness with the original trumpet-call of the symphony. In this guise of the first dance-theme the movements are bound together. The *envoi* phrase is here evident throughout.

At this mystic stage, to pure dance trip of low strings the waltz reënters very softly in constant growing motion, soon attaining the old pace and a new fulness of sound. A fresh spur is given by a wild motion of strings, as in the fugal episode; a new height of tempest is reached where again the distorted shreds of first dance appear, with phrases of the second. From it like sunshine from the clouds breaks quickly the original merry trip of dance.

The full cycle of main Scherzo returns with all stress of storm and tragedy. But so fierce is the tempest that we wonder how the glad mood can prevail. And the sad *envoi* returns and will not be shaken off. The sharp clash of fugue is rung again and again, as if the cup must be drained to the drop. Indeed, the serious later strain does prevail, all but the final blare of the saucy call of brass.*

III.—4. Adagietto.† "Very slowly" first violins carry the expressive song that is repeated by the violas.

---

* In the Scherzo are chimes, accenting the tune of the dance, and even castanets, besides triangle and other percussion. The second movement employs the harp and triangle.

† The Adagietto is scored simply for harp and strings; nor are the latter unusually divided.

A climax is reached by all the violins in unison. A new glow, with quicker motion, is in the episode, where the violins are sharply answered by the violas, rising to a dramatic height and dying away in a vein of rare lyric utterance.

It is all indeed a pure lyric in tones.

III.—5. Rondo-Finale. The whole has the dainty, light-treading humor that does not die of its own vehemence. Somewhat as in the Ninth Symphony of Beethoven,—tyrant of classical traditions, the themes appear right in the beginning as if on muster-roll, each in separate, unattended song. A last chance cadence passes down the line of voices and settles into a comfortable rhythm as prevailing theme, running in melodious extension, and merging after a

(Clarinets, horns and bassoons) (Flutes and oboes)

hearty conclusion in the jovially garrulous fugue.

Here the counter-theme proves to be one of the initial tunes and takes a leading rôle until another charming strain appears on high,—a pure nursery rhyme crowning the learned fugue. Even this is a guise of one of the original motives in the mazing medley, where it seems we could trace the ancestry of each if we could linger and if it really mattered. And yet there is a rare charm in these subtle turns; it is the secret relevance that counts the most.

The fugue reaches a sturdy height with one of the first themes in lusty horns, and suddenly falls into a pleasant jingle, prattling away in the train of important figures, the kind that is pertinent with no outer likeness.

(Strings, bassoons and horns)

Everywhere, to be sure, the little rhythmic cadence appears; the whole sounds almost like the old children's canon on "Three Blind Mice"; indeed the themal inversion is here the main tune. Then in the bass the phrase sounds twice as slow as in the horns. There are capers and horseplay; a sudden shift of tone; a false alarm of fugue; suddenly we are back in the first placid verse of the rhythmic motive.

Here is a new augmentation in resonant horns and middle strings, and the melodious extension. A

former motive that rings out in high reed, seems to
have the function of concluding each episode.

A new stretch of fugue appears with new counter-
theme, that begins in long-blown notes of horns.   It
really is no longer a fugue; it has lapsed into mere
smooth-rolling motion underneath a verse of primal
tune.   And presently another variant of graceful episode brings a delicious lilt,—*tender, but expressive.*

With all the subtle design there is no sense of the
lamp, in the gentle murmur of quicker figure or melodious flow of upper theme.   Moving is the lyric power
and sweetness of this multiple song.   As to themal
relation,—one feels like regarding it all as inspired
madrigal, where the maze and medley is the thing,
where the tunes are not meant to be distinguished.
It becomes an abandoned orgy of clearest counterpoint.   Throughout is a blending of fugue and of
children's romp, anon with the tenderness of lullaby
and even the glow of love-song.   A brief mystic verse,
with slow descending strain in the high wood, preludes the returning gambol of running strings, where

the maze of fugue or canon is in the higher flowing song, with opposite course of answering tune, and a height of jolly revel, where the bright trumpet pours out the usual concluding phrase. The rhythmic episode, in whimsical change, here sings with surprise of lusty volume. So the merry round goes on to a big resonant *Amen* of final acclaim, where the little phrase steals out as naturally as in the beginning.

Then in quicker pace it sounds again all about, big and little, and ends, after a touch of modern Gallic scale, in opposing runs, with a last light, saucy fling.

Mahler, we feel again, realizes all the craving that Bruckner breeds for a kernel of feeling in the shell of counterpoint. Though we cannot deny a rude breach of ancient rule and mode, there is in Mahler a genuine, original, individual quality of polyphonic art that marks a new stage since the first in Bach and a second in Beethoven. It is this bold revel in the neglected sanctuary of the art that is most inspiriting for the future. And as in all true poetry, this o'erleaping audacity of design is a mere expression of simplest gaiety.

CHAPTER XVIII

RICHARD STRAUSS *

MUCH may be wisely written on the right limits of music as a depicting art. The distinction is well drawn between actual delineation, of figure or event, and the mere suggestion of a mood. It is no doubt a fine line, and fortunately; for the critic must beware of mere negative philosophy, lest what he says cannot be done, be refuted in the very doing. If Lessing had lived a little later, he might have extended the principles of his "Laocöon" beyond poetry and sculpture into the field of music. Difficult and ungrateful as is the task of the critical philosopher, it must be performed. There is every reason here as elsewhere why men should see and think clearly.

It is perhaps well that audiences should cling to the simple verdict of beauty, that they should not be led astray by the vanity of finding an answer; else the composer is tempted to create mere riddles. So we may decline to find precise pictures, and content ourselves with the music. The search is really time wasted; it is like a man digging in vain for gold and missing the sunshine above.

Strauss may have his special meanings. But the

---

* Born in 1864.

beauty of the work is for us all-important. We may expect him to mark his scenes. We may not care to crack that kind of a nut.* It is really not good eating. Rather must we be satisfied with the pure beauty of the fruit, without a further hidden kernel. There is no doubt, however, of the ingenuity of these realistic touches. It is interesting, here, to contrast Strauss with Berlioz, who told his stories largely by extra-musical means, such as the funeral trip, the knell of bells, the shepherd's reed. Strauss at this point joins with the Liszt-Wagner group in the use of symbolic motives. Some of his themes have an effect of tonal word-painting. The roguish laugh of Eulenspiegel is unmistakable.

It is in the harmonic rather than the melodic field that the fancy of Strauss soars the freest. It is here that his music bears an individual stamp of beauty. Playing in and out among the edges of the main harmony with a multitude of ornamental phrases, he gains a new shimmer of brilliancy. Aside from instrumental coloring, where he seems to outshine all others in dazzling richness and startling contrasts, he adds to the lustre by a deft playing in the overtones of his harmonies, casting the whole in warmest hue.

If we imagine the same riotous license in the realm of tonal noise,—cacophony, that is, where the aim is not to enchant, but to frighten, bewilder, or amaze;

---

* Strauss remarked that in *Till Eulenspiegel* he had given the critics a hard nut to crack.

to give some special foil to sudden beauty; or, last of all, for graphic touch of story, we have another striking element of Strauss's art. The anticipation of a Beethoven in the drum of the Scherzo of the Fifth Symphony, or the rhythmic whims of a Schumann in his Romantic piano pieces suggest the path of much of this license. Again, as passing notes may run without heed of harmony, since ancient days, so long sequences of other figures may hold their moving organ-point against clashing changes of tonality.

Apart from all this is the modern " counterpoint," where, if it is quite the real thing, Strauss has outdone the boldest dreams of ancient school men. But with the lack of cogent form, and the multitude of small motives it seems a different kind of art. We must get into the view-point of romantic web of infinite threads, shimmering or jarring in infinite antagonism (of delayed harmony). By the same process comes always the tremendous accumulation towards the end. As the end and essence of the theme seems a graphic quality rather than intrinsic melody, so the main pith and point of the music lies in the weight and power of these final climaxes.

TOD UND VERKLÄRUNG (DEATH AND TRANS-FIGURATION), TONE POEM

It may be well to gather a few general impressions before we attempt the study of a work radical in its departure from the usual lines of tonal design.

There can be no doubt of the need of vigilance if

we are to catch the relevance of all the strains. To be sure, perhaps this perception is meant to be subconscious. In any case the consciousness would seem to ensure a full enjoyment.

It is all based on the motif of the Wagner drama and of the Liszt symphonies, and it is carried to quite as fine a point. Only here we have no accompanying words to betray the label of the theme. But in the quick flight of themes, how are we to catch the subtle meaning? The inter-relation seems as close as we care to look, until we are in danger of seeing no woods for the trees.

Again the danger of preconception is of the greatest. We may get our mind all on the meaning and all off the music. The clear fact is the themes do have a way of entering with an air of significance which they challenge us to find. The greatest difficulty is to distinguish the themes that grow out of each other, as a rose throws off its early petals, from those that have a mere chance similarity. Even this likeness may have its own intended meaning, or it may be all beside the mark. But we may lose not merely the musical, but even the dramatic sequence in too close a poring over themal derivation. On the other hand we may defy the composer himself and take simply what he gives, as if on first performance, before the commentators have had a chance to breed. And this may please him best in the end.

We must always attend more to the mood than to themal detail as everywhere in real music, after

264

all. Moments of delight and triumph we know there
are in this work. But they are mere instants. For
it is all the feverish dream of death. There can be
no earlier rest. Snatches they are of fancy, of illusion, as, says the priest in Œdipus, is all of life.

It may be worth while, too, to see how pairs of
themes ever occur in Strauss, the second in answer,
almost in protest, to the first. (It is not unlike the
pleading in the Fifth Symphony of the second theme
with the sense of doom in the first.) So we seem to
find a motive of fate, and one of wondering, and
striving; a theme of beauty and one of passion,—if
we cared to tread on such a dangerous, tempting
ground. Again, we may find whole groups of phrases
expressive of one idea, as of beauty, and another of
anxious pursuit. Thus we escape too literal a themal
association.

Trying a glimpse from the score pure and simple,
we find a poem, opposite the first page, that is said
to have been written after the first production. So,
reluctantly, we must wait for the mere reinforcement of its evidence.

Largo, in uncertain key, begins the throb of irregular rhythm (in strings) that Bach and Chopin and
Wagner have taught us to associate with suffering.
The first figure is a gloomy descent of pairs of chords,
with a hopeless cry above (in the flutes). In the recurrence, the turn of chord is at last upward. A
warmer hue of waving sounds (of harps) is poured
about, and a gentle vision appears on high, shadowed

quickly by a theme of fearful wondering. The chords
return as at first. A new series of descending tones

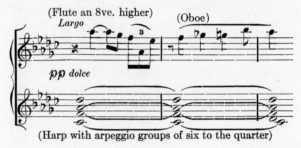

intrude, with a sterner sense of omen, and yield to a
full melodic utterance of longing (again with the

soothing play of harp), and in the midst a fresh theme of wistful fear. For a moment there is a brief glimpse of the former vision. Now the song, less of longing than of pure bliss, sings free and clear its descending lay in solo violin, though an answering phrase (in the horns) of upward striving soon rises from below. The vision now appears again, the wondering monitor close beside. The melancholy chords return to dim the beauty. As the descending theme recedes, the rising motive sings a fuller course on high with a new note of eager, anxious fear.

All these themes are of utmost pertinence in this evident prologue of the story. Or at least the germs of all the leading melodies are here.

In sudden turn of mood to high agitation, a stress of wild desire rings out above in pairs of sharp ascending chords, while below the wondering theme rises in growing tumult. A whirling storm of the two phrases ends in united burst like hymn of battle, on the line of the wondering theme, but infused with

267

resistless energy. Now sings a new discourse of warring phrases that are dimly traced to the phase of the blissful melody, above the theme of upward striv-

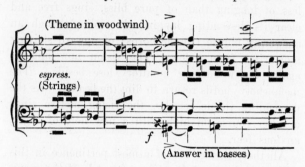

ing. They wing an eager course, undaunted by the harsh intruding chords. Into the midst presses the forceful martial theme. All four elements are clearly evident. The latest gains control, the other voices for the nonce merely trembling in obedient rhythm. But a new phase of the wistful motive appears, masterful but not o'ermastering, fiercely pressing upwards,—and a slower of the changed phrase of blissful song. The former attains a height of sturdy ascending stride.

In spite of the ominous stress of chords that grow louder with the increasing storm, something of assurance comes with the ascending stride. More and more this seems the dominant idea.

A new paroxysm of the warring themes rises to the first great climax where the old symbol of wondering and striving attains a brief moment of assured ecstatic triumph.

In a new scene (*meno mosso*), to murmuring strings (where the theme of striving can possibly be caught) the blissful melody sings in full song, undisturbed save by the former figure that rises as if to grasp,—sings later, too, in close sequence of voices. After a short intervening verse—*leicht bewegt*—where the first vision appears for a moment, the song is resumed, still in a kind of shadowy chase of slow flitting voices, *senza espressione*. The rising, eager phrase is disguised in dancing pace, and grows to a graceful turn of tune. An end comes, *poco agitato,* with rude intrusion of the hymnal march in harsh contrast of rough discord; the note of anxious fear, too, strikes in again. But suddenly, *etwas breiter,* a new joyous mood frightens away the birds of evil omen.

Right in the midst of happenings, we must be warned against too close a view of individual theme. We must not forget that it is on the contrasted pairs and again the separate groups of phrases, where all have a certain common modal purpose, that lies the main burden of the story. Still if we must be curious for fine derivation, we may see in the new tune of exultant chorus the late graceful turn that now, reversing, ends in the former rising phrase. Against it sings the first line of blissful theme. And the first tune of graceful beauty also finds a place. But they

all make one single blended song, full of glad bursts
and cadences.

Hardly dimmed in mood, it turns suddenly into a
phase of languorous passion, in rich setting of pulsing
harp, where now the later figures, all but the blissful
theme, vanish before an ardent song of the wondering
phrase. The motive of passionate desire rises and
falls, and soars in a path of " endless melody," returning on its own line of flight, playing as if with its
shadow, catching its own echo in the ecstasy of chase.
And every verse ends with a new stress of the insistent upward stride, that grows ever in force and
closes with big reverberating blasts. The theme of
the vision joins almost in rough guise of utmost
speed, and the rude marching song breaks in; somehow, though they add to the maze, they do not dispel
the joy. The ruling phase of passion now rumbles
fiercely in lowest depths. The theme of beauty rings
in clarion wind and strings, and now the whole strife
ends in clearest, overwhelming hymn of triumphant
gladness, all in the strides of the old wondering,
striving phrase.

The whole battle here is won. Though former moments are fought through again (and new melodies grow out of the old plaint), the triumphant shout is near and returns (ever from a fresh tonal quarter) to chase away the doubt and fear. All the former phrases sing anew, merging the tale of their strife in the recurring verse of united pæan. The song at last dies away, breaking like setting sun into glinting rays of celestial hue, that pale away into dullest murmur.

Still one returning paroxysm, of wild striving for eluding bliss, and then comes the close. From lowest depths shadowy tones sing herald phrases against dim, distorted figures of the theme of beauty,—that lead to a soft song of the triumphant hymn, *tranquillo*, in gentlest whisper, but with all the sense of gladness and ever bolder straying of the enchanting dream. After a final climax the song ends in slow vanishing echoes.

The poet Ritter is said to have added, after the production of the music, the poem printed on the score, of which the following is a rather literal translation:

> In the miserable chamber,
> Dim with flick'ring candlelight,
> Lies a man on bed of sickness.
> Fiercely but a moment past
> Did he wage with Death the battle;
> Worn he sinks back into sleep.
> Save the clock's persistent ticking
> Not a sound invades the room,

SYMPHONIES AND THEIR MEANING

Where the gruesome quiet warns us
Of the neighborhood of Death.
O'er the pale, distended features
Plays a melancholy smile.
Is he dreaming at life's border
Of his childhood golden days?

But a paltry shrift of sleep
Death begrudges to his victim.
Cruelly he wakes and shakes him,
And the fight begins anew,—
Throb of life and power of death,
And the horror of the struggle.
Neither wins the victory.
Once again the stillness reigns.

Worn of battle, he relapses
Sleepless, as in fevered trance.
Now he sees before him passing
Of his life each single scene:
First the glow of childhood dawn,
Bright in purest innocence,
Then the bolder play of youth
Trying new discovered powers,
Till he joins the strife of men,
Burning with an eager passion
For the high rewards of life.—
To present in greater beauty
What his inner eye beholds,
This is all his highest purpose
That has guided his career.

Cold and scornful does the world
Pile the barriers to his striving.
Is he near his final goal,
Comes a thund'rous " Halt! " to meet him.

" Make the barrier a stepping,
Ever higher keep your path."
Thus he presses on and urges,
Never ceasing from his aim.—
What he ever sought of yore
With his spirit's deepeth longing,
Now he seeks in sweat of death,
Seeks—alas! and finds it never.
Though he grasps it clearer now,
Though it grows in living form,
He can never all achieve it,
Nor create it in his thought.
Then the final blow is sounded
From the hammer-stroke of Death,
Breaks the earthly frame asunder,
Seals the eye with final night.
But a mighty host of sounds
Greet him from the space of heaven
With the song he sought below:
Man redeemed,—the world transfigured.

DON JUAN. (TONE POEM.)

A score or more of lines from Lenau's poem of
the same title stand as the subject of the music.

O magic realm, illimited, eternal,
Of gloried woman,—loveliness supernal!
Fain would I, in the storm of stressful bliss,
Expire upon the last one's lingering kiss!
Through every realm, O friend, would wing my flight,
Wherever Beauty blooms, kneel down to each,
And, if for one brief moment, win delight!

. . . .

I flee from surfeit and from rapture's cloy,
Keep fresh for Beauty service and employ,
Grieving the One, that All I may enjoy.

18   273

My lady's charm to-day hath breath of spring,
To-morrow may the air of dungeon bring.
  When with the new love won I sweetly wander,
No bliss is ours upfurbish'd and regilded;
  A different love has This to That one yonder,—
Not up from ruins be my temple builded.
  Yea Love life is, and ever must be now,
Cannot be changed or turned in new direction;
It must expire—here find a resurrection;
  And, if 'tis real, it nothing knows of rue!
Each Beauty in the world is sole, unique;
So must the love be that would Beauty seek!
So long as Youth lives on with pulse afire,
Out to the chase! To victories new aspire!

. . . .

It was a wond'rous lovely storm that drove me:
Now it is o'er; and calm all round, above me;
  Sheer dead is every wish; all hopes o'ershrouded,—
It was perhaps a flash from heaven descended,
Whose deadly stroke left me with powers ended,
  And all the world, so bright before, o'erclouded;
Yet perchance not! Exhausted is the fuel;
And on the hearth the cold is fiercely cruel.*

In the question of the composer's intent, of general
plan and of concrete detail, it is well to see that the
quotation from Lenau's poem is twice broken by
lines of omission; that there are thus three principal
divisions. It cannot be wise to follow a certain kind
of interpretation † which is based upon the plot of
Mozart's opera. The spirit of Strauss's music is

---

* Translation by John P. Jackson.

† In a complex commentary William Mauke finds Zerlina,
Anna and " The Countess " in the music.

clearly a purely subjective conception, where the symbolic figure of fickle desire moves through scenes of enchantment to a climax of—barren despair.

To some extent Strauss clearly follows the separate parts of his quotation. Fervent desire, sudden indifference are not to be mistaken.

The various love scenes may be filled with special characters without great harm, save that the mind is diverted from a higher poetic view to a mere concrete play of events. The very quality of the pure musical treatment thus loses nobility and significance. Moreover the only thematic elements in the design are the various "motives" of the hero.

Allegro molto con brio begins the impetuous main theme in dashing ascent,

whimsical play

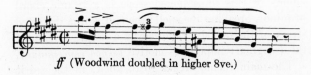

and masterful career.

(Doubled in higher 8ve.)

The various phases are mingled in spirited song; only the very beginning seems reserved as a special symbol of a turn in the chase, of the sudden flame of desire that is kindled anew.

In the midst of a fresh burst of the main phrase are gentle strains of plaint (*flebile*). And now a tenderly sad motive in the wood sings against the marching phrase, amidst a spray of light, dancing chords. Another song of the main theme is spent in a vanishing tremolo of strings and harp, and buried in a rich chord whence rises a new song (*molto espressivo*) or rather a duet, the first of the longer love-passages.

The main melody is begun in clarinet and horn and instantly followed (as in canon) by violins. The climax of this impassioned scene is a titanic chord of minor, breaking the spell; the end is in a distorted strain of the melody, followed by a listless refrain of the (original) impetuous motive (*senza espressione*).

The main theme breaks forth anew, in the spirit

of the beginning. It yields suddenly before the next episode, a languorous song of lower strings (*molto appassionato*), strangely broken into by sighing phrases in the high wood (*flebile*). After further interruption, the love song is crowned by a broad flowing melody (*sehr getragen und ausdrucksvoll*) — the main lyric utterance of all. It has a full length of extended song, proportioned to its distinguished beauty. The dual quality is very clear throughout the scene. Much of the song is on a kindred phrase of the lyric melody sung by the clarinet with dulcet chain of chords of harp.

Here strikes a climatic tune in forte unison of the four horns (*molto espressivo e marcato*). It is the clear utterance of a new mood of the hero,—a purely

subjective phase. With a firm tread, though charged with pathos, it seems what we might venture to call a symbol of renunciation. It is broken in upon by a strange version of the great love song, *agitato* in oboes, losing all its queenly pace. As though in final answer comes again the ruthless phrase of horns, followed now by the original theme. *Rapidamente* in full force of strings comes the coursing strain of impetuous desire. The old and the new themes of the hero are now in stirring encounter, and the latter seems to prevail.

The mood all turns to humor and merrymaking. In gay dancing trip serious subjects are treated jokingly (the great melody of the horns is mockingly sung by the harp),—in fits and gusts. At the height the (first) tempestuous motive once more dashes upwards and yields to a revel of the (second) whimsical phrase. A sense of fated renunciation seems to pervade the play of feelings of the hero. In the lull, when the paroxysm is spent, the various figures of his past romances pass in shadowy review; the first tearful strain, the melody of the first of the longer episodes,—the main lyric song (*agitato*).

In the last big flaming forth of the hero's passion victory is once more with the theme of renunciation,—or shall we say of grim denial where there is no choice.

Strauss does not defy tradition (or providence) by ending his poem with a triumph. A final elemental burst of passion stops abruptly before a long pause. The end is in dismal, dying harmonies,—a mere dull sigh of emptiness, a void of joy and even of the solace of poignant grief.

TILL EULENSPIEGEL'S MERRY PRANKS
In the Manner of Ancient Rogues—In Rondo Form

Hardly another subject could have been more happy for the revelling in brilliant pranks and conceits of a modern vein of composition. And in the

elusive humor of the subject is not the least charm
and fitness. Too much stress has been laid on the
graphic purpose. There is always a tendency to con-
strue too literally. While we must be in full sympathy with the poetic story, there is small need to look
for each precise event. We are tempted to go further,
almost in defiance, and say that music need not be
definite, even despite the composer's intent. In other
words, if the tonal poet designs and has in mind a
group of graphic figures, he may nevertheless achieve
a work where the real value and beauty lie in a certain
interlinear humor and poetry,—where the labels can
in some degree be disregarded.

Indeed, it is this very abstract charm of music that
finds in such a subject its fullest fitness. If we care
to know the pranks exactly, why not turn to the text?
Yet, reading the book, in a way, destroys the spell.
Better imagine the ideal rogue, whimsical, spritely,
all of the people too. But in the music is the real
Till. The fine poetry of ancient humor is all there,
distilled from the dregs of folk-lore that have to us
lost their true essence. There is in the music a
dæmonic quality, inherent in the subject, that somehow vanishes with the concrete tale. So we might
say the tonal picture is a faithful likeness precisely
in so far as it does not tell the facts of the story.

Indeed, in this mass of vulgar stories we cannot
help wondering at the reason for their endurance
through the centuries, until we feel something of the
spirit of the people in all its phases. A true mirror

it was of stupidity and injustice, presented by a sprite of owlish wisdom, sporting, teasing and punishing * all about. It is a kind of popular satire, with a strong personal element of a human Puck, or an impish Robin Hood, with all the fairy restlessness, mocking at human rut and empty custom.

It is perhaps in the multitude of the stories, paradoxical though it seem, that lies the strength. In the number of them (ninety-two " histories " there are) is an element of universality. It is like the broom: one straw does not make, nor does the loss of one destroy it; somewhere in the mass lies the quality of broom.

In a way Till is the Ulysses of German folk-lore, the hero of trickery, a kind of *Reinecke Fuchs* in real life. But he is of the soil as none of the others. A satyr, in a double sense, is Till; only he is pure Teuton, of the latter middle ages.

He is every sort of tradesman, from tailor to doctor. Many of the stories, perhaps the best, are not stories at all, but merely clever sayings. In most of the tricks there is a Roland for an Oliver. Till stops at no estate; parsons are his favorite victims. He is, on the whole, in favor with the people, though he played havoc with entire villages. Once he was

---

* On leaving the scene of some special mischief, Till would draw a chalk picture of an owl on the door, and write below, *Hic fuit*. The edition of 1519 has a woodcut of an owl resting on a mirror, that was carved in stone, the story goes, over Till's grave.

condemned to death by the Lübeck council. But even here it was his enemies, whom he had defrauded, that sought revenge. The others excused the tricks and applauded his escape. Even in death the scandal and mischief do not cease.

The directions in Strauss' music are new in their kind and dignity. They belong quite specially to this new vein of tonal painting. In a double function, they not merely guide the player, but the listener as well. The humor is of utmost essence; the humor is the thing, not the play, nor the story of each of the pranks, in turn, of our jolly rogue. And the humor lies much in these words of the composer, that give the lilt of motion and betray a sense of the intended meaning.

The tune, sung at the outset *gemächlich* (comfortably), is presumably the rogue *motif*, first in pure innocence of mood. But quickly comes another, quite opposed in rhythm, that soon hurries into highest speed. These are not the "subjects" of old tradition.

(Horn)

And first we are almost inclined to take the " Rondo form " as a new roguish prank. But we may find a form where the subjects are independent of the basic themes that weave in and out unfettered by rule— where the subjects are rather new grouping of the fundamental symbols.*

After a pause in the furious course of the second theme, a quick piping phrase sounds *lustig* (merrily) in the clarinet, answered by a chord of ominous

token. But slowly do we trace the laughing phrase to the first theme.

And here is a new whim. Though still in full tilt, the touch of demon is gone in a kind of ursine clog of the basses. Merely jaunty and clownish it would be but for the mischievous scream (of high flute) at the end. And now begins a rage of pranks, where

* It is like the Finale of Brahms' Fourth Symphony, where an older form (of *passacaglia*) is reared together with a later, one within the other.

the main phrase is the rogue's laugh, rising in brilliant gamut of outer pitch and inner mood.

At times the humor is in the spirit of a Jean Paul, playing between rough fun and sadness in a fine spectrum of moods. The lighter motive dances harmlessly about the more serious, intimate second phrase. There is almost the sense of lullaby before the sudden plunge to wildest chaos, the only portent being a constant trembling of low strings. All Bedlam is let loose, where the rogue's shriek is heard through a confused cackling and a medley of voices here and there on the running phrase (that ever ends the second theme). The sound of a big rattle is added to the scene,—where perhaps the whole village is in an uproar over some wholesale trick of the rogue.

And what are we to say to this simplest swing of folk-song that steals in naïvely to enchanting strum of rhythm. We may speculate about the Till as the

people saw him, while elsewhere we have the personal view. The folk-tunes may not have a special dramatic rôle. Out of the text of folk-song, to be sure,

all the strains are woven. Here and there we have
the collective voice. If we have watched keenly, we
have heard how the tune, simply though it begins, has
later all the line of Till's personal phrase. Even in
the bass it is, too. Of the same fibre is this demon
mockery and the thread of folk legend.

We cannot pretend to follow all the literal whims.
And it is part of the very design that we are ever
surprised by new tricks, as by this saucy trip of dancing phrase. The purely human touches are clear,
and almost moving in contrast with the impish humor.

An earlier puzzle is of the second theme. As the
composer has refused to help us, he will not quarrel
if we find our own construction. A possible clue there
is. As the story proceeds, aside from the mere
abounding fun and poetry, the more serious theme
prevails. Things are happening. And there come
the tell-tale directions. *Liebeglühend,* aflame with
love, a melody now sings in urgent pace, ending with

a strange descending note. Presently in quieter mood, *ruhiger,* it gains a new grace, merely to dash again, *wütend,* into a fiercer rage than before. Before long we cannot escape in all this newer melody a mere slower outline of the second theme. A guess then, such as the composer invites us to make, is this: It is not exactly a Jekyll and Hyde, but not altogether different. Here (in the second theme, of horn) is Till himself,—not the rogue, but the man in his likes and loves and suffering. The rogue is another, a demon that possesses him to tease mankind, to tease himself out of his happiness. During the passionate episode the rogue is banned, save for a grimace now and then, until the climax, when all in disguise of long passionate notes of resonant bass the demon theme has full control. But for once it is in earnest, in dead earnest, we might say. And the ominous chord has a supreme moment, in the shadow of the fulfilment.

A new note sounds in solemn legend of lowest wood, sadly beautiful, with a touch of funeral pace.*

The impish laugh still keeps intruding. But throughout the scene it is the Till motive, not the rogue, that fits the stride of the death-march. To be sure the rogue anon laughs bravely. But the other figure is in full view.

---

* Strauss told the writer that this was the march of the jurymen,—"*der Marsch der Schöffen.*" Reproached for killing Till, he admitted that he had taken a license with the story and added: "In the epilogue,—there he lives."

(Lowest woodwind)

The sombre legend is, indeed, in a separate phase, its beauty now distorted in a feverish chase of voices on the main phrase. It is all a second climax, of a certain note of terror,—of fate. In the midst is a dash of the rogue's heartiest laugh, amid the echoes of the fearful chord, while the growing roar of the mob can be heard below. Once again it rings out undaunted, and then to the sauciest of folk-tunes, *leichtfertig,* Till dances gaily and jauntily. Presently, in a mystic passage, *schnell und schattenhaft*

Leichtfertig

(Strings reinforced by clarinets and horns)

286

(like fleeting shadow) a phantom of the rogue's figure passes stealthily across the horizon.

Etwas gemächlicher, a graceful duet weaves prettily out of the Till motive, while the other roars very gently in chastened tones of softest horns.

The first course of themes now all recurs, though some of the roguery is softened and soon trips into purest folk-dance. And yet it is all built of the rascal theme. It might (for another idle guess) be a general rejoicing. Besides the tuneful dance, the personal phrase is laughing and chuckling in between.

The rejoicing has a big climax in the first folk-song of all, that now returns in full blast of horns against a united dance of strings and wood. After a roll of drum loud clanging strokes sound threatening (*dro-hend*) in low bass and strings, to which the rascal pipes his theme indifferently (*gleichgültig*). The third time, his answer has a simulated sound (*ent-stellt*). Finally, on the insistent thud comes a piteous phrase (*kläglich*) in running thirds. The dread chords at last vanish, in the strings. It is very like an actual, physical end. There is no doubt that the composer here intends the death of Till, in face of the tradition.

Follows the epilogue, where in the comfortable swing of the beginning the first melody is extended in full beauty and significance. All the pleasantry of the rogue is here, and at the end a last fierce burst of the demon laugh.

"*SINFONIA DOMESTICA.*"

The work followed a series of tone-poems where the graphic aim is shown far beyond the dreams even of a Berlioz. It may be said that Strauss, strong evidence to the contrary, does not mean more than a suggestion of the mood,—that he plays in the humor and poetry of his subject rather than depicts the full story. It is certainly better to hold to this view as long as possible. The frightening penalty of the game of exact meanings is that if there is one here, there must be another there and everywhere. There is no blinking the signs of some sort of plot in our domestic symphony, with figures and situations. The best way is to lay them before the hearer and leave him to his own reception.

In the usual sense, there are no separate movements. Though "Scherzo" is printed after the first appearance of the three main figures, and later "Adagio" and "Finale," the interplay and recurrence of initial themes is too constant for the traditional division. It is all a close-woven drama in one act, with rapidly changing scenes. Really more important than the conventional Italian names are such headings as "Wiegenlied" (Cradle-song), and above all, the numerous directions. Here is an almost conclusive proof of definite intent. To be sure, even a figure on canvas is not the man himself. Indeed, as music approaches graphic realism, it is strange how painting goes the other way. Or rather, starting from opposite points, the two arts are nearing each other. As modern painting tends to give the feeling of a subject, the subjective impression rather than the literal outline, we can conceive even in latest musical realism the "atmosphere" as the principal aim. In other words, we may view Strauss as a sort of modern impressionist tone-painter, and so get the best view of his pictures.

Indeed, cacophony is alone a most suggestive subject. In the first place the term is always relative, never absolute,—relative in the historic period of the composition, or relative as to the purpose. One can hardly say that any combination of notes is unusable. Most striking it is how the same group of notes makes hideous waste in one case, and a true tonal logic in another. Again, what was impossible in Mozart's time, may be commonplace to-day.

You cannot stamp cacophony as a mere whim of modern decadence. Beethoven made the noblest use of it and suffered misunderstanding. Bach has it in his scores with profound effect. And then the license of one age begets a greater in the next. It is so in poetry, though in far less degree. For, in music, the actual tones are the integral elements of the art. They are the idea itself; in poetry the words merely suggest it.

A final element, independent of the notes themselves, is the official numbering of themes. Strauss indicates a first, second and third theme, obviously of the symphony, not of a single movement. The whole attitude of the composer, while it does not compel, must strongly suggest some sort of guess of intending meaning.*

---

* At the first production, in New York, in obedience to the composer's wish, no descriptive notes were printed. When the symphony was played, likewise under the composer's direction, in Berlin in December, 1904, a brief note in the program-book mentions the three groups of themes, the husband's, the wife's and the child's, in the first movement. The other movements are thus entitled:

II.—*Scherzo.* Parents' happiness. Childish play. Cradle-song (the clock strikes seven in the evening).

III.—*Adagio.* Creation and contemplation. Love scene. Dreams and cares (the clock strikes seven in the morning).

IV.—*Finale.* Awakening and merry dispute (double fugue). Joyous conclusion.

The " first theme " in " comfortable " pace, gliding

1st Theme
Pleasantly

(Cellos and fagots)

Dreamily
(Oboe)

pp
(Cellos, bassoons and horns)

into a " dreamy " phrase, begins the symphony. Pres-

Peevishly

(Clarinets)
mf

ently a " peevish " cry breaks in, in sudden altered
key; then on a second, soothing tonal change, a
strain sings " ardently " in upward wing to a bold
climax and down to gentler cadence, the " peevish "
cry still breaking in. The trumpet has a short cheery

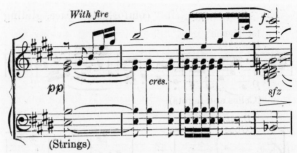

(Strings)

call (*lustig*), followed by a brisk, rousing run in wood and strings (*frisch*). A return of the " comfortable " phrase is quickly overpowered by the " second theme," in very lively manner (*sehr lebhaft*), with an answering phrase, *grazioso,* and light trills above.

2d Theme *With great spirit*

(Strings, wood, horns and harps)

292

The incidental phrases are thus opposed to the main humor of each theme. The serene first melody has "peevish" interruptions; the assertive second yields to graceful blandishments. A little later a strain appears *gefühlvoll,* "full of feeling," (that plays a frequent part), but the main (second) theme breaks in "angrily." Soon a storm is brewing; at the height the same motive is sung insistently. In the lull, the first phrase of all sings gaily (*lustig*), and then serenely (*gemächlich*) in tuneful tenor. Various

parts of the first theme are now blended in mutual discourse.

Amidst trembling strings the oboe d'amore plays the "third theme." "Very tenderly," "quietly," the

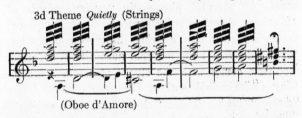

second gives soothing answer, and the third sings a full melodious verse.

Here a loud jangling noise tokens important arrivals. Fierce, hearty pulling of the door-bell excites the parents, especially the mother, who is quite in hysterics. The father takes it decidedly more calmly. The visitors presently appear in full view, so to speak; for " the aunts," in the trumpets, exclaim: " Just like Papa," and the uncles, in the trombones, cry: "Just like Mama " (*ganz die Mama*). There can be no questioning; it is all written in the book.

It is at least not hazardous to guess the three figures in the domestic symphony. Now in jolly Scherzo (*munter*) begin the tricks and sport of babyhood. There is of course but one theme, with mere com-

ments of parental phrases in varying accents of affection. Another noisy scene mars all the peace; father and child have a strong disagreement; the latter is " defiant "; the paternal authority is enforced. Bed-time comes with the stroke of seven, a cradle-song (Wiegenlied) (where the child's theme hums faintly below). Then, " slowly and very quietly " sings the " dreamy " phrase of the first theme, where

the answer, in sweeping descent, gives one of the principal elements of the later plot. It ends in a moving bit of tune, " very quietly and expressively " (*sehr ruhig und innig*).

Adagio, a slow rising strain plays in the softer

wood-notes of flute, oboe d'amore, English horn, and the lower clarinets; below sings gently the second theme, quite transformed in feeling. Those upper notes, with a touch of impassioned yearning, are not new to our ears. That very rising phrase (the "dreamy" motive), if we strain our memory, was at first below the more vehement (second) figure. So

now the whole themal group is reversed outwardly and in the inner feeling. Indeed, in other places crops out a like expressive symbol, and especially in the phrase, marked *gefühlvoll*, that followed the second theme in the beginning. All these motives here find a big concerted song in quiet motion, the true lyric spot of the symphony.

Out of it emerges a full climax, bigger and broader now, of the first motive. At another stage the second has the lead; but at the height is a splendid verse of the maternal song. At the end the quiet, blissful tune sings again *" sehr innig."*

Appassionato re-enters the second figure. Mingled

296

in its song are the latest tune and an earlier expressive phrase (*gefühlvoll*). The storm that here ensues is not of dramatic play of opposition. There are no "angry" indications. It is the full blossoming in richest madrigal of all the themes of tenderness and passion in an aureole of glowing harmonies. The morning comes with the stroke of seven and the awakening cry of the child.

The Finale begins in lively pace (*sehr lebhaft*) with

a double fugue, where it is not difficult to see in the first theme a fragment of the "baby" motive. The second is a remarkably assertive little phrase from the cadence of the second theme (quoted above). The son is clearly the hero, mainly in sportive humor, although he is not free from parental interference. The maze and rigor of the fugue do not prevent a frequent appearance of all the other themes, and even of the full melodies, of which the fugal motives are built. At the climax of the fugue, in the height of speed and noise, something very delightful is happening, some furious romp, perhaps, of father and son, the mother smiling on the game. At the close a new melody that we might trace, if we cared, in earlier origin, has a full verse " quietly and simply " (*ruhig und einfach*) in wood and horns, giving the crown

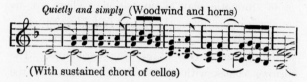

Quietly and simply (Woodwind and horns)

(With sustained chord of cellos)

and seal to the whole. The rest is a final happy refrain of all the strains, where the husband's themes are clearly dominant.

CHAPTER XIX

ITALIAN SYMPHONIES

THE present estate of music in Italy is an instance
of the danger of prophecy in the broad realm
of art. Wise words are daily heard on the rise and
fall of a nation in art, or of a form like the symphony, as though a matter of certain fate, in strict
analogy to the life of man.

Italy was so long regnant in music that she seems
even yet its chosen land. We have quite forgotten
how she herself learned at the feet of the masters
from the distant North. For music is, after all, the
art of the North; the solace for winter's desolation;
an utterance of feeling without the model of a visible
Nature.

And yet, with a prodigal stream of native melody
and an ancient passion of religious rapture, Italy
achieved masterpieces in the opposite fields of the
Mass and of Opera. But for the more abstract plane
of pure tonal forms it has somehow been supposed
that she had neither a power nor a desire for expression. An Italian symphony seems almost an anomaly,
—as strange a product as was once a German opera.

The blunt truth of actual events is that to-day a
renascence has begun, not merely in melodic and
dramatic lines; there is a new blending of the racial

299

gift of song with a power of profound design.* Despite all historical philosophy, here is a new gushing forth from ancient fount, of which the world may rejoice and be refreshed.

In a SYMPHONY BY GIOVANNI SGAMBATI,† IN D MAJOR, the form flows with such unpremeditated ease that it seems all to the manner born. It may be a new evidence that to-day national lines, at least in art, are vanishing; before long the national quality will be imperceptible and indeed irrelevant.

To be sure we see here an Italian touch in the simple artless stream of tune, the warm resonance, the buoyant spring of rhythm. The first movement stands out in the symphony with a subtler design than all the rest, though it does not lack the ringing note of jubilation.

The Andante is a pure lyric somewhat new in design and in feeling. It shows, too, an interesting contrast of opposite kinds of slower melody,—the one dark-hued and legend-like, from which the poet wings his flight to a hymnal rhapsody on a clear choral

---

* In the field of the *Lied* the later group of Italians, such as Sinigaglia and Bossi, show a melodic spontaneity and a breadth of lyric treatment that we miss in the songs of modern French composers.

In his Overture " *Le Baruffe Chiozzote* " (The Disputes of the People of Chiozza) Sinigaglia has woven a charming piece with lightest touch of masterly art; a delicate humor of melody plays amid a wealth of counterpoint that is all free of a sense of learning.

† Born in 1843.

theme, with a rich setting of arpeggic harmonies. A strange halting or limping rhythm is continued throughout the former subject. In the big climax the feeling is strong of some great chant or rite, of vespers or Magnificat. Against convention the ending returns to the mood of sad legend.

The Scherzo is a sparkling chain of dancing tunes of which the third, of more intimate hue, somehow harks back to the second theme of the first movement.

A Trio, a dulcet, tender song of the wood, precedes the return of the Scherzo that ends with the speaking cadence from the first Allegro.

A Serenata must be regarded as a kind of Intermezzo, in the Cantilena manner, with an accompanying rhythm suggesting an ancient Spanish dance. It stands as a foil between the gaiety of the Scherzo and the jubilation of the Finale.

The Finale is one festive idyll, full of ringing tune and almost bucolic lilt of dance. It reaches one of those happy jingles that we are glad to hear the composer singing to his heart's content.

GIUSEPPE MARTUCCI. SYMPHONY IN D MINOR.

The very naturalness, the limpid flow of the melodic thought seem to resist analysis of the design. The listener's perception must be as naïve and spontaneous as was the original conception.

There is, on the one hand, no mere adoption of a

---

* Giuseppe Martucci, 1856–1911.

classical schedule of form, nor, on the other, the over-subtle workmanship of modern schools. Fresh and resolute begins the virile theme with a main charm in the motion itself. It lies not in a tune here or there, but in a dual play of responsive phrases at the start, and then a continuous flow of further melody on the fillip of the original rhythm, indefinable of outline in a joyous chanting of bass and treble.

A first height reached, an expressive line in the following lull rises in the cellos, that is the essence of the contrasting idea, followed straightway by a brief phrase of the kind, like some turns of peasant song, that we can hear contentedly without ceasing.

Again, as at the beginning, such a wealth of melodies sing together that not even the composer could know which he intended in chief. We merely feel, instead of the incisive ring of the first group, a quieter power of soothing beauty. Yet, heralded by a prelude of sweet strains, the expressive line now enters like a queenly figure over a new rhythmic motion, and flows on through delighting glimpses of new harmony to a striking climax.

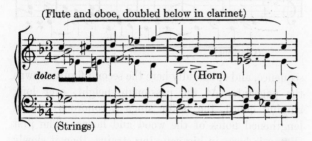

The story, now that the characters have appeared, continues in the main with the second browsing in soft lower strings, while the first (in its later phase) sings above in the wood transformed in mildness, though for a nonce the first motive strikes with decisive vigor. Later is a new heroic mood of minor, quickly softened when the companion melody appears. A chapter of more sombre hue follows, all with the lilt and pace of romantic ballad. At last the main hero returns as at the beginning, only in more splendid panoply, and rides on 'mid clattering suite to passionate triumph. And then, with quieter charm, sings again the second figure, with the delighting strains again and again rehearsed, matching the other with the power of sweetness.

One special idyll there is of carolling soft horn and clarinet, where a kind of lullaby flows like a distilled essence from the gentler play—of the heroic tune, before its last big verse, with a mighty flow of

303

sequence, and splendidly here the second figure crowns the pageant. At the passionate height, over long ringing chord, the latter sings a sonorous line in lengthened notes of the wood and horns. The first climax is here, in big coursing strains, then it slowly lulls, with a new verse of the idyll, to a final hush.

The second movement is a brief lyric with one main melody, sung at first by a solo cello amidst a weaving of muted strings; later it is taken up by the first violins. The solo cello returns for a further song in duet with the violins, where the violas, too, entwine their melody, or the cello is joined by the violins.

Now the chief melody returns for a richer and varied setting with horns and woodwind. At last the first violins, paired in octave with the cello, sing the full melody in a madrigal of lesser strains.

An epilogue answers the prologue of the beginning.

Equally brief is the true Scherzo, though merely entitled Allegretto,—a dainty frolic without the heavy brass, an indefinable conceit of airy fantasy, with here and there a line of sober melody peeping between the mischievous pranks. There is no contrasting Trio in the middle; but just before the end comes a quiet pace as of mock-gravity, before a final scamper.

A preluding fantasy begins in the mood of the early Allegro; a wistful melody of the clarinet plays more slowly between cryptic reminders of the first theme of the symphony. In sudden *Allegro risoluto* over rumbling bass of strings, a mystic call of horns, harking far back, spreads its echoing ripples all about till it rises in united tones, with a clear, descending answer, much like the original first motive. The latter now continues in the bass in large and smaller pace beneath a new tuneful treble of violins, while the call still roams a free course in the wind. Oft repeated is this resonation in paired harmonies, the lower phrase like an " obstinate bass."

Leaving the fantasy, the voices sing in simple choral lines a hymnal song in triumphal pace, with firm cadence and answer, ending at length in the descend-

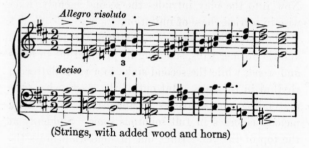

(Strings, with added wood and horns)

ing phrase. The full song is repeated, from the entrance of the latter, as though to stress the two main melodies. The marching chorus halts briefly

20   305

when the clarinet begins again a mystic verse on the strain of the call, where the descending phrase is intermingled in the horns and strings.

There is a new horizon here. We can no longer speak with half-condescension of Italian simplicity, though another kind of primal feeling is mingled in a breadth of symphonic vein. We feel that our Italian poet has cast loose his leading strings and is revealing new glimpses through the classic form.

Against a free course of quicker figures rises in the horns the simple melodic call, with answer and counter-tunes in separate discussion. Here comes storming in a strident line of the inverted melody in the bassoon, quarrelling with the original motive in the clarinet. Then a group sing the song in dancing trip, descending against the stern rising theme of violas; or one choir follows on the heels of another. Now into the play intrudes the second melody, likewise in serried chase of imitation.

The two themes seem to be battling for dominance, and the former wins, shouting its primal tune in brass and wood, while the second sinks to a rude clattering rhythm in the bass. But out of the clash, where the descending phrase recurs in the basses, the second melody emerges in full sonorous song. Suddenly at the top of the verse rings out in stentorian brass the first theme of all the symphony to the opening chord of the Finale, just as it rang at the climax in the beginning.

A gentle duet of violins and clarinet seems to bring back the second melody of the first movement, and somehow, in the softer mood, shows a likeness with the second of the Finale. For a last surprise, the former idyll (of the first Allegro) returns and clearly proves the original guise of our latest main melody. As though to assure its own identity as prevailing motto, it has a special celebration in the final joyous revel.

CHAPTER XX

EDWARD ELGAR. AN ENGLISH SYMPHONY*

THERE is a rare nobility in the simple melody, the vein of primal hymn, that marks the invocation,—in solemn wood against stately stride of

(*Andante nobilmente e semplice*)
(Woodwind)

p dolce

Con 8ve.
(Basses of strings, *staccato*)

lower strings. A true ancient charm is in the tune, with a fervor at the high point and a lilt almost of lullaby,—till the whole chorus begins anew as though the song of marching hosts. Solemnity is the essence here, not of artificial ceremony nor of rhymeless chant, —rather of prehistoric hymn.

In passionate recoil is the upward storming song (Allegro) where a group of horns aid the surging crest of strings and wood,—a resistless motion of massed melody. Most thrilling after the first climax is the sonorous, vibrant stroke of the bass in the

---

* Symphony in A flat. Edward Elgar, born in 1857.

(Strings, wood and horns)

(See page 308, line 10.)

recurring melody. As it proceeds, a new line of
bold tune is stirred above, till the song ends at the
highest in a few ringing, challenging leaps of chord,—
ends or, rather merges in a relentless, concluding
descent. Here, in a striking phrase of double

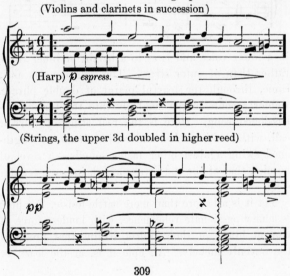

309

song, is a touch of plaint that, hushing, heralds
the coming gentle figure. We are sunk in a sweet
romance, still of ancientest lore, with a sense of lost
bliss in the wistful cadence. Or do these entrancing
strains lead merely to the broader melody that moves
with queenly tread (of descending violins) above a
soft murmuring of lower figures? It is taken up

in a lower voice and rises to a height of inner throb
rather than of outer stress. The song departs as it
came, through the tearful plaint of double phrase.
Bolder accents merge suddenly into the former impassioned song. Here is the real sting of warrior
call, with shaking brass and rolling drum, in lengthened swing against other faster sounds,—a revel of
heroics, that at the end breaks afresh into the regular
song.

Yet it is all more than mere battle-music. For here
is a new passionate vehemence, with loudest force of
vibrant brass, of those dulcet strains that preceded
the queenly melody. An epic it is, at the least, of

ancient flavor, and the sweeter romance here rises to a tempest more overpowering than martial tumult.

It is in the harking back to primal lore that we seem to feel true passion at its best and purest, as somehow all truth of legend, proverb and fable has come from those misty ages of the earth. The drooping harmonies merge in the returning swing of the first solemn hymn,—a mere line that is broken by a new tender appeal, that, rising to a moving height,

yields to the former plaint (of throbbing thirds).

A longer elegy sings, with a fine poignancy, bold and new in the very delicacy of texture, in the sharp impinging of these gentlest sounds. In the depths of the dirge suddenly, though quietly, sounds the herald melody high in the wood, with ever firmer cheer, soon in golden horns, at last in impassioned strings, followed by the wistful motive.

A phase here begins as of dull foreboding, with a new figure stalking in the depths and, above, a brief sigh in the wind. In the growing stress these figures

311

sing from opposite quarters, the sobbing phrase below, when suddenly the queenly melody stills the tumult. It is answered by a dim, slow line of the ominous motive. Quicker echoes of the earlier despond still flit here and there, with gleams of joyous light. The plaintive (dual) song returns and too the tender appeal, which with its sweetness at last wakens the buoyant spirit of the virile theme.

And so pass again the earlier phases of resolution with the masterful conclusion; the tearful accents; the brief verse of romance, and the sweep of queenly figure, rising again to almost exultation. But here, instead of tears and recoil, is the brief sigh over sombre harmonies, rising insistent in growing volume that somehow conquers its own mood. A return of the virile motive is followed at the height by the throbbing dual song with vehement stress of grief, falling to lowest echoes.

Here begins the epilogue with the original solemn hymn. Only it is now entwined with shreds and memories of romance, flowing tranquilly on through gusts of passion. And there is the dull sob with the sudden gleam of joyous light. But the hymn returns like a sombre solace of oblivion,—though there is a final strain of the wistful romance, ending in sad harmony.

II.—Allegro molto. The Scherzo (as we may venture to call it) begins with a breath of new harmony, or is it a blended magic of rhythm, tune and chord? Far more than merely bizarre, it calls

up a vision of Celtic warriors, the wild, free spirit of
Northern races. The rushing jig or reel is halted

(Strings with
kettle-drum)

anon by longer notes in a drop of the tune and instantly returns to the quicker run. Below plays a
kind of drum-roll of rumbling strings. Other revelling pranks appear, of skipping wood, rushing harp
and dancing strings, till at last sounds a clearer tune,
a restrained war-march with touch of terror in the
soft subdued chords, suddenly growing to expressive

volume as it sounds all about, in treble and in bass.

At last the war-song rings in full triumphant blast,
where trumpets and the shrill fife lead, and the lower
brass, with cymbals and drums (big and little) mark

the march. Then to the returning pranks the tune roars in low basses and reeds, and at last a big conclusive phrase descends from the height to meet the rising figure of the basses.

Now the reel dances in furious tumult (instead of the first whisper) and dies down through the slower cadence.

An entirely new scene is here. To a blended tinkle of harp, reeds and high strings sounds a delicate air, quick and light, yet with a tinge of plaint that may be a part of all Celtic song. It were rude to spoil

(Woodwind, with a triplet
pulse of harp and rhythmic strings)

its fine fragrance with some rough title of meaning; nor do we feel a strong sense of romance, rather a whim of Northern fantasy.

Over a single note of bass sings a new strain of elegy, taken up by other voices, varying with the

(Clarinets)

tinkling air. Suddenly in rushes the first reel, softly as at first; but over it sings still the new sad tune, then yields to the wild whims and pranks that lead to the war-song in resonant chorus, joined at the height

by the reel below. They change places, the tune
ringing in the bass. In the martial tumult the tinkling air is likewise infected with saucy vigor, but
suddenly retires abashed into its shell of fairy sound,
and over it sings the elegy in various choirs. The
tinkling melody falls suddenly into a new flow of
moving song, rising to pure lyric fervor. The soft
air has somehow the main say, has reached the high
point, has touched the heart of the movement. Expressively it slowly sinks away amid echoing phrases
and yields to the duet of elegy and the first reel.
But a new spirit has appeared. The sting of war-song
is gone. And here is the reel in slow reluctant pace.
After another verse of the fairy tune, the jig plays
still slower, while above sings a new melody. Still
slower the jig has fallen almost to funeral pace, has
grown to a new song of its own, though, to be sure,
brief reminders of the first dance jingle softly here
and there. And now the (hushed) shadow of the
war-song in quite slower gait strides in lowest basses
and passes quietly straight into the Adagio.

III.—Assured peace is in the simple sincere melody, rising to a glow of passion. But—is this a jest of our poet? Or rather now we see why there was no halt at the end of the Scherzo. For the soothing melody is in the very notes of the impish reel,—is the same tune.* Suddenly hushing, the song hangs on high over delicate minor harmonies.

In exquisite hues an intimate dialogue ensues, almost too personal for the epic vein, a discourse or madrigal of finest fibre that breaks (like rays of setting sun) into a melting cadence of regret. We are doubly thrilled in harking back to the sweet, wistful romance, the strain of the first movement.

(Harp, wood and strings)

Across the gauzy play, horns and wood blow a slow phrase, like a motto of Fate in the sombre harmony, with one ardent burst of pleading.

---

* There seems to be shown in this feat at once the versatility of music as well as the musician in expressing opposite moods by the same theme. The author does not feel bound to trace all such analogies, as in the too close pursuit we may lose the forest in the jungle.

In clearer articulation sings a dual song, still softly o'ercast with sweet sadness, ever richer in the harmonies of multiple strings, tipped with the light mood,—and again the wistful cadence. Siren figures of entrancing grace that move amid the other melody, bring enchantment that has no cheer, nor escape the insistent sighing phrase. Once more come the ominous call and the passionate plea, then assurance with the returning main melody in renewed fervor. Phases of dual melody end again with the wistful cadence. The tranquil close is like one sustained fatal farewell, where the fairy figures but stress the sad burden.

IV.—The beginning is in lowest depths (Largo). First is the stalking figure of earliest movement, from the moment of despond. It is answered by a steadily striding theme, almost martial, save for the

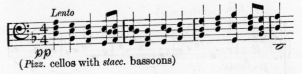

(*Pizz.* cellos with *stacc.* bassoons)

slowness of pace. Not unlike the hymn of the first prologue in line of tune, it bears a mood of dark resignation that breaks presently into the touching plea of the wistful cadence.

The whole is a reflective prologue to the Finale: a deep meditation from which the song may roll forth on new spring. The hymn has suddenly entered with a subtly new guise; for the moment it seems part of the poignant sigh; it is as yet submerged in a flood of gloom and regret; and the former phrases still stride and stalk below. In a wild climax of gloom we hear the former sob, earlier companion of the stalking figure.

Hymnal strains return,—flashes of heavenly light in the depths of hell, and one passionate sigh of the melting cadence.

Allegro,—we are carried back to the resolute vigor of the earlier symphony, lacking the full fiery charm, but ever striving and stirring, like Titans rearing mountain piles, not without the cheer of toil itself. At the height comes a burst of the erst yearning cadence, but there is a new masterful accent; the wistful edge does not return till the echoing phrases sink away in the depths.

A new melody starts soaring on the same wing of

blended striving and yearning of which all this song is fraught. In its broader sweep and brighter cheer it is like the queenly melody of the first movement.

The Titan toil stirs strongly below the soft cadence:

the full, fierce ardor mounts heavenward. Phases now alternate of insistent rearing on the strenuous motive and of fateful submission in the marching strain, that is massed in higher and bigger chorus. As gathers the stress of climax, the brass blowing a defiant blast, the very vehemence brings a new resolution that is uttered in the returning strenuous phrase.

Again rises the towering pile. At the thickest the high horns blow loud a slow, speaking legend,—the farewell motive, it seems, from the end of Adagio, fierce energy struggling with fatal regret gnawing at the heart.

Gripping is the appeal of the sharp cry almost of anguish into which the toiling energy is suddenly resolved. Again the fateful march enters, now in heroic fugue of brass and opposite motion of strings and reed,—all overwhelmed with wild recurring pangs of regret.

And so " double, double, toil and trouble," on goes the fugue and follows the arduous climb (into the sad motto in the horns), each relieving the other, till both yield again to the heart-breaking cry.

The cheerier melody here re-enters and raises the mood for the nonce. Soon it falls amid dim harmonies. Far in the depths now growls the dull tread, answered by perverted line of the hymn.

A mystic verse sounds over pious chords of harp in the tune of the march, which is sung by antiphonal choirs of strings,—later with fuller celestial chorus, almost in rapture of heavenly resignation. Only it is not final; for once again returns the full struggle of the beginning, with the farewell-legend, and in highest passion the phrase of regret rung again and again—till it is soothed by the tranquil melody. The relentless stride of march too reaches a new height, and one last, moving plaint. When the fast chasing cries are in closest tangle, suddenly the hymn pours out its benediction, while the cries have changed to angelic acclaim. Here is the transfigured song in full climactic verse that fulfils the promise of the beginning. A touch of human (or earthly joy) is added in an exultant strain of the sweeping melody that unites with the hymn at the close.

CHAPTER XXI

SYMPHONIES IN AMERICA

WHEN we come to a view of modern music in symphonic design, written in America, we are puzzled by a new phase of the element of nationalism. For here are schools and styles as different as of far corners of Europe. Yet they can be called nothing else than American, if they must have a national name. In the northern centre whence a model orchestra has long shed a beneficent influence far afield, the touch of new French conceits has colored some of the ablest works. Elsewhere we have cited a symphony more in line with classical tradition.*

Perhaps most typical is a symphony of Hadley where one feels, with other modern tradition, the mantle of the lamented MacDowell, of whom it may be said that he was first to find in higher reaches of the musical art an utterance of a purely national temper.

HENRY HADLEY. SYMPHONY NO. 3, B. MINOR.†

With virile swing the majestic melody strides in the strings, attended by trooping chords of wood and brass, all in the minor, in triple rhythm. In

---

* A symphony by Wm. W. Gilchrist. Vol. II, Appendix.
† Opus 60, Henry Hadley, American, born 1871.

the bass is a frequent retort to the themal phrase. For a moment a dulcet line steals in, quickly broken by the returning martial stride of stentorian horns, and of the main theme in full chords. Strange, though, how a softer, romantic humor is soon spread over the very discussion of the martial theme, so that it seems the rough, vigorous march is but the shell for the kernel of tender romance,—the pageant that precedes the queenly figure. And presently, *piu tranquillo,* comes the fervent lyric song that may indeed be the chief theme in poetic import, if not in outer rank. After a moving verse in the strings,

322

with an expressive strain in some voice of the wood-wind or a ripple of the harp, it is sung in tense chorus of lower wood and horns,—soon joined by all the voices but the martial brass, ending with a soft echo of the strings.

Now in full majesty the stern stride of first theme is resumed, in faster insistence,—no longer the mere tune, but a spirited extension and discussion, with retorts between the various choirs. Here the melodious march is suddenly felt in the bass (beneath our feet, as it were) of lowest brass and strings, while the noisy bustle continues above; then, changing places, the theme is above, the active motion below.

Long continues the spirited clatter as of war-like march till again returns the melting mood of the companion melody, now sung by the expressive horn, with murmuring strings. And there are enchanting flashes of tonal light as the song passes to higher choirs. The lyric theme wings its rapturous course to a blissful height, where an intrusion of the main motive but halts for the moment the returning tender verse.

When the first vigorous phrase returns in full career, there is somehow a greater warmth, and the dulcet after-strain is transfigured in a glow greater almost than of the lyric song that now follows with no less response of beauty. In the final spirited blending of both melodies the trumpets sound a quicker pace of the main motive.

In the Andante (*tranquillo*) the sweet tinkle of

church-bells with soft chanting horns quickly de-
fines the scene. Two voices of the strings, to the

(Bells and harp in continuous repetition)

(Strings, with added choir of lower reeds)

continuing hum of the bells, are singing a responsive song that rises in fervor as the horns and later
the woodwind join the strings. Anon will sound
the simple tune of the bells with soft harmonies, like
echoes of the song,—or even the chant without the
chimes.

In more eager motion,—out of the normal measure
of bells and hymn, breaks a new song in minor with
a touch of passion, rising to a burst of ardor. But it
passes, sinking away before a new phase,—a bucolic

fantasy of trilling shepherd's reed (in changed, even pace), supported by strumming strings. The sacred calm and later passion have yielded to a dolorous plaint, like the dirge of the Magyar plains. Suddenly the former fervor returns with strains of the second melody amidst urging motion (in the triple pace) and startling rushes of harp-strings. At the height, trumpets blare forth the first melody, transformed from its earlier softness, while the second presses on in higher wood and strings; the trombones relieve the trumpets, with a still larger chorus in the romantic song; in final exaltation, the basses of brass and strings sound the first melody, while the second still courses in treble voices.

Of a sudden, after a lull, falls again the tinkle of sacred chimes, with a verse each of the two main melodies.

The Scherzo begins with a Saltarello humor, as of airy faun, with a skipping theme ever accompanied by a lower running phrase and a prancing trip of

strings, with a refrain, too, of chirruping woodwind.
Later the skipping phrase gains a melodic cadence.
But the main mood is a revel of gambols and pranks
of rhythm and harmony on the first phase.

In the middle is a sudden shift of major tone and
intimate humor, to a slower pace. With still a
semblance of dance, a pensive melody sings in the
cellos; the graceful cadence is rehearsed in a choir

of woodwind, and the song is taken up by the whole
chorus. As a pretty counter-tune grows above, the
melody sings below, with a blending of lyric feeling
and the charm of dance. At a climactic height the
horns, with clumsy grace, blare forth the main lilting
phrase.

The song now wings along with quicker tripping
counter-tunes that slowly lure the first skipping tune
back into the play after a prelude of high festivity.
New pranks appear,—as of dancing strings against
a stride of loud, muted horns. Then the second
(pensive) melody returns, now above the running
counter-tune. At last, in faster gait, to the coursing
of quicker figures, the (second) melody rings out in

choir of brass in twice slower, stately pace. But
the accompanying bustle is merely heightened until
all four horns are striking together the lyric song. At
the end is a final revel of the first dancing tune.

The Finale, which bears the unusual mark *Allegro
con giubilio,* begins with a big festive march that may
seem to have an added flavor of old English merry-
making. But as in the other cantos of the poem there

(Basses in 8ve.)

is here, too, an opposite figure and feeling. And the
more joyous the gaiety, the more sweetly wistful is
the recoil. Nay there is in this very expressive strain,
beautifully woven in strings, harp, woodwind and
horns, a vein of regret that grows rather than lessens,
whenever the melody appears alone. It is like the
memory, in the midst of festival, of some blissful
moment lost forever.

Indeed, the next phase seems very like a dis-
ordered chase of stray memories; for here a line of
martial air is displaced by a pensive strain which in

327

(Cello and harp with harmony of wood, horns and strings)

turn yields to the quick, active tune that leads to a height of celebration.

But here is a bewildering figure on the scene: Lustily the four horns (helped by the strings) blow in slow notes against the continuing motive an expressive melody. Slowly it breaks upon our ears as the wistful air that followed the chimes of Sunday bells. It has a stern, almost sombre guise, until it suddenly glows in transfigured light, as of a choir of celestial brass.

Slowly we are borne to the less exalted pitch of the first festive march, and here follows, as at first, the expressive melody where each hearer may find his own shade of sadness. It does seem to reach a true passion of regret, with poignant sweet sighs.

At length the sadness is overcome and there is a new animation as separate voices enter in fugal manner in the line of the march. Now the festive tune holds sway in lower pace in the basses; but then rings on high in answer—the wistful melody again and again, in doubled and twice redoubled pace.

When we hear the *penseroso* melody once more at the end, we may feel with the poet a state of resigned cheer.

A remarkable work that shows the influence of modern French harmony rather than its actual traits, is a SYMPHONY BY GUSTAV STRUBE.* It is difficult to resist the sense of a strain for bizarre harmony, of a touch of preciosity. The real business of these harmonies is for incidental pranks, with an after-touch that confesses the jest, or softens it to a lyric utterance. It cannot be denied that the moving moments in this work come precisely in the release of the strain of dissonance, as in the returning melody of the Adagio. Only we may feel we have been waiting too long. The desert was perhaps too long for the oasis. *Est modus in rebus:* the poet seems niggardly with his melody; he may weary us with too long waiting, with too little staying comfort. He does not escape the modern way of symbolic, infinitesimal

* Of Boston,—born in Germany in 1867.

melody, so small that it must, of course, reappear. It is a little like the wonderful arguments from ciphers hidden in poetry.

It cannot be denied that the smallness of phrase does suggest a smallness of idea. The plan of magic motive will not hold *ad infinitesimum*. As the turn of the triplet, in the first movement, twists into a semblance of the Allegro theme, we feel like wondering with the old Philistine:

> . . . "How all this difference can be
> 'Twixt tweedle-dum and tweedle-dee!"

But there is the redeeming vein of lyric melody with a bold fantasy of mischievous humor and a true climax of a clear poetic design. One reason seems sometimes alone to justify this new license, this new French revolution: the deliverance from a stupid slavery of rules,—if we would only get the spirit of them without the inadequate letter. Better, of course, the rules than a fatal chaos. But there is here in the bold flight of these harmonies, soaring as though on some hidden straight path, a truly Promethean utterance.

It is significant, in the problem of future music, that of the symphonies based upon recent French ideas, the most subtly conceived and designed should have been written in America.

I.—In pale tint of harmony sways the impersonal phrase that begins with a descending tone. We may

330

Andante (Melody in flute and violas)
(Violins)

ppp

(Cellos with basses
in lower 8ve.)

remember * how first with the symphony came a clear
sense of tonal residence. It was like the age in
painting when figures no longer hung in the gray air,
when they were given a resting-place, with trees and
a temple.

Here we find just the opposite flight from clear
tonality, as if painting took to a Japanese manner,
sans aught of locality. Where an easy half-step leads
gently somewhere, a whole tone sings instead. Nothing obvious may stand.

It marks, in its reaction, the excessive stress of
tonality and of simple colors of harmony. The basic
sense of residence is not abandoned; there is merely
a bolder search for new tints, a farther straying
from the landmarks.

Soon our timid tune is joined by a more expressive
line that rises in ardent reaches to a sudden tumult,
with a fiery strain of trumpets where we catch a
glimpse of the triplet figure. After a dulcet lullaby

* See Vol I, Chapter I.

(Flute with *tremolo* of high strings)

p espress.

(New melody in ob. and violas)

(Cellos with sustained lower B of basses)

of the first air, the second flows in faster pace (*Allegro commodo*) as the real text, ever with new blossoming variants that sing together in a madrigal of tuneful voices, where the descending note still has a part in a smooth, gliding pace of violins.

In gayer mood comes a verse of the inverted (Allegro) tune, with other melodic guises hovering about. When the theme descends to the bass, the original Andante phrase sings in the trumpet, and there is a chain of entering voices, in growing agitation, in the main legend with the quicker sprites

332

dancing about. At the height, after the stirring
song of trumpets, we feel a passionate strife of resolve
and regret; and immediately after, the descending
tone is echoed everywhere.

A balancing (second) theme now appears, in tran-

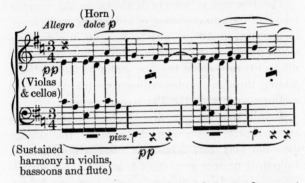

quil flow, but pressing on, at the end, in steady ascent
as to Parnassian summit. Later comes a new rejoinder in livelier mood, till it is lost in a big,
moving verse of the Andante song. But pert retorts
from the latest new tune again fill the air, then yield
in attendance upon the returning Allegro theme.
Of subtle art is the woof of derived phrases. A companion melody, that seems fraught of the text of the
second subject, sings with rising passion, while the
lower brass blow lustily in eccentric rhythm of the
Allegro phrase and at the height share in the dual
triumph.

We feel a kinship of mood rather than of theme,

a coherence that we fear to relate to definite figures, though the descending symbol is clear against the ascending. An idyllic dialogue, with the continuing guise of the Allegro phrase turns to a gayer revel in the original pace, with a brilliant blare of trumpets.

The free use of themes is shown in the opposite moods of the triplet phrase, of sadness, as in Andante, or buoyant, in Allegro. Here are both in close transition as the various verses return from the beginning, entwined about the first strain of the Andante, gliding through the descending tone into the second soothing song with the Parnassian ascent.

A full verse of the first Andante melody sings at the heart of the plot, followed by the strange dæmonic play that keeps the mood within bounds. Indeed, it returns once more as at first, then springs into liveliest trip and rises to an Olympian height, with a final revel of the triplet figure.

II.—With a foreshadowing drop of tone begins the prelude, not unlike the first notes of the sym-

334

phony, answered with a brief phrase. On the descending motive the main melody is woven.

Tenderly they play together, the melody with the main burden, the lighter prelude phrase in graceful accompaniment. But now the latter sings in turn a serious verse, rises to a stormy height, the horns proclaiming the passionate plea amid a tumultuous accord of the other figures, and sinks in subdued temper. In a broader pace begins a new line, though on the thread of the descending motive, and with the entering phrase of the prelude winds to a climax of passion. The true episode, of refuge and solace from the stress of tempest, is in a song of the trumpet through a shimmering gauze of strings with glinting harp, to a soft murmuring in the reeds.

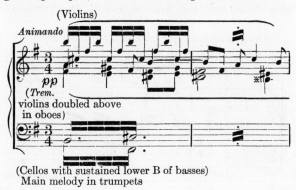

(Cellos with sustained lower B of basses)
Main melody in trumpets

In a new shade of tone it is echoed by the horn, then in a fervent close it is blended with a guise of the prelude phrase, that now heralds the main melody, in a duet of clarinet and violins. At last in the home tone the horn sings amid the sweet tracery the parting verse, and all about sounds the trist symbol of the first (descending) motive.

III.—The Scherzo is in one view a mad revel of demon pranks in a new field of harmonies. Inconsequential though they may seem, there is a real coherence, and, too, a subtle connection with the whole design.

To be sure, with the vagueness of tune that belongs to a school of harmonic exploits a certain mutual relation of themes is a kind of incident. The less defined the phrases, the easier it is to make them similar.

Undoubted likeness there is between the main elfin figure and the first phrase of the symphony.

(Oboes, with lower 8ve. and higher 8ve. of piccolo)

The triplet is itself a kind of password throughout. With this multiple similarity is a lack of the inner bond of outer contrast.

236

The mood of demon humor finds a native medium in the tricks of new Gallic harmony. Early in the prelude we hear the descending tone, a streak of sadness in the mirth. Answering the first burst is a strange stroke of humor in the horn, and as if in

serious balance, a smooth gliding phrase in the wood. Now the first figure grows more articulate, romping and galloping into an ecstasy of fun. A certain spirit of Till Eulenspiegel hovers about.

Out of the maze blows a new line in muted trumpets, that begins with the inverted triplet figure, and in spite of the surrounding bedlam rises almost into a tune. At the height the strange jest of the horns reigns supreme.

From the mad gambols of the first figure comes a relief in sparkling calls of the brass and stirring retorts in pure ringing harmonies. In the next episode is a fall into a lyric mood as the latest figure glides into even pace, singing amid gentlest pranks.

Most tuneful of all sounds is the answer in dulcet
trumpet while, above, the first theme intrudes softly.
The heart of the idyll comes in a song of the clari-

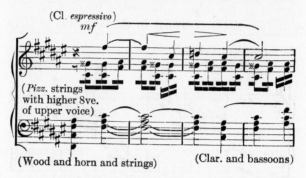

net against strange, murmuring strings, ever with a
soft answer of the lower reed.

New invading sprites do not hem the flight of
the melody. But at the height a redoubled pace
turns the mood back to revelling mirth with broken
bits of the horn tune. Indeed the crisis comes with
a new rage of this symbol of mad abandon, in demonic strife with the fervent song that finally
prevails.

The first theme returns with a new companion
in the highest wood. A fresh strain of serious melody
is now woven about the former dulcet melody of
trumpet in a stretch of delicate poesy, of mingled
mirth and tenderness.—The harmonies have something of the infinitesimal sounds that only insects
hear. With all virtuous recoil, here we must confess
is a masterpiece of cacophonic art, a new world of

tones hitherto unconceived, tinkling and murmuring
with the eerie charm of the forest.—In the return
of the first prelude is a touch of the descending tone.
From the final revelling tempest comes a sudden
awakening. In strange moving harmony sings slowly
the descending symbol, as if confessing the unsuccess-
ful flight from regret. Timidly the vanquished
sprites scurry away.

IV.—The first notes of the Finale blend and bring
back the main motives. First is the descending tone,
but firm and resolute, with the following triplet in

inversion of the Scherzo theme.

It is all in triumphant spirit. From the start the
mood reigns, the art for once is quite subordinate.
Resonant and compelling is the motive of horns and
trumpets, new in temper, though harking back to
the earlier text, in its cogent ending. Splendid is

the soaring flight through flashes of new chords.
There is, we must yield, something Promethean, of
new and true beauty, in the bold path of harmonies
that the French are teaching us after a long age of
slavish rules.

The harking back is here better than in most
modern symphonies with their pedantic subtleties:
in the resurgence of joyous mood, symbolized by the
inversion of phrase, as when the prankish elfin theme
rises in serious aspiration.

Out of these inspiriting reaches sings a new melody
in canon of strings (though it may relate to some
shadowy memory), while in the bass rolls the former
ending phrase; then they romp in jovial turn of
rhythm.

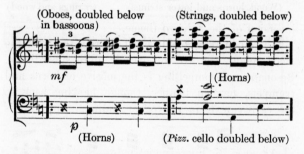

A vague and insignificant similarity of themes is
a fault of the work and of the style, ever in high
disdain of vernacular harmony, refreshing to be sure,
in its saucy audacity, and anon enchanting with a
ring of new, fiery chord. As the sonorous theme

sings in muted brass, picking strings mockingly play quicker fragments, infecting the rest with frivolous retorts, and then a heart-felt song pours forth, where the accompanying cries have softened their mirth. Back they skip to a joyous trip with at last pure ringing harmonies.

At the fervent pitch a blast of trumpets rises in challenging phrase, in incisive clash of chord, with the early sense of Parnassian ascent. At the end of this brave fanfare we hear a soft plea of the descending tone that prompts a song of true lyric melody, with the continuing gentlest touch of regret, all to a sweetly bewildering turn of pace. So tense

and subtle an expression would utterly convert us to the whole harmonic plan, were it not that just here, in these moving moments, we feel a return to clearer tonality. But it is a joy to testify to so devoted a work of art.

With the last notes of melody a new frisking tune

plays in sauciest clashes of chord, with an enchanting stretch of ringing brass. A long merriment ensues in the jovial trip, where the former theme of horns has a rising cadence; or the tripping tune sings in united chorus and again through its variants. After a noisy height the dulcet melody (from the descending tone) sings in linked sweetness. In the later tumult we rub our eyes to see a jovial theme of the bass take on the lines of the wistful melody. Finally, in majestic tread amid general joyous clatter the brass blow the gentle song in mellowed tones of richest harmony.

CHADWICK.* SUITE SYMPHONIQUE (IN E FLAT).

With a rush of harp and higher strings the Suite begins on ardent wing in exultant song of trumpets (with horns, bassoons and cellos) to quick palpitating violins that in its higher flight is given over to upper reeds and violas. It is answered by gracefully drooping melody of strings and harps topped by the oboes, that lightly descends from the heights with a cadence long delayed, like the circling flight of a great bird before he alights. Straightway begins a more pensive turn of phrase (of clarinet and lower strings) in distant tonal scene where now the former (descending) answer sings timidly in alternating groups. The pensive melody returns for a greater reach, blending with the original theme (in all the basses) in a glowing duet of two moods as well as

---

* George W. Chadwick, American, born in 1854.

melodies, rising to sudden brilliant height, pressing on to a full return of the first exultant melody with long, lingering, circling descent.

The listener on first hearing may be warned to have a sharp ear for all kinds of disguises of the stirring theme and in a less degree, of the second subject. What seems a new air in a tranquil spot, with strum of harp,—and new it is as expression,— is our main melody in a kind of inversion. And so a new tissue of song continues, all of the original fibre, calming more and more from the first fierce glow. A tuneful march-like strain now plays gently in the horns while the (inverted) expressive air still sounds above.

When all has quieted to dim echoing answers between horn and reed, a final strain bursts forth (like the nightingale's voice in the surrounding stillness) in full stress of its plaint. And so. in most natural course, grows and flows the main balancing melody that now pours out its burden in slower, broader pace, in joint choirs of wood and strings.

It is the kind of lyric spot where the full stream of warm feeling seems set free after the storm of the first onset. In answer is a timid, almost halting strain in four parts of the wood, echoed in strings. A new agitation now stirs the joint choirs (with touches of brass), and anon comes a poignant line of the inverted (main) theme. It drives in rising stress under the spurring summons of trumpets and horns to a celebration of the transfigured second melody, with triumphant cadence. Nor does the big impulse halt here. The trumpets sound on midst a spirited duet of inverted and original motives until the highest point is reached, where, to quicker calls of the brass, in broadest pace the main subject strikes its inverted tune in the trebles, while the bass rolls its majestic length in a companion melody; trombones, too, are blaring forth the call of the second theme.

Brief interludes of lesser agitation bring a second chorus on the reunited melodies in a new tonal quarter.

In mystic echoing groups on the former descending answer of main theme the mood deepens in darkening scene. Here moves in slow strides of lowest brass a shadowy line of the second melody answered by a poignant phrase of the first. Striking again and again in higher perches the dual song reaches a climax of feeling in overpowering burst of fullest brass. In masterful stride, still with a burden of sadness, it has a solacing tinge as it ends in a chord with pulsing harp, that twice repeated leads back to the stirring first song of main theme.

Thence the whole course is clear in the rehearsal of former melodies. Only the pensive air has lost its melancholy. Here is again the lyric of warm-hued horns with plaintive higher phrase, and the full romance of second melody with its timid answer, where the nervous trip rouses slowly the final exultation. Yet there is one more descent into the depths where the main melody browses in dim searching. Slowly it wings its flight upwards until it is greeted by a bright burst of the second melody in a chorus of united brass. And this is but a prelude to the last joint song, with the inverted theme above. A fanfare of trumpets on the second motive ends the movement.

The Romanze is pure song in three verses where we cannot avoid a touch of Scottish, with the little acclaiming phrases. The theme is given to the saxophone (or cello) with obligato of clarinet and violas; the bass is in bassoons and *pizzicato* of lower strings. One feels a special gratitude to the composer who will write in these days a clear, simple, original and beautiful melody.

The first interlude is a fantasy, almost a variant on the theme in a minor melody of the wood, with a twittering phrase of violins. Later the strings take up the theme in pure *cantilena* in a turn to the major,—all in expressive song that rises to a fervent height. Though it grows out of the main theme, yet the change is clear in a return to the subject, now in true variation, where the saxophone has the longer notes and the clarinet and oboe sing in concert.

There follows a pure interlude, vague in motive, full of dainty touches. The oboe has a kind of *arioso* phrase with trilling of flutes and clarinets, answered in trumpets and harp.

Later the first violins (on the G string) sing the main air with the saxophone.

A double character has the third movement as the title shows, though in a broadest sense it could all be taken as a Humoreske.

With a jaunty lilt of skipping strings the lower reeds strike the capricious tune, where the full chorus soon falls in. The answering melody, with more of sentiment, though always in graceful swing with tricksy attendant figures, has a longer song. Not least charm has the concluding tune that leads back to the whole melodious series. Throughout are certain chirping notes that form the external connection with the Humoreske that begins with strident theme (*molto robusto*) of low strings, the whole chorus, xylophon and all, clattering about, the high wood' echoing like a band of giant crickets,—all in whimsical, varying pace. The humor grows more graceful when the first melody of the Intermezzo is lightly touched. The strange figure returns (in roughest strings and clarinet) somewhat in ancient manner of imitation. Later the chirruping answer recurs. Diminishing trills are echoed between the groups.

Slowly the scene grows stranger. Suddenly in eerie harmonies of newest French or oldest Tartar, here are the tricks and traits where meet the extremes of latest Romantic and primeval barbarian. In this motley cloak sounds the typical Yankee tune, first piping in piccolo, then grunting in tuba. Here is Uncle Sam disporting himself merrily in foreign garb and scene, quite as if at home. If we wished, we might see a political satire as well as musical.

After a climax of the clownish mood we return to the Intermezzo melodies.

The Finale begins in the buoyant spirit of the beginning and seems again to have a touch of Scotch in the jaunty answer. The whole subject is a group of phrases rather than a single melody.

Preluding runs lead to the simple descending line of treble with opposite of basses, answered by the jovial phrase. In the farther course the first theme prevails, answered with an ascending brief motive of long notes in irregular ascent. Here follows a freer flow of the jolly lilting tune, blending with the sterner descending lines.

Balancing this group is an expressive melody of different sentiment. In its answer we have again the weird touch of neo-barbarism in a strain of the reed, with dancing overtones of violins and harp, and strumming chords on lower strings. Or is there a hint of ancient Highland in the drone of alternating horns and bassoons?

Its brief verse is answered by a fervent conclusive line where soon the old lilting refrain appears with new tricks and a big celebration of its own and then of the whole madrigal of martial melody. It simmers down with whims and turns of the skipping phrase into the quiet (*tranquillo*) episode in the midst of the other stress.

The heart of the song is in the horns, with an upper air in the wood, while low strings guard a gentle rhythm. A brief strain in the wind in ardent temper is followed by another in the strings, and still a third in joint strings and wood. (Again we must rejoice in the achievement of true, simple, sincere melody.) The final glowing height is reached in all the choirs together,—final that is before the brass is added with a broader pace, that leads to the moving climax. As the horns had preluding chords to the whole song, so a single horn sings a kind of epilogue amid harmony of strings and other horns. Slowly a more vigorous pulse is stirred, in an interlude of retorting trumpets.

Suddenly in the full energy of the beginning the whole main subject sounds again, with the jolly lilt dancing through all its measures, which are none too many. The foil of gentle melody returns with its answer of eerie tune and harmonies. It seems as if the poet, after his rude jest, wanted, half in amends, half on pure impulse, to utter a strain of true fancy in the strange new idiom.

A new, grateful sound has again the big conclusive phrase that merges into more pranks of the jaunty tune in the biggest revel of all, so that we suspect the jolly jester is the real hero and the majestic figures are, after all, mere background. And yet here follows the most tenderly moving verse, all unexpected, of the quiet episode.

The end is a pure romp, *molto vivace,* mainly on the skipping phrase. To be sure the stately figures after a festive height march in big, lengthened pace; but so does the jolly tune, as though in mockery. He breaks into his old rattling pace (in the Glockenspiel) when all the figures appear together,—the big ones changing places just before the end, where the main theme has the last say, now in the bass, amidst the final festivities.

SYMPHONIES IN AMERICA

LOEFFLER.* LA VILLANELLE DU DIABLE
(The Devil's Round)

(After a poem by M. Rollinat. Symphonic poem for Orchestra and Organ)

Few pieces of program music are so closely associated with the subject as this tone picture of the Devil's Round. The translation of M. Rollinat's "Villanelle," printed in the score is as follows: †

Hell's a-burning, burning, burning. Chuckling in clear staccato, the Devil prowling, runs about.

He watches, advances, retreats like zig-zag lightning; Hell's a-burning, burning, burning.

In dive and cell, underground and in the air, the Devil, prowling, runs about.

Now he is flower, dragon-fly, woman, black-cat, green snake; Hell's a-burning, burning, burning.

---

* Charles Martin Loeffler, born in Alsace in 1861.

† A few translated verses may give an idea of the original rhythm:

Hell's a-burning, burning, burning.
Cackling in his impish play,
Here and there the Devil's turning,

Forward here and back again,
Zig-zag as the lightning's ray,
While the fires burn amain.

In the church and in the cell
In the caves, in open day,
Ever prowls the fiend of hell.

But in the original the first and last lines of the first verse are used as refrains in the succeeding verses, recurring alternately as the last line. In the final verse they are united.—The prose translation is by Philip Hale.

351

And now, with pointed moustache, scented with vetiver, the Devil, prowling, runs about.

Wherever mankind swarms, without rest, summer and winter, Hell's a-burning, burning, burning.

. From alcove to hall, and on the railways, the Devil, prowling, runs about.

He is Mr. Seen-at-Night, who saunters with staring eyes. Hell's a-burning, burning, burning.

There floating as a bubble, here squirming as a worm, the Devil, prowling, runs about.

He's grand seigneur, tough, student, teacher. Hell's a-burning, burning, burning.

He inoculates each soul with his bitter whispering: the Devil, prowling, runs about.

He promises, bargains, stipulates in gentle or proud tones. Hell's a-burning, burning, burning.

Mocking pitilessly the unfortunate whom he destroys, the Devil, prowling, runs about.

He makes goodness ridiculous and the old man futile. Hell's a-burning, burning, burning.

At the home of the priest or sceptic, whose soul or body he wishes, the Devil, prowling, runs about.

Beware of him to whom he toadies, and whom he calls " my dear sir." Hell's a-burning, burning, burning.

Friend of the tarantula, darkness, the odd number, the Devil, prowling, runs about.

—My clock strikes midnight. If I should go to see Lucifer?—Hell's a-burning, burning, burning; the Devil, prowling, runs about.

In the maze of this modern setting of demon antics (not unlike, in conceit, the capers of Till Eulen- spiegel), with an eloquent use of new French strokes of harmony, one must be eager to seize upon definite figures. In the beginning is a brief wandering or

flickering motive in furious pace of harp and strings,
ending ever in a shriek of the high wood. Answering

is a descending phrase mainly in the brass, that ends
in a rapid jingle.

There are various lesser motives, such as a minor
scale of ascending thirds, and a group of crossing figures that seem a guise of the first motive.
To be sure the picture lies less in the separate
figures than in the mingled color and bustle. Special
in its humor is a soft gliding or creeping phrase of
three voices against a constant trip of cellos.

After a climax of the first motive a frolicking
theme begins (in English horn and violas). If
we were forced to guess, we could see here the dandy

devil, with pointed mustachios, frisking about. It is probably another guise of the second motive which presently appears in the bass. A little later, *dolce amabile* in a madrigal of wood and strings, we may see the gentlemanly devil, the gallant. With a crash of chord and a role of cymbals re-enters the first motive, to flickering harmonies of violins, harp and flutes, taken up by succeeding voices, all in the whole-tone scale. Hurrying to a clamorous height, the pace glides into a *Movimento di Valzer,* in massed volume, with the frolicking figure in festive array.

To softest tapping of lowest strings and drums, a shadow of the second figure passes here and there, with a flash of harp. Soon, in returning merriment, it is coursing in unison strings (against an opposite motion in the wood).

At the height of revel, as the strings are holding a trembling chord, a sprightly Gallic tune of the street pipes in the reed, with intermittent flash of the harp, and, to be sure, an unfamiliar tang of harmonies and strange perversions of the tune.* In

---

* "A la villette," a popular song of the Boulevard. Mr. Philip Hale, who may have been specially inspired, associates the song with the word "crapule," "tough," as he connects the following revolutionary songs, in contrapuntal use, with the word "magister," "teacher,"—the idea of the pedagogue in music. It may be less remote to find in these popular airs merely symbols or graphic touches of the swarming groups among which the Devil plies his trade.

the midst is the original flickering figure. As the whole chorus is singing the tune at the loudest, the brass breaks into another traditional air of the Revolutionary Song of 1789.* While the trip is still ringing in the strings, a lusty chorus breaks into the song † " La Carmagnole," against a blast of the horns in a guise of the first motive.

Grim guises of the main figures (in inverted profile) are skulking about to uncanny harmonies. A revel of new pranks dies down to chords of muted horns, amid flashing runs of the harp, with a long roll of drums. Here *Grave* in solemn pace, violas and bassoon strike an ecclesiastical incantation, answered by the organ. Presently a Gregorian plain chant begins solemnly in the strings aided by the organ while a guise of the second profane motive intrudes. Suddenly in quick pace against a fugal tread of lower voices, a light skipping figure dances in the high wood. And now loud trumpets are saucily blowing the chant to the quick step, echoed by the wood. And we catch the wicked song of the

---

* The famous " Ça ira."

† In the wealth of interesting detail furnished by Mr. Hale is the following: " The Carmagnole was first danced in Paris about the liberty-tree, and there was then no bloody suggestion. . . . The word *'Carmagnole'* is found in English and Scottish literature as a nickname for a soldier in the French Revolutionary army, and the term was applied by Burns to the Devil as the author of ruin, ' that curst carmagnole, auld Satan.' "

street (in the English horn) against a legend of hell in lower voices.*

In still livelier pace the reeds sound the street song against a trip of strings, luring the other voices into a furious chorus. All at once, the harp and violins strike the midnight hour to a chord of horns, while a single impish figure dances here or there. To trembling strings and flashing harp the high reed pipes again the song of the Boulevard, echoed by low bassoons.

In rapidest swing the original main motives now sing a joint verse in a kind of *reprise*, with the wild shriek at the end of the line, to a final crashing height. The end comes with dashes of the harp, betwixt pausing chords in the high wood, with a final stifled note.

---

* The religious phrases are naturally related to the "priest or sceptic." In the rapid, skipping rhythm, Mr. Hale finds the tarentella suggested by the "friend of the tarantula."

INDEX

357

INDEX

INDEX

Foster, Stephen, 198
Franck, 72 *et seq.;* symphony in D minor, 75 *et seq.*
Francke, Kuno, 231
French, modern school, 8, 9, 95 *et seq*, 253, 321, 330, 337,
    340, 347
Frenssen, 13
Freytag, 13
Fux, 95

Gade, 4 (See Vol. II)
Gelder, Martinus van, 4
German art, modern, 12–14, 217–218; music, modern, 14,
    143, 230
Gilchrist, 321 (See Vol. II)
Glazounow, 3
Gluck, 94
Goethe, 2, 11, 13, 45; "The Sorcerer's Apprentice," 106
    et seq., 231
Graphic music (See Program music)
Grieg, 72

Hadley, Symphony No. 3, 321–329
Hale, Philip, 231, 354, 355, 356
Harmony, 73, 95 *et seq.*, 262, 338–339 (See Scale; see
    French modern school)
"Heldenleben," by Strauss, 44 (See Vol. II)
"Heldenlied," by Dvôrák, 44
Heine, 13
"Hercules, The Youth of," by Saint-Saëns, 65 *et seq.* (See
    "Omphale")
Hoffmansthal, 13
Hucbald, 91
Hugo, Victor, 39; "Mazeppa" poem, 50 *et seq.*
Hungarian music, 46, 47, 48, 52, 189, 198
"Huns, Battle of the," 53 *et seq.*

INDEX

INDEX

INDEX

INDEX

THE "MOONLIGHT SONATA"

Beethoven loved solitary walks in the country where he could forget the world. He received the inspiration for many a wonderful work in this way. One fine night when he walked in the environs of Bonn on the Rhine he heard suddenly some piano music which came from a country home. He stopped in surprise. Played by an excellent musician, the sound of one of his compositions came to him. Following an irresistible attraction, he entered the villa, went up the stair and opened the door of the room from which the music came. Beethoven stopped as though nailed to the floor.

A poetic scene was in front of him. In the room which was flooded by the moonlight, a young girl of about 16 sat at the piano. "Is that you, father?" the girl asked, but did not turn around, continuing to play. When she had finished the piece of music, she arose and did a few hesitating steps: "Come, father and let me kiss you. Oh, I can't go up to you."

Beethoven approached and stopped, deeply sorrowful. A pair of wide-open, dead eyes stared at him from the delicate and beautiful face of the girl. Now he knew that he stood in front of a blind girl.

. as mpassion filled the heart of the ub. d made him utter an exclamation .... which the blind girl heard. She now that a stranger stood in front . Her childlike voice trembled when ..ed anxiously: "Who are you? Are y father?"

ethoven replied, "but don't be my child, for I am a friend who cause I was attracted by your beautiful playing. I want to thank you for the beautiful way in which you played my composition."

"Oh, are you Beethoven?" said the girl with joy while tears came into her blind eyes. "Oh, I am unfortunate that I come so near to you whose works I admire so much, and yet cannot see you. Music is the only thing that consoles me since two years ago an illness deprived me of my sight. Without music I would have died of despair. And your compositions especially make me forget my sorrow and transport me to higher spheres."

Beethoven replied: "Poor child, if you cannot see me, you shall at least hear me." And he sat down at the piano, and the very melancholy feelings which filled his heart were turned into the beautiful melodies of the "Moonlight Sonata" which grew up from his creative mind in that solemn hour.—Translated from Les Dernieres Nouvelles, Strasbourg, France.